THE FACTS ON FILE
Visual Dictionary

Jean~Claude Corbeil

THE FACTS ON FILE
Visual Dictionary

Facts On File
Publications

New York • Oxford

PUBLISHED UNDER LICENSE IN UNITED STATES OF AMERICA BY **FACTS ON FILE**, NEW YORK

Library of Congress Cataloging -in-Publication Data:

Corbeil, Jean-Claude.
  The Facts On File Visual Dictionary

  Includes index.
  I. Picture dictionaries, English.   2. Handbooks, vade-mecums, etc.   I. Archambault, Ariane.
  II. Title.

AG250.C63 1986   423′.1   86-6261
ISBN 0-8160-1544-9

Printed in Canada

EDITORIAL STAFF

Jacques Fortin
publisher

Jean-Claude Corbeil
editor-in-chief

Ariane Archambault
assistant editor

ASSOCIATE RESEARCH EDITORS
Edith Girard
René Saint-Pierre
Christiane Vachon
Marielle Hébert
Ann Céro

GRAPHICS STAFF
Sylvie Lévesque
Francine Giroux
Emmanuelle Rousseau

COPY EDITORS
Jean-Pierre Fournier
Philip Stratford
Michel Veyron
Diane Martin
Ann Céro
Guy Connolly

Joseph Reilly

The editors are grateful for the assistance provided by the following manufacturers and organizations:

Air Canada — **Archambault Musique** — Aréo-feu Ltée — **ASEA Inc.** — Atelier Lise Dubois — **Atomic Energy of Canada Ltd** — Automobiles Renault Canada Ltée — **Banque de terminologie du Québec** — Bell Canada — **Bombardier Inc.** — Botanical Garden of Montreal — **Camco Inc.** — Canada Mortgage and Housing Corporation — **Canadian Broadcasting Corporation** — Canadian Coleman Supply Inc. — **Canadian General Electric Company Ltd** — Canadian Government Terminology Bank — **Canadian National** — Canadian Pacific — **François Caron Inc.** — CKAC Radio — **CNCP Telecommunications** — Control Data Canada Ltd — **Department of National Defence** — Dow Planetarium — **Eaton** — Fédération québécoise de badminton — **Fédération québécoise de canot-camping** — Fédération québécoise de handball olympique — **Fédération québécoise de la montagne** — Fédération québécoise de ski nautique — **Fédération québécoise de soccer football** — Fédération québécoise des sports aériens Inc. — **Fédération québécoise de tennis** — Fédération de tennis de table du Québec — **Ford du Canada Ltée** — General Motors of Canada Ltd — **G.T.E. Sylvania Canada Ltée** — Gulf Canada Ltd — **Hewitt Equipment Ltd** — Hippodrome Blue Bonnets Inc. — **Honeywell Ltd** — Hudson's Bay Company — **Hydro-Québec** — IBM Canada Ltd — **Imperial Oil Ltd** — Institut de recherche d'Hydro-Québec (IREQ) — **Institut Teccart Inc.** — Institut de tourisme et d'hôtellerie du Québec — **International Civil Aviation Organization** — Johnson & Johnson Inc. — **La Maison Casavant** — Office de la langue française du Québec — **J. Pascal Inc.** — Petro-Canada Inc. — **Quebec Cartier Mining Company** — RCA Inc. — **Shell Canada Products Company Ltd** — Smith-Corona Division of SMC (Canada) Ltd — **Société d'énergie de la Baie James** — Société de transport de la Communauté Urbaine de Montréal — **Teleglobe Canada** — Translation Bureau: Department of the Secretary of State of Canada — **Via Rail Canada Inc.** — Volvo Canada Ltd — **Wild Leitz Canada Ltd** — Xerox Canada Inc. — **Yamaha Canada Music Ltd.**

TABLE OF CONTENTS

PREFACE 15

INTRODUCTION.................................. 17

THE FACTS ON FILE
VISUAL DICTIONARY
USAGE GUIDE 23

ASTRONOMY 25
  Earth coordinate system........................ 27
  Celestial coordinate system.................... 27
  Seasons of the year 27
  Planets of the solar system..................... 28
  Symbols of the planets 28
  Sun 29
    Structure of the Sun, solar eclipse
  Moon 30
    Lunar features, lunar eclipse, phases of the Moon
  Galaxy, Hubble's classification................ 31
  Comet 31
  Constellations of the northern hemisphere 32
  Constellations of the southern hemisphere 33
  Astronomical observatory...................... 34
  Planetarium 35
  Planetarium projector........................... 35

GEOGRAPHY....................................... 37
  Structure of the Earth.......................... 39
  Profile of the Earth's atmosphere 39
  Space achievements 39
  Section of the Earth's crust 40
  Configuration of the continents............... 41
  Ocean floor.. 42
  Wave.. 43
  Common coastal features 43
  Clouds and meteorological symbols 44
  Volcano 45
  Earthquake 45
  Mountain... 46
  Cave 46
  Desert 47
  Glacier 48

Water forms 49
  Classification of snow crystals, kinds of precipi-
  tation
Hydrologic cycle................................... 50
Climates of the world 51
International weather symbols 52
  Meteors, fronts, sky coverage, wind
Meteorology.. 54
  Weather map, station model, meteorological
  ground
Meteorological measuring instruments 56
  Direct-reading rain gauge, sunshine recorder
Meteorological satellite......................... 57

VEGETABLE KINGDOM........................... 59
  Structure of a plant 61
    Root, stem, leaf, leaf margin, types of leaves,
    simple leaves, compound leaves
  Structure of a tree 63
    Tree, cross section of a trunk, stump
  Structure of a flower 64
    Types of inflorescences
  Mushrooms.. 65
    Structure of a mushroom, edible mushrooms,
    poisonous mushroom, deadly mushroom
  Fleshy fruits : berry fruits 66
    Section of a berry : grape, major types of berries
  Compound fleshy fruits......................... 66
    Section of a strawberry, section of a wild black-
    berry or raspberry
  Stone fleshy fruits 67
    Section of a stone fruit : peach, major types of
    stone fruits
  Pome fleshy fruits 68
    Section of a pome fruit : apple, principal types
    of pome fruits
  Fleshy fruits : citrus fruits 69
    Section of a citrus fruit : orange, major types of
    citrus fruits
  Dry fruits : nuts 70
    Section of a hazelnut, section of a walnut, major
    types of nuts
  Various dry fruits 71
    Section of a follicle : star anise, section of a
    legume : pea, section of a silique : mustard, sec-
    tion of a capsule : poppy, section of a grain of
    wheat

Table of Contents

Tropical fruits 72
  Major types of tropical fruits
Vegetables...................................... 73
  Fruit vegetables, inflorescent vegetables, leaf
  vegetables, section of a bulb, bulb vegetables,
  tuber vegetables, root vegetables, stalk vegetables, seed vegetables

ANIMAL KINGDOM 79
  Deer family 81
    Deer antlers, kinds of deer
  Types of jaws.................................. 82
    Carnivore's jaw: leopard, rodent's jaw: beaver,
    herbivore's jaw: horse
  Horse 83
    Morphology, skeleton, hoof, plantar surface of
    the hoof, horseshoe
  Cat 86
    Head, foreleg, retracted claw, extended claw
  Bird 87
    Morphology, wing, contour feather, principal
    types of bills, principal types of feet, egg
  Fish 90
    Morphology, gills, anatomy
  Butterfly....................................... 92
    Caterpillar, pupa, butterfly
  Univalve shell 93
  Bivalve shell 93
    Left valve, dorsal view
  Mollusk.. 94
    Oyster, principal edible mollusks
  Crustacean 95
    Lobster, principal edible crustaceans
  Gastropod 96
    Snail, principal edible gastropods
  Batrachian..................................... 97
    Frog, life cycle of the frog, skeleton of the
    hindlimb
  Honeybee...................................... 98
    Worker, queen, drone, hind legs of the worker,
    hive, honeycomb section
  Bat 100
  Reptile.. 101
    Venomous snake's head, turtle

HUMAN BEING 103
  Cell 105
    Plant cell, animal cell
  Human body................................... 106
    Anterior view, posterior view
  Genital organs, male.......................... 108
    Sagittal section, spermatozoon
  Genital organs, female........................ 109
    Sagittal section, anterior view
  Breast, sagittal section....................... 109
  Muscles 110
    Anterior view, posterior view
  Skeleton...................................... 112
    Anterior view, posterior view
  Osteology of skull 114
    Lateral view, anterior view, superior view, inferior
    view

Teeth 115
  Cross section of a molar, human denture
Blood circulation 116
  Schema of circulation, heart, principal veins and
  arteries
Respiratory system, lungs..................... 118
Digestive system.............................. 119
Urinary system................................ 120
Nervous system 121
  Peripheral nervous system, central nervous sys-
  tem, medullar axis of lumbar vertebra
Sense organs : sight 123
  Eye, eyeball
Sense organs : hearing 124
  External ear, internal and middle ear
Sense organs : smell 125
  External nose, nasal fossae, sense of smell and
  taste
Sense organs : taste 126
  Mouth, dorsum of tongue
Sense organs : touch 127
  Skin, sensory impulse
Neuron.. 127
Skin... 128
Nail 129
Hair 129
Family ties 130

FOOD 133
  Herbs 135
  Pasta... 136
  Bread 138
  Veal 139
    North American cut, Parisian cut
  Beef.. 140
    North American cut, Parisian cut
  Pork.. 142
    North American cut, Parisian cut
  Lamb 143
    North American cut, Parisian cut
  North American cheeses 144
  French cheeses 144
  Desserts...................................... 146

FARM 149
  Buildings..................................... 151
  Agricultural machinery 152

ARCHITECTURE.............................. 157
  Traditional houses............................ 159
  Architecture styles 160
    Doric order, ionic order, corinthian order, column
    base
  Greek temple................................. 161
    Basic plan of the Greek temple
  Arches 162
    Semicircular arch, types of arches
  Roman house 163
  Gothic cathedral.............................. 164
    Cathedral, plan, façade, vault
  Vauban fortification 166
  Castle.. 167
  Downtown 168

Theater...................................... 169
Hall, wings, cross section of a stage
Elevator.................................... 171
Escalator................................... 172
City houses................................. 173
HOUSE 175
Exterior of a house 177
Plan reading............................... 178
Lot plan, ground floor, upper floor
Rooms of the house 179
Ground floor, upper floor, basement
Structure of the house 180
Roof structure, types of roofs, frame, foundations
Building materials 183
Wood flooring.............................. 186
Wood flooring on wooden structure, wood floor-
ing on cement screed, wood flooring arrange-
ments
Stairs 187
Door 188
Exterior door, types of doors, plan symbols
Window 189
Structure, types of windows
Heating.................................... 190
Fireplace, wood stove, firetending tools, log car-
rier, andiron, forced warm-air system, chimney,
forced hot-water system, heating unit, convector,
column radiator, baseboard radiator, boiler, split
system heating pump, electric furnace, oil burner
Air conditioning............................ 196
Room air conditioner, ceiling fan, dehumidifier
HOUSE FURNITURE 197
Table 199
Drop-leaf table, major types of tables
Armchair................................... 200
Parts, principal types of armchairs
Seats...................................... 202
Side chair.................................. 203
Parts, stretchers, types of chairs
Bed 204
Parts, linen
Storage furniture 205
Window accessories 207
Curtain, pole, rod, track, roller shade, roll-up
blind, shutters, Venetian blind
Lights...................................... 210
Glassware.................................. 212
Dinnerware................................. 213
Silverware.................................. 214
Knife, major types of knives, fork, major types of
forks, spoon, major types of spoons
Kitchen utensils 217
Kitchen knife, types of kitchen knives, utensils
for straining and draining, utensils for grinding
and grating, set of utensils, utensils for opening,
utensils for measuring, baking utensils, miscellaneous utensils
Cooking utensils............................ 222
Coffee makers.............................. 224
Domestic appliances........................ 225
Blender, table mixer, hand mixer, hand blender,
beaters, food processor, ice-cream freezer, juicer,
citrus juicer, microwave oven, grill and waffle
baker, toaster, griddle, electric range, frost-free
refrigerator, washer, dryer, dishwasher, steam
iron, can opener, kettle, canister vacuum cleaner,
cleaning tools
GARDENING 235
Pleasure garden 237
Tools and equipment 238
Chainsaw 243
DO-IT-YOURSELF............................. 245
Carpentry : tools............................ 247
Carpenter's hammer, mallet, plane, screwdriver,
wrenches, pliers, vise, C-clamp, brace, hand
drill, router, drill press, electric drill, bench saw,
hacksaw, handsaw, circular saw
Carpentry : fasteners 254
Nail, screw, bolt, nut, washer
Carpentry.................................. 255
Board, peeled veneer, panel, plywood
Lock 256
Mortise lock, cylinder, tubular lock
Plumbing................................... 257
Plumbing system, toilet, bathroom, sink, faucet,
branching, electric water-heater tank, connectors,
union, fittings, plumbing tools, septic tank, sump
pump
Painting upkeep 268
Ladders and stepladders, spray paint gun, brush,
scraper, paint roller
Soldering and welding....................... 271
Soldering iron, soldering gun, soldering torch,
oxyacetylene welding, arc welding, welding torch,
cutting torch, butt welding, pressure regulator,
protective clothing
Electricity 274
Incandescent lamp, mercury-vapor lamp, fluorescent lamp, electrical supplies, electrician's
tools, distribution board
CLOTHING 279
Men's clothing 281
Trench coat, raincoat, sheepskin jacket, duffle
coat, parka, inverness cape, three-quarter coat,
vest, double-breasted jacket, single-breasted coat,
pants, suspenders, belt, shirt, collar, necktie, ascot
tie, bow tie, V-neck cardigan, pullovers, sock,
underwear, headgear
Glove 289
Women's clothing 290
Coats, dresses, skirts, pockets, blouses, sleeves,
vests and pullovers, types of collars, necklines
and necks, pants, nightwear, hoses, underwear,
headwear
Children's clothing 305
Christening set, wraparound diaper shirt bathing
wrap, grow sleepers, blanket sleepers, nylon
rumba thigts, plastic pants, diaper, vest, bib,
crisscross back straps overall, high-back overall,
jumpsuit, bunting bag, sleeper, body stocking,
polojama, gym rompers, jumper, Eton suit, snowsuit

Table of Contents

Shoes.. 308
  Parts of a shoe, principal types of shoes, accessories for shoes
Costumes.................................... 311
  Bullfighter, ballerina, diving suit, clown

PERSONAL ADORNMENT 313
Jewelry..................................... 315
  Diversity of jewelry, bracelets, charms, rings, necklaces, cuts for gemstones, brilliant cut facets
Eyeglasses.................................. 318
  Front, temple, nose pad, principal types of eyeglasses
Hair styles 320
  Kinds of hair, components of hair styles, wigs and hairpieces
Makeup...................................... 322
  Makeup kit, makeup products, makeup accessories

PERSONAL ARTICLES 325
Razors...................................... 327
Scissors.................................... 328
Combs...................................... 328
Hairbrushes 328
Toothbrush 329
Oral hygiene center 329
Hair dryer.................................. 330
Lighted mirror.............................. 330
Salon-style hair dryer 330
Curling iron................................ 331
Curling brush 331
Hairsetter.................................. 331
Manicure set................................ 332
Manicuring instruments 333
Hairstyling implements 333
Smoking accessories 334
Umbrella 336
Luggage..................................... 337
Handbags.................................... 338
Leather goods............................... 340

COMMUNICATIONS 343
Writing systems of the world................ 345
Braille alphabet 346
Deaf-mute alphabet 347
Punctuation marks 347
Diacritic symbols 347
International phonetic alphabet.............. 348
Typical letter 349
Proofreading 350
Writing instruments 352
Photography 353
  Single-lens reflex camera, still cameras, objective and accessories, Polaroid Land camera, films, flash unit, exposure meter, spotmeter, studio lighting, photographic accessories, studio accessories, darkroom, enlarger, slide projector, projection screen
Sound reproducing system 363
  System elements amplifier-tuner, turntable, record, tape deck
Video tape recorder 367

Cinematography.............................. 368
  Sound camera, sound projector, video camera, dynamic microphone
Telegraph................................... 370
  Diagram of a circuit, receiver, transmitter, Morse code
Telex: teleprinter.......................... 371
Telephone set 372
  Receiver, transmitter, types of telephones, telephone answering machine
Television 374
  Studio and control rooms, studio floor, production control room, television set, picture tube
Telecommunication satellites................ 378
  Hermes satellite, examples of satellites, trajectory of a satellite, telecommunications network

TRANSPORTATION 381
Transportation by Road 383
Automobile 383
  Body, types of bodies, headlight, back of a station wagon, windshield wiper, dashboard, instrument board, door, steering, seats
Service station 387
  Gasoline pump
Semitrailer 388
  Platform, truck trailer
Engines 390
  Diesel engine, turbo-compressor engine, gasoline engine
Battery 392
Radiator 392
Spark plug 392
Exhaust system 392
Tires 393
Brakes...................................... 393
Snowmobile 394
Motorcycle.................................. 395
Bicycle 397
Cross section of a street................... 399
Cross section of a road 399
Fixed bridges............................... 400
Movable bridges 403

Transportation by Railroad 404
Diesel-electric locomotive.................. 404
Box car 405
Types of cars............................... 406
Types of passenger cars..................... 407
  Coach car, sleeping car, dining car
Railroad track 408
Highway crossing 409
Railroad station 410
Train yard.................................. 411
Container 411
Station hall 412
Station platform............................ 413

Transportation by Subway.................. 414
Subway station.............................. 414
Underground railway 415
  Subway train, passenger car interior, truck and track

Transportation by Sea............................ 416
Four-masted bark................................ 416
   Masting and rigging, sails
Types of sails...................................... 418
Types of rigs 418
Passenger liner 419
Ferry.. 420
Container ship 420
Hovercraft 421
Hydrofoil boat.................................... 422
Bathyscaphe 423
Submarine.. 424
Frigate.. 425
Canal lock 426
Harbor.. 427
Navigation devices 428
   Echo sounder, sextant, liquid compass
Maritime signals 430
   Buoys, lighthouse, lantern of lighthouse, cardinal
   system of marking, lateral system of marking
Anchor 433
   Ship's anchor, types of anchors

Transportation by Air........................... 434
Long-range jet 434
Wing structure 435
Wing shape....................................... 435
Tail shape.. 435
Turbo-jet engine................................. 436
Flight deck....................................... 437
Airport... 438
   Ground airport equipment
Passenger terminal.............................. 440
Helicopter.. 441

Space Transportation 442
Rocket.. 442
Space shuttle..................................... 443
   Space shuttle at takeoff, space shuttle in orbit
Space suit.. 444

OFFICE SUPPLIES AND EQUIPMENT........ 445
Stationery.. 447
Office furniture................................... 451
Typewriter.. 452
Microcomputer 454
   Functions in a system, configuration of a system,
   keyboard, peripheral equipment, dot matrix
   printer, acoustic coupler, joystick
Computer room 458

MUSIC 459
Musical notation 461
Stringed instruments............................ 463
   Violin family, violin, bow, harp
Keyboard instruments 465
   Upright piano, upright piano action
Organ.. 467
   Production of sound, console, mechanism of the
   organ, organ pipes
Wind instruments................................ 469
   Woodwind family, saxophone, reeds, brass family,
   trumpet

Percussion instruments.......................... 471
Traditional musical instruments................ 473
Instrumental groups............................. 476
Musical accessories.............................. 478
Symphony orchestra............................. 479
Electric and electronic instruments........... 480
   Electric guitar, synthesizer

CREATIVE LEISURE ACTIVITIES............... 483
Sewing 485
   Sewing machine: tension block, presser foot,
   needle, sewing accessories, fasteners, zipper,
   fabric structure, underlying fabrics, pattern
Knitting.. 490
   Knitting machine: tension block, needle bed,
   carriage, latch needle
Bobbin lace...................................... 492
Embroidery...................................... 493
   Frame, groups of stitches
Weaving.. 494
   Low warp loom, high warp loom, accessories,
   diagram of weaving principle, basic weaves
Fine bookbinding................................. 498
   Bound book
Intaglio printing process 501
Relief printing process........................... 502
   Equipment, etching press
Lithography 503
   Equipment, lithographic press
Printing.. 504
   Diagram of letterpress printing, diagram of in-
   taglio printing, diagram of planographic printing
Pottery 505
   Turning wheel, tools, baking
Stained glass 507

SPORTS 509
Team Games..................................... 511
Baseball.. 511
   Field, catcher, player, bat, glove
Football 513
   Playing field for Canadian football, playing field
   for American football, scrimmage in American
   football, scrimmage in Canadian football, protec-
   tive equipment, uniform, football
Rugby 517
   Field, team, ball
Soccer.. 518
   Field, ball
Ice hockey 519
   Rink, goalkeeper, ice hockey player, player's
   stick, goalkeeper's stick, puck
Basketball.. 521
   Court, basket
Volleyball 522
   Court, volleyball
Tennis.. 523
   Court, tennis players, tennis racket
Handball 525
   Court, handball
Squash 526
   International singles court, squash racket
Racquetball....................................... 527
   Four-wall court, racquetball racket

Table of Contents

Badminton.............................. 528
   Court, shuttlecock
Table tennis 529
   Table
Curling 530
   Curling rink

Water Sports 531
Water polo 531
   Playing area
Swimming 532
   Swimming competition, starting position, types of strokes
Diving 534
   Diving installations, starting positions, groups of dives
Skin diving....................................... 536
Sailboard.. 537
Dinghy 538
   Points of sailing, upperworks
Water skiing 540

Aerial Sports 541
Parachuting 541
   Parachute, free fall
Gliding 542
   Glider, cockpit
Hang gliding...................................... 543
   Hang glider

Winter Sports 544
Skiing... 544
   Ski resort, alpine skier, ski boot, safety binding
Cross-country skiing.......................... 547
   Cross-country skier, cross-country ski
Skating 548
   Figure skate, hockey skate, speed skate, roller skate
Snowshoes 549
   Michigan snowshoe, snowshoe types
Bobsleigh 550
Toboggan.. 550

Equestrian Sports 551
Riding 551
   Dress and equipment, obstacles, course of obstacles, bridle, saddle
Harness racing 554
   Standardbred pacer, racing program, stand and track

Athletics 556
Track and field athletics 556
   Arena, throwings
Gymnastics....................................... 559
   Men's apparatus, women's apparatus, trampoline
Weightlifting...................................... 561

Combat Sports 562
Fencing 562
   Piste, fencer, parts of the weapon, fencing weapons, positions
Judo 564
   Mat, judo suit, holds

Boxing.. 565
   Ring
Leisure Sports 566
Fishing 566
   Fly rod, spinning rod, fly reel, open-face spinning reel, fishhook, float, lures, accessories
Billiards 568
   Billiards equipment, pool and carom billiards, English billiards and snooker
Golf.. 571
   Course, hole, types of golf clubs, golf accessories
Mountaineering 574
   Equipment, mountaineer
Bowling 576
Parlor Games.................................... 577
Chess... 577
   Men, chessboards, chess notation
Backgammon 578
Card games....................................... 578
Dice... 579
Dominoes.. 579
Mah-jongg 579
Roulette table 580
   Roulette wheel, betting layout
Slot machine 581

Camping 582
Tents 582
   Family tents, pup tent, major types of tents
Sleeping bags 584
Bed-mattress and accessories................ 584
Propane accessories 585
Cook kit 585
Combination knife............................... 585
Tools 586
Knots 587

MEASURING DEVICES 589
Measure of time................................. 591
   Mechanical watch, tuning fork watch, hourglass, sundial, weight-driven clock mechanism, grandfather clock
Measure of weight.............................. 594
   Steelyard, beam balance, spring balance, Roberval's balance, analytical balance, self-indicating scale, bathroom scale, electronic scale
Measure of heat................................. 597
   Bimetallic thermometer, clinical thermometer, room thermostat
Measure of pressure 598
   Aneroid barometer, sphygmomanometer
Tape measure.................................... 599
Pedometer... 599
Micrometer caliper 599
Theodolite 600
Watt-hour meter 601
Horizontal seismograph 602
Vertical seismograph........................... 602

OPTICAL INSTRUMENTS........................ 603
Binocular microscope 605
Electron microscope............................ 606

Prism binocular 607
Hunting scope 607
Reflector 608
Refracting telescope 609
Radar 610
Lens 611
  Conveging lens, diverging lens
Magnetic compass 611

HEALTH 613
First aid kit...................................... 615
Syringes... 615
Walking aids.................................... 616
  Crutches, canes
Wheelchair...................................... 617

ENERGY... 619
Coal mine.. 621
  Open-pit mine, strip mine, mining, underground mine, pithead, pneumatic hammer, jackleg drill
Oil... 626
  Drilling rig, beam pump, gas lift, Christmas tree, offshore drilling, production platform, pipeline, tanker, tank car, tank trailer, tank truck, floating-roof tank, fixed-roof tank, refinery, refinery products, oil sands mining plant
Electricity 637
  Hydroelectric complex, cross section of an embankment dam, cross section of a concrete dam, major types of dams, steps in production of electricity, cross section of an hydroelectric power station, generator, cross section of an hydraulic turbine, tower, overhead connection, tidal power plant
Nuclear energy................................. 647
  Candu nuclear generating station, Candu reactor, nuclear reactor, fuel bundle, generating station flow diagram, fuel handling sequence, control room, production of electricity by nuclear energy, nuclear fuel cycle
Solar energy.................................... 654
  Solar furnace, tower-type solar power station, solar house, solar cell, solar collector
Windmill.. 657
  Tower mill, post mill
Wind turbine..................................... 658
  Horizontal-axis wind turbine, vertical-axis wind turbine, wind turbine electricity production

HEAVY MACHINERY 659
Dragline.. 661
Fire engine...................................... 662
  Aerial ladder truck, pumper
Bulldozer.. 664
Backhoe loader 665
Grader... 666

Hydraulic shovel................................ 667
Scraper... 668
Dump truck...................................... 668
Material handling 669
  Crane, forklift truck, forklift reach truck, handling engines

WEAPONS 673
Stone Age arms................................. 675
African warrior.................................. 675
Roman legionary 675
Armor... 676
Bows and crossbow............................ 677
Swords... 678
Bayonets... 679
  Major types of bayonets, parts of a hilted bayonet
Seventeenth century cannon 680
  Muzzle loading, tube, projectiles, accessories for firing
Arquebus 682
  Flintlock, loading
Hand grenade................................... 682
Mortar 683
  Modern, seventeenth century
Submachine gun................................ 683
Modern howitzer................................ 684
Automatic rifle 685
Bazooka.. 686
Recoilless rifle 686
Heavy machine gun 687
Light machine gun 687
Hunting weapons............................... 688
  Rifle, shotgun, cartridge
Pistol 689
Revolver.. 689
Tank 690
Combat aircraft 691
Missiles... 692
  Structure of a missile, command system, major types of missiles

SYMBOLS.. 693
Heraldry.. 695
  Parts of a flag, shield, examples of symbols, flag shapes
Signs of the zodiac 698
Notice symbols 699
  Graphic elements for symbols, international road signs, common symbols, fabric care
Common scientific symbols 709

GENERAL INDEX 711
THEMATIC INDEXES 745
SPECIALIZED INDEXES....................... 781
SELECTIVE BIBLIOGRAPHY.................. 795
CONTENTS...................................... 797

PREFACE

There are a number of dictionaries on the market whose titles readily spring to mind and whose merits are beyond question. Why then a new dictionary?

First, there is in every language a notable absence of dictionaries that provide a reliable modern terminology for the many objects, devices, machines, instruments or tools of everyday life. Secondly, bilingual Canada, and particularly Quebec, have long carried out and achieved world renown in the field of terminological research. Linguistic boards and organizations are maintained by governments; highly-skilled terminologists, linguists and translators are trained by universities; and efficient, competent terminology and translation services thrive within large corporations.

Given this context, it was only logical for Éditions Québec/Amérique to engage in the great adventure of compiling a dictionary. In four years, terminologists, linguists, researchers, translators, illustrators and graphic artists, under the supervision of prominent terminologist and linguist Jean-Claude Corbeil, have devised and composed an impressive work of reference. No dictionary had yet been specifically designed to cope with this era of information where high technology pervades every facet of our daily life. This one fills a tremendous gap.

Its novel presentation, carefully selected content, didactic illustrations and simplicity of use make it a unique tool for anyone concerned with using the right term in all circumstances. It is a work intended for clear, efficient communication serving to develop and enrich everyone's vocabulary.

Jacques Fortin
Publisher
Éditions Québec/Amérique

INTRODUCTION

PURPOSE OF THE DICTIONARY

Initially, we set ourselves two goals:

a) List all the terms and notions which designate or portray the many elements of everyday life in an industrial, post-industrial or developing society, and which one needs to know to buy an object, discuss a repair, read a book or a newspaper, etc.

b) Visualize them through graphic representation; i.e., assign to an illustration the role played by the written definition in a conventional dictionary.

The latter implies a constraint: The selected notions must lend themselves to graphic representation. Hence, the list must omit abstract words, adjectives, verbs and adverbs, even though they are part of the specialized vocabulary. Terminologists have not yet adequately solved this problem.

Following a series of tests and consultations, technical graphics were deemed the best form of visual presentation because they stress the essential features of a notion and leave out the accessories, like the fashion details of clothing. The resulting illustration gains in conceptual clarity what it loses in detail and provides a better definition.

To achieve our goals, we assembled two production teams, one of terminologists and another of graphic artists, who worked together under one scientific supervisor.

THE INTENDED USER

The VISUAL DICTIONARY is meant for the active member of the modern industrial society who needs to be acquainted with a wide range of technical terms from many assorted areas, but not to be specialist in any.

The profile of the typical user guided our selection of items in every category. We included what may be of use to everybody and deliberately left out what is in the exclusive realm of the specialist.

Varying levels of specialization will be noted from one category to another, however, depending on one's degree of familiarity with a subject or the very constraints of specialization. Thus, the vocabulary of clothing or electricity is more familiar to us than that of nuclear energy. Or again, to describe the human anatomy, one is confined to medical terminology but to describe the structure of a fruit, one may use both the scientific and popular terms. Familiarity with a subject also varies from one user to another or with the degree of penetration of a specialty. The best example no doubt is the propagation of the vocabulary of data processing brought on by the widespread use of the personal computer.

Be that as it may, the aim was to reflect as best as possible the specialized vocabulary currently used in every field.

CHARACTERISTICS OF THE DICTIONARY

What distinguishes THE FACTS ON FILE VISUAL DICTIONARY from other lexicons?

Conventional works

Dictionaries come in four basic types:

a) Language dictionaries

Language dictionaries are divided into two parts.

The first is the nomenclature, i.e., the list of words that are the object of a lexicographical commentary. It forms the macrostructure of the dictionary. For practical purposes, words are

Introduction

listed in alphabetical order. The nomenclature generally includes words of the common modern language, archaic words — often incorporated in a text — whose knowledge is useful to understand the language's history, and some technical terms that are fairly widespread.

The second is a lexicographical commentary whose microstructure varies according to lexicographical tradition. It generally deals with the word's grammatical category, its gender (if the case may be), its pronunciation in the international phonetic alphabet, its etymology, its various meanings, often in chronological order, and, finally, its uses according to a rather impressionistic typology that includes the *colloquial*, the *popular* and the *vulgar*.

b) Encyclopedic dictionaries

These add on to, the former type of dictionary commentaries on the nature, the function or the history of things, allowing the layman or the specialist to better understand the import of a word. They devote much more space to technical terms and closely follow the development of science and technology. Illustrations are assigned an important role. These works are more or less bulky, depending on the extent of the nomenclature, the importance of the commentaries and the space allotted to proper nouns.

c) Encyclopedias

Contrary to the preceding, encyclopedias do not include a full word list. They are essentially concerned with the scientific, technical, geographical, historical and economic aspects of their subjects. The structure of the nomenclature is arbitrary since every classification, be it alphabetical, notional, chronological or otherwise, is legitimate. The number of such works is potentially unlimited as are the activities of civilization, although a distinction must be drawn between universal and specialized encyclopedias.

d) Specialized lexicons or vocabularies

These works are generally meant to enhance communications or to answer particular needs arising from the evolution of science or technology. They vary from one another in every respect: the method of compilation, the relationship of the authors to the subject, the size of the nomenclature, the number of languages dealt with at once and the manner of establishing equivalents, either through translation or comparison between unilingual terminologies. There is intense activity in this field nowadays. Works abound in every area and in every language combination deemed useful.

THE FACTS ON FILE VISUAL DICTIONARY is not an encyclopedia. For one, it does not describe but names items. Secondly, it avoids the enumeration of items within a category. Rather than list the different types of trees, for instance, it selects a typical representative of the tree family and lists each of its parts.

It is even less a language dictionary. It contains only substantives — without written definitions — few adjectives, and very often complex terms, which is common to all terminologies.

Neither is it a compendium of specialized vocabularies —, as it favors words useful to the average person over terms known only to specialists, who may find it too elementary.

The VISUAL DICTIONARY is the first basic dictionary of terminological orientation, comprising within a single volume, with high regard for accuracy and easy access, thousands of more or less technical terms for which knowledge becomes a necessity in this modern world where science, technology and their by-products permeate and influence daily life.

METHODOLOGY

The preparation of this dictionary followed the methodology of systematic and comparative terminological research developed in Quebec in the early Seventies, now widespread in the whole of Canada, Europe, South America, North Africa and Sub-Saharan Africa.

We worked in the two languages, English and French, that are the most widely used throughout the world. The research available in both languages ensures a comprehensive stock of notions and terms, thanks to the interrelationship of approaches and specialties proper to

each language and their different perception and expression of the same realities. Eventually, we propose to apply the same methods to other languages, particularly Arab and Spanish.

The methodology of systematic terminological research involves many stages that follow one another in logical order. This progression applies to each language under study, their comparison intervening only at the end of the process with the compilation of terminological files. Thus, the pitfalls of literal translation are avoided.

A brief description of each stage follows:

Field delimitation

First, the content and size of the project must be carefully determined according to its goals and its prospective users.

In the case of the VISUAL DICTIONARY, we selected the major themes we felt should be dealt with, then divided each one into categories and sub-categories, keeping sight of our initial goal to steer clear of encyclopedism and ultraspecialization. The result was a detailed interim table of contents, providing the structure of the dictionary, to be used as a guide and refined in subsequent stages. The actual table of contents emerged from this process.

A dummy was then submitted to the contributing editors, lexicographers and terminologists, for their opinion on the content and the graphic style of the illustrations. Enriched from their comments, the project moved onto the production stage.

The collection of documentary sources

The production plan first called for researching and collecting the material likely to yield the required information on each subject. The research covered both French and English texts.

Here, without prejudice, is the list of documentary sources in order of the confidence placed in them for reflecting correct usage:

— English-French language dictionaries.
— Specialized dictionaries or vocabularies, whether unilingual, bilingual (French-English) or multilingual, whose quality and reliability should be carefully appraised.
— Encyclopedias or encyclopedic dictionaries, language dictionaries.
— Catalogues, commercial texts, advertisements in specialized magazines and large dailies.
— Technical documents from the International Standard Organization (ISO), the American Standard Association (ASA) and the Association française de normalisation (AFNOR); directions for use of commercial products; comparative product analyses; technical information supplied by manufacturers; official government publications, etc.
— French or English articles or works by specialists with an adequate level of competence in their field. In translation, these prove highly instructive as to word usage, although caution should be exercized.

On the whole, some four to five thousand references. The selective bibliography contained in the dictionary lists only the general reference works, not the specialized sources.

Sifting through the documentation

For every subject, the terminologist must sift through the documentation, searching for specific notions and the words used by various authors to express them. From this process emerges the notional structure of the subject, its standard or differing designations. In the latter case, the terminologist pursues his research, recording each term with supporting references, until he has formed a well-documented opinion on each of the competing terms.

Since the dictionary is visual, terminologists at this stage searched for appropriate ways of graphically depicting each coherent group of notions in one or several illustrations

Introduction

depending on the subject. The graphic artists drew from these elements to design each page of the dictionary.

The make-up of documentary files

The elements of each terminological file were assembled from the mass of documentation.

Once identified and defined through illustration, each notion was assigned the term most frequently used by the best authors and the most reliable sources to express it. If the terminological file suggested competing terms, one was selected upon discussion and agreement between the terminologist and the scientific director.

Specialists were called upon to discuss highly technical files subject to a greater risk of error.

Graphic visualization

The terminological file, along with a proposal for graphic representation, was then turned over to the graphics team for the design and production of the final illustrated page.

Each terminologist revised the plates pertaining to his files to ensure the accuracy of illustrations, terms and spelling.

General revision of plates

The terminological research was carried out subject by subject following a plan, but not necessarily in order.

The final version of the dictionary underwent two complete verifications. Three revisers in each language were first asked to proofread the entire work, with emphasis on the spelling, without disregarding the terminology. With the help of their commentaries, the written form was standardized throughout the dictionary. Each instance of every word or notion was checked to insure the greatest possible degree of coherence.

All the documentation and terminological files on which the dictionary is based remain in archives.

PARTICULAR PROBLEMS

Users of THE FACTS ON FILE VISUAL DICTIONARY may want to know how regional disparities in English usage were resolved.

American, Canadian or British English ?

English usage, particularly spelling, but also vocabulary, varies with every region.

We elected to follow American standards, using the various editions of Webster's and the Random House Dictionary of the English Language, Unabridged Edition (1983), as our basic references.

In a later edition of the dictionary, it might be worthwhile to list the terms in usage in each English-language community.

Terminological variation

Our research revealed a number of cases of terminological variation, i.e., designation of a notion by different terms.

Here is a partial list of such cases:

- A particular term may have been used by only one author or occurred only once throughout the documentation; we then chose the most frequent competing term;
- Technical terms are often in compound form, hyphenated or not, incorporating a preposition or preceded by a noun. This characteristic gives rise to at least two types of terminological variants:

a) The compound technical term may be shortened by the deletion of one or many of its elements, especially when the context is significant. Within limits, the shorter term becomes the usual designation of the notion. For instance, *objective lens* becomes *objective*, *fine adjustment knob* becomes *fine adjustment*, *revolving nose piece*, *nose piece*. We retained the compound form, leaving it to the user to shorten it according to the context.

b) One of the elements of the compound may itself have equivalent forms, generally synonyms in the common language. For instance, *magnetic needle* is equivalent to *magnetized needle*, *eye lens* to *ocular lens*. We then retained the most frequent form.

— Finally, the variation may stem from a difference of opinion, with no bearing on terminology, making it unnecessary to give up the best known term. For instance, the *first condenser lens* and *second condenser lens* of the electronic microscope are called *upper condenser lens* and *lower condenser lens* by some authors. The difference is not sufficient to cause a problem. In these cases, the most frequent or best known form was preferred.

Terminological sense

This calls for a brief commentary on the terminological sense as compared to the lexicographical sense.

The long history of language dictionaries, the fact that they are familiar reference works, known and used by everyone from schooldays, means that a certain tradition has been set that is known and accepted by all. We know how variants designating the same notion are classified and treated; therefore, we know how to interpret the dictionary and how to use the information it gives or does not give us.

Terminological dictionaries are either recent or intended for a specialized few. There is no real tradition guiding the preparation of such dictionaries. If the specialist knows how to interpret a dictionary pertaining to his own area of expertise because he is familiar with its terminology, the same cannot be said of the layman who may be confused by variants. Finally, language dictionaries have to some extent disciplined their users to a standard vocabulary. But since they relate to recent specialties, the terms listed in specialized vocabularies are far from set.

This aspect of the vocabulary sciences must be taken into account in the evaluation of the VISUAL DICTIONARY.

Spelling variations

The spelling of English words varies considerably. It sometimes differs according to the variety of English: for instance, *center* is American while *centre* is British. Often, the problem lies in determining whether a word should be written as a single word or in two words, with or without a hyphen: for example, *wave length* and *wavelength*, *grand-mother* and *grandmother*, *cross bar* and *crossbar*. Finally, there is some question as to the doubling of consonants in words like *levelling* and *traveller*. In every case, we used the spelling favored by Merriam Webster's and the Random House Dictionary.

Jean-Claude CORBEIL

THE FACTS ON FILE VISUAL DICTIONARY
FOR A *NEW* DICTIONARY A *NEW* USAGE GUIDE

THE FACTS ON FILE VISUAL DICTIONARY is divided into three parts:
- — TABLE OF CONTENTS
- — ILLUSTRATIONS depicting the ENTRIES
- — ALPHABETICAL INDEXES
    - — GENERAL
    - — THEMATIC
    - — SPECIALIZED

There are two ways of finding what you are looking for. You may refer either to the illustration or the word.

Starting from the **illustration**	Starting from the **word**
You want to know what an object is called	You want to know what a word stands for
Look in the **table of contents** for the **theme** which best corresponds to your query	Look for the word in the **general** index or in the **thematic** or **specialized** indexes, depending on the area of research
You will find **references** to **illustrations**	You will find **references** to the **illustrations** in which the word appears
Alongside the illustration, you will find the corresponding **word**	You will see from the **illustration** what the word stands for

ASTRONOMY

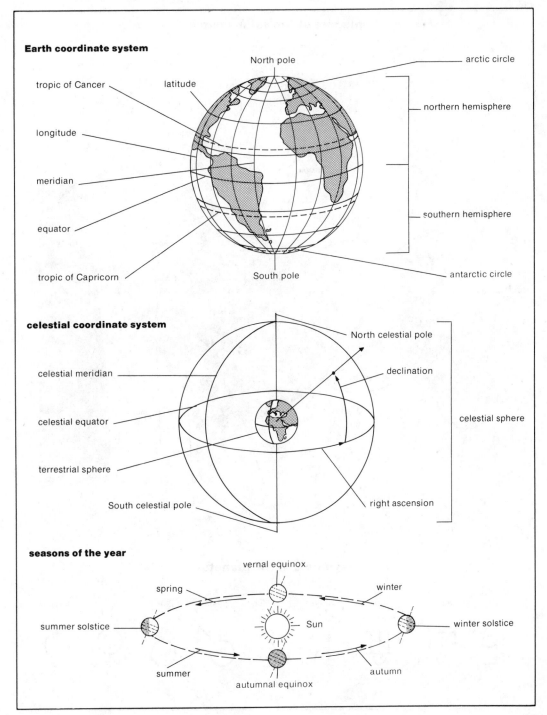

Earth coordinate system

North pole
arctic circle
tropic of Cancer
latitude
northern hemisphere
longitude
meridian
equator
southern hemisphere
tropic of Capricorn
South pole
antarctic circle

celestial coordinate system

North celestial pole
celestial meridian
declination
celestial equator
celestial sphere
terrestrial sphere
South celestial pole
right ascension

seasons of the year

vernal equinox
spring
winter
summer solstice
Sun
winter solstice
summer
autumn
autumnal equinox

planets of the solar system

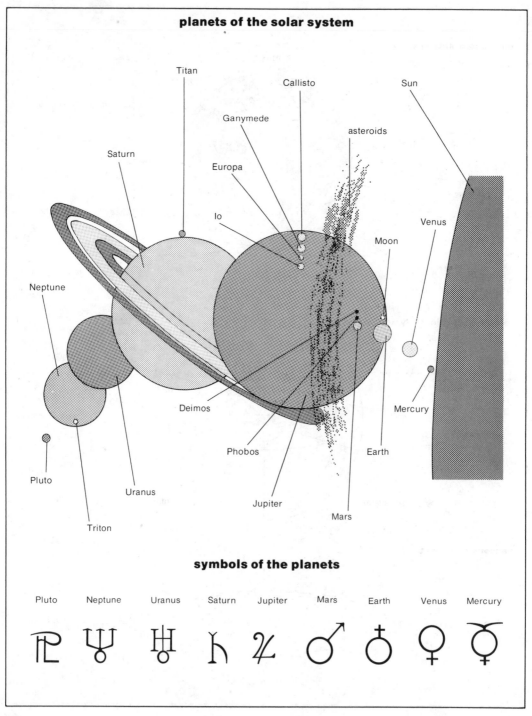

Titan
Callisto
Sun
Ganymede
asteroids
Saturn
Europa
Venus
Io
Moon
Neptune
Deimos
Mercury
Phobos
Earth
Pluto
Jupiter
Uranus
Mars
Triton

symbols of the planets

Pluto	Neptune	Uranus	Saturn	Jupiter	Mars	Earth	Venus	Mercury

Sun

structure of the Sun

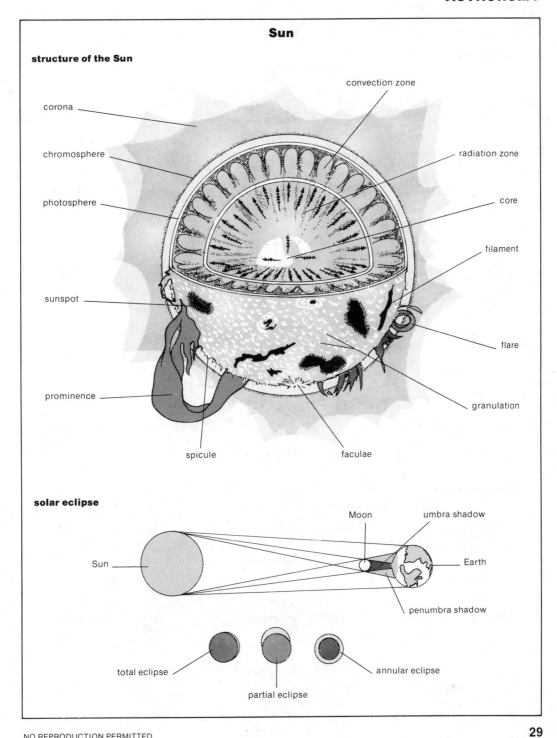

convection zone

corona

radiation zone

chromosphere

core

photosphere

filament

sunspot

flare

prominence

granulation

spicule

faculae

solar eclipse

Moon

umbra shadow

Sun

Earth

penumbra shadow

total eclipse

partial eclipse

annular eclipse

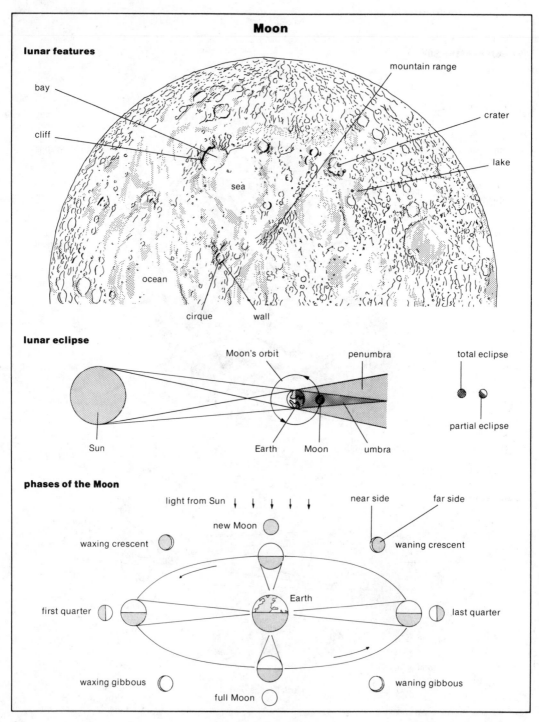

Moon

lunar features

- mountain range
- bay
- cliff
- crater
- lake
- sea
- ocean
- cirque
- wall

lunar eclipse

- Moon's orbit
- penumbra
- total eclipse
- partial eclipse
- Sun
- Earth
- Moon
- umbra

phases of the Moon

- light from Sun
- new Moon
- near side
- far side
- waxing crescent
- waning crescent
- first quarter
- Earth
- last quarter
- waxing gibbous
- waning gibbous
- full Moon

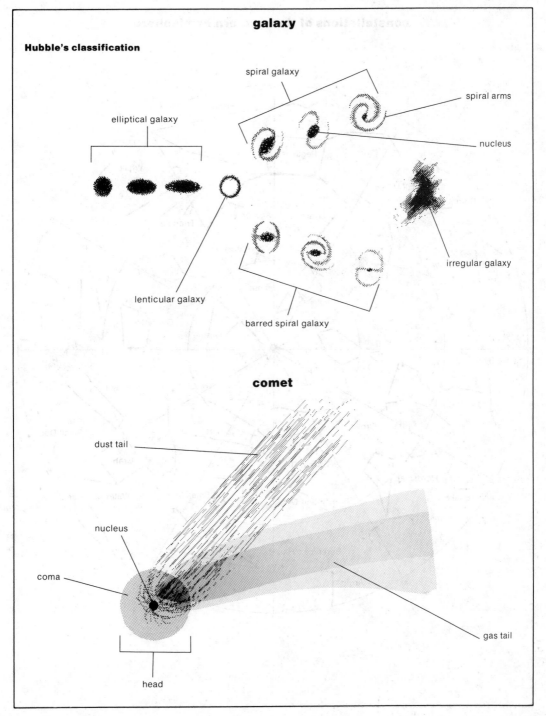

galaxy

Hubble's classification

spiral galaxy

spiral arms

elliptical galaxy

nucleus

irregular galaxy

lenticular galaxy

barred spiral galaxy

comet

dust tail

nucleus

coma

gas tail

head

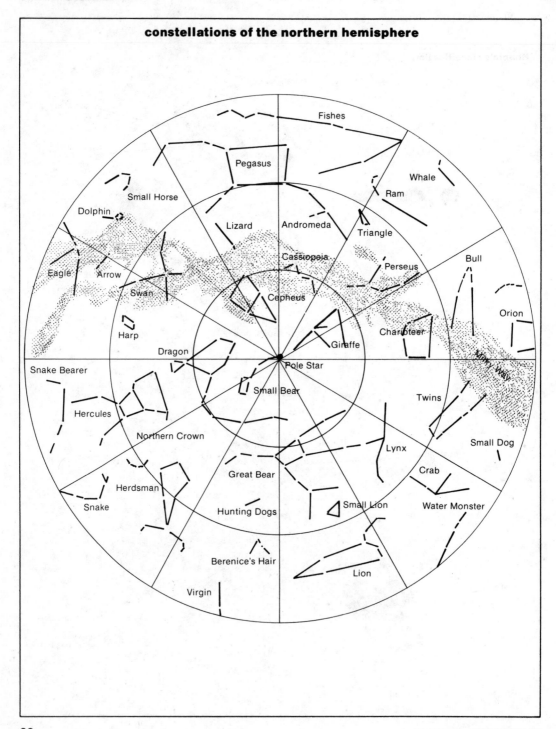

constellations of the northern hemisphere

Fishes

Pegasus

Small Horse

Whale

Dolphin

Ram

Lizard

Andromeda

Triangle

Cassiopeia

Perseus

Bull

Eagle

Arrow

Swan

Cepheus

Harp

Giraffe

Charioteer

Orion

Dragon

MILKY WAY

Pole Star

Snake Bearer

Small Bear

Twins

Hercules

Small Dog

Northern Crown

Lynx

Great Bear

Crab

Herdsman

Snake

Hunting Dogs

Small Lion

Water Monster

Berenice's Hair

Lion

Virgin

constellations of the southern hemisphere

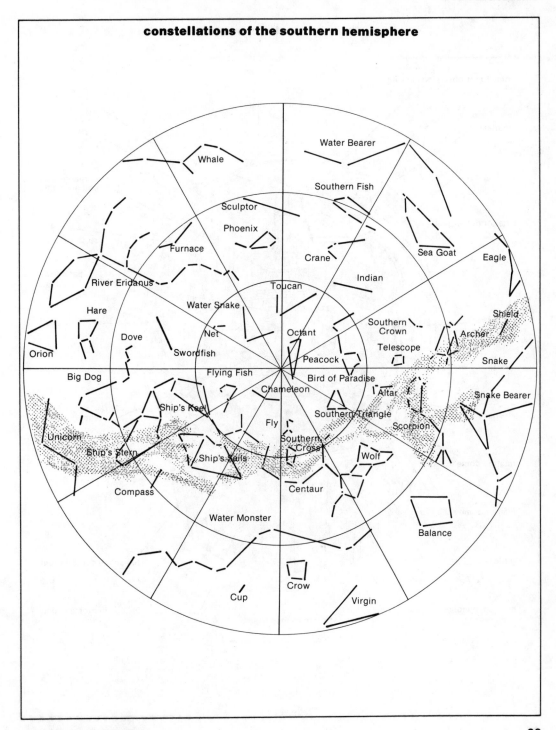

astronomical observatory

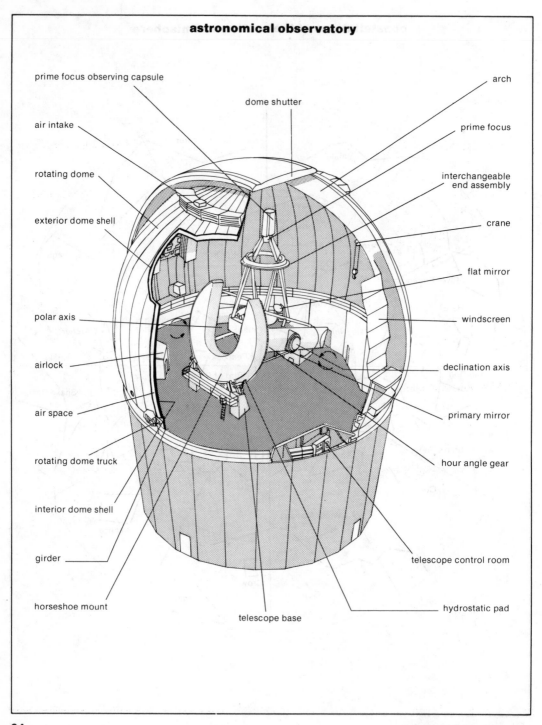

prime focus observing capsule

arch

dome shutter

air intake

prime focus

rotating dome

interchangeable
end assembly

exterior dome shell

crane

flat mirror

polar axis

windscreen

airlock

declination axis

air space

primary mirror

rotating dome truck

hour angle gear

interior dome shell

girder

telescope control room

horseshoe mount

hydrostatic pad

telescope base

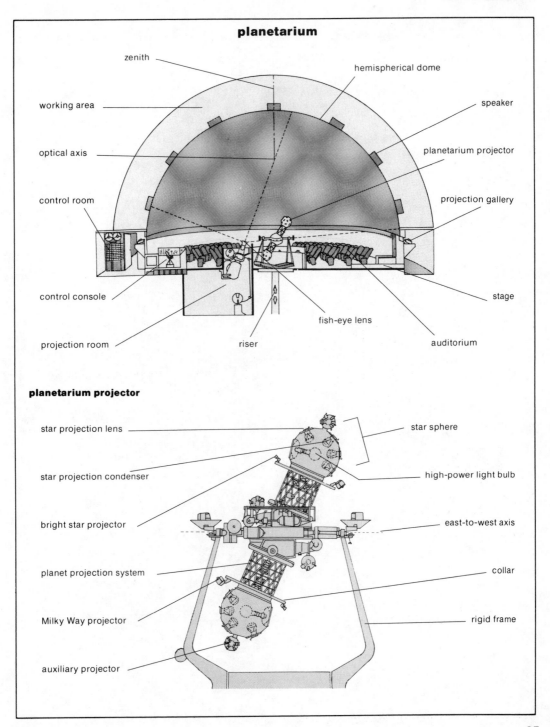

planetarium

- zenith
- hemispherical dome
- working area
- speaker
- optical axis
- planetarium projector
- control room
- projection gallery
- control console
- stage
- projection room
- fish-eye lens
- riser
- auditorium

planetarium projector

- star projection lens
- star sphere
- star projection condenser
- high-power light bulb
- bright star projector
- east-to-west axis
- planet projection system
- collar
- Milky Way projector
- rigid frame
- auxiliary projector

GEOGRAPHY

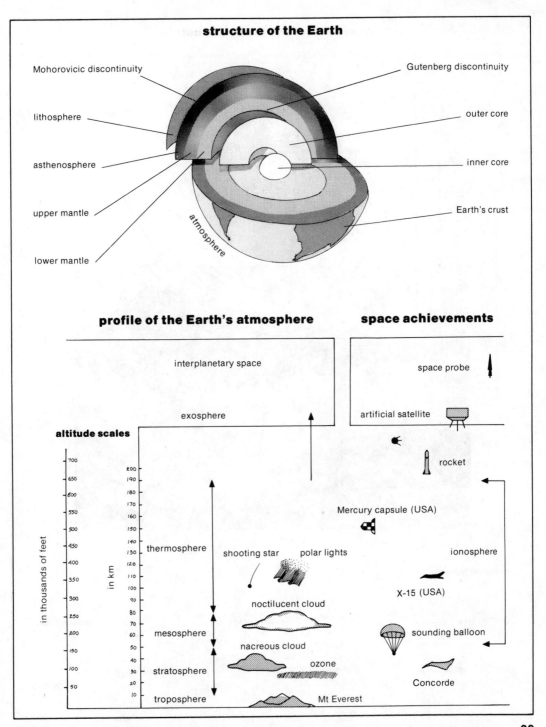

structure of the Earth

Mohorovicic discontinuity

Gutenberg discontinuity

lithosphere

outer core

asthenosphere

inner core

upper mantle

Earth's crust

lower mantle

atmosphere

profile of the Earth's atmosphere

space achievements

interplanetary space

space probe

exosphere

artificial satellite

altitude scales

rocket

in thousands of feet

in km

Mercury capsule (USA)

thermosphere

shooting star   polar lights

ionosphere

X-15 (USA)

noctilucent cloud

mesosphere

sounding balloon

nacreous cloud

stratosphere

ozone

Concorde

troposphere

Mt Everest

altitude scale (thousands of feet): 700, 650, 600, 550, 500, 450, 400, 350, 300, 250, 200, 150, 100, 50

altitude scale (km): 200, 190, 180, 170, 160, 150, 140, 130, 120, 110, 100, 90, 80, 70, 60, 50, 40, 30, 20, 10

section of the Earth's crust

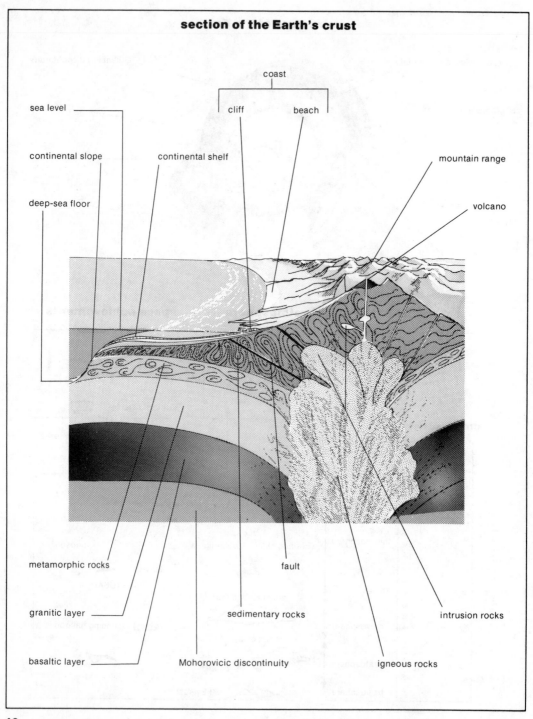

coast

sea level

cliff

beach

continental slope

continental shelf

mountain range

deep-sea floor

volcano

metamorphic rocks

fault

granitic layer

sedimentary rocks

intrusion rocks

basaltic layer

Mohorovicic discontinuity

igneous rocks

configuration of the continents

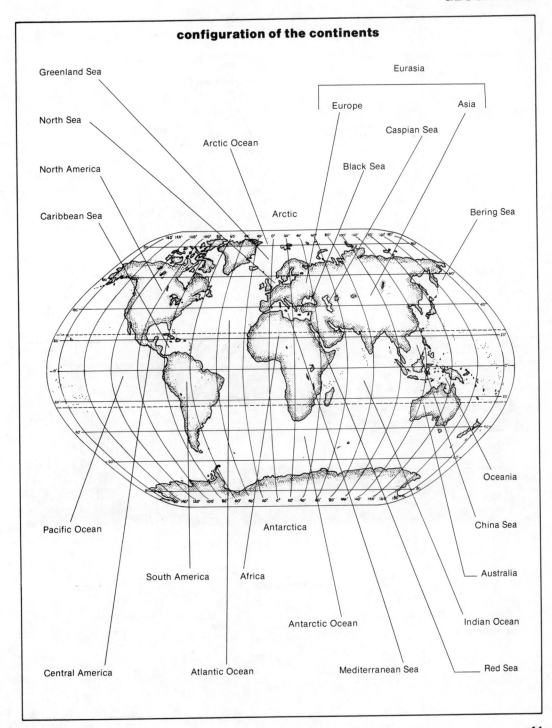

Greenland Sea

North Sea

Arctic Ocean

North America

Caribbean Sea

Arctic

Eurasia

Europe

Asia

Caspian Sea

Black Sea

Bering Sea

Oceania

China Sea

Australia

Pacific Ocean

Antarctica

South America

Africa

Antarctic Ocean

Indian Ocean

Central America

Atlantic Ocean

Mediterranean Sea

Red Sea

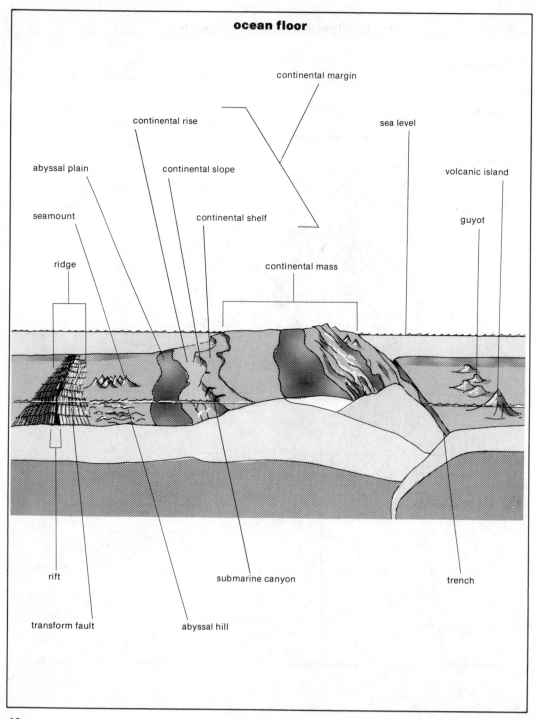

ocean floor

continental margin

continental rise

sea level

abyssal plain

continental slope

volcanic island

seamount

continental shelf

guyot

ridge

continental mass

rift

submarine canyon

trench

transform fault

abyssal hill

wave

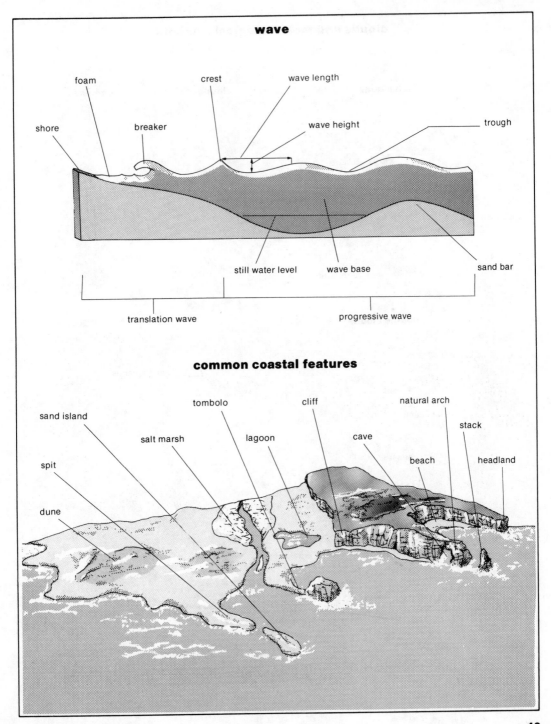

common coastal features

clouds and meteorological symbols

high clouds

clouds of vertical development

cirrus

cirrocumulus

cirrostratus

middle clouds

altostratus

cumulonimbus

altocumulus

stratocumulus

low clouds

nimbostratus

cumulus

stratus

volcano

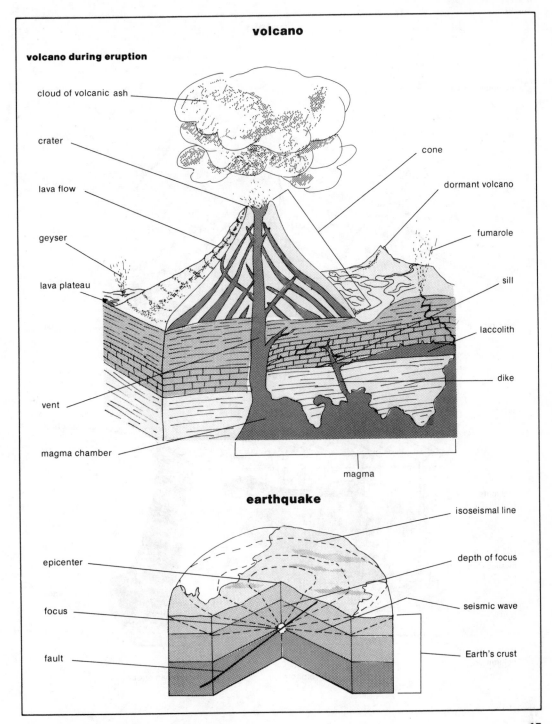

volcano during eruption

cloud of volcanic ash

crater

lava flow

geyser

lava plateau

vent

magma chamber

cone

dormant volcano

fumarole

sill

laccolith

dike

magma

earthquake

isoseismal line

epicenter

depth of focus

focus

seismic wave

fault

Earth's crust

GEOGRAPHY

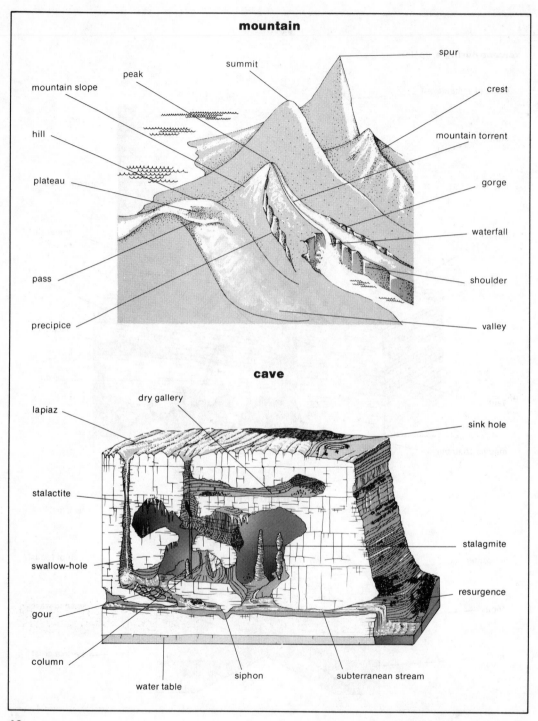

mountain

spur

summit

peak

mountain slope

crest

hill

mountain torrent

plateau

gorge

waterfall

pass

shoulder

precipice

valley

cave

dry gallery

lapiaz

sink hole

stalactite

stalagmite

swallow-hole

resurgence

gour

column

siphon

subterranean stream

water table

desert

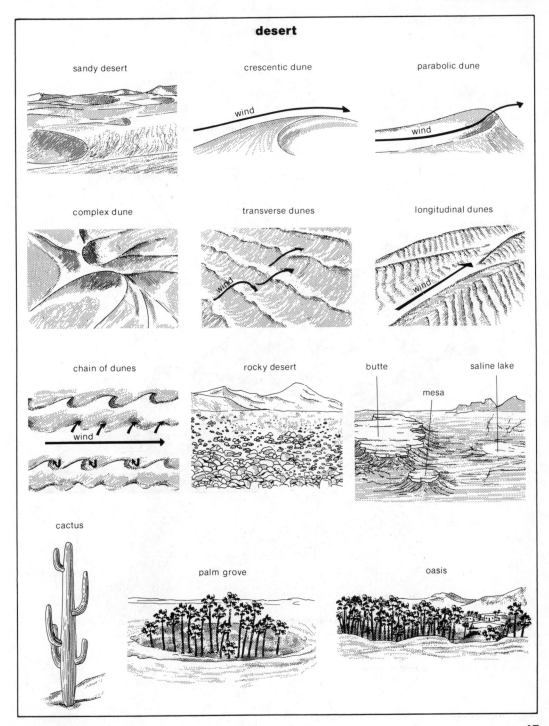

sandy desert

crescentic dune

wind

parabolic dune

wind

complex dune

transverse dunes

wind

longitudinal dunes

wind

chain of dunes

wind

rocky desert

butte

mesa

saline lake

cactus

palm grove

oasis

glacier

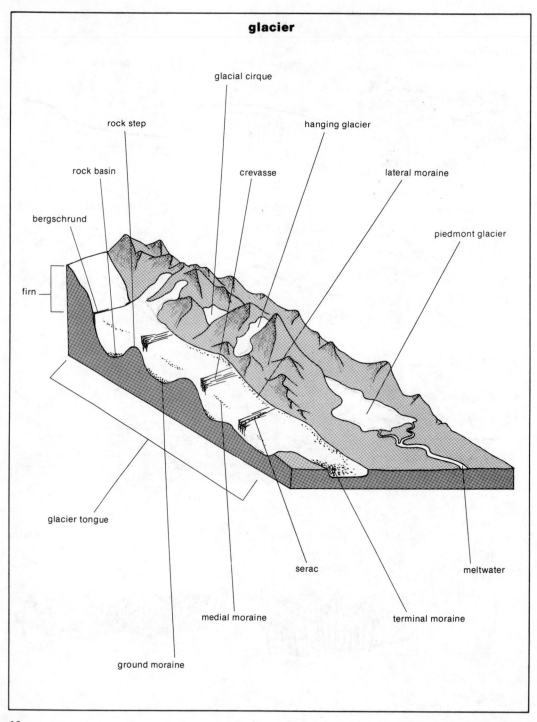

glacial cirque

rock step

rock basin

bergschrund

firn

hanging glacier

crevasse

lateral moraine

piedmont glacier

glacier tongue

serac

meltwater

medial moraine

terminal moraine

ground moraine

water forms

classification of snow crystals

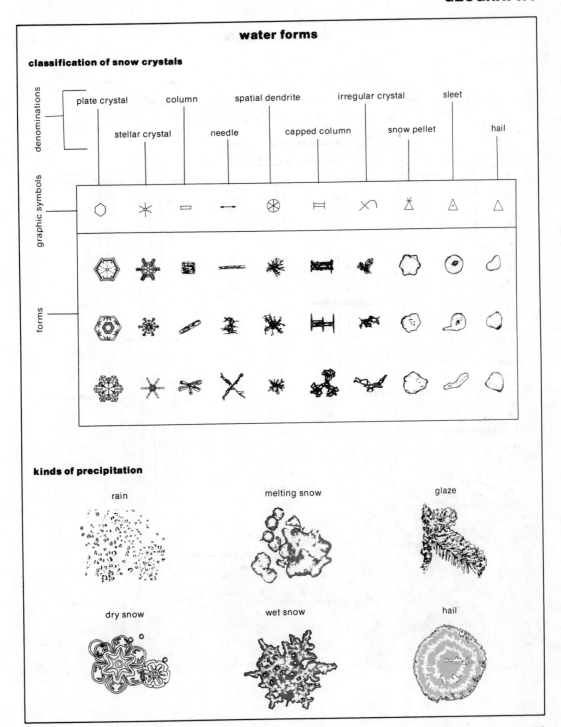

denominations

plate crystal · stellar crystal · column · needle · spatial dendrite · capped column · irregular crystal · snow pellet · sleet · hail

graphic symbols

forms

kinds of precipitation

rain

melting snow

glaze

dry snow

wet snow

hail

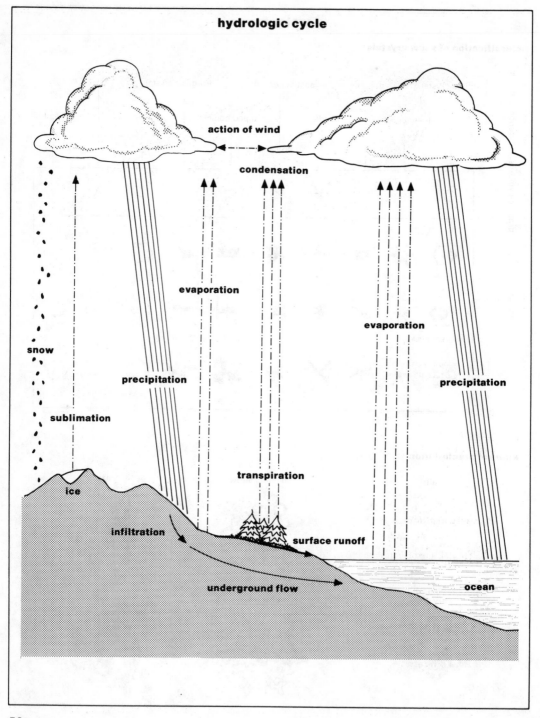

hydrologic cycle

action of wind

condensation

evaporation

evaporation

snow

precipitation

precipitation

sublimation

transpiration

ice

infiltration

surface runoff

underground flow

ocean

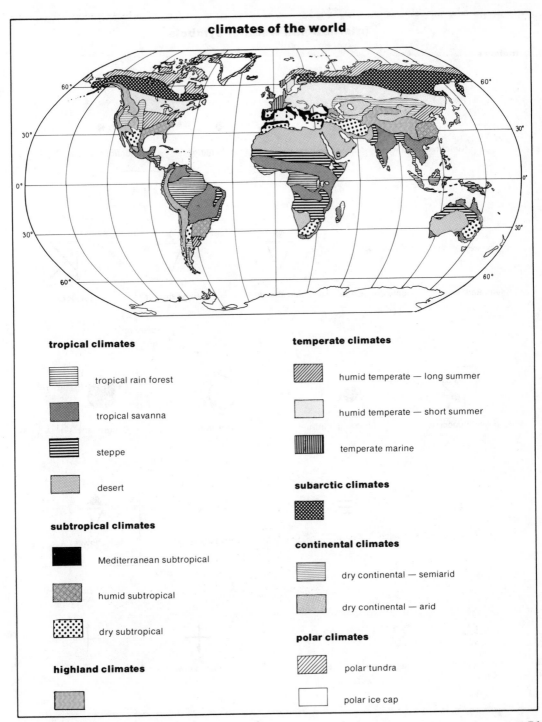

climates of the world

tropical climates

tropical rain forest

tropical savanna

steppe

desert

subtropical climates

Mediterranean subtropical

humid subtropical

dry subtropical

highland climates

temperate climates

humid temperate — long summer

humid temperate — short summer

temperate marine

subarctic climates

continental climates

dry continental — semiarid

dry continental — arid

polar climates

polar tundra

polar ice cap

international weather symbols

meteors

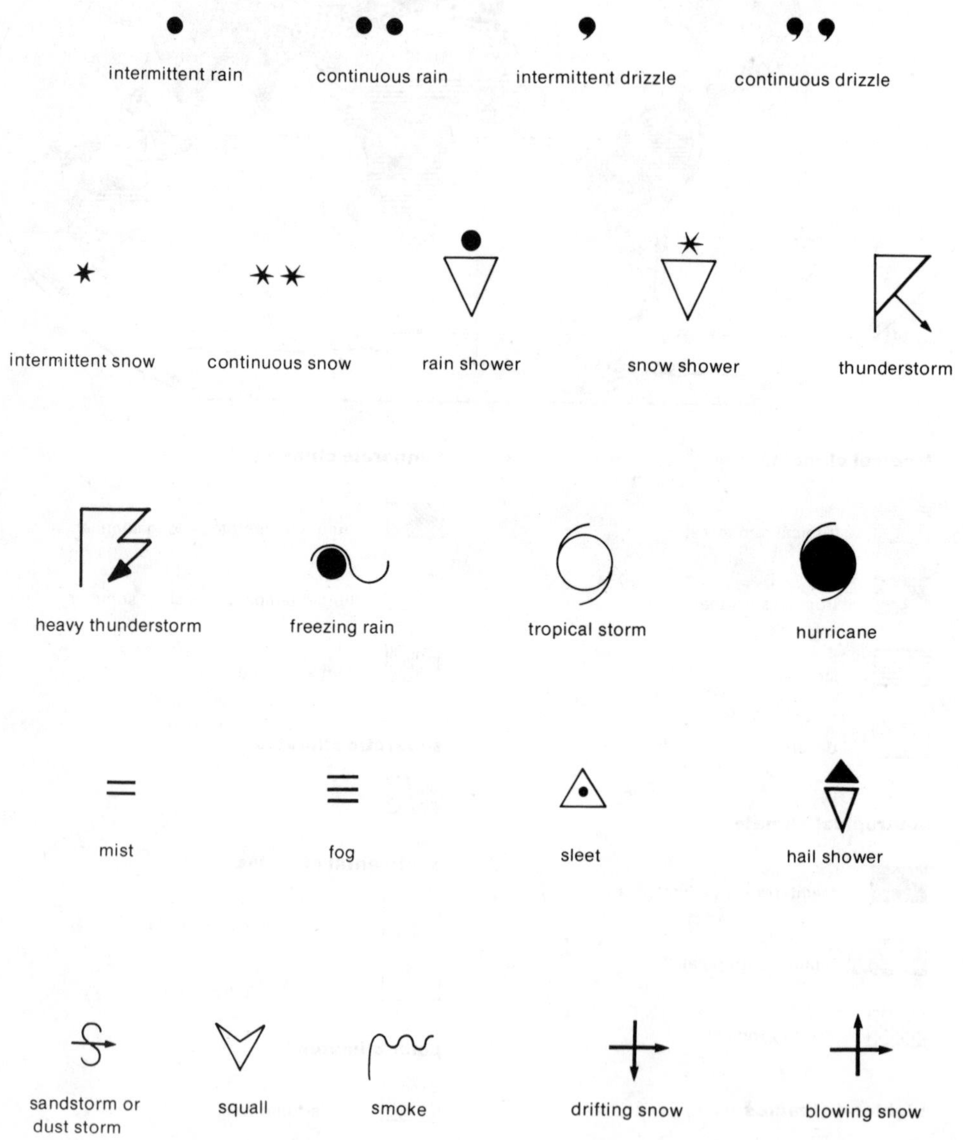

●	●●	❜	❜❜
intermittent rain	continuous rain	intermittent drizzle	continuous drizzle

✶	✶ ✶	▽ (with dot above)	▽ (with star above)	↘ (thunderstorm symbol)
intermittent snow	continuous snow	rain shower	snow shower	thunderstorm

↯	freezing rain symbol	tropical storm symbol	hurricane symbol
heavy thunderstorm	freezing rain	tropical storm	hurricane

═	≡	△ (with dot)	▲▽
mist	fog	sleet	hail shower

sandstorm symbol	⋁	∿	↓✛	→✛
sandstorm or dust storm	squall	smoke	drifting snow	blowing snow

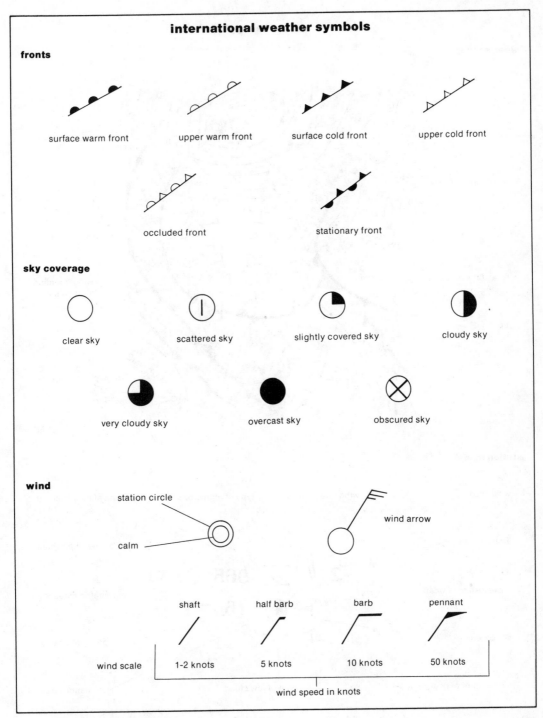

international weather symbols

fronts

surface warm front · upper warm front · surface cold front · upper cold front

occluded front · stationary front

sky coverage

clear sky · scattered sky · slightly covered sky · cloudy sky

very cloudy sky · overcast sky · obscured sky

wind

station circle · calm · wind arrow

shaft · half barb · barb · pennant

wind scale · 1-2 knots · 5 knots · 10 knots · 50 knots

wind speed in knots

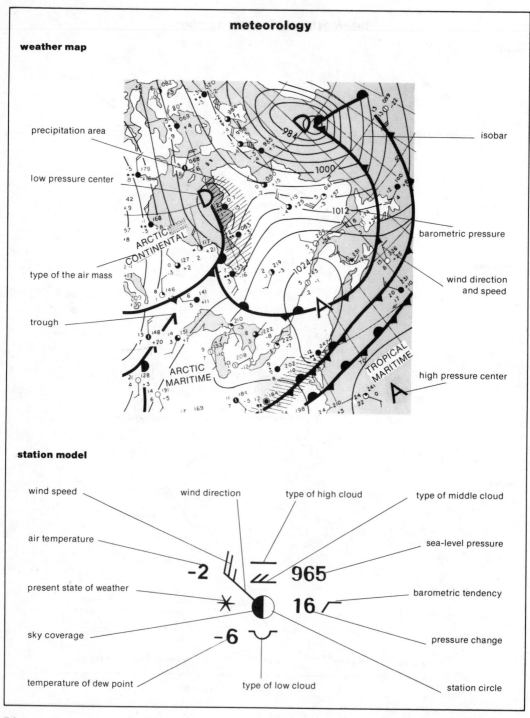

meteorology

weather map

- precipitation area
- low pressure center
- type of the air mass
- trough

ARCTIC CONTINENTAL

ARCTIC MARITIME

TROPICAL MARITIME

- isobar
- barometric pressure
- wind direction and speed
- high pressure center

station model

- wind speed
- air temperature
- present state of weather
- sky coverage
- temperature of dew point
- wind direction
- type of high cloud
- type of low cloud
- type of middle cloud
- sea-level pressure
- barometric tendency
- pressure change
- station circle

-2   965

16

-6

meteorology

meteorological ground

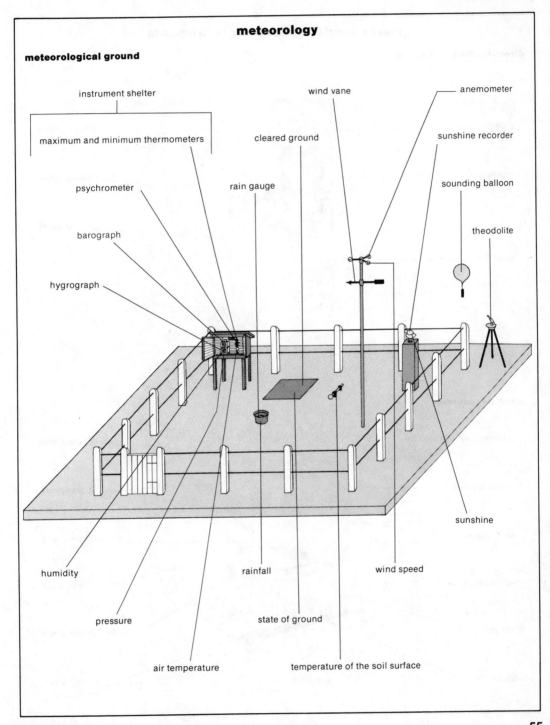

instrument shelter

wind vane

anemometer

maximum and minimum thermometers

cleared ground

sunshine recorder

psychrometer

rain gauge

sounding balloon

barograph

theodolite

hygrograph

humidity

rainfall

wind speed

sunshine

pressure

state of ground

air temperature

temperature of the soil surface

meteorological measuring instruments

direct-reading rain gauge

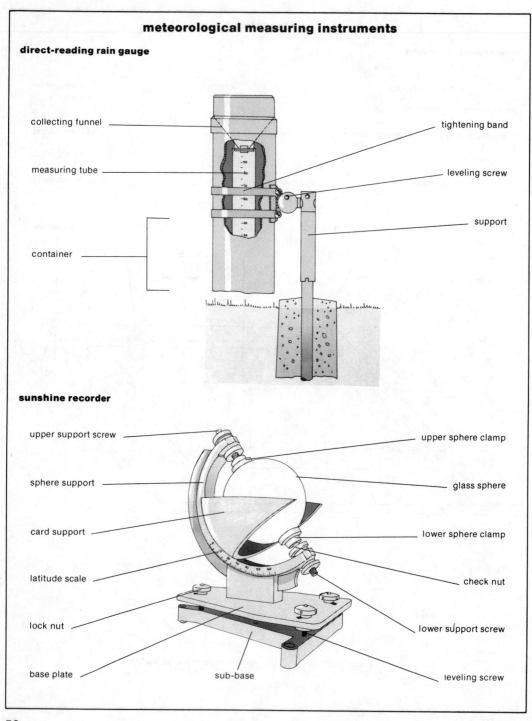

collecting funnel

measuring tube

container

tightening band

leveling screw

support

sunshine recorder

upper support screw

sphere support

card support

latitude scale

lock nut

base plate

upper sphere clamp

glass sphere

lower sphere clamp

check nut

lower support screw

sub-base

leveling screw

NIMBUS III meteorological satellite

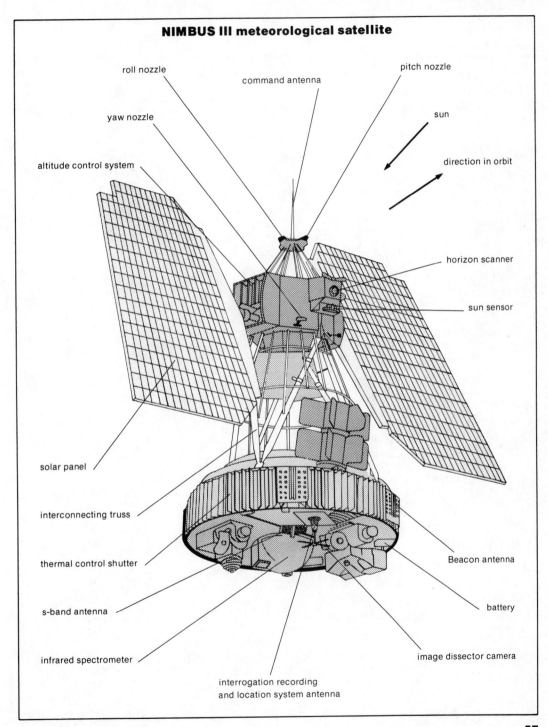

roll nozzle

command antenna

pitch nozzle

yaw nozzle

sun

altitude control system

direction in orbit

horizon scanner

sun sensor

solar panel

interconnecting truss

Beacon antenna

thermal control shutter

battery

s-band antenna

infrared spectrometer

image dissector camera

interrogation recording
and location system antenna

VEGETABLE KINGDOM

structure of a plant

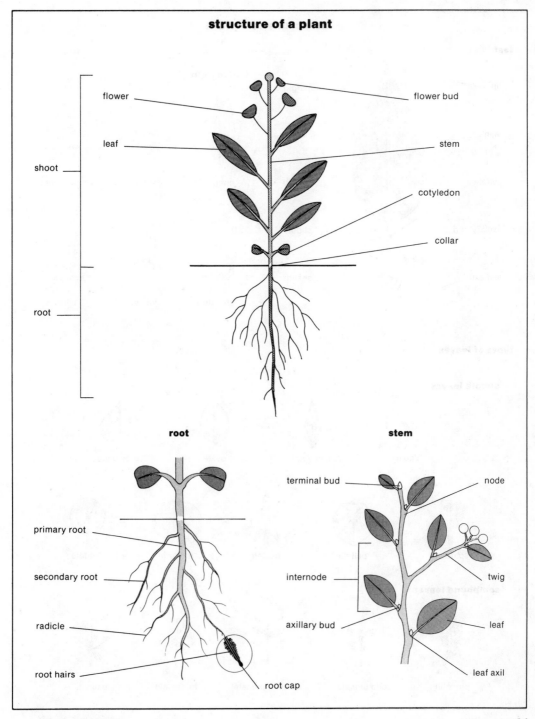

flower

flower bud

leaf

stem

shoot

cotyledon

collar

root

root

stem

primary root

terminal bud

node

secondary root

internode

twig

radicle

axillary bud

leaf

root hairs

leaf axil

root cap

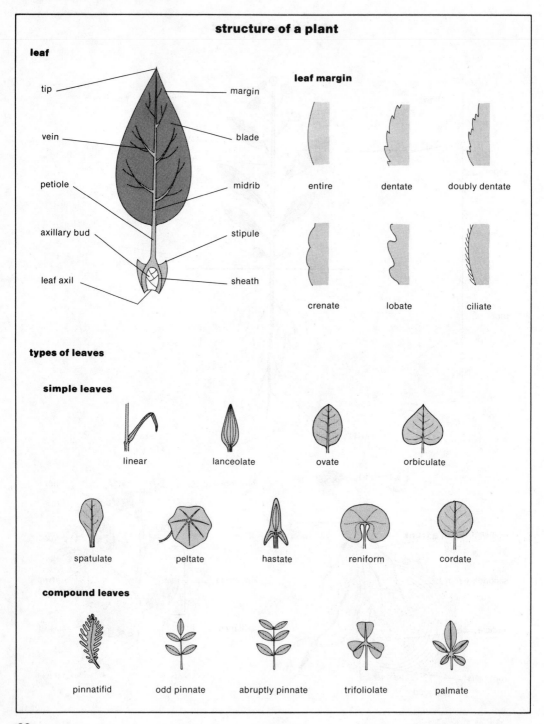

structure of a plant

leaf

tip • margin • vein • blade • petiole • midrib • axillary bud • stipule • leaf axil • sheath

leaf margin

entire • dentate • doubly dentate • crenate • lobate • ciliate

types of leaves

simple leaves

linear • lanceolate • ovate • orbiculate • spatulate • peltate • hastate • reniform • cordate

compound leaves

pinnatifid • odd pinnate • abruptly pinnate • trifoliolate • palmate

structure of a tree

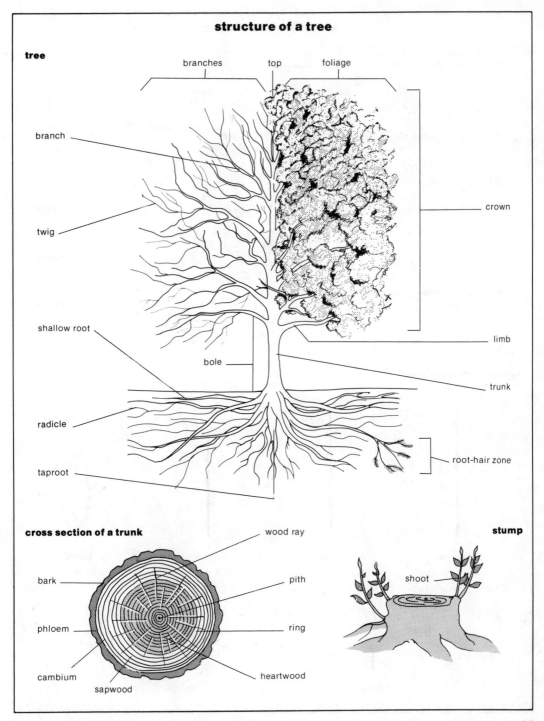

tree

branches   top   foliage

branch

twig

crown

shallow root

limb

bole

trunk

radicle

root-hair zone

taproot

cross section of a trunk

wood ray

stump

bark

pith

shoot

phloem

ring

cambium

heartwood

sapwood

VEGETABLE KINGDOM

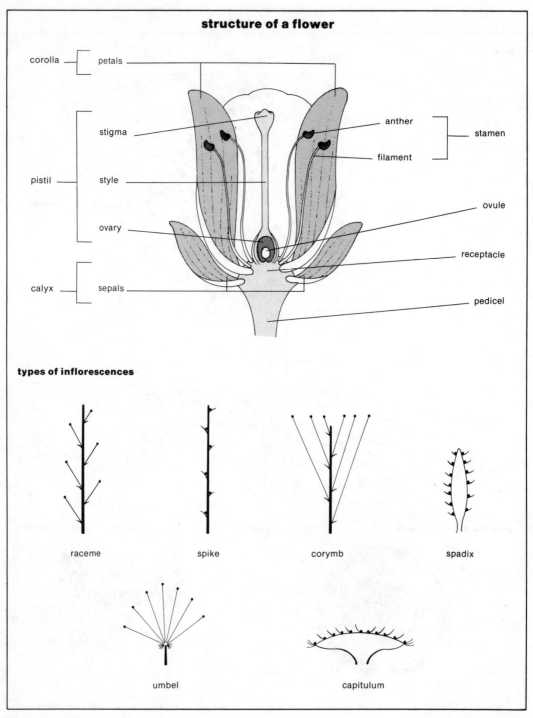

structure of a flower

corolla — petals

pistil

stigma

anther

stamen

style

filament

ovary

ovule

receptacle

calyx — sepals

pedicel

types of inflorescences

raceme

spike

corymb

spadix

umbel

capitulum

mushrooms

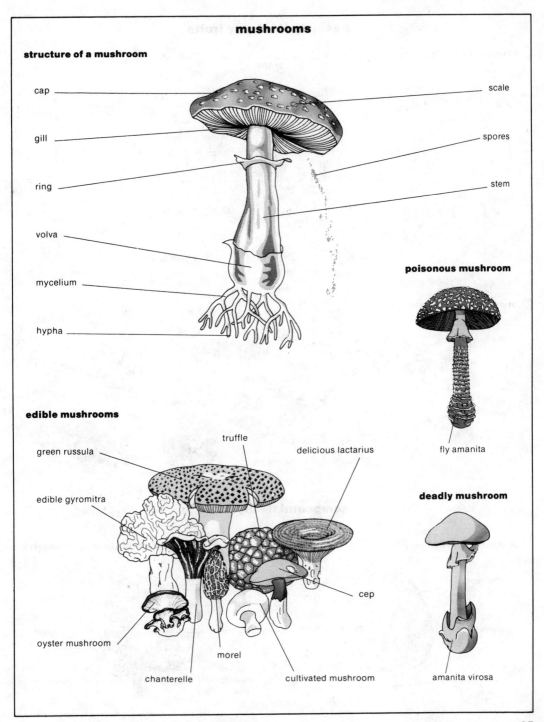

structure of a mushroom

cap

gill

ring

volva

mycelium

hypha

scale

spores

stem

poisonous mushroom

fly amanita

edible mushrooms

truffle

green russula

delicious lactarius

edible gyromitra

cep

oyster mushroom

morel

chanterelle

cultivated mushroom

deadly mushroom

amanita virosa

fleshy fruits : berry fruits

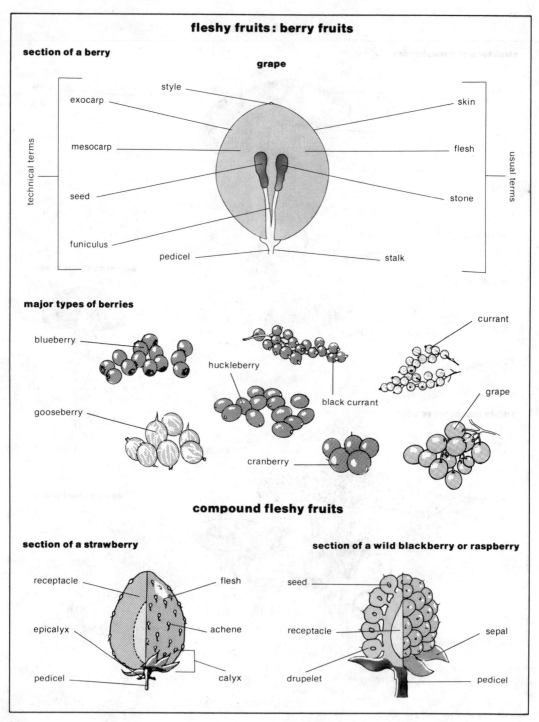

section of a berry

grape

technical terms

- style
- exocarp
- mesocarp
- seed
- funiculus
- pedicel

usual terms

- skin
- flesh
- stone
- stalk

major types of berries

- blueberry
- huckleberry
- black currant
- currant
- gooseberry
- cranberry
- grape

compound fleshy fruits

section of a strawberry

- receptacle
- flesh
- epicalyx
- achene
- pedicel
- calyx

section of a wild blackberry or raspberry

- seed
- receptacle
- sepal
- drupelet
- pedicel

stone fleshy fruits

section of a stone fruit

peach

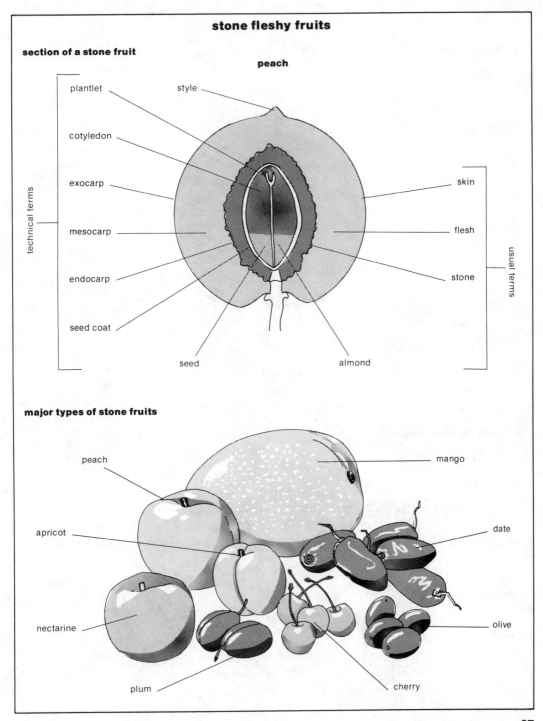

technical terms

plantlet

cotyledon

exocarp

mesocarp

endocarp

seed coat

style

skin

flesh

stone

usual terms

seed

almond

major types of stone fruits

peach

apricot

nectarine

plum

mango

date

olive

cherry

VEGETABLE KINGDOM

pome fleshy fruits

section of a pome fruit

apple

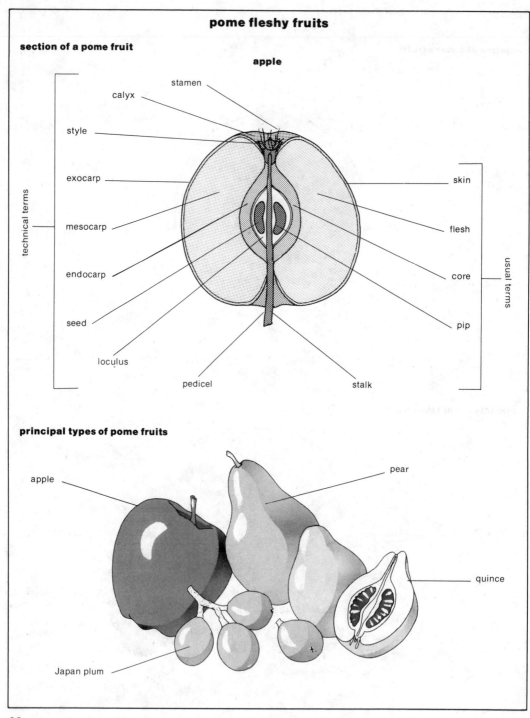

technical terms

- calyx
- stamen
- style
- exocarp
- mesocarp
- endocarp
- seed
- loculus
- pedicel

usual terms

- skin
- flesh
- core
- pip
- stalk

principal types of pome fruits

- apple
- pear
- quince
- Japan plum

fleshy fruits: citrus fruits

section of a citrus fruit

orange

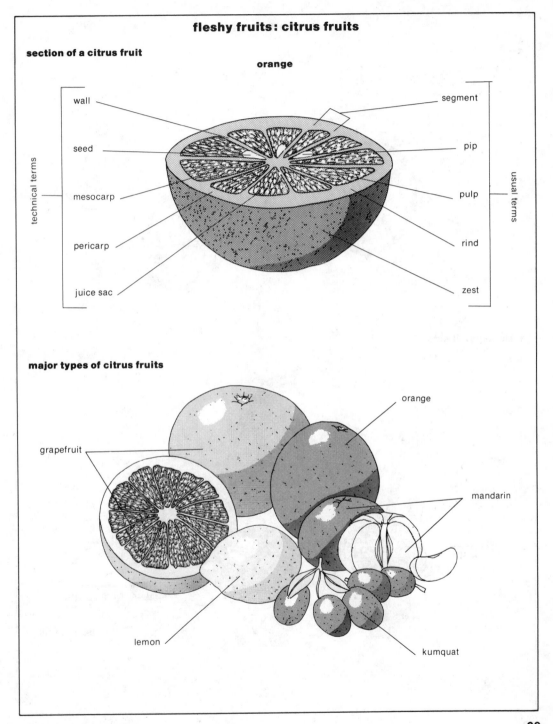

technical terms

wall
seed
mesocarp
pericarp
juice sac

usual terms

segment
pip
pulp
rind
zest

major types of citrus fruits

orange
grapefruit
mandarin
lemon
kumquat

dry fruits : nuts

section of a hazelnut

section of a walnut

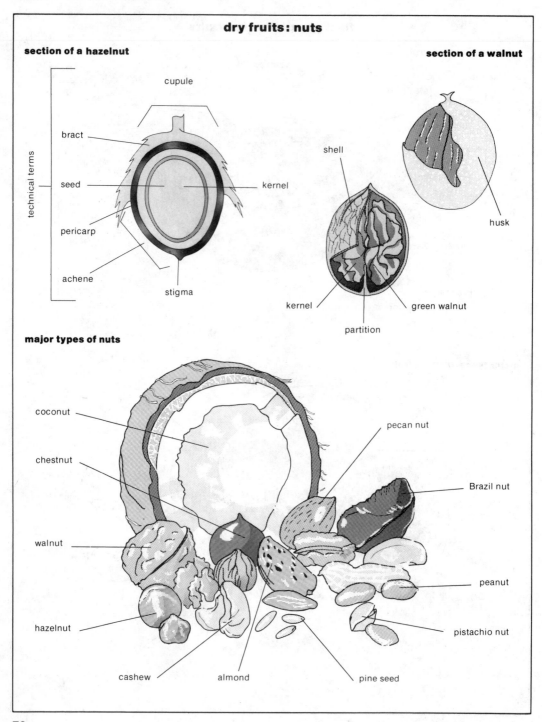

technical terms

- cupule
- bract
- seed
- pericarp
- achene
- stigma
- kernel

- shell
- husk
- kernel
- partition
- green walnut

major types of nuts

- coconut
- chestnut
- walnut
- hazelnut
- cashew
- almond
- pine seed
- pecan nut
- Brazil nut
- peanut
- pistachio nut

various dry fruits

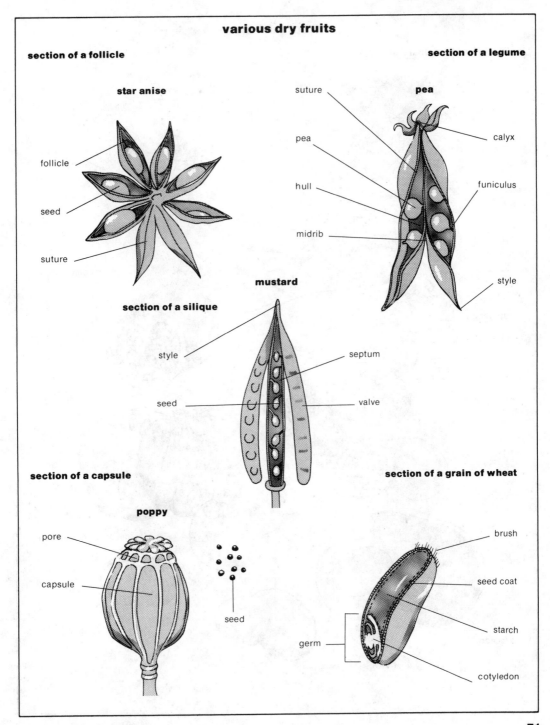

section of a follicle

star anise

follicle

seed

suture

section of a legume

pea

suture

pea

hull

midrib

calyx

funiculus

style

mustard

section of a silique

style

seed

septum

valve

section of a capsule

poppy

pore

capsule

seed

section of a grain of wheat

brush

seed coat

starch

germ

cotyledon

VEGETABLE KINGDOM

tropical fruits

major types of tropical fruits

pineapple

banana

pomegranate

papaya

Indian fig

cherimoya

guava

Japanese persimmon

avocado

litchi

kiwi

vegetables

fruit vegetables

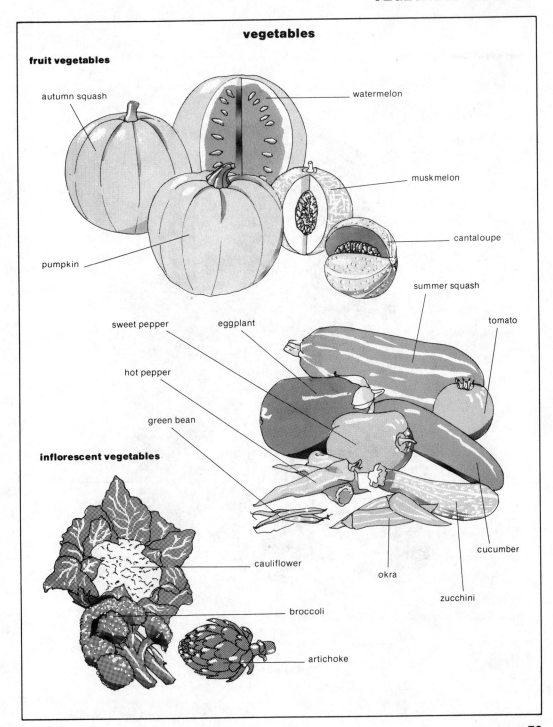

autumn squash

watermelon

muskmelon

cantaloupe

pumpkin

summer squash

sweet pepper

eggplant

tomato

hot pepper

green bean

inflorescent vegetables

cauliflower

okra

cucumber

zucchini

broccoli

artichoke

vegetables

leaf vegetables

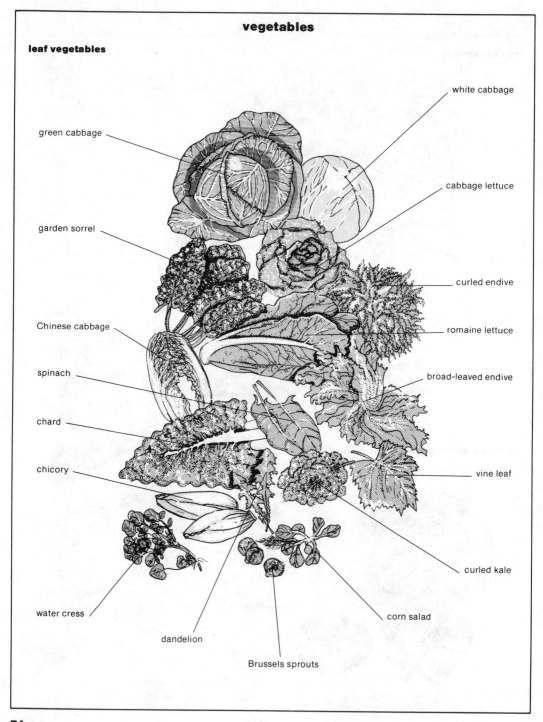

white cabbage

green cabbage

cabbage lettuce

garden sorrel

curled endive

Chinese cabbage

romaine lettuce

spinach

broad-leaved endive

chard

chicory

vine leaf

curled kale

water cress

corn salad

dandelion

Brussels sprouts

vegetables

section of a bulb

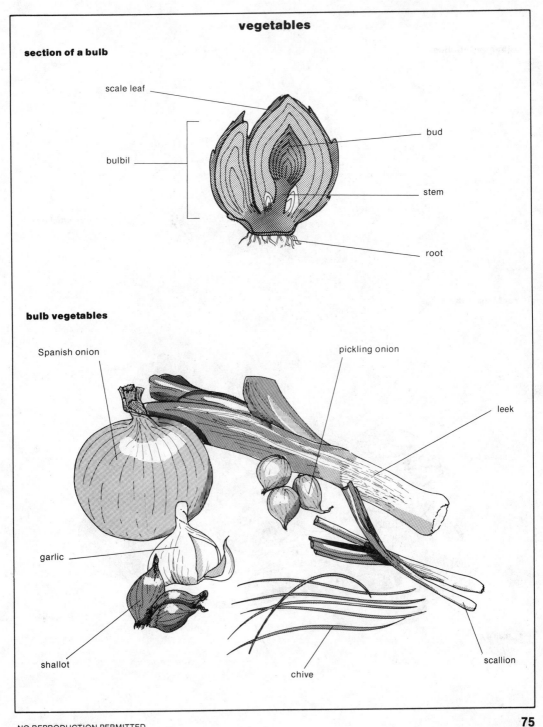

scale leaf

bud

bulbil

stem

root

bulb vegetables

Spanish onion

pickling onion

leek

garlic

shallot

chive

scallion

VEGETABLE KINGDOM

vegetables

tuber vegetables

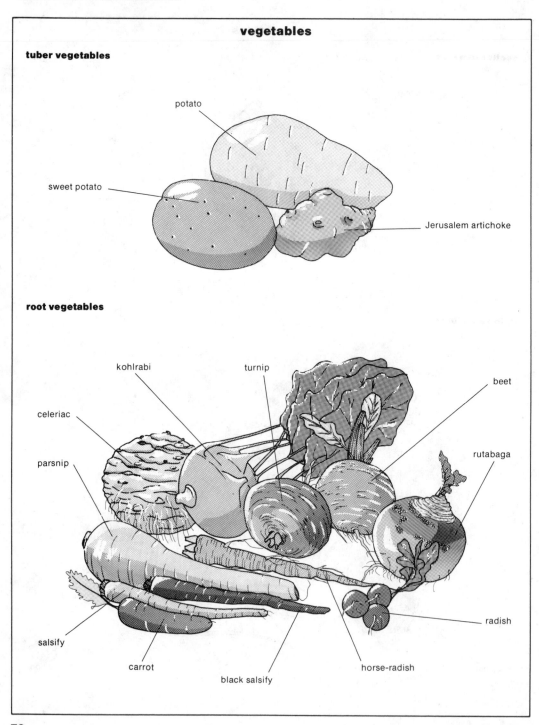

potato

sweet potato

Jerusalem artichoke

root vegetables

kohlrabi

turnip

beet

celeriac

rutabaga

parsnip

salsify

carrot

black salsify

horse-radish

radish

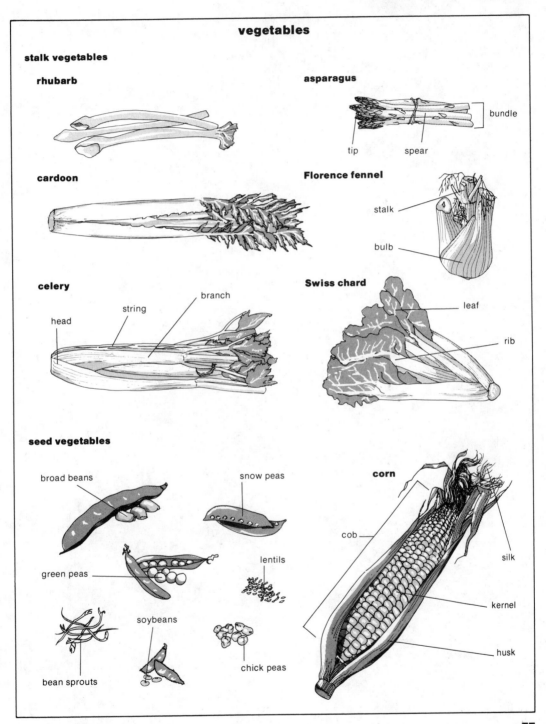

vegetables

stalk vegetables

rhubarb

asparagus

bundle

tip   spear

cardoon

Florence fennel

stalk

bulb

celery

branch

string

head

Swiss chard

leaf

rib

seed vegetables

broad beans

snow peas

corn

cob

silk

green peas

lentils

kernel

bean sprouts

soybeans

chick peas

husk

ANIMAL KINGDOM

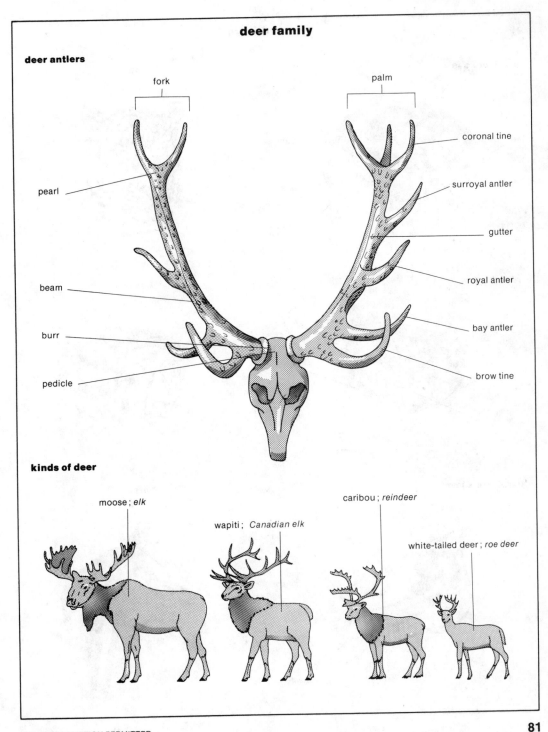

deer family

deer antlers

fork

palm

coronal tine

pearl

surroyal antler

gutter

beam

royal antler

burr

bay antler

pedicle

brow tine

kinds of deer

moose ; *elk*

caribou ; *reindeer*

wapiti ; *Canadian elk*

white-tailed deer ; *roe deer*

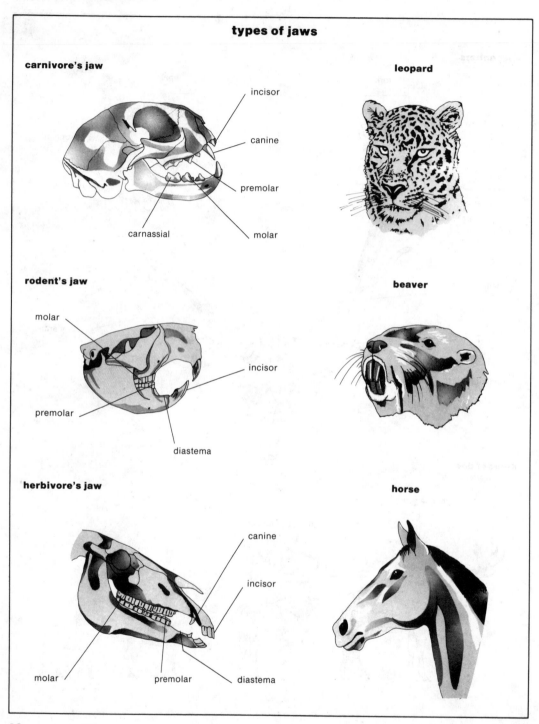

types of jaws

carnivore's jaw

incisor

canine

premolar

carnassial

molar

leopard

rodent's jaw

molar

premolar

incisor

diastema

beaver

herbivore's jaw

canine

incisor

molar

premolar

diastema

horse

horse

morphology

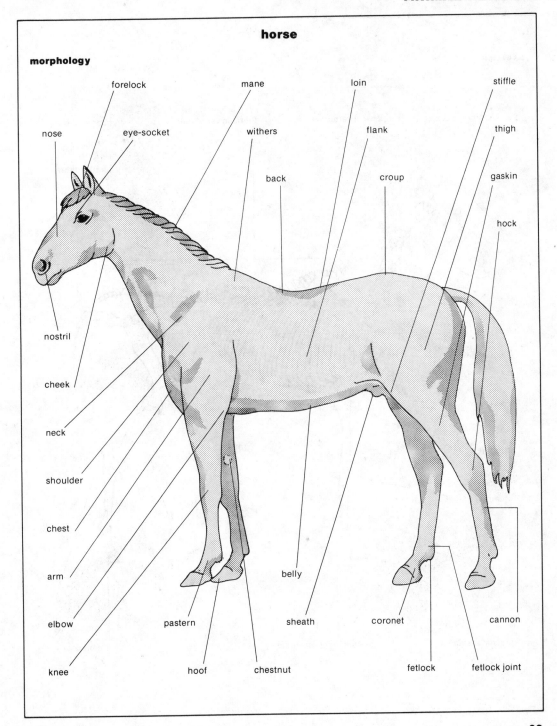

forelock

mane

loin

stiffle

nose

eye-socket

withers

flank

thigh

back

croup

gaskin

hock

nostril

cheek

neck

shoulder

chest

arm

belly

elbow

pastern

sheath

coronet

cannon

knee

hoof

chestnut

fetlock

fetlock joint

horse

skeleton

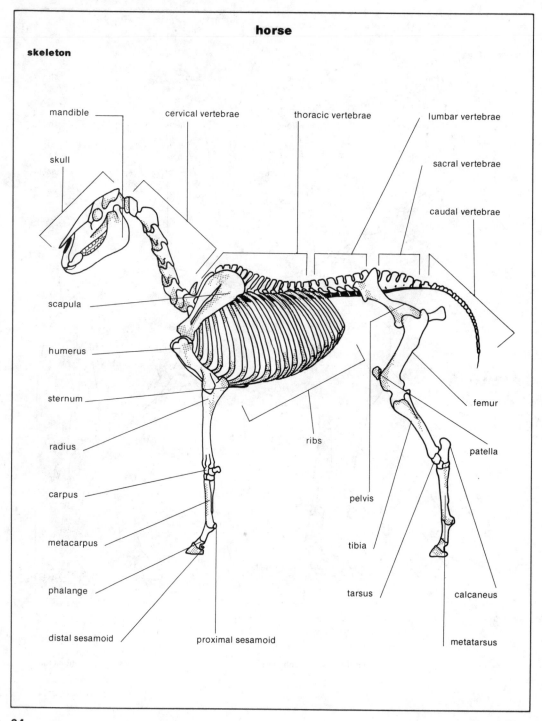

mandible

cervical vertebrae

thoracic vertebrae

lumbar vertebrae

skull

sacral vertebrae

caudal vertebrae

scapula

humerus

sternum

femur

radius

ribs

patella

carpus

metacarpus

pelvis

phalange

tibia

distal sesamoid

proximal sesamoid

tarsus

calcaneus

metatarsus

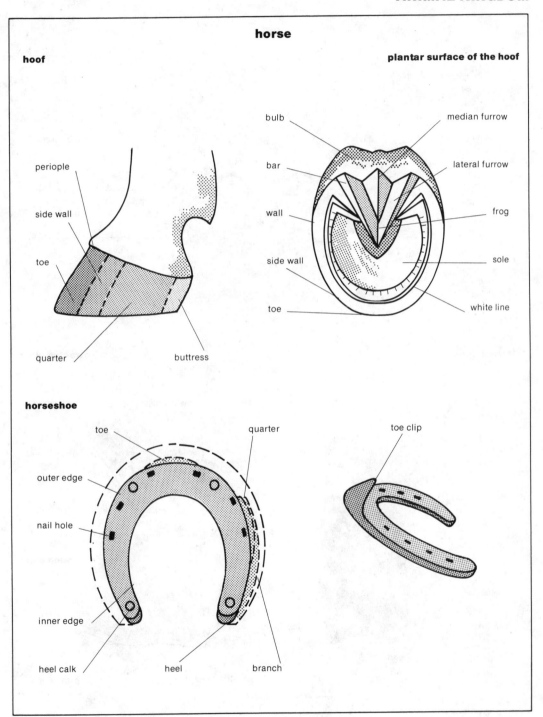

horse

hoof

plantar surface of the hoof

periople

side wall

toe

quarter

buttress

bulb

bar

wall

side wall

toe

median furrow

lateral furrow

frog

sole

white line

horseshoe

toe

quarter

toe clip

outer edge

nail hole

inner edge

heel calk

heel

branch

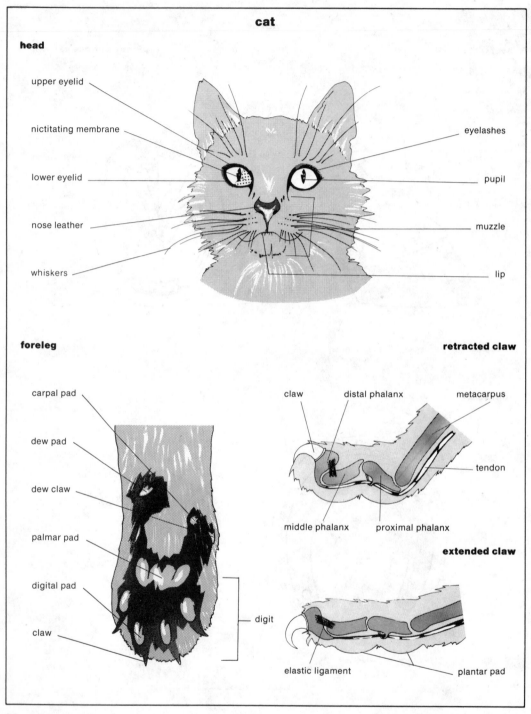

cat

head

upper eyelid

nictitating membrane

lower eyelid

nose leather

whiskers

eyelashes

pupil

muzzle

lip

foreleg

carpal pad

dew pad

dew claw

palmar pad

digital pad

claw

digit

retracted claw

claw

distal phalanx

metacarpus

tendon

middle phalanx

proximal phalanx

extended claw

elastic ligament

plantar pad

bird

morphology

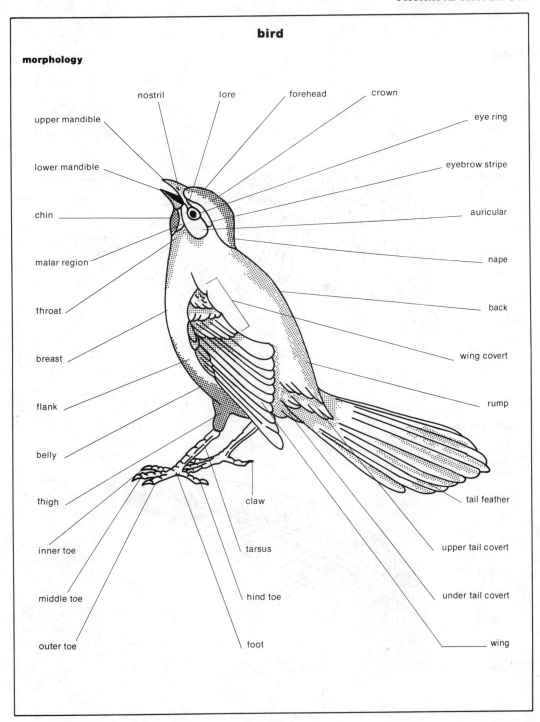

nostril

lore

forehead

crown

upper mandible

eye ring

lower mandible

eyebrow stripe

chin

auricular

malar region

nape

throat

back

breast

wing covert

flank

rump

belly

thigh

claw

inner toe

tarsus

tail feather

middle toe

hind toe

upper tail covert

outer toe

foot

under tail covert

wing

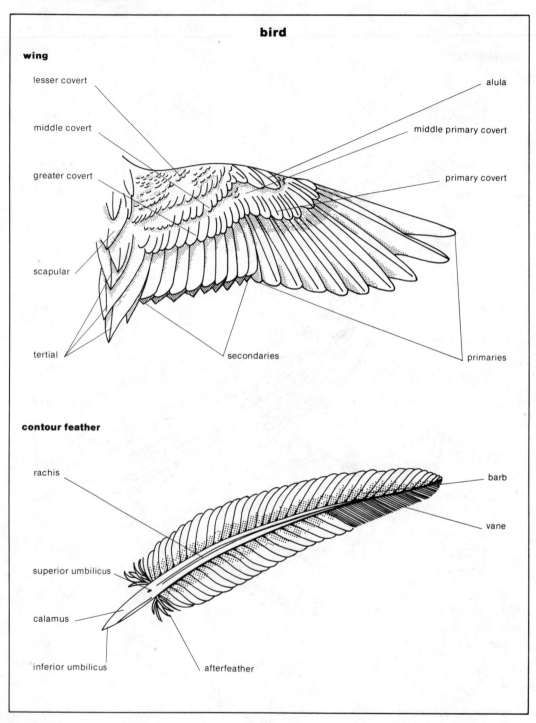

bird

wing

lesser covert

alula

middle covert

middle primary covert

greater covert

primary covert

scapular

tertial

secondaries

primaries

contour feather

rachis

barb

vane

superior umbilicus

calamus

inferior umbilicus

afterfeather

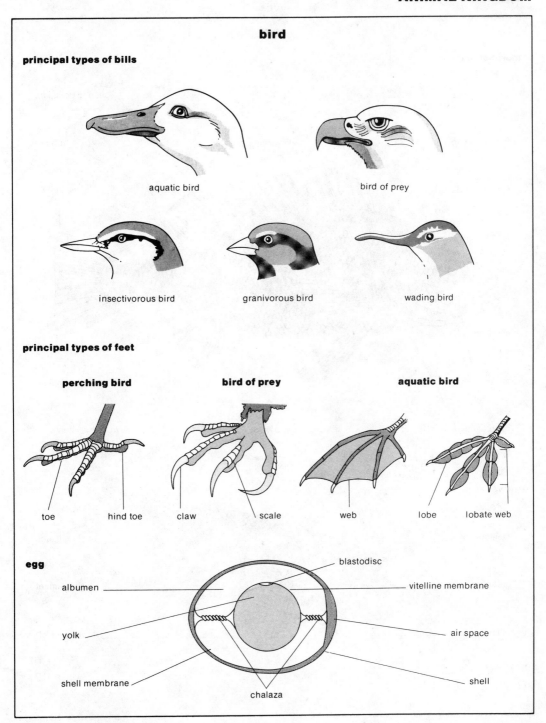

bird

principal types of bills

aquatic bird

bird of prey

insectivorous bird

granivorous bird

wading bird

principal types of feet

perching bird

bird of prey

aquatic bird

toe

hind toe

claw

scale

web

lobe

lobate web

egg

albumen

blastodisc

vitelline membrane

yolk

air space

shell membrane

chalaza

shell

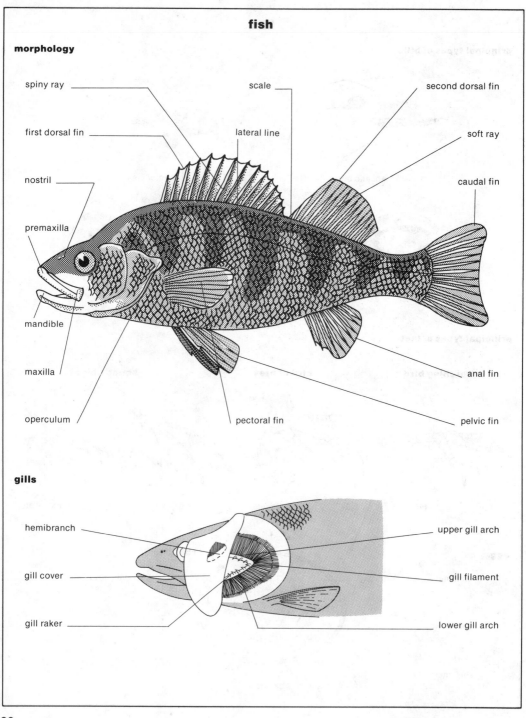

fish

morphology

spiny ray

first dorsal fin

nostril

premaxilla

mandible

maxilla

operculum

scale

lateral line

pectoral fin

second dorsal fin

soft ray

caudal fin

anal fin

pelvic fin

gills

hemibranch

gill cover

gill raker

upper gill arch

gill filament

lower gill arch

fish

anatomy

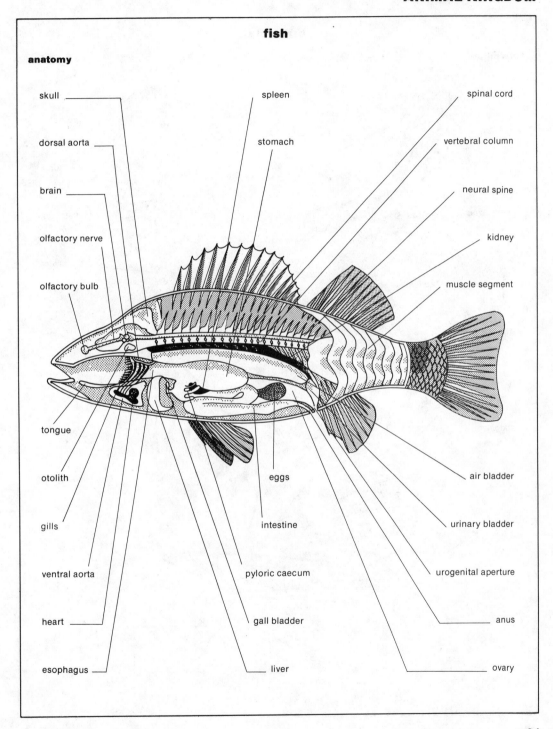

skull

dorsal aorta

brain

olfactory nerve

olfactory bulb

tongue

otolith

gills

ventral aorta

heart

esophagus

spleen

stomach

eggs

intestine

pyloric caecum

gall bladder

liver

spinal cord

vertebral column

neural spine

kidney

muscle segment

air bladder

urinary bladder

urogenital aperture

anus

ovary

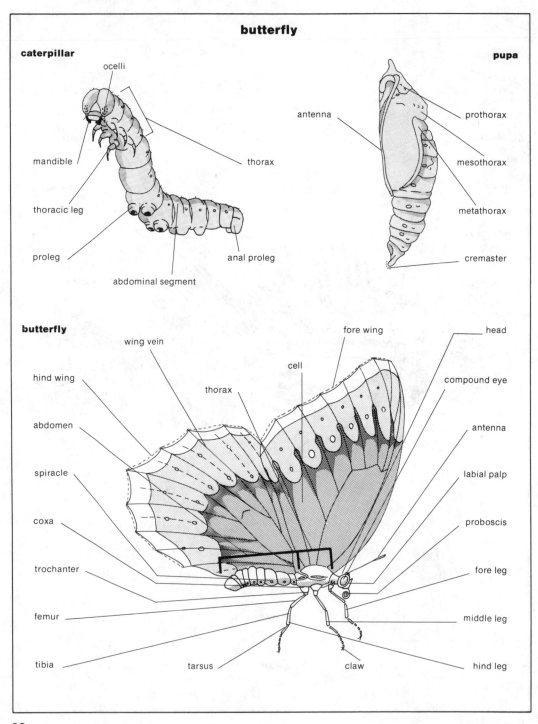

butterfly

caterpillar

ocelli

thorax

mandible

thoracic leg

proleg

anal proleg

abdominal segment

pupa

antenna

prothorax

mesothorax

metathorax

cremaster

butterfly

wing vein

fore wing

head

cell

compound eye

hind wing

thorax

antenna

abdomen

labial palp

spiracle

proboscis

coxa

trochanter

fore leg

femur

middle leg

tibia

tarsus

claw

hind leg

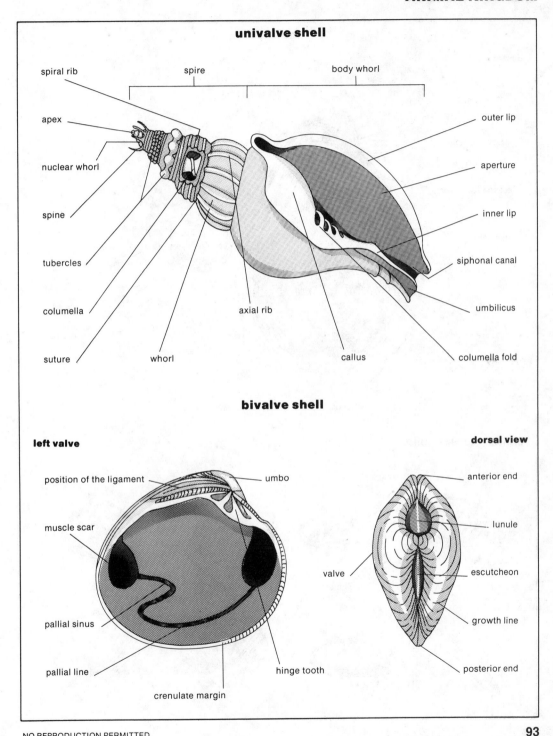

univalve shell

spiral rib

spire

body whorl

apex

outer lip

nuclear whorl

aperture

spine

inner lip

tubercles

siphonal canal

columella

axial rib

umbilicus

suture

whorl

callus

columella fold

bivalve shell

left valve

dorsal view

position of the ligament

umbo

anterior end

muscle scar

lunule

valve

escutcheon

pallial sinus

growth line

pallial line

hinge tooth

posterior end

crenulate margin

mollusk

oyster

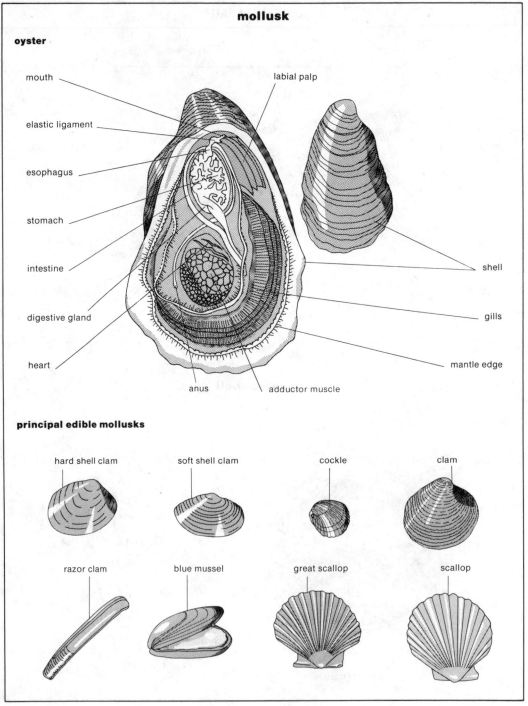

mouth

labial palp

elastic ligament

esophagus

stomach

intestine

digestive gland

heart

anus

adductor muscle

shell

gills

mantle edge

principal edible mollusks

hard shell clam

soft shell clam

cockle

clam

razor clam

blue mussel

great scallop

scallop

crustacean

lobster

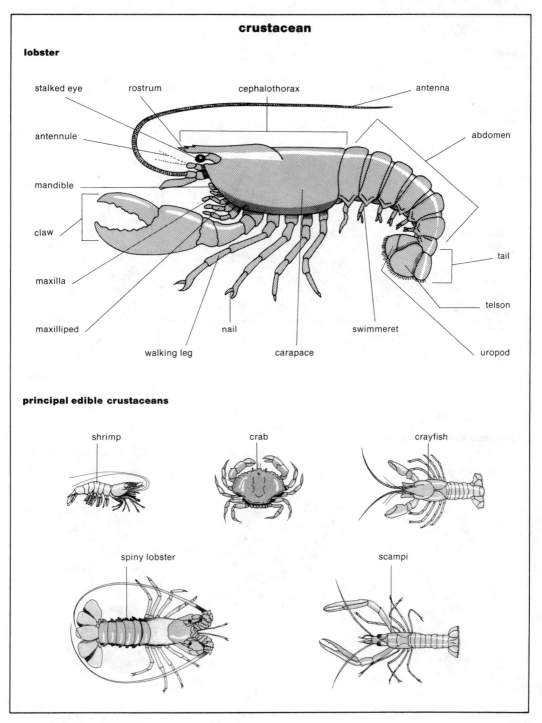

stalked eye

rostrum

cephalothorax

antenna

antennule

abdomen

mandible

claw

maxilla

tail

maxilliped

telson

nail

swimmeret

uropod

walking leg

carapace

principal edible crustaceans

shrimp

crab

crayfish

spiny lobster

scampi

gastropod

snail

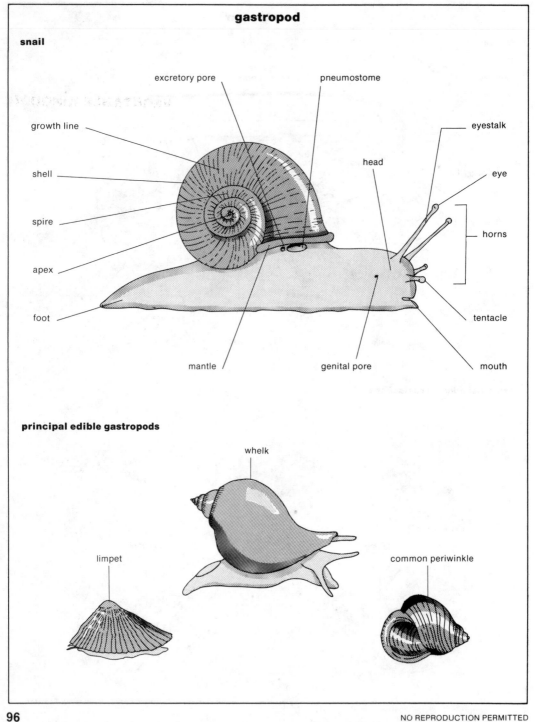

excretory pore

pneumostome

growth line

eyestalk

head

eye

shell

spire

horns

apex

tentacle

foot

mantle

genital pore

mouth

principal edible gastropods

whelk

limpet

common periwinkle

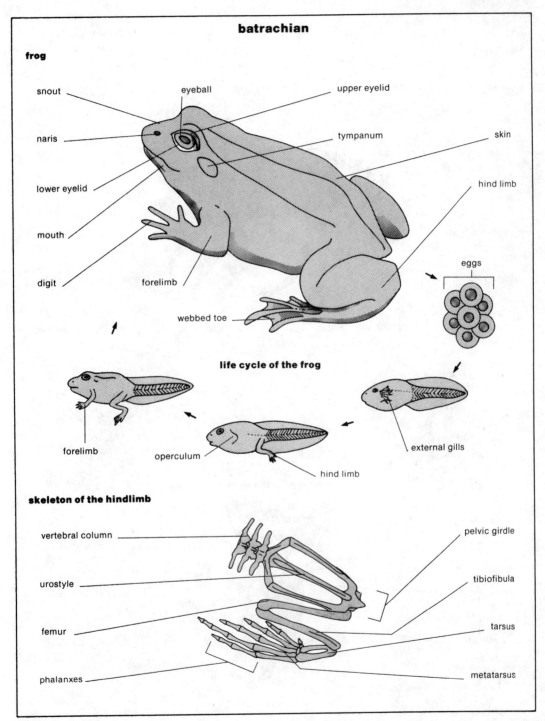

batrachian

frog

snout

eyeball

upper eyelid

naris

tympanum

skin

lower eyelid

hind limb

mouth

eggs

digit

forelimb

webbed toe

life cycle of the frog

external gills

forelimb

operculum

hind limb

skeleton of the hindlimb

vertebral column

pelvic girdle

urostyle

tibiofibula

femur

tarsus

phalanxes

metatarsus

ANIMAL KINGDOM

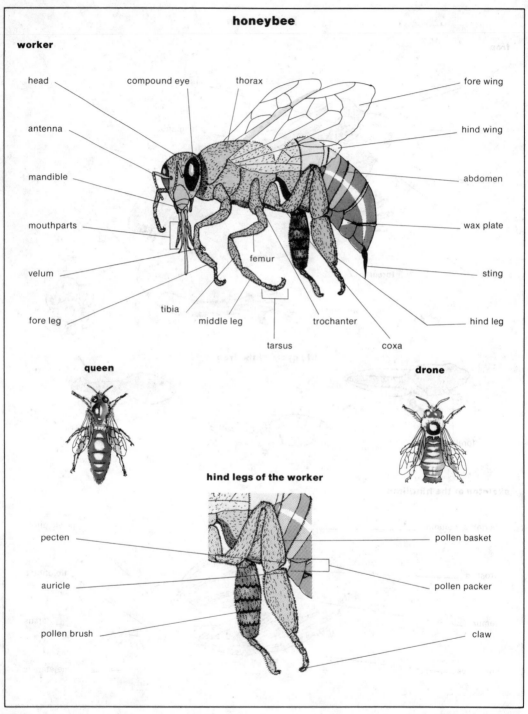

honeybee

worker

head
compound eye
thorax
fore wing
antenna
hind wing
mandible
abdomen
mouthparts
wax plate
velum
femur
sting
fore leg
tibia
middle leg
trochanter
hind leg
tarsus
coxa

queen

drone

hind legs of the worker

pecten
pollen basket
auricle
pollen packer
pollen brush
claw

honeybee

hive

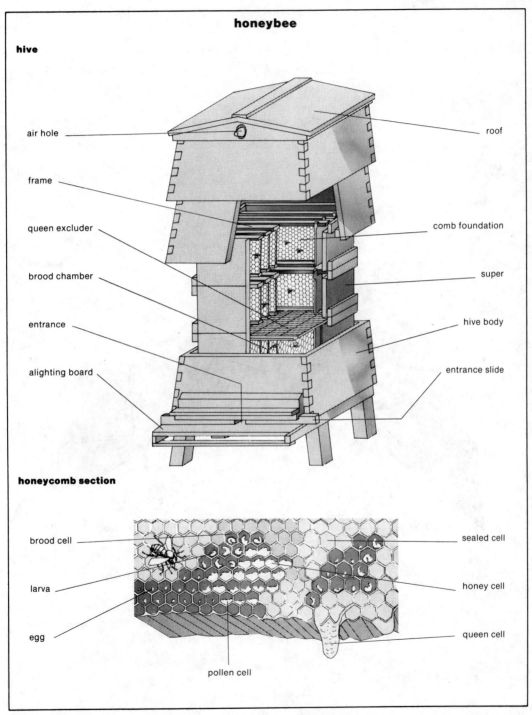

air hole — roof

frame

queen excluder — comb foundation

brood chamber — super

entrance — hive body

alighting board — entrance slide

honeycomb section

brood cell — sealed cell

larva — honey cell

egg — queen cell

pollen cell

bat

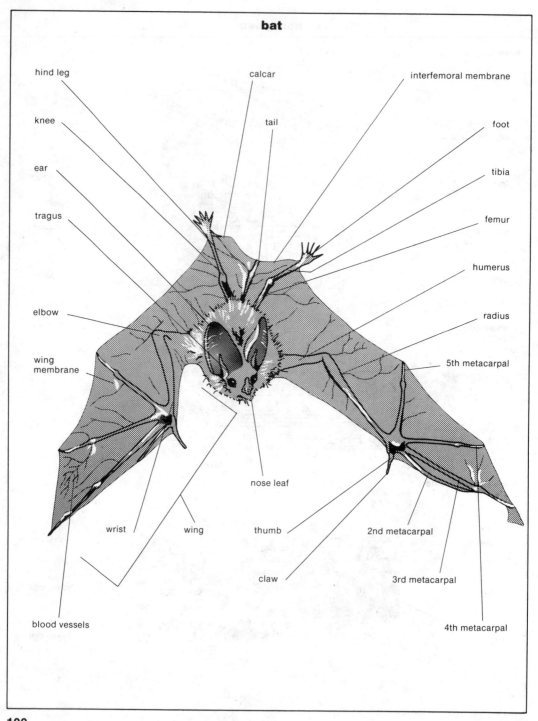

hind leg

calcar

interfemoral membrane

knee

tail

foot

ear

tibia

tragus

femur

humerus

elbow

radius

wing
membrane

5th metacarpal

nose leaf

wrist

wing

thumb

2nd metacarpal

claw

3rd metacarpal

blood vessels

4th metacarpal

reptile

venomous snake's head

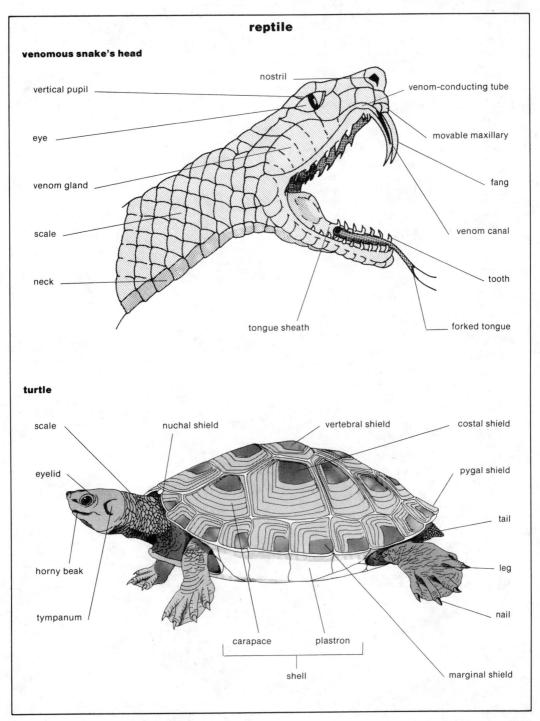

vertical pupil

nostril

venom-conducting tube

eye

movable maxillary

venom gland

fang

scale

venom canal

neck

tooth

tongue sheath

forked tongue

turtle

scale

nuchal shield

vertebral shield

costal shield

eyelid

pygal shield

tail

horny beak

leg

tympanum

nail

carapace

plastron

marginal shield

shell

HUMAN BEING

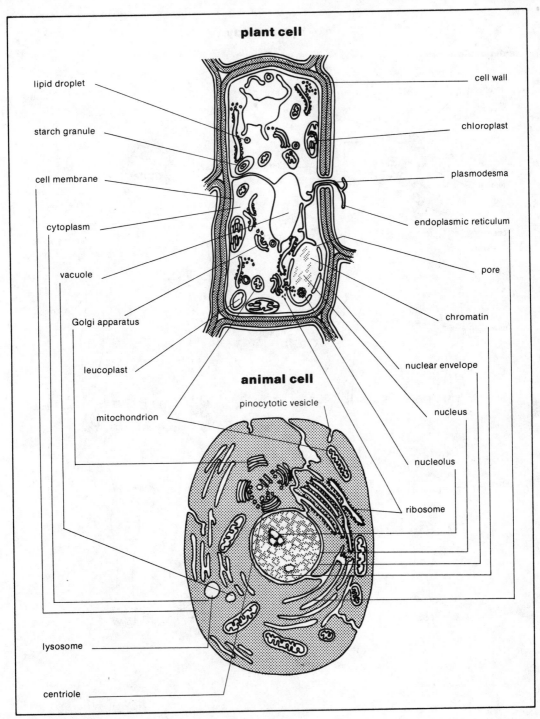

plant cell

lipid droplet

starch granule

cell membrane

cytoplasm

vacuole

Golgi apparatus

leucoplast

mitochondrion

cell wall

chloroplast

plasmodesma

endoplasmic reticulum

pore

chromatin

nuclear envelope

animal cell

pinocytotic vesicle

nucleus

nucleolus

ribosome

lysosome

centriole

human body

anterior view

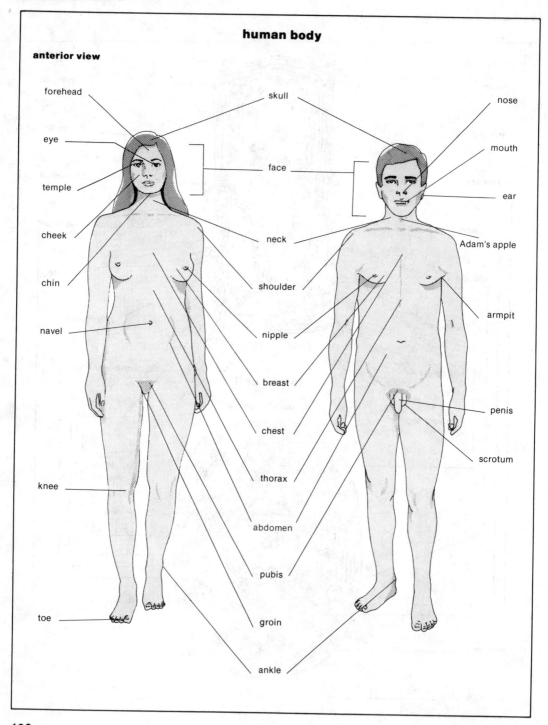

forehead

skull

nose

eye

mouth

temple

face

ear

cheek

Adam's apple

chin

neck

navel

shoulder

armpit

knee

nipple

breast

penis

scrotum

chest

toe

thorax

abdomen

pubis

groin

ankle

human body

posterior view

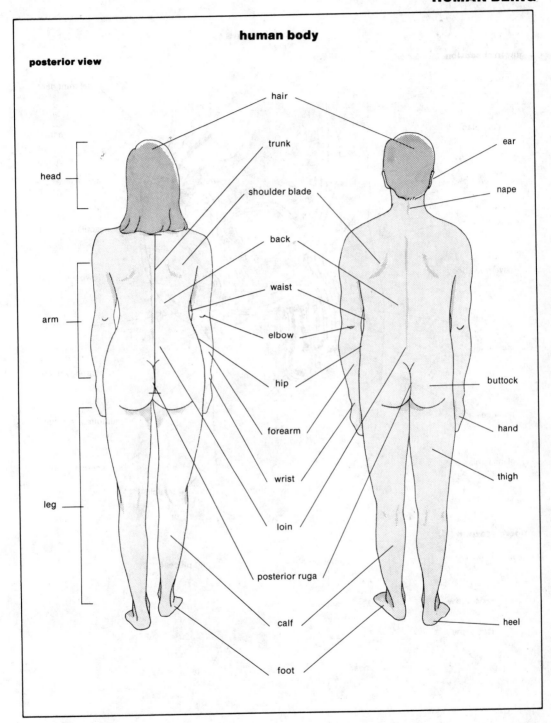

hair

trunk

shoulder blade

back

waist

elbow

hip

forearm

wrist

loin

posterior ruga

calf

foot

head

arm

leg

ear

nape

buttock

hand

thigh

heel

genital organs
male

sagittal section

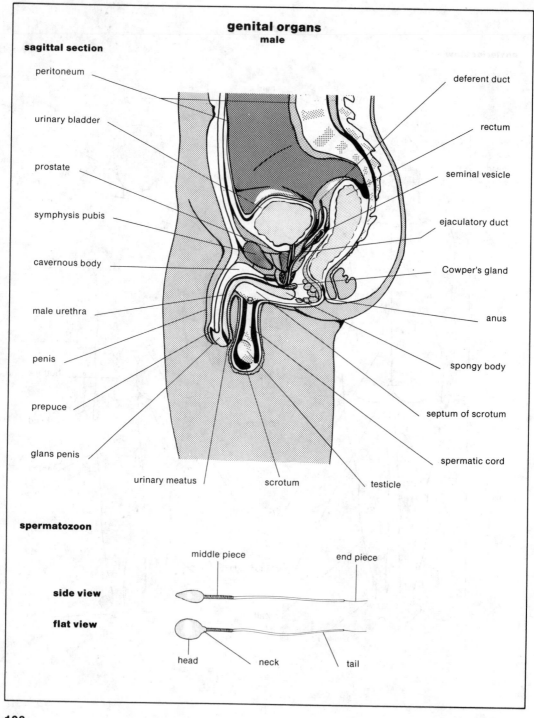

peritoneum

deferent duct

urinary bladder

rectum

prostate

seminal vesicle

symphysis pubis

ejaculatory duct

cavernous body

Cowper's gland

male urethra

anus

penis

spongy body

prepuce

septum of scrotum

glans penis

spermatic cord

urinary meatus

scrotum

testicle

spermatozoon

middle piece

end piece

side view

flat view

head

neck

tail

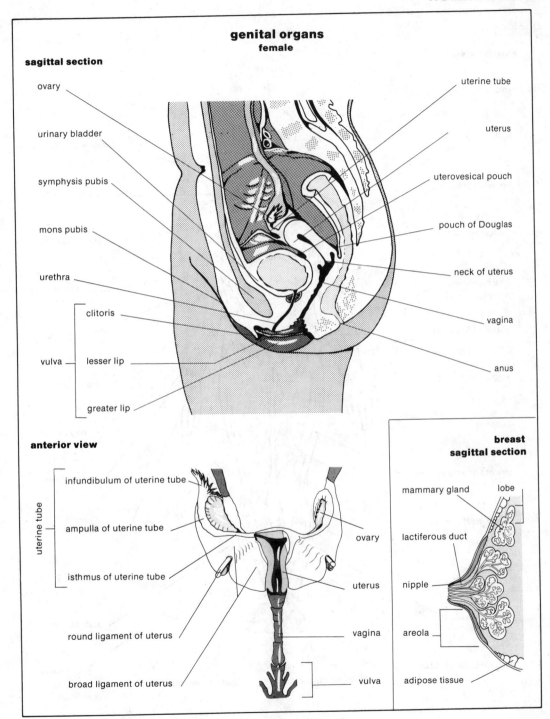

genital organs
female

sagittal section

ovary

urinary bladder

symphysis pubis

mons pubis

urethra

vulva {
  clitoris
  lesser lip
  greater lip
}

uterine tube

uterus

uterovesical pouch

pouch of Douglas

neck of uterus

vagina

anus

anterior view

uterine tube {
  infundibulum of uterine tube
  ampulla of uterine tube
  isthmus of uterine tube
}

round ligament of uterus

broad ligament of uterus

ovary

uterus

vagina

vulva

breast
sagittal section

mammary gland

lactiferous duct

nipple

areola

adipose tissue

lobe

muscles

anterior view

frontal

masseter

orbicular of eye

deltoid

sternocleidomastoid

external oblique

trapezius

abdominal rectus

greater pectoral

brachioradial

biceps of arm

tensor of fascia lata

brachial

long adductor

round pronator

sartorius

long palmar

straight muscle of thigh

short palmar

lateral great

ulnar flexor of wrist

anterior tibial

medial great

long peroneal

gastrocnemius

long extensor of toes

soleus

short extensor of toes

plantar interosseous

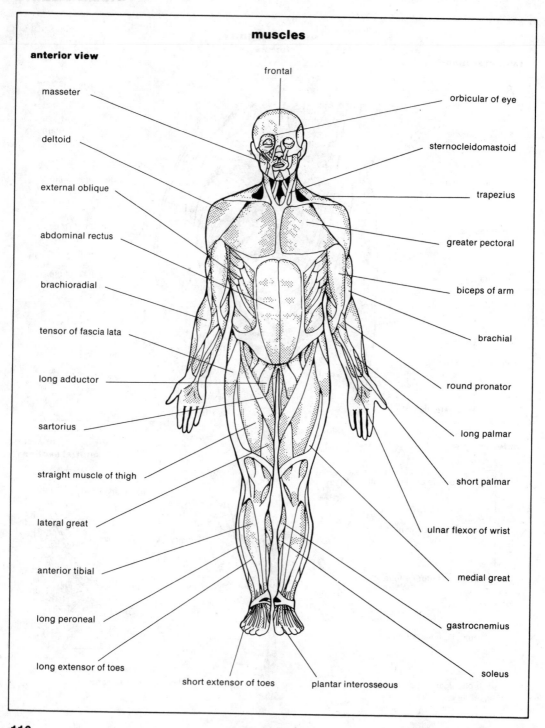

muscles

posterior view

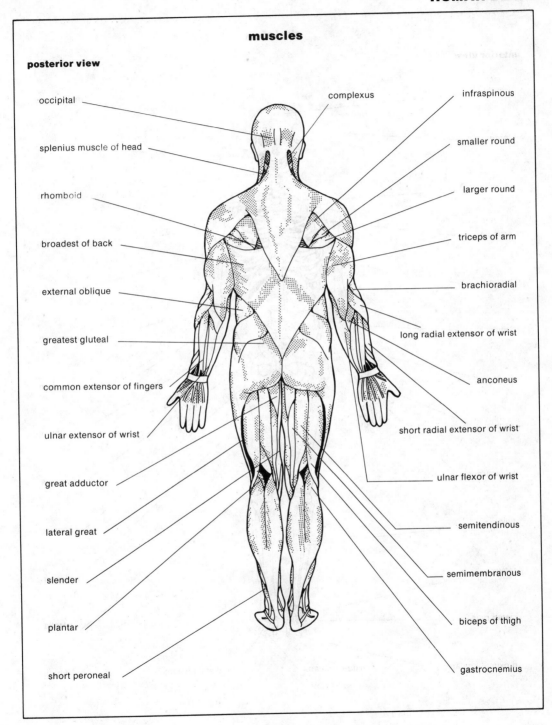

occipital

complexus

infraspinous

splenius muscle of head

smaller round

rhomboid

larger round

broadest of back

triceps of arm

external oblique

brachioradial

greatest gluteal

long radial extensor of wrist

common extensor of fingers

anconeus

ulnar extensor of wrist

short radial extensor of wrist

great adductor

ulnar flexor of wrist

lateral great

semitendinous

slender

semimembranous

plantar

biceps of thigh

short peroneal

gastrocnemius

skeleton

anterior view

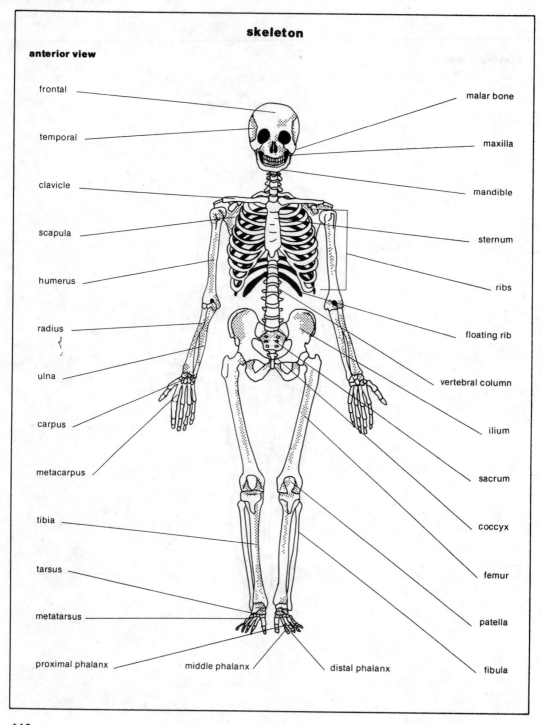

frontal

temporal

clavicle

scapula

humerus

radius

ulna

carpus

metacarpus

tibia

tarsus

metatarsus

proximal phalanx

malar bone

maxilla

mandible

sternum

ribs

floating rib

vertebral column

ilium

sacrum

coccyx

femur

patella

fibula

middle phalanx

distal phalanx

skeleton

posterior view

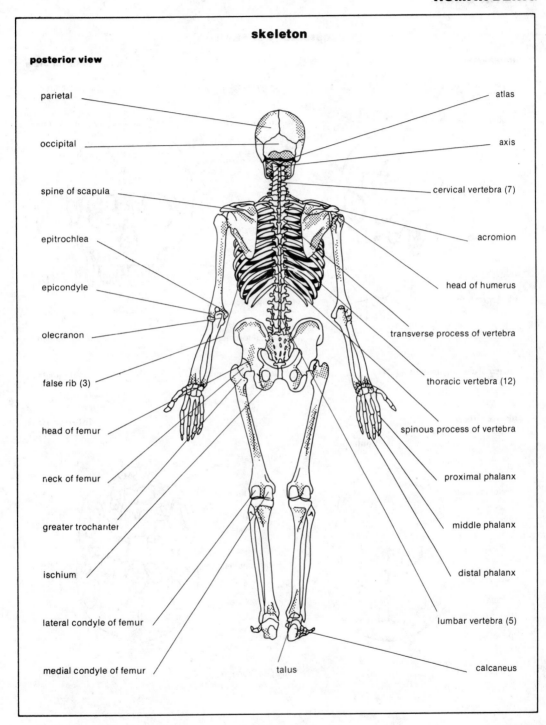

parietal

occipital

spine of scapula

epitrochlea

epicondyle

olecranon

false rib (3)

head of femur

neck of femur

greater trochanter

ischium

lateral condyle of femur

medial condyle of femur

talus

atlas

axis

cervical vertebra (7)

acromion

head of humerus

transverse process of vertebra

thoracic vertebra (12)

spinous process of vertebra

proximal phalanx

middle phalanx

distal phalanx

lumbar vertebra (5)

calcaneus

osteology of skull

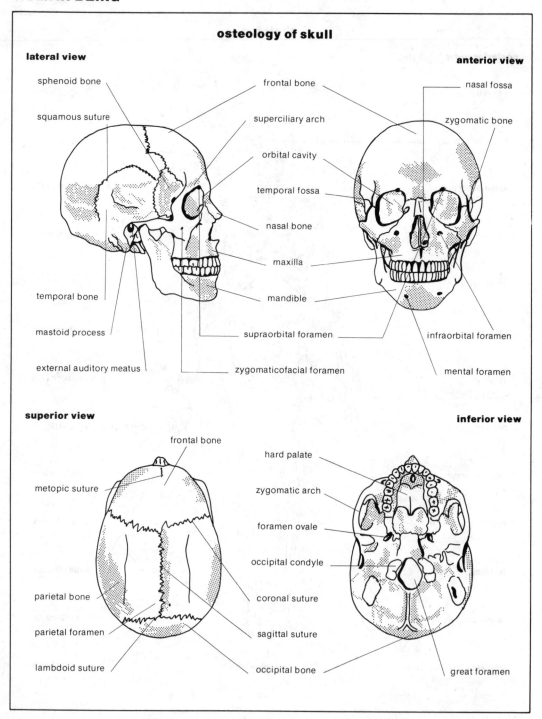

lateral view

- sphenoid bone
- squamous suture
- temporal bone
- mastoid process
- external auditory meatus

- frontal bone
- superciliary arch
- orbital cavity
- temporal fossa
- nasal bone
- maxilla
- mandible
- supraorbital foramen
- zygomaticofacial foramen

anterior view

- nasal fossa
- zygomatic bone
- infraorbital foramen
- mental foramen

superior view

- metopic suture
- parietal bone
- parietal foramen
- lambdoid suture

- frontal bone
- coronal suture
- sagittal suture
- occipital bone

inferior view

- hard palate
- zygomatic arch
- foramen ovale
- occipital condyle
- great foramen

teeth

cross section of a molar

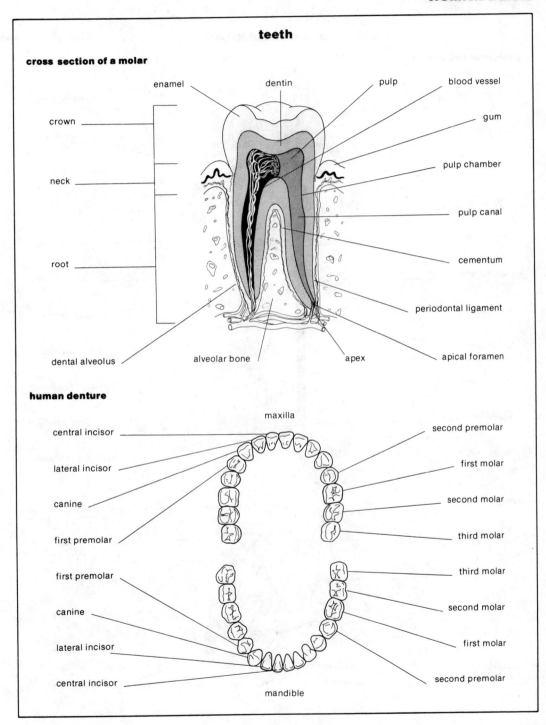

enamel
dentin
pulp
blood vessel
crown
gum
neck
pulp chamber
pulp canal
cementum
root
periodontal ligament
apical foramen
dental alveolus
alveolar bone
apex

human denture

maxilla

central incisor
second premolar

lateral incisor
first molar

canine
second molar

first premolar
third molar

first premolar
third molar

canine
second molar

lateral incisor
first molar

central incisor
second premolar

mandible

blood circulation

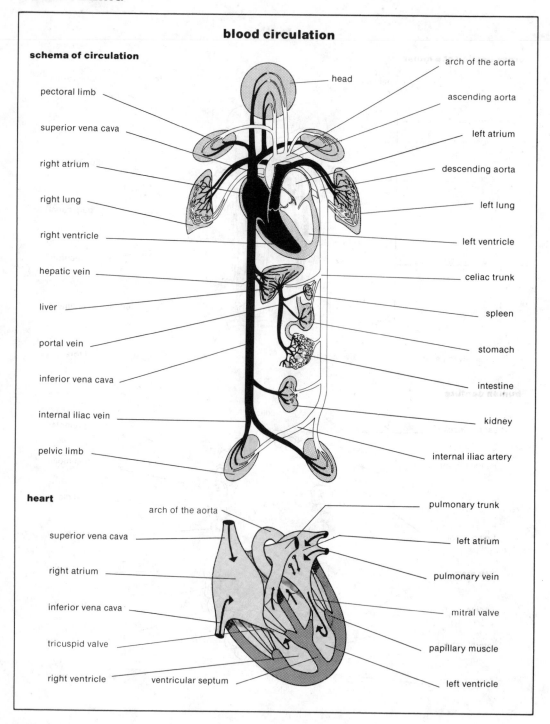

schema of circulation

pectoral limb

superior vena cava

right atrium

right lung

right ventricle

hepatic vein

liver

portal vein

inferior vena cava

internal iliac vein

pelvic limb

head

arch of the aorta

ascending aorta

left atrium

descending aorta

left lung

left ventricle

celiac trunk

spleen

stomach

intestine

kidney

internal iliac artery

heart

arch of the aorta

superior vena cava

right atrium

inferior vena cava

tricuspid valve

right ventricle

ventricular septum

pulmonary trunk

left atrium

pulmonary vein

mitral valve

papillary muscle

left ventricle

blood circulation

principal veins and arteries

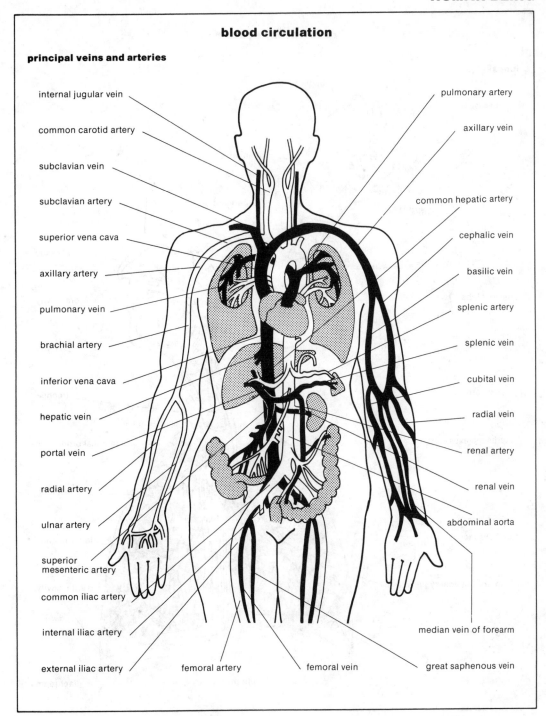

internal jugular vein

common carotid artery

subclavian vein

subclavian artery

superior vena cava

axillary artery

pulmonary vein

brachial artery

inferior vena cava

hepatic vein

portal vein

radial artery

ulnar artery

superior
mesenteric artery

common iliac artery

internal iliac artery

external iliac artery

femoral artery

femoral vein

pulmonary artery

axillary vein

common hepatic artery

cephalic vein

basilic vein

splenic artery

splenic vein

cubital vein

radial vein

renal artery

renal vein

abdominal aorta

median vein of forearm

great saphenous vein

respiratory system

lungs

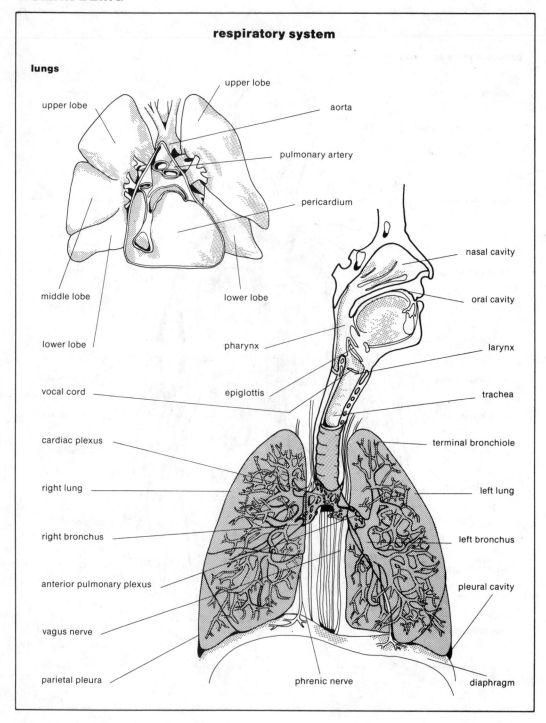

upper lobe

upper lobe

aorta

pulmonary artery

pericardium

nasal cavity

oral cavity

middle lobe

lower lobe

pharynx

larynx

lower lobe

vocal cord

epiglottis

trachea

cardiac plexus

terminal bronchiole

right lung

left lung

right bronchus

left bronchus

anterior pulmonary plexus

pleural cavity

vagus nerve

parietal pleura

phrenic nerve

diaphragm

digestive system

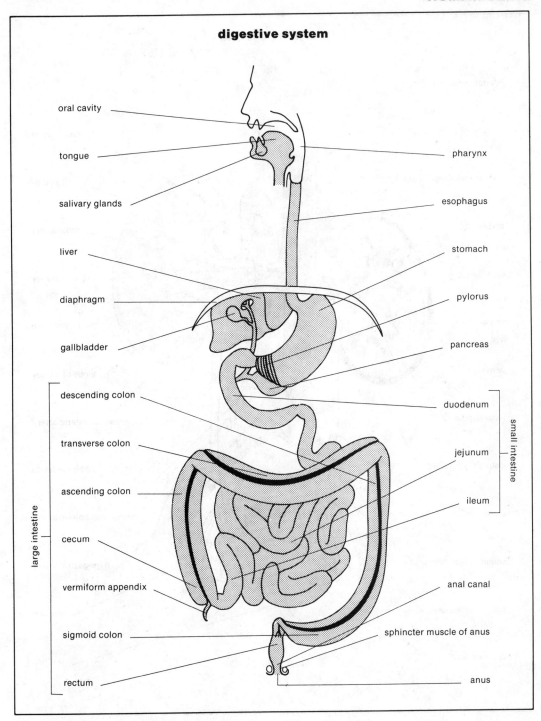

oral cavity

tongue

salivary glands

liver

diaphragm

gallbladder

descending colon

transverse colon

ascending colon

cecum

vermiform appendix

sigmoid colon

rectum

large intestine

pharynx

esophagus

stomach

pylorus

pancreas

duodenum

jejunum

ileum

small intestine

anal canal

sphincter muscle of anus

anus

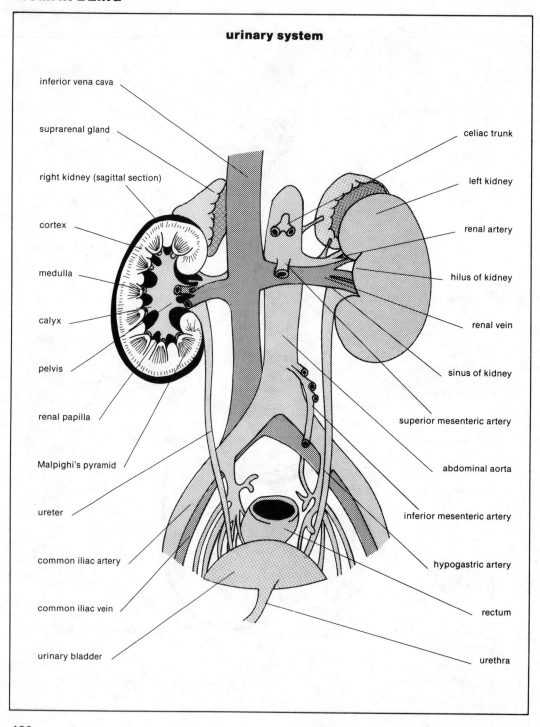

urinary system

inferior vena cava

suprarenal gland

celiac trunk

right kidney (sagittal section)

left kidney

cortex

renal artery

medulla

hilus of kidney

calyx

renal vein

pelvis

sinus of kidney

renal papilla

superior mesenteric artery

Malpighi's pyramid

abdominal aorta

ureter

inferior mesenteric artery

common iliac artery

hypogastric artery

common iliac vein

rectum

urinary bladder

urethra

nervous system

peripheral nervous system

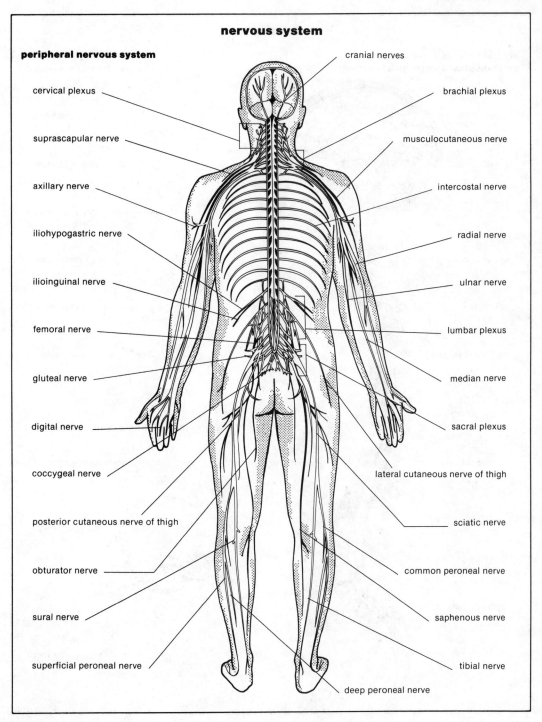

cranial nerves

cervical plexus

brachial plexus

suprascapular nerve

musculocutaneous nerve

axillary nerve

intercostal nerve

iliohypogastric nerve

radial nerve

ilioinguinal nerve

ulnar nerve

femoral nerve

lumbar plexus

gluteal nerve

median nerve

digital nerve

sacral plexus

coccygeal nerve

lateral cutaneous nerve of thigh

posterior cutaneous nerve of thigh

sciatic nerve

obturator nerve

common peroneal nerve

sural nerve

saphenous nerve

superficial peroneal nerve

tibial nerve

deep peroneal nerve

HUMAN BEING

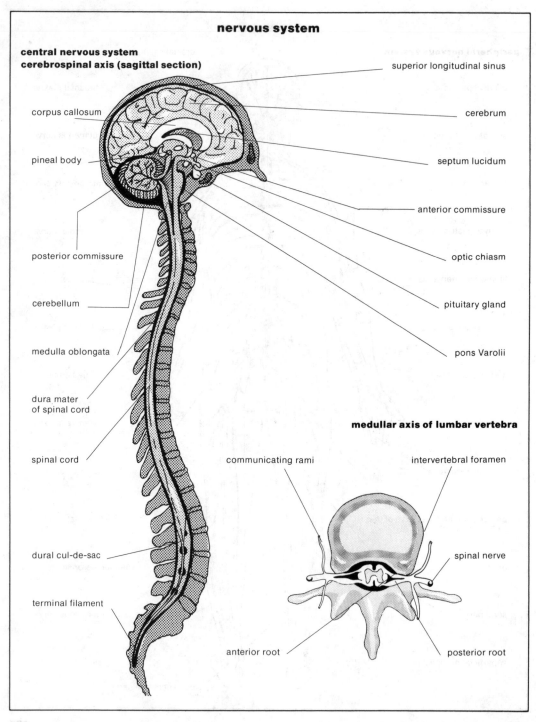

nervous system

central nervous system
cerebrospinal axis (sagittal section)

- corpus callosum
- pineal body
- posterior commissure
- cerebellum
- medulla oblongata
- dura mater of spinal cord
- spinal cord
- dural cul-de-sac
- terminal filament

- superior longitudinal sinus
- cerebrum
- septum lucidum
- anterior commissure
- optic chiasm
- pituitary gland
- pons Varolii

medullar axis of lumbar vertebra

- communicating rami
- intervertebral foramen
- spinal nerve
- anterior root
- posterior root

sense organs : sight

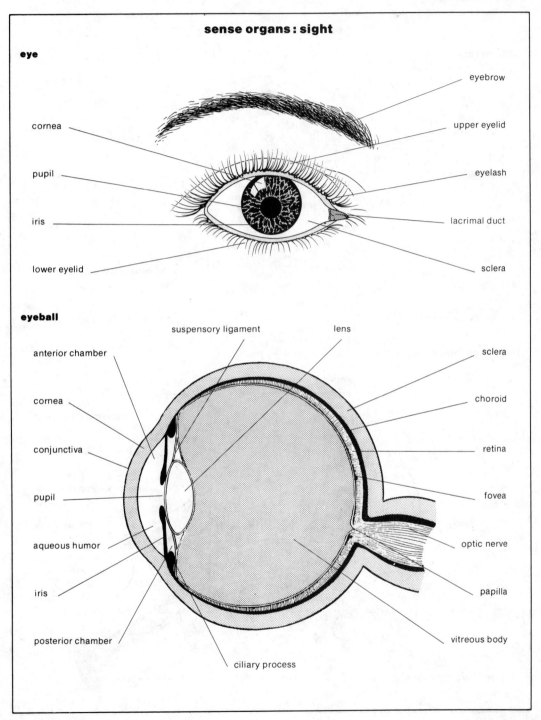

eye

eyebrow

cornea

upper eyelid

pupil

eyelash

iris

lacrimal duct

lower eyelid

sclera

eyeball

suspensory ligament

lens

anterior chamber

sclera

cornea

choroid

conjunctiva

retina

pupil

fovea

aqueous humor

optic nerve

iris

papilla

posterior chamber

vitreous body

ciliary process

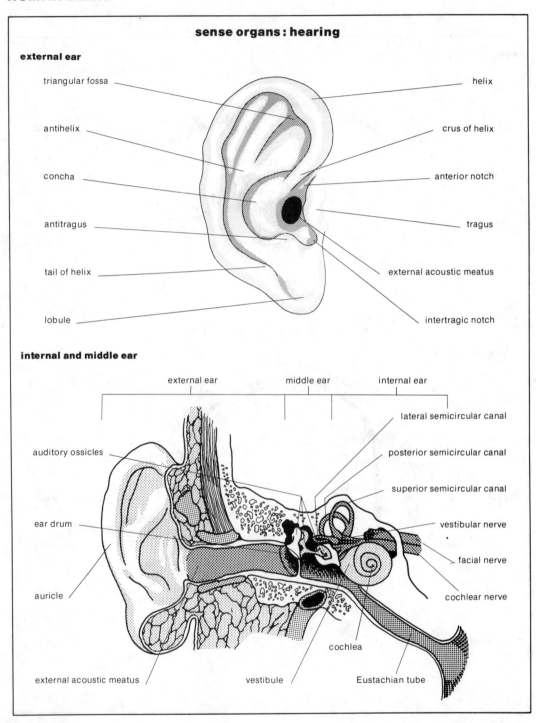

sense organs : hearing

external ear

triangular fossa

helix

antihelix

crus of helix

concha

anterior notch

antitragus

tragus

tail of helix

external acoustic meatus

lobule

intertragic notch

internal and middle ear

external ear — middle ear — internal ear

auditory ossicles

lateral semicircular canal

posterior semicircular canal

superior semicircular canal

ear drum

vestibular nerve

facial nerve

auricle

cochlear nerve

cochlea

external acoustic meatus

vestibule

Eustachian tube

sense organs : smell

external nose

root of nose

dorsum of nose

naris

tip of nose

ala

mobile septum of nose

philtrum

frontal sinus

nasal fossae

cribriform plate of ethmoid

superior nasal concha

middle nasal concha

inferior nasal concha

sphenoidal sinus

Eustachian tube

nasal bone

greater alar cartilage

maxilla

nasopharynx

uvula

palate

septal cartilage of nose

senses of smell and taste

olfactory bulb

Brunn s membrane

rhinencephalon

olfactory membrane

tongue

olfactory nerve

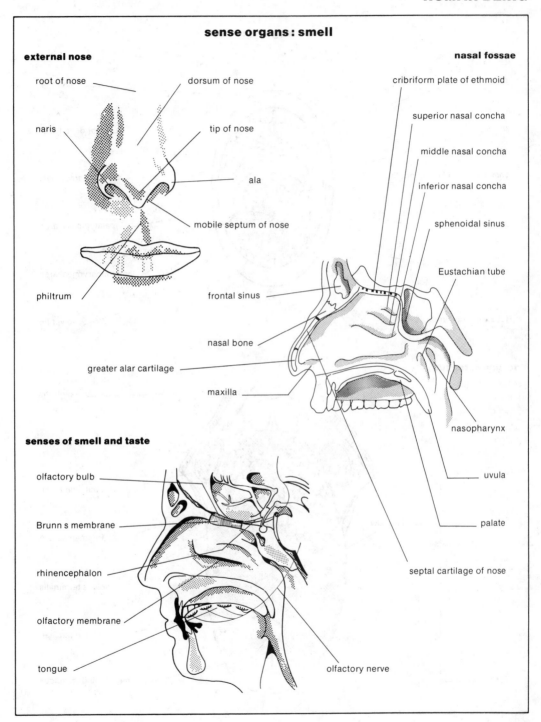

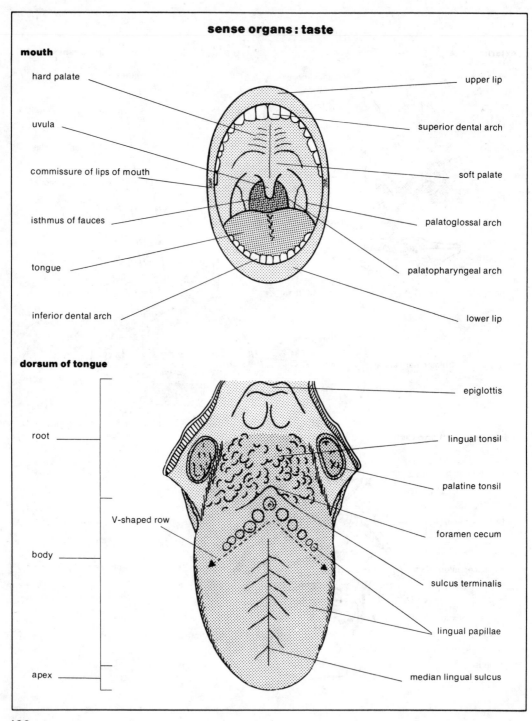

sense organs : taste

mouth

hard palate

uvula

commissure of lips of mouth

isthmus of fauces

tongue

inferior dental arch

upper lip

superior dental arch

soft palate

palatoglossal arch

palatopharyngeal arch

lower lip

dorsum of tongue

root

V-shaped row

body

apex

epiglottis

lingual tonsil

palatine tonsil

foramen cecum

sulcus terminalis

lingual papillae

median lingual sulcus

sense organs : touch

skin

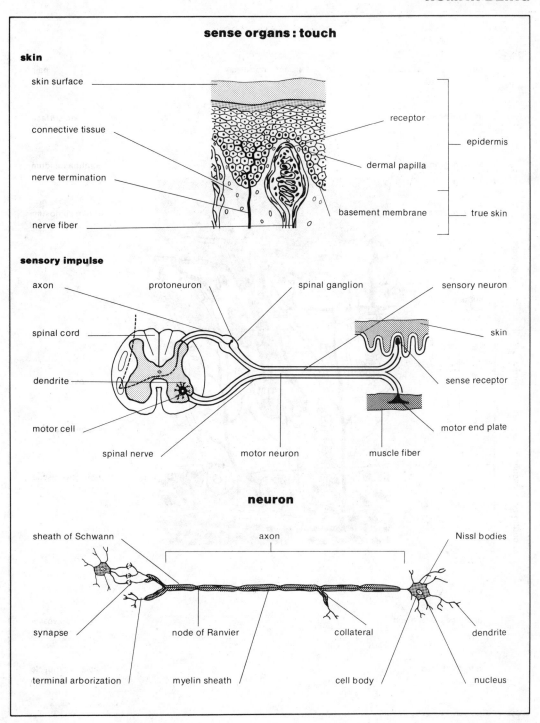

skin surface

connective tissue

nerve termination

nerve fiber

receptor

dermal papilla

basement membrane

epidermis

true skin

sensory impulse

axon

protoneuron

spinal ganglion

sensory neuron

spinal cord

skin

dendrite

sense receptor

motor cell

motor end plate

spinal nerve

motor neuron

muscle fiber

neuron

sheath of Schwann

axon

Nissl bodies

synapse

node of Ranvier

collateral

dendrite

terminal arborization

myelin sheath

cell body

nucleus

skin

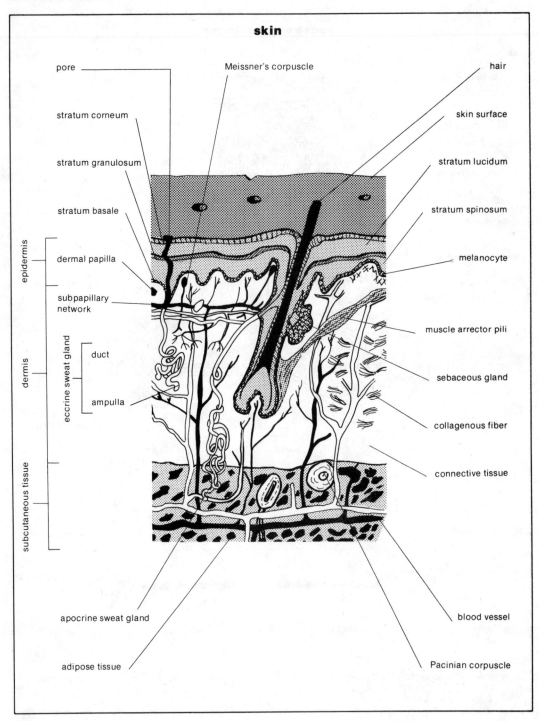

pore

Meissner's corpuscle

hair

stratum corneum

skin surface

stratum granulosum

stratum lucidum

stratum basale

stratum spinosum

epidermis

dermal papilla

melanocyte

subpapillary network

muscle arrector pili

dermis

eccrine sweat gland

duct

sebaceous gland

ampulla

collagenous fiber

subcutaneous tissue

connective tissue

apocrine sweat gland

blood vessel

adipose tissue

Pacinian corpuscle

nail

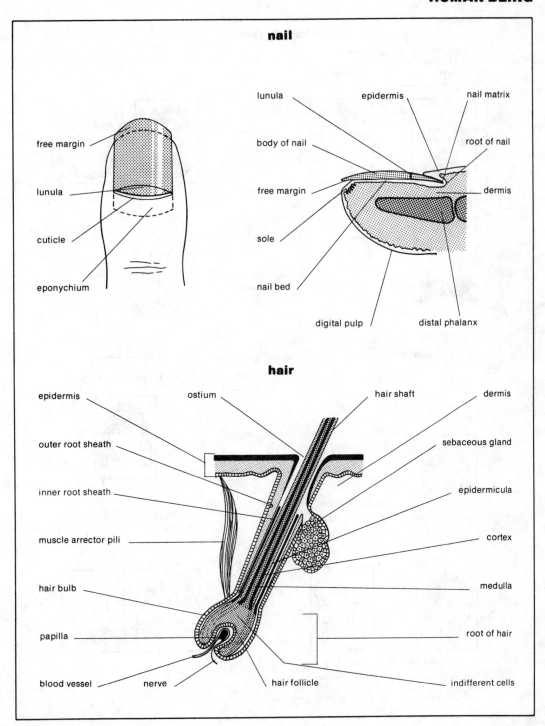

free margin

lunula

cuticle

eponychium

lunula — epidermis — nail matrix

body of nail — root of nail

free margin — dermis

sole

nail bed

digital pulp — distal phalanx

hair

epidermis — ostium — hair shaft — dermis

outer root sheath — sebaceous gland

inner root sheath — epidermicula

muscle arrector pili — cortex

hair bulb — medulla

papilla — root of hair

blood vessel — nerve — hair follicle — indifferent cells

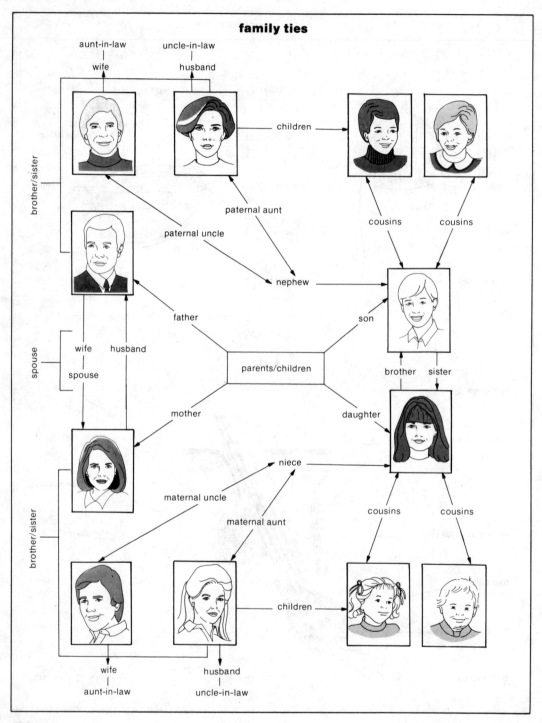

family ties

aunt-in-law   uncle-in-law

wife   husband

children

brother/sister

paternal aunt

paternal uncle

cousins   cousins

nephew

father

son

spouse

wife   husband

spouse

parents/children

brother   sister

mother

daughter

niece

maternal uncle

maternal aunt

cousins   cousins

children

wife   husband

aunt-in-law   uncle-in-law

brother/sister

family ties

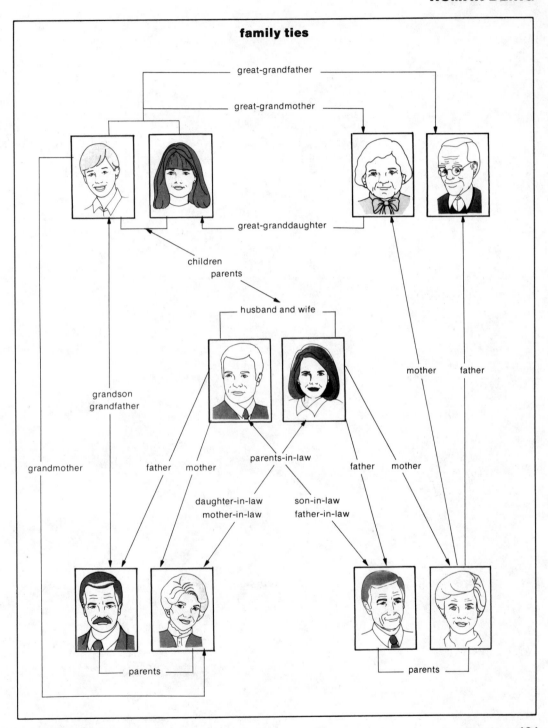

great-grandfather

great-grandmother

great-granddaughter

children

parents

husband and wife

grandson
grandfather

grandmother

mother   father

father   mother

parents-in-law

father   mother

daughter-in-law
mother-in-law

son-in-law
father-in-law

parents

parents

FOOD

herbs

basil

tarragon

chervil

parsley

marjoram

oregano

sage

rosemary

savory

thyme

sweet bay

dill

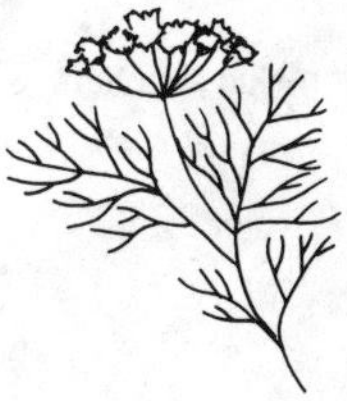

mint

lovage

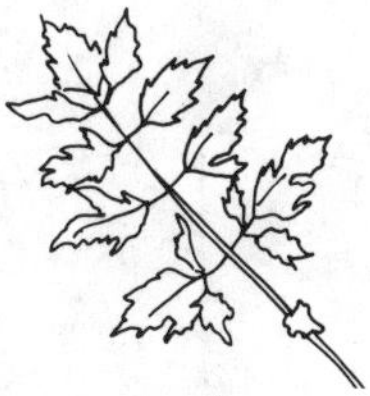

hyssop

borage

pasta

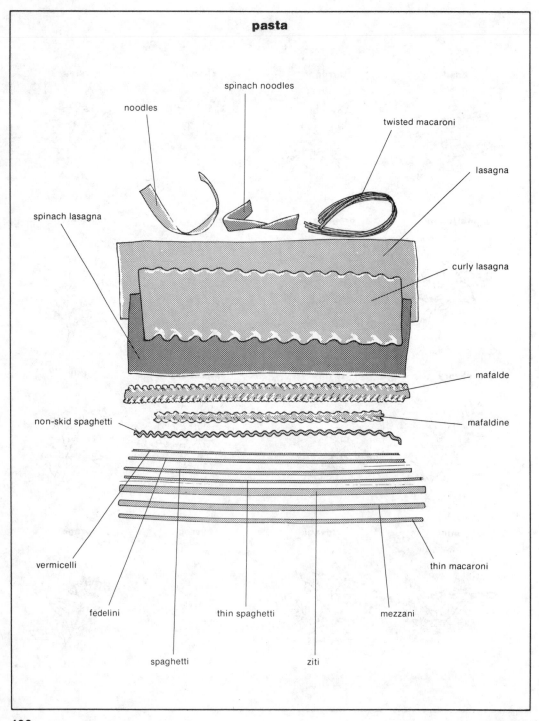

pasta

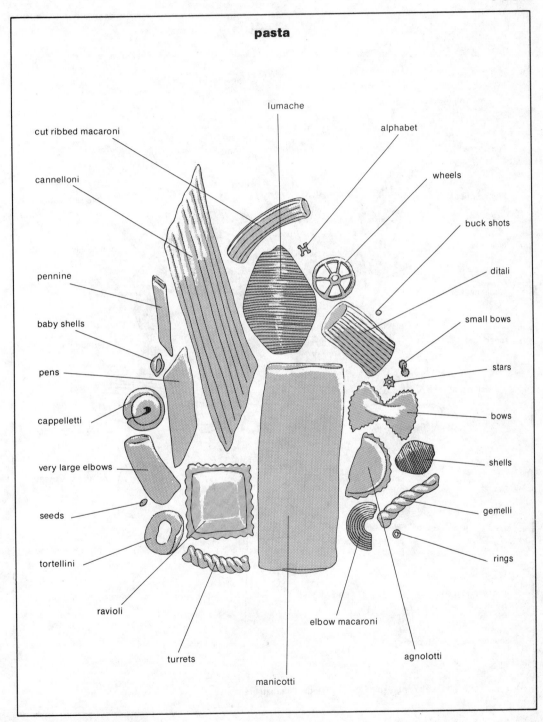

lumache

cut ribbed macaroni

alphabet

cannelloni

wheels

buck shots

pennine

ditali

baby shells

small bows

pens

stars

cappelletti

bows

very large elbows

shells

seeds

gemelli

tortellini

rings

ravioli

turrets

elbow macaroni

agnolotti

manicotti

bread

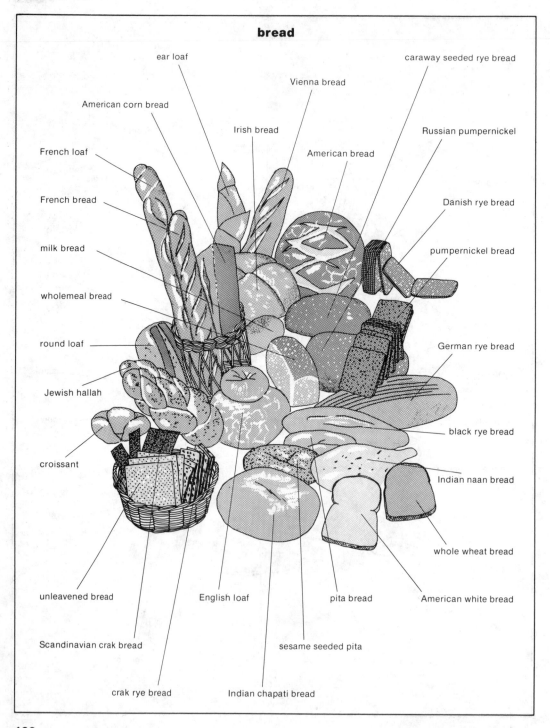

ear loaf

caraway seeded rye bread

Vienna bread

American corn bread

Irish bread

American bread

Russian pumpernickel

French loaf

French bread

Danish rye bread

milk bread

pumpernickel bread

wholemeal bread

round loaf

German rye bread

Jewish hallah

black rye bread

croissant

Indian naan bread

whole wheat bread

unleavened bread

English loaf

pita bread

American white bread

Scandinavian crak bread

sesame seeded pita

crak rye bread

Indian chapati bread

veal

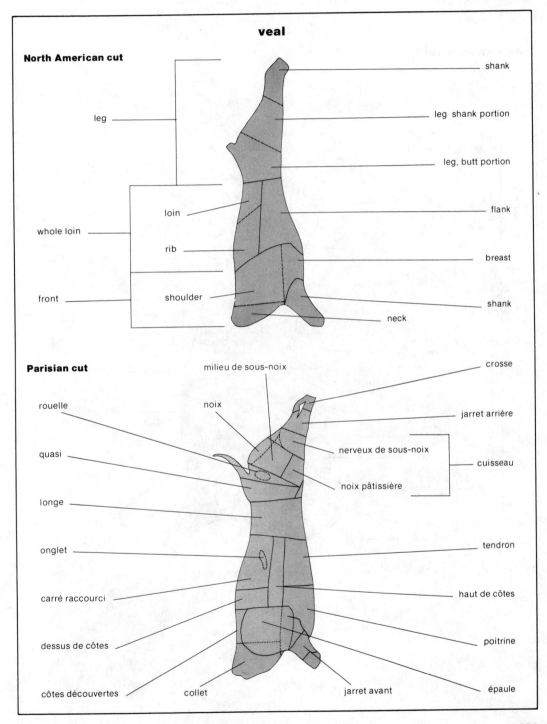

North American cut

- shank
- leg
- leg shank portion
- leg, butt portion
- flank
- whole loin
- loin
- rib
- breast
- front
- shoulder
- shank
- neck

Parisian cut

- milieu de sous-noix
- crosse
- rouelle
- noix
- jarret arrière
- quasi
- nerveux de sous-noix
- cuisseau
- noix pâtissière
- longe
- onglet
- tendron
- carré raccourci
- haut de côtes
- dessus de côtes
- poitrine
- côtes découvertes
- collet
- jarret avant
- épaule

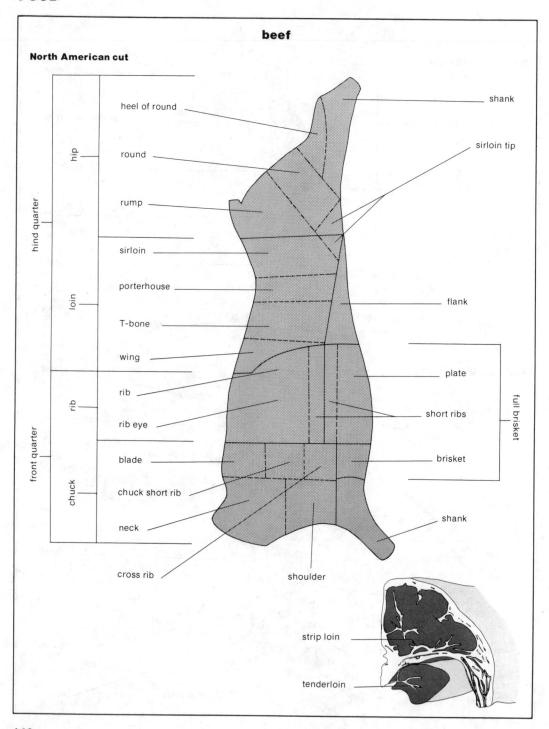

beef

North American cut

hip

hind quarter

loin

front quarter

rib

chuck

heel of round

round

rump

sirloin

porterhouse

T-bone

wing

rib

rib eye

blade

chuck short rib

neck

cross rib

shoulder

shank

sirloin tip

flank

plate

short ribs

brisket

full brisket

shank

strip loin

tenderloin

beef

Parisian cut

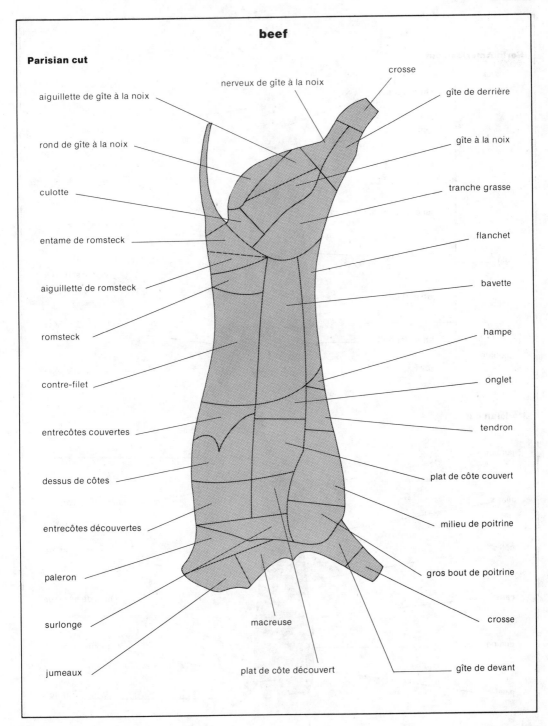

aiguillette de gîte à la noix

nerveux de gîte à la noix

crosse

gîte de derrière

rond de gîte à la noix

gîte à la noix

culotte

tranche grasse

entame de romsteck

flanchet

aiguillette de romsteck

bavette

romsteck

hampe

contre-filet

onglet

entrecôtes couvertes

tendron

dessus de côtes

plat de côte couvert

entrecôtes découvertes

milieu de poitrine

paleron

gros bout de poitrine

surlonge

crosse

macreuse

jumeaux

plat de côte découvert

gîte de devant

pork

North American cut

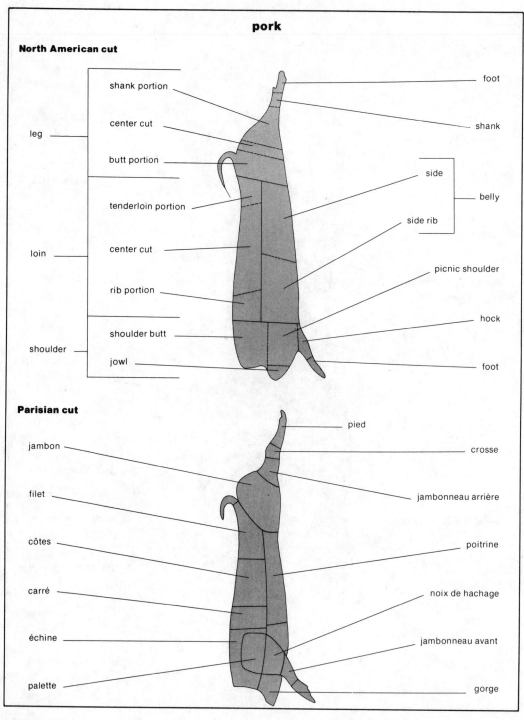

leg
- shank portion
- center cut
- butt portion

loin
- tenderloin portion
- center cut
- rib portion

shoulder
- shoulder butt
- jowl

foot

shank

side

belly

side rib

picnic shoulder

hock

foot

Parisian cut

jambon

filet

côtes

carré

échine

palette

pied

crosse

jambonneau arrière

poitrine

noix de hachage

jambonneau avant

gorge

lamb

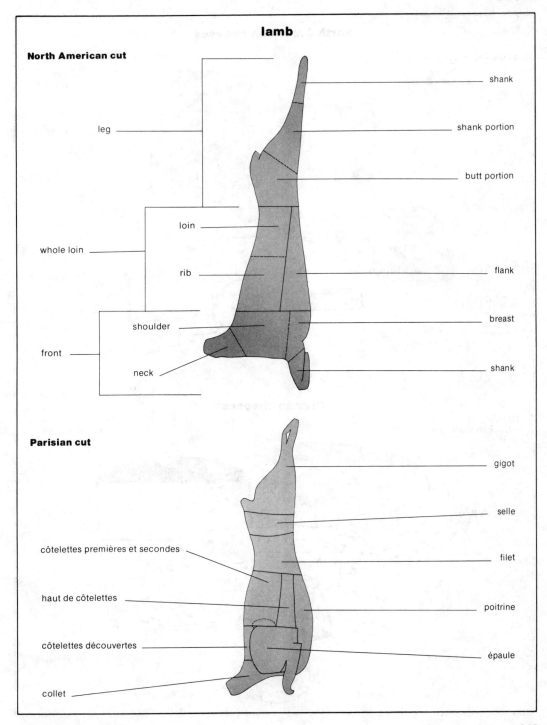

North American cut

shank

leg

shank portion

butt portion

whole loin

loin

rib

flank

breast

shoulder

front

neck

shank

Parisian cut

gigot

selle

côtelettes premières et secondes

filet

haut de côtelettes

poitrine

côtelettes découvertes

épaule

collet

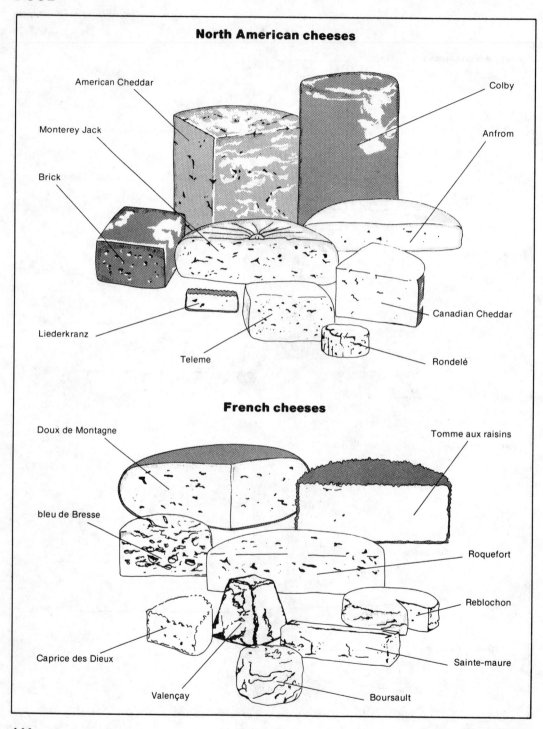

North American cheeses

American Cheddar

Colby

Monterey Jack

Anfrom

Brick

Canadian Cheddar

Liederkranz

Teleme

Rondelé

French cheeses

Doux de Montagne

Tomme aux raisins

bleu de Bresse

Roquefort

Reblochon

Caprice des Dieux

Sainte-maure

Valençay

Boursault

French cheeses

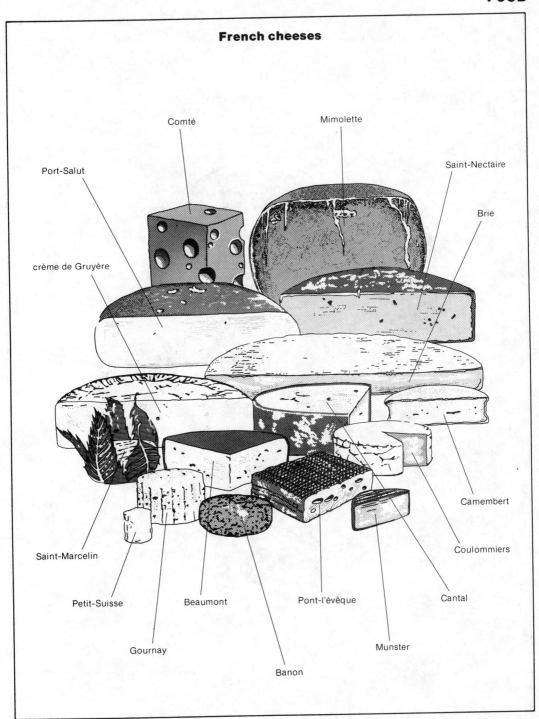

Comté

Mimolette

Saint-Nectaire

Port-Salut

Brie

crème de Gruyère

Camembert

Saint-Marcelin

Coulommiers

Petit-Suisse

Beaumont

Pont-l'évêque

Cantal

Gournay

Munster

Banon

desserts

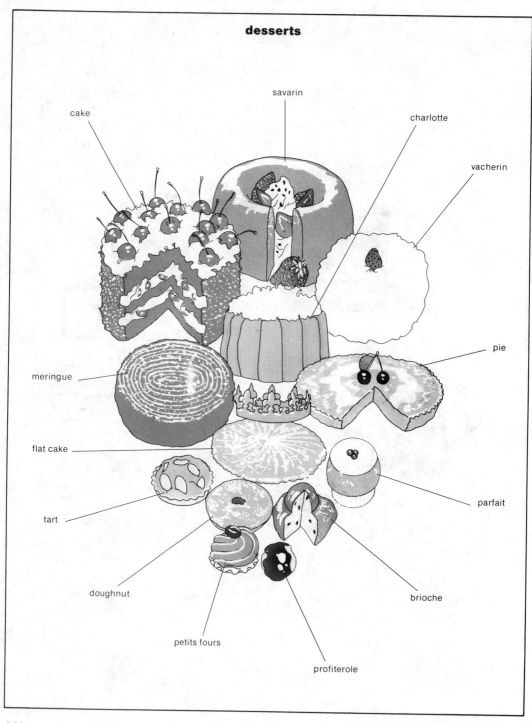

savarin

charlotte

vacherin

cake

meringue

pie

flat cake

parfait

tart

doughnut

brioche

petits fours

profiterole

desserts

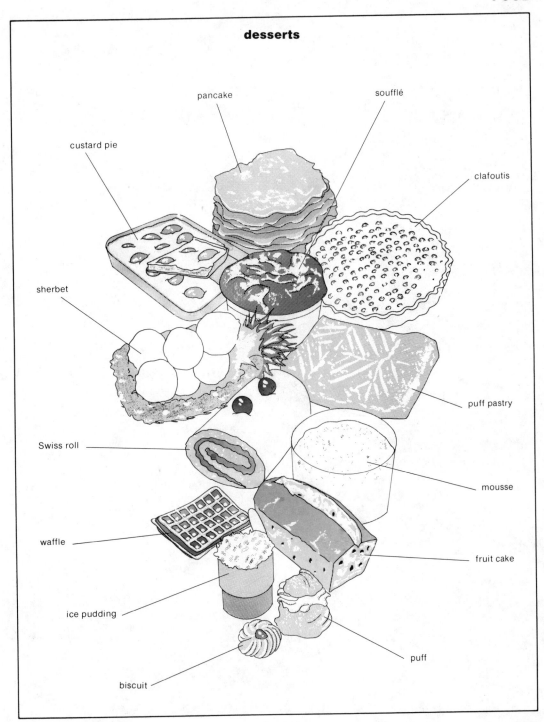

pancake

soufflé

custard pie

clafoutis

sherbet

puff pastry

Swiss roll

mousse

waffle

fruit cake

ice pudding

puff

biscuit

FARM

buildings

open housing

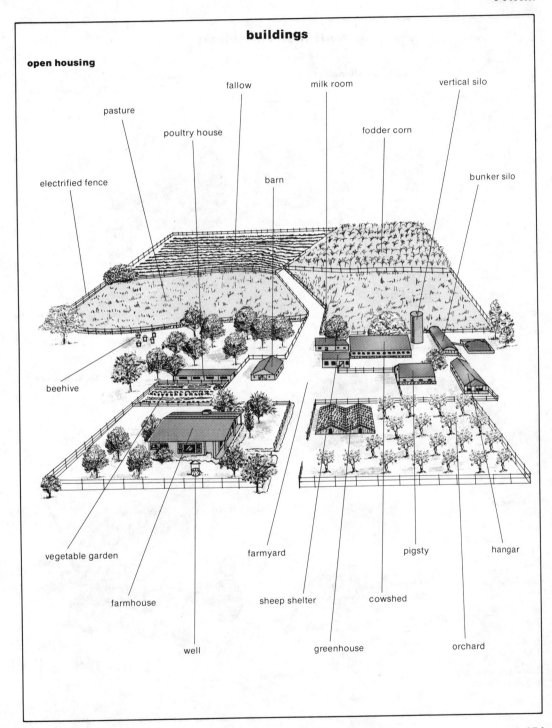

fallow

milk room

vertical silo

pasture

poultry house

fodder corn

electrified fence

barn

bunker silo

beehive

vegetable garden

pigsty

hangar

farmhouse

farmyard

sheep shelter

cowshed

well

greenhouse

orchard

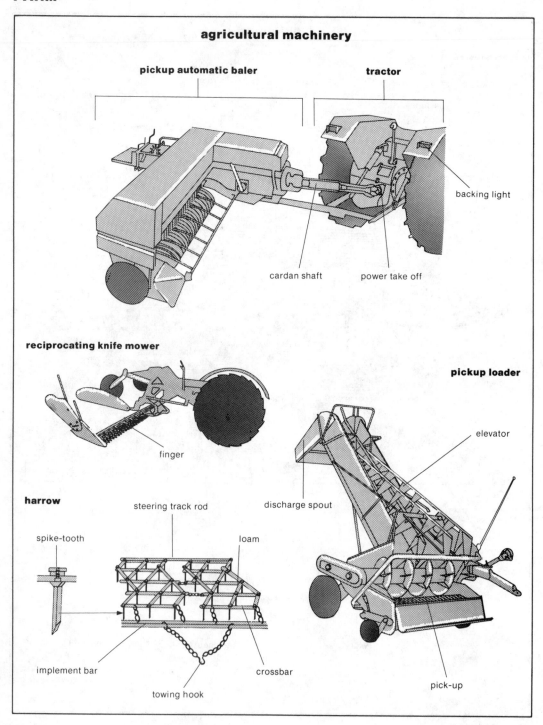

agricultural machinery

pickup automatic baler

tractor

backing light

cardan shaft

power take off

reciprocating knife mower

pickup loader

finger

elevator

harrow

steering track rod

discharge spout

spike-tooth

loam

implement bar

crossbar

towing hook

pick-up

agricultural machinery

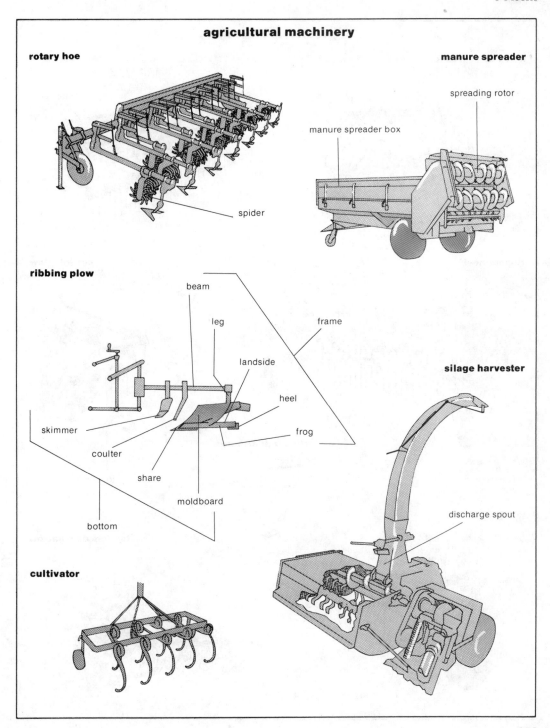

rotary hoe

spider

manure spreader

spreading rotor

manure spreader box

ribbing plow

beam

leg

frame

landside

silage harvester

heel

skimmer

frog

coulter

share

discharge spout

moldboard

bottom

cultivator

agricultural machinery

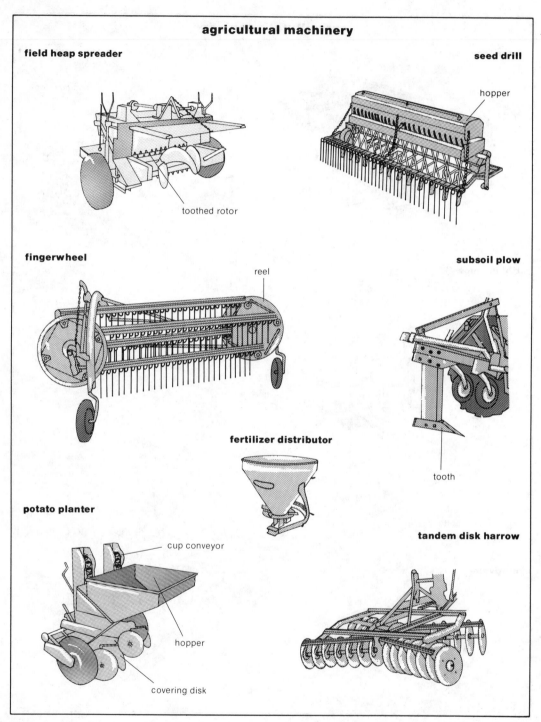

field heap spreader

seed drill

hopper

toothed rotor

fingerwheel

reel

subsoil plow

fertilizer distributor

tooth

potato planter

cup conveyor

hopper

covering disk

tandem disk harrow

machinery

combine harvester

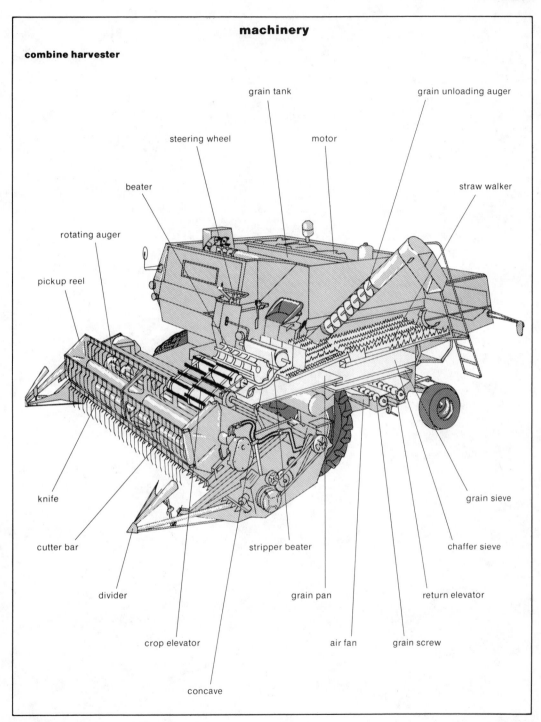

grain tank

grain unloading auger

steering wheel

motor

beater

straw walker

rotating auger

pickup reel

knife

cutter bar

grain sieve

divider

chaffer sieve

stripper beater

grain pan

return elevator

crop elevator

air fan

grain screw

concave

ARCHITECTURE

traditional houses

hut

wigwam

hut

igloo

yurt

tepee

isba

ARCHITECTURE

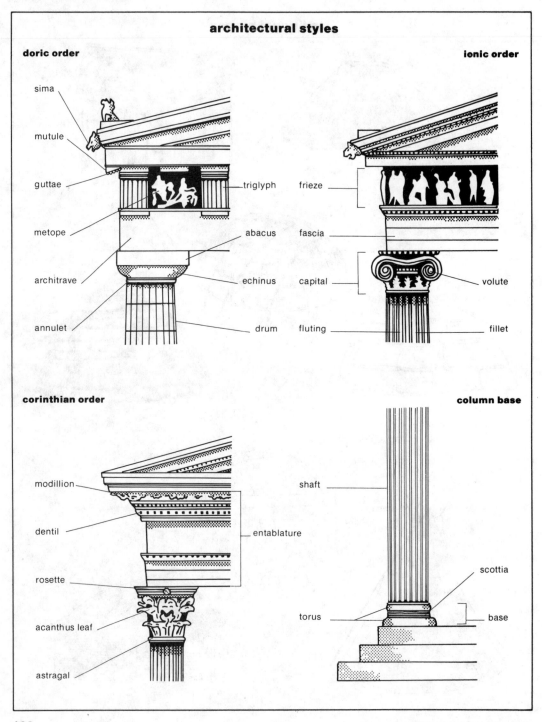

architectural styles

doric order

sima
mutule
guttae
metope
architrave
annulet

triglyph
abacus
echinus
drum

ionic order

frieze
fascia
capital

volute
fillet

corinthian order

modillion
dentil
rosette
acanthus leaf
astragal

entablature

column base

shaft
scottia
torus
base

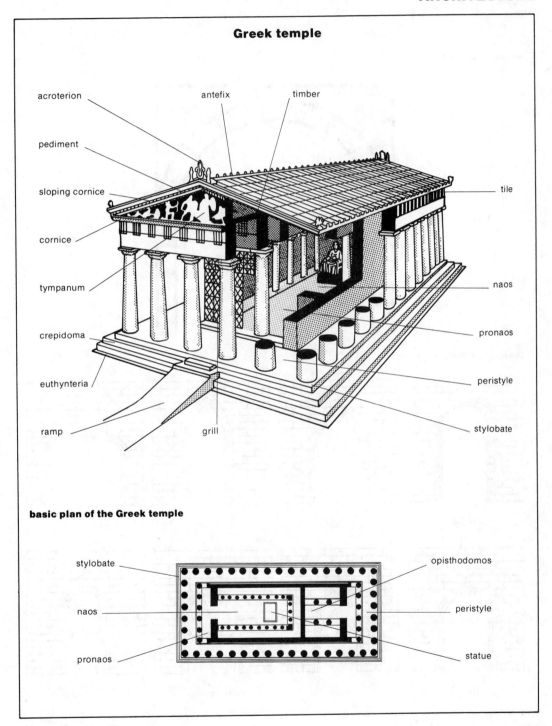

Greek temple

acroterion
antefix
timber
pediment
sloping cornice
tile
cornice
tympanum
naos
crepidoma
pronaos
euthynteria
peristyle
ramp
grill
stylobate

basic plan of the Greek temple

stylobate
opisthodomos
naos
peristyle
pronaos
statue

ARCHITECTURE

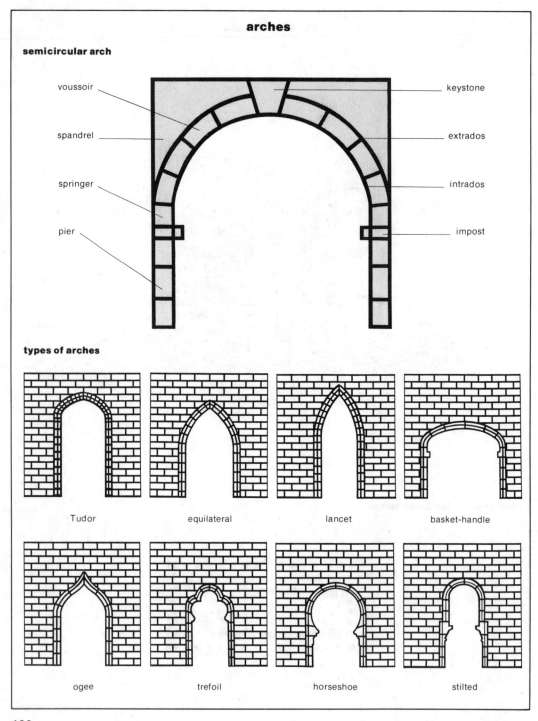

arches

semicircular arch

voussoir

spandrel

springer

pier

keystone

extrados

intrados

impost

types of arches

Tudor

equilateral

lancet

basket-handle

ogee

trefoil

horseshoe

stilted

Roman house

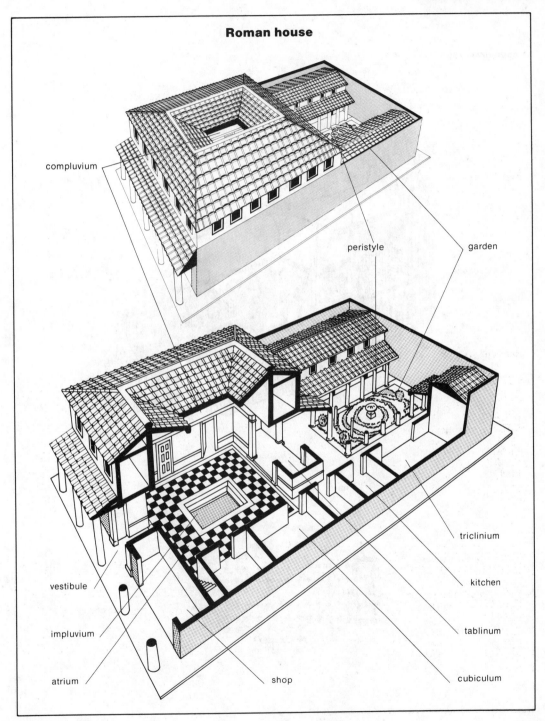

compluvium

peristyle

garden

triclinium

kitchen

tablinum

cubiculum

vestibule

impluvium

atrium

shop

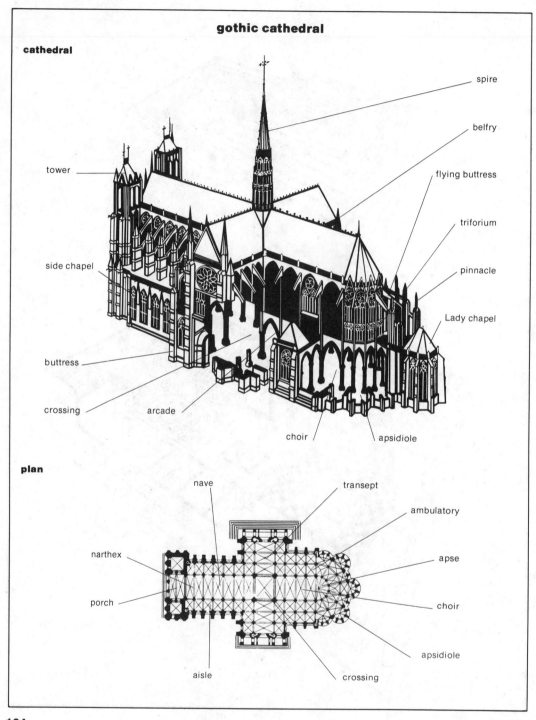

gothic cathedral

cathedral

spire

belfry

tower

flying buttress

triforium

side chapel

pinnacle

Lady chapel

buttress

crossing

arcade

choir

apsidiole

plan

nave

transept

ambulatory

narthex

apse

porch

choir

apsidiole

aisle

crossing

gothic cathedral

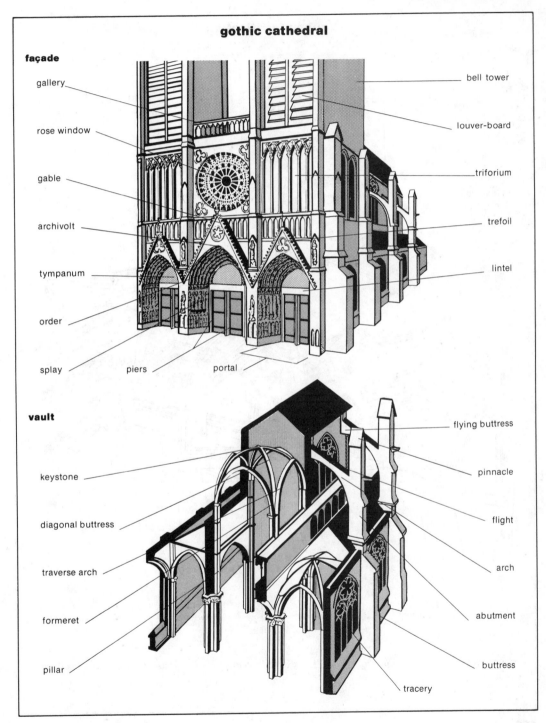

façade

gallery

rose window

gable

archivolt

tympanum

order

splay

piers

portal

bell tower

louver-board

triforium

trefoil

lintel

vault

keystone

diagonal buttress

traverse arch

formeret

pillar

flying buttress

pinnacle

flight

arch

abutment

buttress

tracery

Vauban fortification

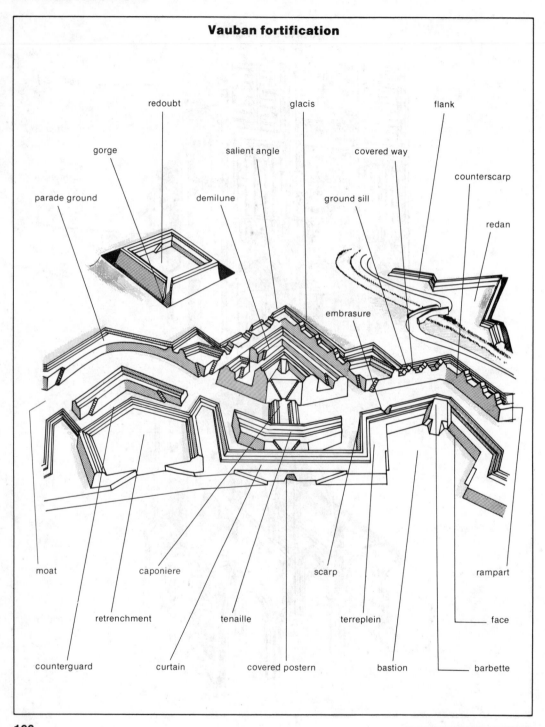

redoubt

glacis

flank

gorge

salient angle

covered way

counterscarp

parade ground

demilune

ground sill

redan

embrasure

moat

caponiere

scarp

rampart

retrenchment

tenaille

terreplein

face

counterguard

curtain

covered postern

bastion

barbette

castle

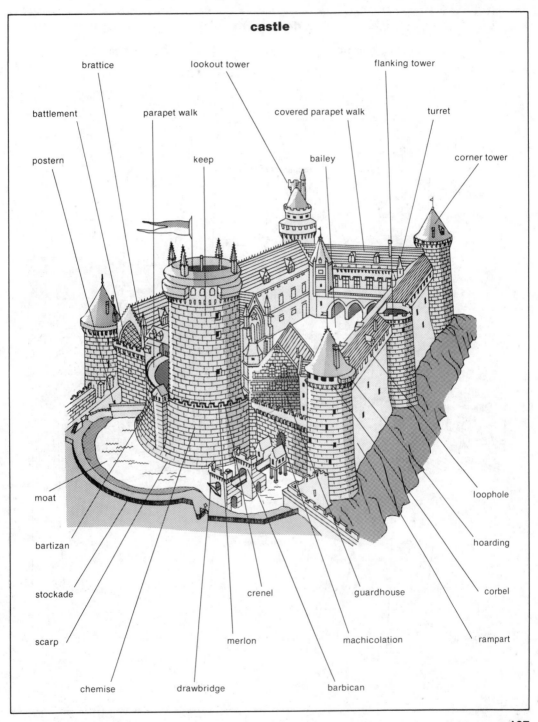

brattice

lookout tower

flanking tower

battlement

parapet walk

covered parapet walk

turret

postern

keep

bailey

corner tower

moat

loophole

bartizan

hoarding

stockade

crenel

guardhouse

corbel

scarp

merlon

machicolation

rampart

chemise

drawbridge

barbican

ARCHITECTURE

downtown

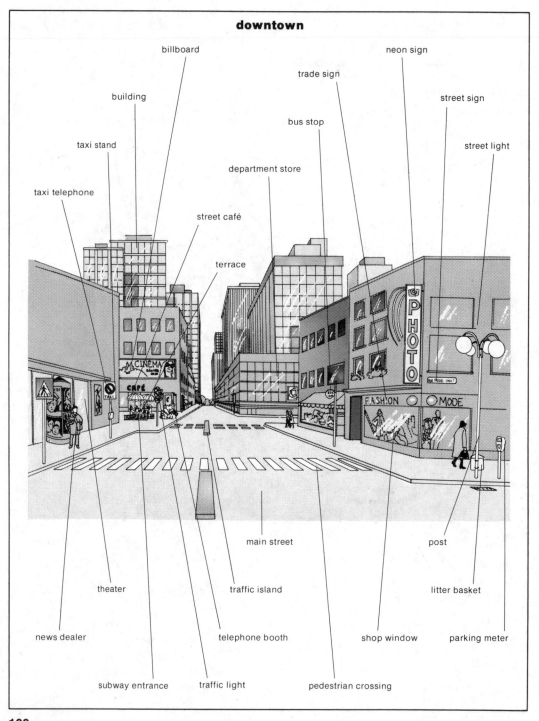

billboard

neon sign

trade sign

building

street sign

taxi stand

bus stop

street light

taxi telephone

department store

street café

terrace

main street

post

theater

traffic island

litter basket

news dealer

telephone booth

shop window

parking meter

subway entrance

traffic light

pedestrian crossing

theater

hall

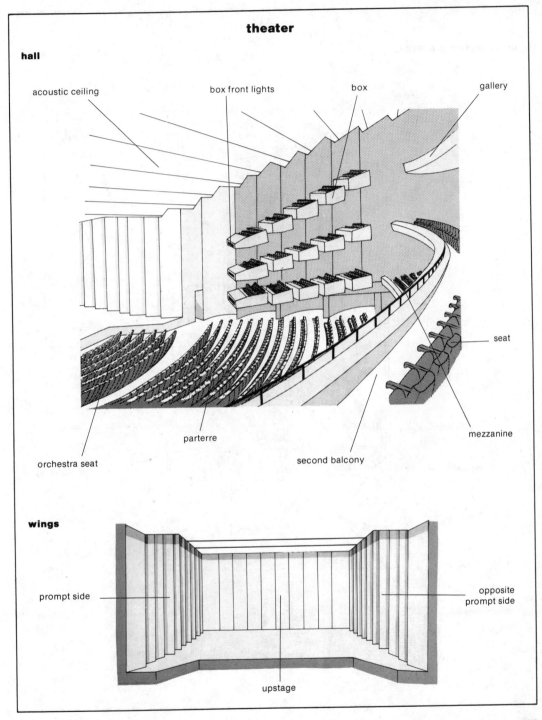

acoustic ceiling

box front lights

box

gallery

seat

mezzanine

parterre

orchestra seat

second balcony

wings

prompt side

opposite
prompt side

upstage

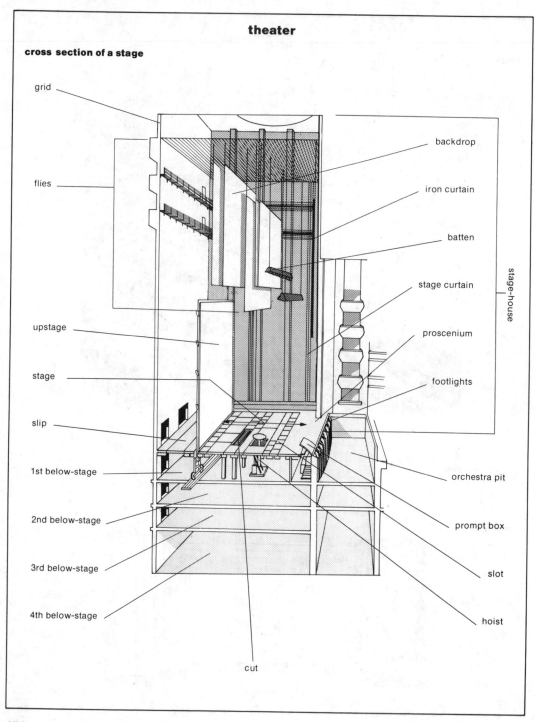

theater

cross section of a stage

grid

flies

backdrop

iron curtain

batten

stage curtain

proscenium

footlights

stage-house

upstage

stage

slip

1st below-stage

2nd below-stage

3rd below-stage

4th below-stage

cut

orchestra pit

prompt box

slot

hoist

elevator

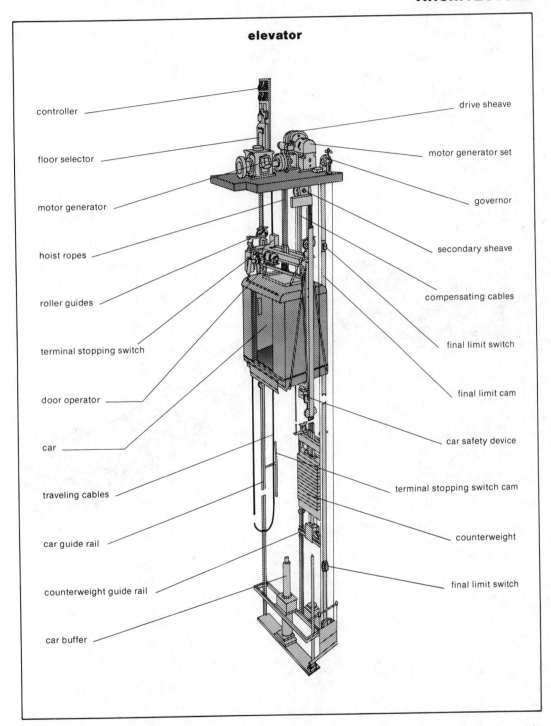

controller

floor selector

motor generator

hoist ropes

roller guides

terminal stopping switch

door operator

car

traveling cables

car guide rail

counterweight guide rail

car buffer

drive sheave

motor generator set

governor

secondary sheave

compensating cables

final limit switch

final limit cam

car safety device

terminal stopping switch cam

counterweight

final limit switch

escalator

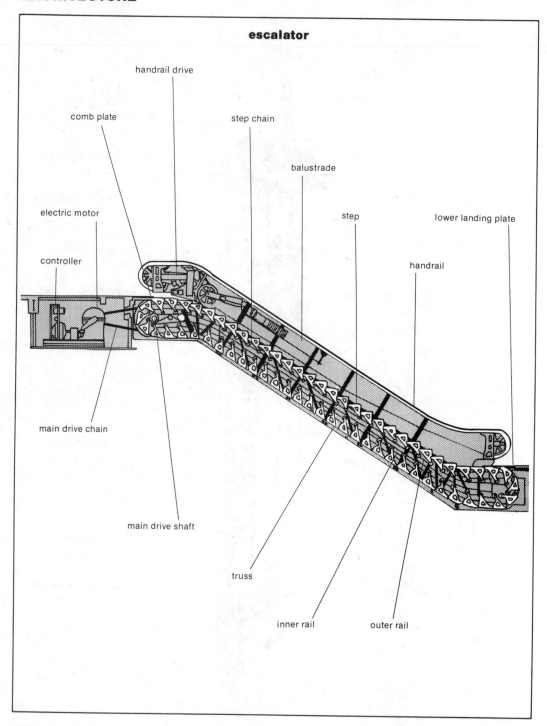

handrail drive

comb plate

step chain

balustrade

electric motor

step

lower landing plate

controller

handrail

main drive chain

main drive shaft

truss

inner rail

outer rail

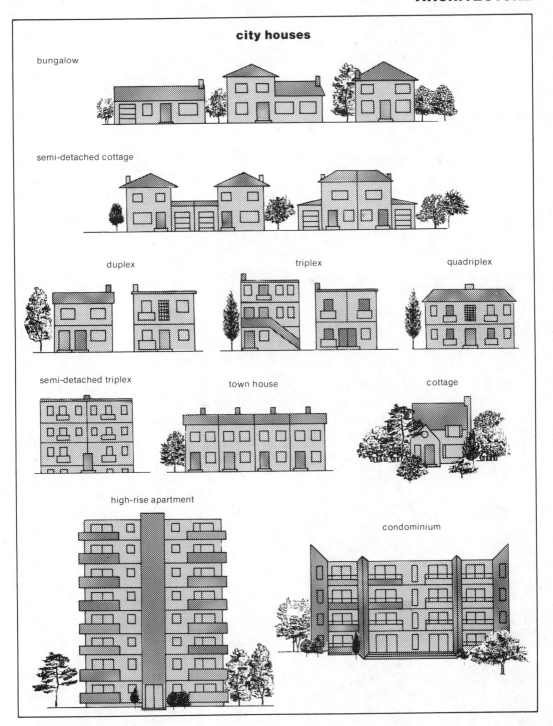

city houses

bungalow

semi-detached cottage

duplex

triplex

quadriplex

semi-detached triplex

town house

cottage

high-rise apartment

condominium

HOUSE

exterior of a house

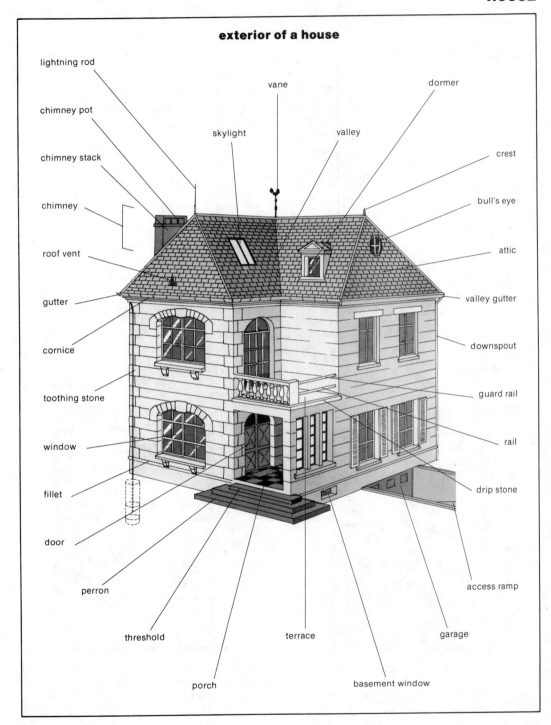

lightning rod

vane

dormer

chimney pot

skylight

valley

crest

chimney stack

bull's eye

chimney

attic

roof vent

valley gutter

gutter

downspout

cornice

guard rail

toothing stone

rail

window

drip stone

fillet

door

access ramp

perron

threshold

terrace

garage

porch

basement window

HOUSE

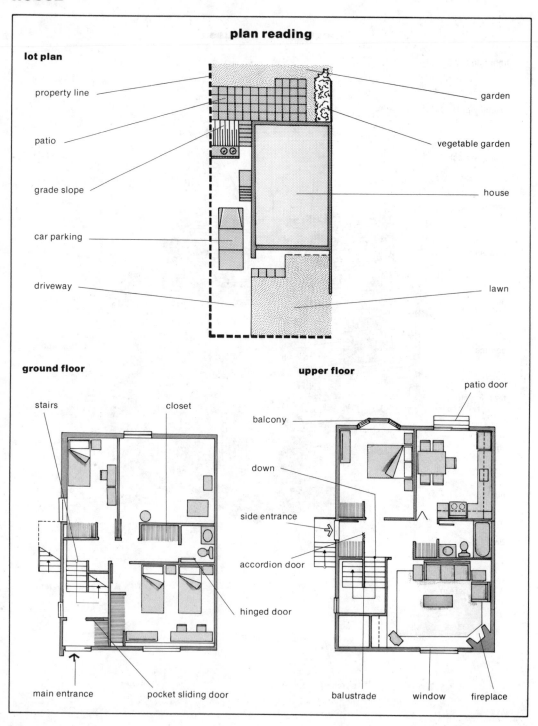

plan reading

lot plan

property line

garden

patio

vegetable garden

grade slope

house

car parking

driveway

lawn

ground floor

upper floor

stairs

closet

patio door

balcony

down

side entrance

accordion door

hinged door

main entrance

pocket sliding door

balustrade

window

fireplace

rooms of the house

ground floor   **upper floor**

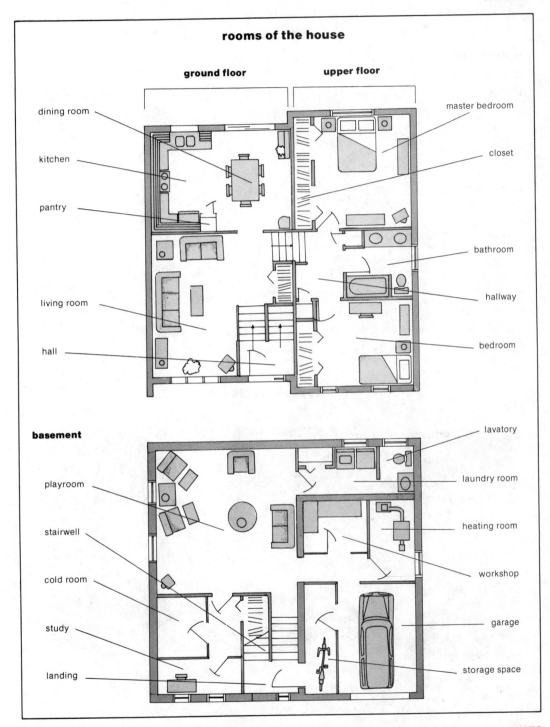

dining room

kitchen

pantry

living room

hall

master bedroom

closet

bathroom

hallway

bedroom

basement

lavatory

playroom

laundry room

stairwell

heating room

cold room

workshop

study

garage

landing

storage space

HOUSE

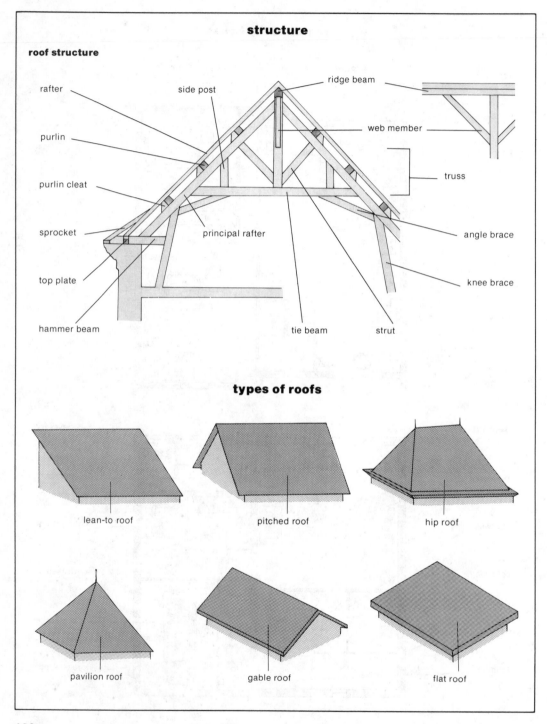

structure

roof structure

- rafter
- side post
- ridge beam
- purlin
- web member
- purlin cleat
- truss
- sprocket
- principal rafter
- angle brace
- top plate
- knee brace
- hammer beam
- tie beam
- strut

types of roofs

- lean-to roof
- pitched roof
- hip roof
- pavilion roof
- gable roof
- flat roof

types of roofs

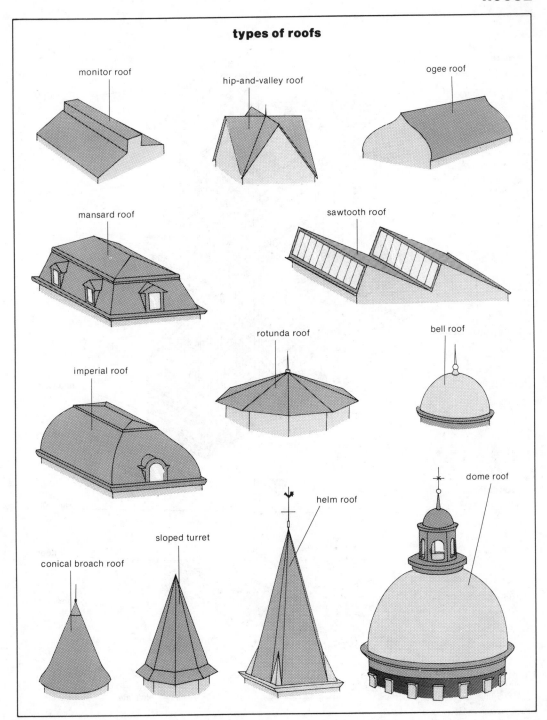

monitor roof

hip-and-valley roof

ogee roof

mansard roof

sawtooth roof

imperial roof

rotunda roof

bell roof

conical broach roof

sloped turret

helm roof

dome roof

HOUSE

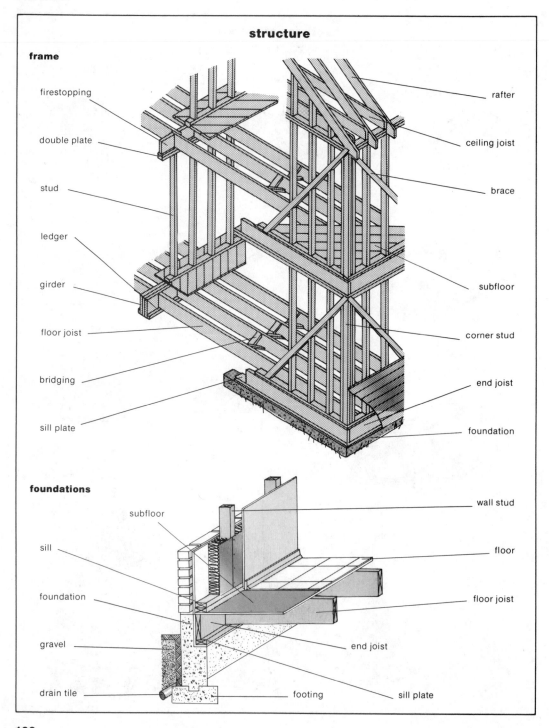

structure

frame

- firestopping
- double plate
- stud
- ledger
- girder
- floor joist
- bridging
- sill plate

- rafter
- ceiling joist
- brace
- subfloor
- corner stud
- end joist
- foundation

foundations

- subfloor
- sill
- foundation
- gravel
- drain tile
- footing

- wall stud
- floor
- floor joist
- end joist
- sill plate

building materials

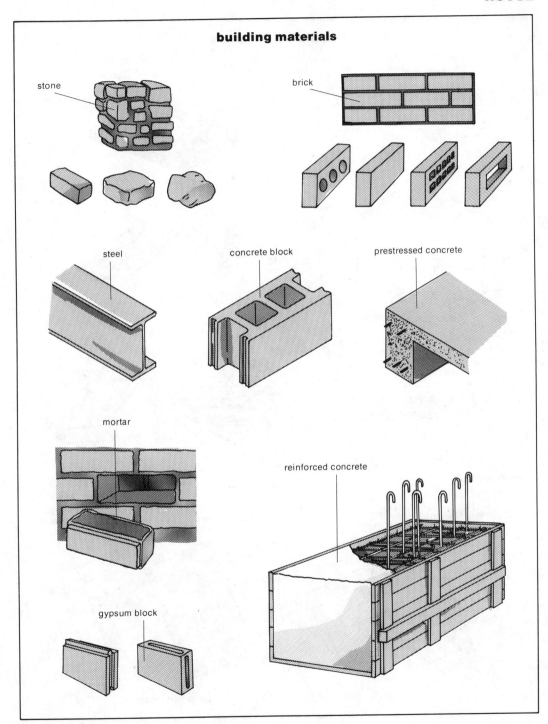

stone

brick

steel

concrete block

prestressed concrete

mortar

reinforced concrete

gypsum block

building materials

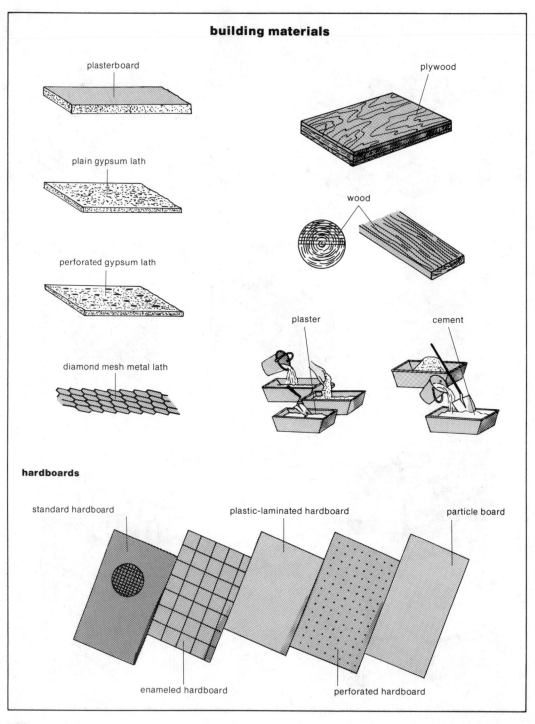

plasterboard

plywood

plain gypsum lath

wood

perforated gypsum lath

plaster

cement

diamond mesh metal lath

hardboards

standard hardboard

plastic-laminated hardboard

particle board

enameled hardboard

perforated hardboard

building materials

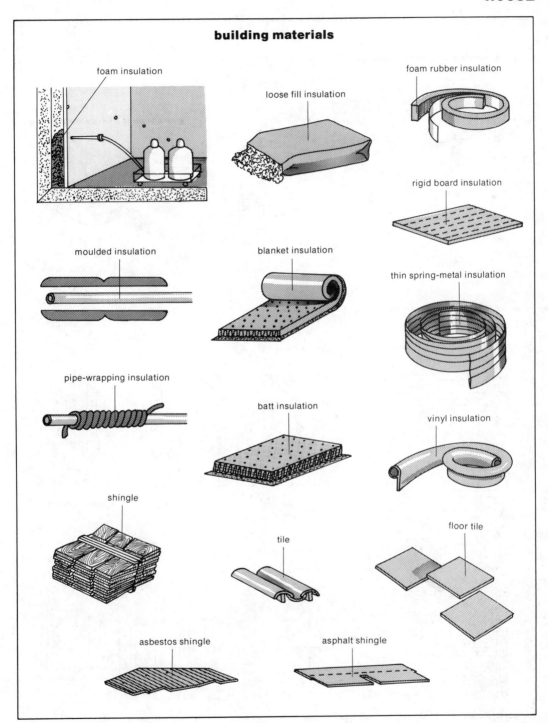

foam insulation

loose fill insulation

foam rubber insulation

rigid board insulation

moulded insulation

blanket insulation

thin spring-metal insulation

pipe-wrapping insulation

batt insulation

vinyl insulation

shingle

tile

floor tile

asbestos shingle

asphalt shingle

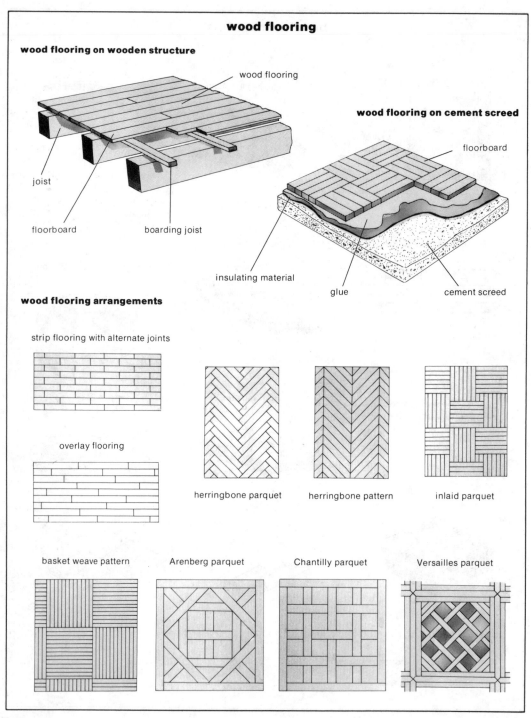

wood flooring

wood flooring on wooden structure

wood flooring

wood flooring on cement screed

floorboard

joist

floorboard

boarding joist

insulating material

glue

cement screed

wood flooring arrangements

strip flooring with alternate joints

overlay flooring

herringbone parquet

herringbone pattern

inlaid parquet

basket weave pattern

Arenberg parquet

Chantilly parquet

Versailles parquet

stairs

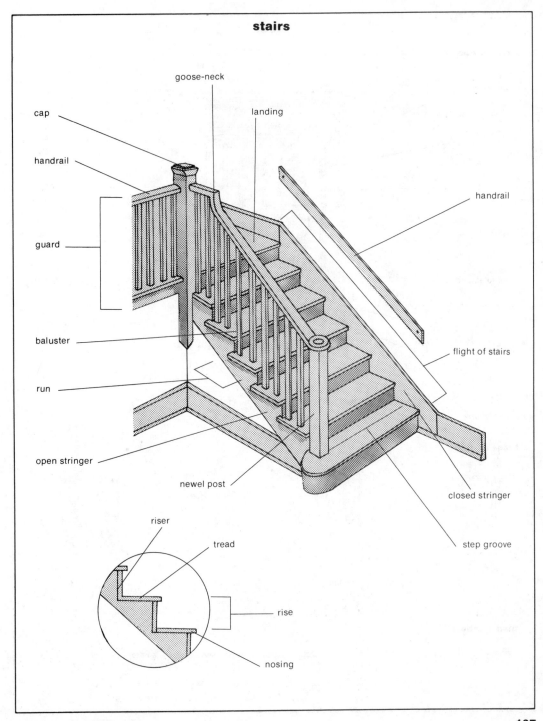

goose-neck

cap

landing

handrail

handrail

guard

baluster

run

open stringer

newel post

flight of stairs

closed stringer

step groove

riser

tread

rise

nosing

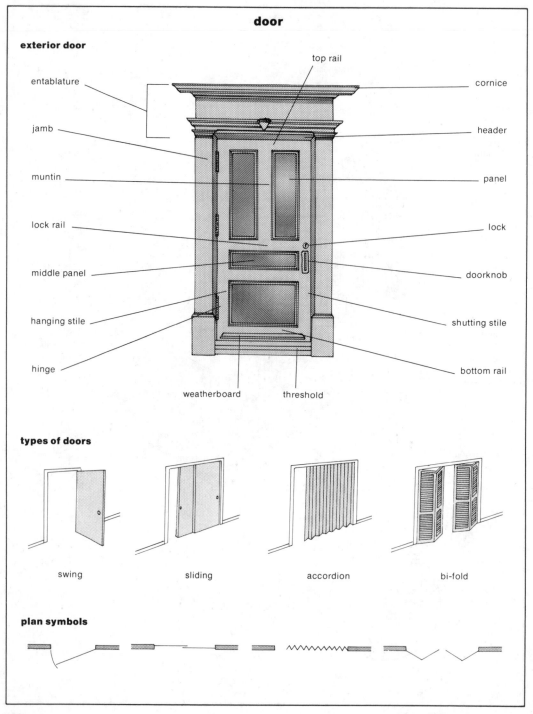

door

exterior door

entablature

jamb

muntin

lock rail

middle panel

hanging stile

hinge

top rail

cornice

header

panel

lock

doorknob

shutting stile

bottom rail

weatherboard   threshold

types of doors

swing   sliding   accordion   bi-fold

plan symbols

window

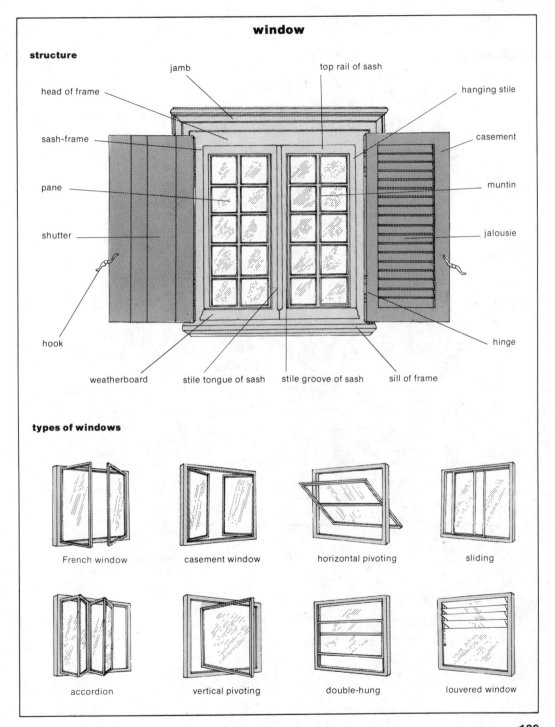

structure

jamb · top rail of sash · head of frame · hanging stile · sash-frame · casement · pane · muntin · shutter · jalousie · hook · hinge · weatherboard · stile tongue of sash · stile groove of sash · sill of frame

types of windows

French window · casement window · horizontal pivoting · sliding

accordion · vertical pivoting · double-hung · louvered window

heating

fireplace

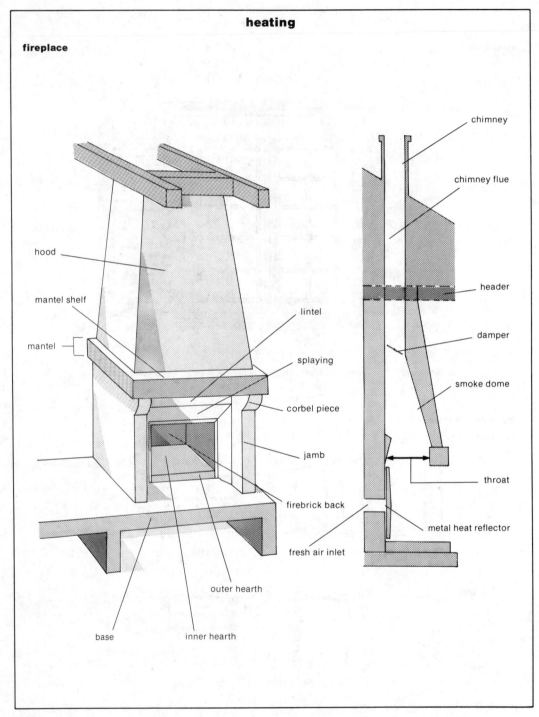

chimney

chimney flue

hood

mantel shelf

lintel

header

mantel

splaying

damper

corbel piece

smoke dome

jamb

firebrick back

throat

fresh air inlet

metal heat reflector

outer hearth

base

inner hearth

heating

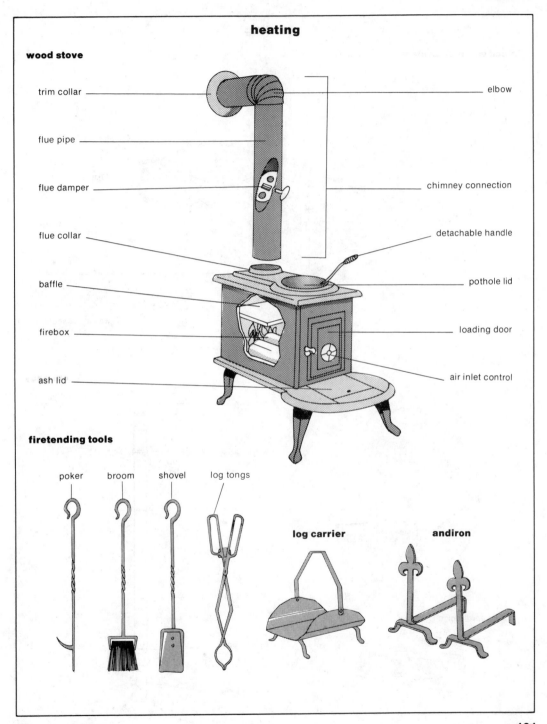

wood stove

trim collar — elbow

flue pipe

flue damper — chimney connection

flue collar — detachable handle

baffle — pothole lid

firebox — loading door

ash lid — air inlet control

firetending tools

poker broom shovel log tongs

log carrier **andiron**

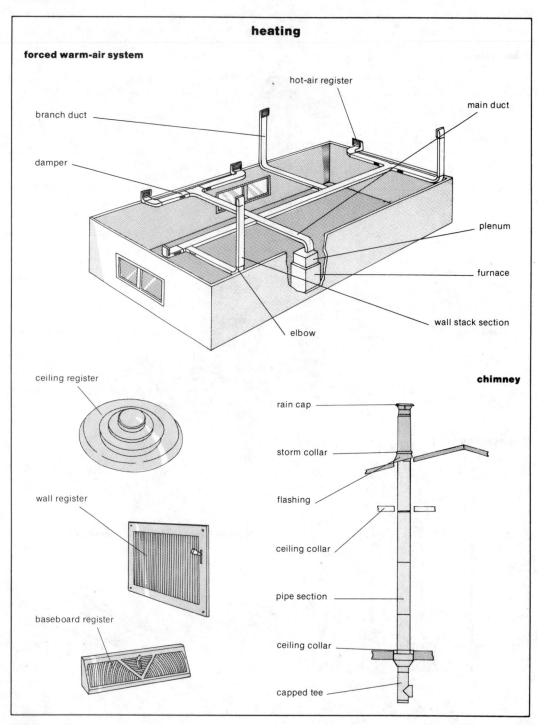

heating

forced warm-air system

hot-air register

branch duct

main duct

damper

plenum

furnace

wall stack section

elbow

ceiling register

chimney

rain cap

storm collar

flashing

ceiling collar

pipe section

wall register

ceiling collar

baseboard register

capped tee

heating

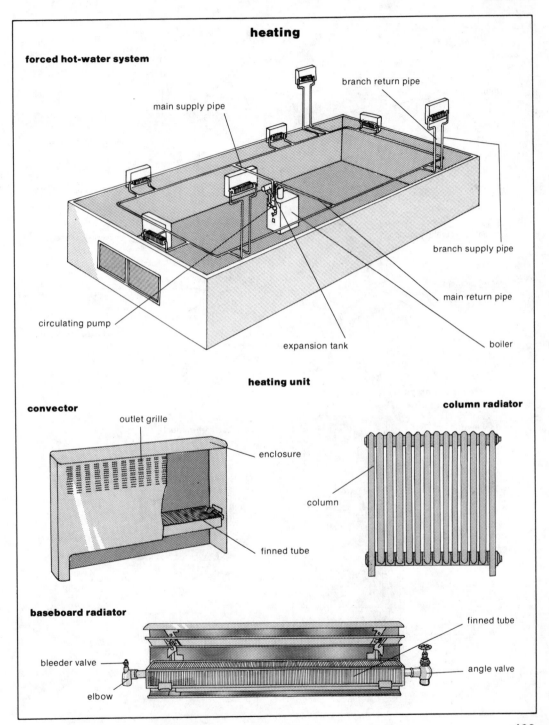

forced hot-water system

branch return pipe

main supply pipe

branch supply pipe

main return pipe

circulating pump

expansion tank

boiler

heating unit

convector

column radiator

outlet grille

enclosure

column

finned tube

baseboard radiator

finned tube

bleeder valve

angle valve

elbow

heating

boiler

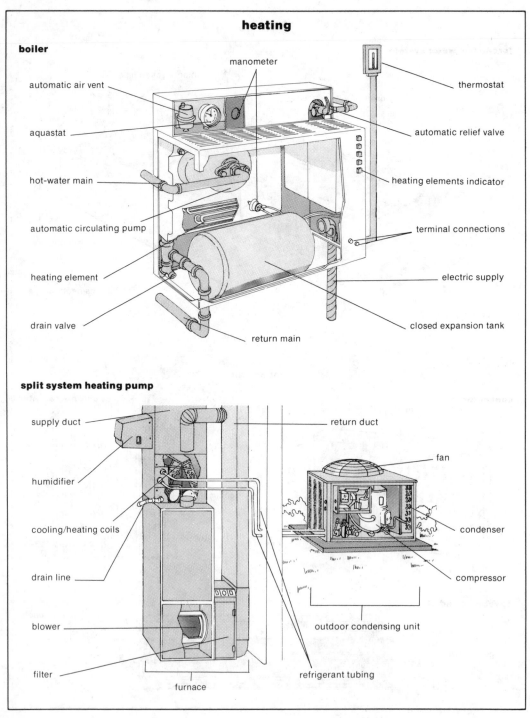

manometer

automatic air vent

thermostat

aquastat

automatic relief valve

hot-water main

heating elements indicator

automatic circulating pump

terminal connections

heating element

electric supply

drain valve

closed expansion tank

return main

split system heating pump

supply duct

return duct

fan

humidifier

cooling/heating coils

condenser

drain line

compressor

blower

outdoor condensing unit

filter

refrigerant tubing

furnace

heating

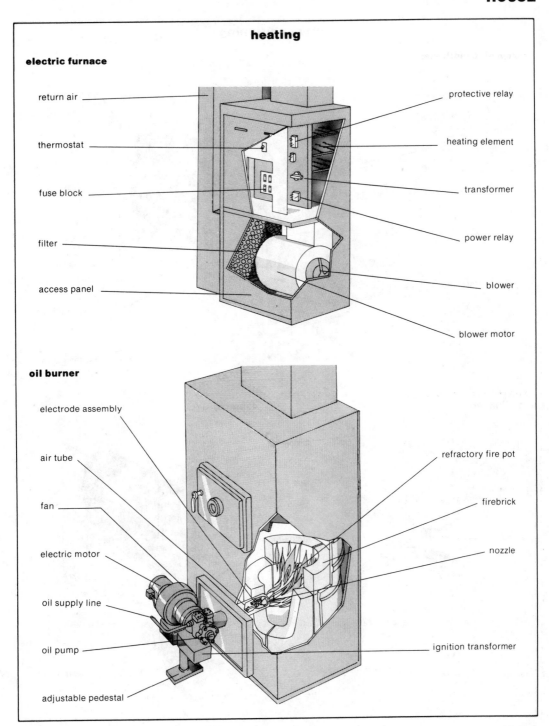

electric furnace

return air

thermostat

fuse block

filter

access panel

protective relay

heating element

transformer

power relay

blower

blower motor

oil burner

electrode assembly

air tube

fan

electric motor

oil supply line

oil pump

adjustable pedestal

refractory fire pot

firebrick

nozzle

ignition transformer

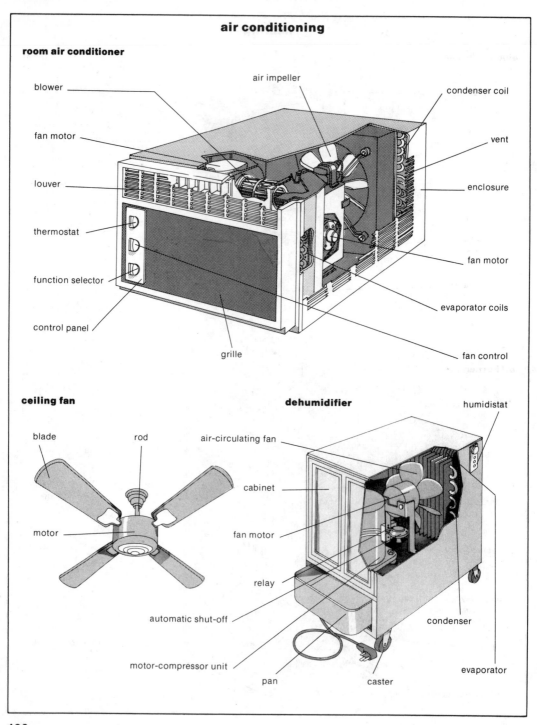

air conditioning

room air conditioner

blower

air impeller

condenser coil

fan motor

vent

louver

enclosure

thermostat

function selector

fan motor

evaporator coils

control panel

fan control

grille

ceiling fan

dehumidifier

humidistat

blade

rod

air-circulating fan

cabinet

motor

fan motor

relay

automatic shut-off

motor-compressor unit

pan

caster

condenser

evaporator

HOUSE FURNITURE

table

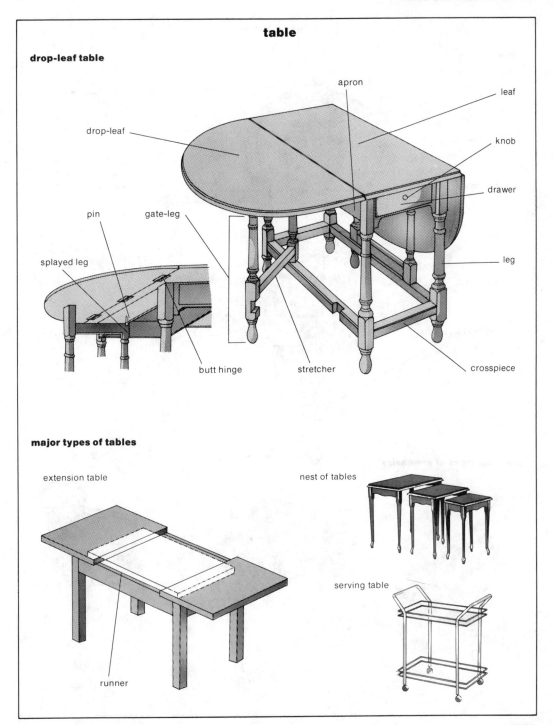

drop-leaf table

apron

leaf

drop-leaf

knob

drawer

pin

gate-leg

splayed leg

leg

butt hinge

stretcher

crosspiece

major types of tables

extension table

nest of tables

serving table

runner

armchair

parts

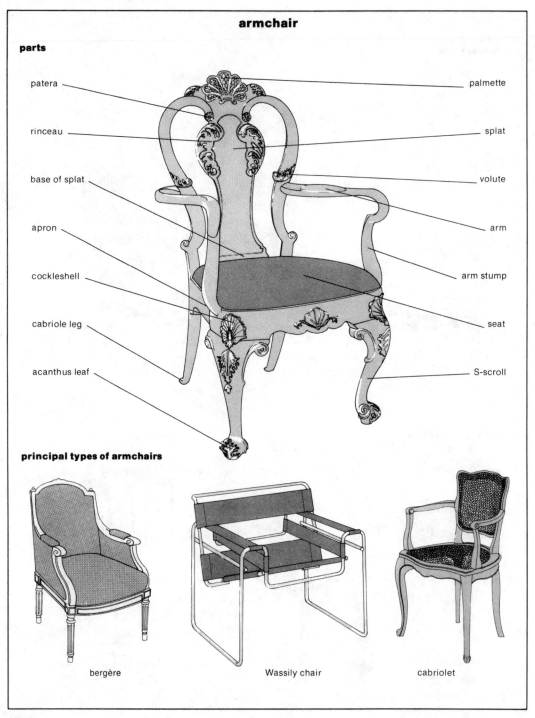

patera

rinceau

base of splat

apron

cockleshell

cabriole leg

acanthus leaf

palmette

splat

volute

arm

arm stump

seat

S-scroll

principal types of armchairs

bergère

Wassily chair

cabriolet

armchairs

principal types of armchairs

récamier

sofa

love seat

director's chair

club chair

chesterfield

rocking chair

méridienne

seats

banquette

hassock

bean bag chair

bench

step chair

stool

ottoman

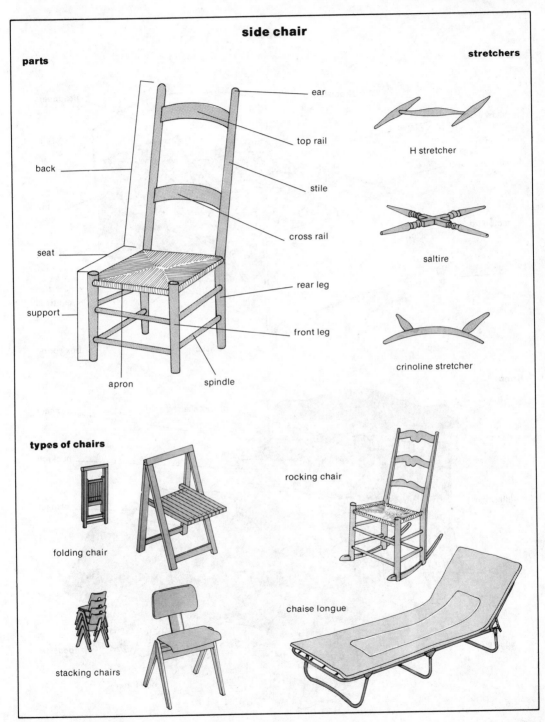

side chair

parts

stretchers

ear

top rail

back

stile

cross rail

H stretcher

seat

saltire

rear leg

support

front leg

crinoline stretcher

apron

spindle

types of chairs

rocking chair

folding chair

stacking chairs

chaise longue

HOUSE FURNITURE

bed

parts

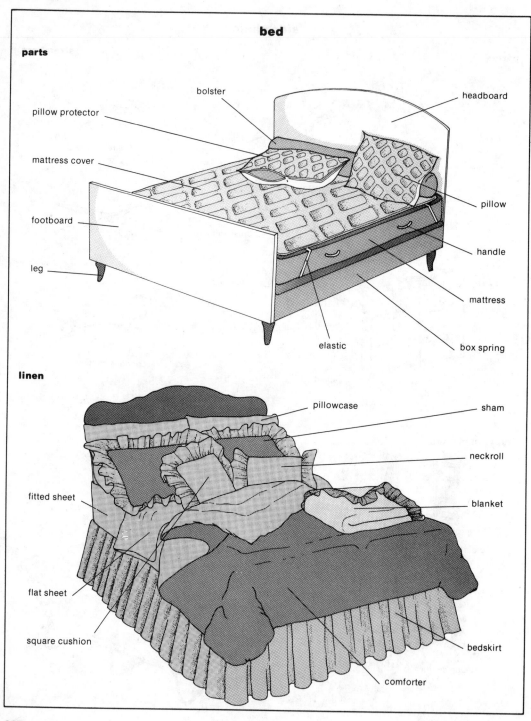

bolster

pillow protector

mattress cover

footboard

leg

headboard

pillow

handle

mattress

box spring

elastic

linen

pillowcase

sham

neckroll

blanket

fitted sheet

flat sheet

square cushion

bedskirt

comforter

storage furniture

armoire

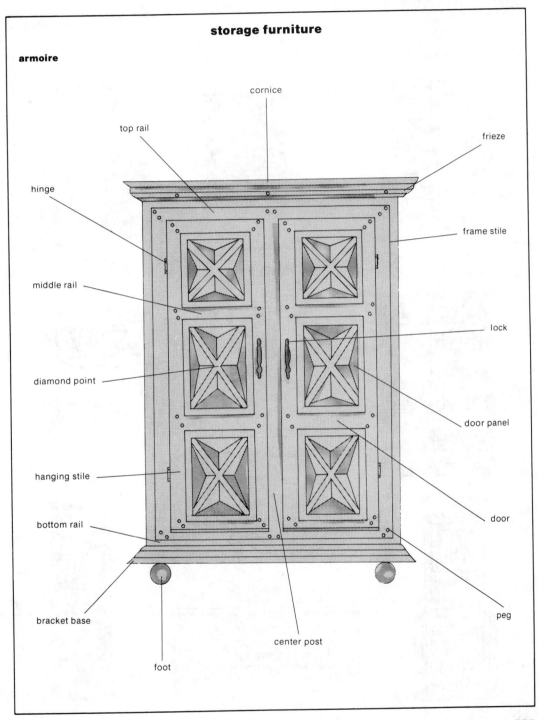

cornice

top rail

frieze

hinge

frame stile

middle rail

lock

diamond point

door panel

hanging stile

door

bottom rail

peg

bracket base

center post

foot

HOUSE FURNITURE

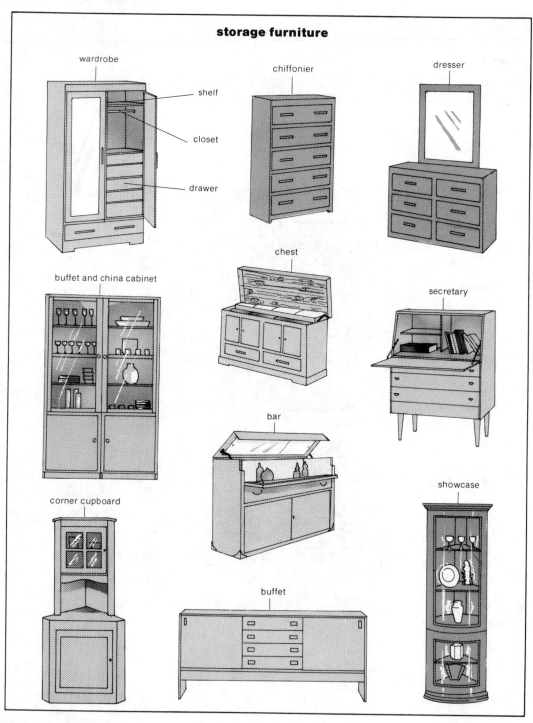

storage furniture

wardrobe

shelf

closet

drawer

chiffonier

dresser

buffet and china cabinet

chest

secretary

bar

corner cupboard

showcase

buffet

206

window accessories

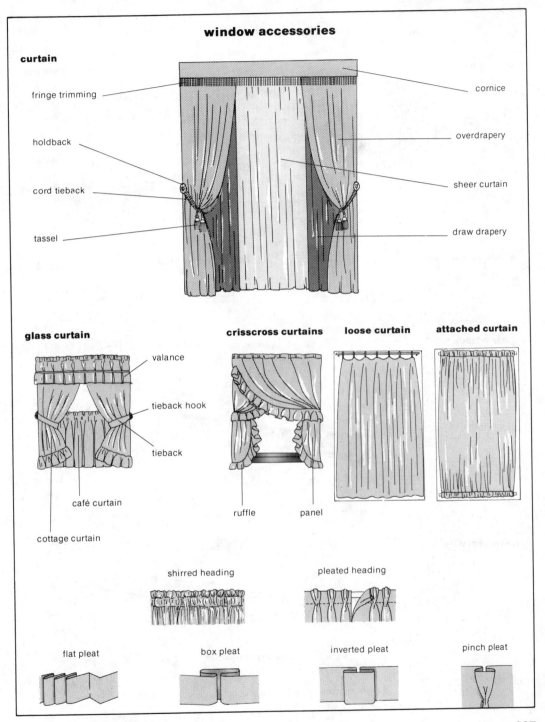

curtain

fringe trimming

cornice

holdback

overdrapery

cord tieback

sheer curtain

tassel

draw drapery

glass curtain

valance

tieback hook

tieback

café curtain

cottage curtain

crisscross curtains

ruffle   panel

loose curtain

attached curtain

shirred heading

pleated heading

flat pleat

box pleat

inverted pleat

pinch pleat

HOUSE FURNITURE

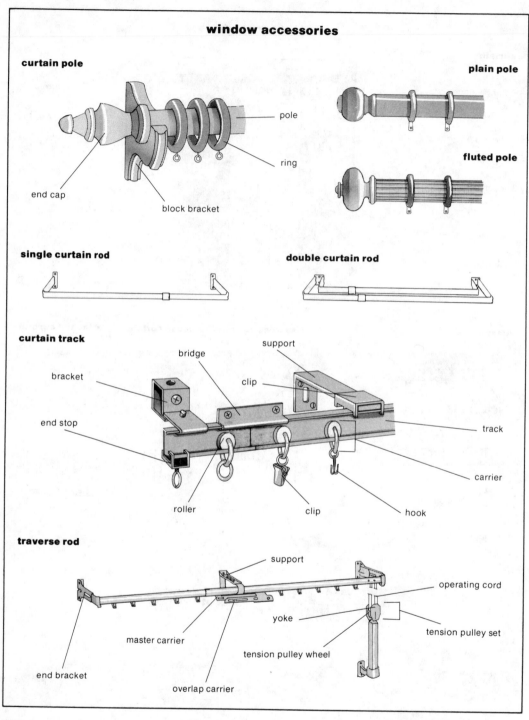

window accessories

curtain pole

pole

ring

end cap

block bracket

plain pole

fluted pole

single curtain rod

double curtain rod

curtain track

bridge

support

bracket

clip

end stop

track

carrier

roller

clip

hook

traverse rod

support

operating cord

yoke

tension pulley set

master carrier

tension pulley wheel

end bracket

overlap carrier

window accessories

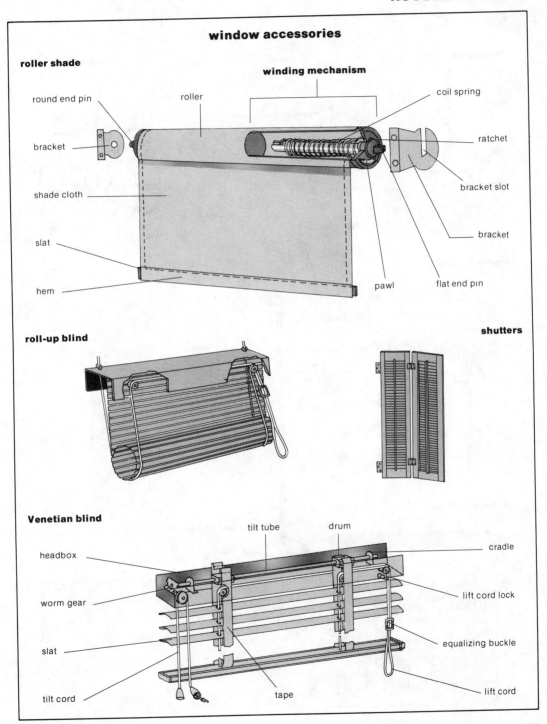

roller shade

round end pin

roller

winding mechanism

coil spring

bracket

ratchet

shade cloth

bracket slot

slat

bracket

hem

pawl

flat end pin

roll-up blind

shutters

Venetian blind

tilt tube

drum

cradle

headbox

worm gear

lift cord lock

slat

equalizing buckle

tilt cord

tape

lift cord

lights

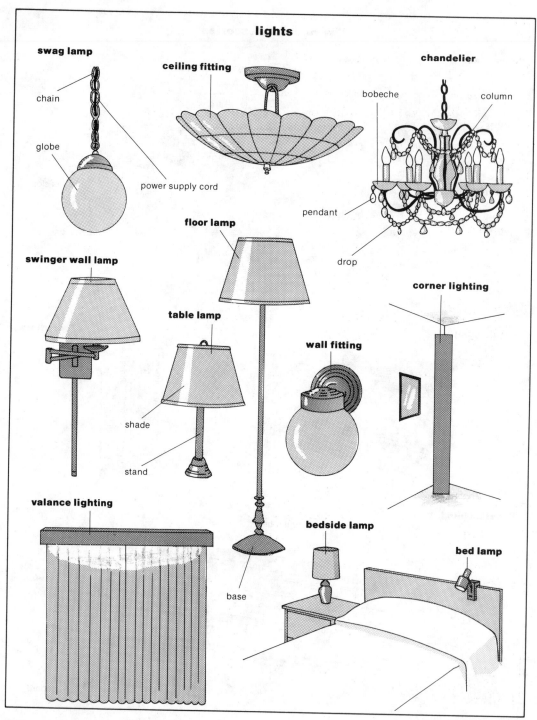

swag lamp

chain

globe

ceiling fitting

power supply cord

chandelier

bobeche

column

pendant

drop

floor lamp

swinger wall lamp

table lamp

wall fitting

corner lighting

shade

stand

valance lighting

bedside lamp

bed lamp

base

lights

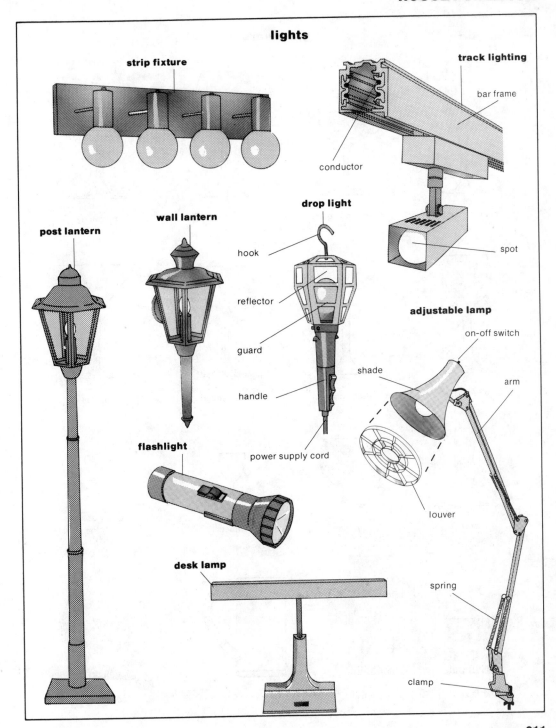

strip fixture

track lighting

bar frame

conductor

drop light

wall lantern

post lantern

hook

reflector

guard

handle

spot

adjustable lamp

on-off switch

shade

arm

flashlight

power supply cord

louver

desk lamp

spring

clamp

glassware

champagne flute

champagne glass

bordeaux

burgundy

white wine

Alsace glass

water goblet

cocktail

port

brandy

liqueur

old-fashioned

highball

beer mug

decanter

dinnerware

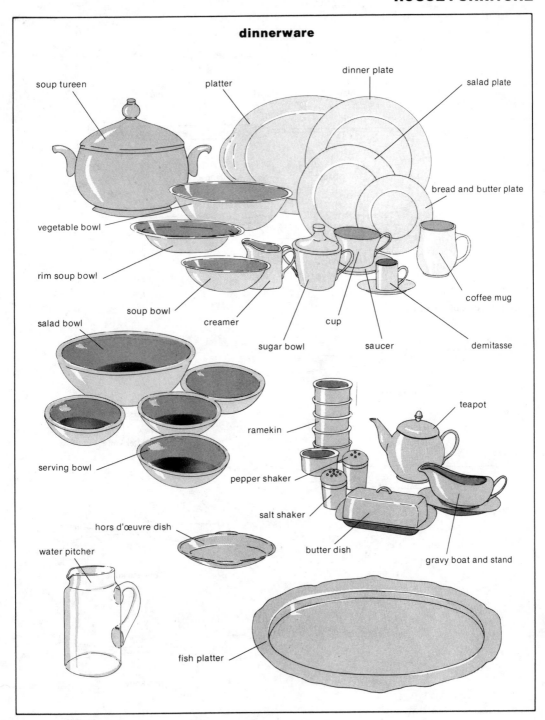

soup tureen

platter

dinner plate

salad plate

bread and butter plate

vegetable bowl

rim soup bowl

soup bowl

creamer

sugar bowl

cup

saucer

coffee mug

demitasse

salad bowl

serving bowl

ramekin

pepper shaker

salt shaker

teapot

butter dish

gravy boat and stand

hors d'œuvre dish

water pitcher

fish platter

HOUSE FURNITURE

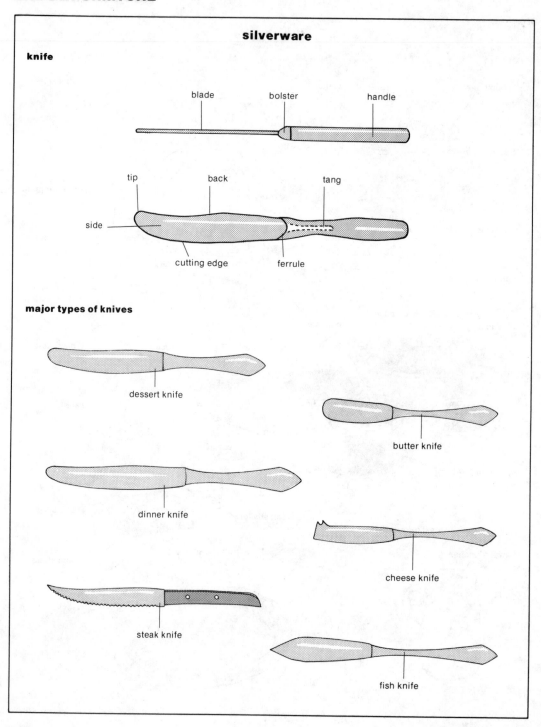

silverware

knife

blade   bolster   handle

tip   back   tang

side

cutting edge   ferrule

major types of knives

dessert knife

butter knife

dinner knife

cheese knife

steak knife

fish knife

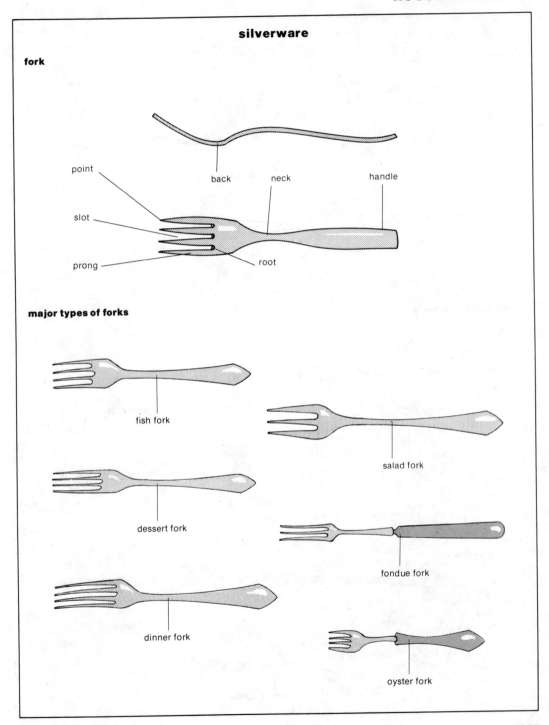

silverware

fork

point
back
neck
handle
slot
prong
root

major types of forks

fish fork

salad fork

dessert fork

fondue fork

dinner fork

oyster fork

HOUSE FURNITURE

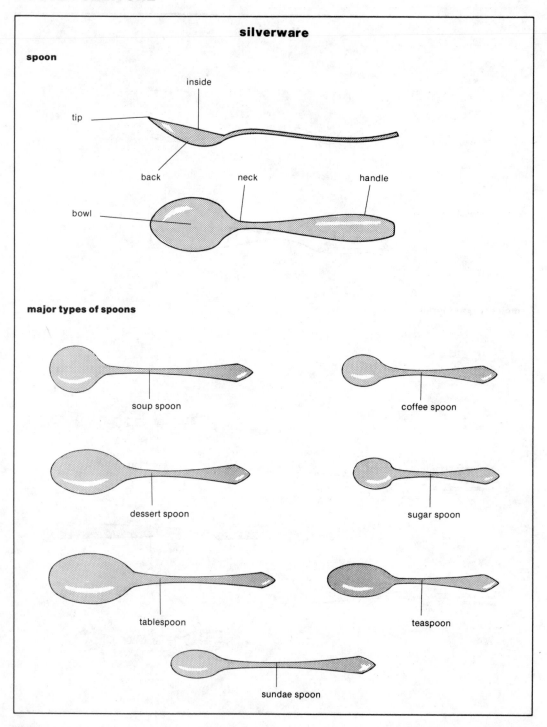

silverware

spoon

inside

tip

back   neck   handle

bowl

major types of spoons

soup spoon

coffee spoon

dessert spoon

sugar spoon

tablespoon

teaspoon

sundae spoon

kitchen utensils

kitchen knife

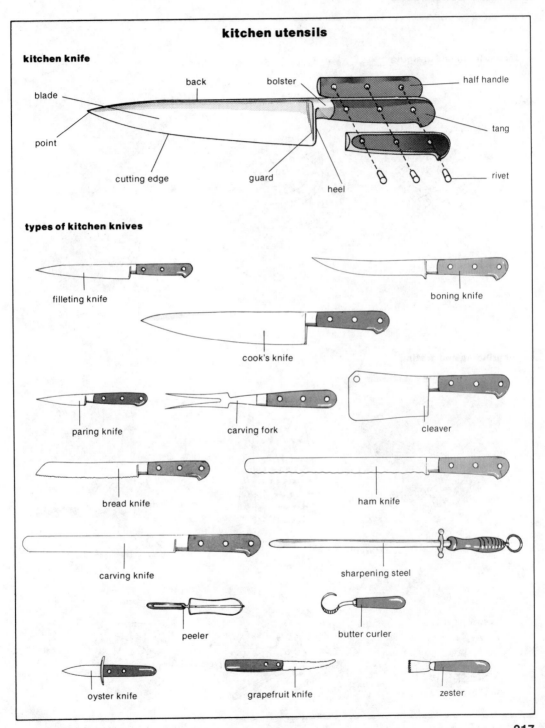

blade

point

back

bolster

half handle

tang

cutting edge

guard

heel

rivet

types of kitchen knives

filleting knife

boning knife

cook's knife

paring knife

carving fork

cleaver

bread knife

ham knife

carving knife

sharpening steel

peeler

butter curler

oyster knife

grapefruit knife

zester

kitchen utensils

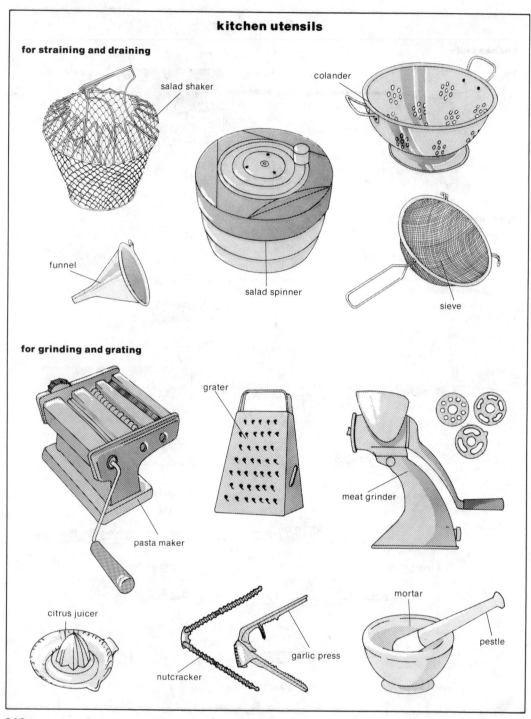

for straining and draining

salad shaker

colander

funnel

salad spinner

sieve

for grinding and grating

grater

pasta maker

meat grinder

citrus juicer

nutcracker

garlic press

mortar

pestle

kitchen utensils

set of utensils

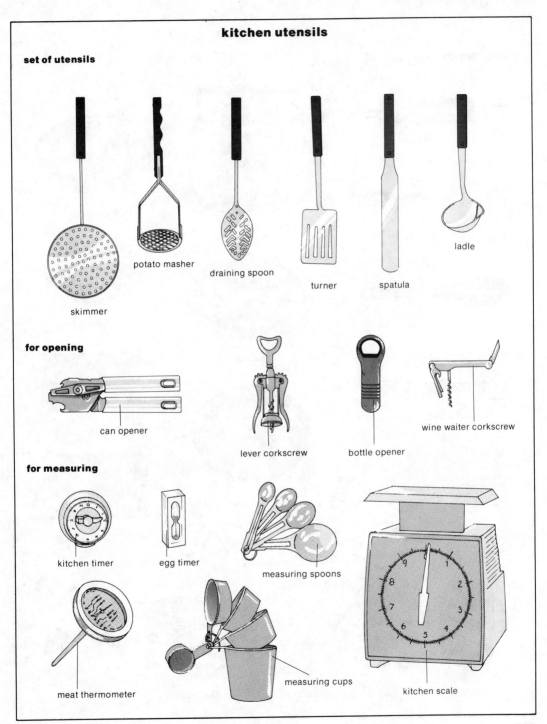

skimmer

potato masher

draining spoon

turner

spatula

ladle

for opening

can opener

lever corkscrew

bottle opener

wine waiter corkscrew

for measuring

kitchen timer

egg timer

measuring spoons

meat thermometer

measuring cups

kitchen scale

HOUSE FURNITURE

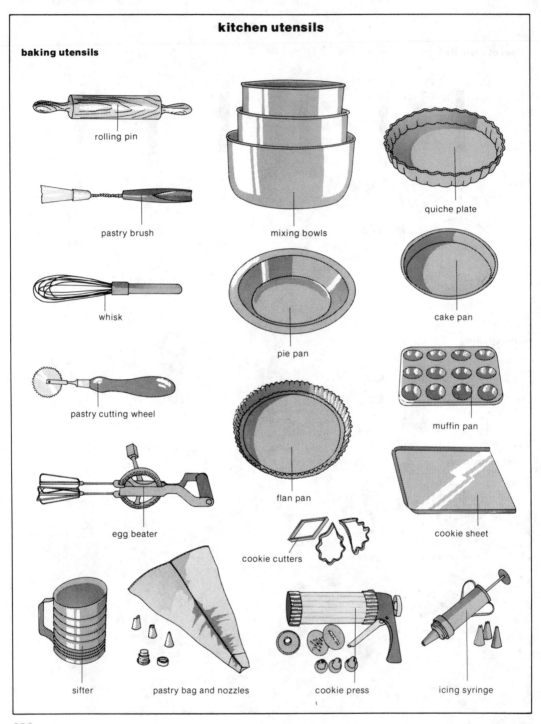

kitchen utensils

baking utensils

rolling pin

pastry brush

whisk

pastry cutting wheel

egg beater

sifter

pastry bag and nozzles

mixing bowls

pie pan

flan pan

cookie cutters

cookie press

quiche plate

cake pan

muffin pan

cookie sheet

icing syringe

kitchen utensils

miscellaneous utensils

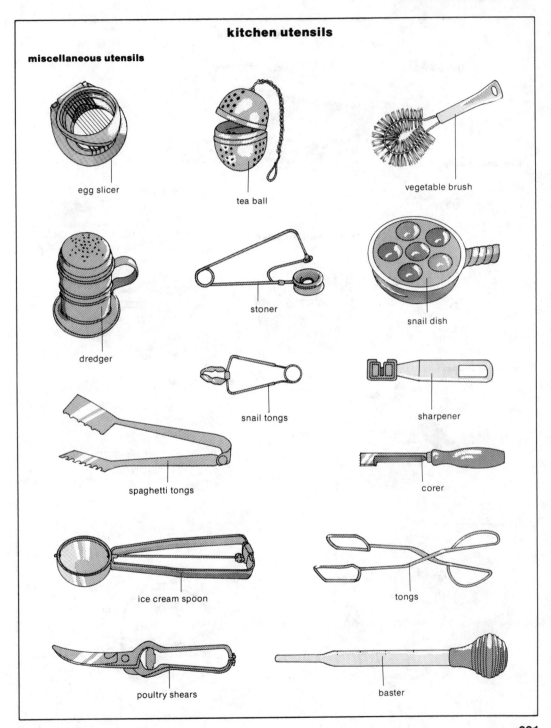

egg slicer

tea ball

vegetable brush

dredger

stoner

snail dish

spaghetti tongs

snail tongs

sharpener

corer

ice cream spoon

tongs

poultry shears

baster

cooking utensils

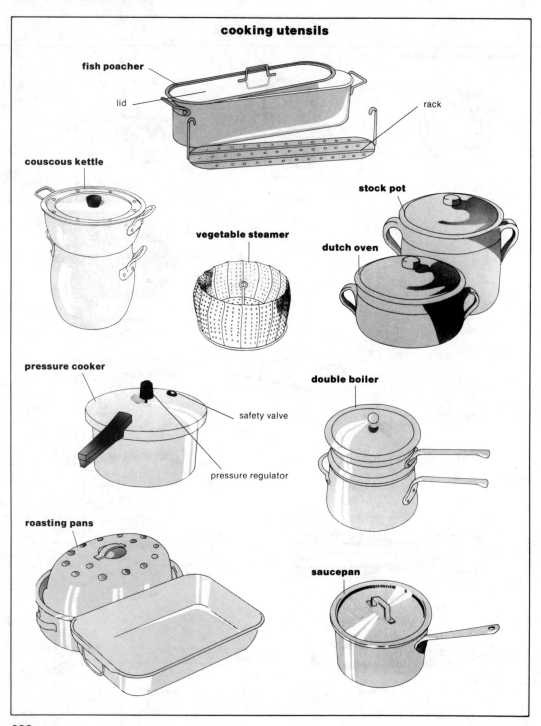

fish poacher

lid

rack

couscous kettle

stock pot

vegetable steamer

dutch oven

pressure cooker

safety valve

pressure regulator

double boiler

roasting pans

saucepan

cooking utensils

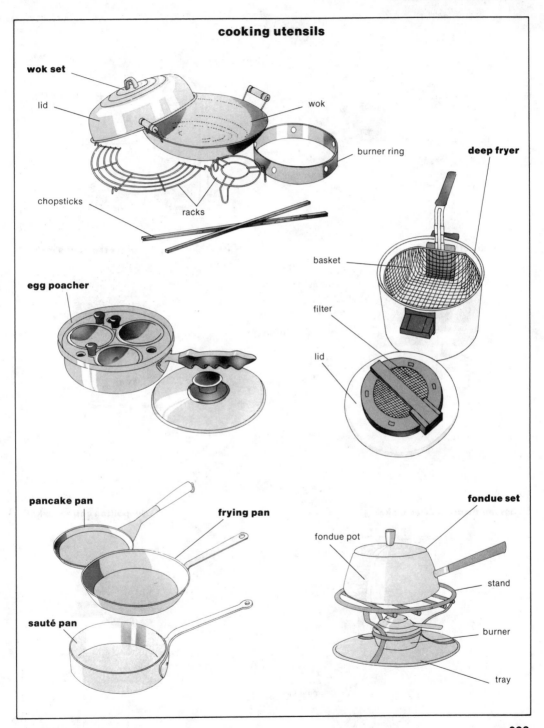

wok set

lid

wok

burner ring

chopsticks

racks

deep fryer

basket

filter

lid

egg poacher

pancake pan

frying pan

fondue pot

fondue set

stand

sauté pan

burner

tray

HOUSE FURNITURE

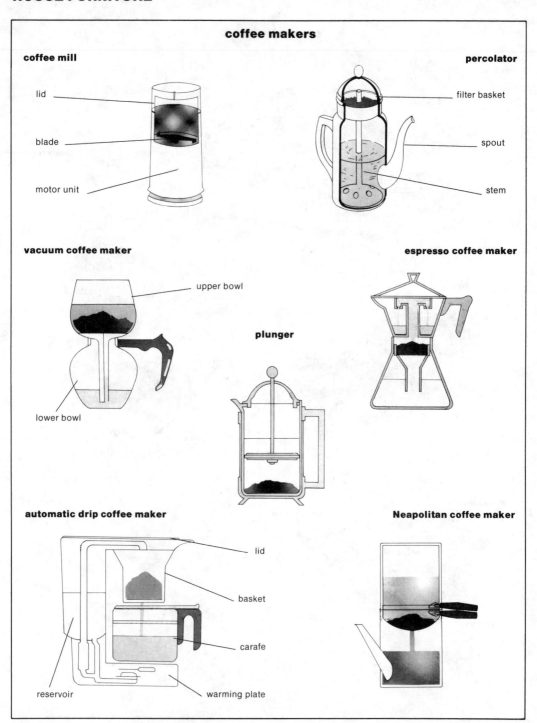

coffee makers

coffee mill

- lid
- blade
- motor unit

percolator

- filter basket
- spout
- stem

vacuum coffee maker

- upper bowl
- lower bowl

plunger

espresso coffee maker

automatic drip coffee maker

- lid
- basket
- carafe
- reservoir
- warming plate

Neapolitan coffee maker

domestic appliances

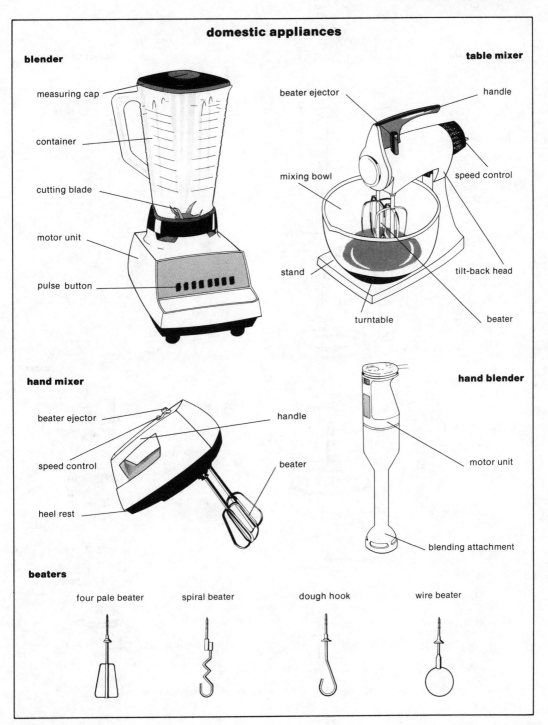

blender

measuring cap

container

cutting blade

motor unit

pulse button

table mixer

beater ejector

handle

mixing bowl

speed control

stand

tilt-back head

turntable

beater

hand mixer

beater ejector

handle

speed control

beater

heel rest

hand blender

motor unit

blending attachment

beaters

four pale beater

spiral beater

dough hook

wire beater

domestic appliances

food processor

ice-cream freezer

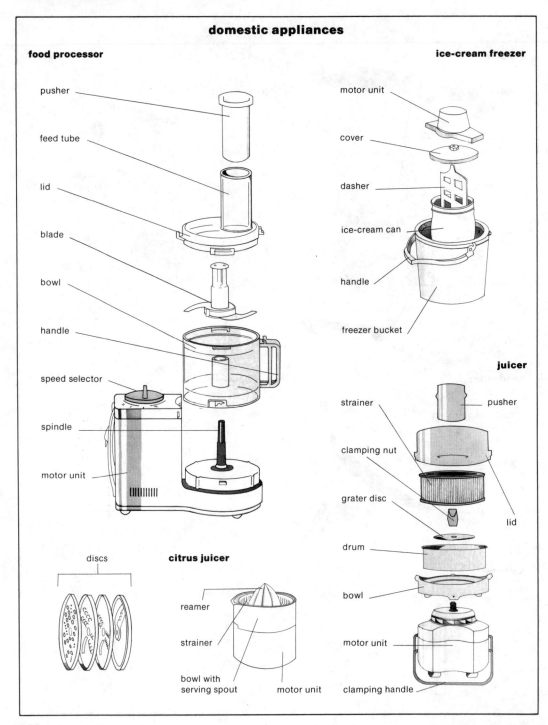

pusher

feed tube

lid

blade

bowl

handle

speed selector

spindle

motor unit

discs

citrus juicer

reamer

strainer

bowl with
serving spout

motor unit

motor unit

cover

dasher

ice-cream can

handle

freezer bucket

juicer

strainer

pusher

clamping nut

grater disc

lid

drum

bowl

motor unit

clamping handle

domestic appliances

microwave oven

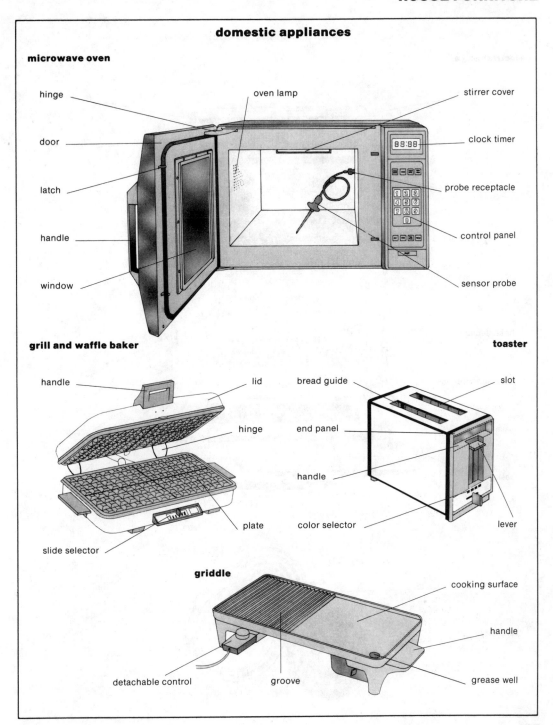

hinge

oven lamp

stirrer cover

door

clock timer

latch

probe receptacle

handle

control panel

window

sensor probe

grill and waffle baker

toaster

handle

lid

bread guide

slot

hinge

end panel

handle

plate

color selector

lever

slide selector

griddle

cooking surface

handle

detachable control

groove

grease well

domestic appliances

electric range

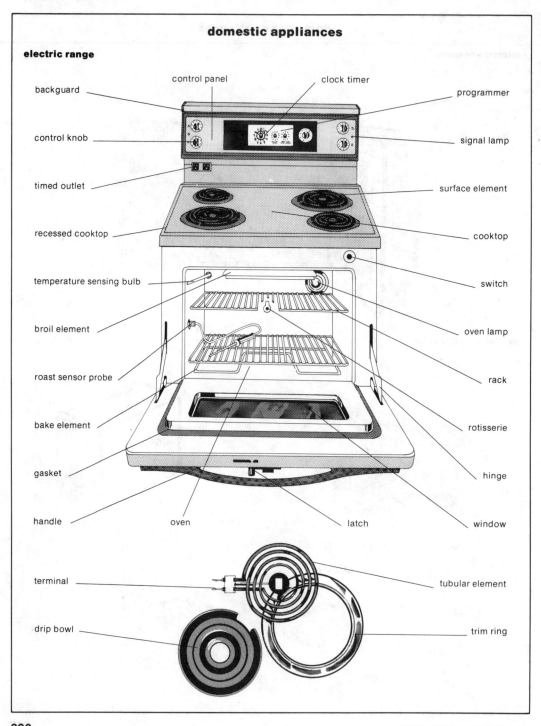

control panel

clock timer

backguard

programmer

control knob

signal lamp

timed outlet

surface element

recessed cooktop

cooktop

temperature sensing bulb

switch

broil element

oven lamp

roast sensor probe

rack

bake element

rotisserie

gasket

hinge

handle

oven

latch

window

terminal

tubular element

drip bowl

trim ring

domestic appliances

frost-free refrigerator

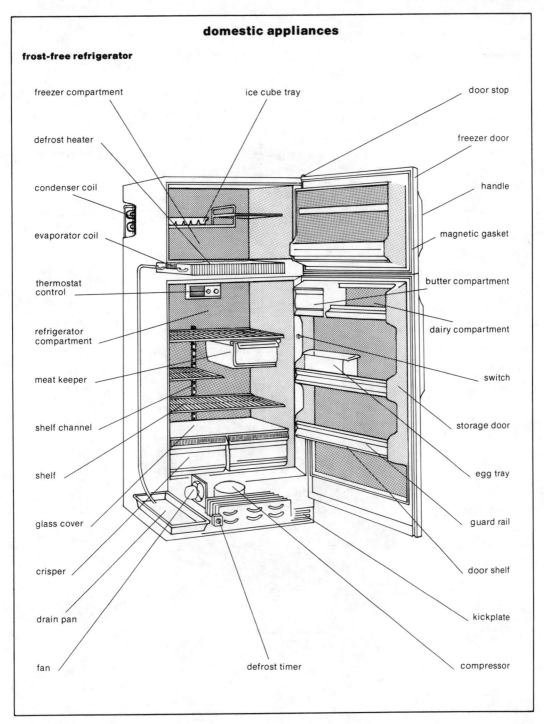

freezer compartment

ice cube tray

door stop

defrost heater

freezer door

condenser coil

handle

evaporator coil

magnetic gasket

thermostat control

butter compartment

refrigerator compartment

dairy compartment

meat keeper

switch

shelf channel

storage door

shelf

egg tray

glass cover

guard rail

crisper

door shelf

drain pan

kickplate

fan

defrost timer

compressor

domestic appliances

washer

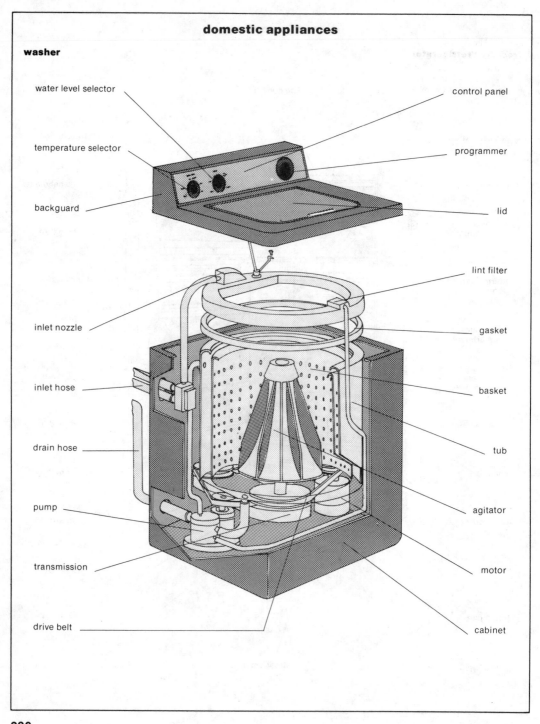

water level selector

control panel

temperature selector

programmer

backguard

lid

lint filter

inlet nozzle

gasket

inlet hose

basket

drain hose

tub

pump

agitator

transmission

motor

drive belt

cabinet

domestic appliances

dryer

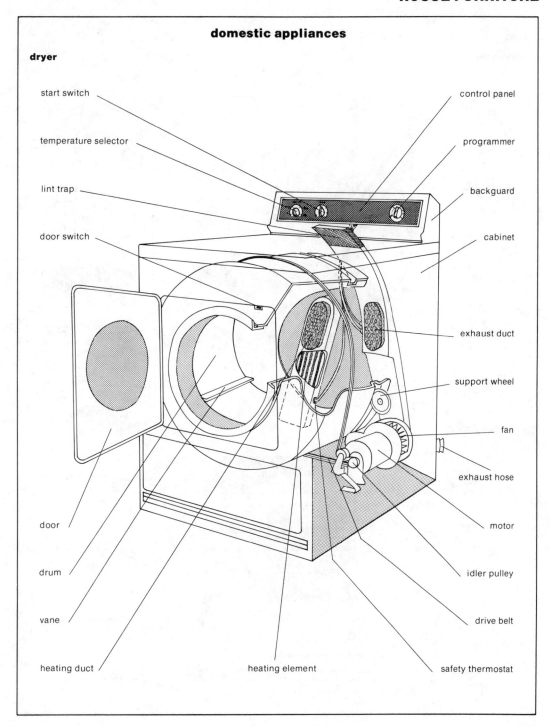

start switch

temperature selector

lint trap

door switch

control panel

programmer

backguard

cabinet

exhaust duct

support wheel

fan

exhaust hose

motor

idler pulley

drive belt

safety thermostat

door

drum

vane

heating duct

heating element

HOUSE FURNITURE

domestic appliances

dishwasher

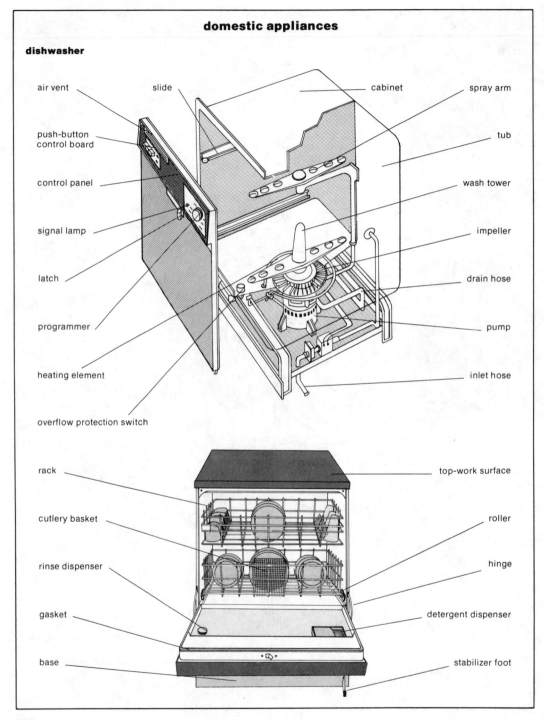

air vent

slide

cabinet

spray arm

push-button control board

tub

control panel

wash tower

signal lamp

impeller

latch

drain hose

programmer

pump

heating element

inlet hose

overflow protection switch

rack

top-work surface

cutlery basket

roller

rinse dispenser

hinge

gasket

detergent dispenser

base

stabilizer foot

domestic appliances

steam iron

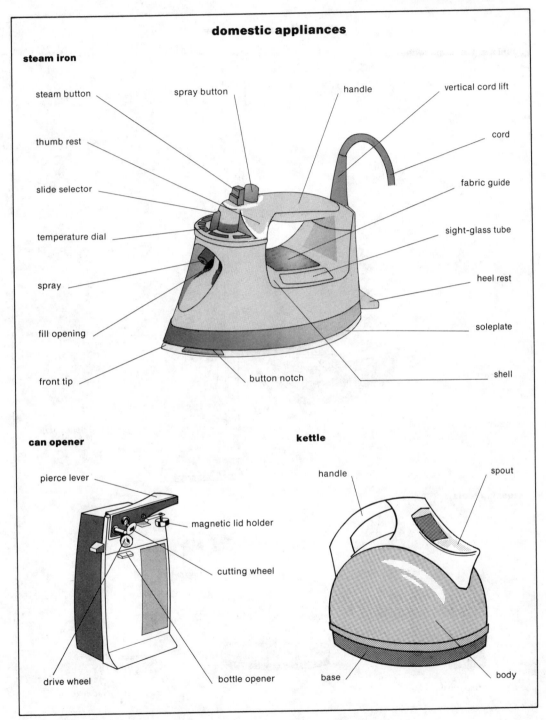

steam button

spray button

handle

vertical cord lift

thumb rest

cord

slide selector

fabric guide

temperature dial

sight-glass tube

spray

heel rest

fill opening

soleplate

front tip

button notch

shell

can opener

kettle

pierce lever

handle

spout

magnetic lid holder

cutting wheel

drive wheel

bottle opener

base

body

HOUSE FURNITURE

domestic appliances

canister vacuum cleaner

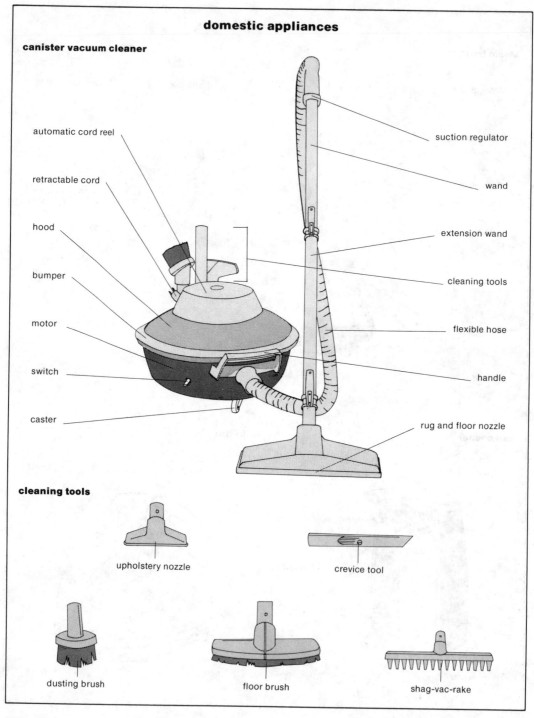

automatic cord reel

retractable cord

hood

bumper

motor

switch

caster

suction regulator

wand

extension wand

cleaning tools

flexible hose

handle

rug and floor nozzle

cleaning tools

upholstery nozzle

crevice tool

dusting brush

floor brush

shag-vac-rake

GARDENING

pleasure garden

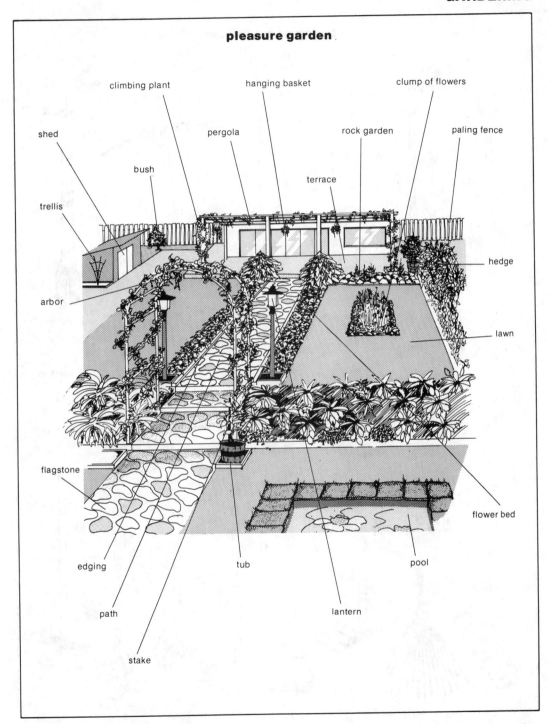

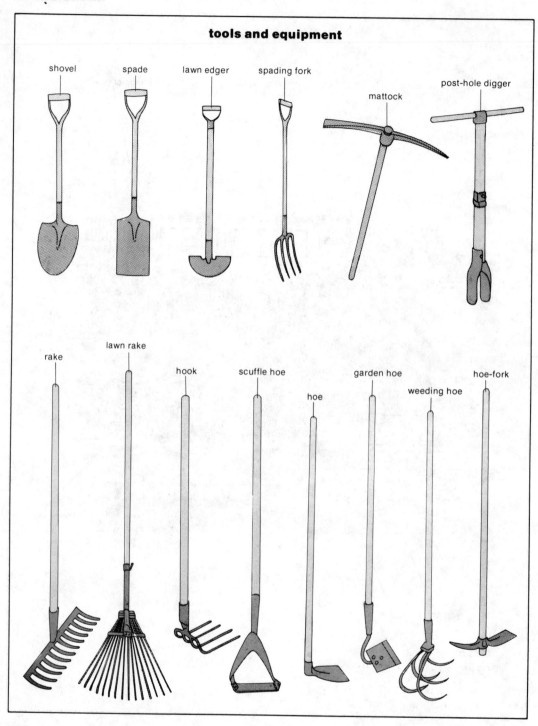

tools and equipment

shovel

spade

lawn edger

spading fork

mattock

post-hole digger

rake

lawn rake

hook

scuffle hoe

hoe

garden hoe

weeding hoe

hoe-fork

tools and equipment

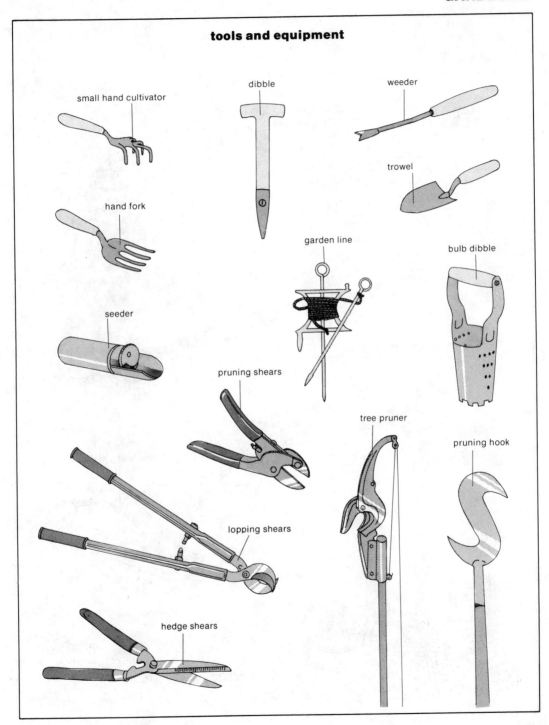

small hand cultivator

dibble

weeder

trowel

hand fork

garden line

bulb dibble

seeder

pruning shears

tree pruner

pruning hook

lopping shears

hedge shears

GARDENING

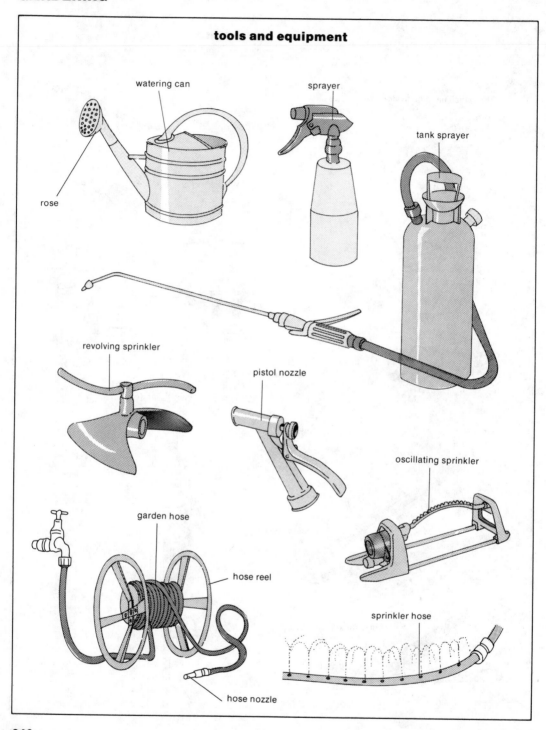

tools and equipment

watering can

sprayer

tank sprayer

rose

revolving sprinkler

pistol nozzle

oscillating sprinkler

garden hose

hose reel

sprinkler hose

hose nozzle

tools and equipment

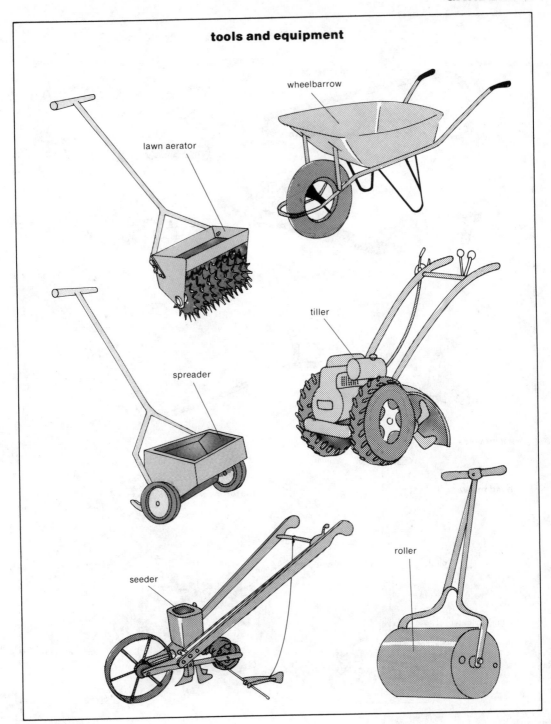

wheelbarrow

lawn aerator

spreader

tiller

seeder

roller

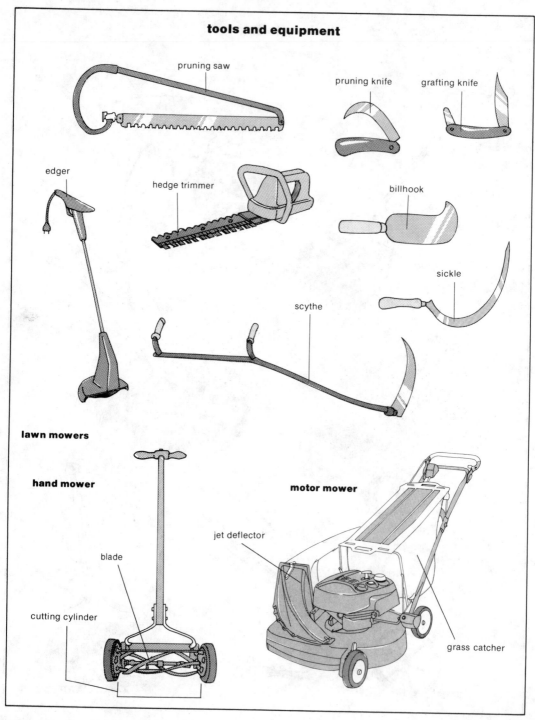

tools and equipment

pruning saw

pruning knife

grafting knife

edger

hedge trimmer

billhook

sickle

scythe

lawn mowers

hand mower

motor mower

jet deflector

blade

cutting cylinder

grass catcher

chainsaw

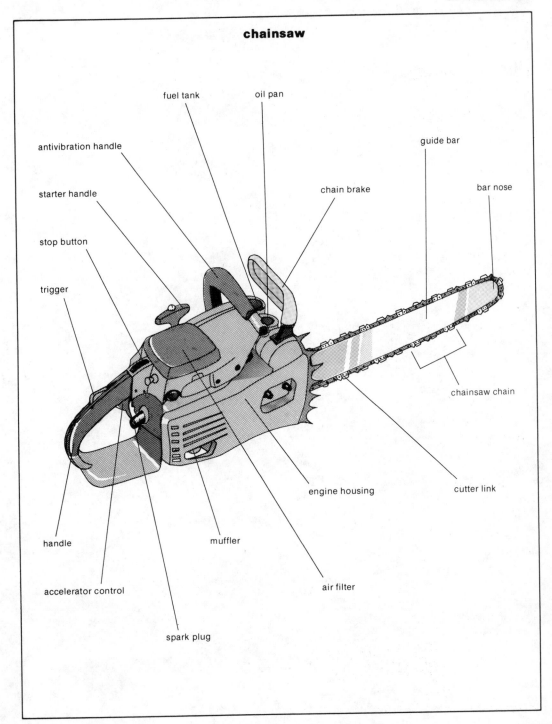

fuel tank

oil pan

guide bar

antivibration handle

chain brake

bar nose

starter handle

stop button

trigger

chainsaw chain

engine housing

cutter link

handle

muffler

accelerator control

air filter

spark plug

DO-IT-YOURSELF

carpentry: tools

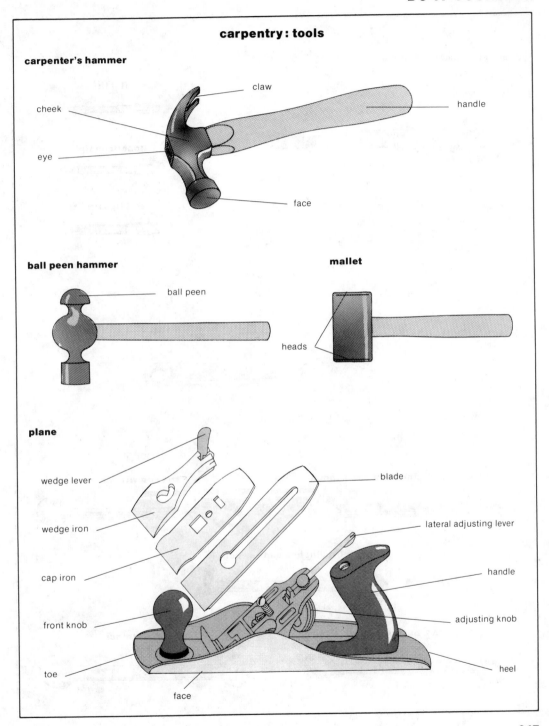

carpenter's hammer

claw

cheek

handle

eye

face

ball peen hammer

ball peen

mallet

heads

plane

wedge lever

blade

wedge iron

lateral adjusting lever

cap iron

handle

front knob

adjusting knob

toe

heel

face

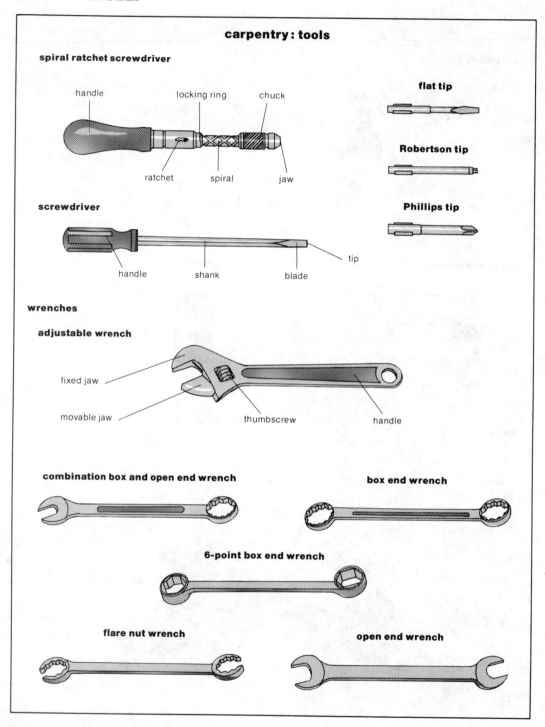

carpentry : tools

spiral ratchet screwdriver

handle   locking ring   chuck

ratchet   spiral   jaw

flat tip

Robertson tip

screwdriver

handle   shank   blade   tip

Phillips tip

wrenches

adjustable wrench

fixed jaw

movable jaw   thumbscrew   handle

combination box and open end wrench

box end wrench

6-point box end wrench

flare nut wrench

open end wrench

carpentry: tools

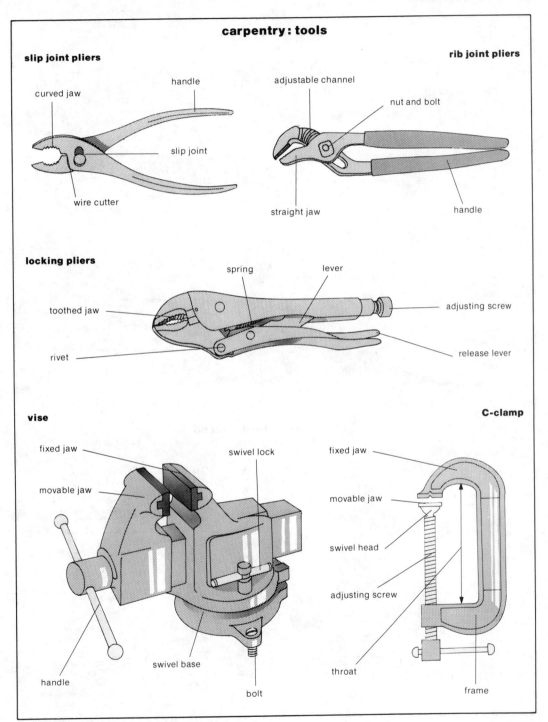

slip joint pliers

handle

curved jaw

slip joint

wire cutter

rib joint pliers

adjustable channel

nut and bolt

straight jaw

handle

locking pliers

spring

lever

toothed jaw

adjusting screw

rivet

release lever

vise

fixed jaw

swivel lock

movable jaw

handle

swivel base

bolt

C-clamp

fixed jaw

movable jaw

swivel head

adjusting screw

throat

frame

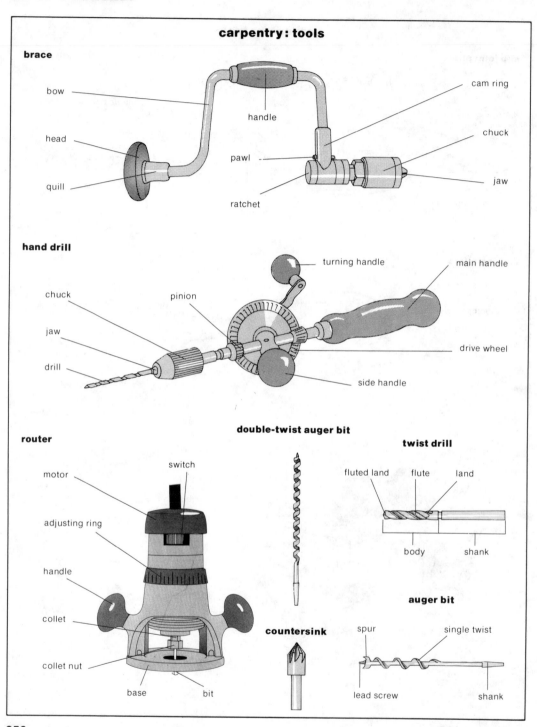

carpentry: tools

brace

bow

head

quill

handle

pawl

ratchet

cam ring

chuck

jaw

hand drill

chuck

jaw

drill

pinion

turning handle

main handle

drive wheel

side handle

router

motor

adjusting ring

handle

collet

collet nut

switch

base

bit

double-twist auger bit

countersink

twist drill

fluted land

flute

land

body

shank

auger bit

spur

single twist

lead screw

shank

carpentry : tools

drill press

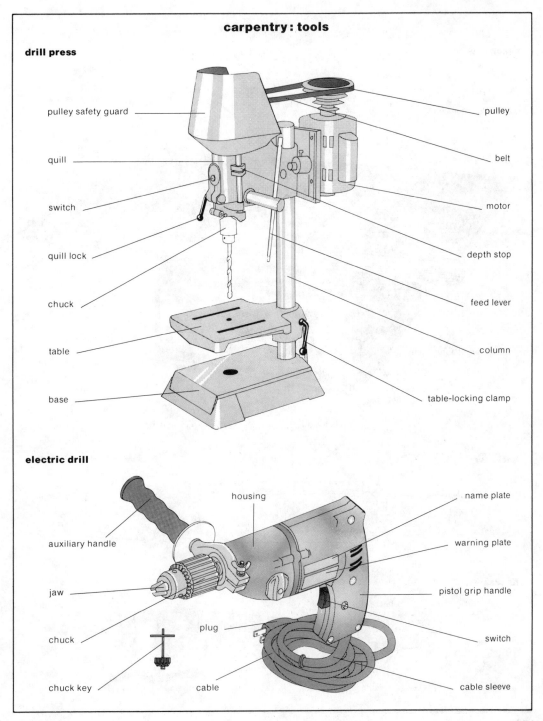

pulley safety guard

quill

switch

quill lock

chuck

table

base

pulley

belt

motor

depth stop

feed lever

column

table-locking clamp

electric drill

housing

auxiliary handle

jaw

chuck

chuck key

plug

cable

name plate

warning plate

pistol grip handle

switch

cable sleeve

carpentry : tools

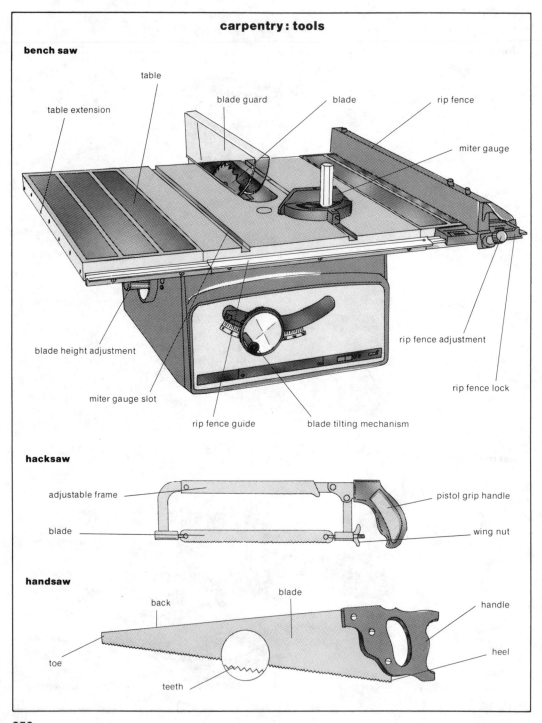

bench saw

table

table extension

blade guard

blade

rip fence

miter gauge

blade height adjustment

rip fence adjustment

miter gauge slot

rip fence lock

rip fence guide

blade tilting mechanism

hacksaw

adjustable frame

pistol grip handle

blade

wing nut

handsaw

back

blade

handle

toe

heel

teeth

carpentry : tools

circular saw

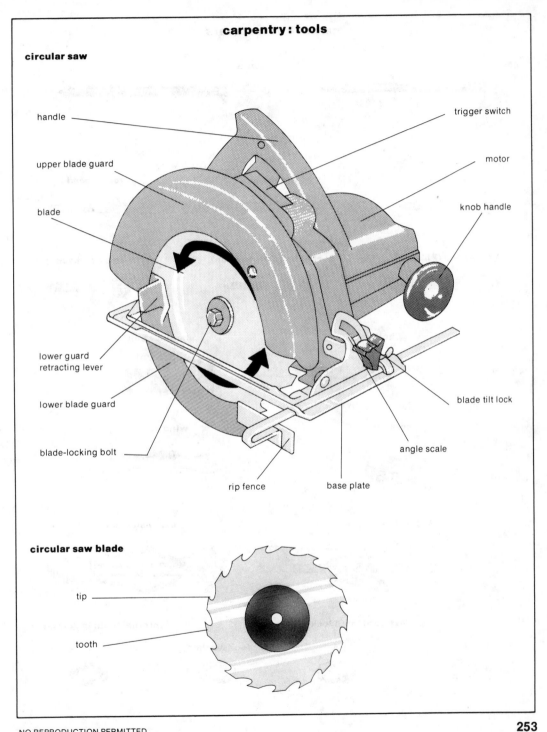

handle

trigger switch

upper blade guard

motor

blade

knob handle

lower guard
retracting lever

lower blade guard

blade-locking bolt

blade tilt lock

angle scale

rip fence

base plate

circular saw blade

tip

tooth

253

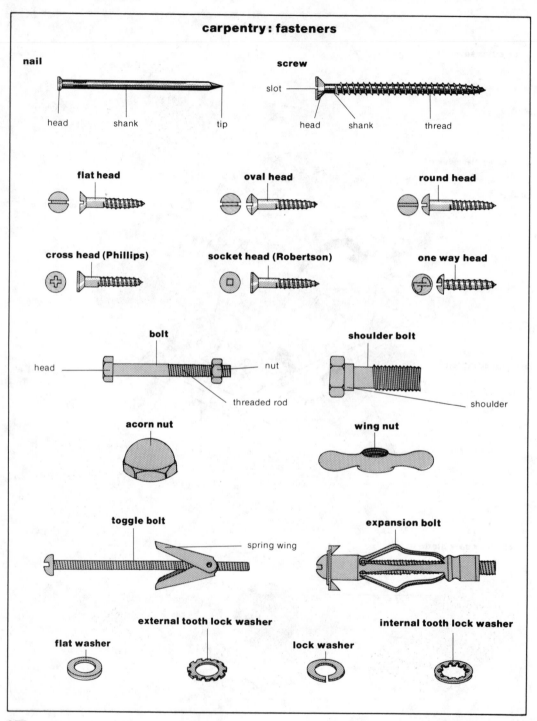

carpentry: fasteners

nail

head   shank   tip

screw

slot   head   shank   thread

flat head

oval head

round head

cross head (Phillips)

socket head (Robertson)

one way head

bolt

head   nut

threaded rod

shoulder bolt

shoulder

acorn nut

wing nut

toggle bolt

spring wing

expansion bolt

external tooth lock washer

internal tooth lock washer

flat washer

lock washer

carpentry

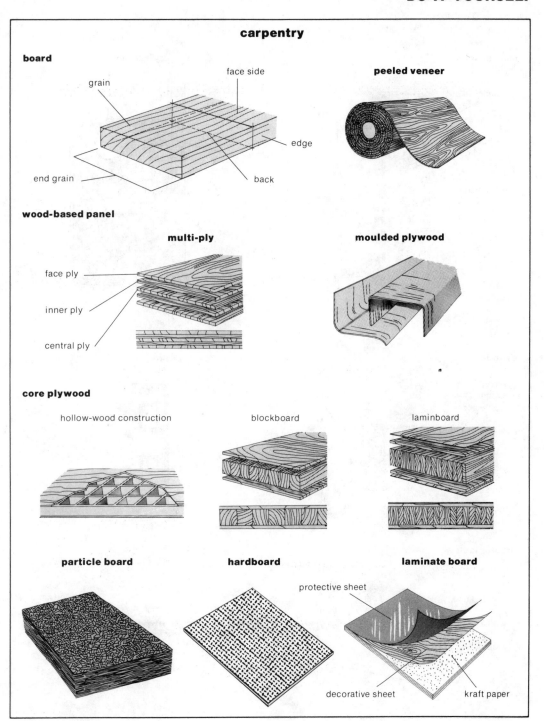

board

grain

face side

edge

end grain

back

peeled veneer

wood-based panel

multi-ply

face ply

inner ply

central ply

moulded plywood

core plywood

hollow-wood construction

blockboard

laminboard

particle board

hardboard

laminate board

protective sheet

decorative sheet

kraft paper

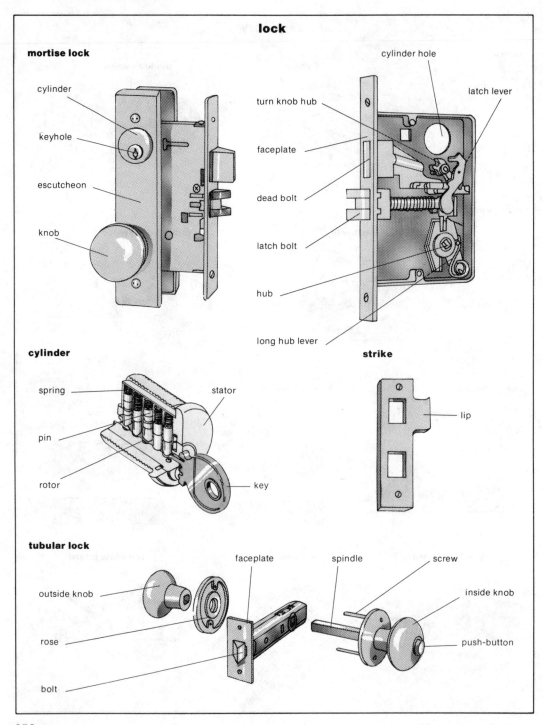

lock

mortise lock

cylinder

keyhole

escutcheon

knob

cylinder hole

turn knob hub

latch lever

faceplate

dead bolt

latch bolt

hub

long hub lever

cylinder

spring

stator

pin

rotor

key

strike

lip

tubular lock

outside knob

faceplate

spindle

screw

inside knob

rose

push-button

bolt

plumbing

plumbing system

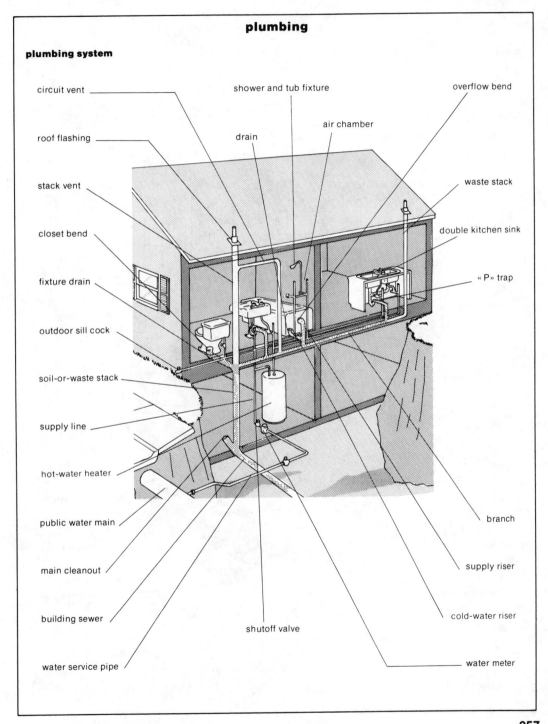

circuit vent

roof flashing

stack vent

closet bend

fixture drain

outdoor sill cock

soil-or-waste stack

supply line

hot-water heater

public water main

main cleanout

building sewer

water service pipe

shower and tub fixture

drain

air chamber

shutoff valve

overflow bend

waste stack

double kitchen sink

« P » trap

branch

supply riser

cold-water riser

water meter

plumbing

toilet

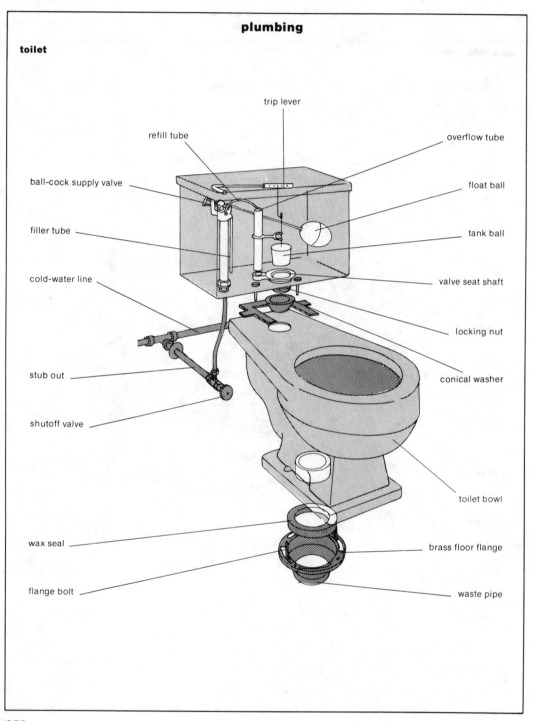

trip lever

refill tube

overflow tube

ball-cock supply valve

float ball

filler tube

tank ball

cold-water line

valve seat shaft

locking nut

stub out

conical washer

shutoff valve

toilet bowl

wax seal

brass floor flange

flange bolt

waste pipe

plumbing

bathroom

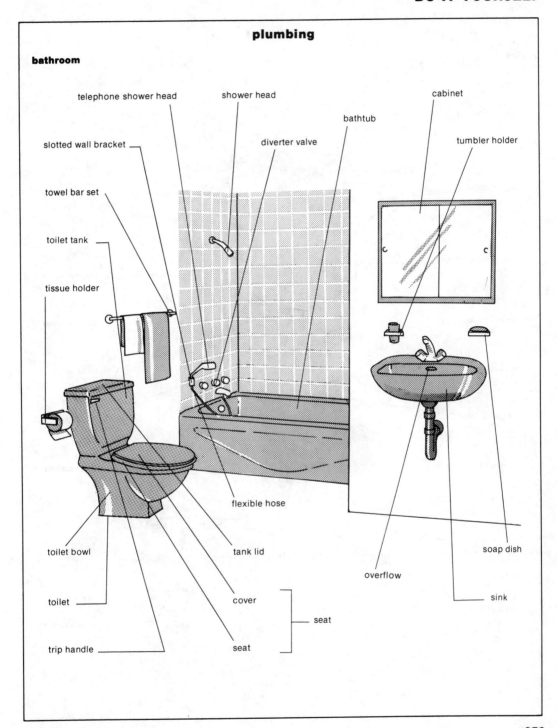

telephone shower head

shower head

cabinet

bathtub

tumbler holder

slotted wall bracket

diverter valve

towel bar set

toilet tank

tissue holder

flexible hose

toilet bowl

tank lid

soap dish

toilet

overflow

sink

cover

seat

trip handle

seat

plumbing

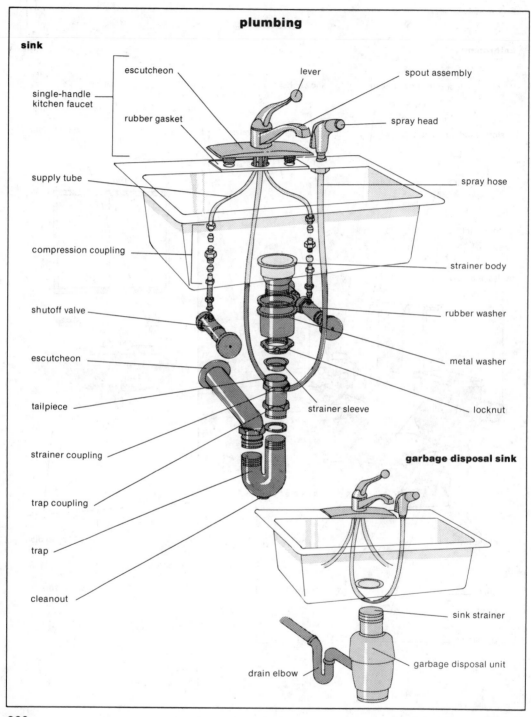

sink

single-handle kitchen faucet

escutcheon

lever

spout assembly

rubber gasket

spray head

supply tube

spray hose

compression coupling

strainer body

shutoff valve

rubber washer

escutcheon

metal washer

tailpiece

strainer sleeve

locknut

strainer coupling

garbage disposal sink

trap coupling

trap

cleanout

sink strainer

garbage disposal unit

drain elbow

plumbing

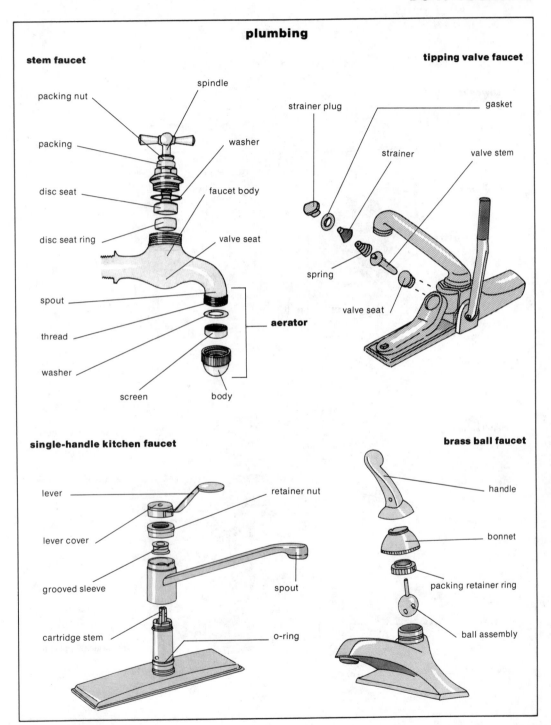

stem faucet

packing nut

spindle

packing

washer

disc seat

faucet body

disc seat ring

valve seat

spout

thread

washer

screen

body

aerator

tipping valve faucet

strainer plug

gasket

strainer

valve stem

spring

valve seat

single-handle kitchen faucet

lever

retainer nut

lever cover

grooved sleeve

spout

cartridge stem

o-ring

brass ball faucet

handle

bonnet

packing retainer ring

ball assembly

plumbing

examples of branching

dishwasher

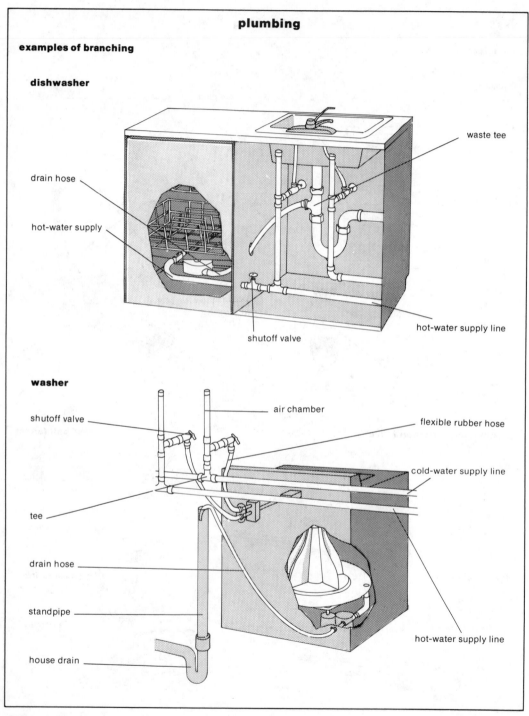

waste tee

drain hose

hot-water supply

hot-water supply line

shutoff valve

washer

shutoff valve

air chamber

flexible rubber hose

cold-water supply line

tee

drain hose

hot-water supply line

standpipe

house drain

plumbing

electric water-heater tank

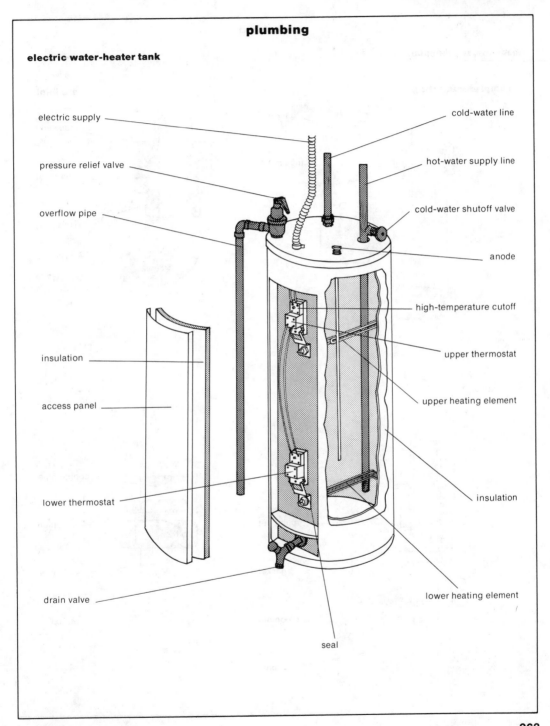

electric supply

pressure relief valve

overflow pipe

insulation

access panel

lower thermostat

drain valve

cold-water line

hot-water supply line

cold-water shutoff valve

anode

high-temperature cutoff

upper thermostat

upper heating element

insulation

lower heating element

seal

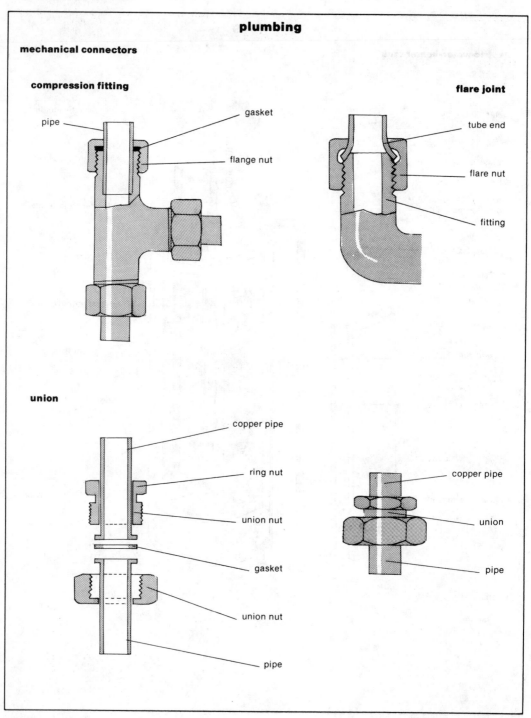

plumbing

mechanical connectors

compression fitting

pipe

gasket

flange nut

flare joint

tube end

flare nut

fitting

union

copper pipe

ring nut

union nut

gasket

union nut

pipe

copper pipe

union

pipe

plumbing

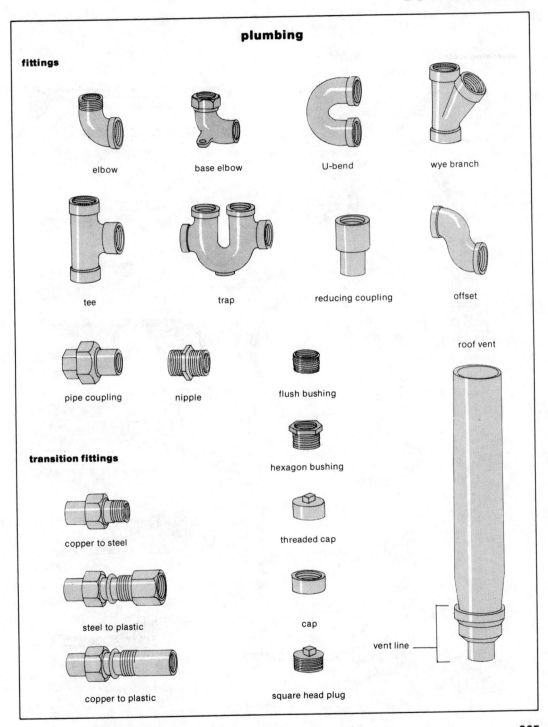

fittings

elbow   base elbow   U-bend   wye branch

tee   trap   reducing coupling   offset

pipe coupling   nipple   flush bushing

hexagon bushing

transition fittings

copper to steel

threaded cap

steel to plastic

cap

copper to plastic

square head plug

roof vent

vent line

plumbing

plumbing tools

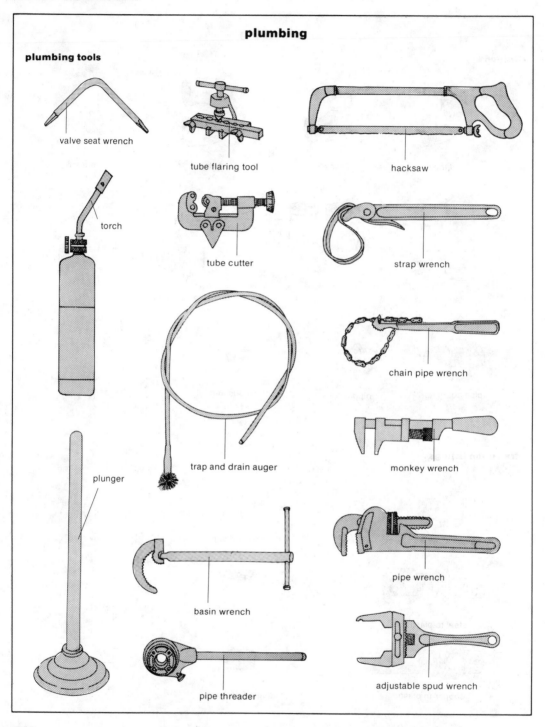

valve seat wrench

tube flaring tool

hacksaw

torch

tube cutter

strap wrench

trap and drain auger

chain pipe wrench

monkey wrench

plunger

pipe wrench

basin wrench

pipe threader

adjustable spud wrench

plumbing

septic tank

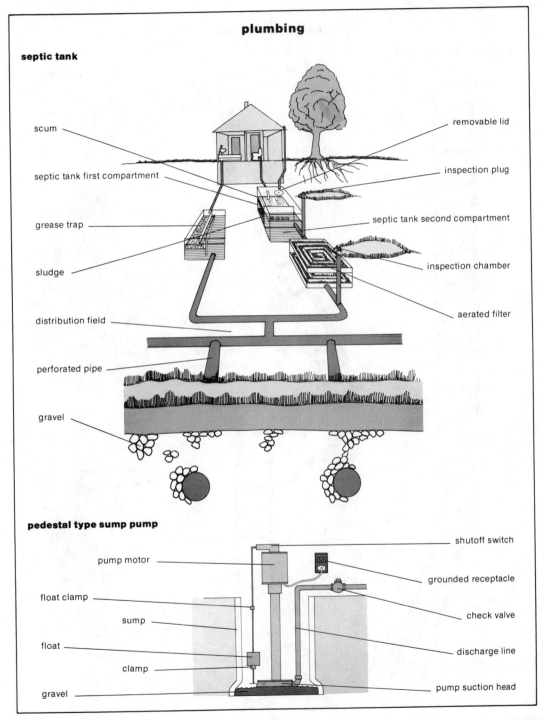

scum

septic tank first compartment

grease trap

sludge

distribution field

perforated pipe

gravel

removable lid

inspection plug

septic tank second compartment

inspection chamber

aerated filter

pedestal type sump pump

pump motor

float clamp

sump

float

clamp

gravel

shutoff switch

grounded receptacle

check valve

discharge line

pump suction head

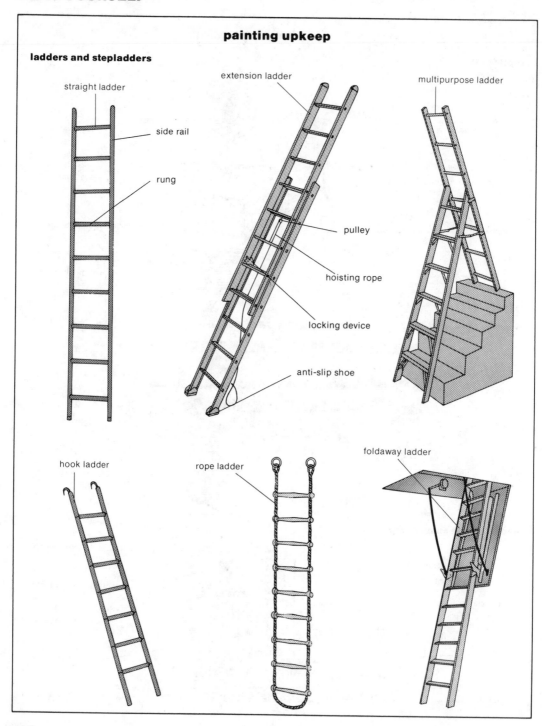

painting upkeep

ladders and stepladders

straight ladder

side rail

rung

extension ladder

pulley

hoisting rope

locking device

anti-slip shoe

multipurpose ladder

hook ladder

rope ladder

foldaway ladder

painting upkeep

ladders and stepladders

rolling ladder

fruit-picking ladder

ladder scaffold

stepladder

tool tray

step

platform ladder

safety rail

step stool

platform

shelf

brace

frame

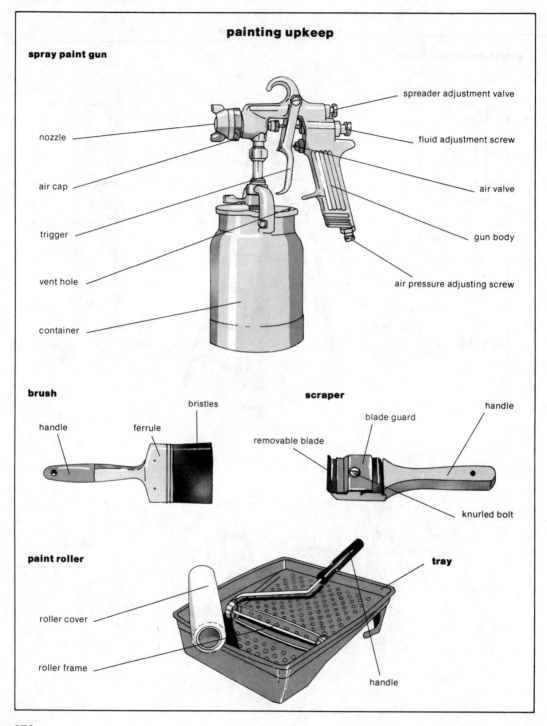

painting upkeep

spray paint gun

nozzle

air cap

trigger

vent hole

container

spreader adjustment valve

fluid adjustment screw

air valve

gun body

air pressure adjusting screw

brush

handle

ferrule

bristles

scraper

removable blade

blade guard

handle

knurled bolt

paint roller

roller cover

roller frame

tray

handle

soldering and welding

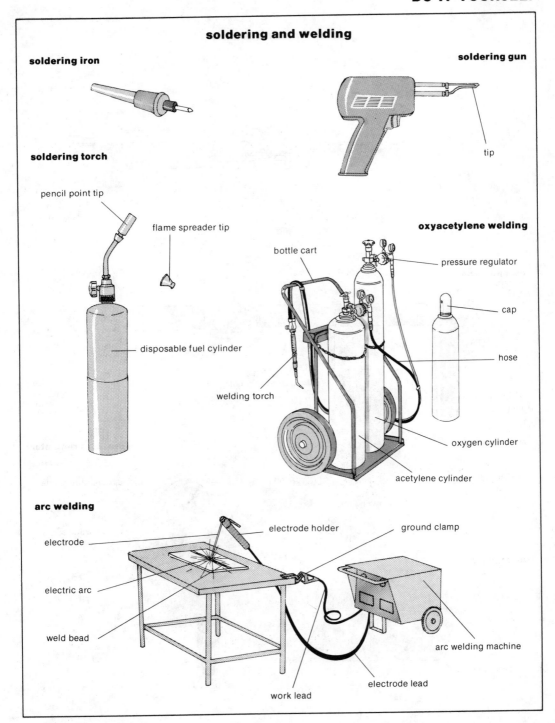

soldering iron

soldering gun

tip

soldering torch

pencil point tip

flame spreader tip

oxyacetylene welding

bottle cart

pressure regulator

cap

disposable fuel cylinder

hose

welding torch

oxygen cylinder

acetylene cylinder

arc welding

electrode holder

ground clamp

electrode

electric arc

weld bead

arc welding machine

work lead

electrode lead

soldering and welding

welding torch

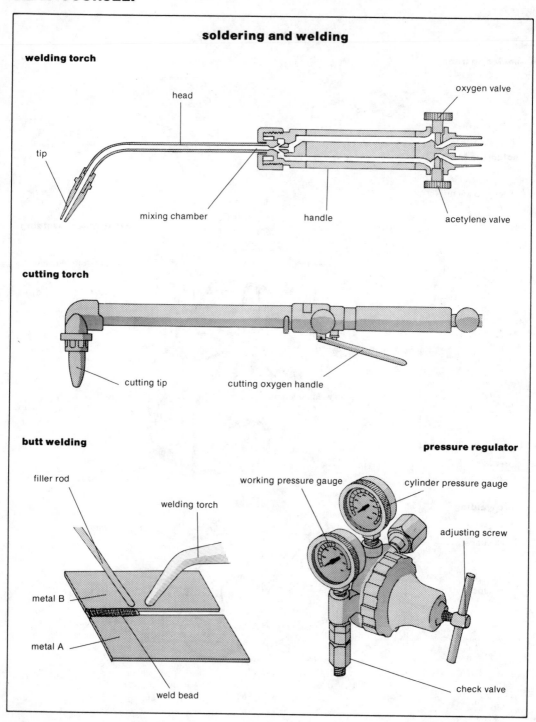

head

oxygen valve

tip

mixing chamber

handle

acetylene valve

cutting torch

cutting tip

cutting oxygen handle

butt welding

pressure regulator

filler rod

working pressure gauge

cylinder pressure gauge

welding torch

adjusting screw

metal B

metal A

check valve

weld bead

soldering and welding

protective clothing

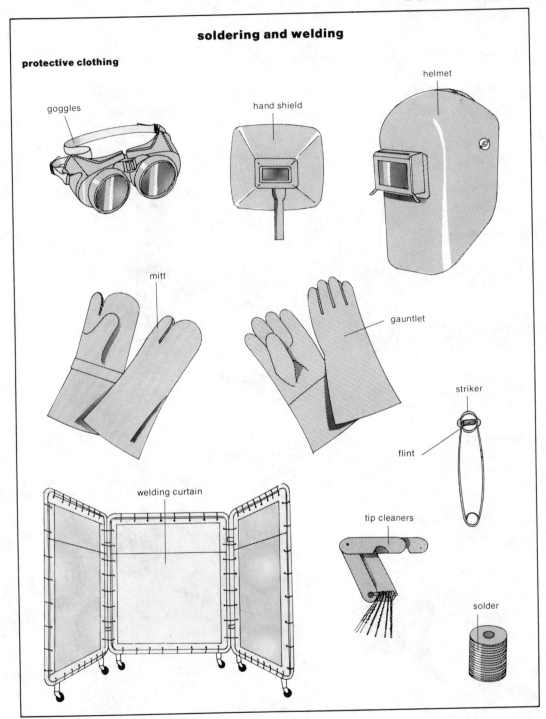

goggles

hand shield

helmet

mitt

gauntlet

striker

flint

welding curtain

tip cleaners

solder

electricity

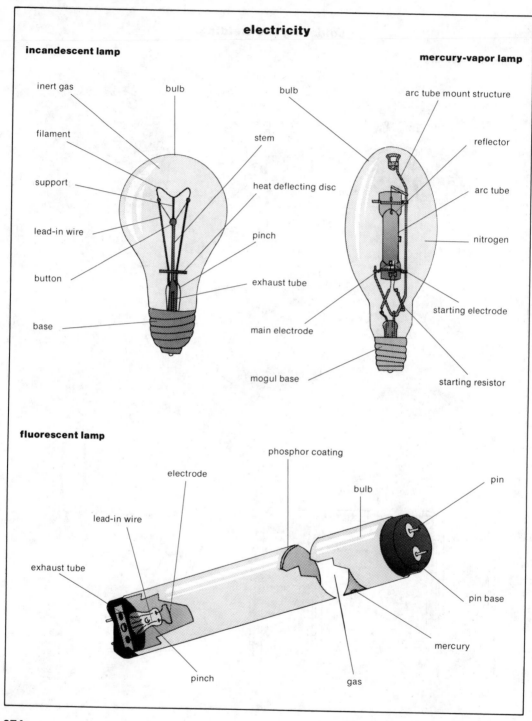

incandescent lamp

inert gas

bulb

filament

stem

support

heat deflecting disc

lead-in wire

pinch

button

exhaust tube

base

main electrode

mercury-vapor lamp

bulb

arc tube mount structure

reflector

arc tube

nitrogen

starting electrode

mogul base

starting resistor

fluorescent lamp

phosphor coating

electrode

bulb

pin

lead-in wire

exhaust tube

pin base

mercury

pinch

gas

274

electricity

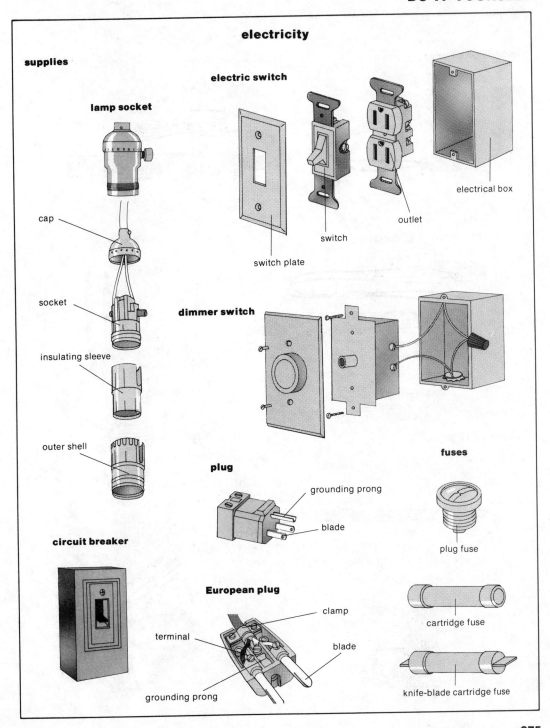

supplies

lamp socket

cap

socket

insulating sleeve

outer shell

circuit breaker

electric switch

switch plate

switch

outlet

electrical box

dimmer switch

plug

grounding prong

blade

European plug

clamp

terminal

blade

grounding prong

fuses

plug fuse

cartridge fuse

knife-blade cartridge fuse

electricity

electrician's tools

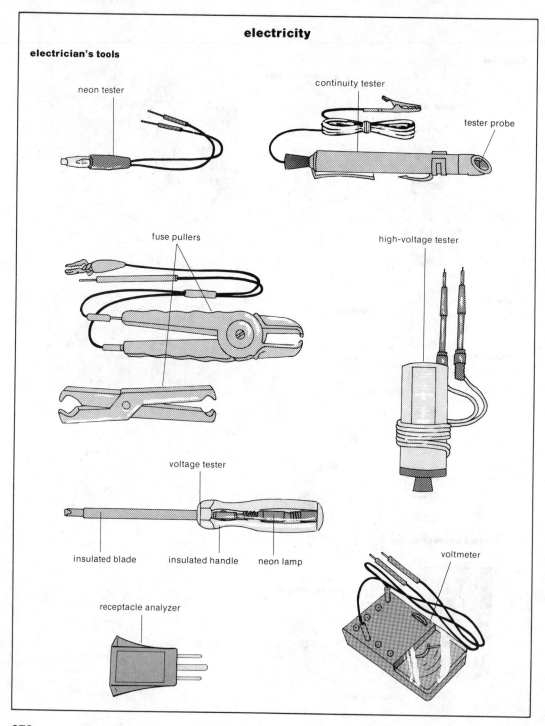

neon tester

continuity tester

tester probe

fuse pullers

high-voltage tester

voltage tester

insulated blade   insulated handle   neon lamp

voltmeter

receptacle analyzer

electricity

electrician's tools

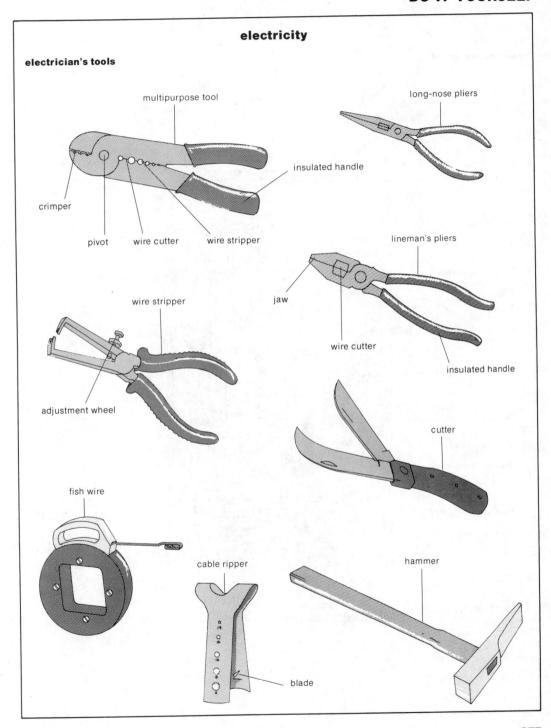

multipurpose tool

long-nose pliers

insulated handle

crimper

pivot   wire cutter   wire stripper

lineman's pliers

jaw

wire stripper

wire cutter

insulated handle

adjustment wheel

cutter

fish wire

cable ripper

hammer

blade

electricity

distribution board

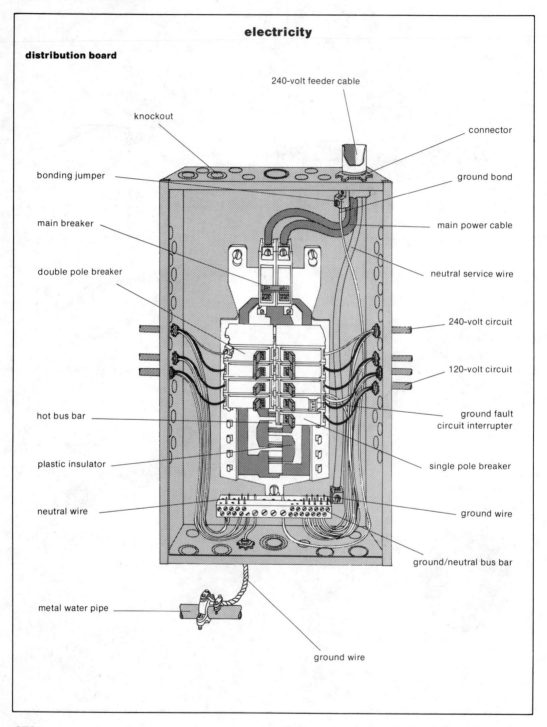

- 240-volt feeder cable
- knockout
- connector
- bonding jumper
- ground bond
- main breaker
- main power cable
- double pole breaker
- neutral service wire
- 240-volt circuit
- 120-volt circuit
- hot bus bar
- ground fault circuit interrupter
- plastic insulator
- single pole breaker
- neutral wire
- ground wire
- ground/neutral bus bar
- metal water pipe
- ground wire

CLOTHING

men's clothing

trench coat

raincoat

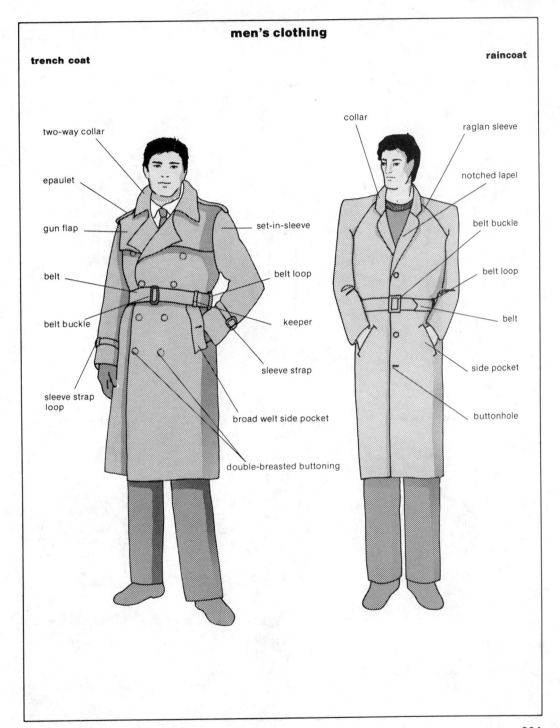

- two-way collar
- epaulet
- gun flap
- belt
- belt buckle
- sleeve strap loop
- set-in-sleeve
- belt loop
- keeper
- sleeve strap
- broad welt side pocket
- double-breasted buttoning
- collar
- raglan sleeve
- notched lapel
- belt buckle
- belt loop
- belt
- side pocket
- buttonhole

CLOTHING

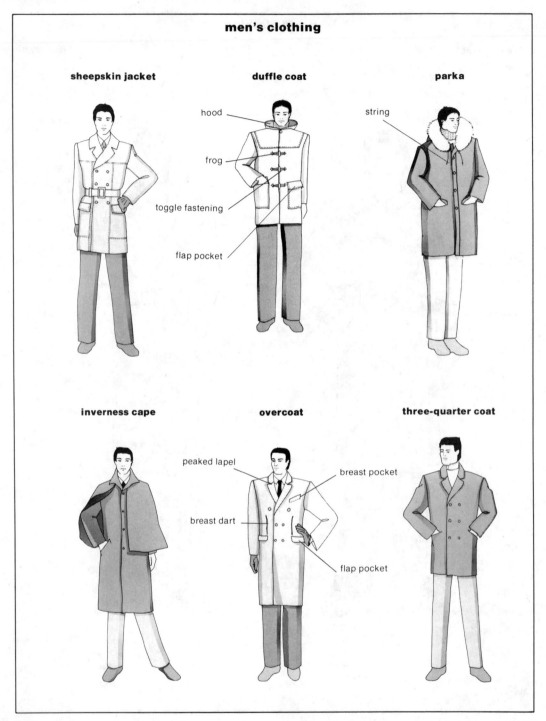

men's clothing

sheepskin jacket

duffle coat

hood

frog

toggle fastening

flap pocket

parka

string

inverness cape

overcoat

peaked lapel

breast dart

breast pocket

flap pocket

three-quarter coat

men's clothing

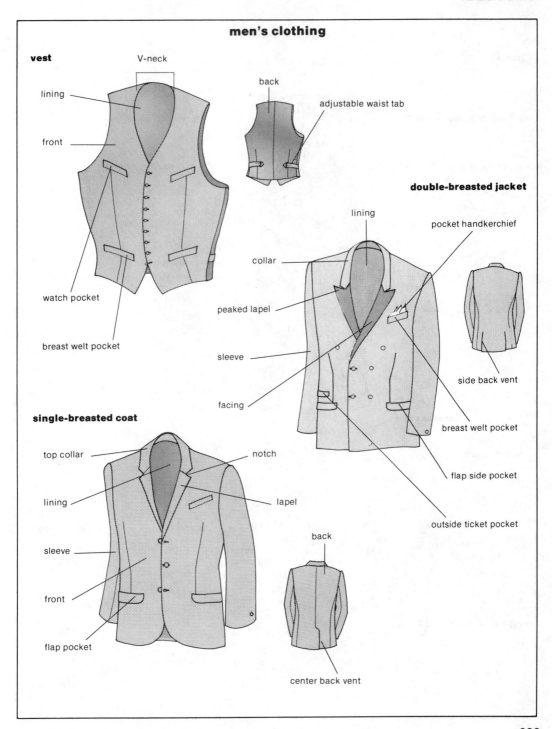

vest

V-neck

lining

front

back

adjustable waist tab

watch pocket

breast welt pocket

double-breasted jacket

lining

pocket handkerchief

collar

peaked lapel

sleeve

facing

side back vent

breast welt pocket

flap side pocket

outside ticket pocket

single-breasted coat

top collar

notch

lining

lapel

sleeve

front

flap pocket

back

center back vent

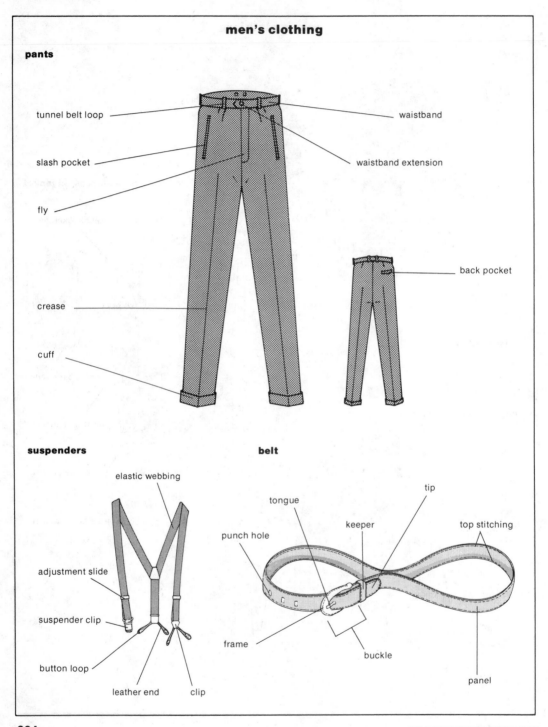

men's clothing

pants

- tunnel belt loop
- waistband
- slash pocket
- waistband extension
- fly
- back pocket
- crease
- cuff

suspenders

- elastic webbing
- adjustment slide
- suspender clip
- button loop
- leather end
- clip

belt

- tongue
- tip
- keeper
- top stitching
- punch hole
- frame
- buckle
- panel

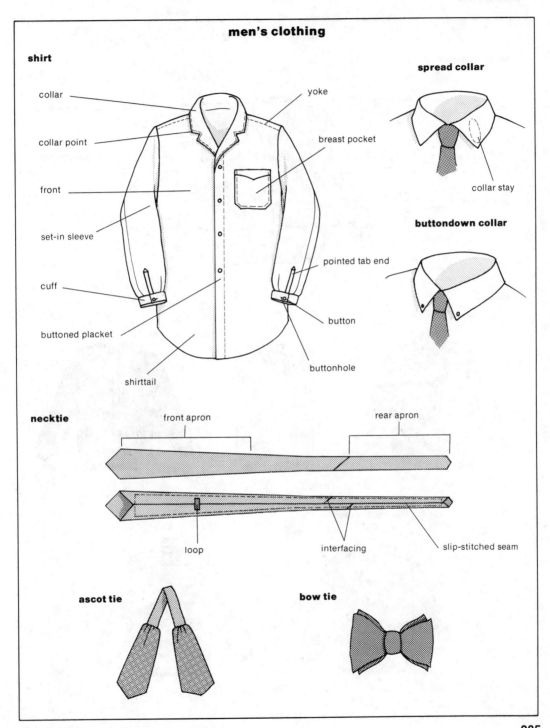

men's clothing

shirt

- collar
- collar point
- front
- set-in sleeve
- cuff
- buttoned placket
- shirttail
- yoke
- breast pocket
- pointed tab end
- button
- buttonhole

spread collar

- collar stay

buttondown collar

necktie

- front apron
- rear apron
- loop
- interfacing
- slip-stitched seam

ascot tie

bow tie

CLOTHING

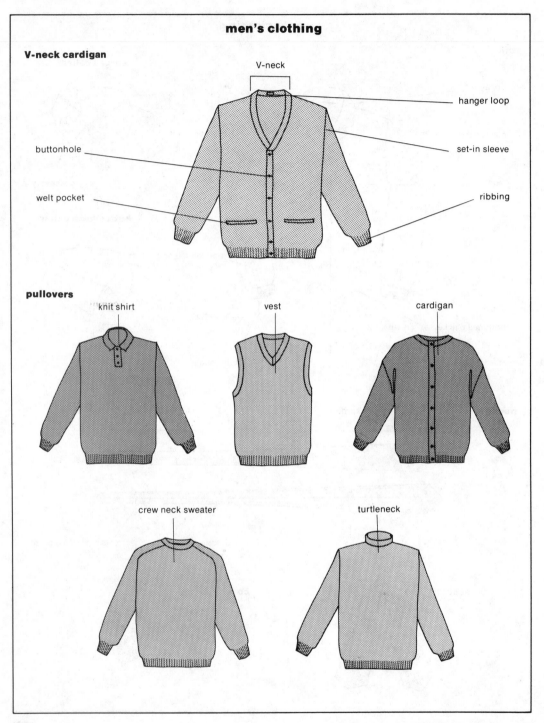

men's clothing

V-neck cardigan

V-neck

hanger loop

buttonhole

set-in sleeve

welt pocket

ribbing

pullovers

knit shirt

vest

cardigan

crew neck sweater

turtleneck

men's clothing

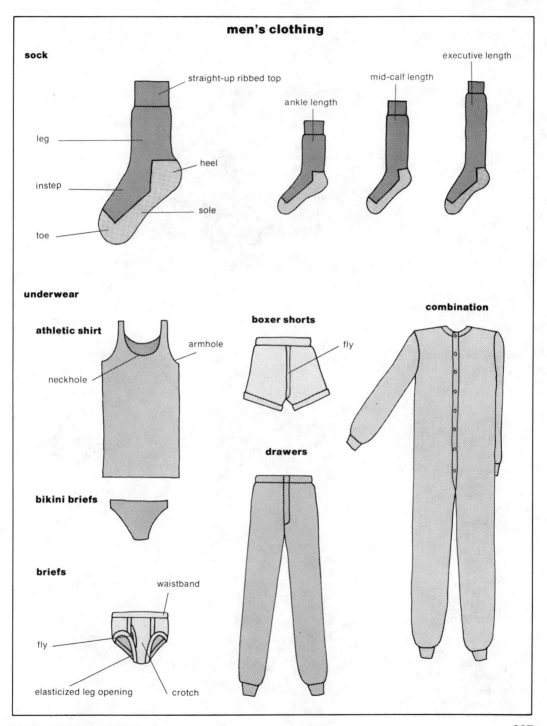

sock

straight-up ribbed top

executive length

mid-calf length

ankle length

leg

heel

instep

sole

toe

underwear

combination

athletic shirt

boxer shorts

armhole

fly

neckhole

bikini briefs

drawers

briefs

waistband

fly

elasticized leg opening

crotch

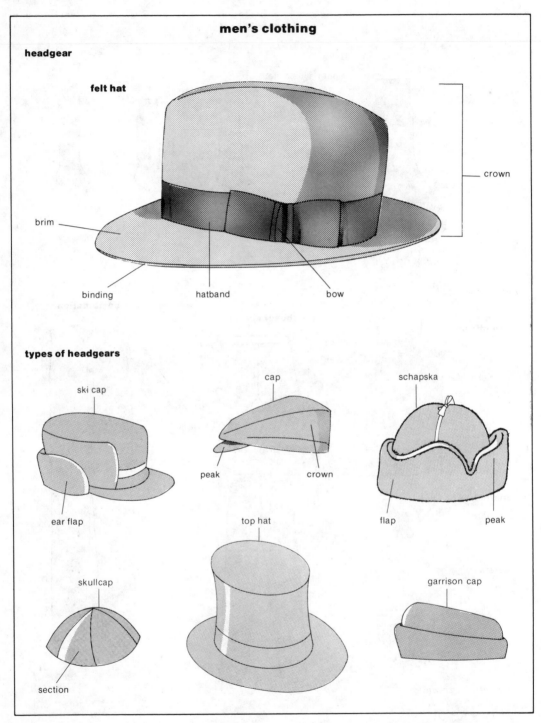

men's clothing

headgear

felt hat

crown

brim

binding hatband bow

types of headgears

ski cap

cap

schapska

peak crown

ear flap

flap peak

skullcap

top hat

garrison cap

section

glove

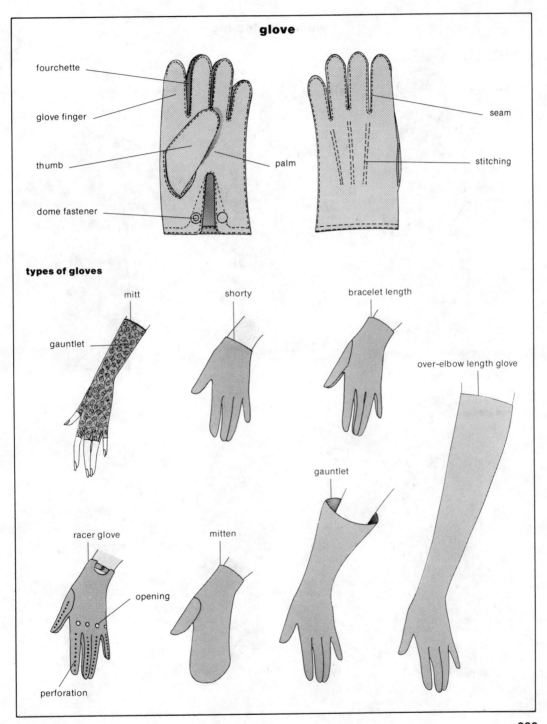

fourchette

glove finger

thumb

dome fastener

palm

seam

stitching

types of gloves

mitt

gauntlet

shorty

bracelet length

over-elbow length glove

gauntlet

racer glove

opening

mitten

perforation

CLOTHING

women's clothing

coats

overcoat

patch pocket with turn-down flap

raglan

raglan sleeve

broad welt

fly front closing

pelerine

pelerine

seam pocket

redingote

seaming

patch pocket

back belt

women's clothing

coats

cape

buttoned placket

arm slit

tailored collar

pea jacket

notched lapel

hand warmer pocket

mock pocket

poncho

double breasted buttoning

windbreaker

windbreaker

ribbing

waistband

women's clothing

dresses

shirtwaist dress

princess dress

coat dress

sheath dress

sundress

drop waist dress

T-shirt dress

maternity dress

jumper

wrap dress

pinafore

tunic

women's clothing

skirts

straight skirt

sheath skirt

wraparound skirt

gather skirt

kilt

ruffled skirt

gored skirt

yoke skirt

sarong

culotte

CLOTHING

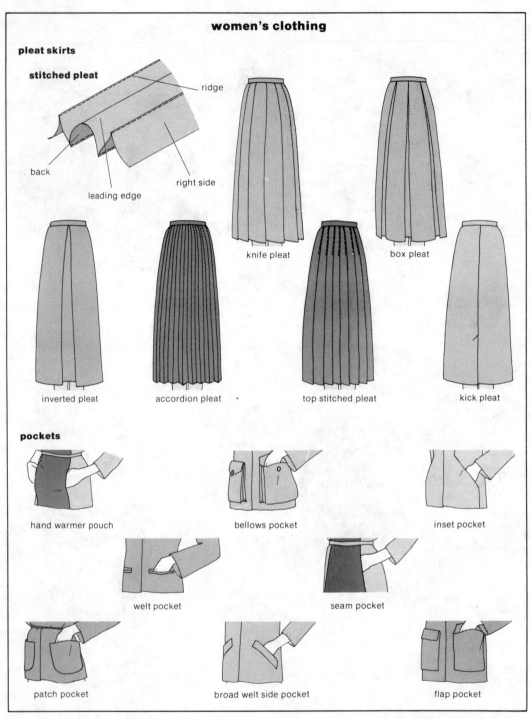

women's clothing

pleat skirts

stitched pleat

ridge

back

leading edge

right side

knife pleat

box pleat

inverted pleat

accordion pleat

top stitched pleat

kick pleat

pockets

hand warmer pouch

bellows pocket

inset pocket

welt pocket

seam pocket

patch pocket

broad welt side pocket

flap pocket

women's clothing

blouses

classic

tunic

middy

smock

yoke

gather

polo shirt

buttoned placket

breast pocket

wrap over top

over-blouse

mini shirtdress

bottom of collar

shirt collar

shirttail

body shirt

shirt sleeve

crotch piece

women's clothing

sleeves

set-in sleeve

unmounted sleeve

armhole

barrel cuff

tailored sleeve

kimono sleeve

shirtwaist sleeve

bishop sleeve

three-quarter sleeve

cutaway armhole

raglan sleeve

narrow cuff

puff sleeve

cap sleeve

pagoda sleeve

batwing sleeve

epaulet sleeve

leg-of-mutton sleeve

French cuff

pointed tab end

women's clothing

vests and pullovers

cardigan

pullover

turtleneck

sweater

twin-set

shrink

crew sweater

bellows pocket

safari

blazer

weskit

vest pocket

bolero

spencer

CLOTHING

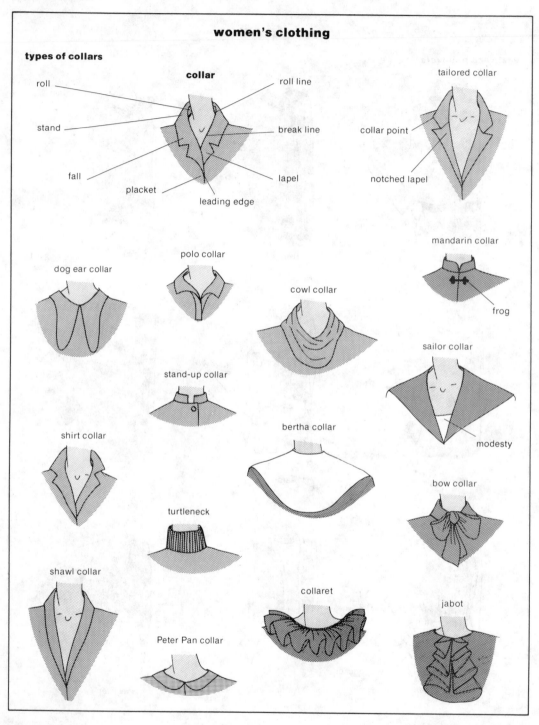

women's clothing

types of collars

collar

roll

roll line

stand

break line

fall

lapel

placket

leading edge

tailored collar

collar point

notched lapel

dog ear collar

polo collar

cowl collar

mandarin collar

frog

stand-up collar

sailor collar

modesty

shirt collar

bertha collar

bow collar

turtleneck

shawl collar

collaret

jabot

Peter Pan collar

women's clothing

necklines and necks

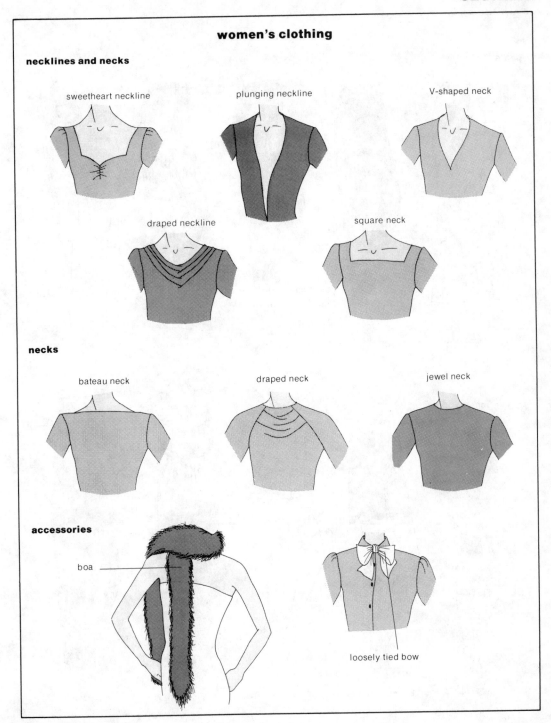

sweetheart neckline

plunging neckline

V-shaped neck

draped neckline

square neck

necks

bateau neck

draped neck

jewel neck

accessories

boa

loosely tied bow

CLOTHING

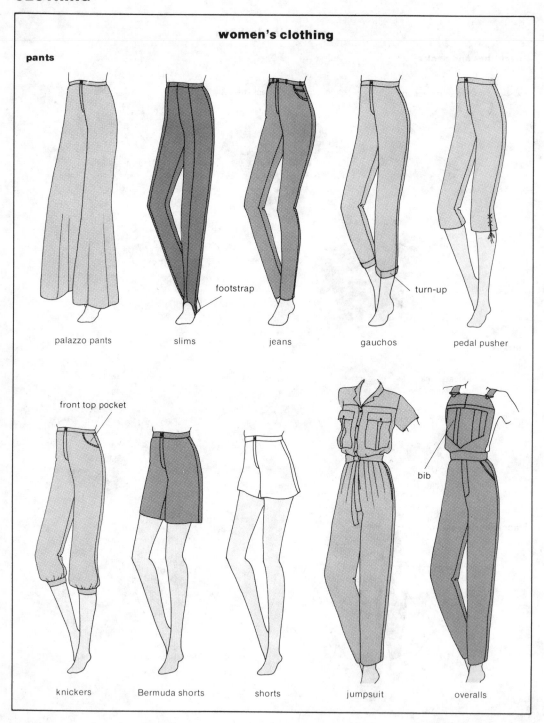

women's clothing

pants

palazzo pants

slims

footstrap

jeans

gauchos

turn-up

pedal pusher

front top pocket

knickers

Bermuda shorts

shorts

jumpsuit

bib

overalls

women's clothing

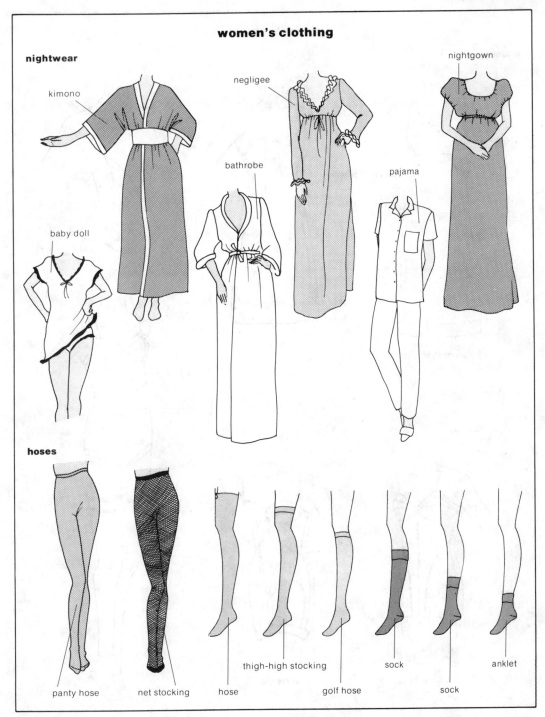

nightwear

kimono

negligee

nightgown

baby doll

bathrobe

pajama

hoses

panty hose

net stocking

hose

thigh-high stocking

golf hose

sock

sock

anklet

CLOTHING

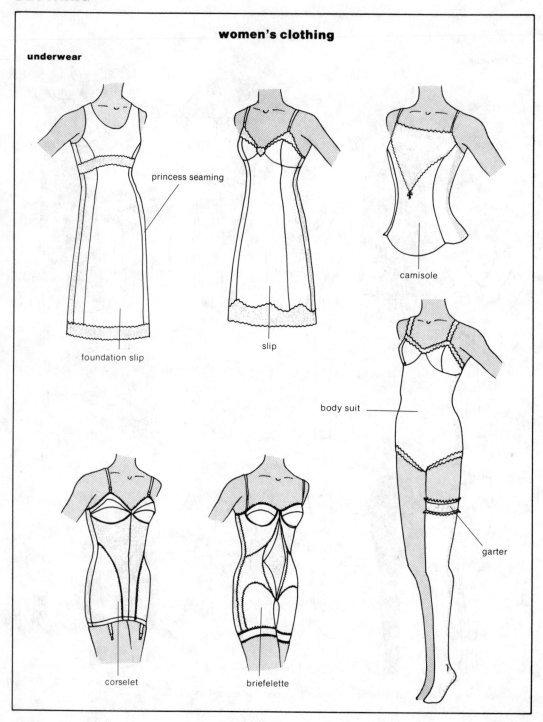

women's clothing

underwear

princess seaming

foundation slip

slip

camisole

body suit

garter

corselet

briefelette

women's clothing

underwear

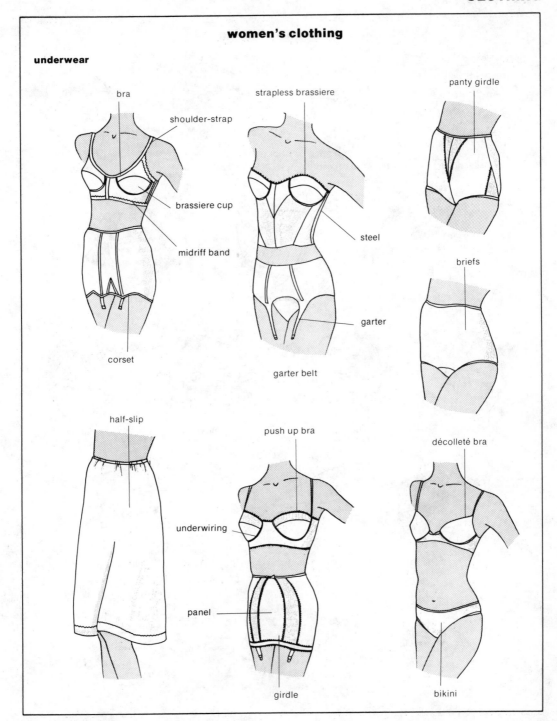

bra

shoulder-strap

brassiere cup

midriff band

corset

strapless brassiere

steel

garter

garter belt

panty girdle

briefs

half-slip

push up bra

underwiring

panel

girdle

décolleté bra

bikini

women's clothing

headgear

crusader hood

crusader cap

stocking cap

kerchief

pompom

head band

tam o'shanter

string

southwester

crown

brim

gob hat

toque

hat veil

pillbox hat

mob-cap

turban

boater

cartwheel hat

felt hat

cap

beret

cloche

children's clothing

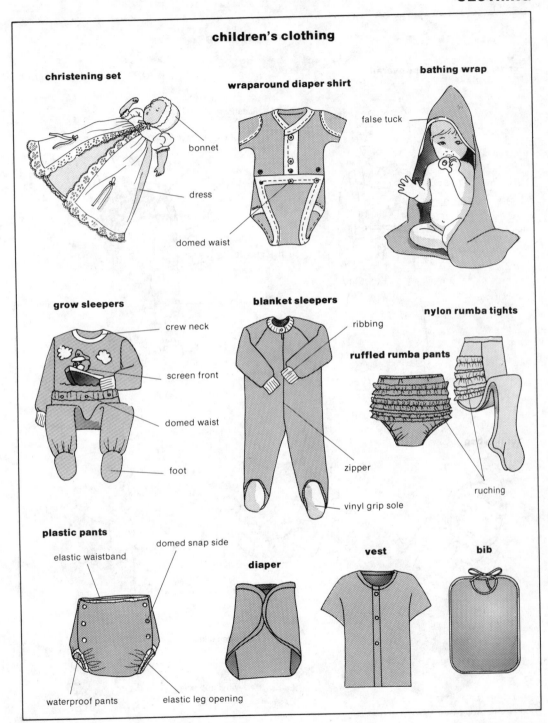

christening set
- bonnet
- dress
- domed waist

wraparound diaper shirt

bathing wrap
- false tuck

grow sleepers
- crew neck
- screen front
- domed waist
- foot

blanket sleepers
- ribbing
- zipper
- vinyl grip sole

nylon rumba tights

ruffled rumba pants
- ruching

plastic pants
- elastic waistband
- domed snap side
- waterproof pants
- elastic leg opening

diaper

vest

bib

children's clothing

crisscross back straps overall

high-back overall

domed adjustable strap

button straps

top stitching

bib

zipper

rope belt

patch pocket

belt loop

domed inseam

ribbing

jumpsuit

dome shoulder closure

sleeper

bunting bag

raglan sleeve

screen print

ribbing

vest

domed front

foot

domed inseam

vinyl grip sole

children's clothing

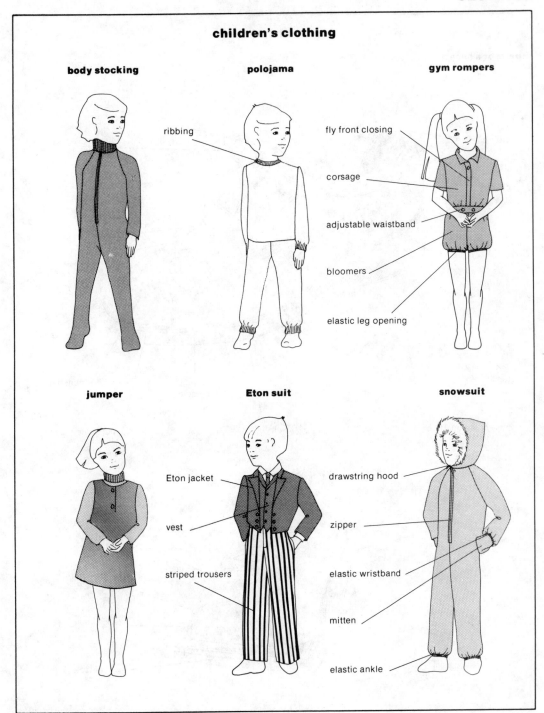

body stocking

polojama

ribbing

gym rompers

fly front closing

corsage

adjustable waistband

bloomers

elastic leg opening

jumper

Eton suit

Eton jacket

vest

striped trousers

snowsuit

drawstring hood

zipper

elastic wristband

mitten

elastic ankle

shoes

parts of a shoe

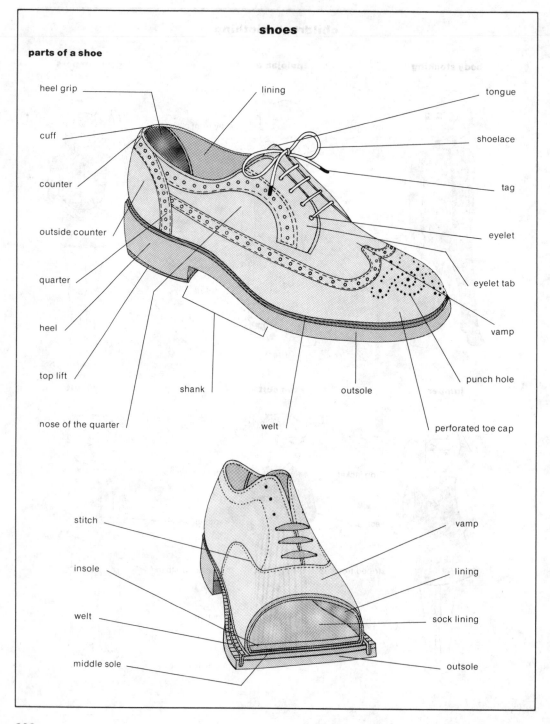

heel grip

lining

tongue

cuff

shoelace

counter

tag

outside counter

eyelet

quarter

eyelet tab

heel

vamp

top lift

punch hole

nose of the quarter

shank

welt

outsole

perforated toe cap

stitch

vamp

insole

lining

welt

sock lining

middle sole

outsole

shoes

principal types of shoes

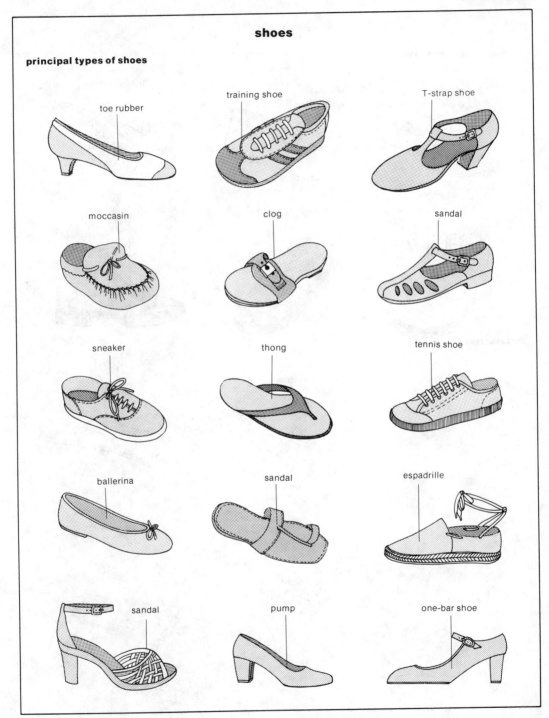

toe rubber

training shoe

T-strap shoe

moccasin

clog

sandal

sneaker

thong

tennis shoe

ballerina

sandal

espadrille

sandal

pump

one-bar shoe

CLOTHING

shoes

principal types of shoes

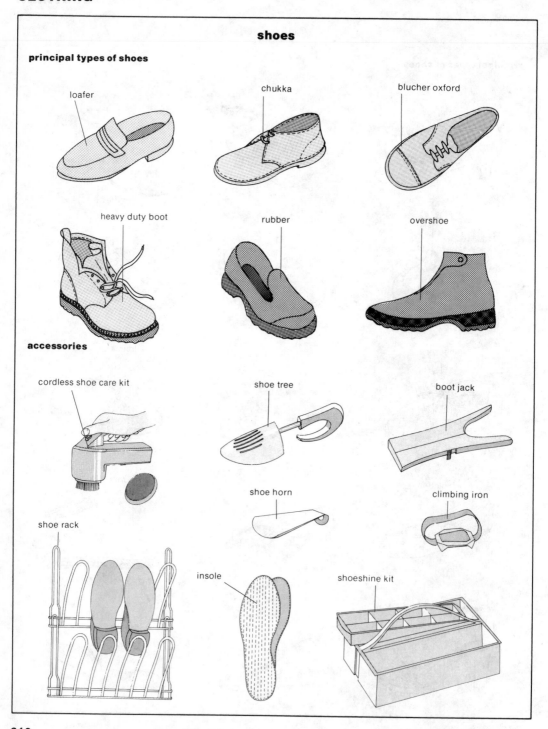

loafer

chukka

blucher oxford

heavy duty boot

rubber

overshoe

accessories

cordless shoe care kit

shoe tree

boot jack

shoe horn

climbing iron

shoe rack

insole

shoeshine kit

costumes

bullfighter

ballerina

shirt

hat

tie

pigtail

vest

epaulet

sash

jacket

frog

cape

pants

tassel

pink stocking

tights

slippers

tutu

ribbon

drawstring

toe

sole

slippers

CLOTHING

costumes

diving suit

cable

telephone line

helmet

glass port

mask

three-branched air tube

steel hook

clown

pointed hat

bulb

whiteface

big bowtie

magnesium alloy

balloon pants

back pack

clown shoe

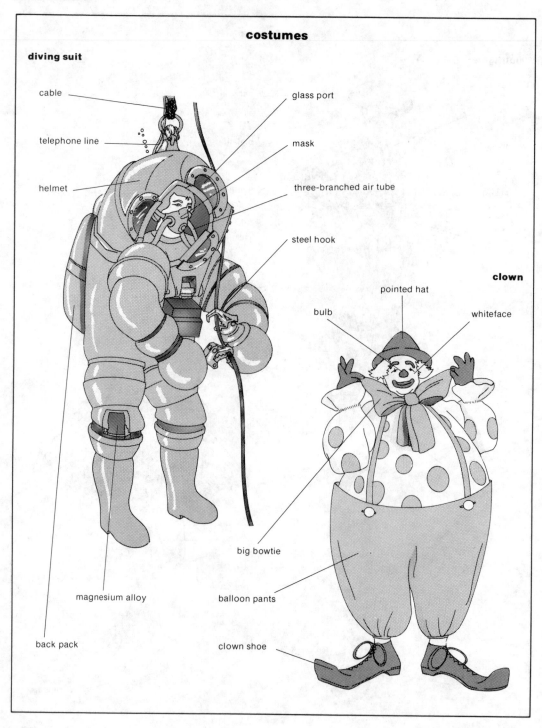

PERSONAL ADORNMENT

jewelry

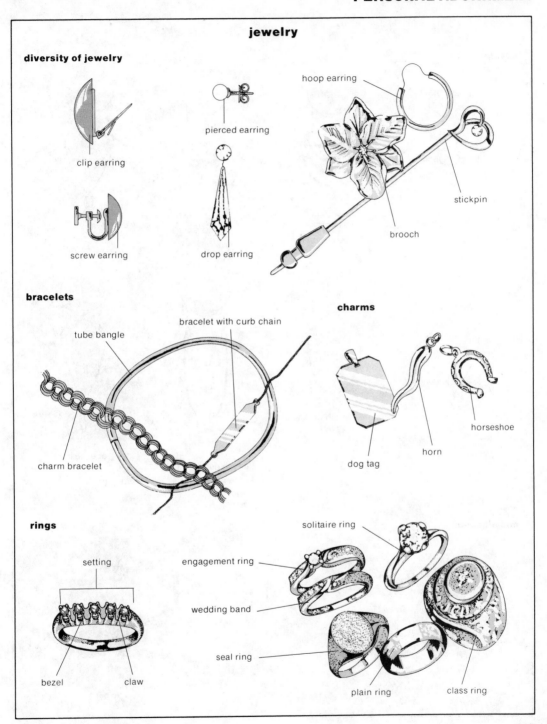

diversity of jewelry

clip earring

screw earring

pierced earring

drop earring

hoop earring

stickpin

brooch

bracelets

tube bangle

bracelet with curb chain

charm bracelet

charms

dog tag

horn

horseshoe

rings

setting

bezel

claw

engagement ring

wedding band

solitaire ring

seal ring

plain ring

class ring

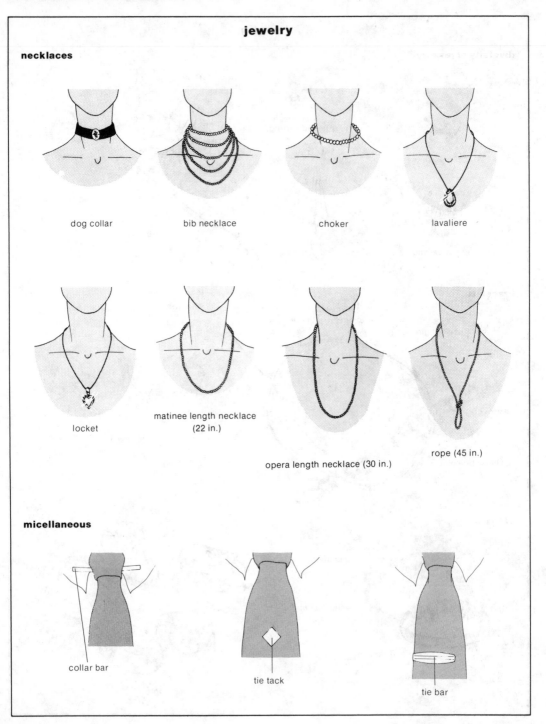

jewelry

necklaces

dog collar

bib necklace

choker

lavaliere

locket

matinee length necklace
(22 in.)

opera length necklace (30 in.)

rope (45 in.)

micellaneous

collar bar

tie tack

tie bar

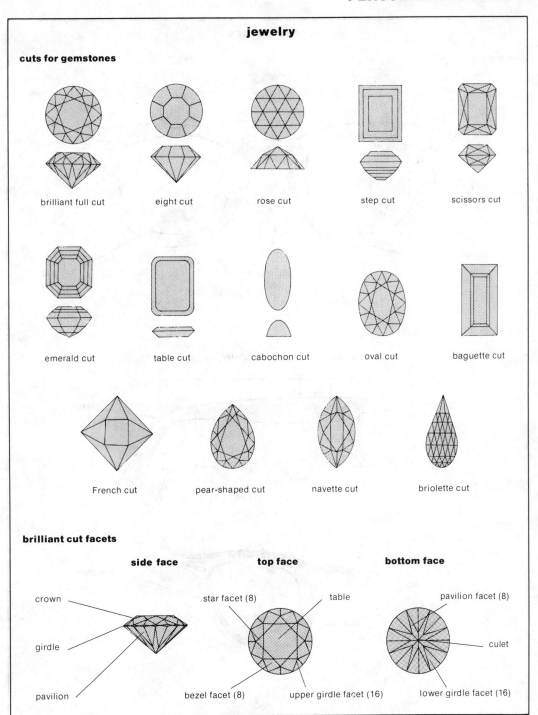

jewelry

cuts for gemstones

brilliant full cut   eight cut   rose cut   step cut   scissors cut

emerald cut   table cut   cabochon cut   oval cut   baguette cut

French cut   pear-shaped cut   navette cut   briolette cut

brilliant cut facets

side face   top face   bottom face

crown

girdle

pavilion

star facet (8)   table

bezel facet (8)   upper girdle facet (16)

pavilion facet (8)

culet

lower girdle facet (16)

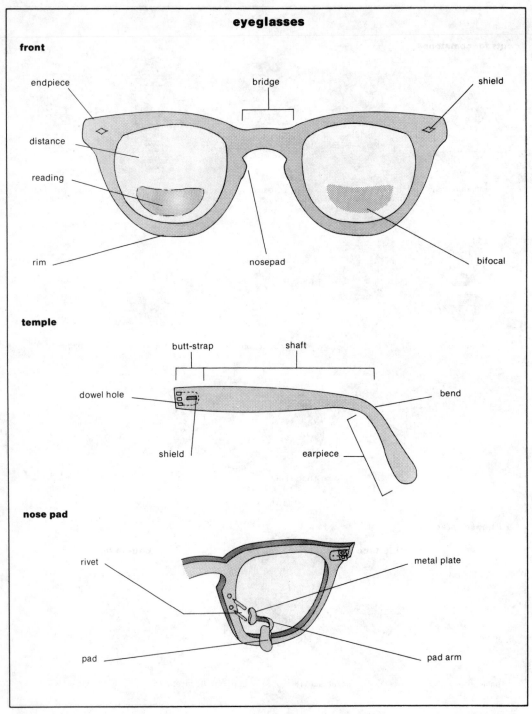

eyeglasses

front

endpiece

bridge

shield

distance

reading

rim

nosepad

bifocal

temple

butt-strap

shaft

dowel hole

bend

shield

earpiece

nose pad

rivet

metal plate

pad

pad arm

eyeglasses

principal types of eyeglasses

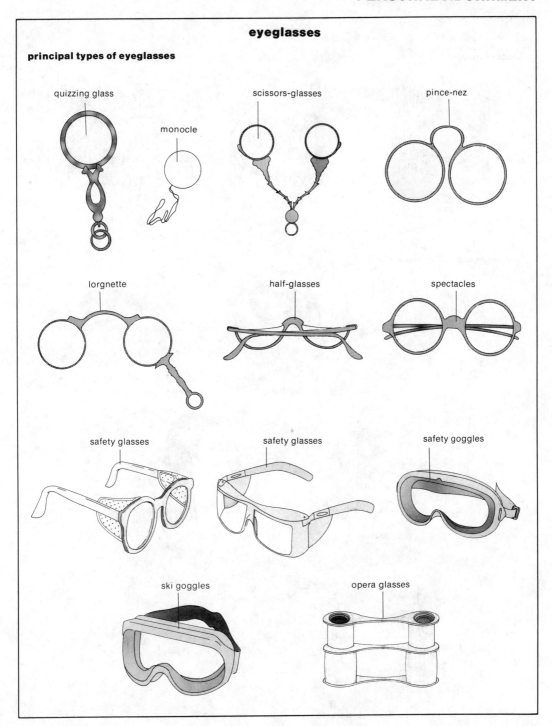

quizzing glass

monocle

scissors-glasses

pince-nez

lorgnette

half-glasses

spectacles

safety glasses

safety glasses

safety goggles

ski goggles

opera glasses

hair styles

kinds of hair

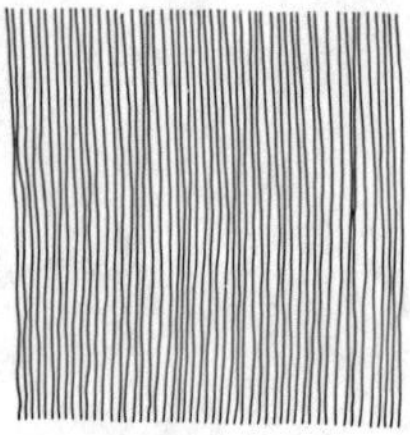

straight hair

wavy hair

curly hair

components of hair styles

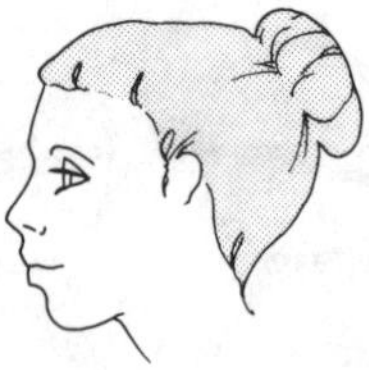

bun

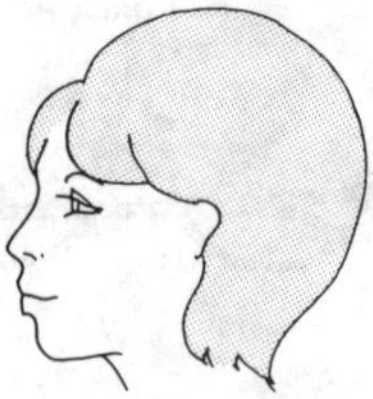

bouffant

page boy

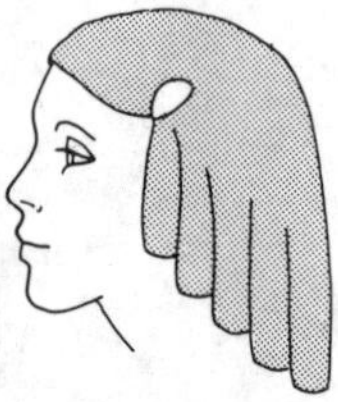

corkscrew curls

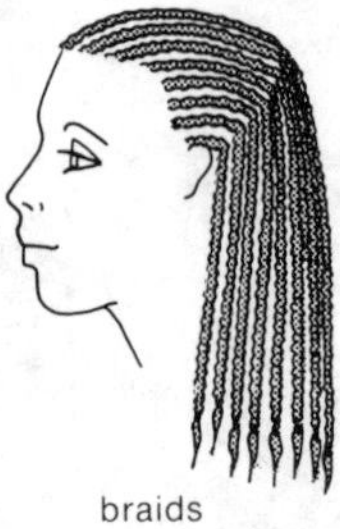

braids

pigtails

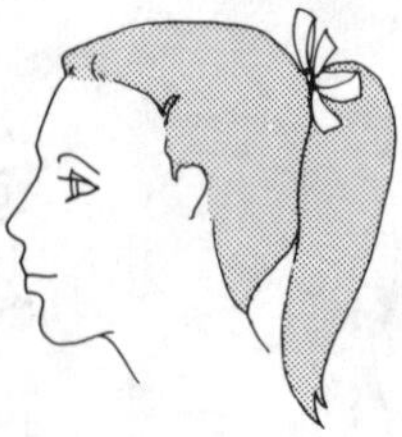

pony tail

fingerwaves

hair styles

components of hair styles

shag

poodle cut

women's pompadour

French twist

bangs

bob

crew cut

Beatle cut

men's pompadour

Afro

wigs and hairpieces

capless wig

hairpieces

toupee

bun

PERSONAL ADORNMENT

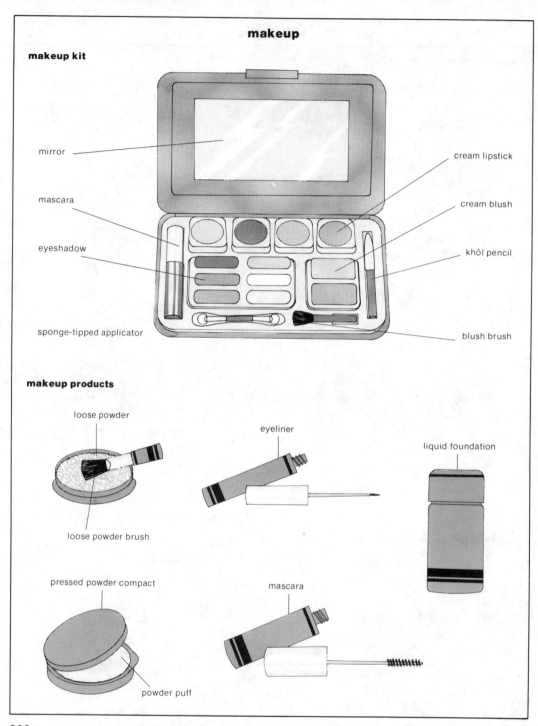

makeup

makeup kit

mirror

mascara

eyeshadow

sponge-tipped applicator

cream lipstick

cream blush

khôl pencil

blush brush

makeup products

loose powder

loose powder brush

pressed powder compact

powder puff

eyeliner

mascara

liquid foundation

makeup

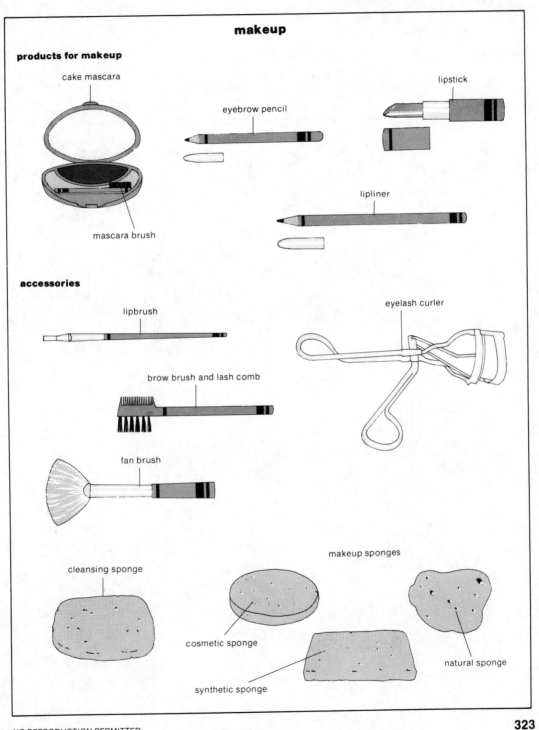

products for makeup

cake mascara

mascara brush

eyebrow pencil

lipstick

lipliner

accessories

lipbrush

eyelash curler

brow brush and lash comb

fan brush

cleansing sponge

makeup sponges

cosmetic sponge

synthetic sponge

natural sponge

PERSONAL ARTICLES

razors

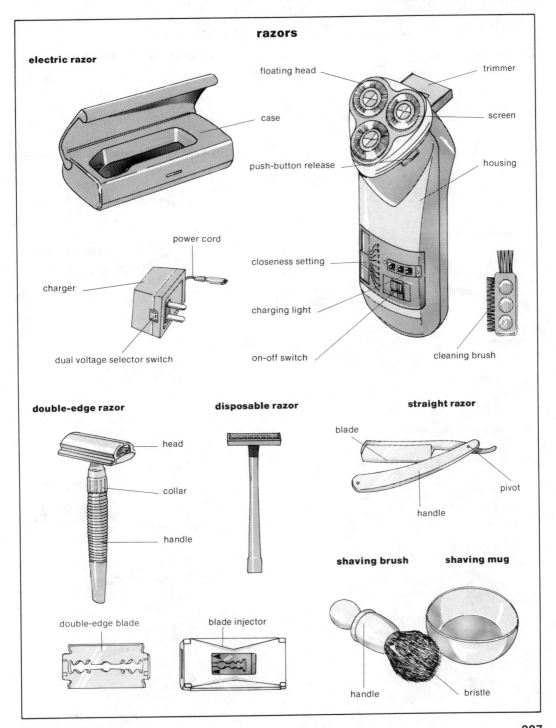

electric razor

floating head

trimmer

case

screen

push-button release

housing

power cord

charger

closeness setting

charging light

dual voltage selector switch

on-off switch

cleaning brush

double-edge razor

head

collar

handle

double-edge blade

disposable razor

blade injector

straight razor

blade

pivot

handle

shaving brush　　**shaving mug**

handle

bristle

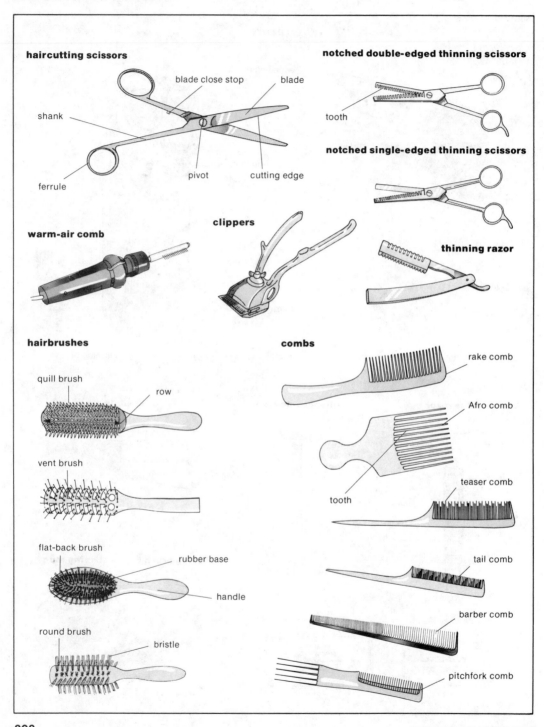

haircutting scissors

blade close stop

blade

shank

pivot

cutting edge

ferrule

notched double-edged thinning scissors

tooth

notched single-edged thinning scissors

warm-air comb

clippers

thinning razor

hairbrushes

quill brush

row

vent brush

flat-back brush

rubber base

handle

round brush

bristle

combs

rake comb

Afro comb

teaser comb

tooth

tail comb

barber comb

pitchfork comb

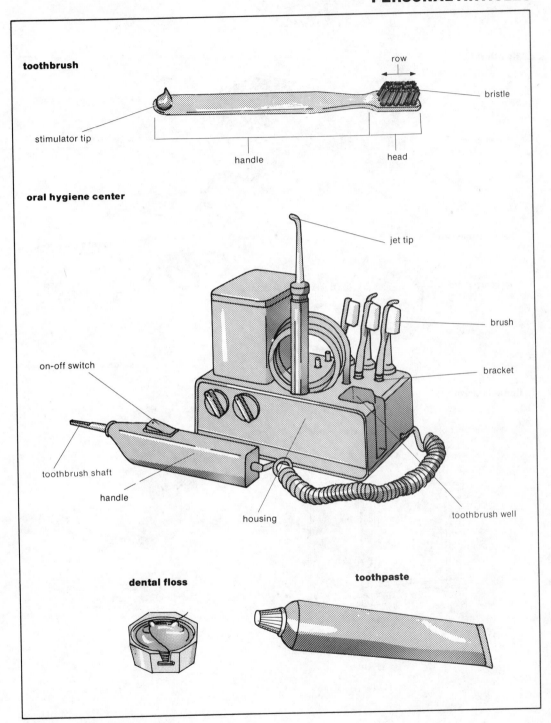

toothbrush

row

bristle

stimulator tip

handle

head

oral hygiene center

jet tip

brush

on-off switch

bracket

toothbrush shaft

handle

housing

toothbrush well

dental floss

toothpaste

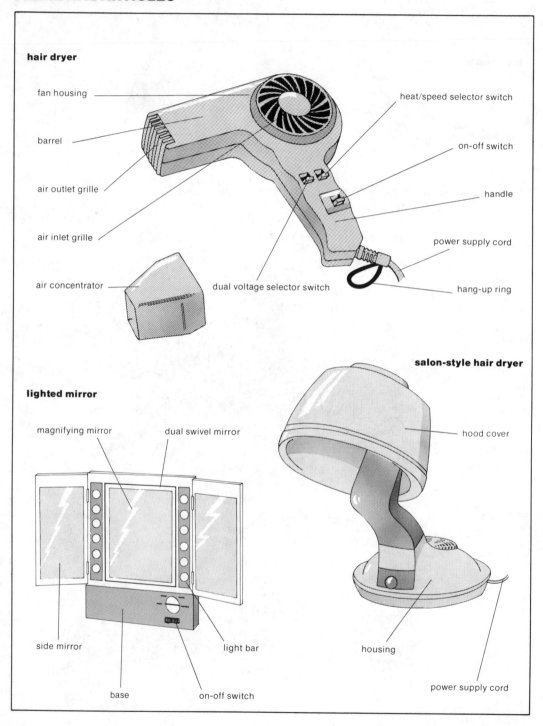

hair dryer

fan housing

barrel

air outlet grille

air inlet grille

air concentrator

dual voltage selector switch

heat/speed selector switch

on-off switch

handle

power supply cord

hang-up ring

lighted mirror

magnifying mirror

dual swivel mirror

side mirror

base

on-off switch

light bar

salon-style hair dryer

hood cover

housing

power supply cord

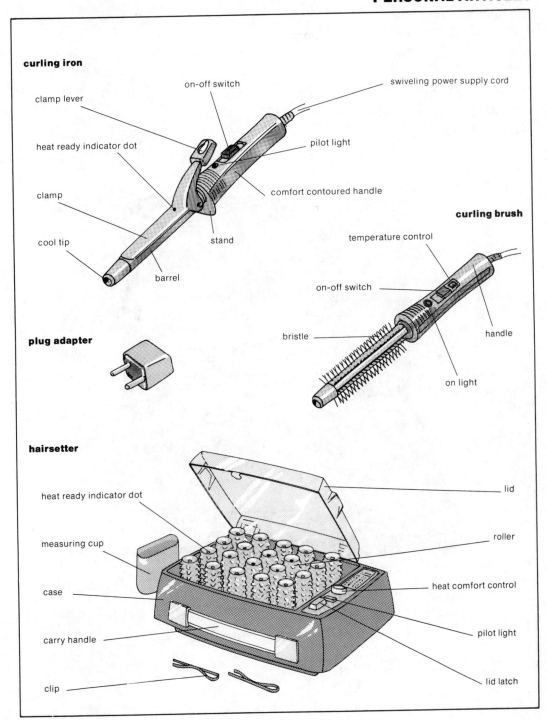

curling iron

on-off switch

clamp lever

swiveling power supply cord

heat ready indicator dot

pilot light

clamp

comfort contoured handle

curling brush

cool tip

stand

temperature control

barrel

on-off switch

handle

plug adapter

bristle

on light

hairsetter

lid

heat ready indicator dot

roller

measuring cup

case

heat comfort control

carry handle

pilot light

clip

lid latch

manicure set

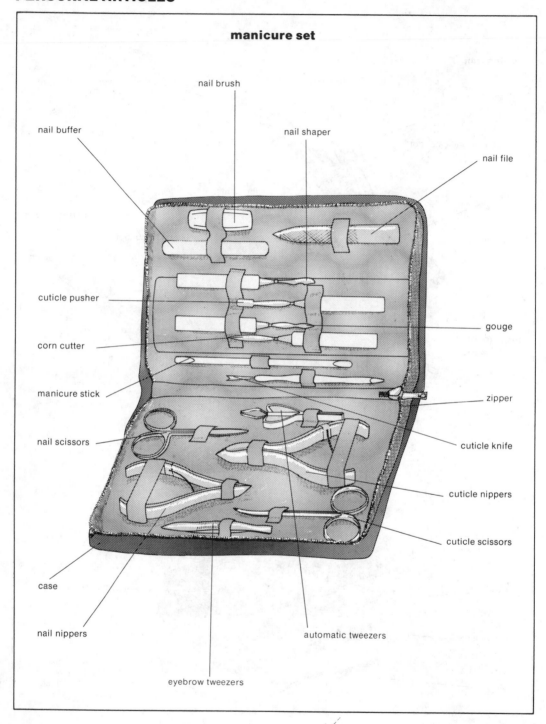

nail brush

nail buffer

nail shaper

nail file

cuticle pusher

gouge

corn cutter

manicure stick

zipper

nail scissors

cuticle knife

cuticle nippers

cuticle scissors

case

nail nippers

automatic tweezers

eyebrow tweezers

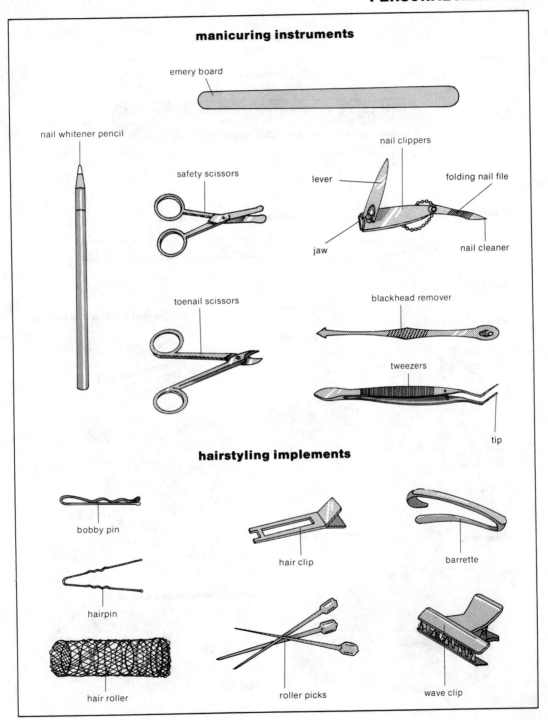

manicuring instruments

emery board

nail whitener pencil

safety scissors

nail clippers

lever

folding nail file

jaw

nail cleaner

toenail scissors

blackhead remover

tweezers

tip

hairstyling implements

bobby pin

hair clip

barrette

hairpin

hair roller

roller picks

wave clip

smoking accessories

cigar

cigar band · wrapper · tobacco · filler · head · bunch · tuck

cigarette holder

cigarette

paper · tobacco · filter tip · seam

gas lighter

striker wheel · valve · butane well · flame adjustment wheel

ashtray

ash · butt

packet of cigarette papers

carton

cigar box

cellophane wrapped packet

tear tape · label

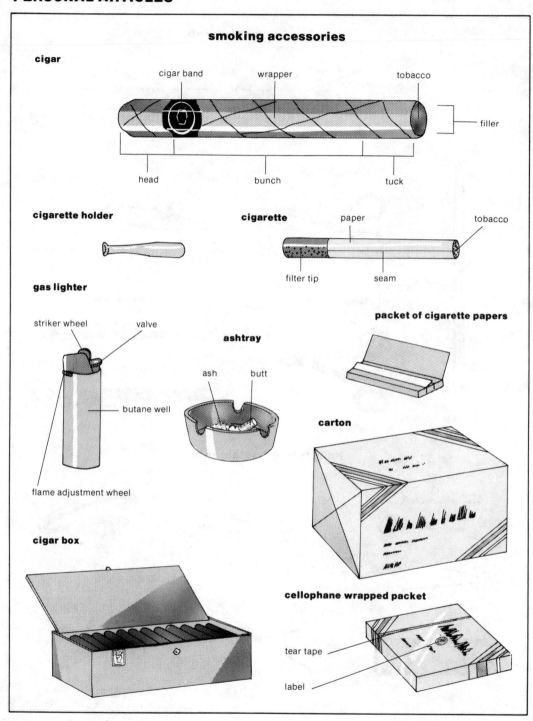

smoking accessories

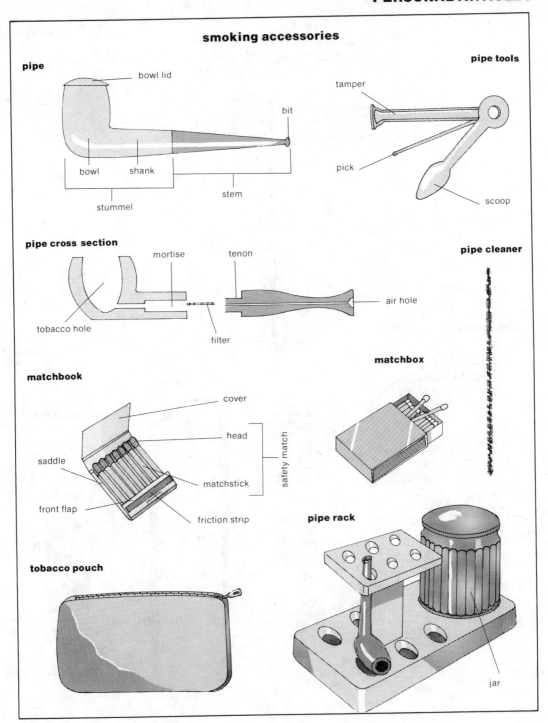

pipe
- bowl lid
- bit
- bowl
- shank
- stem
- stummel

pipe tools
- tamper
- pick
- scoop

pipe cross section
- mortise
- tenon
- tobacco hole
- filter
- air hole

pipe cleaner

matchbook
- cover
- head
- saddle
- matchstick
- front flap
- friction strip
- safety match

matchbox

pipe rack
- jar

tobacco pouch

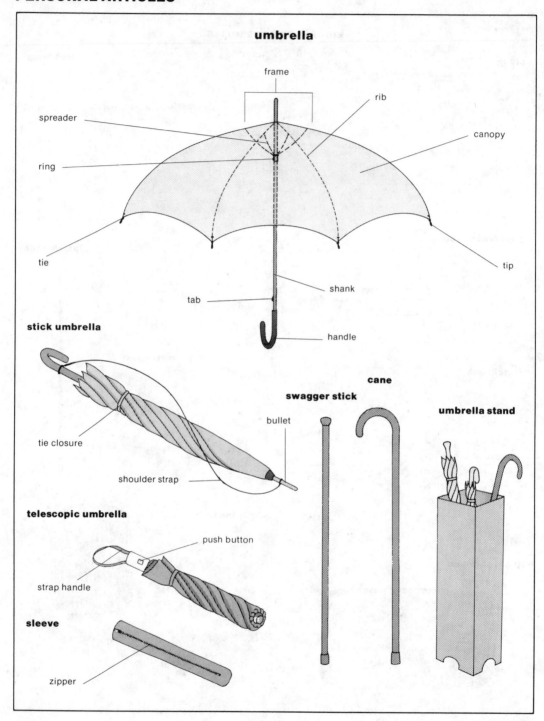

umbrella

frame

rib

spreader

canopy

ring

tie

tip

shank

tab

handle

stick umbrella

bullet

tie closure

shoulder strap

cane

swagger stick

umbrella stand

telescopic umbrella

push button

strap handle

sleeve

zipper

luggage

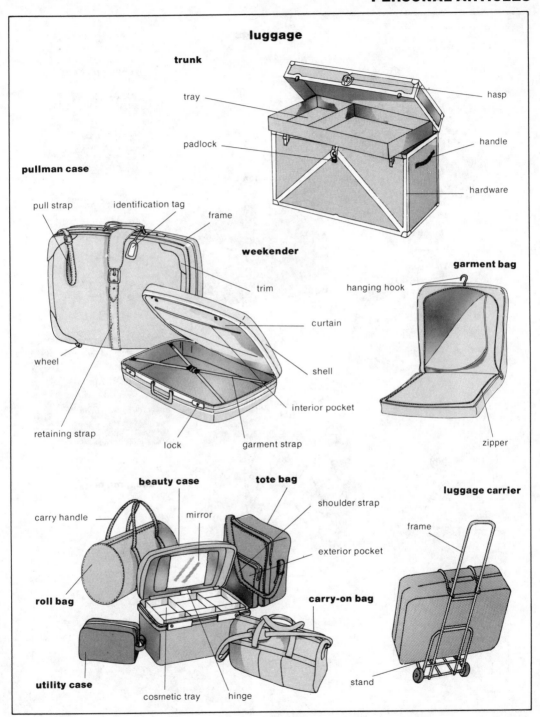

trunk

tray

hasp

padlock

handle

hardware

pullman case

pull strap

identification tag

frame

weekender

trim

garment bag

hanging hook

curtain

shell

wheel

interior pocket

retaining strap

lock

garment strap

zipper

beauty case

tote bag

luggage carrier

carry handle

mirror

shoulder strap

frame

exterior pocket

roll bag

carry-on bag

utility case

cosmetic tray

hinge

stand

handbags

barrel

zipper

envelope bag

press-button

accordion bag

box bag

pocket

tote bag

lining

beach bag

carrier bag

shopping bag

handbags

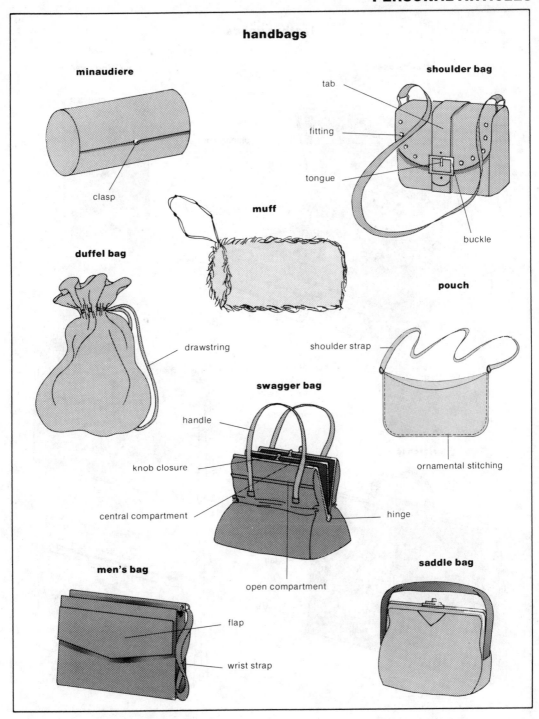

minaudiere

clasp

shoulder bag

tab

fitting

tongue

buckle

muff

duffel bag

drawstring

pouch

shoulder strap

ornamental stitching

swagger bag

handle

knob closure

central compartment

open compartment

hinge

men's bag

flap

wrist strap

saddle bag

leather goods

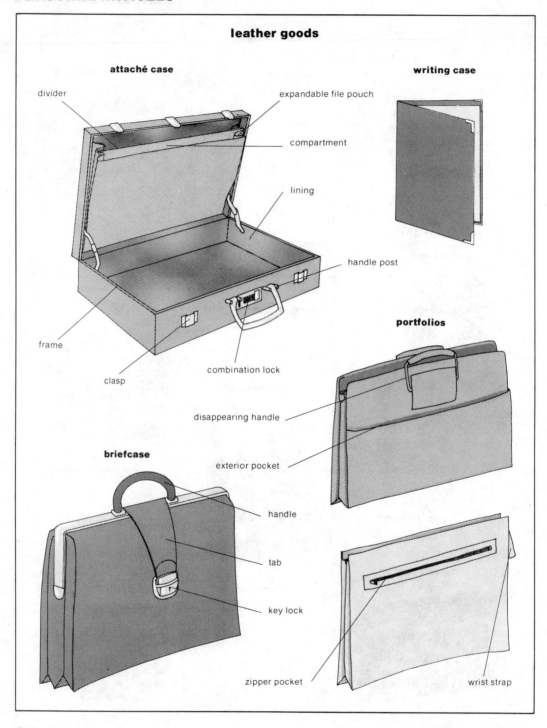

attaché case

divider

expandable file pouch

compartment

lining

handle post

frame

clasp

combination lock

writing case

portfolios

disappearing handle

exterior pocket

briefcase

handle

tab

key lock

zipper pocket

wrist strap

leather goods

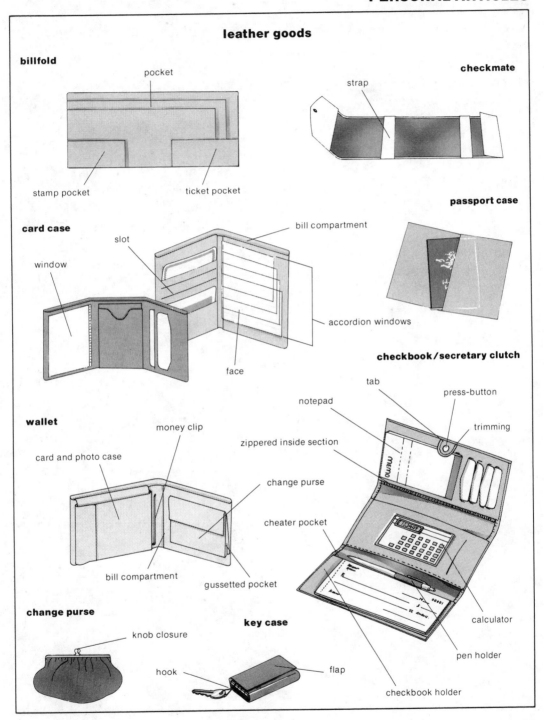

billfold

pocket

stamp pocket

ticket pocket

checkmate

strap

card case

window

slot

bill compartment

accordion windows

face

passport case

checkbook/secretary clutch

tab

press-button

notepad

trimming

wallet

money clip

card and photo case

zippered inside section

change purse

cheater pocket

calculator

bill compartment

gussetted pocket

pen holder

change purse

knob closure

key case

hook

flap

checkbook holder

COMMUNICATIONS

writing systems of the world

Merry Christmas
Happy New Year

English

Joyeux Noël
Bonne année

French

クリスマス
おめでとう　謹賀新年

Japanese

God
Jul
Godt
Nytt Ar

Norwegian

Vrolijk Kerstfeest
en een
Gelukkig Nieuwjaar

Dutch

Feliz
Navidad
Próspero
Año Nuevo

Spanish

С Рождеством
С новым годом

Russian

חג שמח
וברכה

Hebrew

عید شما مبارک
کریسمس مبارک

Iranian

BUON
NATALE
FELICE
ANNO NUOVO

Italian

Glædelig Jul
og
Godt Nytaar

Danish

Hyvaa Joulua Ja
Onnellista
Uutta Vuotta

Finnish

ΚΑΛΑ ΧΡΙΣΤΟΥΓΕΝΝΑ
ΚΑΙ ΕΥΤΥΧΙΣΜΕΝΟΣ Ο
ΚΑΙΝΟΥΡΓΙΟΣ ΧΡΟΝΟΣ

Greek

CHÚC MỪNG GIÁNG SINH
CUNG CHÚC TÂN XUÂN

Vietnamese

God Jul
och
Gott Nytt
År

Swedish

عام سعيد
وكل عام وانتم بخير

Arabic

नव वर्ष की शुभकामनाऐं

Hindi

 Տեառնընդառաջ
Շնորհաւոր

Armenian

SĂRBĂTORI FERICITE
ŞI
LA MULŢI ANI

Rumanian

ХРИСТОС
РОДИВСЯ
ШАСЛИВОГО
НОВОГО РОКУ

Ukrainian

FELIZ NATAL
PROSPERO ANO NOVO

Portuguese

Fröhliche Weihnachten
und alles Gute
zum Neuen Jahr

German

සුභ නත්තලක් වේවා
සුභ අලුත් අවුරුද්දක් වේවා

Sinhalese

Wesołych Świąt
i
Szczęśliwego
Nowego Roku

Polish

聖誕快樂
新年愉快

Chinese

Nadolig Llawen
Blwyddyn Newydd
Dda

Welsh

KELLEMES KARÁCSONYi
ÜNNEPEKE
BOLDOG ÚJÉVET

Hungarian

ᒥᕐᕆ ᖁᕕᐊᓱᒡ ᖁᕕᐊᓱᒡᕕᒃ
ᖁᕕᐊᓱᒡᕕᒃ ᐊᒻᒪᓗ ᐅᑉᐱᕈᕐ

Inuktitut

Braille

letters

a b c d e f g h i j k l m

n o p q r s t u v w x y z

numerals

numeral sign 1 2 3 4 5 6 7 8 9 0

mathematical symbols

: :: + − × / = > < √

punctuation marks

, ; : . ! ( ) " ? *

, — capital sign

French language signs

ì ò ou § æ ç é à è ù

â ê î ô û ë ï ü œ

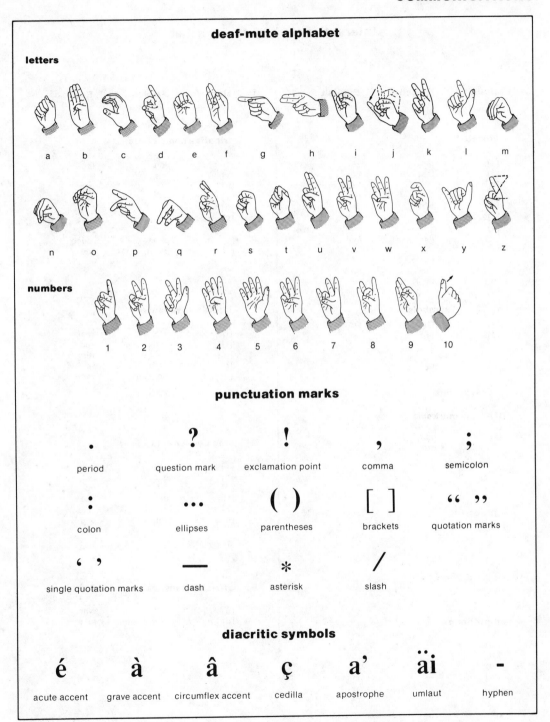

deaf-mute alphabet

letters

a b c d e f g h i j k l m

n o p q r s t u v w x y z

numbers

1 2 3 4 5 6 7 8 9 10

punctuation marks

.	?	!	,	;
period	question mark	exclamation point	comma	semicolon

:	...	( )	[ ]	" "
colon	ellipses	parentheses	brackets	quotation marks

' '	—	*	/
single quotation marks	dash	asterisk	slash

diacritic symbols

é	à	â	ç	a'	äi	-
acute accent	grave accent	circumflex accent	cedilla	apostrophe	umlaut	hyphen

international phonetic alphabet

signs	French	English
vowels		
[a]	lac	—
[ɑ]	mât	arm
[æ]	—	back
[e]	thé	elite
[ɛ]	poète	yet
[ə]	—	ago
[ɜ]	—	earth
[i]	île	beet
[ɪ]	—	bit
[ɔ]	note	ball
[o]	dos	note
[œ]	peur	—
[u]	loup	rule
[ʊ]	—	bull
[ʌ]	—	but
[y]	mur	cure
[ø]	feu	—
nasal vowels		
[ã]	blanc	—
[ɛ̃]	pain	—
[ɔ̃]	bon	—
[œ̃]	brun	—
glides		
[j]	yeux	you
[ɥ]	nuit	—
[w]	oui	we
diphthongs		
[aɪ]	—	my
[aʊ]	—	how
[ɔɪ]	—	toy
[ju]	—	amuse

signs	French	English
fricative consonants		
[f]	fou	life
[v]	vite	live
[θ]	—	thin
[ð]	—	then
[h]	—	hot
[s]	hélas	pass
[z]	gaz	zoo
[ʒ]	page	rouge
[ʃ]	cheval	she
liquid consonants		
[l]	mal	real
[r]	rude	rue
[m]	blême	him
[n]	fanal	in
[ɲ]	agneau	rang
stop consonants		
[p]	pas	mop
[b]	beau	bat
[d]	dur	do
[t]	tu	two
[k]	que	lake
[g]	gare	bag
affricate consonants		
[tʃ]	—	chin
[dʒ]	—	joke

typical letter

American model

letterhead

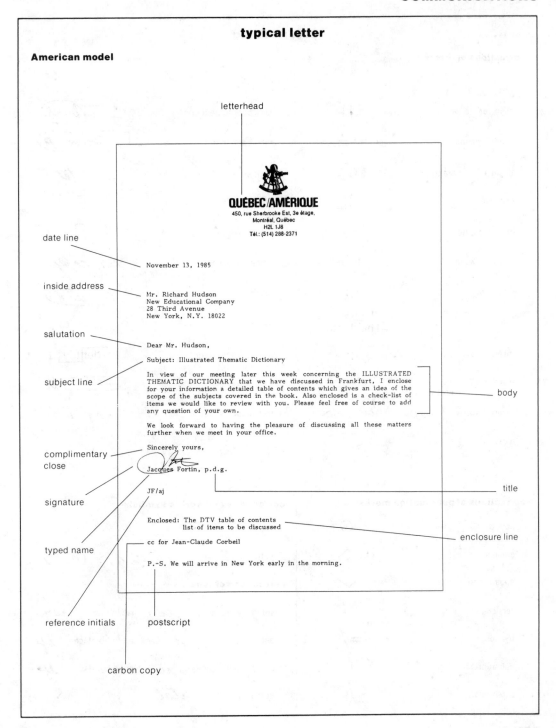

QUÉBEC/AMÉRIQUE
450, rue Sherbrooke Est, 3e étage,
Montréal, Québec
H2L 1J8
Tél.: (514) 288-2371

date line — November 13, 1985

inside address —
Mr. Richard Hudson
New Educational Company
28 Third Avenue
New York, N.Y. 18022

salutation — Dear Mr. Hudson,

subject line — Subject: Illustrated Thematic Dictionary

In view of our meeting later this week concerning the ILLUSTRATED THEMATIC DICTIONARY that we have discussed in Frankfurt, I enclose for your information a detailed table of contents which gives an idea of the scope of the subjects covered in the book. Also enclosed is a check-list of items we would like to review with you. Please feel free of course to add any question of your own. — body

We look forward to having the pleasure of discussing all these matters further when we meet in your office.

complimentary close — Sincerely yours,

Jacques Fortin, p.d.g. — title

signature —

JF/aj

typed name —

Enclosed: The DTV table of contents
        list of items to be discussed — enclosure line

cc for Jean-Claude Corbeil

P.-S. We will arrive in New York early in the morning.

reference initials — postscript

carbon copy —

COMMUNICATIONS

proofreading

corrections of errors

align vertically	$\|\|$	take over to next line	⌐ *break*	
align horizontal	$\equiv$	take back to previous line	⌐ *move up*	
begin a new paragraph	¶	let it stand	.... *stet*	
center	] [	move to left	[	
correct a letter	a/	move to right	]	
correct a word	heel /	something omitted	*see copy*	
insert space	#	reduce space	*reduce #*	
run in	heel.⌐ The doctor	delete	e	
insert here	∧	transpose two words	order the | *tr*	
insert a letter	a ∧	transpose lines	*tr*	
insert a word	*low* ∧	transpose two letters	yo *tr*	
close up	⌣			

corrections of punctuation marks

period	⊙
comma	∧,
apostrophe	∨,
semicolon	; /
hyphen	= /
quotation marks	∨'' / ∨''
parentheses	c / ⊃

corrections of diacritic symbols

superscript	2/ a^2
subscript	∧2 (h_2O)

corrections of type

set in lowercase	*lc*	set in roman	*rom*
set in capitals	*cap*	set in boldface	*bf*
set in small capitals	*sc*	set in lightface	*lf*
set in italic	*ital*		

proofreading

indication of types

italic	<u>bible</u>	*bible*
boldface	<u>bible</u>	**bible**
small capitals	<u>bible</u>	BIBLE
capitals	<u>bible</u>	BIBLE
italic capitals	<u>bible</u>	*BIBLE*
boldface capitals	<u>bible</u>	**BIBLE**
ital. boldface capitals	<u>bible</u>	***BIBLE***
capitals for initials small capitals for the rest	<u>HENRY MILLER</u>	HENRY MILLER

1.1 - <u>The phoneme</u>. It is important to keep in mind that the sounds of human language are more that just *n/* *p/* sounds. The p of pin is explosed with a puff of air *d/* *tu* flolowing it, where as the p of <u>capture</u> is not those *o/* *Two* *s/* sound are quite different as mere sounds. But english *in* we say they are the same, and they are, because they functions as the same unit in the sound system of English.

se The functionning units like English /p/ are called *y/* <u>phonemes</u> by structural linguists and with usually be *will* *s/* enclosed in plant bars in the text. <u>Robert</u> <u>Lado</u>

from <u>Linguistics across cultures</u>

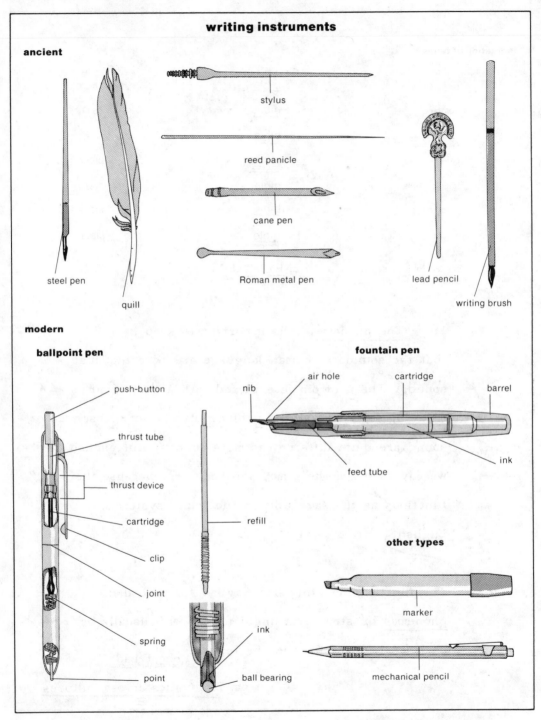

writing instruments

ancient

stylus

reed panicle

cane pen

Roman metal pen

steel pen

quill

lead pencil

writing brush

modern

ballpoint pen

push-button

thrust tube

thrust device

cartridge

clip

joint

spring

point

refill

ink

ball bearing

fountain pen

nib

air hole

cartridge

barrel

feed tube

ink

other types

marker

mechanical pencil

photography

single-lens reflex camera

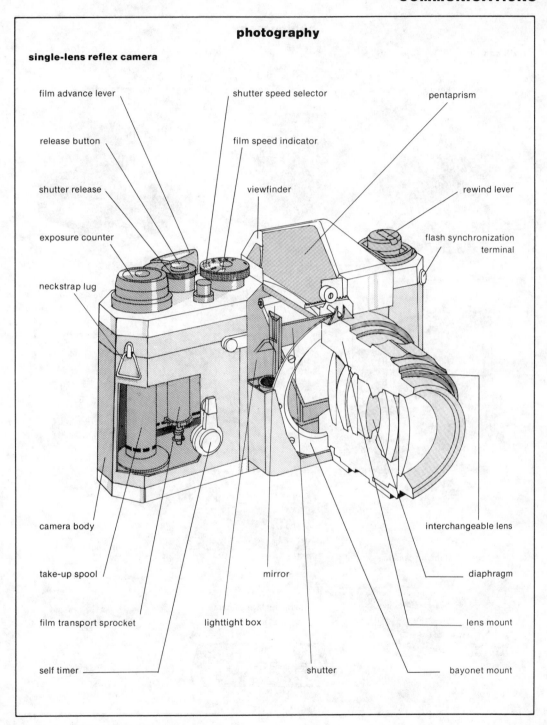

film advance lever

shutter speed selector

pentaprism

release button

film speed indicator

shutter release

viewfinder

rewind lever

exposure counter

flash synchronization terminal

neckstrap lug

camera body

interchangeable lens

take-up spool

mirror

diaphragm

film transport sprocket

lighttight box

lens mount

self timer

shutter

bayonet mount

photography

still cameras

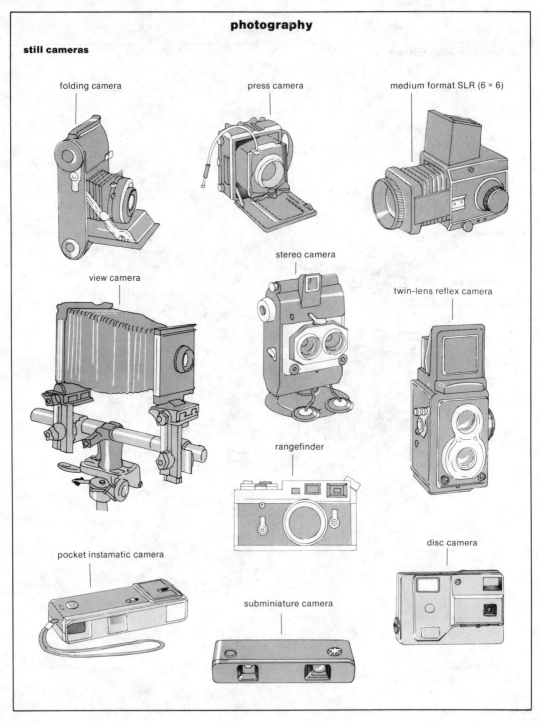

folding camera

press camera

medium format SLR (6 × 6)

view camera

stereo camera

twin-lens reflex camera

rangefinder

pocket instamatic camera

disc camera

subminiature camera

photography

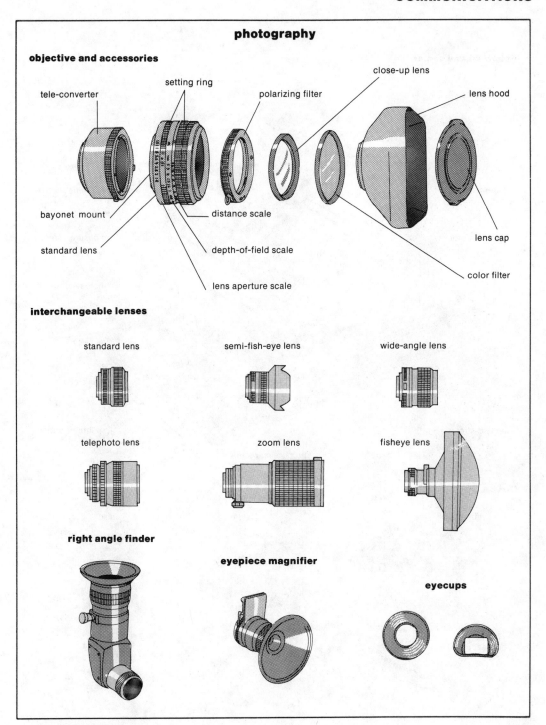

objective and accessories

tele-converter

setting ring

close-up lens

polarizing filter

lens hood

bayonet mount

distance scale

standard lens

depth-of-field scale

lens cap

lens aperture scale

color filter

interchangeable lenses

standard lens

semi-fish-eye lens

wide-angle lens

telephoto lens

zoom lens

fisheye lens

right angle finder

eyepiece magnifier

eyecups

COMMUNICATIONS

photography

Polaroid Land camera

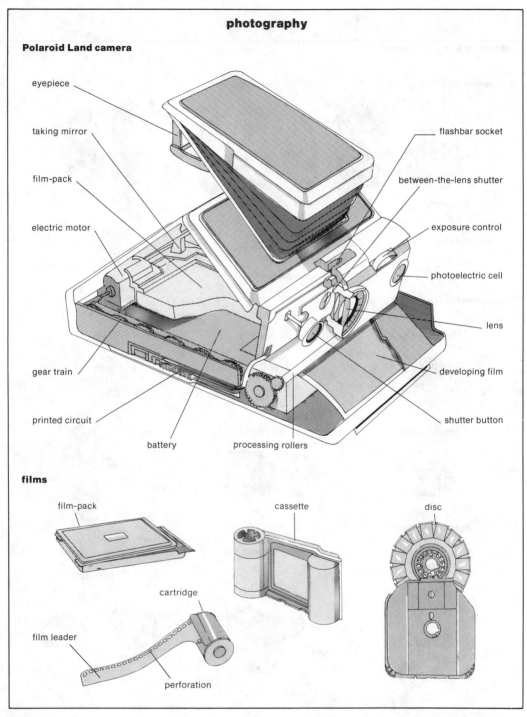

eyepiece

taking mirror

film-pack

electric motor

gear train

printed circuit

battery

processing rollers

flashbar socket

between-the-lens shutter

exposure control

photoelectric cell

lens

developing film

shutter button

films

film-pack

cassette

disc

cartridge

film leader

perforation

photography

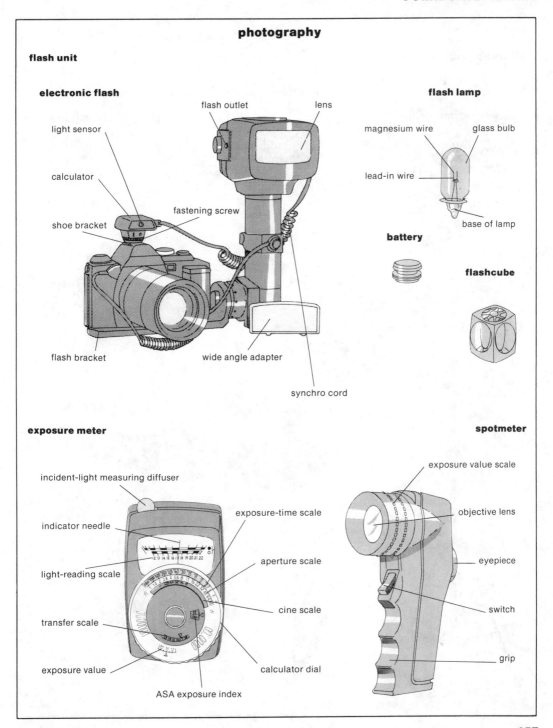

flash unit

electronic flash

flash outlet

lens

light sensor

calculator

fastening screw

shoe bracket

flash bracket

wide angle adapter

synchro cord

flash lamp

magnesium wire

glass bulb

lead-in wire

base of lamp

battery

flashcube

exposure meter

incident-light measuring diffuser

indicator needle

light-reading scale

transfer scale

exposure value

ASA exposure index

exposure-time scale

aperture scale

cine scale

calculator dial

spotmeter

exposure value scale

objective lens

eyepiece

switch

grip

photography

studio lighting

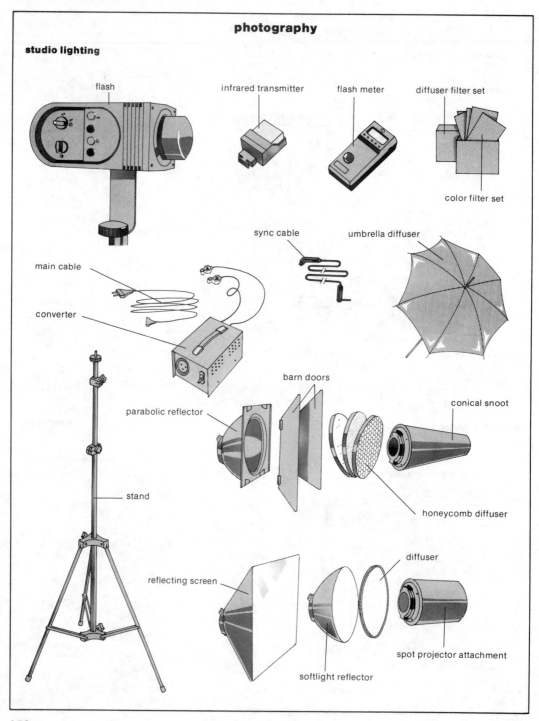

flash

infrared transmitter

flash meter

diffuser filter set

color filter set

sync cable

umbrella diffuser

main cable

converter

barn doors

conical snoot

parabolic reflector

honeycomb diffuser

stand

diffuser

reflecting screen

spot projector attachment

softlight reflector

photography

photographic accessories

air bulb release

cable release

tripod

side-tilt lock

panoramic and tilting head

camera screw

column lock

camera platform

column crank

pan handle

column

telescoping leg

collet

lower pan-head mounting screw

studio accessories

boom

stand

reflector

background

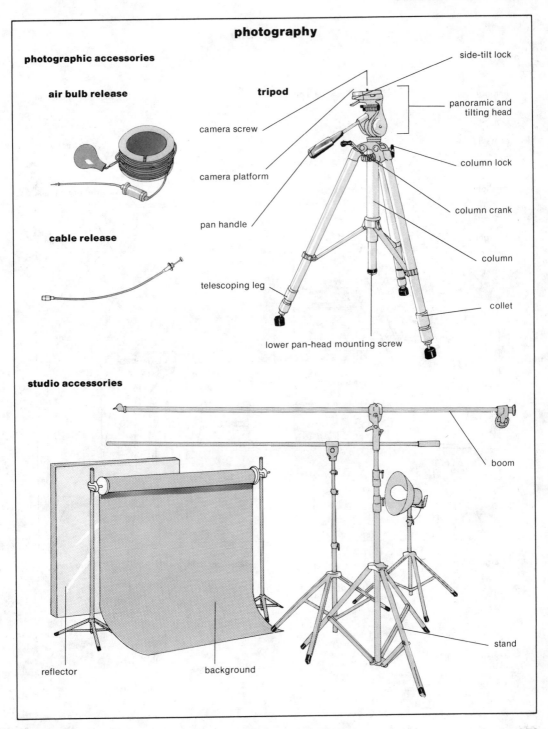

359

photography

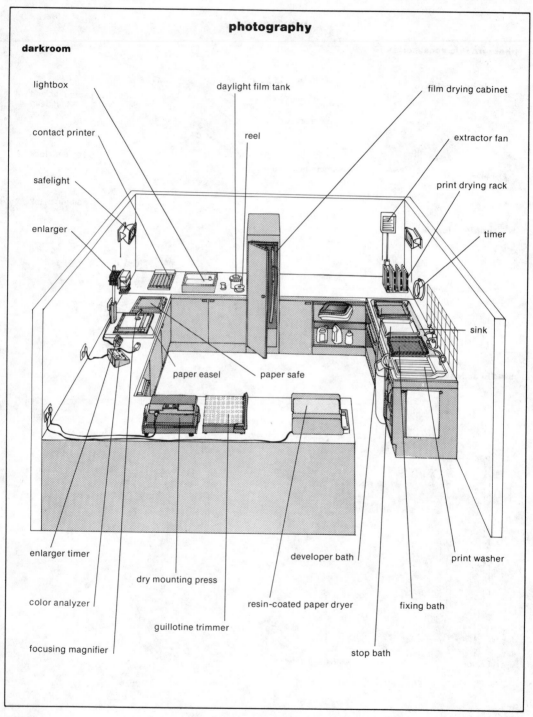

darkroom

lightbox

contact printer

safelight

enlarger

daylight film tank

reel

film drying cabinet

extractor fan

print drying rack

timer

sink

paper easel

paper safe

enlarger timer

dry mounting press

developer bath

print washer

color analyzer

resin-coated paper dryer

fixing bath

guillotine trimmer

focusing magnifier

stop bath

photography

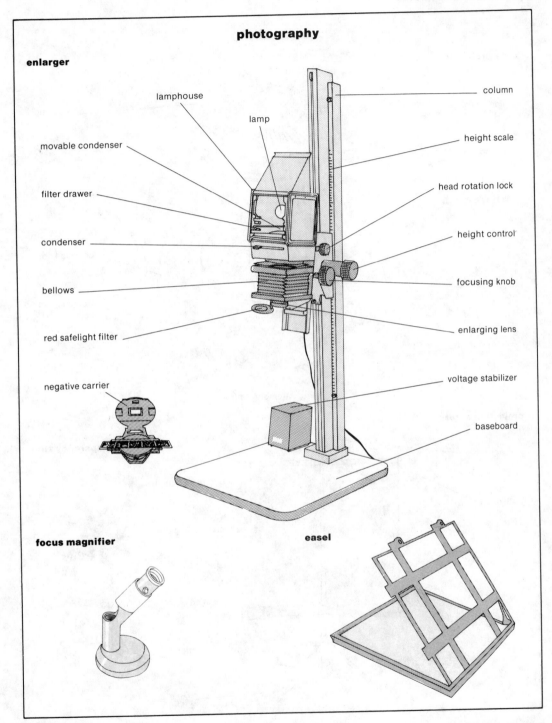

enlarger

- lamphouse
- lamp
- movable condenser
- filter drawer
- condenser
- bellows
- red safelight filter
- negative carrier

- column
- height scale
- head rotation lock
- height control
- focusing knob
- enlarging lens
- voltage stabilizer
- baseboard

focus magnifier

easel

COMMUNICATIONS

photography

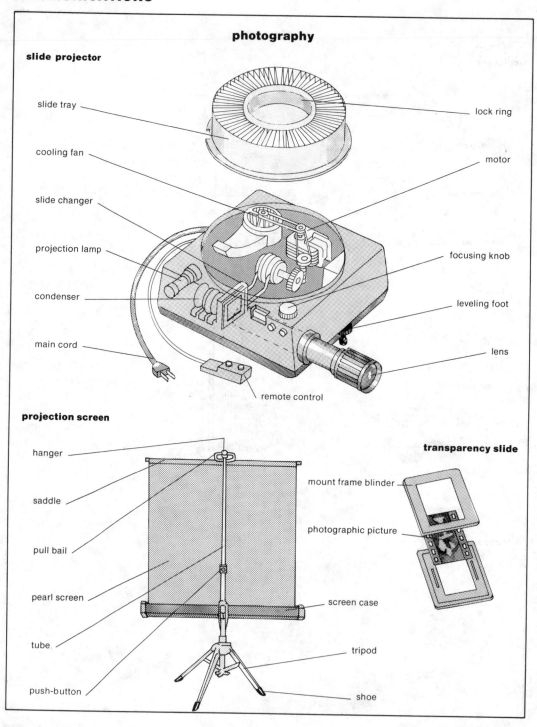

slide projector

slide tray

lock ring

cooling fan

motor

slide changer

projection lamp

focusing knob

condenser

leveling foot

main cord

lens

remote control

projection screen

hanger

transparency slide

mount frame blinder

saddle

photographic picture

pull bail

pearl screen

screen case

tube

tripod

push-button

shoe

sound reproducing system

system elements

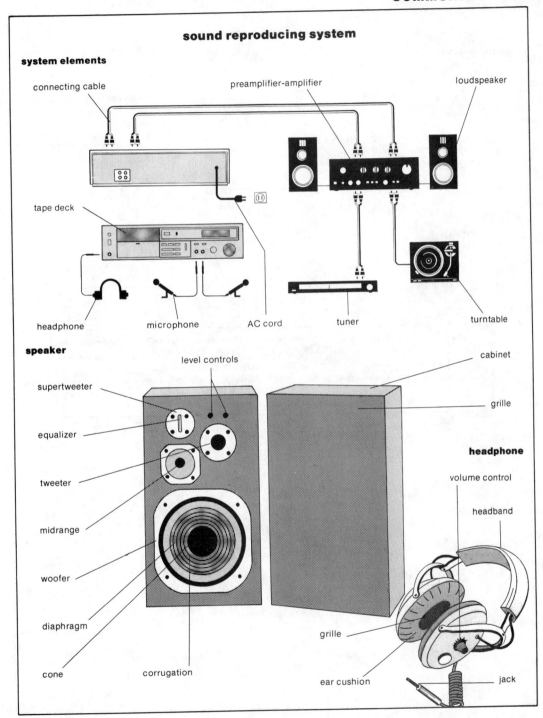

connecting cable

preamplifier-amplifier

loudspeaker

tape deck

headphone

microphone

AC cord

tuner

turntable

speaker

level controls

cabinet

supertweeter

grille

equalizer

headphone

tweeter

volume control

midrange

headband

woofer

diaphragm

grille

cone

corrugation

ear cushion

jack

COMMUNICATIONS

sound reproducing system

amplifier-tuner

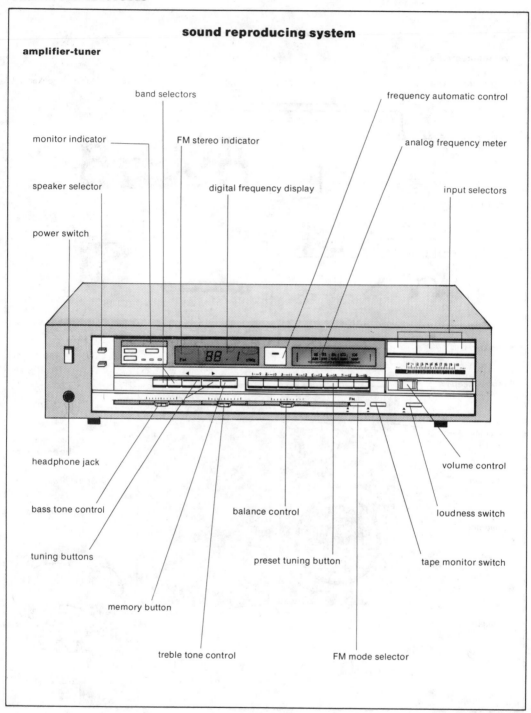

band selectors

frequency automatic control

monitor indicator

FM stereo indicator

analog frequency meter

speaker selector

digital frequency display

input selectors

power switch

headphone jack

volume control

bass tone control

balance control

loudness switch

tuning buttons

preset tuning button

tape monitor switch

memory button

treble tone control

FM mode selector

sound reproducing system

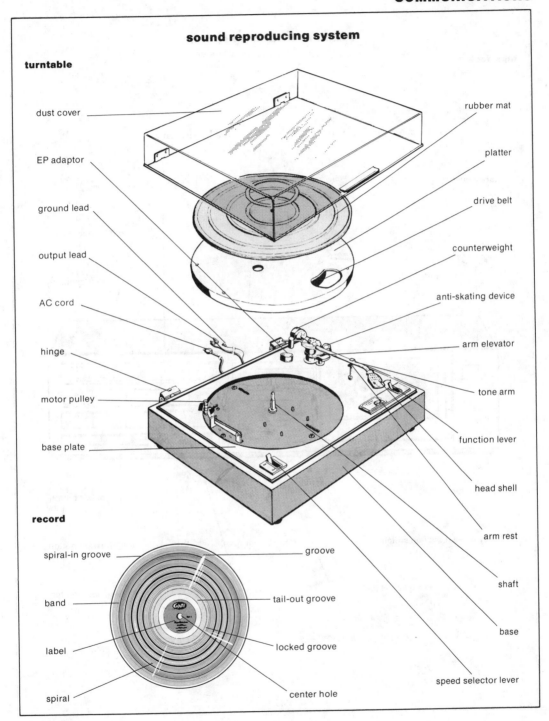

turntable

dust cover

EP adaptor

ground lead

output lead

AC cord

hinge

motor pulley

base plate

rubber mat

platter

drive belt

counterweight

anti-skating device

arm elevator

tone arm

function lever

head shell

arm rest

shaft

base

speed selector lever

record

spiral-in groove

band

label

spiral

groove

tail-out groove

locked groove

center hole

sound reproducing system

tape deck

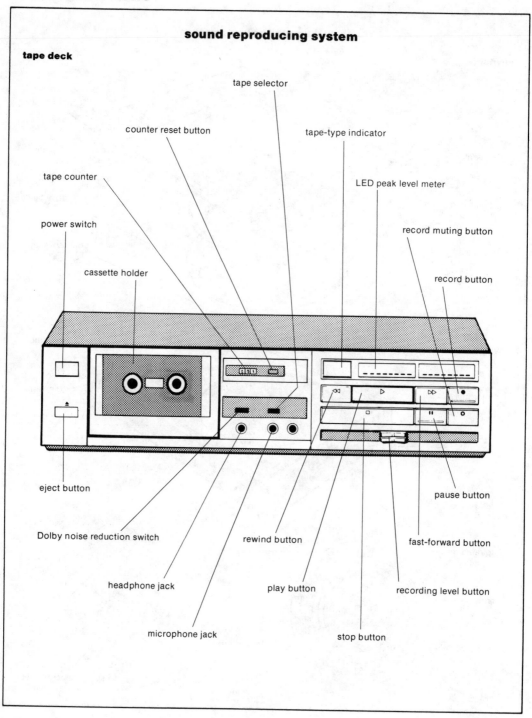

tape selector

counter reset button

tape-type indicator

tape counter

LED peak level meter

power switch

record muting button

cassette holder

record button

eject button

pause button

Dolby noise reduction switch

fast-forward button

headphone jack

rewind button

play button

recording level button

microphone jack

stop button

video tape recorder

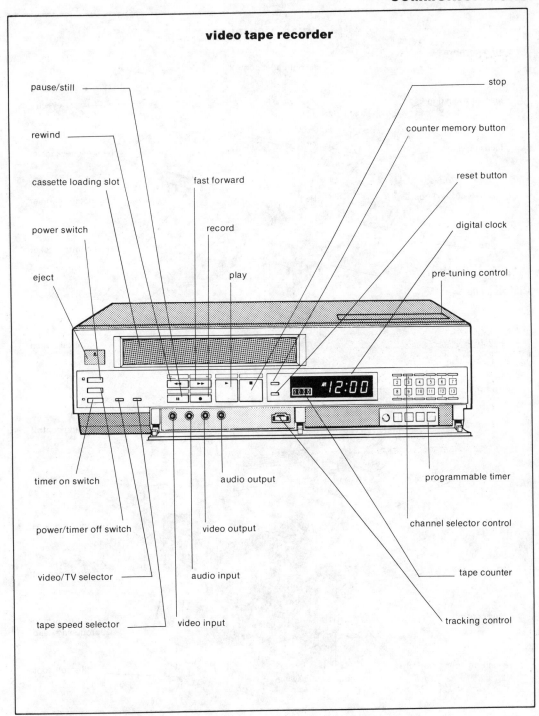

pause/still

stop

rewind

counter memory button

cassette loading slot

fast forward

reset button

power switch

record

digital clock

eject

play

pre-tuning control

timer on switch

audio output

programmable timer

power/timer off switch

video output

channel selector control

video/TV selector

audio input

tape counter

tape speed selector

video input

tracking control

cinematography

sound camera

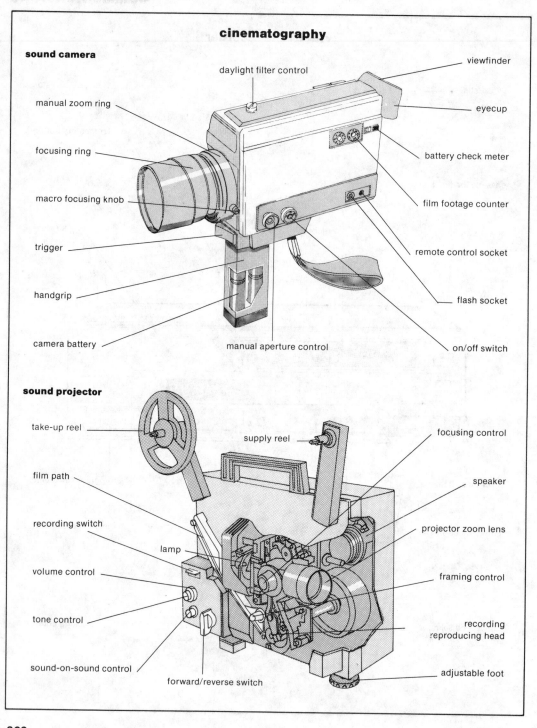

daylight filter control

viewfinder

manual zoom ring

eyecup

focusing ring

battery check meter

macro focusing knob

film footage counter

trigger

remote control socket

handgrip

flash socket

camera battery

manual aperture control

on/off switch

sound projector

take-up reel

supply reel

focusing control

film path

speaker

recording switch

projector zoom lens

lamp

volume control

framing control

tone control

recording reproducing head

sound-on-sound control

forward/reverse switch

adjustable foot

video camera

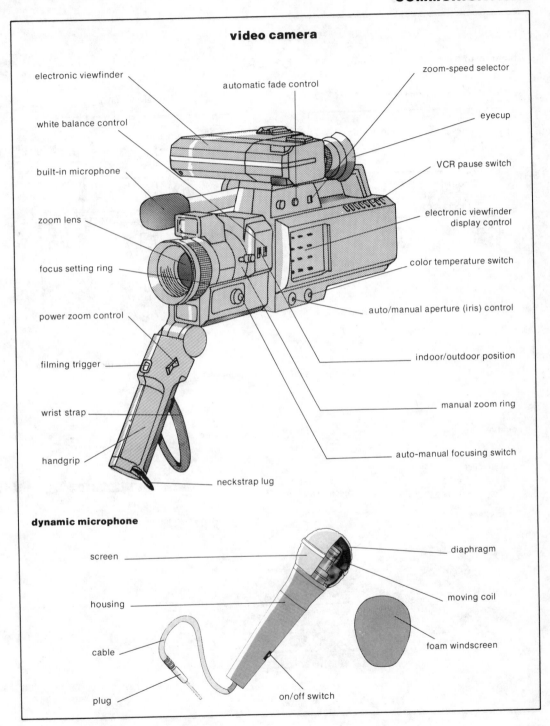

electronic viewfinder

automatic fade control

zoom-speed selector

white balance control

eyecup

built-in microphone

VCR pause switch

zoom lens

electronic viewfinder display control

focus setting ring

color temperature switch

power zoom control

auto/manual aperture (iris) control

filming trigger

indoor/outdoor position

wrist strap

manual zoom ring

handgrip

auto-manual focusing switch

neckstrap lug

dynamic microphone

screen

diaphragm

housing

moving coil

cable

foam windscreen

plug

on/off switch

COMMUNICATIONS

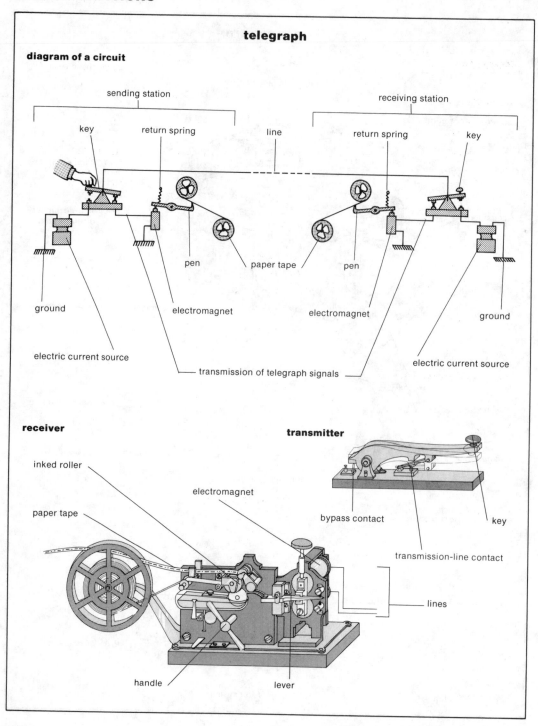

telegraph

diagram of a circuit

sending station

receiving station

key

return spring

line

return spring

key

ground

pen

paper tape

pen

ground

electromagnet

electromagnet

electric current source

electric current source

transmission of telegraph signals

receiver

transmitter

inked roller

electromagnet

bypass contact

key

paper tape

transmission-line contact

lines

handle

lever

telegraph

Morse code

alphabet

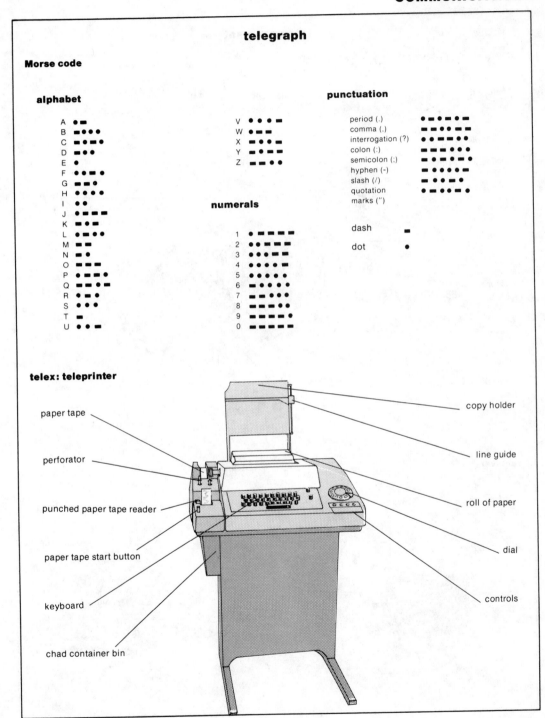

A	● ▬	V	● ● ● ▬
B	▬ ● ● ●	W	● ▬ ▬
C	▬ ● ▬ ●	X	▬ ● ● ▬
D	▬ ● ●	Y	▬ ● ▬ ▬
E	●	Z	▬ ▬ ● ●
F	● ● ▬ ●		
G	▬ ▬ ●		
H	● ● ● ●		
I	● ●		
J	● ▬ ▬ ▬		
K	▬ ● ▬		
L	● ▬ ● ●		
M	▬ ▬		
N	▬ ●		
O	▬ ▬ ▬		
P	● ▬ ▬ ●		
Q	▬ ▬ ● ▬		
R	● ▬ ●		
S	● ● ●		
T	▬		
U	● ● ▬		

numerals

1	● ▬ ▬ ▬ ▬
2	● ● ▬ ▬ ▬
3	● ● ● ▬ ▬
4	● ● ● ● ▬
5	● ● ● ● ●
6	▬ ● ● ● ●
7	▬ ▬ ● ● ●
8	▬ ▬ ▬ ● ●
9	▬ ▬ ▬ ▬ ●
0	▬ ▬ ▬ ▬ ▬

punctuation

period (.)	▬ ● ▬ ● ▬ ●
comma (,)	● ● ▬ ▬ ● ●
interrogation (?)	● ● ▬ ▬ ● ●
colon (:)	▬ ▬ ▬ ● ● ●
semicolon (;)	▬ ● ▬ ● ▬ ●
hyphen (-)	▬ ● ● ● ● ▬
slash (/)	▬ ● ● ▬ ●
quotation marks (")	● ▬ ● ● ▬ ●

dash	▬
dot	●

telex: teleprinter

paper tape

perforator

punched paper tape reader

paper tape start button

keyboard

chad container bin

copy holder

line guide

roll of paper

dial

controls

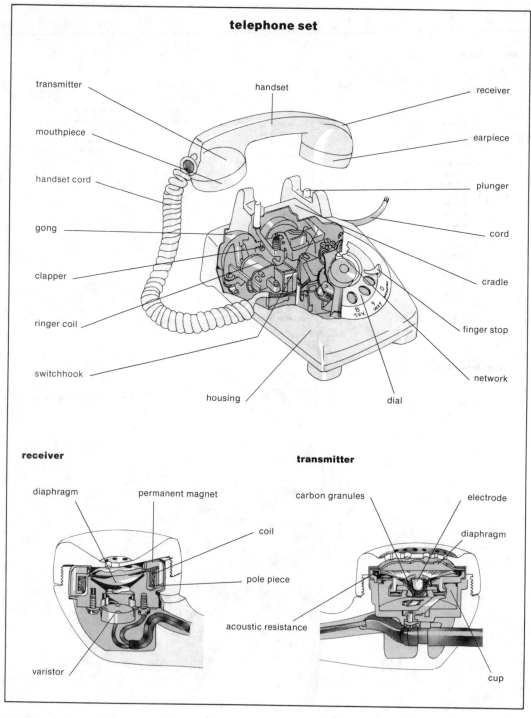

telephone set

transmitter
handset
receiver

mouthpiece
earpiece

handset cord
plunger

gong
cord

clapper
cradle

ringer coil
finger stop

switchhook
network

housing
dial

receiver

diaphragm
permanent magnet

coil

pole piece

acoustic resistance

varistor

transmitter

carbon granules
electrode

diaphragm

cup

types of telephones

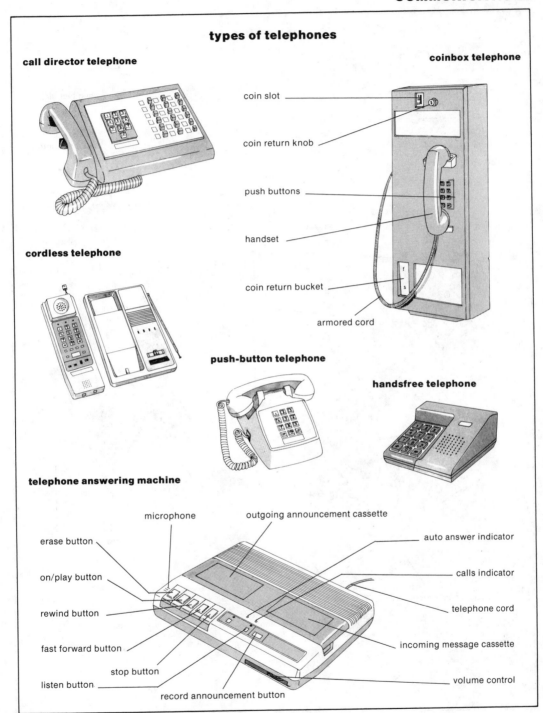

call director telephone

coinbox telephone

coin slot

coin return knob

push buttons

handset

coin return bucket

armored cord

cordless telephone

push-button telephone

handsfree telephone

telephone answering machine

microphone

outgoing announcement cassette

erase button

auto answer indicator

on/play button

calls indicator

rewind button

telephone cord

fast forward button

incoming message cassette

stop button

listen button

volume control

record announcement button

COMMUNICATIONS

television

studio and control rooms

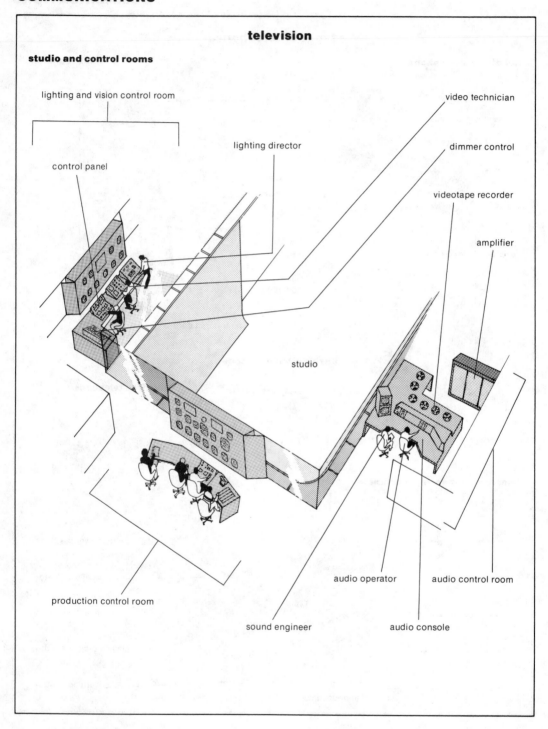

lighting and vision control room

video technician

lighting director

dimmer control

videotape recorder

control panel

amplifier

studio

production control room

audio operator

audio control room

sound engineer

audio console

television

studio floor

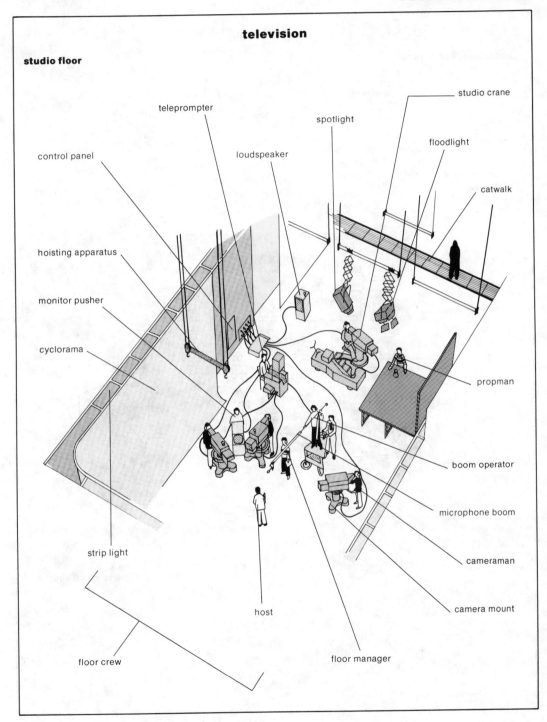

studio crane

teleprompter

spotlight

floodlight

control panel

loudspeaker

catwalk

hoisting apparatus

monitor pusher

cyclorama

propman

boom operator

microphone boom

strip light

cameraman

camera mount

host

floor crew

floor manager

television

production control room

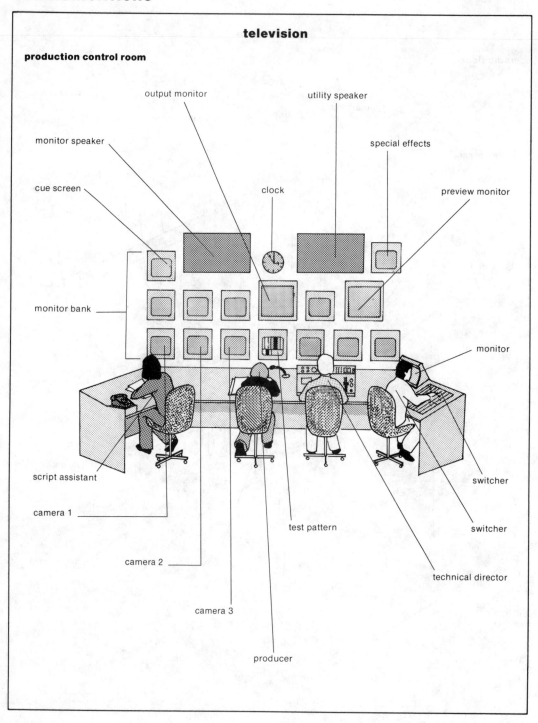

output monitor

utility speaker

monitor speaker

special effects

cue screen

clock

preview monitor

monitor bank

monitor

script assistant

switcher

camera 1

test pattern

switcher

camera 2

technical director

camera 3

producer

television

television set

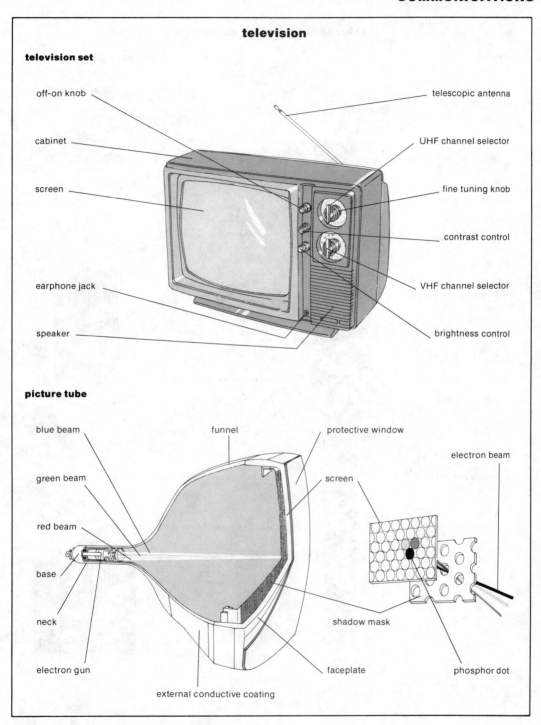

off-on knob

cabinet

screen

earphone jack

speaker

telescopic antenna

UHF channel selector

fine tuning knob

contrast control

VHF channel selector

brightness control

picture tube

blue beam

green beam

red beam

base

neck

electron gun

external conductive coating

funnel

protective window

screen

shadow mask

faceplate

electron beam

phosphor dot

telecommunication satellites

Hermes satellite

examples of satellites

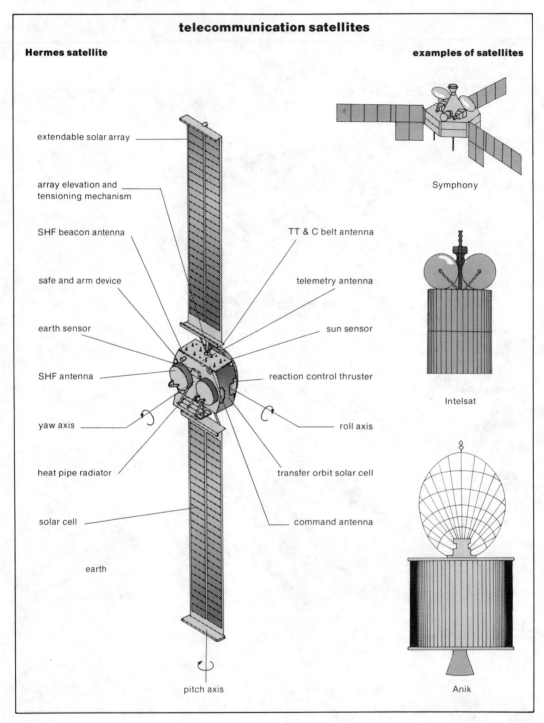

extendable solar array

array elevation and tensioning mechanism

SHF beacon antenna

safe and arm device

earth sensor

SHF antenna

yaw axis

heat pipe radiator

solar cell

earth

pitch axis

TT & C belt antenna

telemetry antenna

sun sensor

reaction control thruster

roll axis

transfer orbit solar cell

command antenna

Symphony

Intelsat

Anik

telecommunication satellites

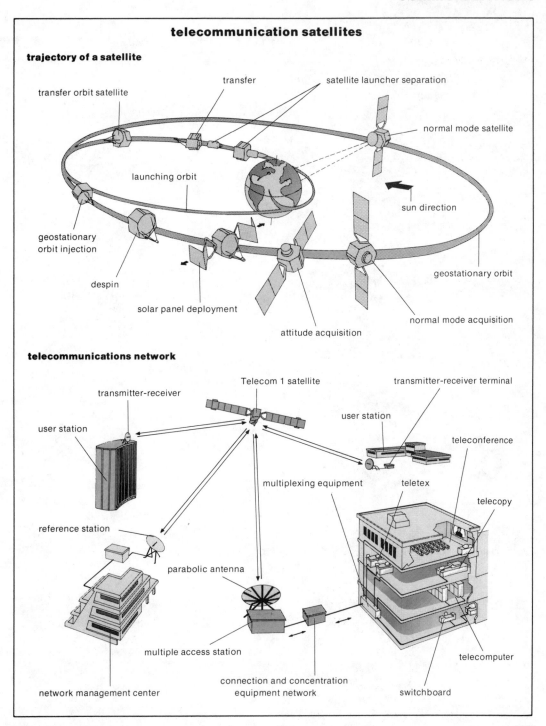

trajectory of a satellite

transfer orbit satellite

transfer

satellite launcher separation

normal mode satellite

launching orbit

sun direction

geostationary orbit injection

geostationary orbit

despin

solar panel deployment

attitude acquisition

normal mode acquisition

telecommunications network

transmitter-receiver

Telecom 1 satellite

transmitter-receiver terminal

user station

user station

teleconference

multiplexing equipment

teletex

telecopy

reference station

parabolic antenna

telecomputer

multiple access station

network management center

connection and concentration equipment network

switchboard

TRANSPORTATION

automobile

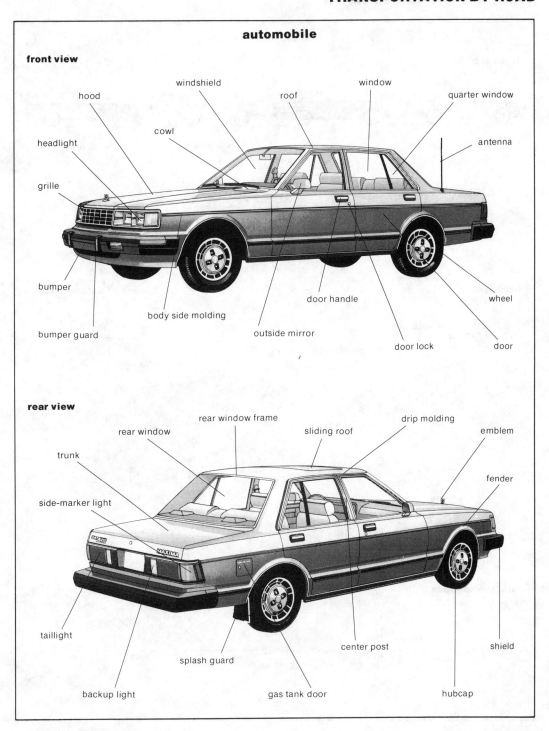

front view

hood

windshield

roof

window

quarter window

cowl

headlight

antenna

grille

bumper

body side molding

door handle

wheel

bumper guard

outside mirror

door lock

door

rear view

rear window frame

sliding roof

drip molding

emblem

rear window

trunk

fender

side-marker light

taillight

splash guard

center post

shield

backup light

gas tank door

hubcap

automobile

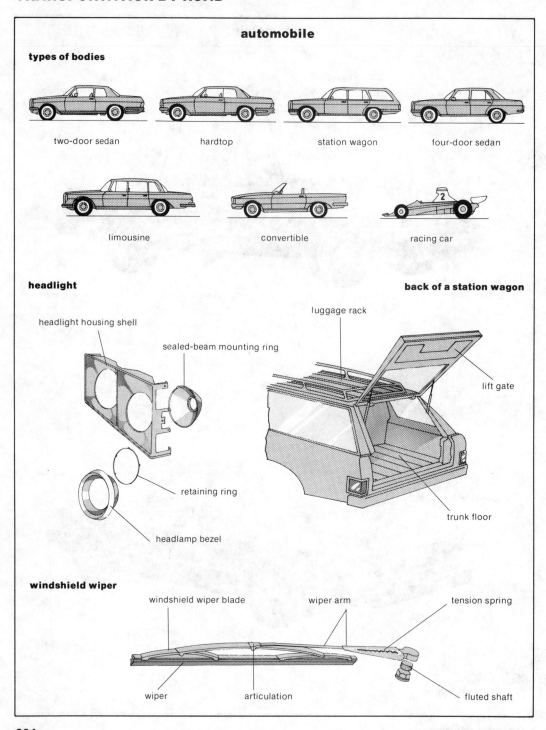

types of bodies

two-door sedan   hardtop   station wagon   four-door sedan

limousine   convertible   racing car

headlight

headlight housing shell

sealed-beam mounting ring

retaining ring

headlamp bezel

back of a station wagon

luggage rack

lift gate

trunk floor

windshield wiper

windshield wiper blade   wiper arm   tension spring

wiper   articulation   fluted shaft

automobile

dashboard

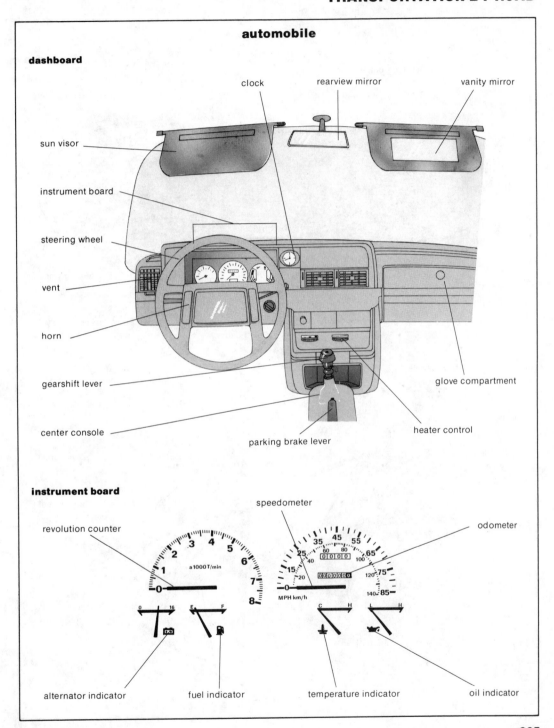

clock

rearview mirror

vanity mirror

sun visor

instrument board

steering wheel

vent

horn

gearshift lever

center console

parking brake lever

glove compartment

heater control

instrument board

speedometer

revolution counter

odometer

a 1000 T/min

MPH km/h

alternator indicator

fuel indicator

temperature indicator

oil indicator

automobile

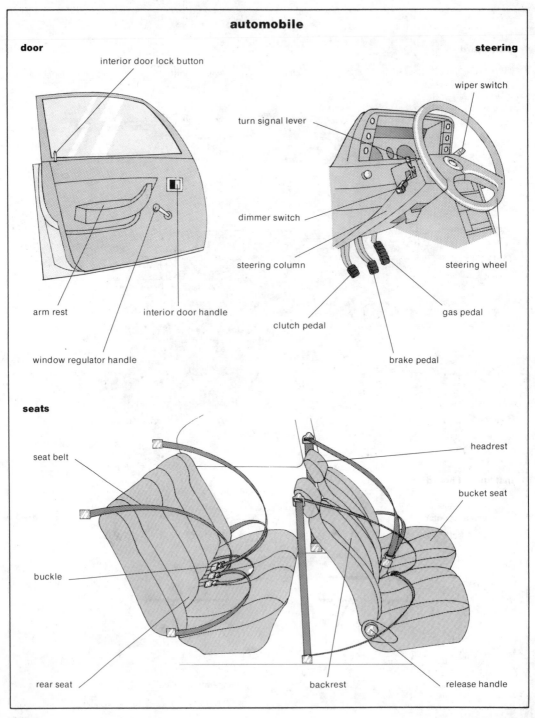

door

interior door lock button

arm rest

interior door handle

window regulator handle

steering

wiper switch

turn signal lever

dimmer switch

steering column

steering wheel

clutch pedal

gas pedal

brake pedal

seats

seat belt

buckle

rear seat

headrest

bucket seat

backrest

release handle

service station

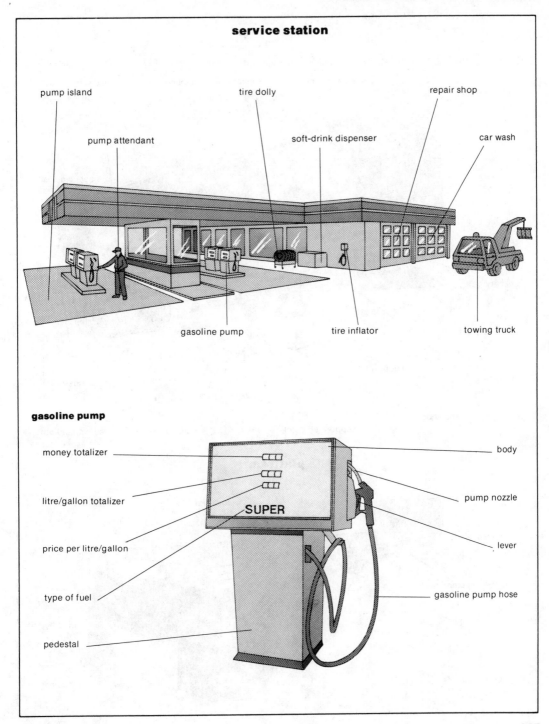

pump island

pump attendant

tire dolly

soft-drink dispenser

repair shop

car wash

gasoline pump

tire inflator

towing truck

gasoline pump

money totalizer

litre/gallon totalizer

price per litre/gallon

type of fuel

pedestal

SUPER

body

pump nozzle

lever

gasoline pump hose

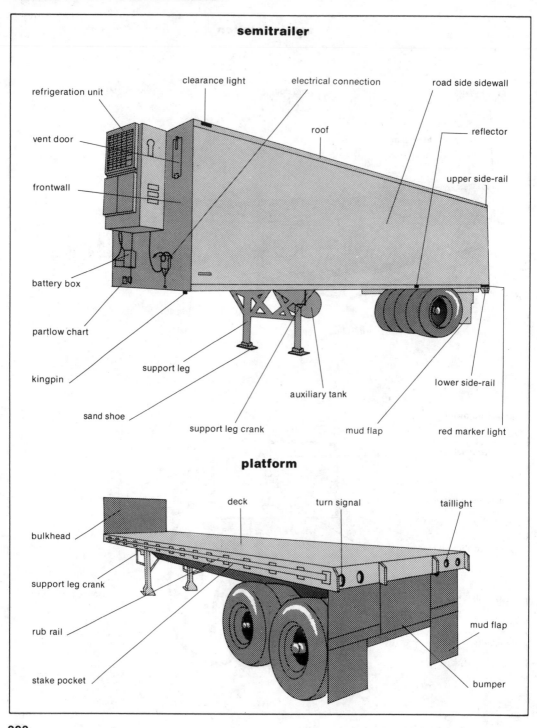

semitrailer

clearance light

electrical connection

road side sidewall

refrigeration unit

roof

reflector

vent door

upper side-rail

frontwall

battery box

partlow chart

support leg

kingpin

auxiliary tank

lower side-rail

sand shoe

support leg crank

mud flap

red marker light

platform

deck

turn signal

taillight

bulkhead

support leg crank

mud flap

rub rail

stake pocket

bumper

truck trailer

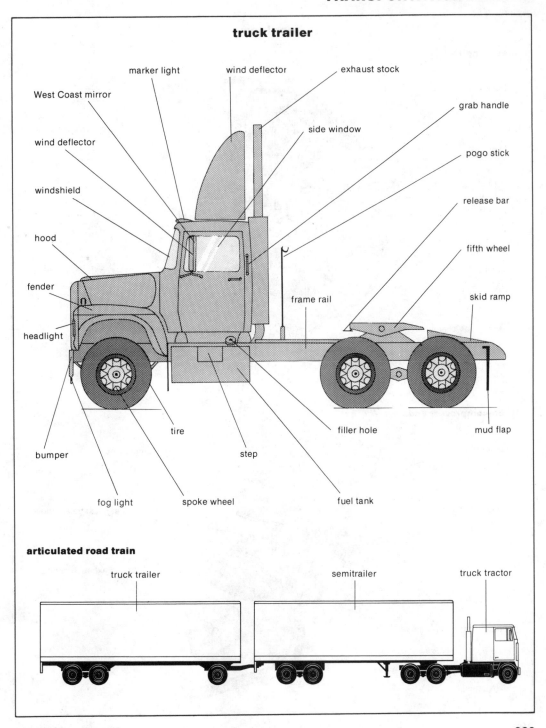

marker light

wind deflector

exhaust stock

West Coast mirror

grab handle

side window

wind deflector

pogo stick

windshield

release bar

hood

fifth wheel

fender

skid ramp

headlight

frame rail

tire

filler hole

mud flap

bumper

step

fog light

spoke wheel

fuel tank

articulated road train

truck trailer

semitrailer

truck tractor

engines

diesel engine

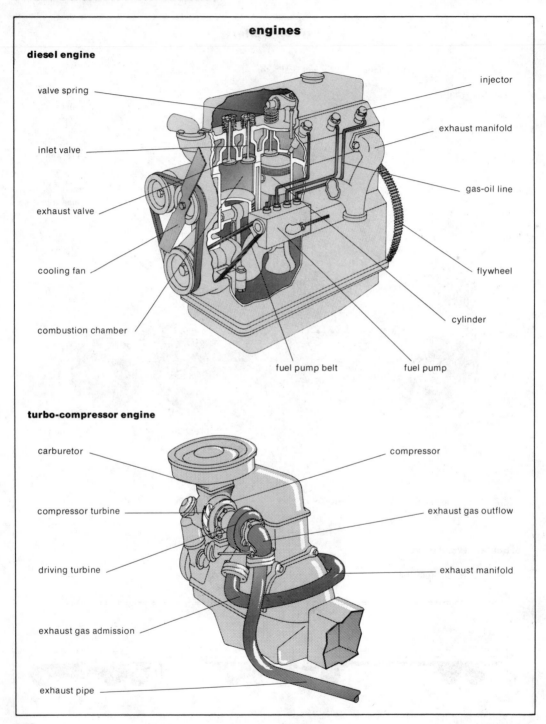

valve spring

injector

inlet valve

exhaust manifold

gas-oil line

exhaust valve

cooling fan

flywheel

combustion chamber

cylinder

fuel pump belt

fuel pump

turbo-compressor engine

carburetor

compressor

compressor turbine

exhaust gas outflow

driving turbine

exhaust manifold

exhaust gas admission

exhaust pipe

engine

gasoline engine

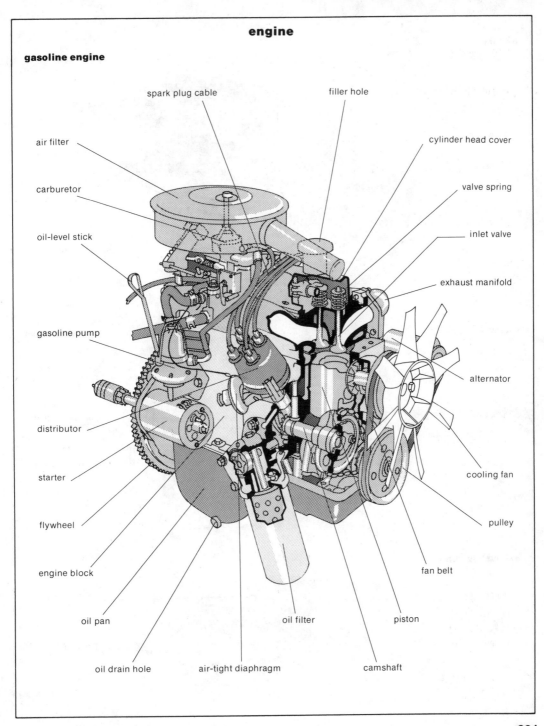

spark plug cable

filler hole

air filter

cylinder head cover

carburetor

valve spring

oil-level stick

inlet valve

exhaust manifold

gasoline pump

alternator

distributor

starter

cooling fan

flywheel

pulley

engine block

fan belt

oil pan

oil filter

piston

oil drain hole

air-tight diaphragm

camshaft

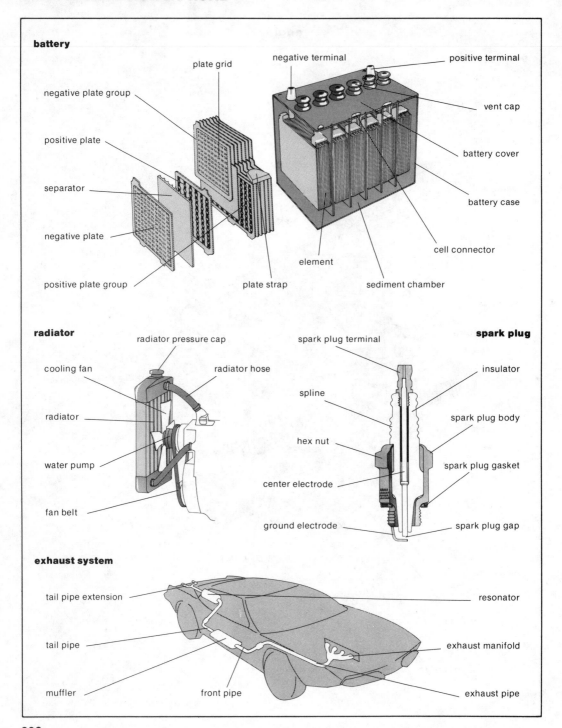

battery

plate grid

negative plate group

positive plate

separator

negative plate

positive plate group

plate strap

element

negative terminal

positive terminal

vent cap

battery cover

battery case

cell connector

sediment chamber

radiator

radiator pressure cap

cooling fan

radiator hose

radiator

water pump

fan belt

spark plug

spark plug terminal

spline

hex nut

center electrode

ground electrode

insulator

spark plug body

spark plug gasket

spark plug gap

exhaust system

tail pipe extension

tail pipe

muffler

front pipe

resonator

exhaust manifold

exhaust pipe

tires

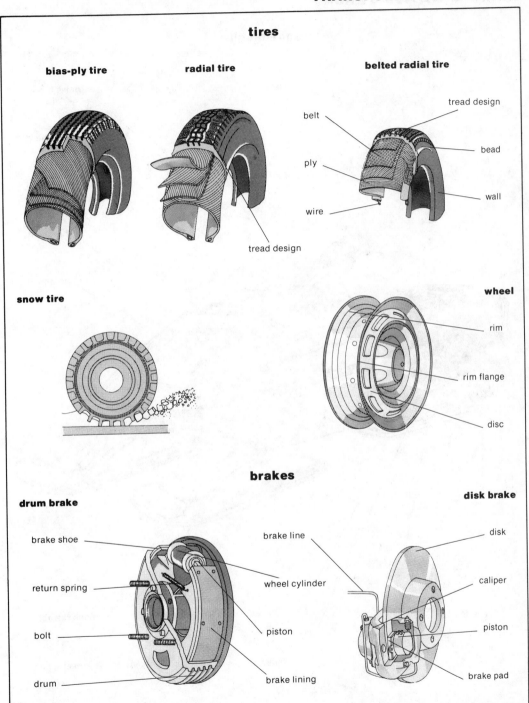

bias-ply tire

radial tire

belted radial tire

tread design

belt

bead

ply

wire

wall

tread design

snow tire

wheel

rim

rim flange

disc

brakes

drum brake

disk brake

brake shoe

brake line

disk

wheel cylinder

return spring

caliper

piston

bolt

piston

brake lining

drum

brake pad

snowmobile

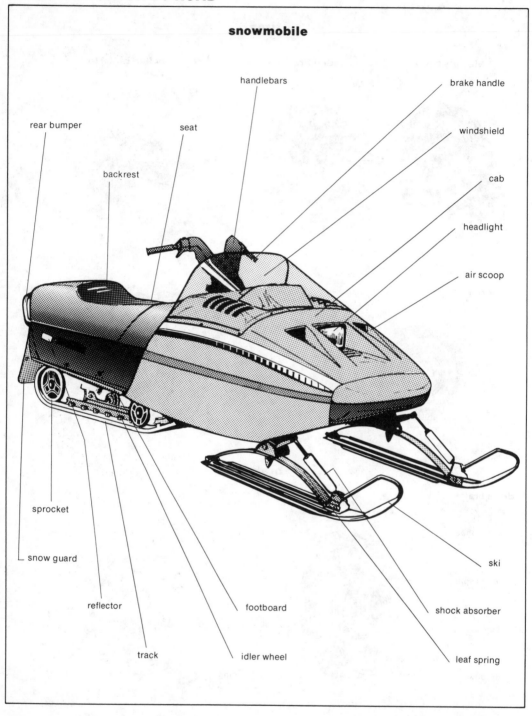

handlebars

brake handle

rear bumper

seat

windshield

backrest

cab

headlight

air scoop

sprocket

snow guard

ski

reflector

shock absorber

track

idler wheel

footboard

leaf spring

motorcycle

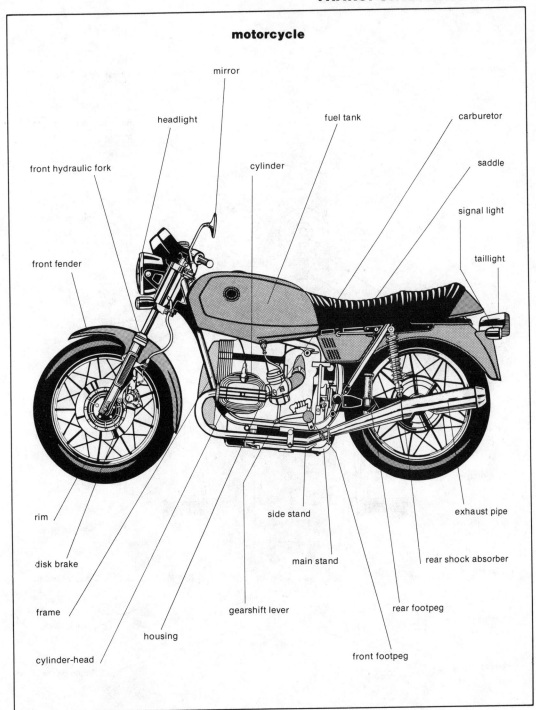

mirror

headlight

fuel tank

carburetor

cylinder

saddle

front hydraulic fork

signal light

front fender

taillight

rim

exhaust pipe

disk brake

rear shock absorber

frame

side stand

main stand

rear footpeg

housing

gearshift lever

cylinder-head

front footpeg

motorcycle

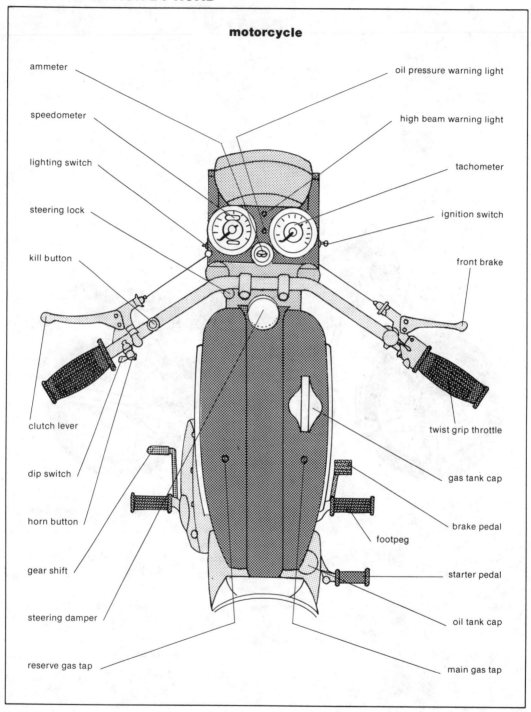

ammeter

oil pressure warning light

speedometer

high beam warning light

lighting switch

tachometer

steering lock

ignition switch

kill button

front brake

clutch lever

twist grip throttle

dip switch

gas tank cap

horn button

brake pedal

footpeg

gear shift

starter pedal

steering damper

oil tank cap

reserve gas tap

main gas tap

bicycle

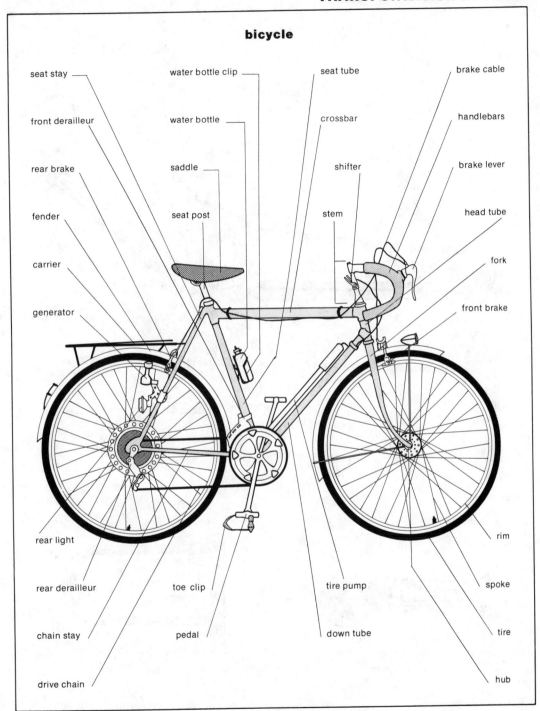

seat stay

water bottle clip

seat tube

brake cable

front derailleur

water bottle

crossbar

handlebars

rear brake

saddle

shifter

brake lever

fender

seat post

stem

head tube

carrier

fork

generator

front brake

rear light

rim

rear derailleur

toe clip

tire pump

spoke

chain stay

pedal

down tube

tire

drive chain

hub

bicycle

power train

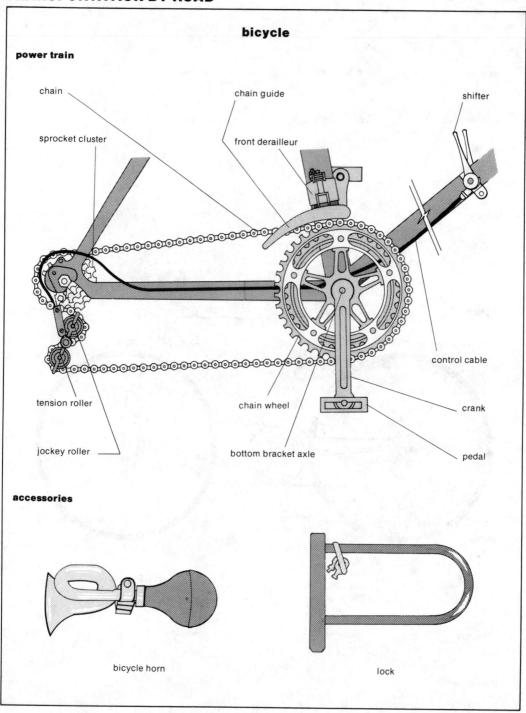

chain

chain guide

shifter

sprocket cluster

front derailleur

control cable

tension roller

chain wheel

crank

jockey roller

bottom bracket axle

pedal

accessories

bicycle horn

lock

cross section of a street

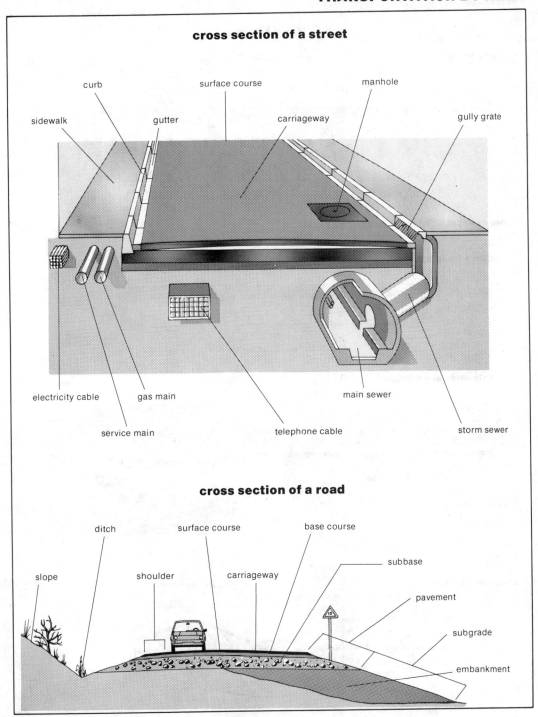

curb

surface course

manhole

sidewalk

gutter

carriageway

gully grate

electricity cable

gas main

main sewer

service main

telephone cable

storm sewer

cross section of a road

ditch

surface course

base course

subbase

slope

shoulder

carriageway

pavement

subgrade

embankment

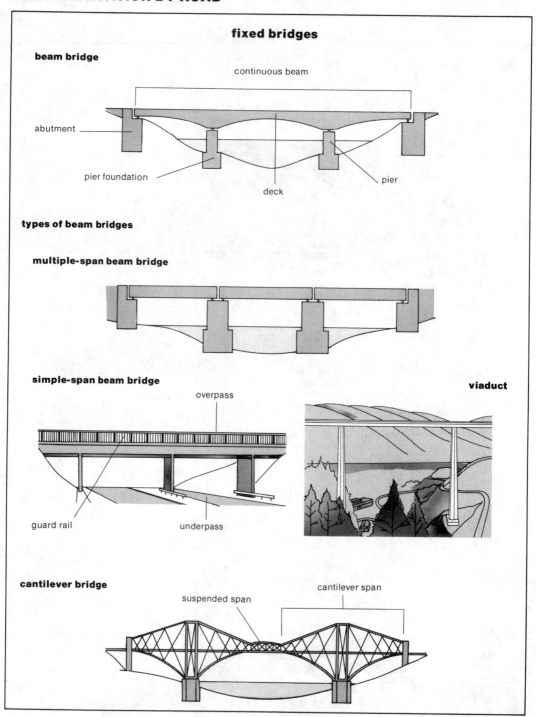

fixed bridges

beam bridge

continuous beam

abutment

pier foundation

deck

pier

types of beam bridges

multiple-span beam bridge

simple-span beam bridge

viaduct

overpass

guard rail

underpass

cantilever bridge

suspended span

cantilever span

fixed bridges

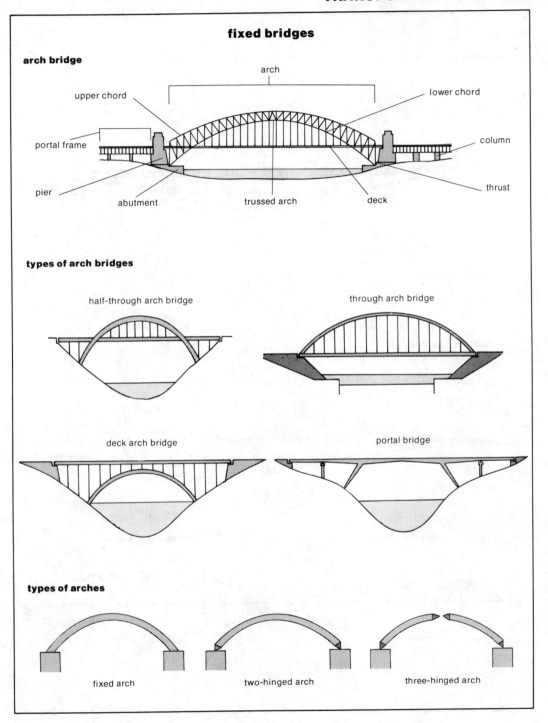

arch bridge

arch

upper chord

lower chord

portal frame

column

pier

thrust

abutment

trussed arch

deck

types of arch bridges

half-through arch bridge

through arch bridge

deck arch bridge

portal bridge

types of arches

fixed arch

two-hinged arch

three-hinged arch

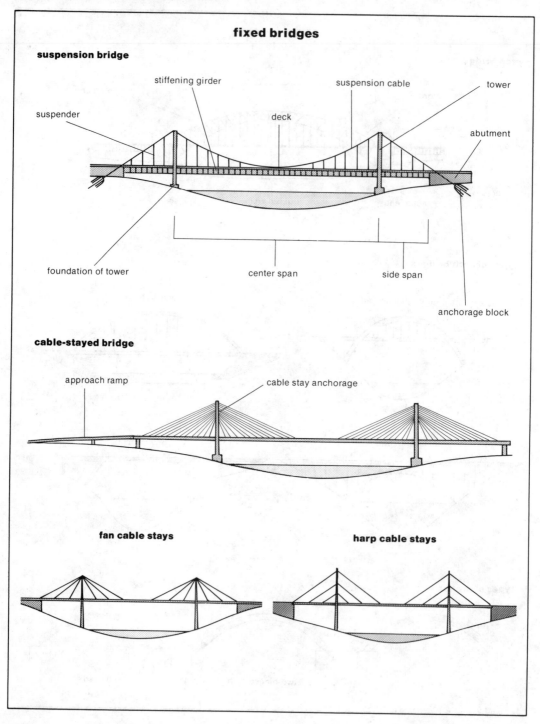

fixed bridges

suspension bridge

stiffening girder

suspension cable

tower

suspender

deck

abutment

foundation of tower

center span

side span

anchorage block

cable-stayed bridge

approach ramp

cable stay anchorage

fan cable stays

harp cable stays

movable bridges

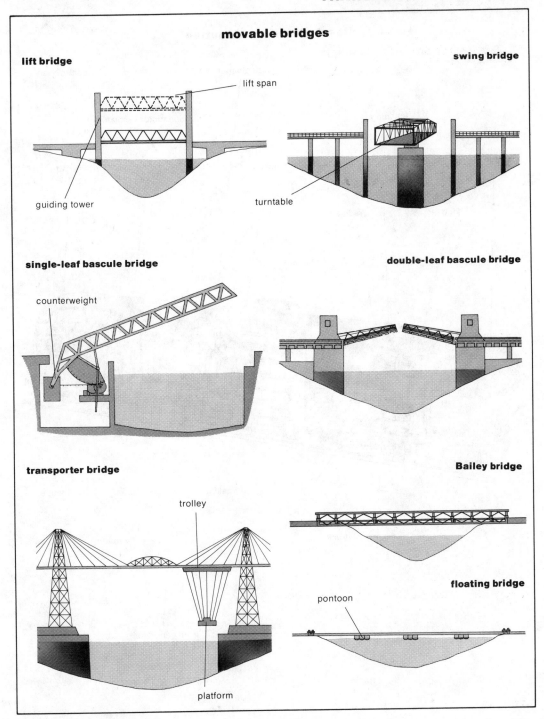

lift bridge

lift span

guiding tower

swing bridge

turntable

single-leaf bascule bridge

counterweight

double-leaf bascule bridge

transporter bridge

trolley

platform

Bailey bridge

floating bridge

pontoon

diesel-electric locomotive

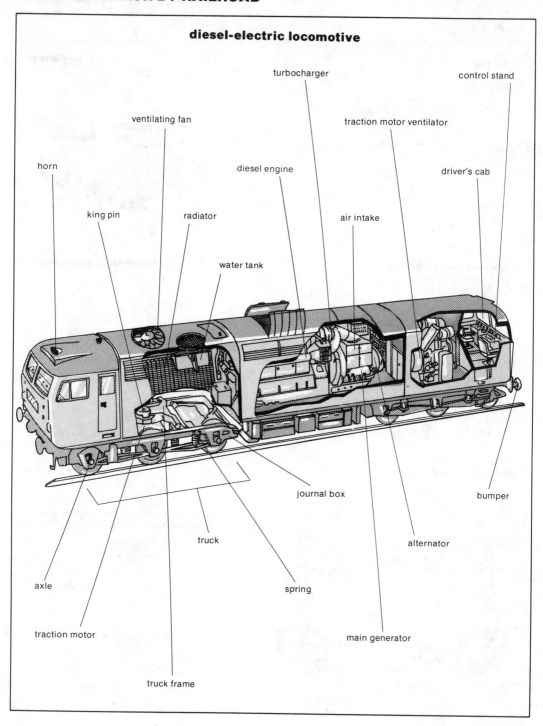

box car

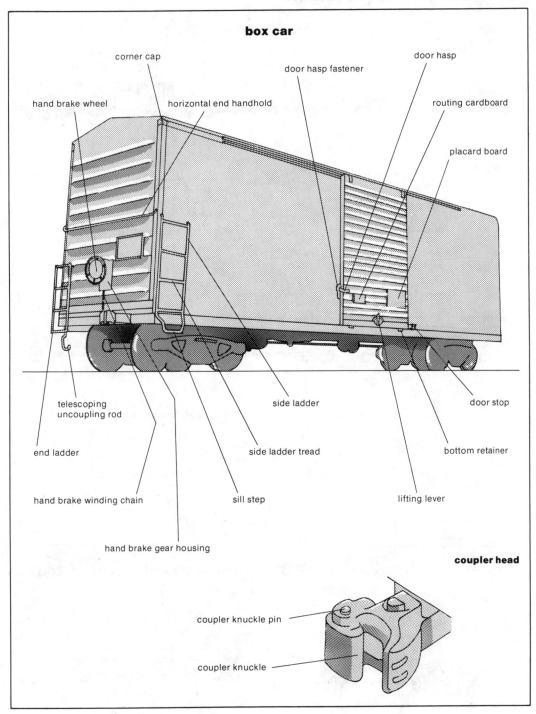

corner cap

door hasp fastener

door hasp

hand brake wheel

horizontal end handhold

routing cardboard

placard board

telescoping uncoupling rod

side ladder

door stop

end ladder

side ladder tread

bottom retainer

hand brake winding chain

sill step

lifting lever

hand brake gear housing

coupler head

coupler knuckle pin

coupler knuckle

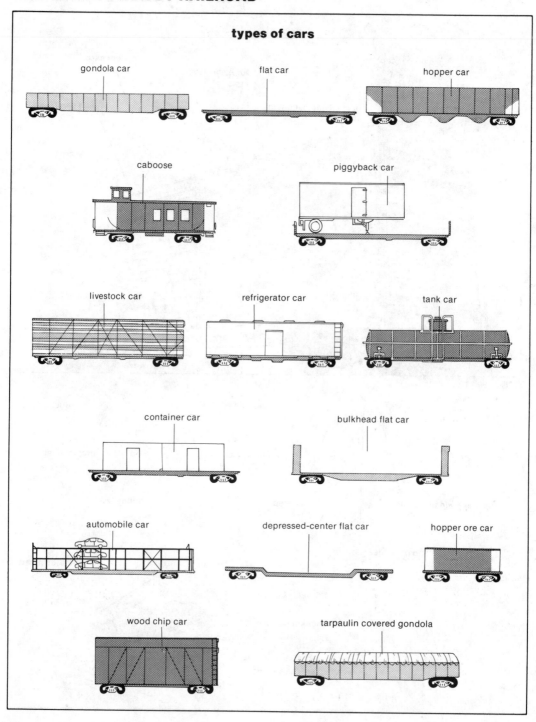

types of cars

gondola car

flat car

hopper car

caboose

piggyback car

livestock car

refrigerator car

tank car

container car

bulkhead flat car

automobile car

depressed-center flat car

hopper ore car

wood chip car

tarpaulin covered gondola

types of passenger cars

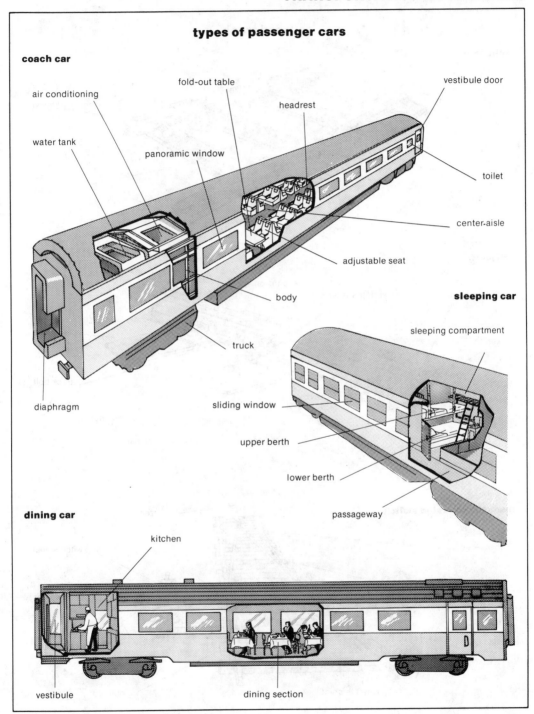

coach car

air conditioning

water tank

fold-out table

panoramic window

headrest

vestibule door

toilet

center-aisle

adjustable seat

body

truck

diaphragm

sleeping car

sleeping compartment

sliding window

upper berth

lower berth

passageway

dining car

kitchen

vestibule

dining section

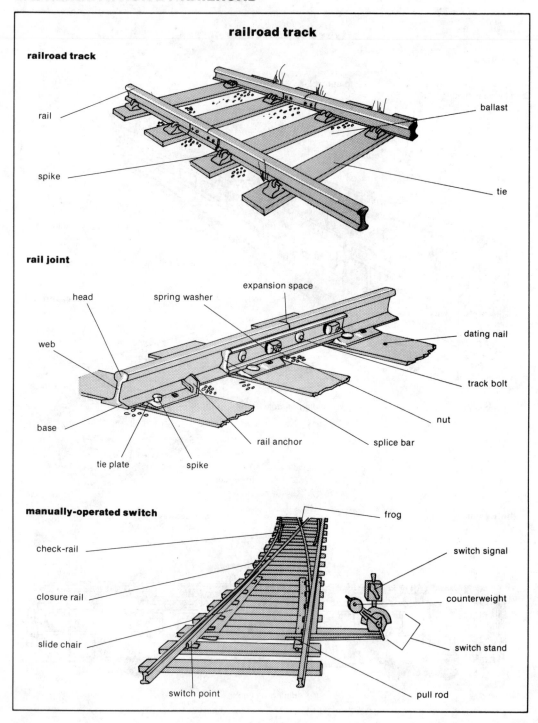

railroad track

railroad track

rail

spike

ballast

tie

rail joint

head

web

base

tie plate

spike

spring washer

expansion space

rail anchor

splice bar

dating nail

track bolt

nut

manually-operated switch

check-rail

closure rail

slide chair

switch point

frog

switch signal

counterweight

switch stand

pull rod

railroad track

remote-controlled switch

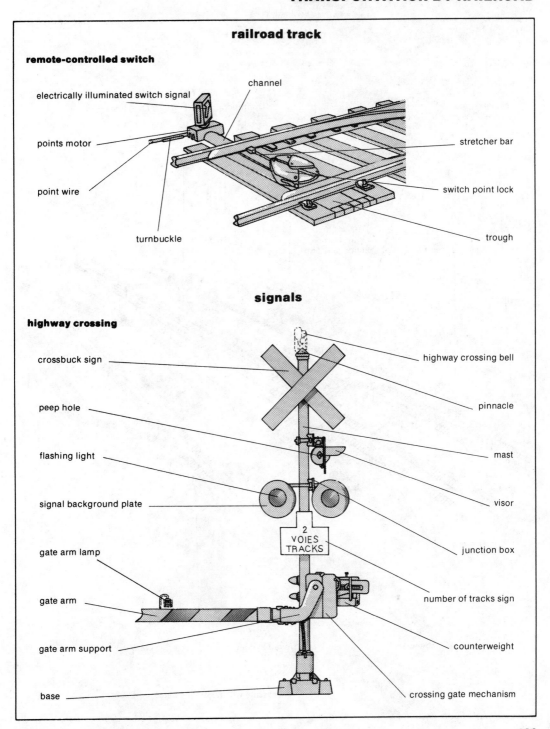

electrically illuminated switch signal

channel

points motor

stretcher bar

point wire

switch point lock

turnbuckle

trough

signals

highway crossing

crossbuck sign

highway crossing bell

peep hole

pinnacle

flashing light

mast

signal background plate

visor

2
VOIES
TRACKS

junction box

gate arm lamp

number of tracks sign

gate arm

counterweight

gate arm support

base

crossing gate mechanism

railroad station

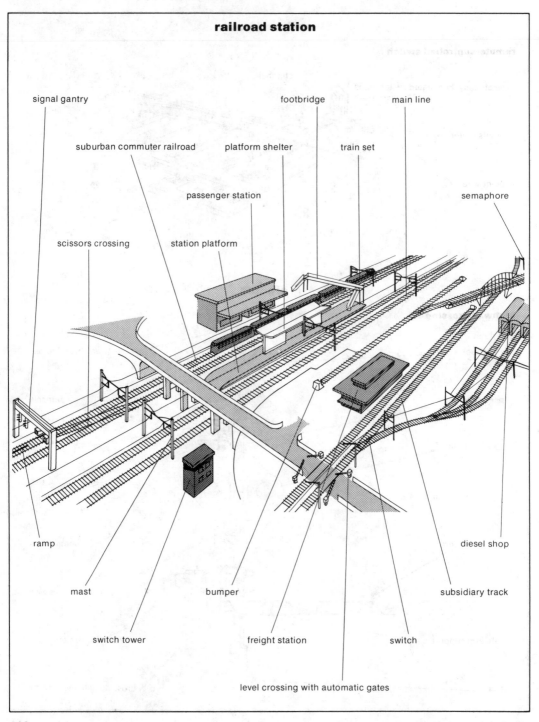

signal gantry

footbridge

main line

suburban commuter railroad

platform shelter

train set

semaphore

passenger station

scissors crossing

station platform

ramp

diesel shop

mast

bumper

subsidiary track

switch tower

freight station

switch

level crossing with automatic gates

container

yard

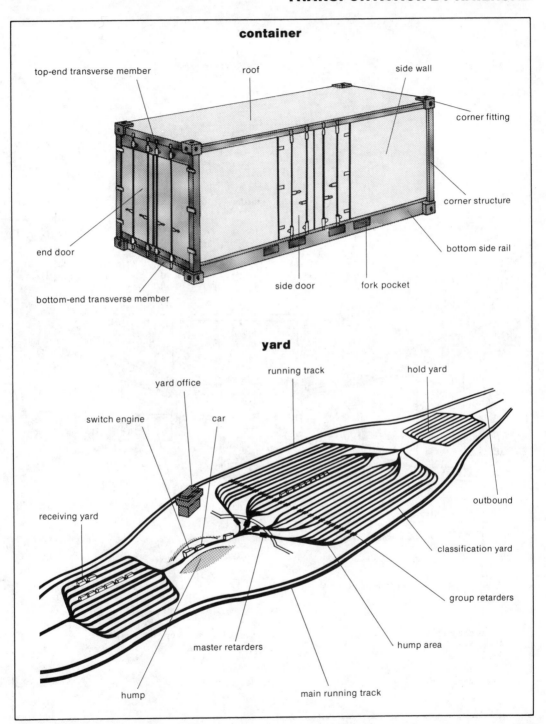

top-end transverse member

roof

side wall

corner fitting

corner structure

bottom side rail

end door

bottom-end transverse member

side door

fork pocket

running track

hold yard

yard office

switch engine

car

outbound

receiving yard

classification yard

group retarders

master retarders

hump area

hump

main running track

station hall

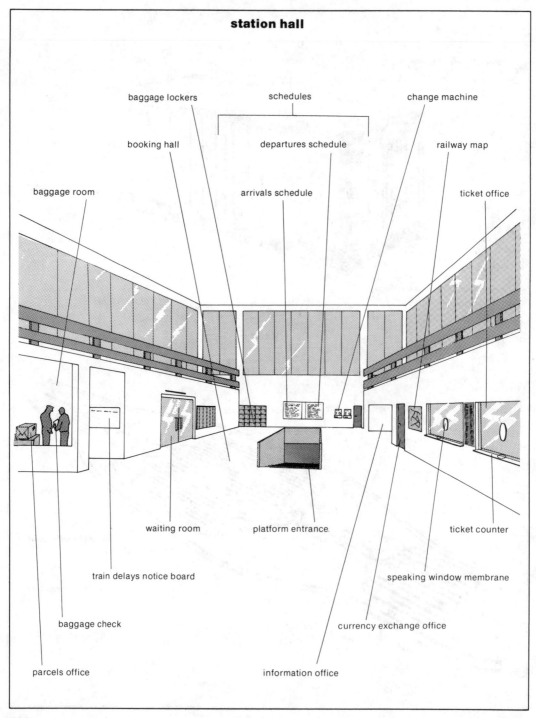

baggage lockers

schedules

change machine

booking hall

departures schedule

railway map

baggage room

arrivals schedule

ticket office

waiting room

platform entrance

ticket counter

train delays notice board

speaking window membrane

baggage check

currency exchange office

parcels office

information office

station platform

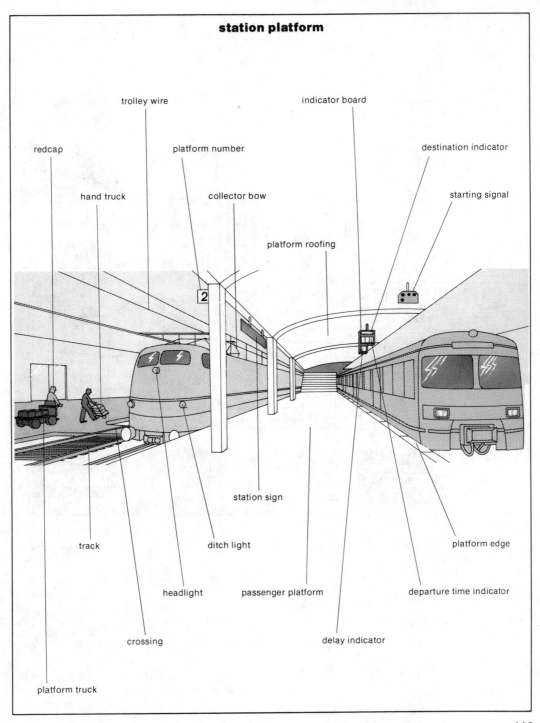

trolley wire

indicator board

redcap

destination indicator

platform number

hand truck

starting signal

collector bow

platform roofing

station sign

track

ditch light

platform edge

headlight

passenger platform

departure time indicator

crossing

delay indicator

platform truck

TRANSPORTATION BY SUBWAY

subway station

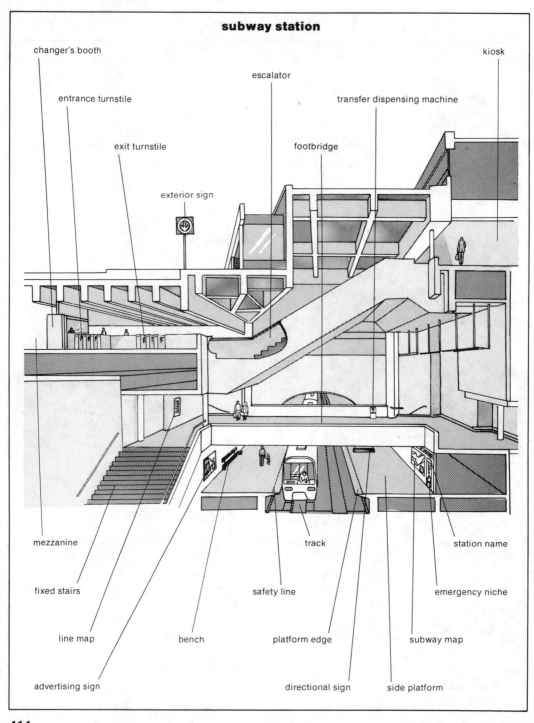

changer's booth

kiosk

escalator

entrance turnstile

transfer dispensing machine

exit turnstile

footbridge

exterior sign

mezzanine

track

station name

fixed stairs

safety line

emergency niche

line map

bench

platform edge

subway map

advertising sign

directional sign

side platform

underground railway

subway train

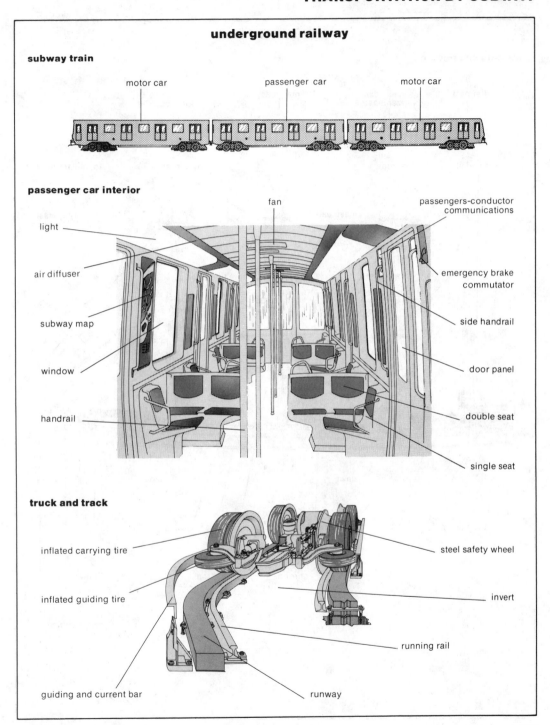

motor car   passenger car   motor car

passenger car interior

light

air diffuser

subway map

window

handrail

fan

passengers-conductor communications

emergency brake commutator

side handrail

door panel

double seat

single seat

truck and track

inflated carrying tire

inflated guiding tire

steel safety wheel

invert

running rail

guiding and current bar   runway

four-masted bark

masting and rigging

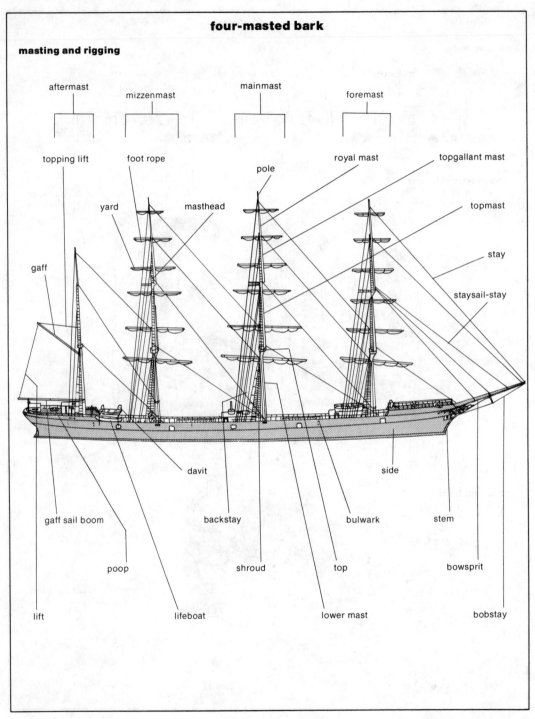

aftermast

mizzenmast

mainmast

foremast

topping lift

foot rope

pole

royal mast

topgallant mast

yard

masthead

topmast

stay

staysail-stay

gaff

davit

side

gaff sail boom

backstay

bulwark

stem

poop

shroud

top

bowsprit

lift

lifeboat

lower mast

bobstay

four-masted bark

sails

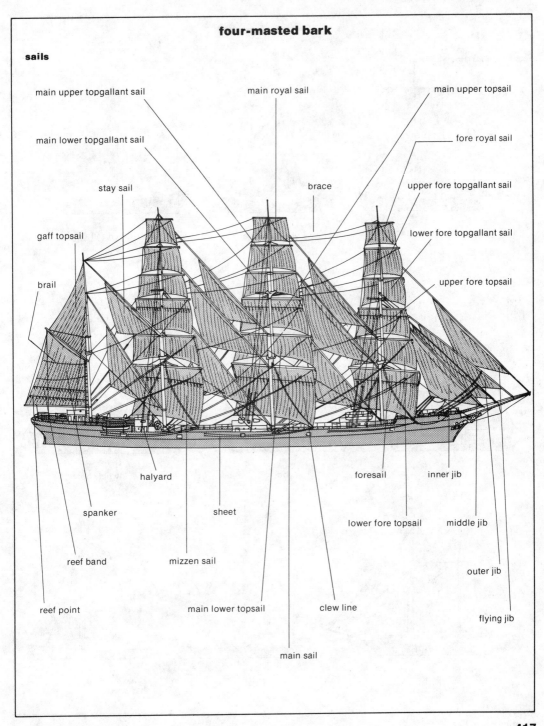

main upper topgallant sail

main royal sail

main upper topsail

main lower topgallant sail

fore royal sail

brace

upper fore topgallant sail

stay sail

lower fore topgallant sail

gaff topsail

upper fore topsail

brail

halyard

foresail

inner jib

spanker

sheet

lower fore topsail

middle jib

reef band

mizzen sail

outer jib

reef point

main lower topsail

clew line

flying jib

main sail

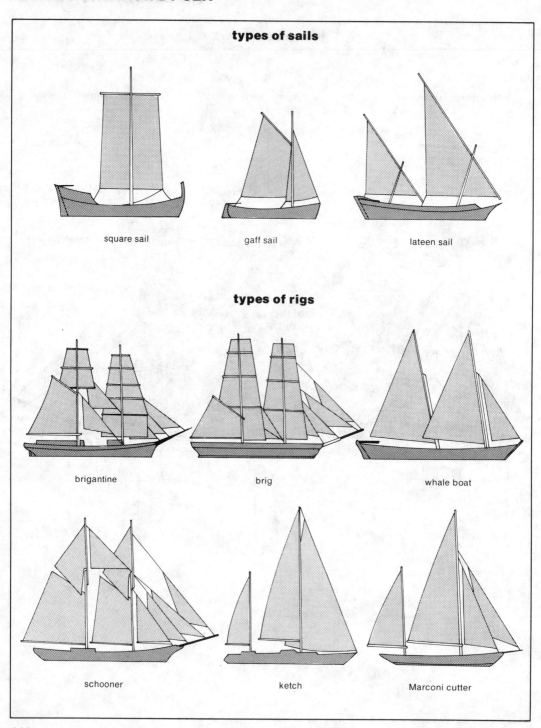

types of sails

square sail

gaff sail

lateen sail

types of rigs

brigantine

brig

whale boat

schooner

ketch

Marconi cutter

passenger liner

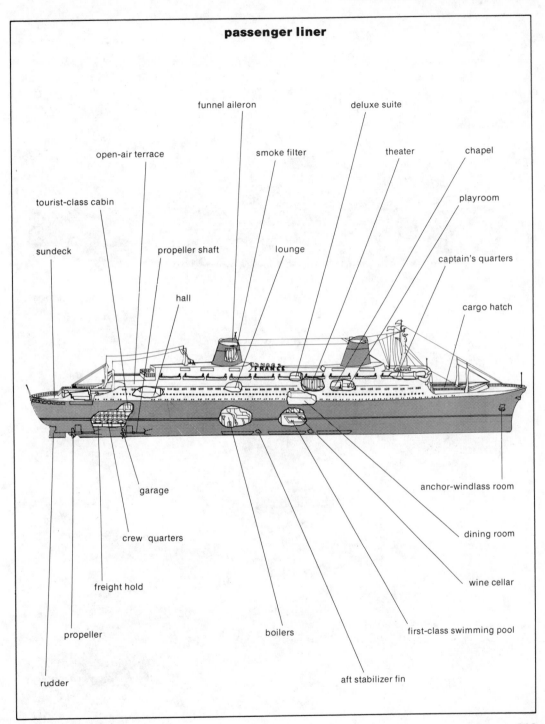

funnel aileron

deluxe suite

open-air terrace

smoke filter

theater

chapel

playroom

tourist-class cabin

sundeck

propeller shaft

lounge

captain's quarters

cargo hatch

hall

garage

crew quarters

anchor-windlass room

dining room

freight hold

wine cellar

propeller

boilers

first-class swimming pool

rudder

aft stabilizer fin

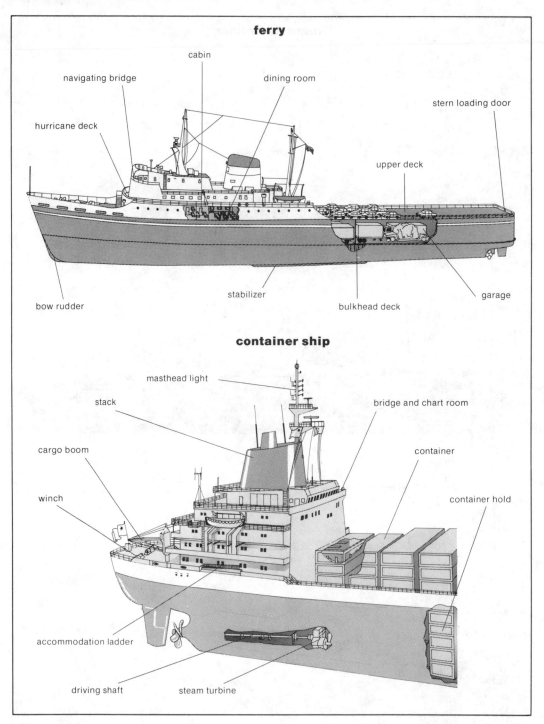

ferry

cabin

navigating bridge

dining room

stern loading door

hurricane deck

upper deck

bow rudder

stabilizer

garage

bulkhead deck

container ship

masthead light

stack

bridge and chart room

cargo boom

container

winch

container hold

accommodation ladder

driving shaft

steam turbine

hovercraft

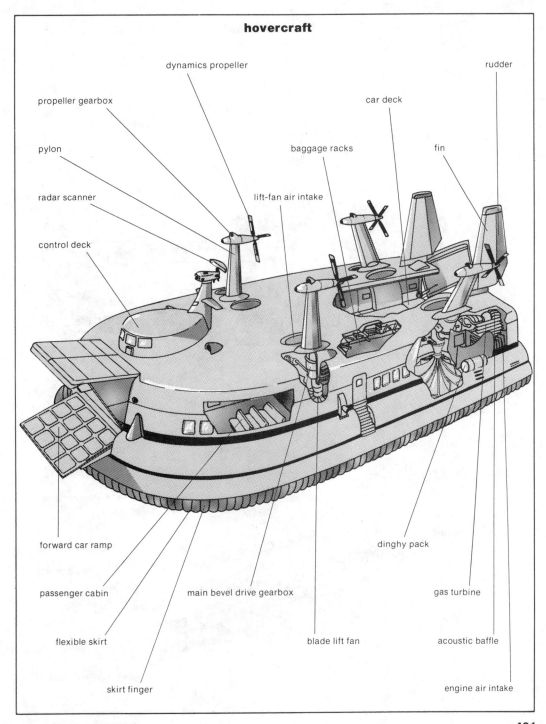

dynamics propeller

rudder

propeller gearbox

car deck

pylon

baggage racks

fin

radar scanner

lift-fan air intake

control deck

forward car ramp

dinghy pack

passenger cabin

main bevel drive gearbox

gas turbine

flexible skirt

blade lift fan

acoustic baffle

skirt finger

engine air intake

hydrofoil boat

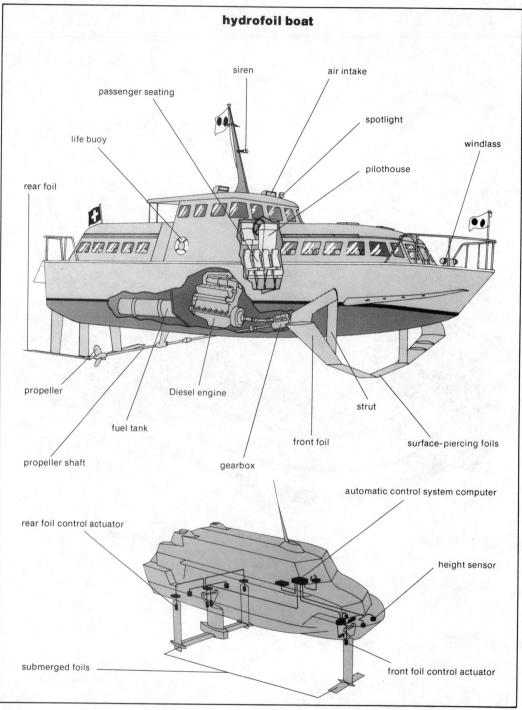

siren

air intake

passenger seating

spotlight

life buoy

windlass

rear foil

pilothouse

propeller

Diesel engine

strut

fuel tank

front foil

surface-piercing foils

propeller shaft

gearbox

automatic control system computer

rear foil control actuator

height sensor

submerged foils

front foil control actuator

bathyscaphe

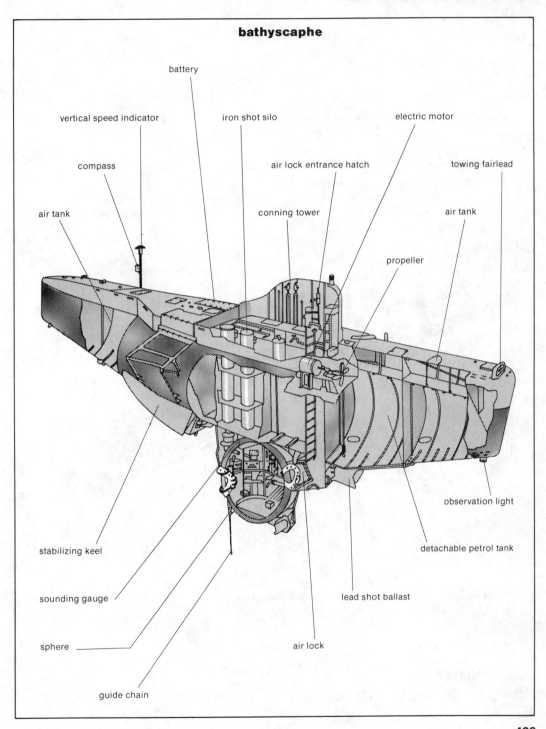

battery

vertical speed indicator

iron shot silo

electric motor

compass

air lock entrance hatch

towing fairlead

air tank

conning tower

air tank

propeller

stabilizing keel

observation light

sounding gauge

detachable petrol tank

sphere

lead shot ballast

air lock

guide chain

submarine

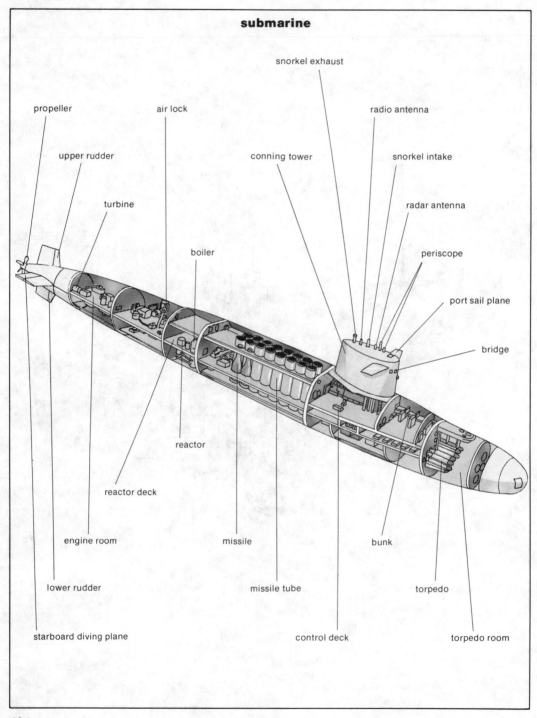

snorkel exhaust

radio antenna

propeller

air lock

snorkel intake

conning tower

upper rudder

radar antenna

turbine

periscope

boiler

port sail plane

bridge

reactor

reactor deck

engine room

missile

bunk

lower rudder

missile tube

torpedo

starboard diving plane

control deck

torpedo room

frigate

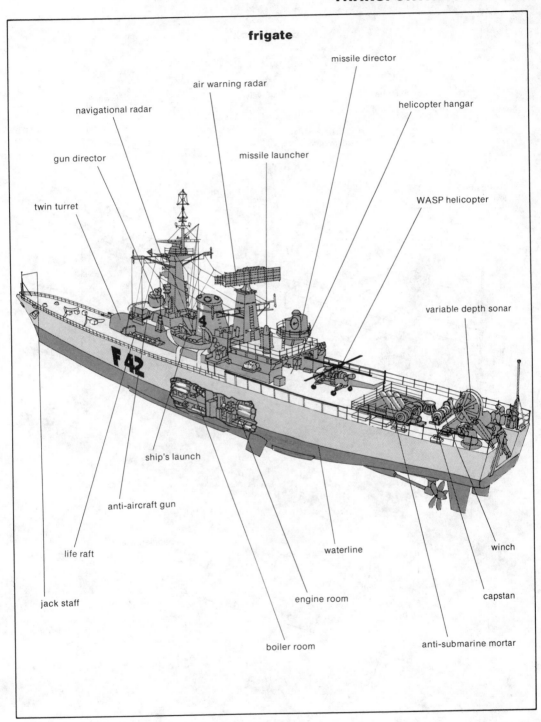

missile director

air warning radar

helicopter hangar

navigational radar

gun director

missile launcher

WASP helicopter

twin turret

variable depth sonar

F 42

ship's launch

anti-aircraft gun

life raft

waterline

winch

jack staff

capstan

engine room

anti-submarine mortar

boiler room

canal lock

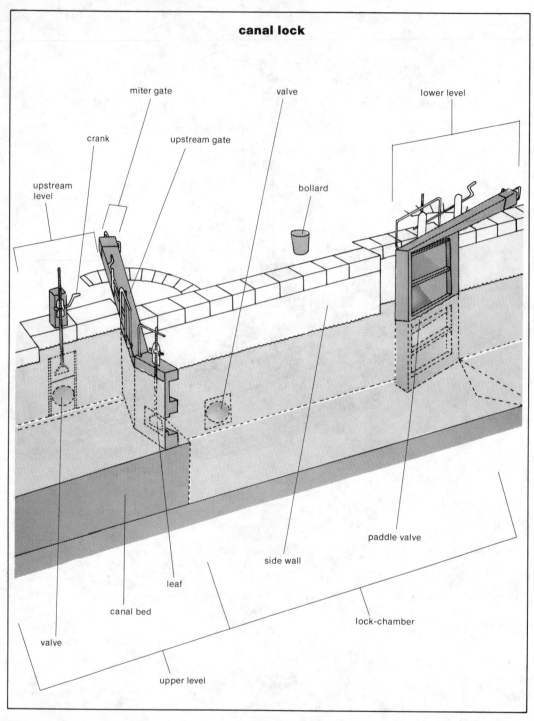

miter gate

valve

lower level

crank

upstream gate

bollard

upstream level

valve

side wall

paddle valve

leaf

canal bed

lock-chamber

upper level

harbor

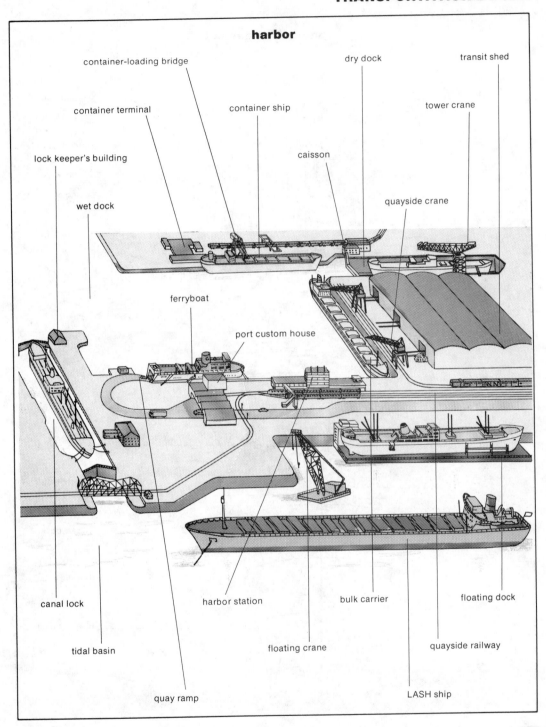

container-loading bridge

dry dock

transit shed

container terminal

tower crane

lock keeper's building

caisson

wet dock

quayside crane

ferryboat

port custom house

canal lock

harbor station

bulk carrier

floating dock

tidal basin

floating crane

quayside railway

quay ramp

LASH ship

navigation devices

echo sounder

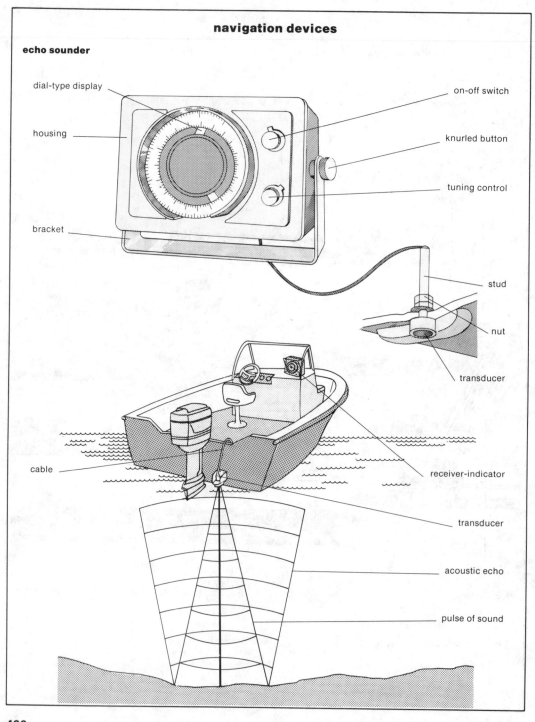

dial-type display

on-off switch

housing

knurled button

tuning control

bracket

stud

nut

transducer

cable

receiver-indicator

transducer

acoustic echo

pulse of sound

navigation devices

sextant

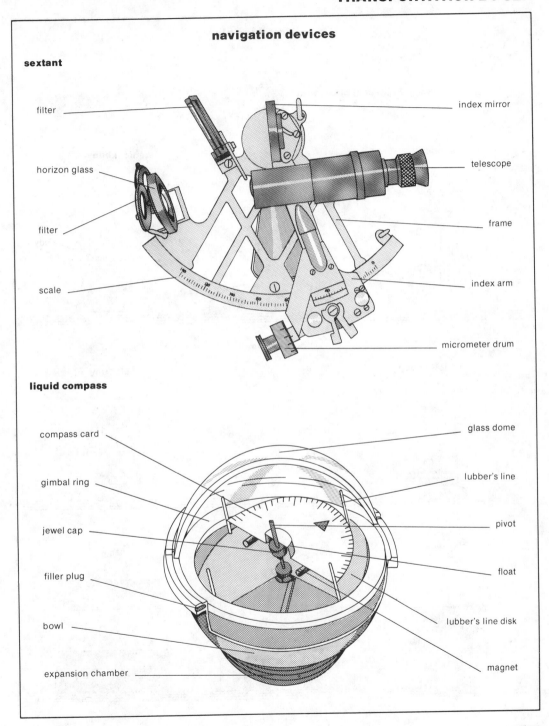

filter — index mirror

horizon glass — telescope

filter — frame

scale — index arm

micrometer drum

liquid compass

compass card — glass dome

gimbal ring — lubber's line

jewel cap — pivot

filler plug — float

bowl — lubber's line disk

expansion chamber — magnet

429

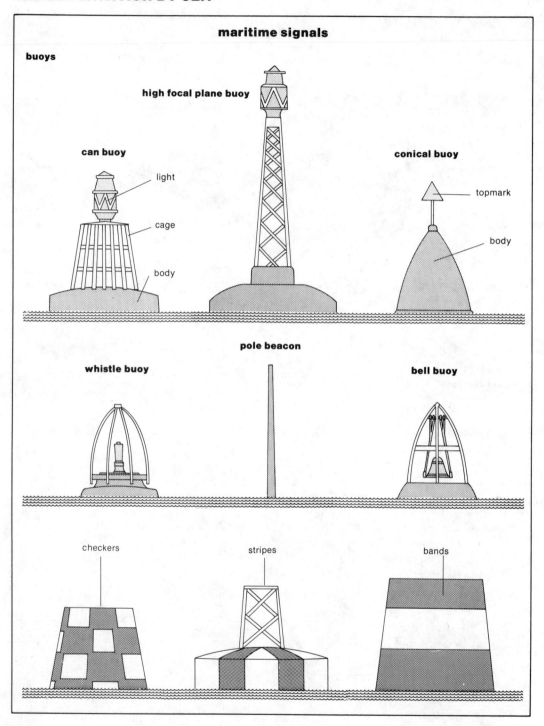

maritime signals

buoys

high focal plane buoy

can buoy

conical buoy

light

cage

body

topmark

body

pole beacon

whistle buoy

bell buoy

checkers

stripes

bands

maritime signals

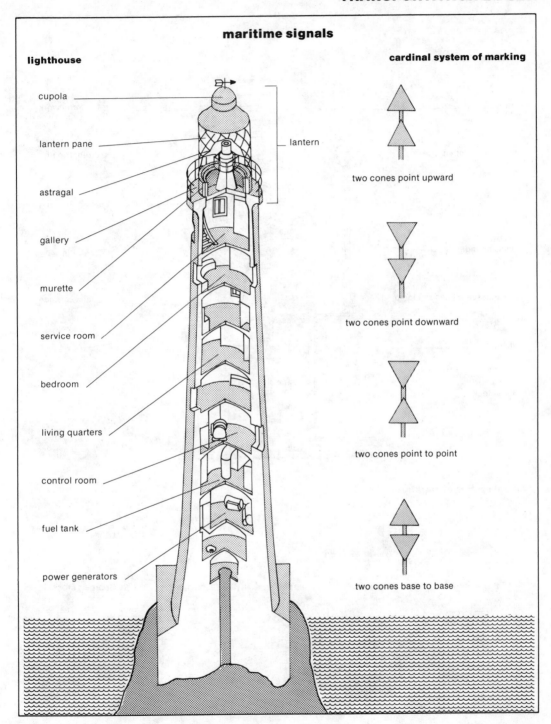

lighthouse

- cupola
- lantern pane
- astragal
- gallery
- murette
- service room
- bedroom
- living quarters
- control room
- fuel tank
- power generators

lantern

cardinal system of marking

two cones point upward

two cones point downward

two cones point to point

two cones base to base

maritime signals

lantern of lighthouse

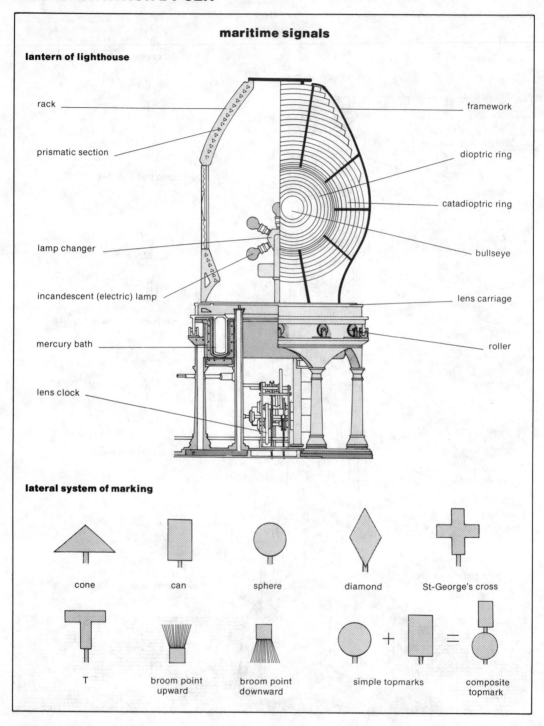

rack

framework

prismatic section

dioptric ring

catadioptric ring

lamp changer

bullseye

incandescent (electric) lamp

lens carriage

mercury bath

roller

lens clock

lateral system of marking

cone

can

sphere

diamond

St-George's cross

T

broom point upward

broom point downward

simple topmarks

composite topmark

anchor

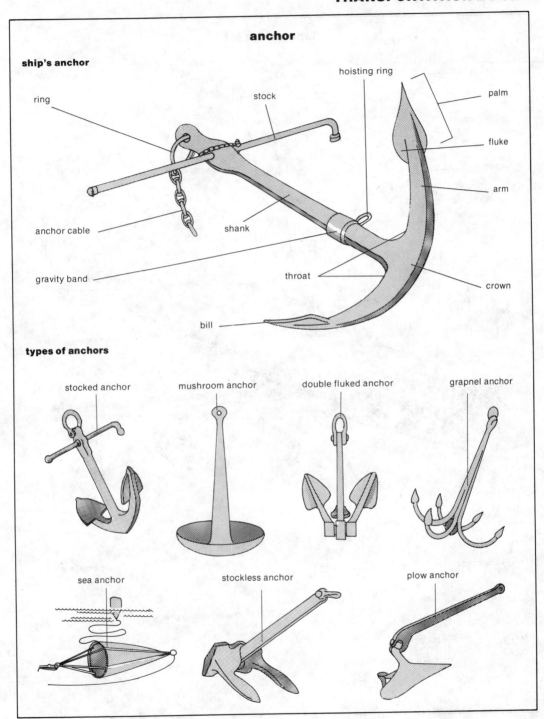

ship's anchor

ring

hoisting ring

stock

palm

fluke

arm

anchor cable

shank

gravity band

throat

crown

bill

types of anchors

stocked anchor

mushroom anchor

double fluked anchor

grapnel anchor

sea anchor

stockless anchor

plow anchor

long-range jet

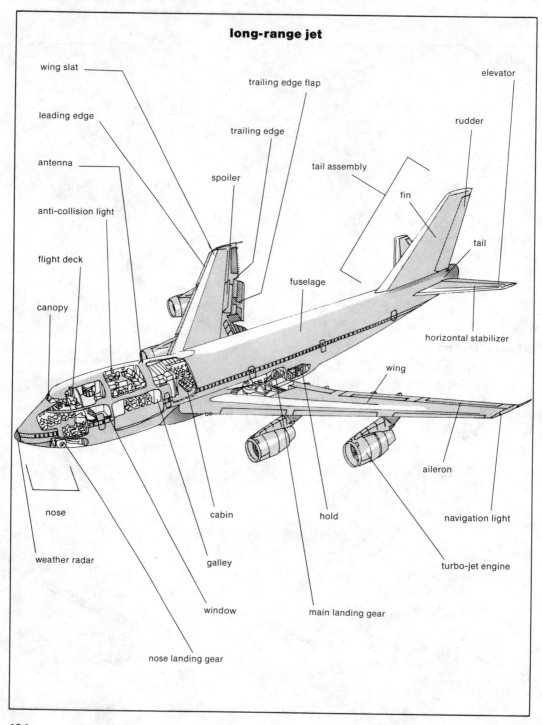

wing slat

leading edge

antenna

anti-collision light

flight deck

canopy

trailing edge flap

trailing edge

spoiler

tail assembly

fin

fuselage

elevator

rudder

tail

horizontal stabilizer

wing

aileron

navigation light

nose

weather radar

cabin

galley

window

hold

main landing gear

turbo-jet engine

nose landing gear

wing structure

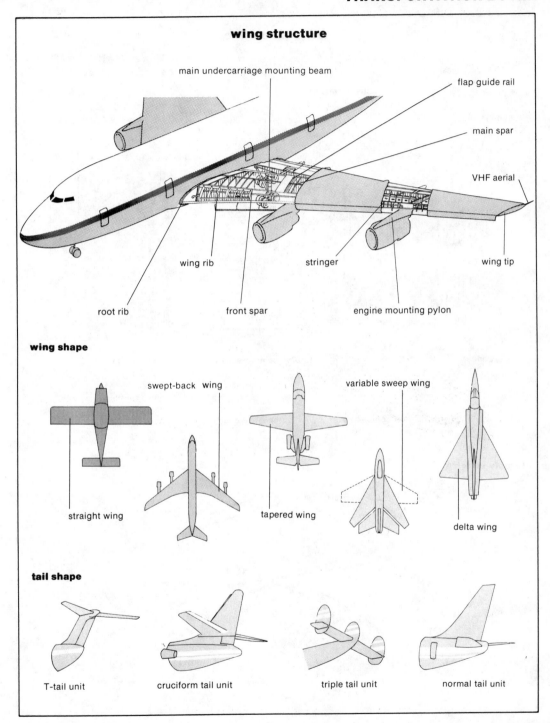

main undercarriage mounting beam

flap guide rail

main spar

VHF aerial

wing rib

stringer

wing tip

root rib

front spar

engine mounting pylon

wing shape

straight wing

swept-back wing

tapered wing

variable sweep wing

delta wing

tail shape

T-tail unit

cruciform tail unit

triple tail unit

normal tail unit

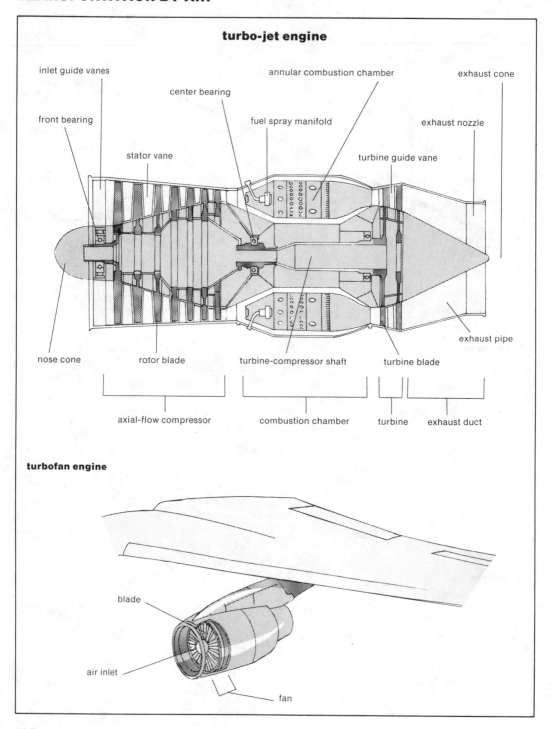

turbo-jet engine

inlet guide vanes

annular combustion chamber

exhaust cone

center bearing

front bearing

fuel spray manifold

exhaust nozzle

stator vane

turbine guide vane

nose cone

rotor blade

turbine-compressor shaft

turbine blade

exhaust pipe

axial-flow compressor

combustion chamber

turbine

exhaust duct

turbofan engine

blade

air inlet

fan

flight deck

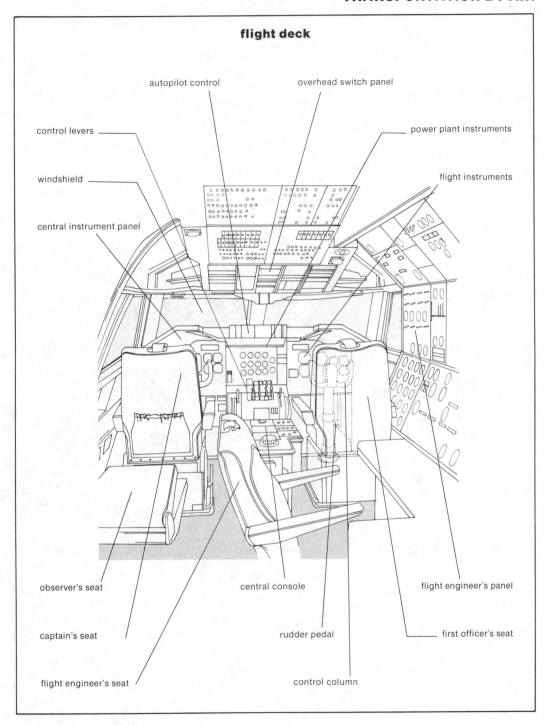

autopilot control

overhead switch panel

control levers

power plant instruments

windshield

flight instruments

central instrument panel

observer's seat

central console

flight engineer's panel

captain's seat

rudder pedal

first officer's seat

flight engineer's seat

control column

airport

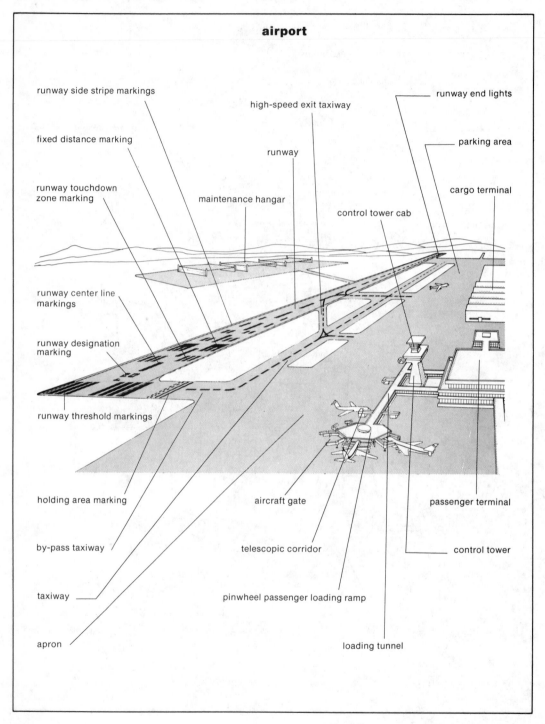

runway side stripe markings

high-speed exit taxiway

runway end lights

fixed distance marking

runway

parking area

runway touchdown zone marking

maintenance hangar

cargo terminal

control tower cab

runway center line markings

runway designation marking

runway threshold markings

holding area marking

aircraft gate

passenger terminal

by-pass taxiway

telescopic corridor

control tower

taxiway

pinwheel passenger loading ramp

apron

loading tunnel

airport

ground airport equipment

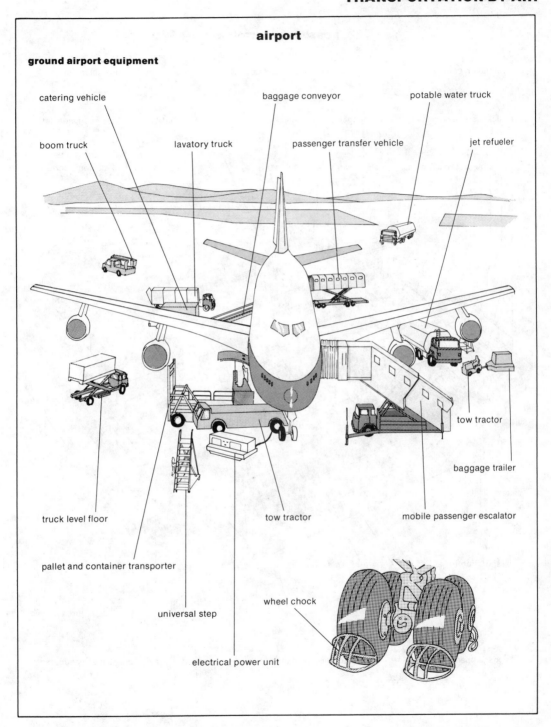

catering vehicle

baggage conveyor

potable water truck

boom truck

lavatory truck

passenger transfer vehicle

jet refueler

tow tractor

baggage trailer

truck level floor

tow tractor

mobile passenger escalator

pallet and container transporter

universal step

wheel chock

electrical power unit

TRANSPORTATION BY AIR

passenger terminal

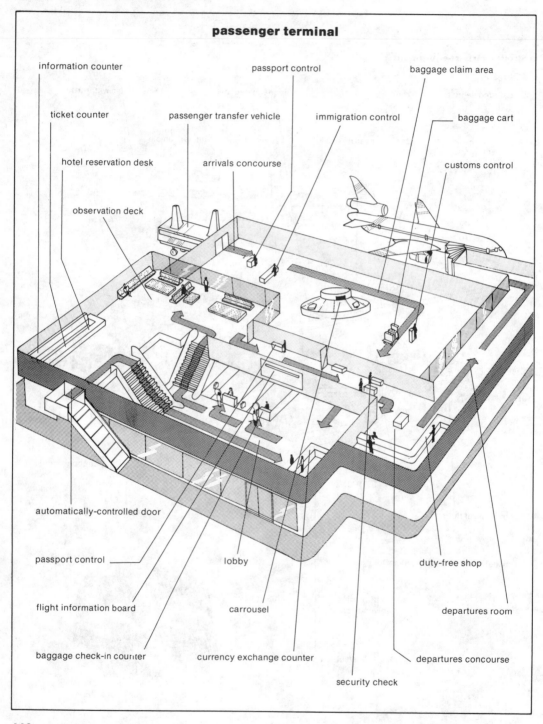

information counter

passport control

baggage claim area

ticket counter

passenger transfer vehicle

immigration control

baggage cart

hotel reservation desk

arrivals concourse

customs control

observation deck

automatically-controlled door

passport control

lobby

duty-free shop

flight information board

carrousel

departures room

baggage check-in counter

currency exchange counter

departures concourse

security check

helicopter

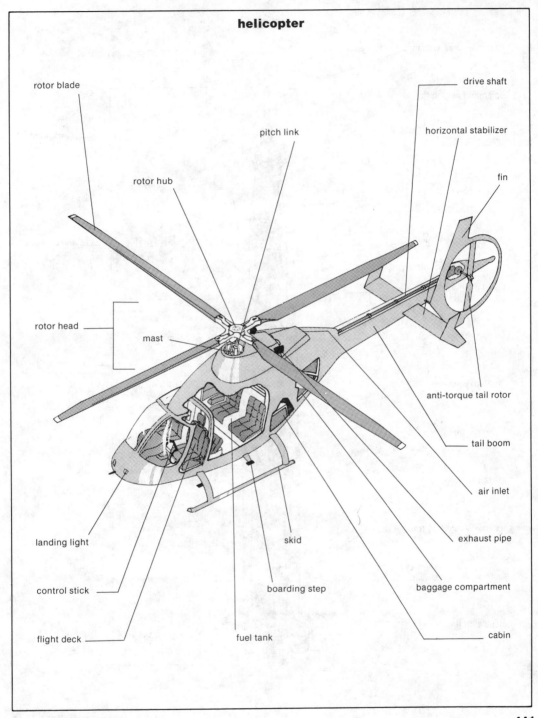

rotor blade

drive shaft

pitch link

horizontal stabilizer

rotor hub

fin

rotor head

mast

anti-torque tail rotor

tail boom

air inlet

landing light

skid

exhaust pipe

control stick

boarding step

baggage compartment

flight deck

fuel tank

cabin

rocket

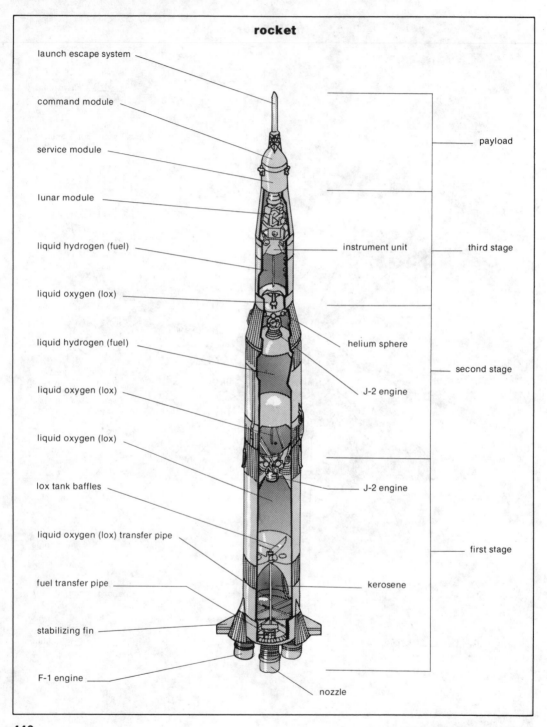

launch escape system

command module

service module

lunar module

liquid hydrogen (fuel)

liquid oxygen (lox)

liquid hydrogen (fuel)

liquid oxygen (lox)

liquid oxygen (lox)

lox tank baffles

liquid oxygen (lox) transfer pipe

fuel transfer pipe

stabilizing fin

F-1 engine

payload

third stage

second stage

first stage

instrument unit

helium sphere

J-2 engine

J-2 engine

kerosene

nozzle

space shuttle

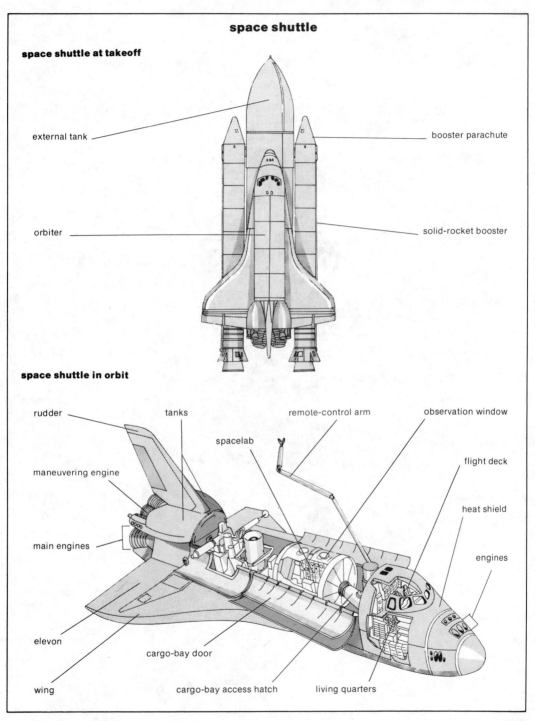

space shuttle at takeoff

external tank

booster parachute

orbiter

solid-rocket booster

space shuttle in orbit

rudder

tanks

remote-control arm

observation window

spacelab

flight deck

maneuvering engine

heat shield

main engines

engines

elevon

cargo-bay door

wing

cargo-bay access hatch

living quarters

space suit

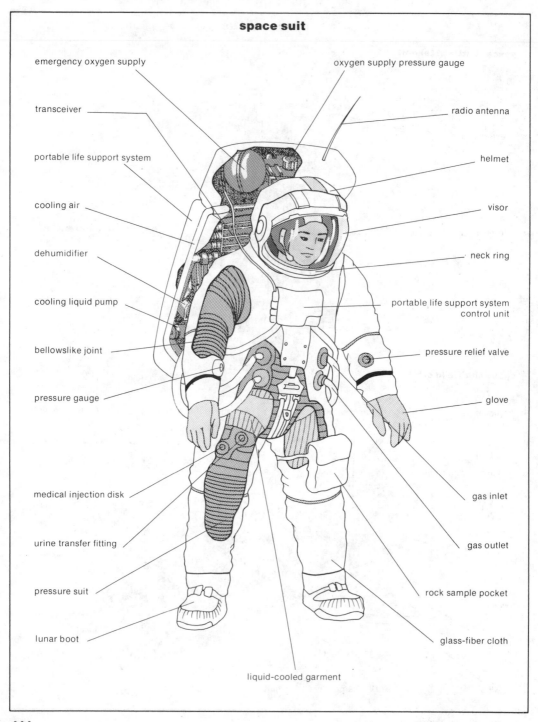

emergency oxygen supply

transceiver

portable life support system

cooling air

dehumidifier

cooling liquid pump

bellowslike joint

pressure gauge

medical injection disk

urine transfer fitting

pressure suit

lunar boot

oxygen supply pressure gauge

radio antenna

helmet

visor

neck ring

portable life support system control unit

pressure relief valve

glove

gas inlet

gas outlet

rock sample pocket

glass-fiber cloth

liquid-cooled garment

OFFICE SUPPLIES AND EQUIPMENT

stationery

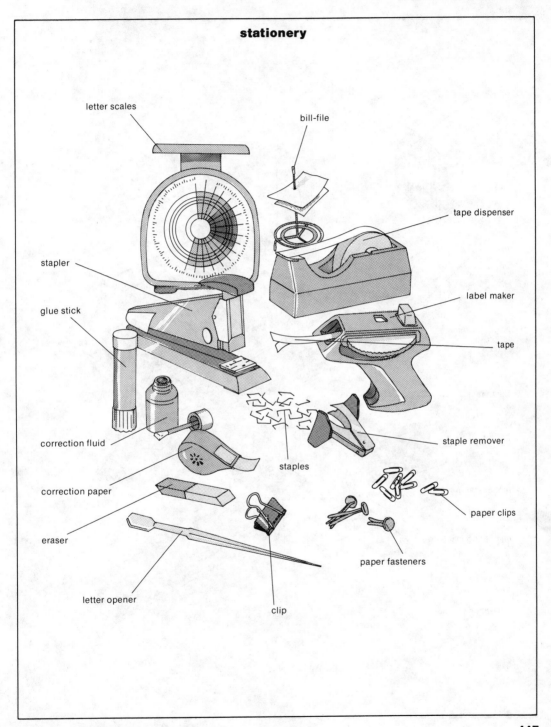

letter scales

bill-file

tape dispenser

stapler

glue stick

label maker

tape

correction fluid

correction paper

staples

staple remover

eraser

paper clips

letter opener

clip

paper fasteners

stationery

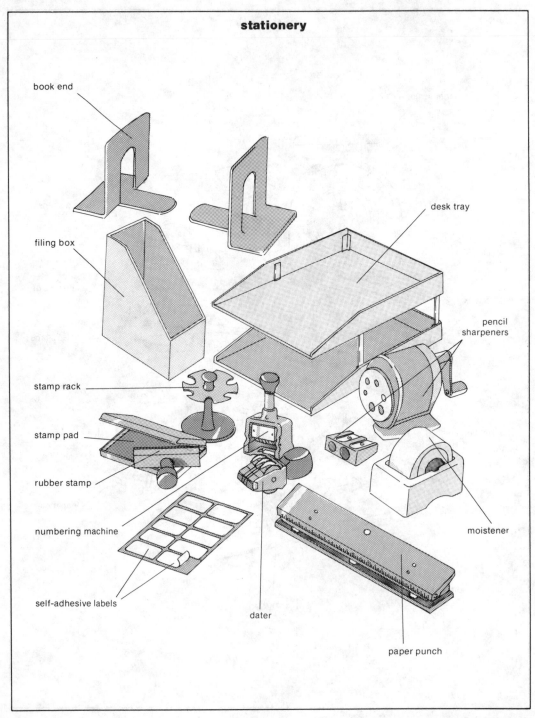

book end

desk tray

filing box

pencil sharpeners

stamp rack

stamp pad

rubber stamp

numbering machine

self-adhesive labels

dater

moistener

paper punch

stationery

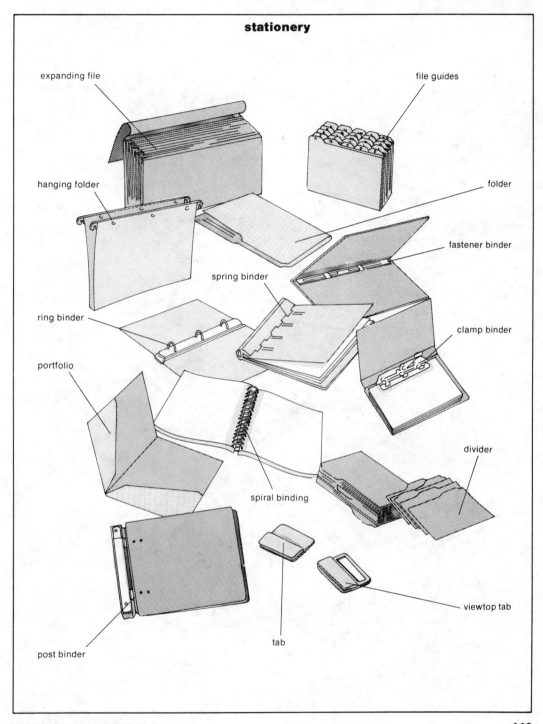

expanding file

file guides

hanging folder

folder

fastener binder

spring binder

ring binder

clamp binder

portfolio

divider

spiral binding

post binder

tab

viewtop tab

stationery

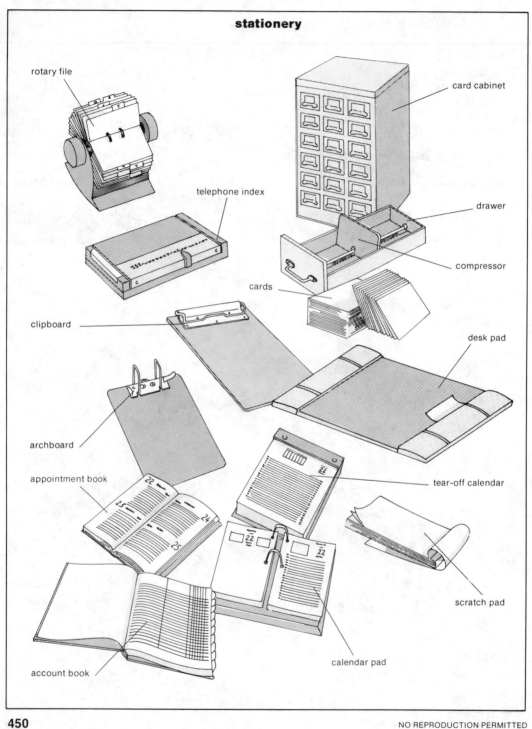

rotary file

card cabinet

telephone index

drawer

compressor

cards

clipboard

desk pad

archboard

appointment book

tear-off calendar

scratch pad

calendar pad

account book

office furniture

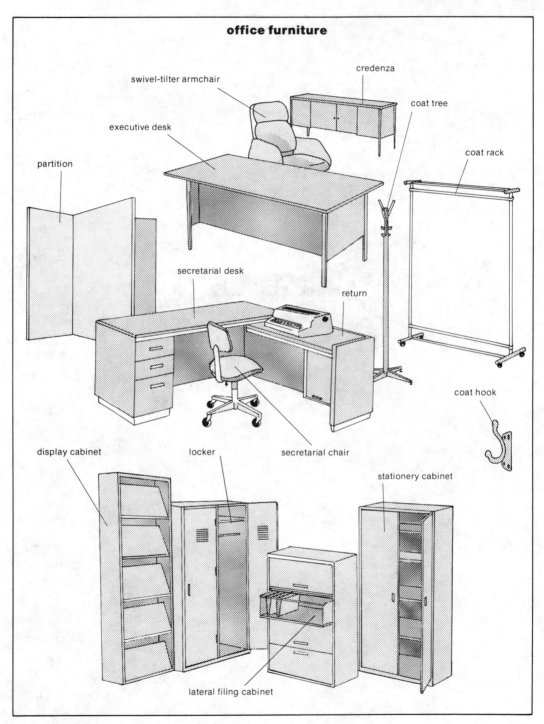

swivel-tilter armchair

credenza

coat tree

executive desk

coat rack

partition

secretarial desk

return

display cabinet

locker

secretarial chair

stationery cabinet

coat hook

lateral filing cabinet

typewriter

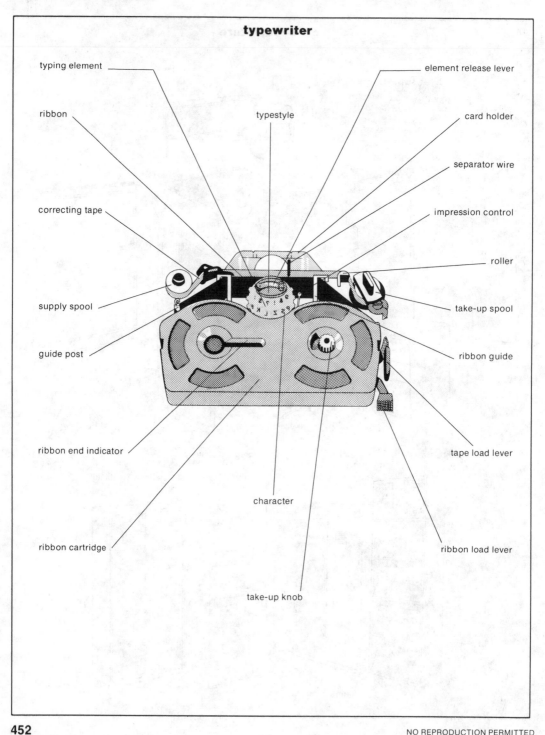

typing element

element release lever

ribbon

typestyle

card holder

separator wire

correcting tape

impression control

roller

supply spool

take-up spool

guide post

ribbon guide

ribbon end indicator

tape load lever

character

ribbon cartridge

ribbon load lever

take-up knob

typewriter

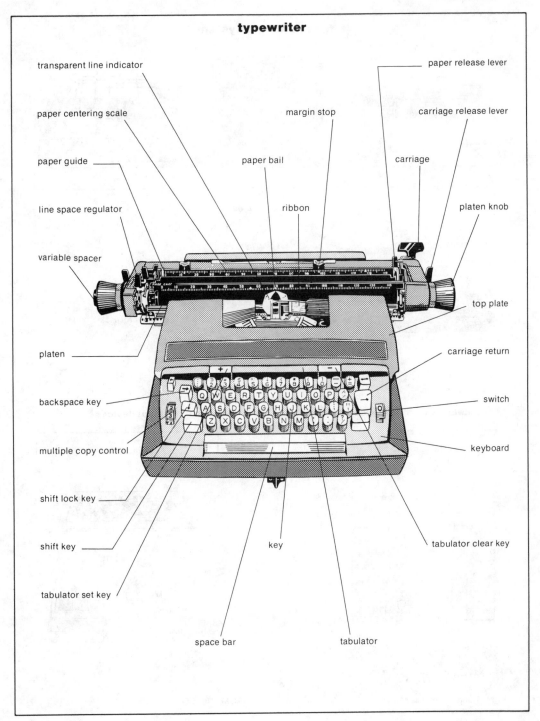

transparent line indicator

paper centering scale

paper guide

line space regulator

variable spacer

platen

backspace key

multiple copy control

shift lock key

shift key

tabulator set key

space bar

key

tabulator

margin stop

paper bail

ribbon

carriage

paper release lever

carriage release lever

platen knob

top plate

carriage return

switch

keyboard

tabulator clear key

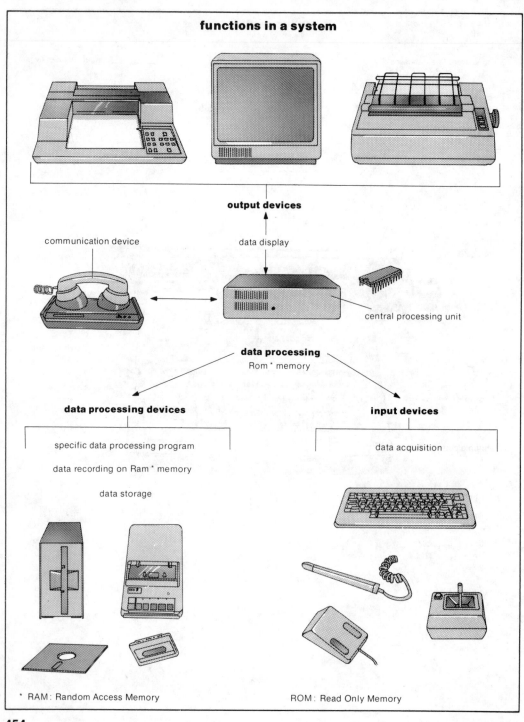

functions in a system

output devices

communication device   data display

central processing unit

data processing
Rom * memory

data processing devices   input devices

specific data processing program   data acquisition

data recording on Ram * memory

data storage

* RAM: Random Access Memory   ROM: Read Only Memory

configuration of a system

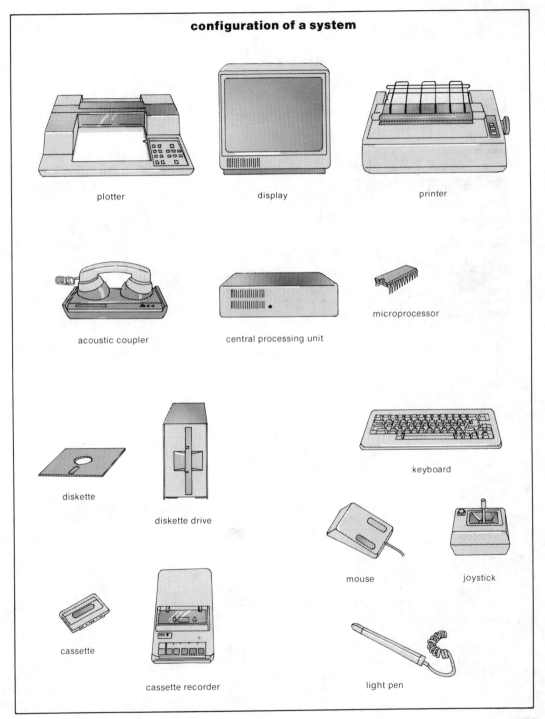

plotter

display

printer

acoustic coupler

central processing unit

microprocessor

diskette

diskette drive

keyboard

mouse

joystick

cassette

cassette recorder

light pen

MICROCOMPUTER

keyboard

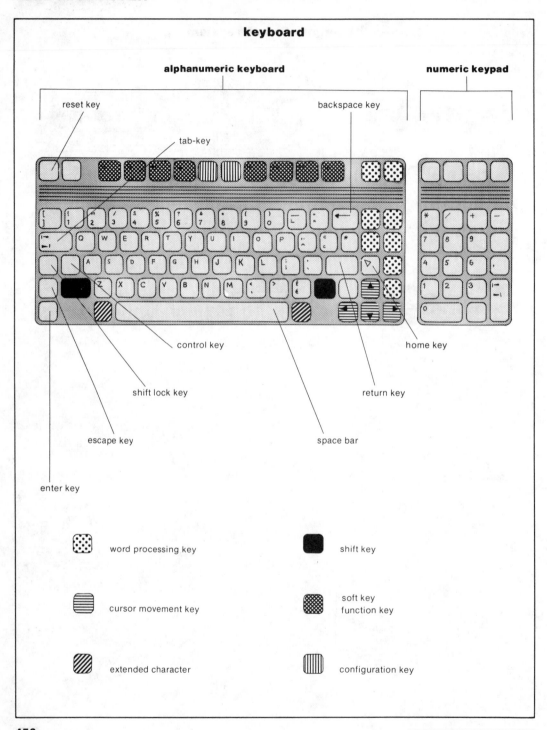

alphanumeric keyboard

numeric keypad

reset key

backspace key

tab-key

control key

home key

shift lock key

return key

escape key

space bar

enter key

▦ word processing key   ■ shift key

▤ cursor movement key   ▨ soft key
function key

▨ extended character   ▥ configuration key

peripheral equipment

dot matrix printer

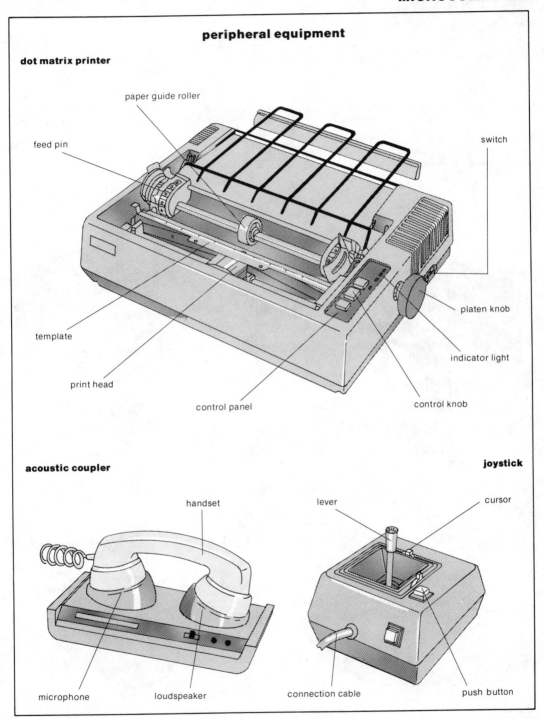

paper guide roller

feed pin

switch

template

print head

control panel

platen knob

indicator light

control knob

acoustic coupler

joystick

handset

lever

cursor

microphone

loudspeaker

connection cable

push button

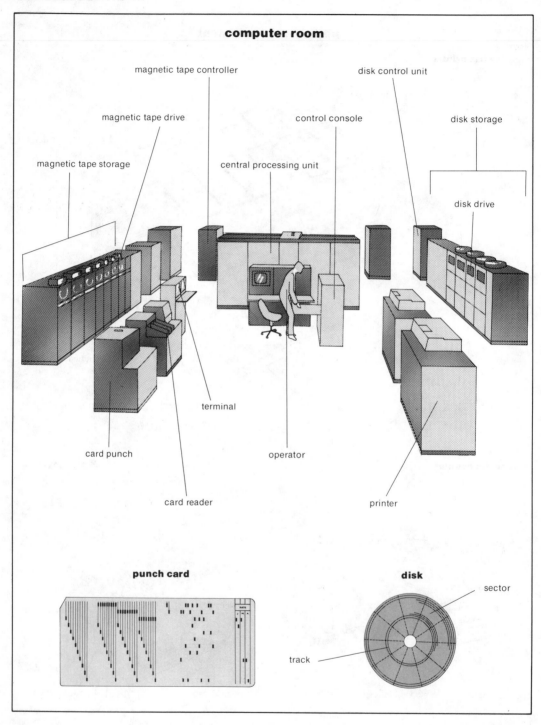

computer room

magnetic tape controller

disk control unit

magnetic tape drive

control console

disk storage

magnetic tape storage

central processing unit

disk drive

terminal

card punch

operator

card reader

printer

punch card

disk

sector

track

MUSIC

musical notation

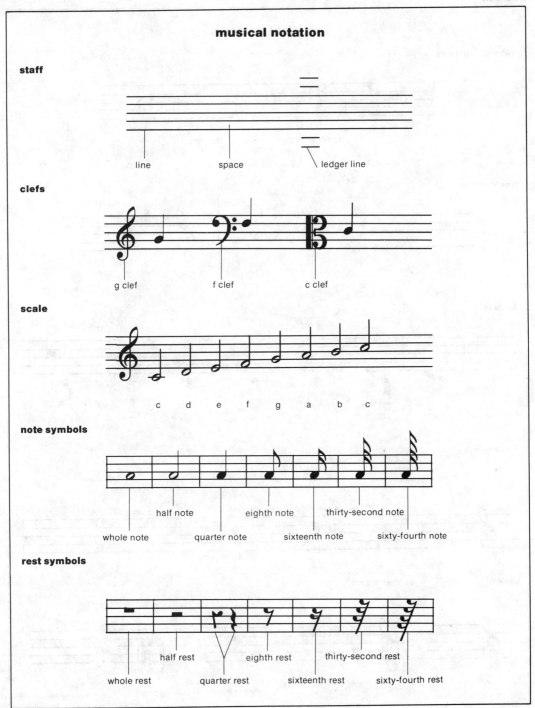

musical notation

time signatures

two-two time
three-four time
four-four time
bar line
repeat mark

accidentals

sharp
flat
natural
double sharp
double flat
key signature

intervals

unison · second · third · fourth · fifth · sixth · seventh · octave

ornaments

appoggiatura · trill · turn · mordent

chord   **other signs**

tie · accent mark · arpeggio · pause

stringed instruments

violin family

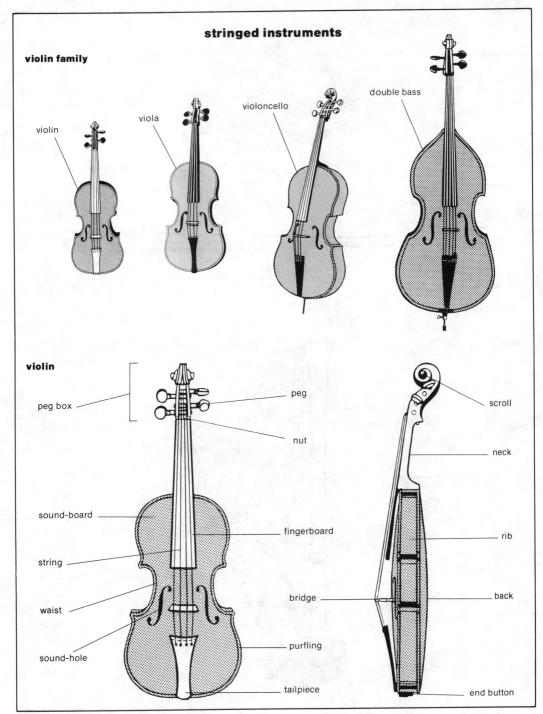

violin

viola

violoncello

double bass

violin

peg box

peg

nut

scroll

neck

sound-board

fingerboard

string

rib

waist

bridge

back

sound-hole

purfling

tailpiece

end button

stringed instruments

violin

bow

harp

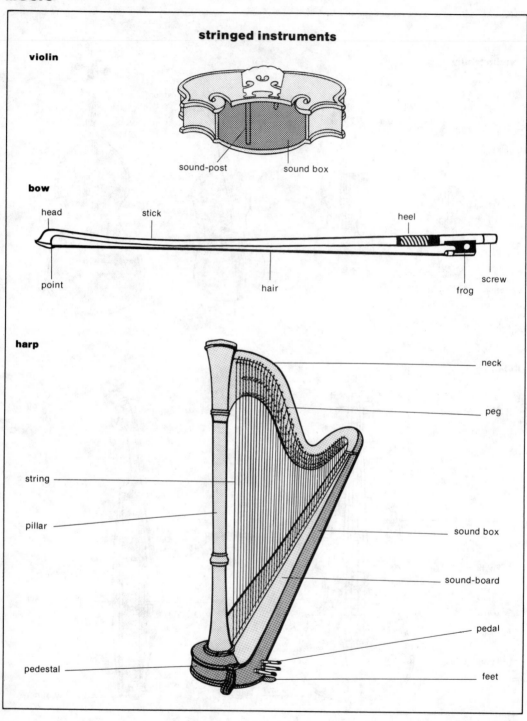

sound-post   sound box

head   stick   heel

point   hair   frog   screw

neck

peg

string

pillar

sound box

sound-board

pedal

pedestal

feet

keyboard instruments

upright piano

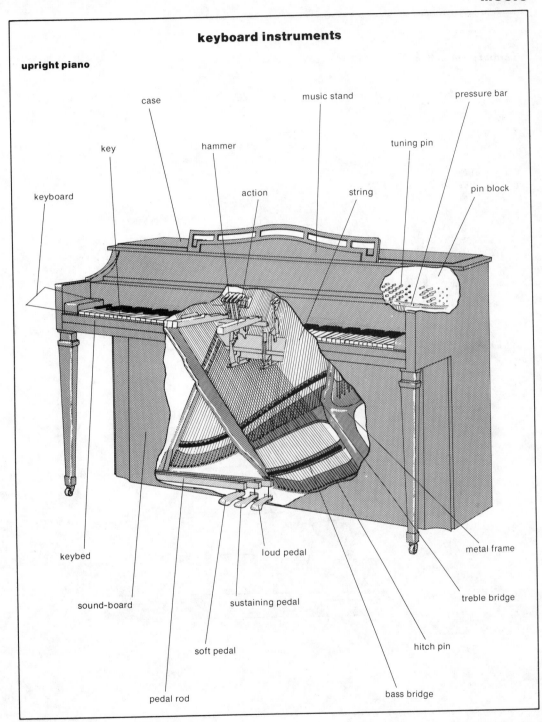

key · keyboard · case · hammer · action · music stand · string · tuning pin · pressure bar · pin block · keybed · sound-board · loud pedal · sustaining pedal · soft pedal · metal frame · treble bridge · hitch pin · pedal rod · bass bridge

keyboard instruments

upright piano action

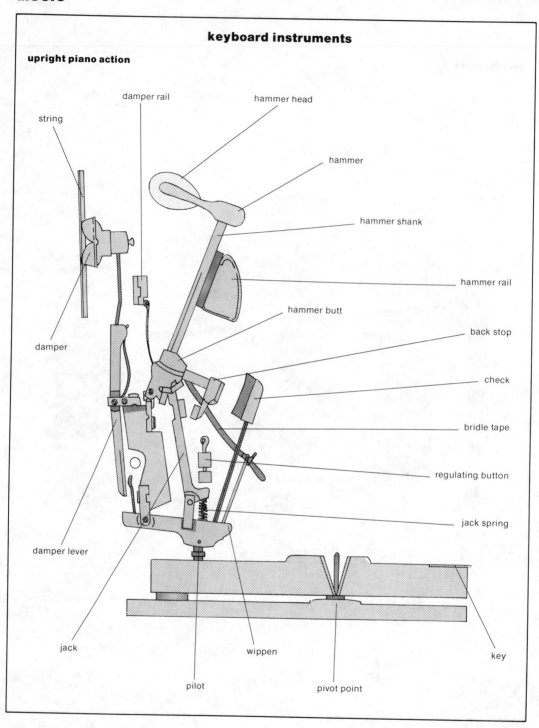

string

damper rail

hammer head

hammer

hammer shank

hammer rail

hammer butt

back stop

damper

check

bridle tape

regulating button

jack spring

damper lever

jack

wippen

key

pilot

pivot point

organ

production of sound

pipework

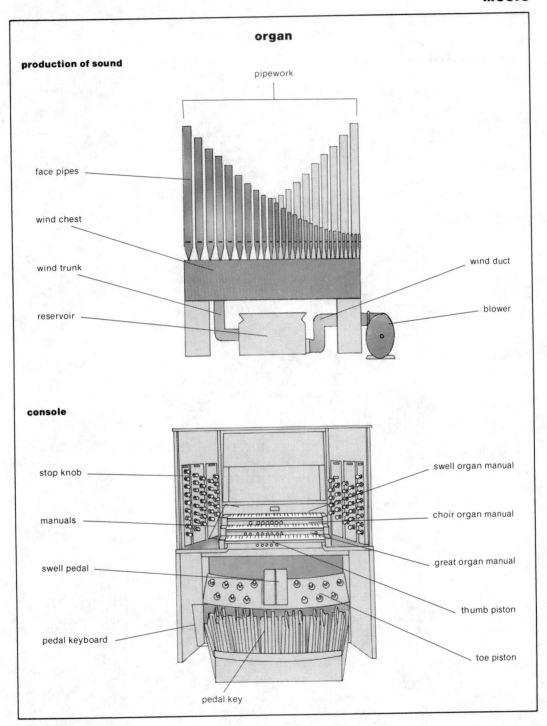

face pipes

wind chest

wind trunk

reservoir

wind duct

blower

console

stop knob

manuals

swell pedal

pedal keyboard

swell organ manual

choir organ manual

great organ manual

thumb piston

toe piston

pedal key

organ

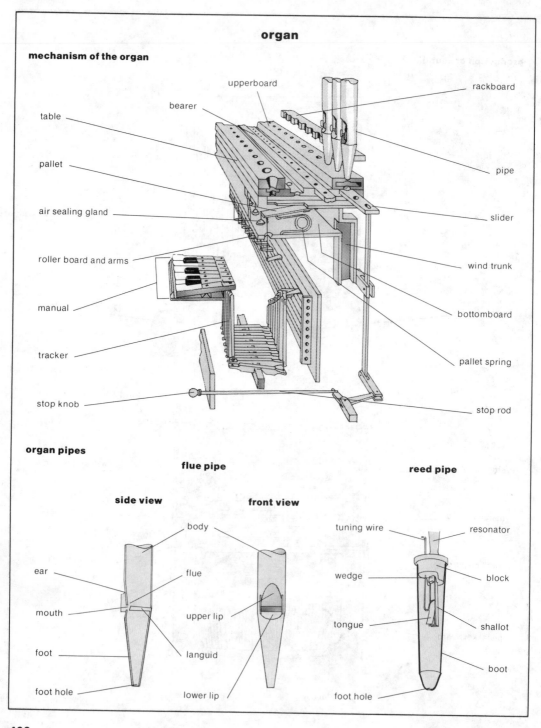

mechanism of the organ

upperboard

rackboard

bearer

table

pipe

pallet

air sealing gland

slider

roller board and arms

wind trunk

manual

bottomboard

tracker

pallet spring

stop knob

stop rod

organ pipes

flue pipe

reed pipe

side view

front view

body

tuning wire

resonator

ear

flue

wedge

block

mouth

upper lip

tongue

shallot

foot

languid

boot

foot hole

lower lip

foot hole

wind instruments

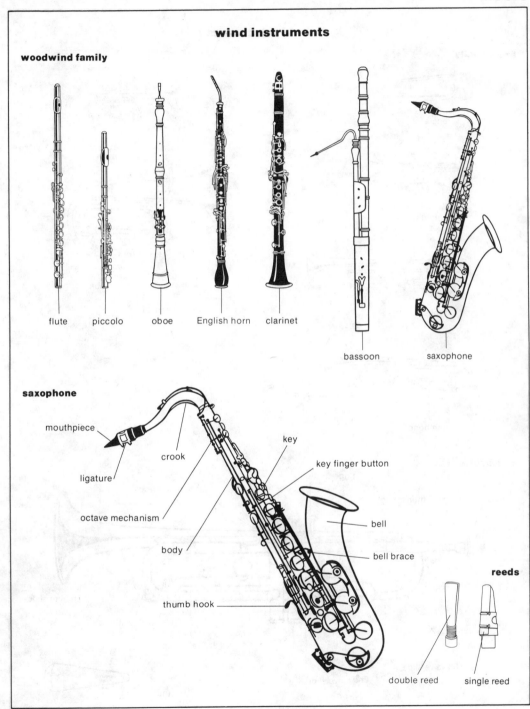

woodwind family

flute piccolo oboe English horn clarinet bassoon saxophone

saxophone

mouthpiece
crook
ligature
octave mechanism
body
thumb hook
key
key finger button
bell
bell brace

reeds

double reed single reed

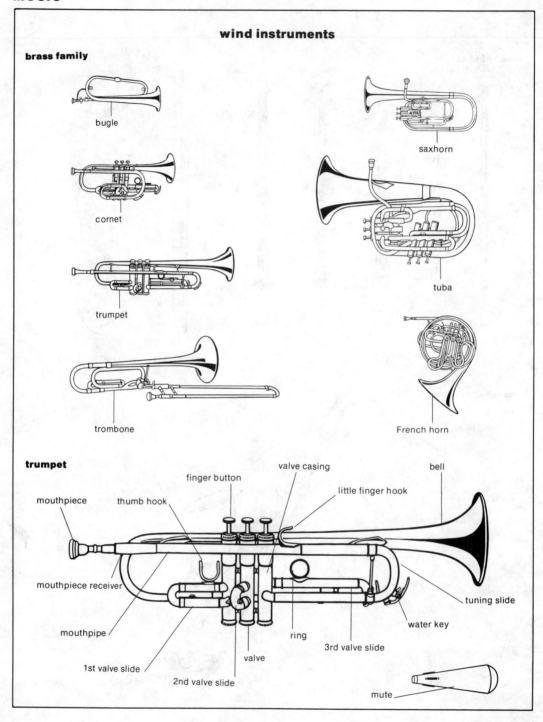

wind instruments

brass family

bugle

cornet

trumpet

trombone

saxhorn

tuba

French horn

trumpet

mouthpiece

thumb hook

finger button

valve casing

little finger hook

bell

mouthpiece receiver

mouthpipe

1st valve slide

2nd valve slide

valve

ring

3rd valve slide

water key

tuning slide

mute

percussion instruments

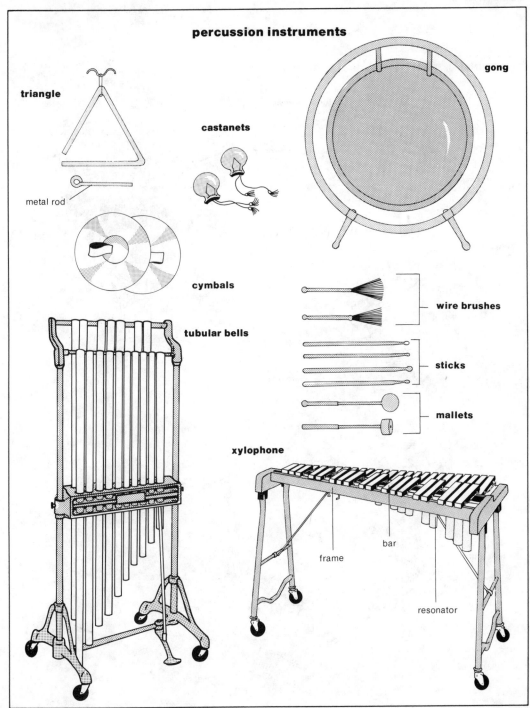

triangle

metal rod

castanets

gong

cymbals

tubular bells

wire brushes

sticks

mallets

xylophone

frame

bar

resonator

percussion instruments

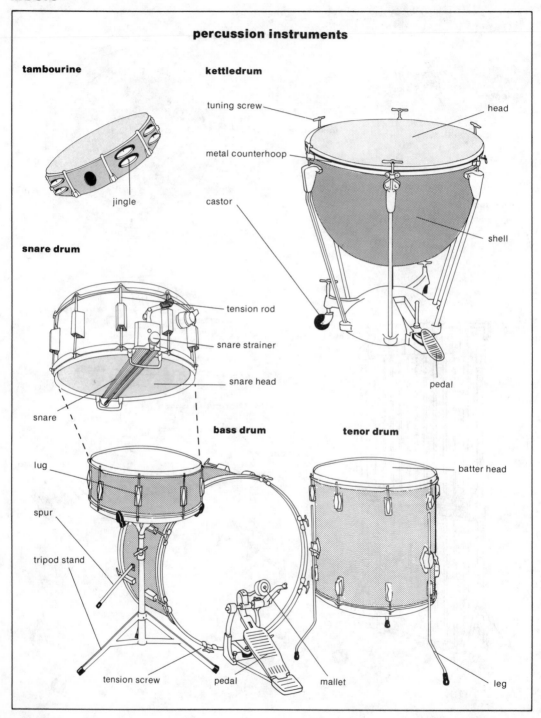

tambourine

jingle

kettledrum

tuning screw

head

metal counterhoop

castor

shell

snare drum

tension rod

snare strainer

snare head

snare

pedal

bass drum

tenor drum

lug

batter head

spur

tripod stand

tension screw

pedal

mallet

leg

traditional musical instruments

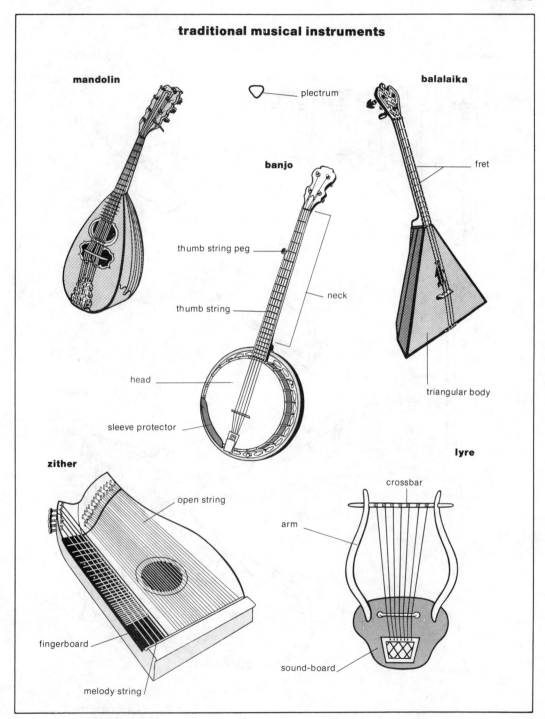

mandolin

plectrum

balalaika

banjo

fret

thumb string peg

neck

thumb string

head

sleeve protector

triangular body

zither

lyre

open string

crossbar

arm

fingerboard

sound-board

melody string

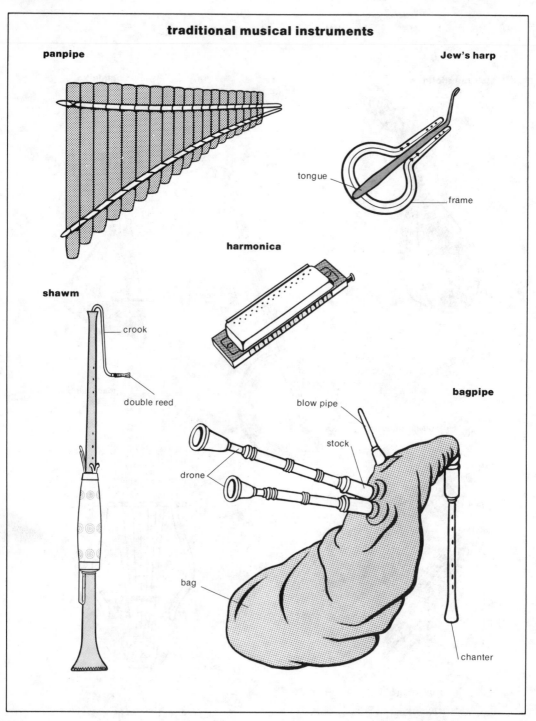

traditional musical instruments

panpipe

Jew's harp

tongue

frame

harmonica

shawm

crook

double reed

bagpipe

blow pipe

stock

drone

bag

chanter

traditional musical instruments

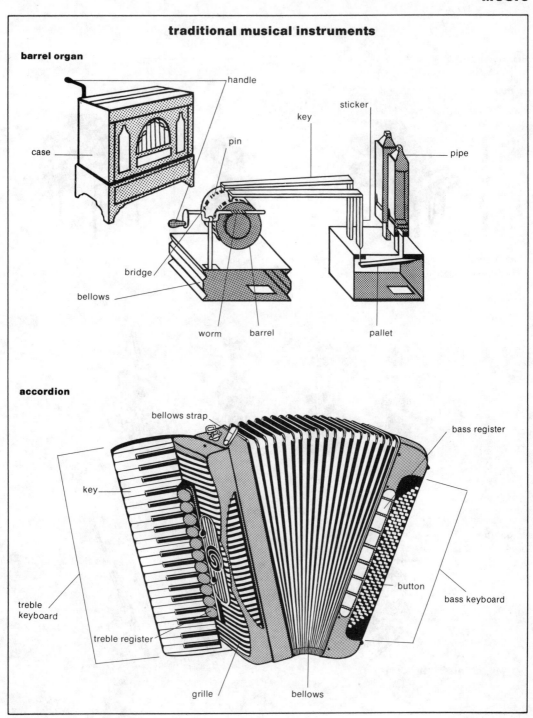

barrel organ

handle

case

sticker

key

pin

pipe

bridge

bellows

worm

barrel

pallet

accordion

bellows strap

bass register

key

treble keyboard

treble register

button

bass keyboard

grille

bellows

examples of instrumental groups

duo

trio

clarinet piano

violoncello oboe harpsichord

quartet

violin violin viola violoncello

quintet

French horn flute oboe clarinet bassoon

examples of instrumental groups

sextet

| clarinet | clarinet | French horn | French horn | bassoon | bassoon |

jazz band

drum kit

| bass drum | tenor drum | snare drum | cymbals | piano |

| double bass | clarinet | saxophone | trombone | trumpet | cornet |

musical accessories

metronome

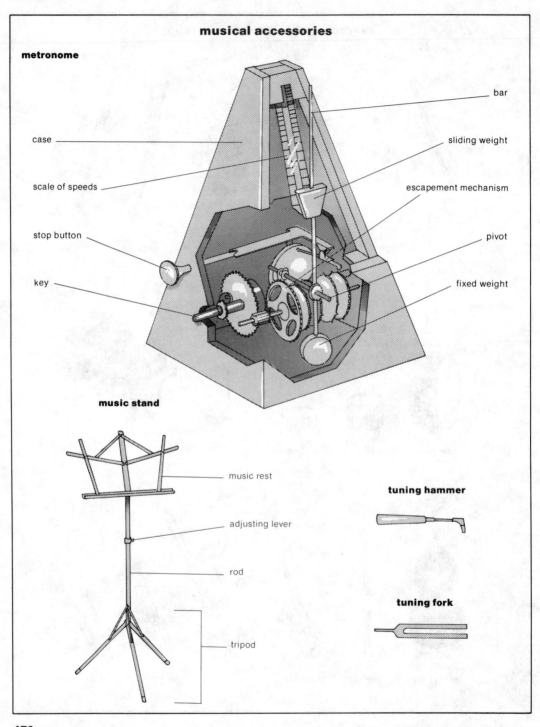

bar

case

sliding weight

scale of speeds

escapement mechanism

stop button

pivot

key

fixed weight

music stand

music rest

tuning hammer

adjusting lever

rod

tuning fork

tripod

symphony orchestra

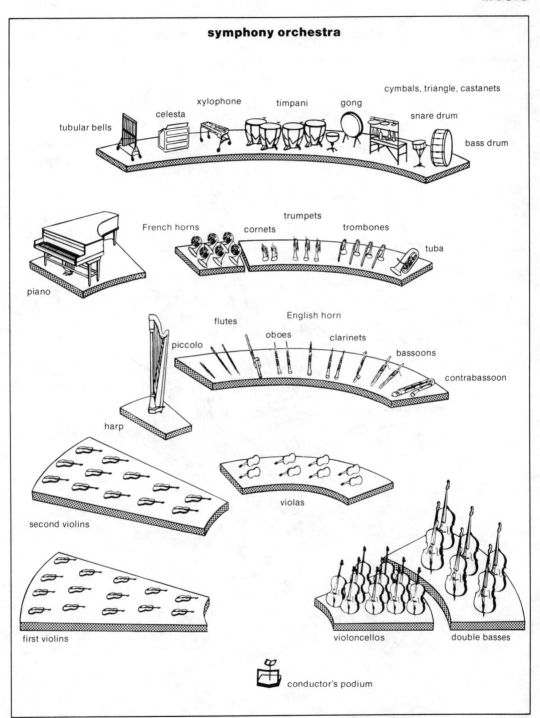

tubular bells

celesta

xylophone

timpani

gong

cymbals, triangle, castanets

snare drum

bass drum

French horns

cornets

trumpets

trombones

tuba

piano

piccolo

flutes

oboes

English horn

clarinets

bassoons

contrabassoon

harp

second violins

violas

first violins

violoncellos

double basses

conductor's podium

electric and electronic instruments

electric guitar

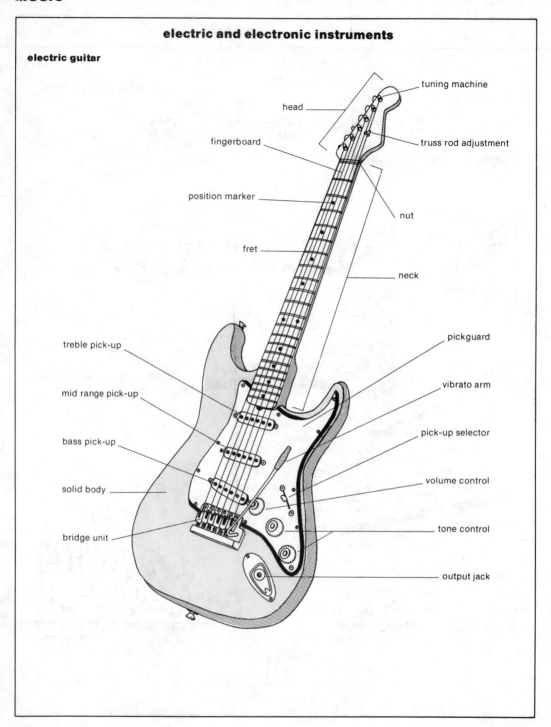

head

tuning machine

fingerboard

truss rod adjustment

position marker

nut

fret

neck

treble pick-up

pickguard

mid range pick-up

vibrato arm

bass pick-up

pick-up selector

solid body

volume control

bridge unit

tone control

output jack

electric and electronic instruments

synthesizer

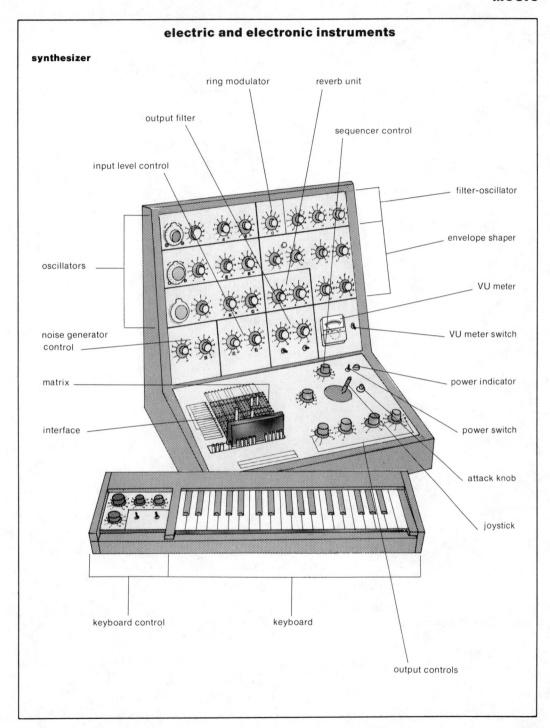

ring modulator

reverb unit

output filter

sequencer control

input level control

filter-oscillator

envelope shaper

oscillators

VU meter

noise generator control

VU meter switch

matrix

power indicator

interface

power switch

attack knob

joystick

keyboard control

keyboard

output controls

CREATIVE LEISURE
ACTIVITIES

sewing

sewing machine

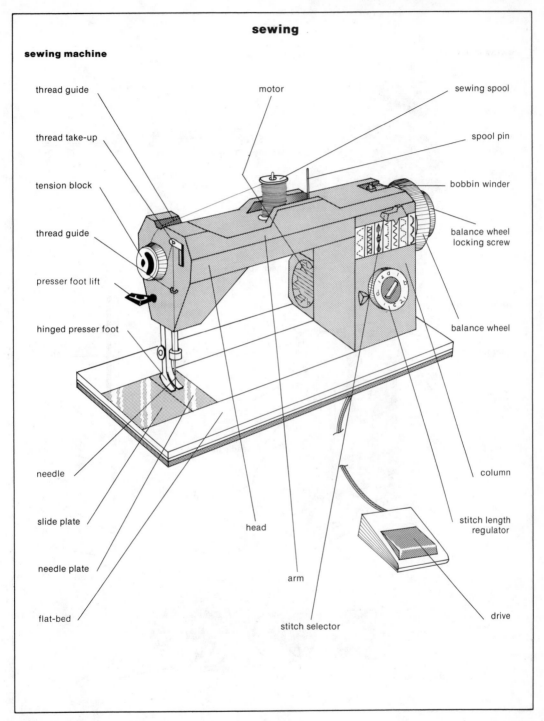

thread guide

motor

sewing spool

thread take-up

spool pin

tension block

bobbin winder

thread guide

balance wheel
locking screw

presser foot lift

hinged presser foot

balance wheel

needle

slide plate

head

column

needle plate

stitch length
regulator

arm

flat-bed

drive

stitch selector

CREATIVE LEISURE ACTIVITIES

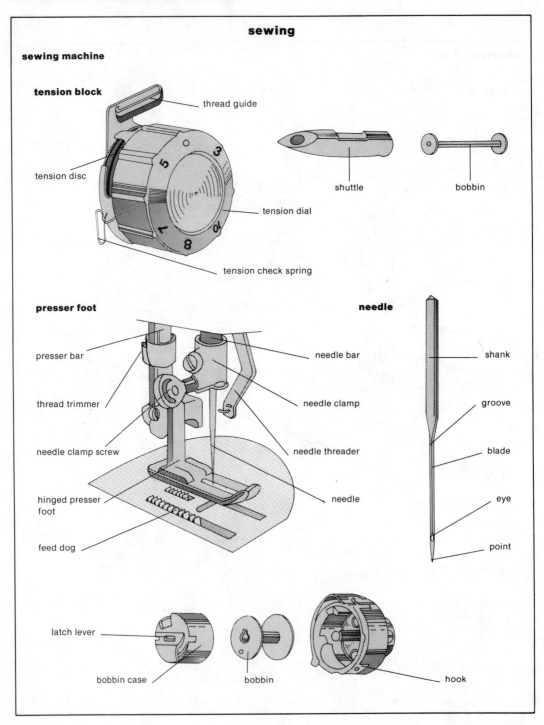

sewing

sewing machine

tension block

thread guide

tension disc

tension dial

tension check spring

shuttle

bobbin

presser foot

needle

presser bar

needle bar

thread trimmer

needle clamp

needle clamp screw

needle threader

hinged presser foot

needle

feed dog

shank

groove

blade

eye

point

latch lever

bobbin case

bobbin

hook

sewing

supplies

pin cushion

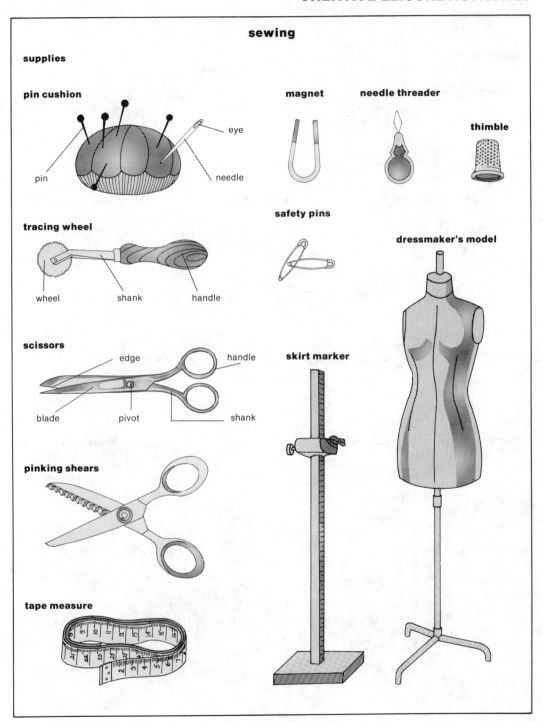

eye

pin

needle

magnet

needle threader

thimble

tracing wheel

wheel   shank   handle

safety pins

dressmaker's model

scissors

edge   handle

blade   pivot   shank

skirt marker

pinking shears

tape measure

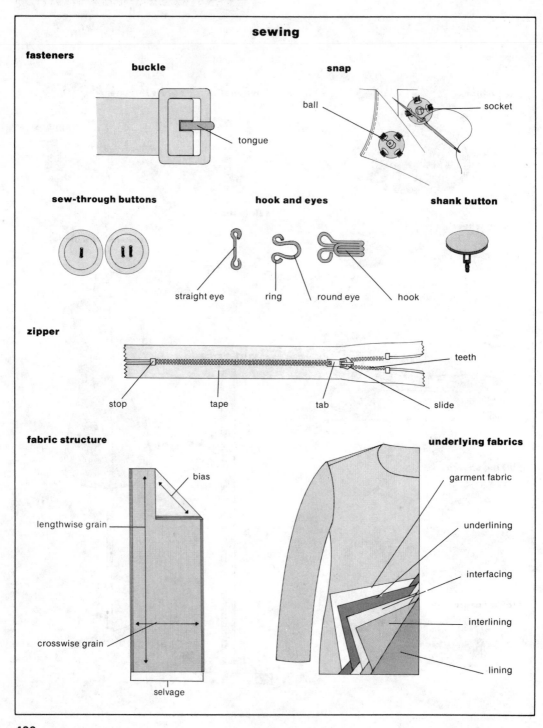

sewing

fasteners

buckle

tongue

snap

ball · socket

sew-through buttons

hook and eyes

straight eye · ring · round eye · hook

shank button

zipper

teeth · stop · tape · tab · slide

fabric structure

bias · lengthwise grain · crosswise grain · selvage

underlying fabrics

garment fabric · underlining · interfacing · interlining · lining

sewing

pattern

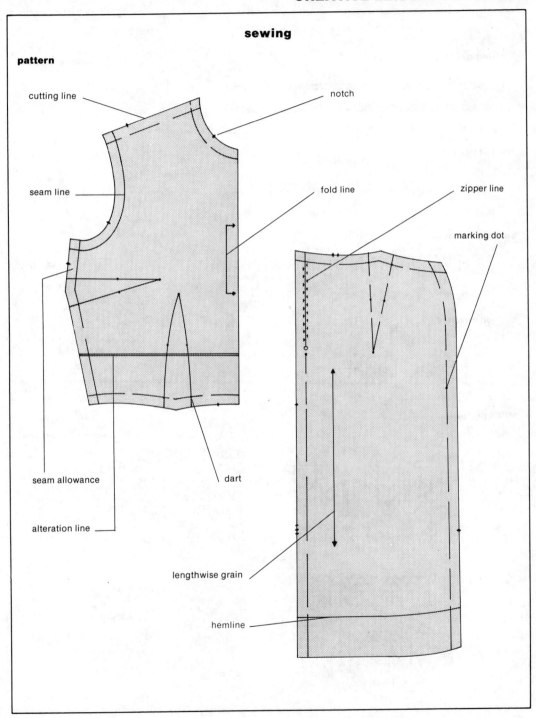

cutting line

notch

seam line

fold line

zipper line

marking dot

seam allowance

dart

alteration line

lengthwise grain

hemline

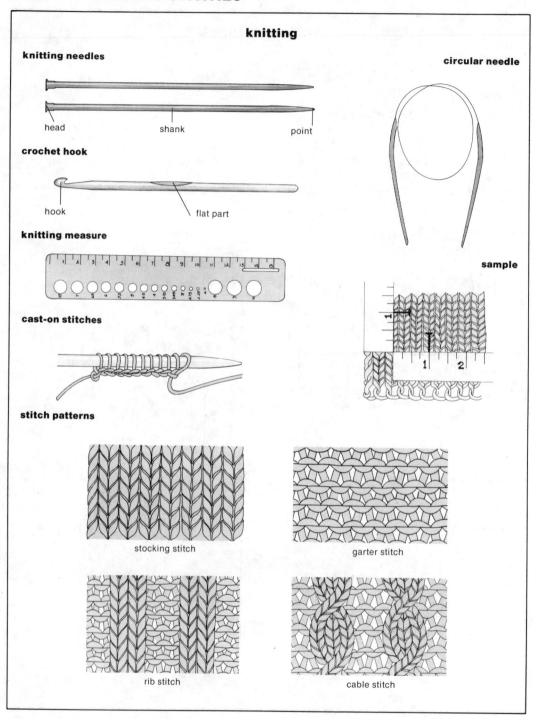

knitting

knitting needles

head
shank
point

circular needle

crochet hook

hook
flat part

knitting measure

sample

cast-on stitches

stitch patterns

stocking stitch

garter stitch

rib stitch

cable stitch

knitting machine

tension block

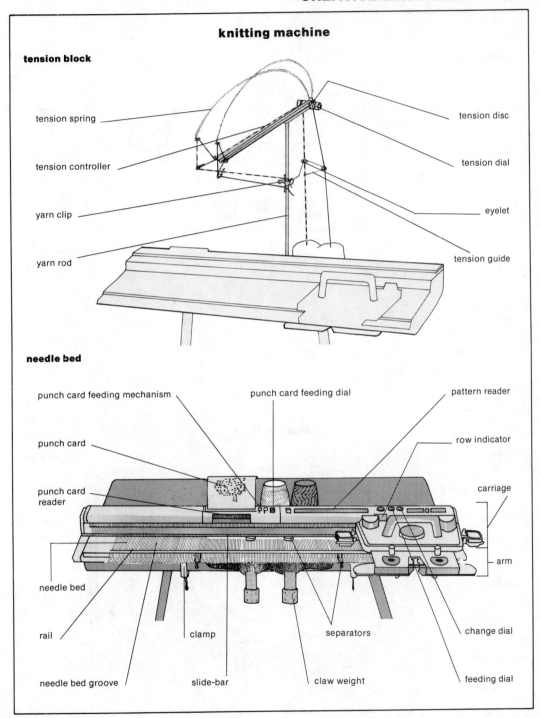

tension spring

tension disc

tension controller

tension dial

yarn clip

eyelet

yarn rod

tension guide

needle bed

punch card feeding mechanism

punch card feeding dial

pattern reader

punch card

row indicator

punch card reader

carriage

arm

needle bed

rail

change dial

needle bed groove

clamp

slide-bar

separators

claw weight

feeding dial

CREATIVE LEISURE ACTIVITIES

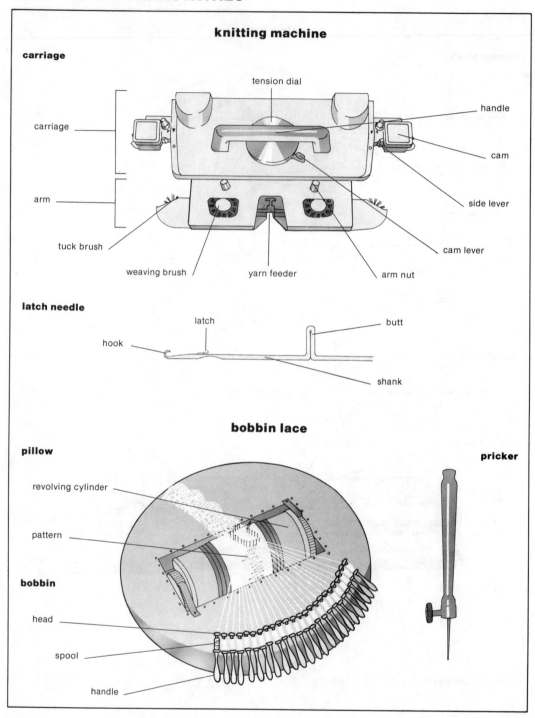

knitting machine

carriage

tension dial

handle

cam

side lever

carriage

arm

cam lever

tuck brush

weaving brush

yarn feeder

arm nut

latch needle

latch

hook

butt

shank

bobbin lace

pillow

pricker

revolving cylinder

pattern

bobbin

head

spool

handle

embroidery

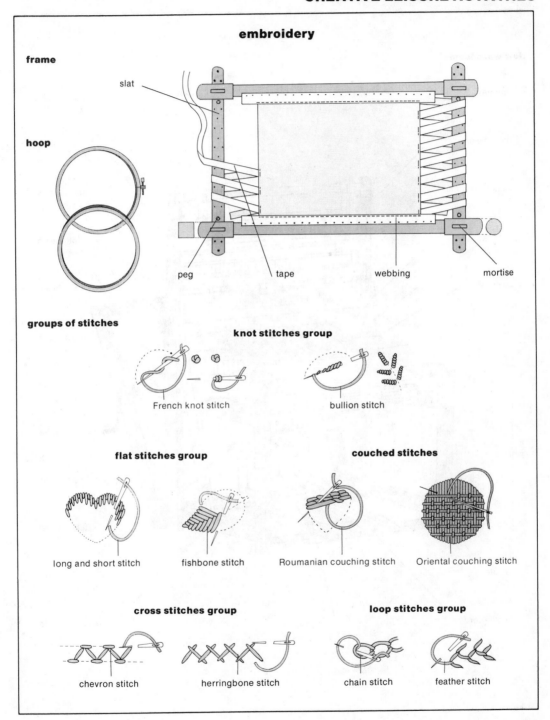

frame

slat

hoop

peg   tape   webbing   mortise

groups of stitches

knot stitches group

French knot stitch   bullion stitch

flat stitches group

long and short stitch   fishbone stitch

couched stitches

Roumanian couching stitch   Oriental couching stitch

cross stitches group

chevron stitch   herringbone stitch

loop stitches group

chain stitch   feather stitch

CREATIVE LEISURE ACTIVITIES

weaving

low warp loom

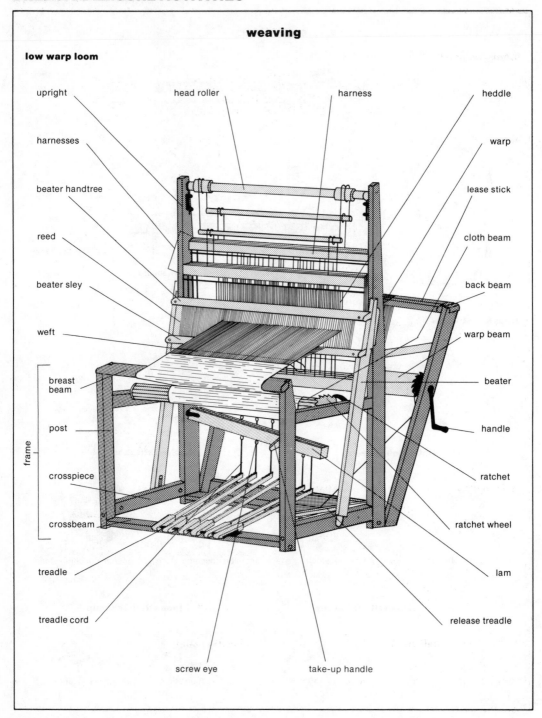

upright

head roller

harness

heddle

harnesses

warp

beater handtree

lease stick

reed

cloth beam

beater sley

back beam

weft

warp beam

breast beam

beater

post

handle

frame

crosspiece

ratchet

crossbeam

ratchet wheel

treadle

lam

treadle cord

release treadle

screw eye

take-up handle

weaving

high warp loom

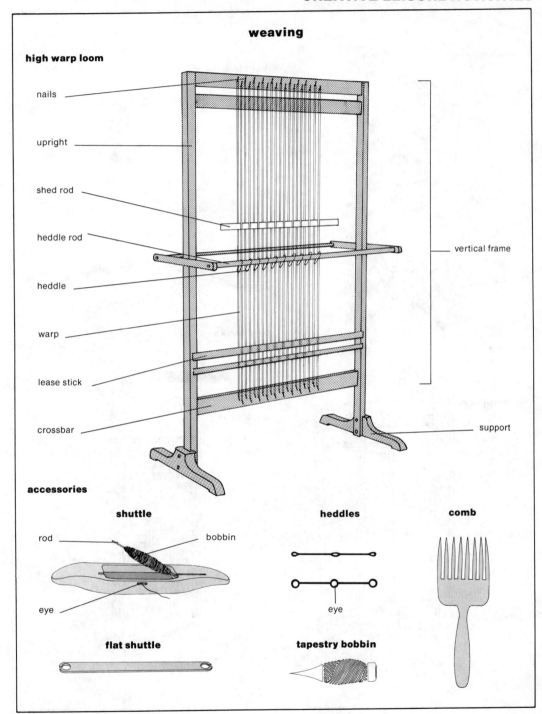

nails

upright

shed rod

heddle rod

heddle

warp

lease stick

crossbar

vertical frame

support

accessories

shuttle

rod

bobbin

eye

flat shuttle

heddles

eye

tapestry bobbin

comb

CREATIVE LEISURE ACTIVITIES

weaving

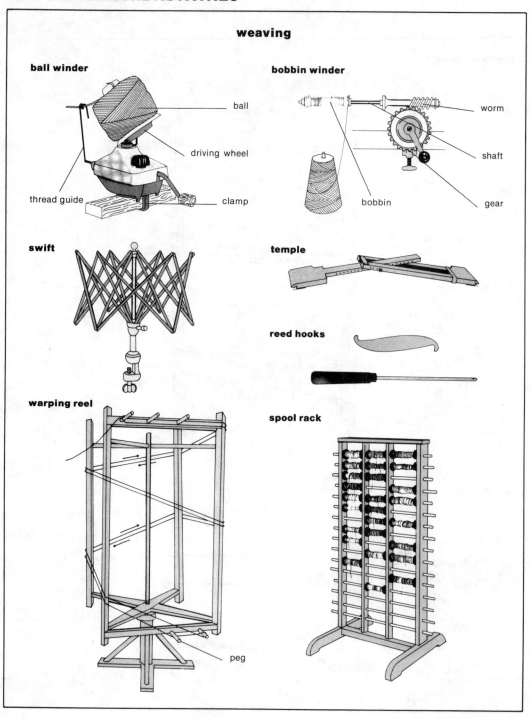

ball winder

ball

driving wheel

thread guide

clamp

bobbin winder

worm

shaft

bobbin

gear

swift

temple

reed hooks

warping reel

peg

spool rack

weaving

diagram of weaving principle

basic weaves

other techniques

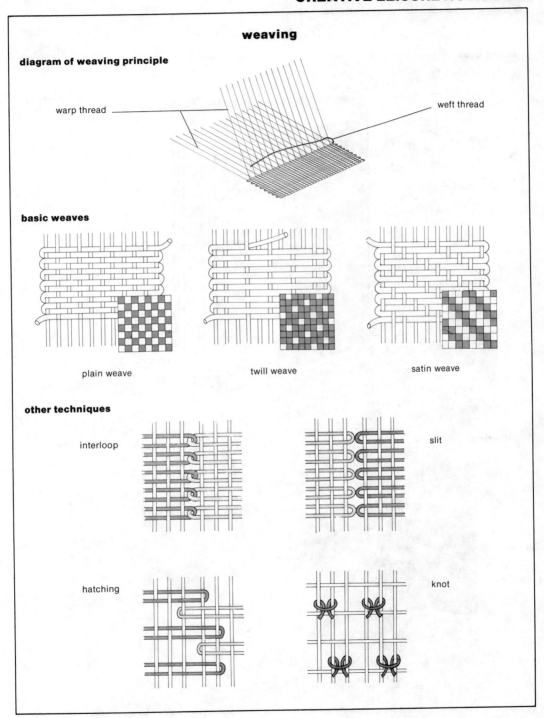

warp thread

weft thread

plain weave

twill weave

satin weave

interloop

slit

hatching

knot

fine bookbinding

bound book

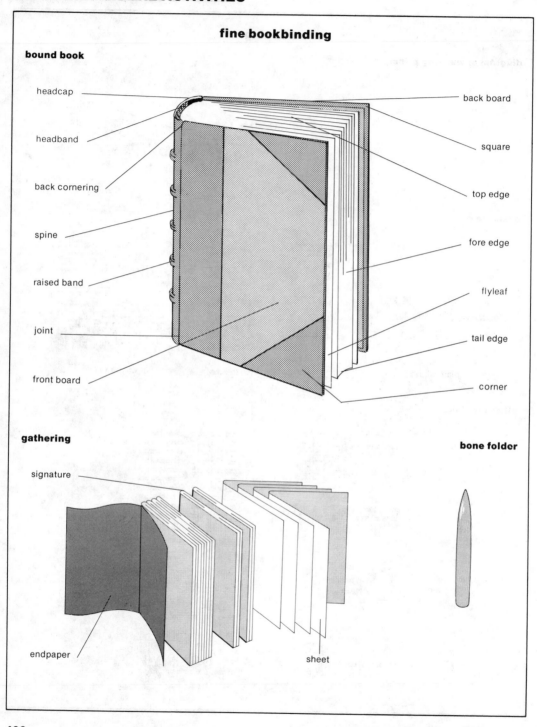

headcap

headband

back cornering

spine

raised band

joint

front board

back board

square

top edge

fore edge

flyleaf

tail edge

corner

gathering

bone folder

signature

endpaper

sheet

fine bookbinding

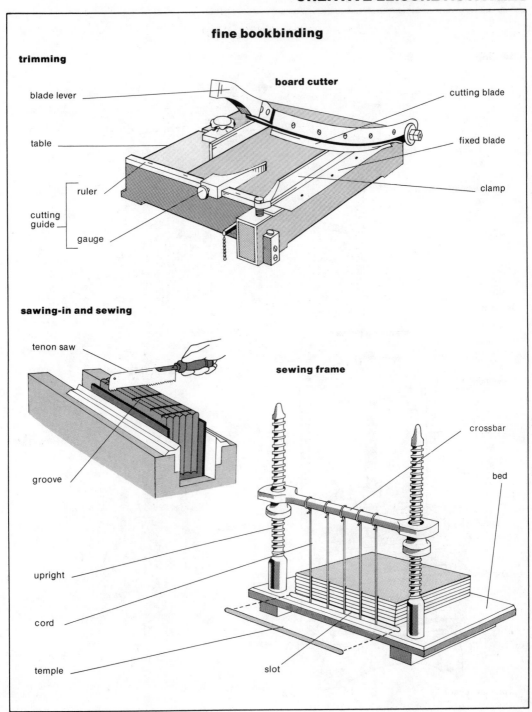

trimming

blade lever

board cutter

cutting blade

table

fixed blade

ruler

cutting guide

gauge

clamp

sawing-in and sewing

tenon saw

sewing frame

crossbar

bed

groove

upright

cord

temple

slot

CREATIVE LEISURE ACTIVITIES

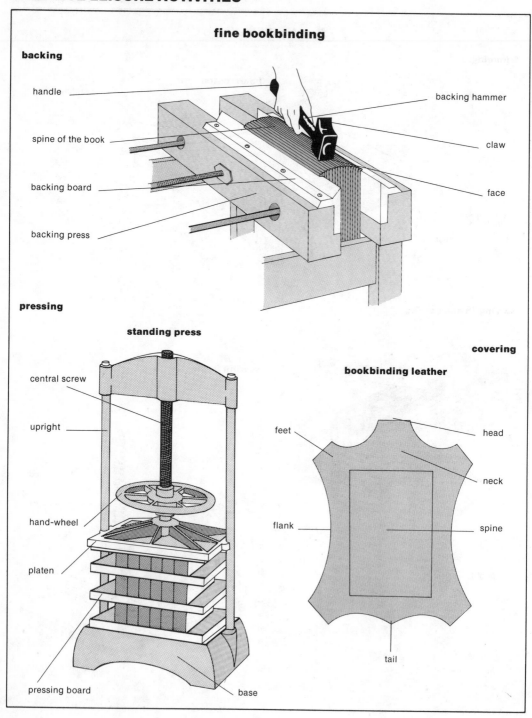

fine bookbinding

backing

handle

spine of the book

backing board

backing press

backing hammer

claw

face

pressing

standing press

central screw

upright

hand-wheel

platen

pressing board

base

covering

bookbinding leather

feet

head

neck

flank

spine

tail

intaglio printing process

equipment

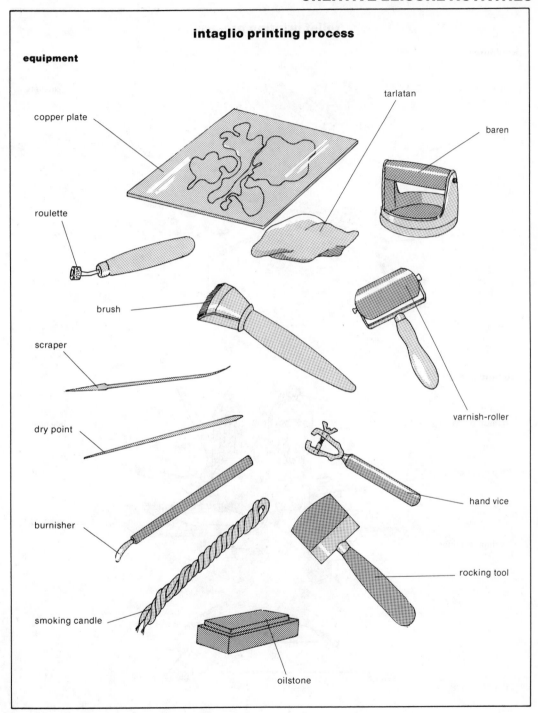

tarlatan

copper plate

baren

roulette

brush

varnish-roller

scraper

dry point

hand vice

burnisher

rocking tool

smoking candle

oilstone

CREATIVE LEISURE ACTIVITIES

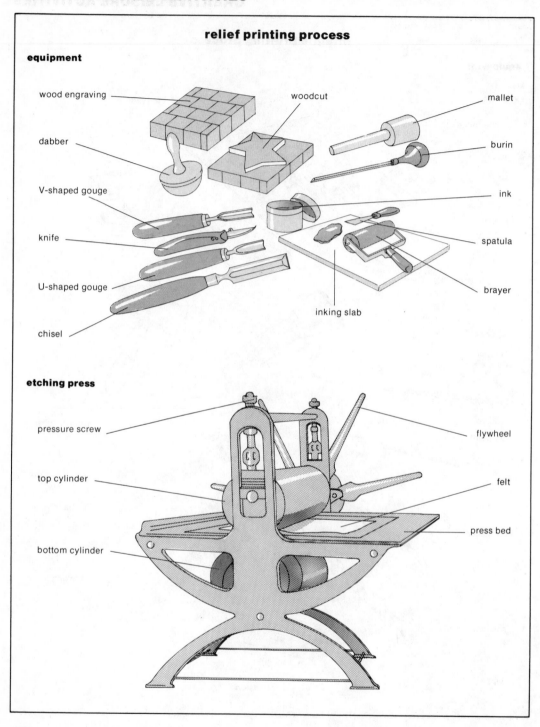

relief printing process

equipment

wood engraving

woodcut

mallet

dabber

burin

V-shaped gouge

ink

knife

spatula

U-shaped gouge

brayer

chisel

inking slab

etching press

pressure screw

flywheel

top cylinder

felt

press bed

bottom cylinder

lithography

equipment

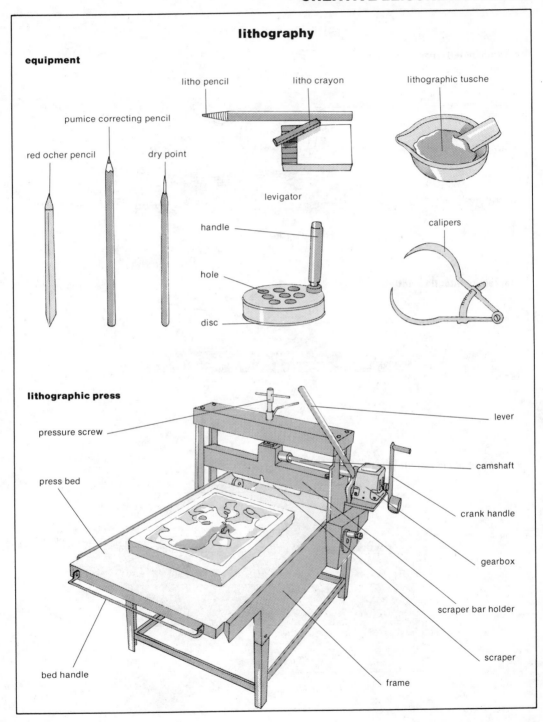

litho pencil

litho crayon

lithographic tusche

pumice correcting pencil

red ocher pencil

dry point

levigator

handle

hole

disc

calipers

lithographic press

pressure screw

press bed

lever

camshaft

crank handle

gearbox

scraper bar holder

scraper

bed handle

frame

printing

diagram of letterpress printing

diagram of intaglio printing

diagram of planographic printing

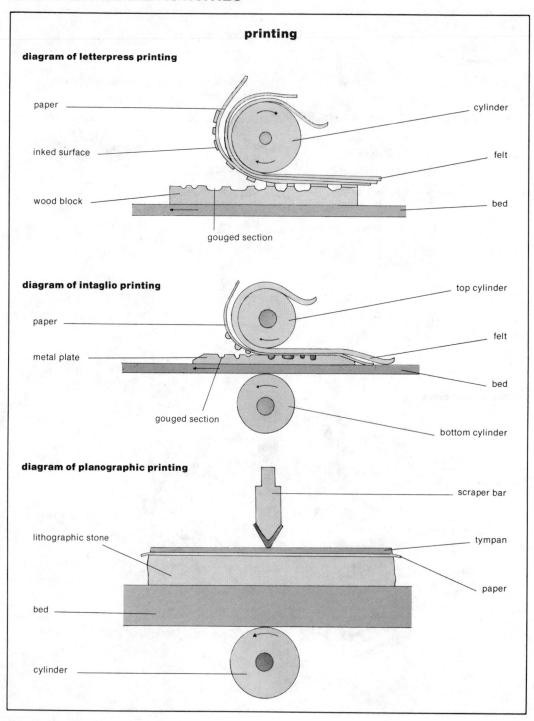

paper — cylinder
inked surface — felt
wood block — bed
gouged section

paper — top cylinder
metal plate — felt
gouged section — bed
bottom cylinder

scraper bar
lithographic stone — tympan
bed — paper
cylinder

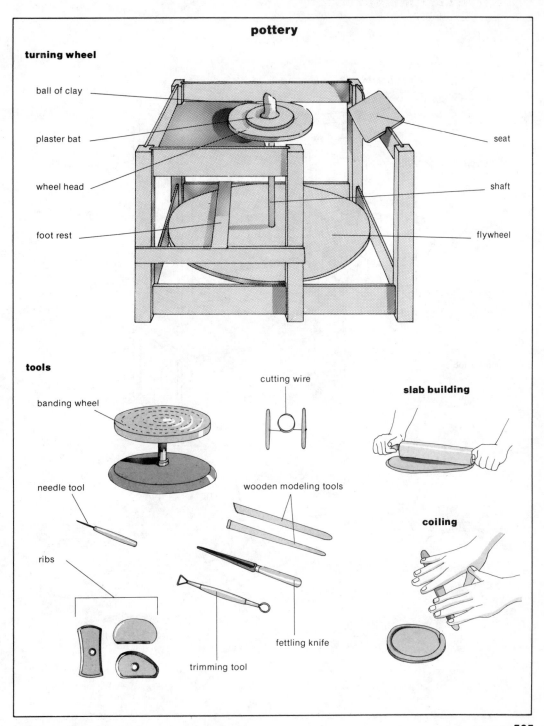

pottery

turning wheel

ball of clay

plaster bat

wheel head

foot rest

seat

shaft

flywheel

tools

cutting wire

slab building

banding wheel

needle tool

wooden modeling tools

coiling

ribs

trimming tool

fettling knife

pottery

baking

electric kiln

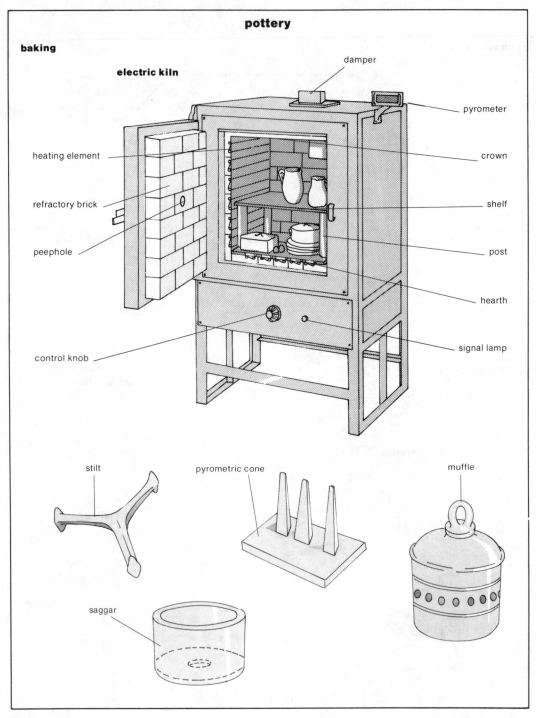

damper

pyrometer

heating element

crown

refractory brick

shelf

peephole

post

hearth

control knob

signal lamp

stilt

pyrometric cone

muffle

saggar

stained glass

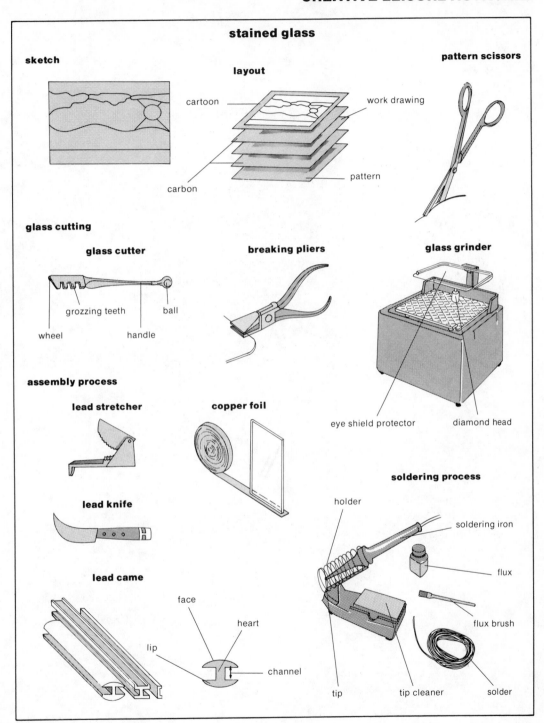

sketch

layout

cartoon

work drawing

carbon

pattern

pattern scissors

glass cutting

glass cutter

grozzing teeth

ball

wheel

handle

breaking pliers

glass grinder

eye shield protector

diamond head

assembly process

lead stretcher

copper foil

lead knife

lead came

face

heart

lip

channel

soldering process

holder

soldering iron

flux

flux brush

tip

tip cleaner

solder

SPORTS

baseball

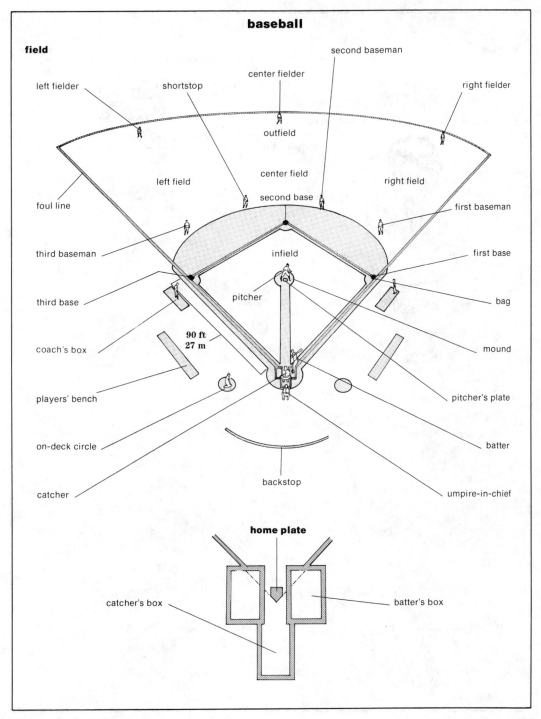

field

left fielder

shortstop

center fielder

second baseman

right fielder

outfield

left field

center field

right field

foul line

second base

first baseman

third baseman

infield

first base

third base

pitcher

bag

coach's box

**90 ft
27 m**

mound

players' bench

pitcher's plate

on-deck circle

batter

catcher

backstop

umpire-in-chief

home plate

catcher's box

batter's box

TEAM GAMES

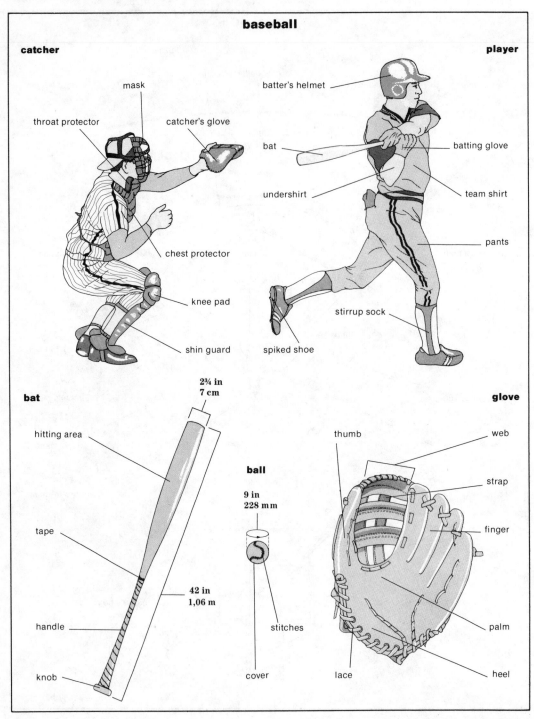

baseball

catcher

player

- mask
- throat protector
- catcher's glove
- batter's helmet
- bat
- batting glove
- undershirt
- team shirt
- chest protector
- pants
- knee pad
- stirrup sock
- shin guard
- spiked shoe

bat

glove

- 2¾ in
  7 cm
- hitting area
- thumb
- web
- **ball**
- strap
- 9 in
  228 mm
- tape
- finger
- 42 in
  1,06 m
- handle
- palm
- stitches
- knob
- cover
- lace
- heel

football

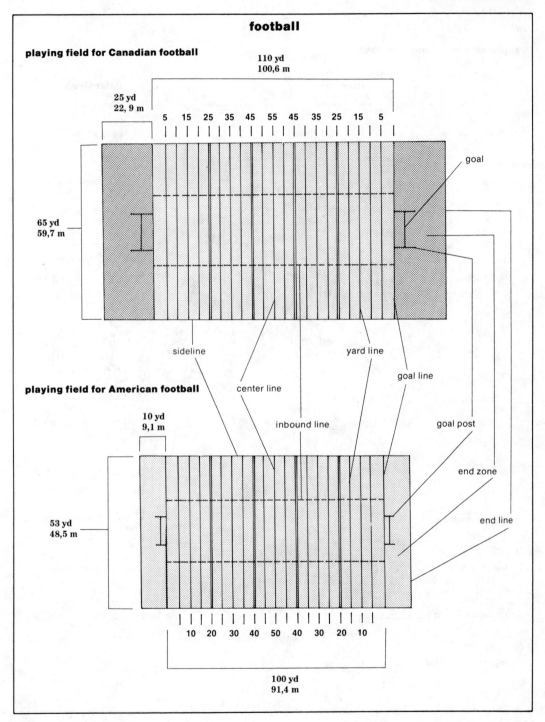

playing field for Canadian football

110 yd
100,6 m

25 yd
22,9 m

5 15 25 35 45 55 45 35 25 15 5

65 yd
59,7 m

goal

playing field for American football

10 yd
9,1 m

sideline

center line

inbound line

yard line

goal line

goal post

end zone

end line

53 yd
48,5 m

10 20 30 40 50 40 30 20 10

100 yd
91,4 m

football

scrimmage in American football

offensive **defensive**

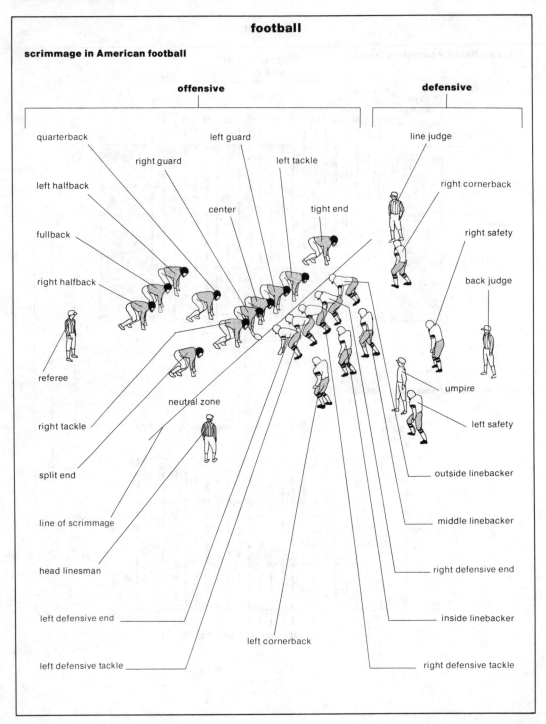

quarterback

left guard

line judge

right guard

left tackle

right cornerback

left halfback

center

tight end

right safety

fullback

back judge

right halfback

referee

umpire

neutral zone

left safety

right tackle

split end

outside linebacker

line of scrimmage

middle linebacker

head linesman

right defensive end

left defensive end

inside linebacker

left cornerback

left defensive tackle

right defensive tackle

football

scrimmage in Canadian football

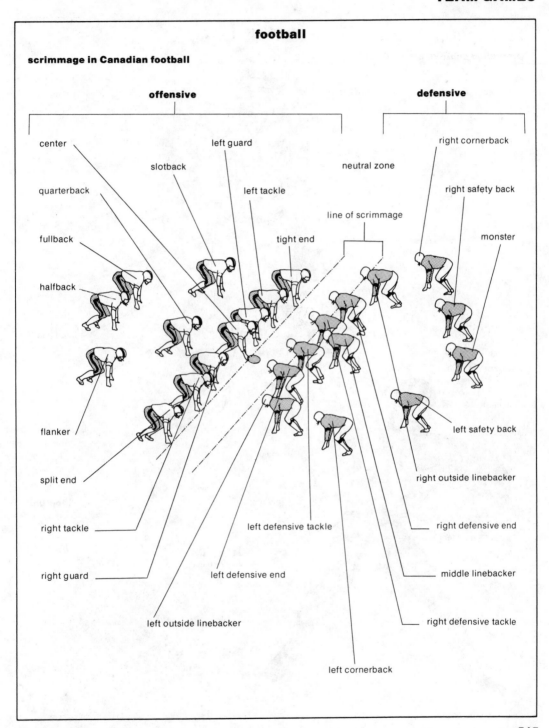

offensive

defensive

center

left guard

right cornerback

slotback

neutral zone

quarterback

left tackle

right safety back

fullback

line of scrimmage

monster

halfback

tight end

flanker

left safety back

split end

right outside linebacker

right tackle

left defensive tackle

right defensive end

right guard

left defensive end

middle linebacker

left outside linebacker

right defensive tackle

left cornerback

football

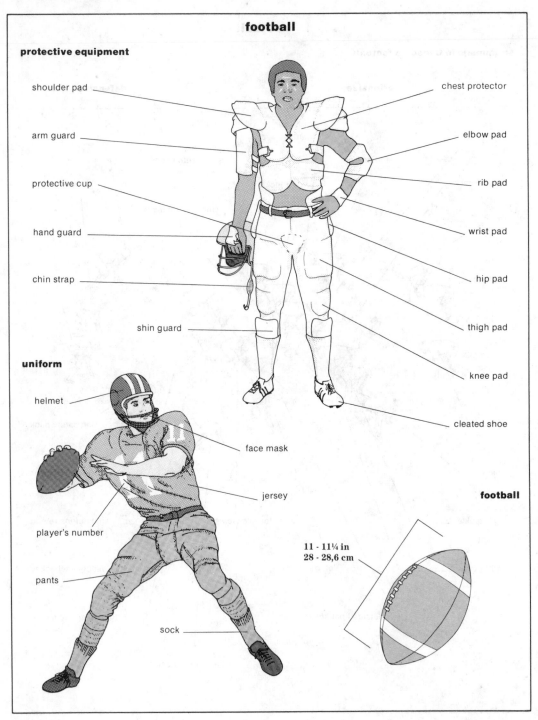

protective equipment

shoulder pad

arm guard

protective cup

hand guard

chin strap

shin guard

chest protector

elbow pad

rib pad

wrist pad

hip pad

thigh pad

knee pad

cleated shoe

uniform

helmet

face mask

jersey

player's number

pants

sock

football

11 - 11¼ in
28 - 28,6 cm

rugby

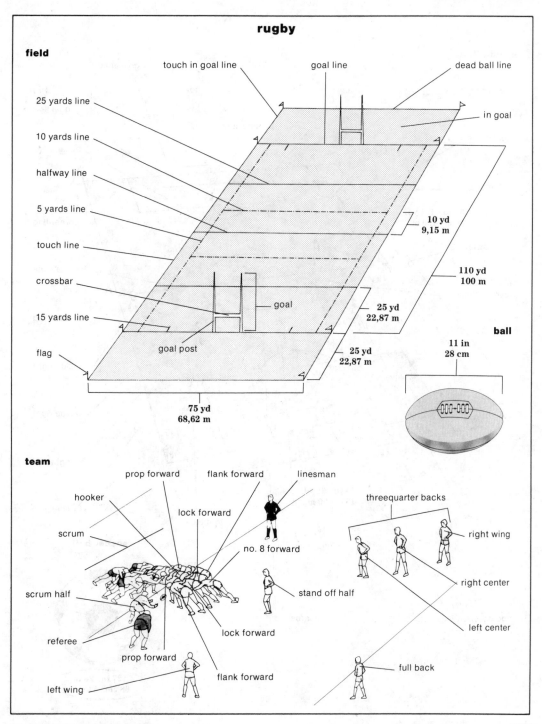

field

touch in goal line

goal line

dead ball line

25 yards line

10 yards line

halfway line

5 yards line

touch line

crossbar

15 yards line

flag

in goal

10 yd
9,15 m

110 yd
100 m

25 yd
22,87 m

25 yd
22,87 m

goal

goal post

75 yd
68,62 m

ball

11 in
28 cm

team

prop forward

flank forward

linesman

hooker

lock forward

scrum

threequarter backs

right wing

no. 8 forward

scrum half

stand off half

right center

referee

lock forward

left center

prop forward

flank forward

full back

left wing

soccer

playing field

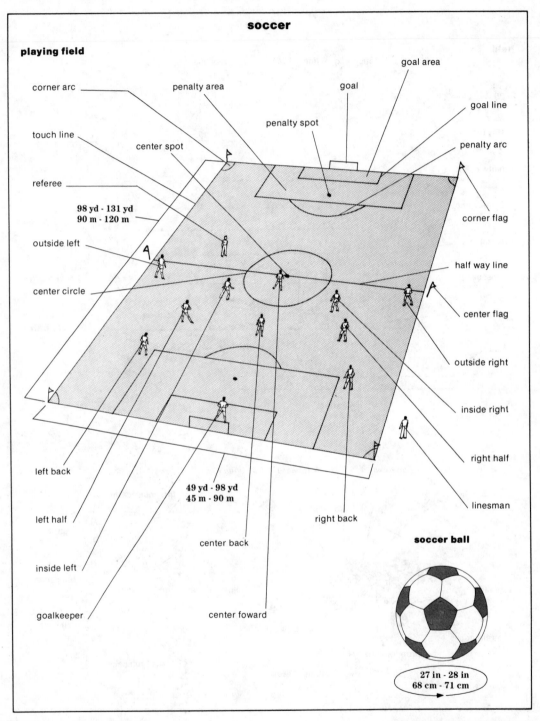

corner arc

penalty area

goal area

goal

goal line

penalty spot

penalty arc

touch line

center spot

referee

98 yd - 131 yd
90 m - 120 m

corner flag

outside left

half way line

center circle

center flag

outside right

inside right

right half

left back

linesman

49 yd - 98 yd
45 m - 90 m

left half

right back

inside left

center back

goalkeeper

center foward

soccer ball

27 in - 28 in
68 cm - 71 cm

ice hockey

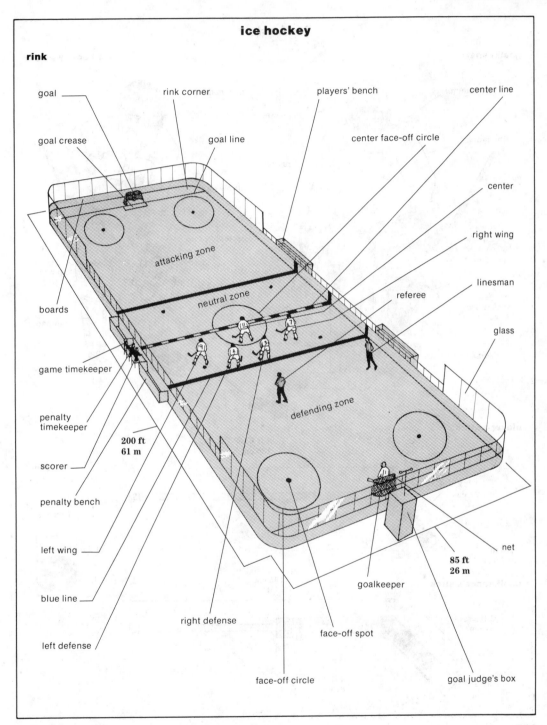

rink

goal
rink corner
players' bench
center line

goal crease
goal line
center face-off circle

center

right wing

attacking zone
linesman

boards
neutral zone
referee
glass

game timekeeper

defending zone

penalty
timekeeper

200 ft
61 m

scorer

penalty bench

left wing
net

blue line
85 ft
26 m

left defense
goalkeeper

right defense

face-off spot

face-off circle
goal judge's box

ice hockey

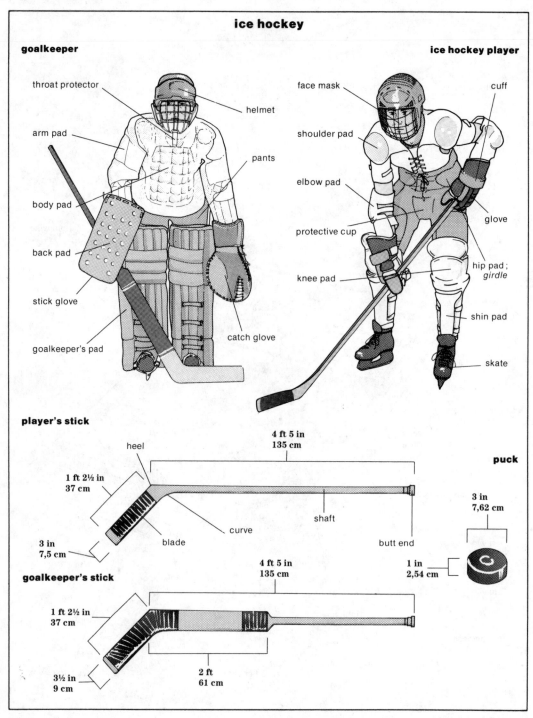

goalkeeper

throat protector

helmet

arm pad

pants

body pad

back pad

stick glove

goalkeeper's pad

catch glove

ice hockey player

face mask

cuff

shoulder pad

elbow pad

glove

protective cup

hip pad; *girdle*

knee pad

shin pad

skate

player's stick

heel

4 ft 5 in
135 cm

1 ft 2½ in
37 cm

puck

3 in
7,62 cm

shaft

3 in
7,5 cm

curve

blade

butt end

1 in
2,54 cm

goalkeeper's stick

4 ft 5 in
135 cm

1 ft 2½ in
37 cm

3½ in
9 cm

2 ft
61 cm

basketball

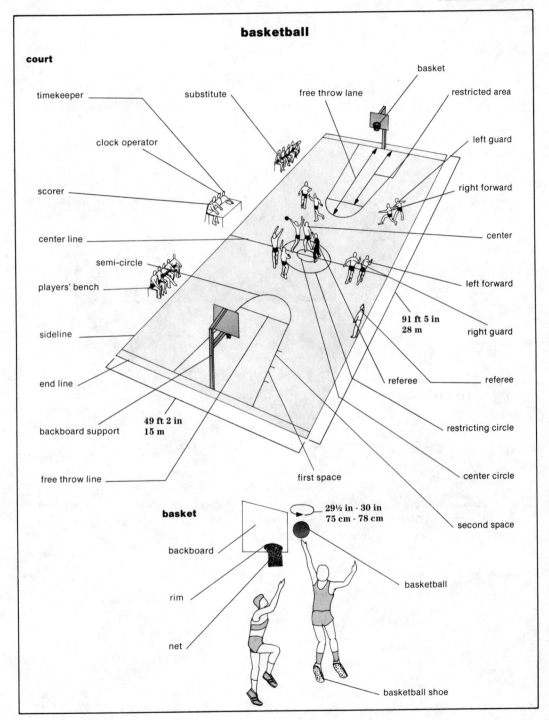

court

- timekeeper
- clock operator
- scorer
- center line
- semi-circle
- players' bench
- sideline
- end line
- backboard support
- free throw line
- substitute
- first space

- basket
- free throw lane
- restricted area
- left guard
- right forward
- center
- left forward
- right guard
- referee
- referee
- restricting circle
- center circle
- second space

91 ft 5 in
28 m

49 ft 2 in
15 m

basket

- backboard
- rim
- net

29½ in - 30 in
75 cm - 78 cm

- basketball
- basketball shoe

TEAM GAMES

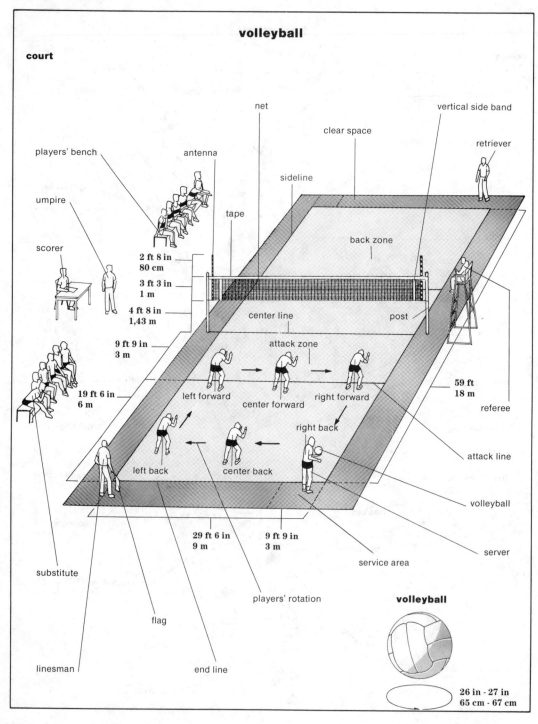

volleyball

court

players' bench

umpire

scorer

antenna

net

clear space

vertical side band

retriever

sideline

tape

back zone

2 ft 8 in
80 cm

3 ft 3 in
1 m

4 ft 8 in
1,43 m

9 ft 9 in
3 m

center line

attack zone

post

left forward

center forward

right forward

59 ft
18 m

referee

19 ft 6 in
6 m

right back

left back

center back

attack line

volleyball

substitute

service area

server

29 ft 6 in
9 m

9 ft 9 in
3 m

players' rotation

flag

end line

linesman

volleyball

26 in - 27 in
65 cm - 67 cm

tennis

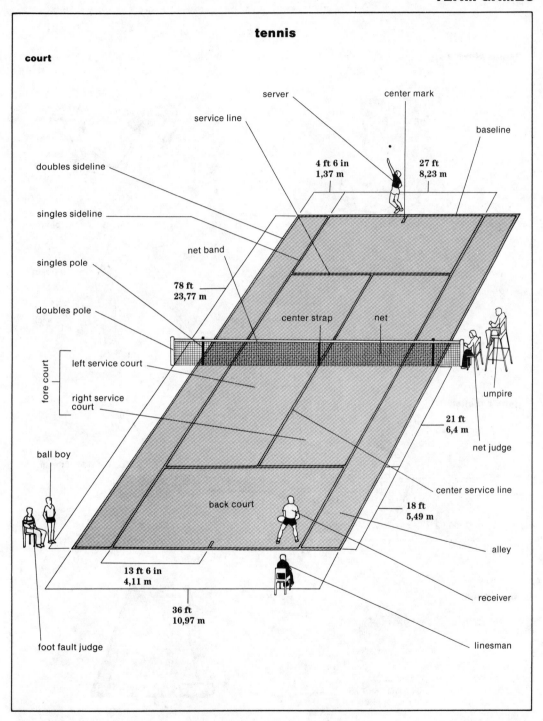

court

server

center mark

service line

baseline

4 ft 6 in
1,37 m

27 ft
8,23 m

doubles sideline

singles sideline

net band

singles pole

78 ft
23,77 m

doubles pole

center strap

net

fore court

left service court

right service
court

umpire

21 ft
6,4 m

net judge

ball boy

center service line

back court

18 ft
5,49 m

alley

13 ft 6 in
4,11 m

receiver

36 ft
10,97 m

linesman

foot fault judge

523

tennis

tennis players

headband

shirt

wristband

shorts

blouse

skirt

tennis shoe

sock

tennis racket

shoulder

throat

top

bevel

frame

flat side of the grip

stringing

butt

handle

head

shaft

tennis ball

press

63,5 mm - 66,7 mm
2½ in - 2⅝ in

handball

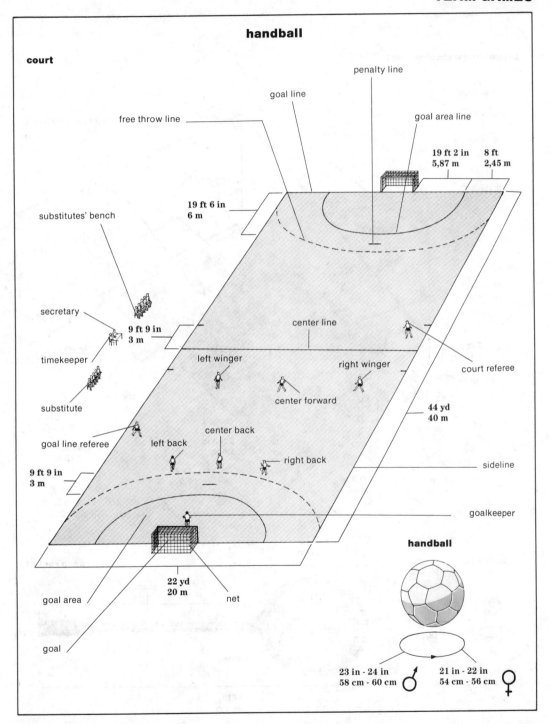

court

penalty line

goal line

goal area line

free throw line

19 ft 2 in
5,87 m

8 ft
2,45 m

19 ft 6 in
6 m

substitutes' bench

secretary

9 ft 9 in
3 m

center line

timekeeper

left winger

right winger

court referee

substitute

center forward

goal line referee

44 yd
40 m

center back

left back

right back

9 ft 9 in
3 m

sideline

goalkeeper

handball

22 yd
20 m

goal area

net

goal

23 in - 24 in
58 cm - 60 cm

21 in - 22 in
54 cm - 56 cm

squash

international singles court

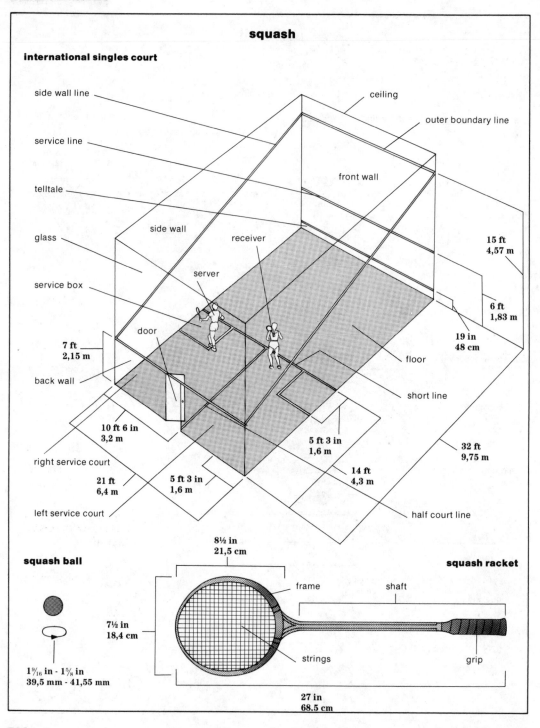

side wall line

service line

telltale

glass

service box

7 ft
2,15 m

back wall

10 ft 6 in
3,2 m

right service court

21 ft
6,4 m

left service court

door

side wall

server

receiver

ceiling

outer boundary line

front wall

15 ft
4,57 m

6 ft
1,83 m

19 in
48 cm

floor

short line

5 ft 3 in
1,6 m

14 ft
4,3 m

32 ft
9,75 m

5 ft 3 in
1,6 m

half court line

squash ball

1⁹⁄₁₆ in - 1⁵⁄₈ in
39,5 mm - 41,55 mm

7½ in
18,4 cm

8½ in
21,5 cm

squash racket

frame

shaft

strings

grip

7½ in
18,4 cm

27 in
68,5 cm

racquetball

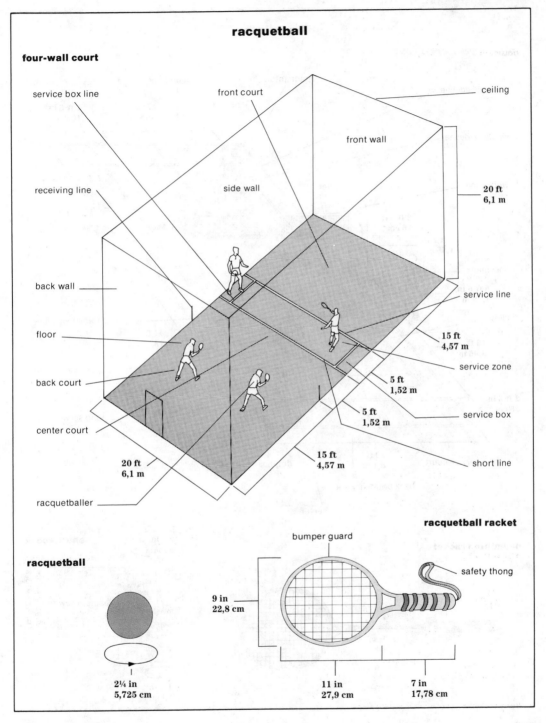

four-wall court

service box line

front court

ceiling

front wall

receiving line

side wall

20 ft
6,1 m

back wall

floor

service line

back court

15 ft
4,57 m

center court

service zone

5 ft
1,52 m

service box

5 ft
1,52 m

20 ft
6,1 m

15 ft
4,57 m

short line

racquetballer

racquetball racket

bumper guard

racquetball

safety thong

9 in
22,8 cm

2¼ in
5,725 cm

11 in
27,9 cm

7 in
17,78 cm

badminton

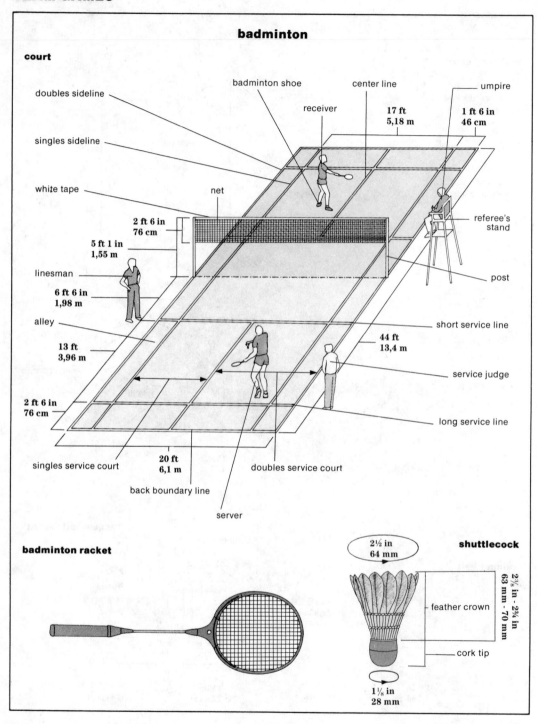

court

doubles sideline

badminton shoe

center line

umpire

receiver

17 ft
5,18 m

1 ft 6 in
46 cm

singles sideline

white tape

net

2 ft 6 in
76 cm

referee's
stand

5 ft 1 in
1,55 m

linesman

6 ft 6 in
1,98 m

post

alley

short service line

13 ft
3,96 m

44 ft
13,4 m

2 ft 6 in
76 cm

service judge

long service line

singles service court

20 ft
6,1 m

doubles service court

back boundary line

server

badminton racket

2½ in
64 mm

shuttlecock

2⅜ in - 2¾ in
63 mm - 70 mm

feather crown

cork tip

1⅛ in
28 mm

table tennis

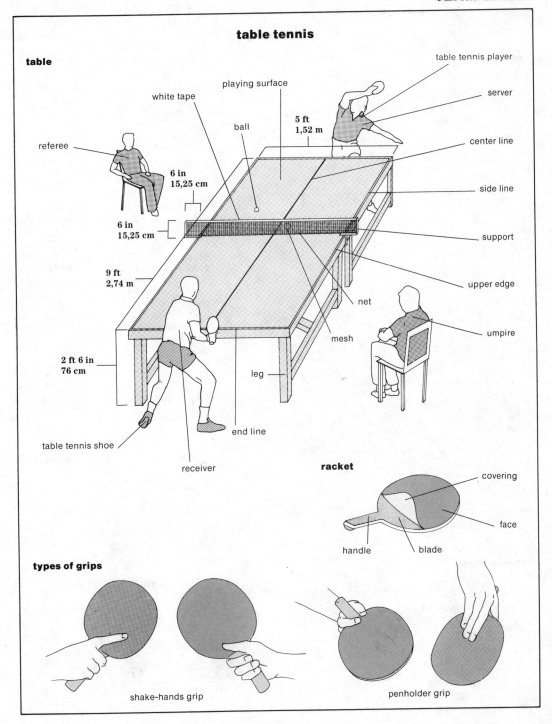

table

table tennis player

server

playing surface

white tape

center line

ball

5 ft
1,52 m

referee

side line

6 in
15,25 cm

support

6 in
15,25 cm

9 ft
2,74 m

upper edge

net

umpire

mesh

2 ft 6 in
76 cm

leg

table tennis shoe

end line

receiver

racket

covering

face

handle

blade

types of grips

shake-hands grip

penholder grip

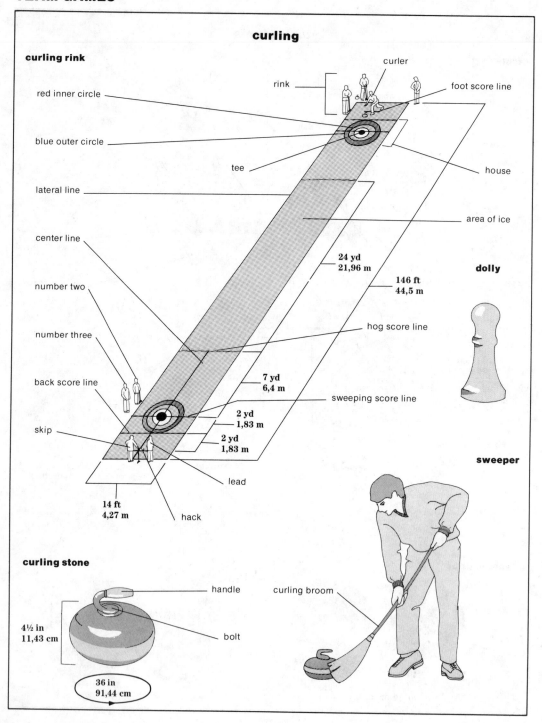

curling

curling rink

curler

rink

red inner circle

blue outer circle

tee

lateral line

center line

number two

number three

back score line

skip

foot score line

house

area of ice

24 yd
21,96 m

146 ft
44,5 m

dolly

hog score line

7 yd
6,4 m

sweeping score line

2 yd
1,83 m

2 yd
1,83 m

sweeper

lead

14 ft
4,27 m

hack

curling stone

handle

curling broom

4½ in
11,43 cm

bolt

36 in
91,44 cm

water polo

playing area

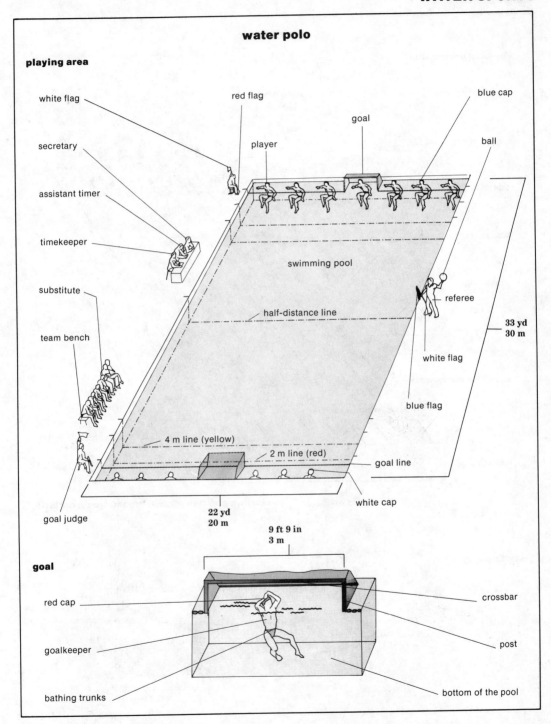

white flag

red flag

blue cap

goal

secretary

player

ball

assistant timer

timekeeper

swimming pool

substitute

half-distance line

33 yd
30 m

team bench

white flag

blue flag

4 m line (yellow)

2 m line (red)

goal line

white cap

goal judge

22 yd
20 m

referee

goal

9 ft 9 in
3 m

red cap

crossbar

goalkeeper

post

bottom of the pool

bathing trunks

swimming

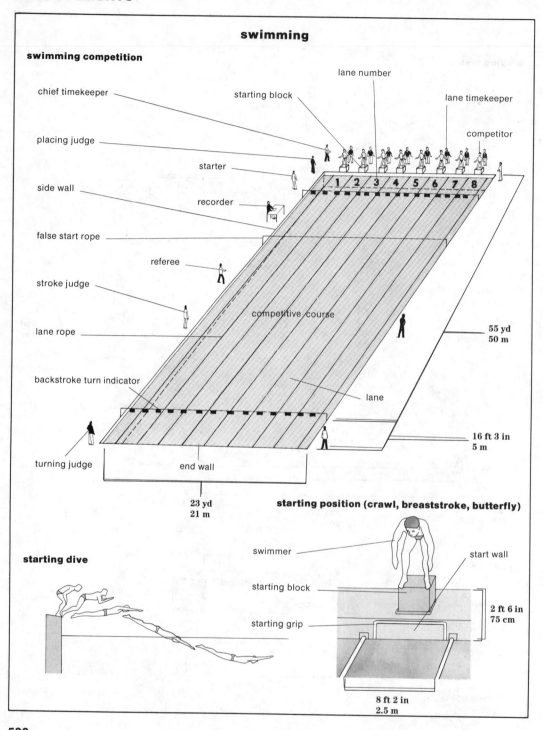

swimming competition

chief timekeeper

placing judge

starter

side wall

recorder

false start rope

referee

stroke judge

lane rope

backstroke turn indicator

turning judge

end wall

starting block

lane number

lane timekeeper

competitor

1 2 3 4 5 6 7 8

competitive course

lane

55 yd
50 m

16 ft 3 in
5 m

23 yd
21 m

starting position (crawl, breaststroke, butterfly)

swimmer

start wall

starting dive

starting block

starting grip

2 ft 6 in
75 cm

8 ft 2 in
2.5 m

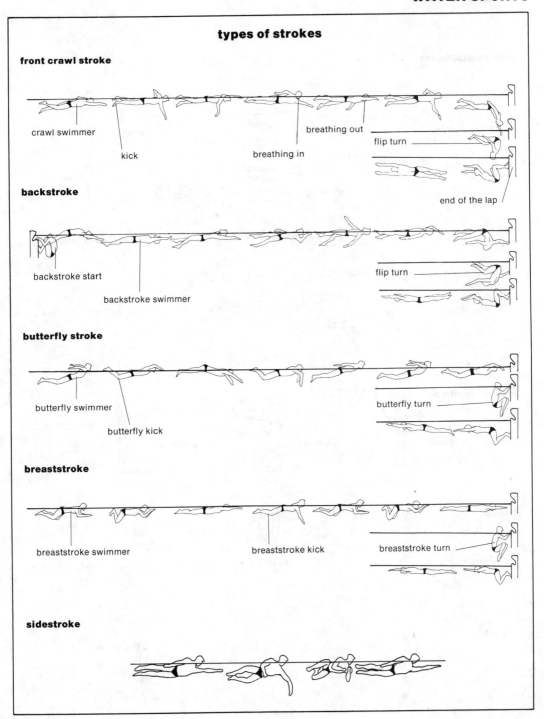

types of strokes

front crawl stroke

crawl swimmer

kick

breathing in

breathing out

flip turn

end of the lap

backstroke

backstroke start

backstroke swimmer

flip turn

butterfly stroke

butterfly swimmer

butterfly kick

butterfly turn

breaststroke

breaststroke swimmer

breaststroke kick

breaststroke turn

sidestroke

WATER SPORTS

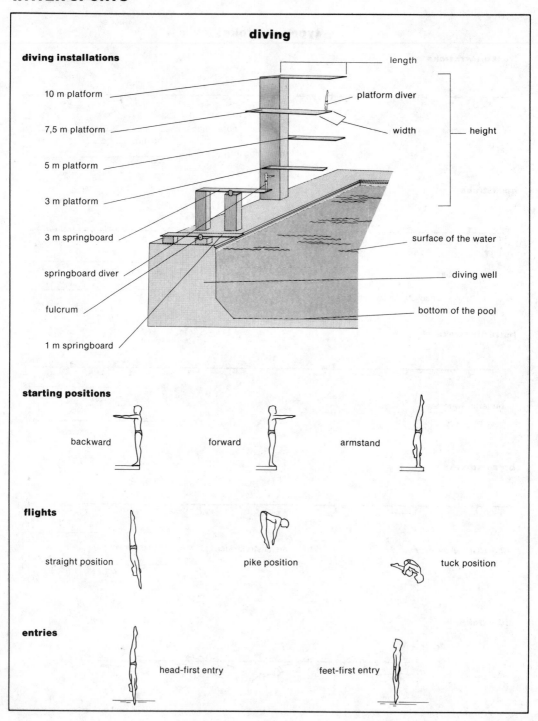

diving

diving installations

- 10 m platform
- 7,5 m platform
- 5 m platform
- 3 m platform
- 3 m springboard
- springboard diver
- fulcrum
- 1 m springboard

- length
- platform diver
- width
- height
- surface of the water
- diving well
- bottom of the pool

starting positions

backward

forward

armstand

flights

straight position

pike position

tuck position

entries

head-first entry

feet-first entry

groups of dives

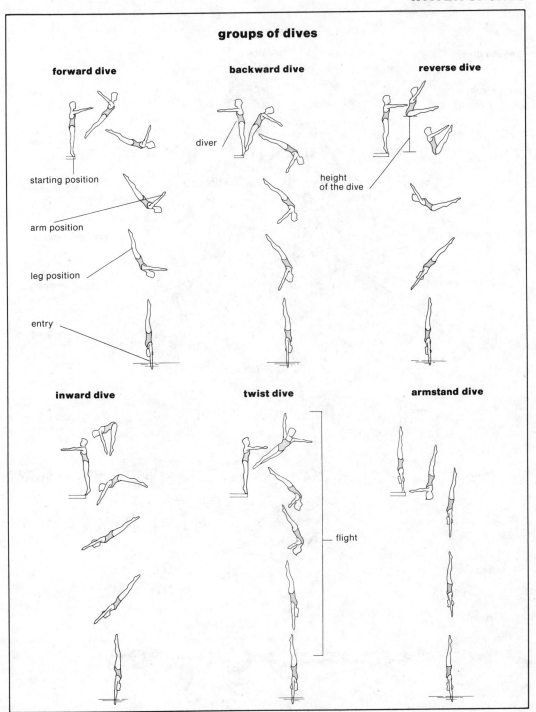

forward dive

starting position

arm position

leg position

entry

backward dive

diver

reverse dive

height
of the dive

inward dive

twist dive

flight

armstand dive

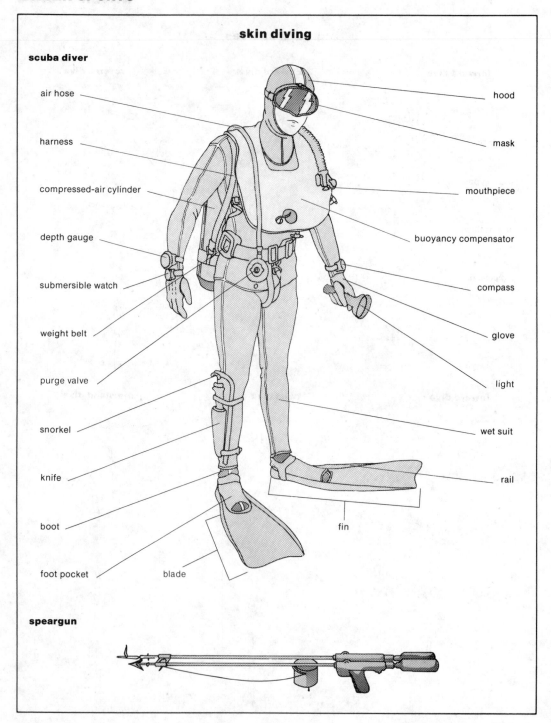

skin diving

scuba diver

- air hose
- harness
- compressed-air cylinder
- depth gauge
- submersible watch
- weight belt
- purge valve
- snorkel
- knife
- boot
- foot pocket
- blade

- hood
- mask
- mouthpiece
- buoyancy compensator
- compass
- glove
- light
- wet suit
- rail
- fin

speargun

sailboard

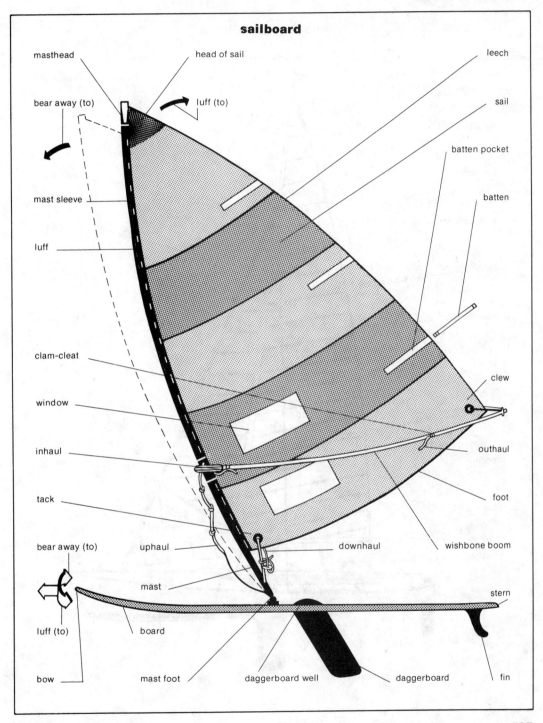

masthead

head of sail

leech

bear away (to)

luff (to)

sail

batten pocket

mast sleeve

batten

luff

clam-cleat

clew

window

inhaul

outhaul

tack

foot

bear away (to)

uphaul

downhaul

wishbone boom

luff (to)

mast

stern

board

bow

mast foot

daggerboard well

daggerboard

fin

one-design sailboat

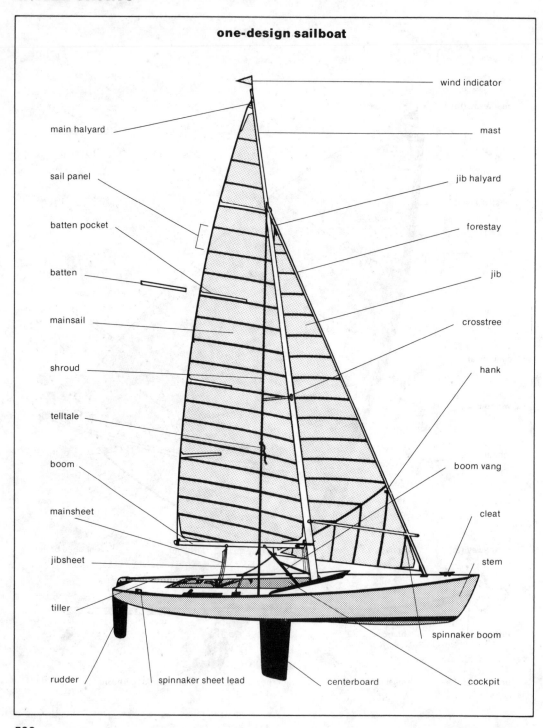

wind indicator

main halyard

mast

sail panel

jib halyard

batten pocket

forestay

batten

jib

mainsail

crosstree

shroud

hank

telltale

boom

boom vang

mainsheet

cleat

jibsheet

stem

tiller

spinnaker boom

rudder

spinnaker sheet lead

centerboard

cockpit

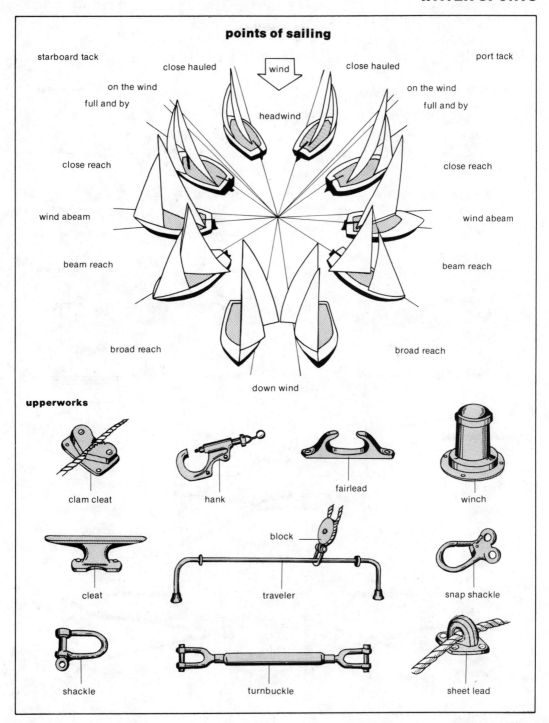

points of sailing

starboard tack

close hauled

wind

close hauled

port tack

on the wind

on the wind

full and by

full and by

headwind

close reach

close reach

wind abeam

wind abeam

beam reach

beam reach

broad reach

broad reach

down wind

upperworks

clam cleat

hank

fairlead

winch

block

cleat

traveler

snap shackle

shackle

turnbuckle

sheet lead

water skiing

types of skis

twin skis

mono-ski

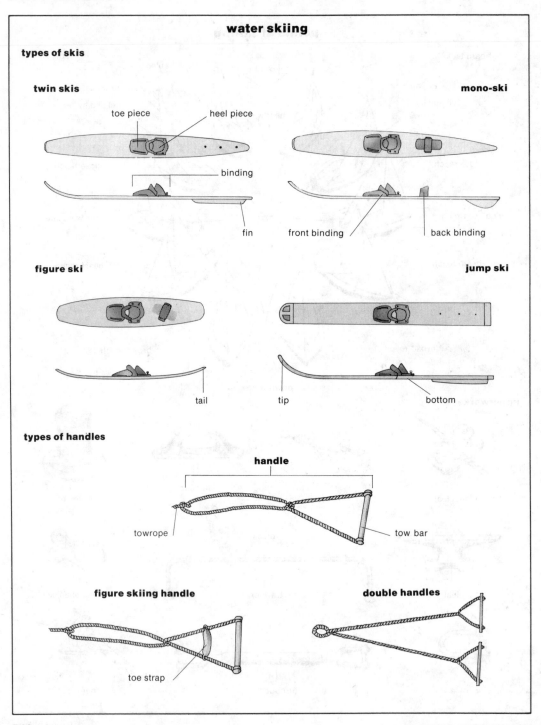

toe piece

heel piece

binding

fin

front binding

back binding

figure ski

jump ski

tail

tip

bottom

types of handles

handle

towrope

tow bar

figure skiing handle

double handles

toe strap

parachuting

parachute

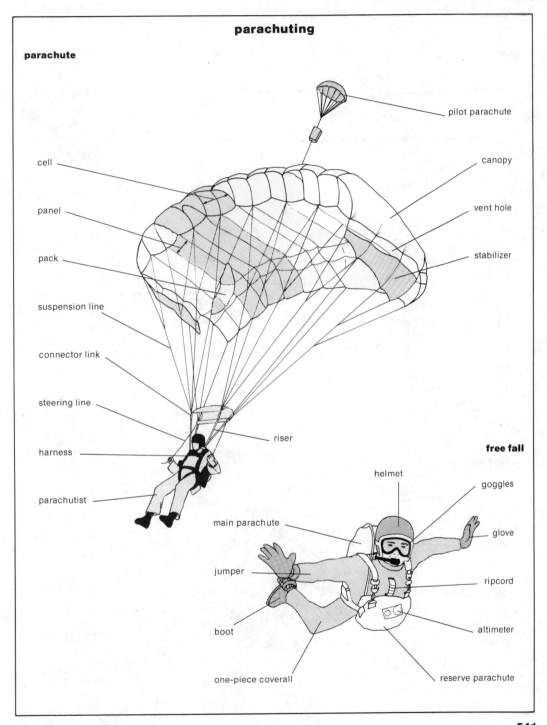

- pilot parachute
- cell
- canopy
- panel
- vent hole
- pack
- stabilizer
- suspension line
- connector link
- steering line
- riser
- harness
- parachutist

free fall

- helmet
- goggles
- main parachute
- glove
- jumper
- ripcord
- boot
- altimeter
- one-piece coverall
- reserve parachute

gliding

glider

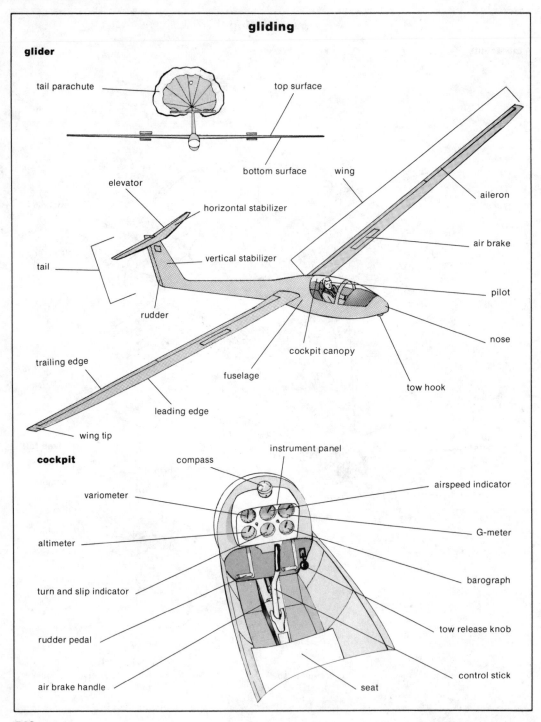

tail parachute

top surface

bottom surface

wing

aileron

air brake

elevator

horizontal stabilizer

vertical stabilizer

pilot

tail

nose

rudder

trailing edge

cockpit canopy

fuselage

tow hook

leading edge

wing tip

cockpit

instrument panel

compass

airspeed indicator

variometer

G-meter

altimeter

barograph

turn and slip indicator

rudder pedal

tow release knob

air brake handle

seat

control stick

hang gliding

hang glider

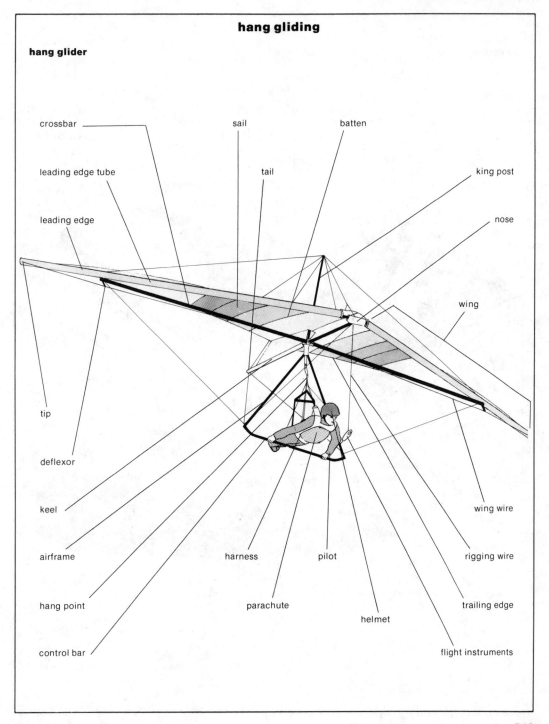

crossbar

sail

batten

leading edge tube

tail

king post

leading edge

nose

wing

tip

deflexor

keel

airframe

harness

pilot

wing wire

rigging wire

hang point

parachute

trailing edge

helmet

control bar

flight instruments

skiing

ski resort

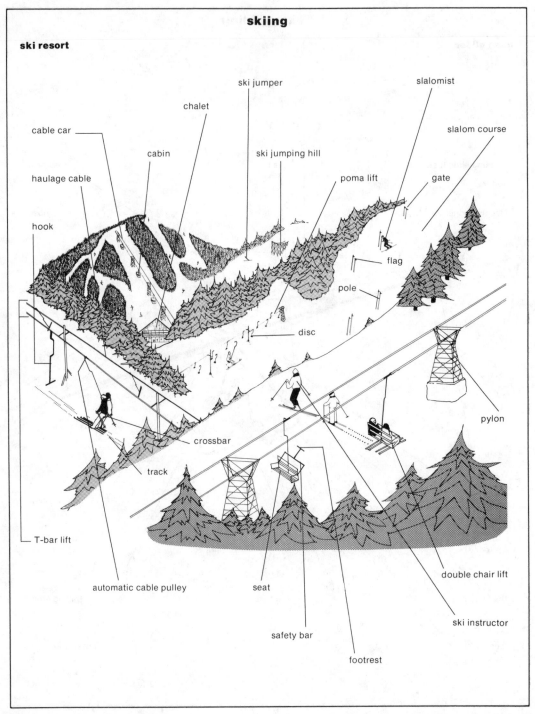

ski jumper

slalomist

chalet

slalom course

cable car

cabin

ski jumping hill

haulage cable

poma lift

gate

hook

flag

pole

disc

pylon

crossbar

track

T-bar lift

automatic cable pulley

seat

double chair lift

ski instructor

safety bar

footrest

alpine skiing

alpine skier

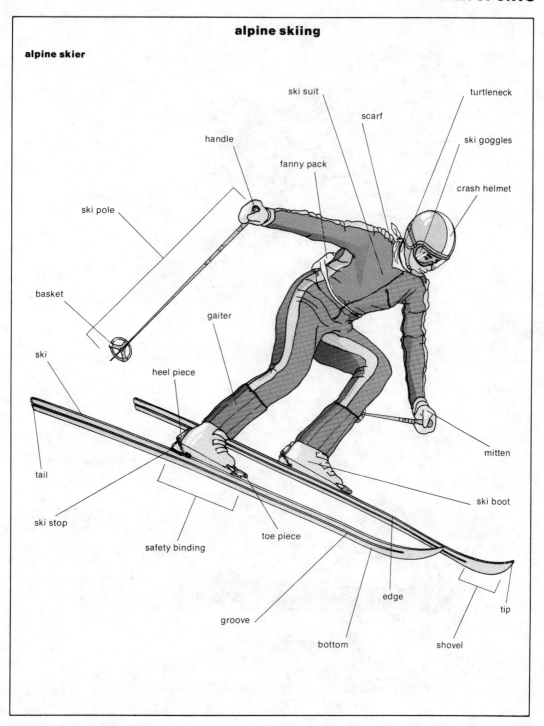

ski suit

turtleneck

scarf

handle

ski goggles

fanny pack

crash helmet

ski pole

basket

gaiter

ski

heel piece

mitten

tail

ski boot

ski stop

toe piece

safety binding

edge

groove

tip

bottom

shovel

alpine skiing

ski boot

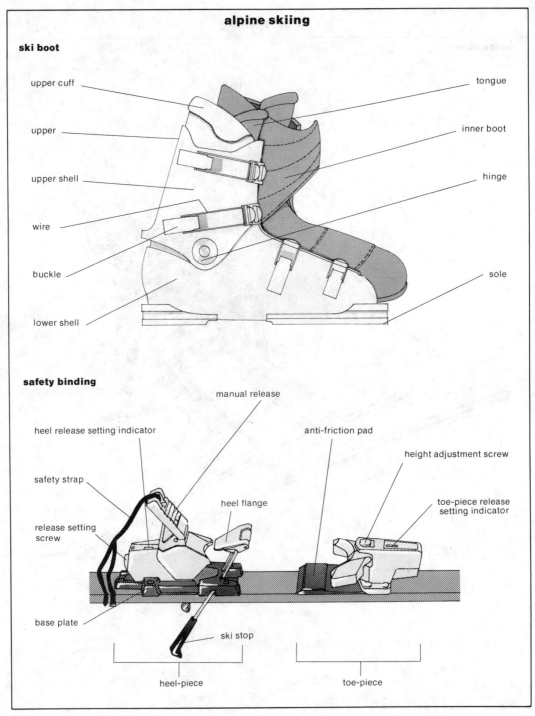

upper cuff

tongue

upper

inner boot

upper shell

hinge

wire

buckle

lower shell

sole

safety binding

manual release

heel release setting indicator

anti-friction pad

height adjustment screw

safety strap

heel flange

toe-piece release setting indicator

release setting screw

base plate

ski stop

heel-piece

toe-piece

cross-country skiing

cross-country skier

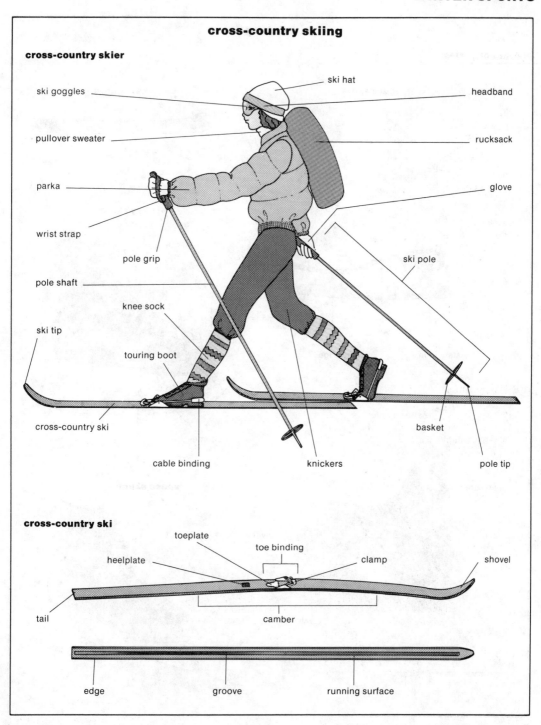

ski hat

ski goggles

headband

pullover sweater

rucksack

parka

glove

wrist strap

pole grip

ski pole

pole shaft

knee sock

ski tip

touring boot

cross-country ski

basket

cable binding

knickers

pole tip

cross-country ski

toeplate

toe binding

heelplate

clamp

shovel

tail

camber

edge

groove

running surface

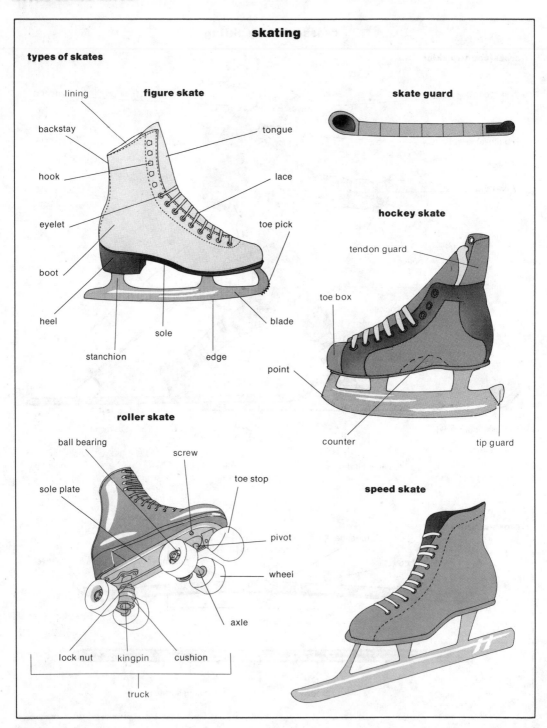

skating

types of skates

figure skate

lining

backstay

hook

eyelet

boot

heel

tongue

lace

toe pick

blade

sole

edge

stanchion

skate guard

hockey skate

tendon guard

toe box

point

counter

tip guard

speed skate

roller skate

ball bearing

screw

toe stop

sole plate

pivot

wheel

axle

lock nut   kingpin   cushion

truck

snowshoes

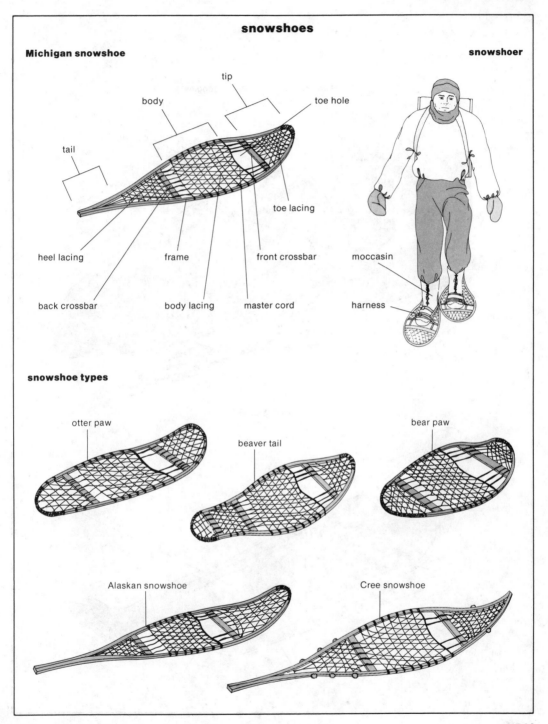

Michigan snowshoe

snowshoer

tip

body

toe hole

tail

toe lacing

heel lacing

frame

front crossbar

moccasin

back crossbar

body lacing

master cord

harness

snowshoe types

otter paw

beaver tail

bear paw

Alaskan snowshoe

Cree snowshoe

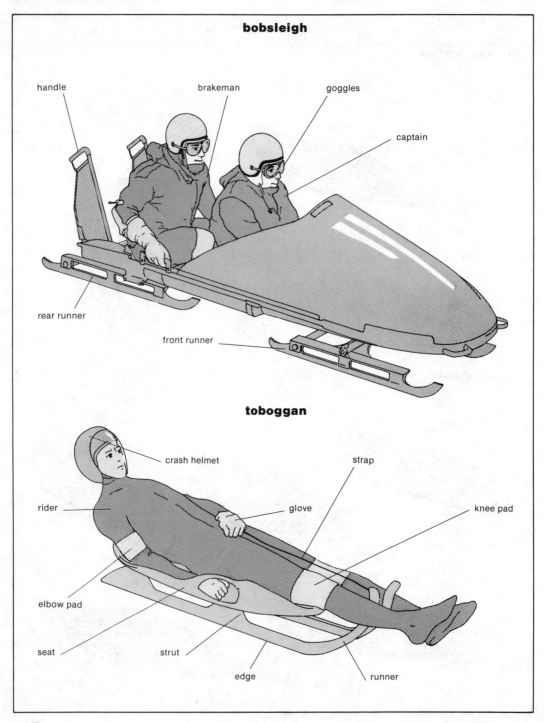

bobsleigh

handle

brakeman

goggles

captain

rear runner

front runner

toboggan

crash helmet

strap

rider

glove

knee pad

elbow pad

seat

strut

edge

runner

riding

dress and equipment

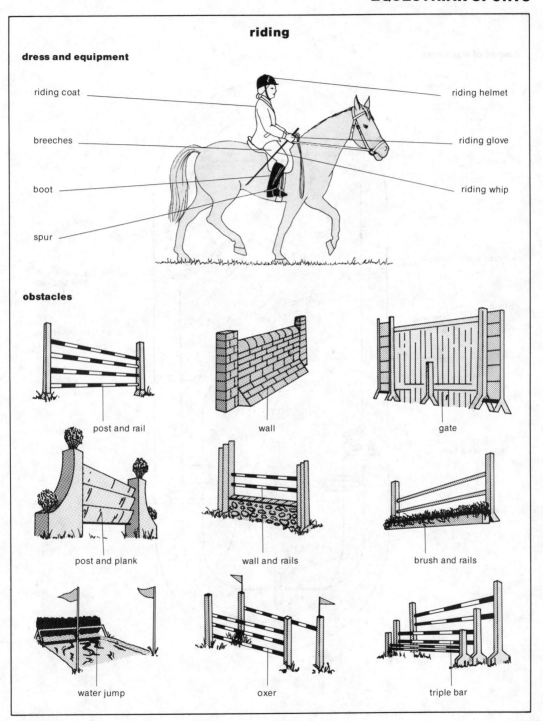

riding coat

breeches

boot

spur

riding helmet

riding glove

riding whip

obstacles

post and rail

wall

gate

post and plank

wall and rails

brush and rails

water jump

oxer

triple bar

riding

course of obstacles

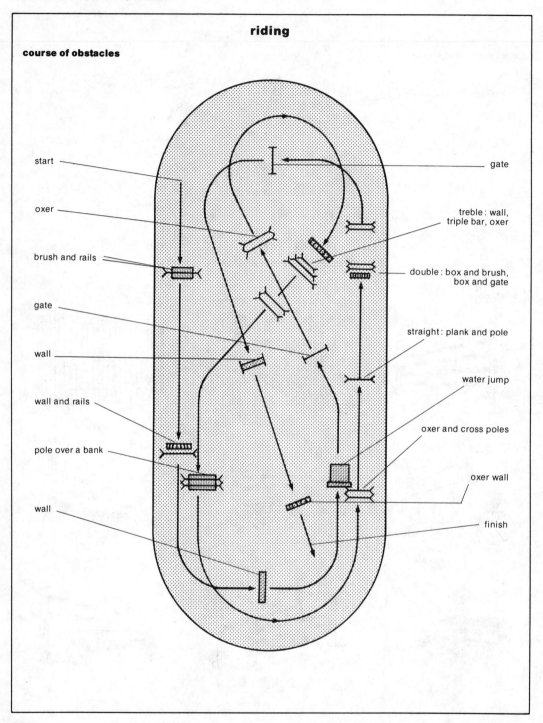

start

oxer

brush and rails

gate

wall

wall and rails

pole over a bank

wall

gate

treble : wall, triple bar, oxer

double : box and brush, box and gate

straight : plank and pole

water jump

oxer and cross poles

oxer wall

finish

riding

bridle

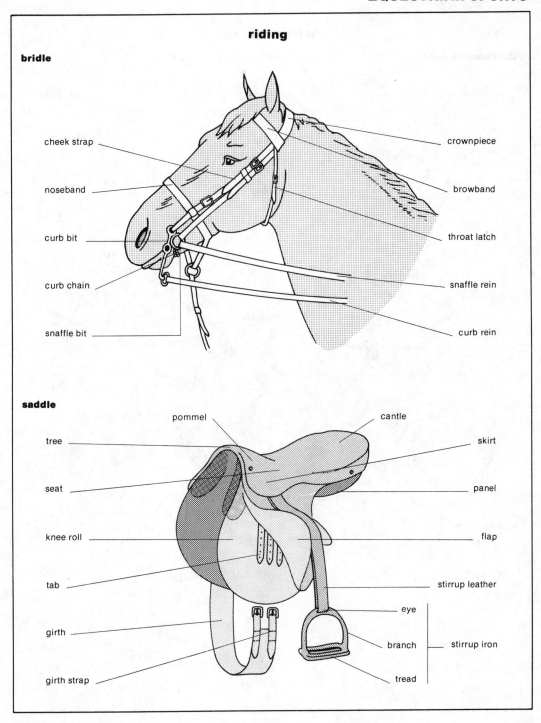

cheek strap

noseband

curb bit

curb chain

snaffle bit

crownpiece

browband

throat latch

snaffle rein

curb rein

saddle

pommel

cantle

tree

seat

knee roll

tab

girth

girth strap

skirt

panel

flap

stirrup leather

eye

branch

tread

stirrup iron

harness racing

standardbred pacer

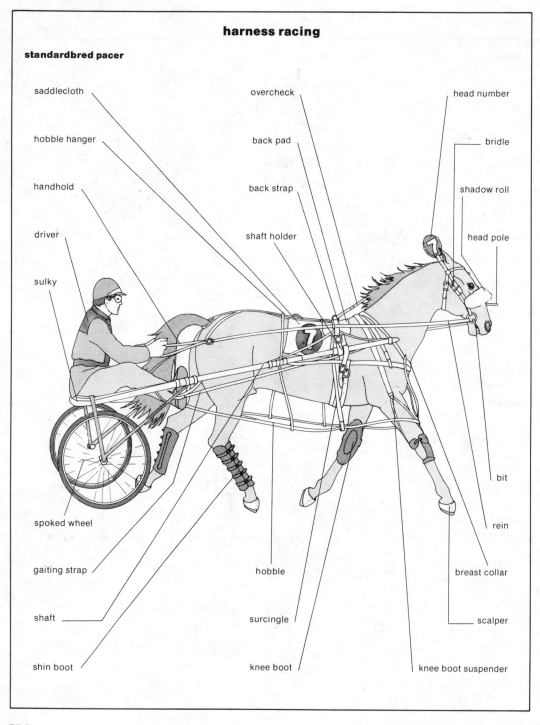

saddlecloth

hobble hanger

handhold

driver

sulky

spoked wheel

gaiting strap

shaft

shin boot

overcheck

back pad

back strap

shaft holder

hobble

surcingle

knee boot

head number

bridle

shadow roll

head pole

bit

rein

breast collar

scalper

knee boot suspender

harness racing

racing programm

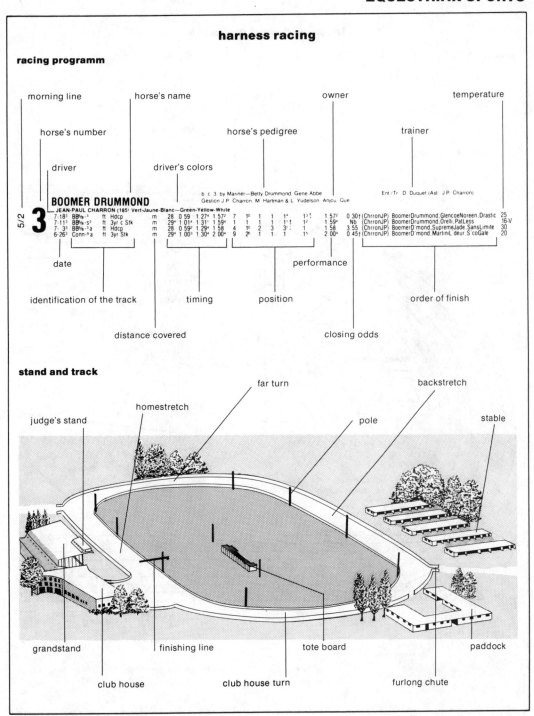

morning line

horse's name

owner

temperature

horse's number

trainer

driver

driver's colors

horse's pedigree

b. c. 3. by Mariner—Betty Drummond. Gene Abbe
Gestion J.P. Charron, M. Hartman & L. Yudelson. Anjou. Que.

Ent./Tr. D. Duquet (Ast. J.P. Charron)

BOOMER DRUMMOND
JEAN-PAUL CHARRON (185) Vert-Jaune-Blanc—Green-Yellow-White

5/2 **3**

7-18³	BB⅝-³	ft	Hdcp	m	28	0.59	1.27⁴	1.57²	7	1⁰	1	1	1⁴	1³¹	1.57²	0.30†	(ChrronJP)	BoomerDrummond,GlencoeNoreen,Drastic	25
7-11³	BB⅝-s³	ft	3yr c Stk	m	29⁴	1.01⁴	1.31¹	1.59⁴	1	1	1	1¹	1¹	1²	1.59⁴	Nb	(ChrronJP)	BoomerDrummond,Orelli,PatLess	16-V
7- 3³	BB⅝-³ a	ft	Hdcp	m	28	0.59²	1.29⁴	1.58	4	1⁰	2	3	3¹	1	1.58	3.55	(ChrronJP)	BoomerD'mond,SupremeJade,SansLimite	30
6-26³	Conn-³ a	ft	3yr Stk	m	29⁴	1.00³	1.30⁴	2.00⁴	9	2⁰	1	1	1⁵		2.00⁴	0.45†	(ChrronJP)	BoomerD'mond,MartiniL.deur,S'coGale	20

date

performance

identification of the track

timing

position

order of finish

distance covered

closing odds

stand and track

far turn

backstretch

homestretch

pole

stable

judge's stand

grandstand

club house

finishing line

club house turn

tote board

furlong chute

paddock

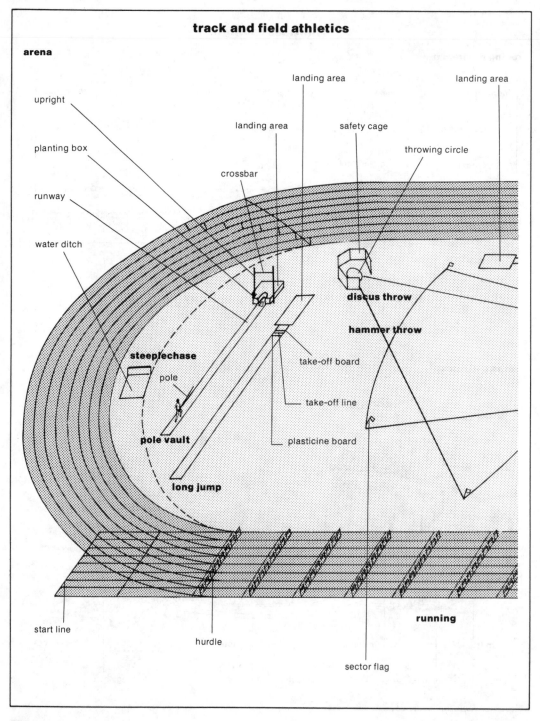

track and field athletics

arena

upright

planting box

runway

water ditch

landing area

landing area

landing area

crossbar

safety cage

throwing circle

discus throw

hammer throw

steeplechase

pole

take-off board

take-off line

pole vault

plasticine board

long jump

start line

hurdle

running

sector flag

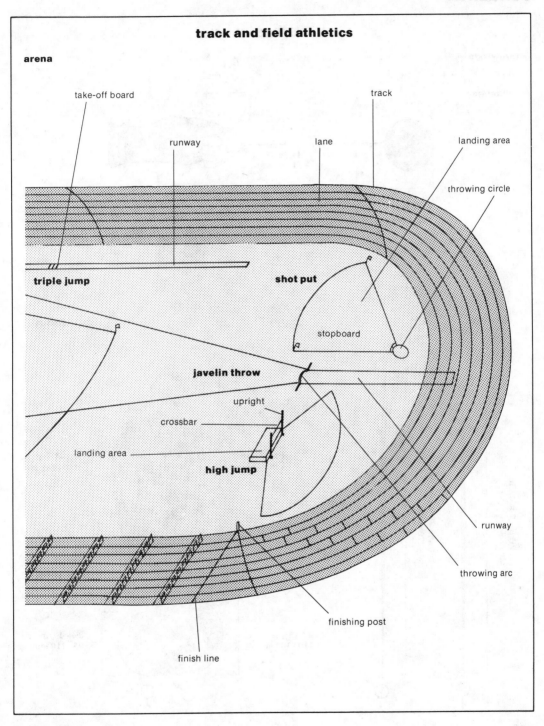

track and field athletics

arena

take-off board

track

runway

lane

landing area

throwing circle

triple jump

shot put

stopboard

javelin throw

upright

crossbar

landing area

high jump

runway

throwing arc

finishing post

finish line

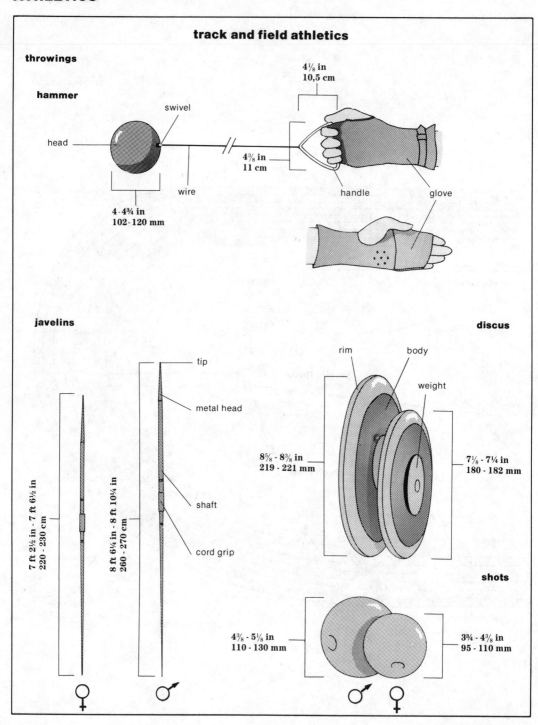

track and field athletics

throwings

hammer

head
swivel
wire
4 - 4¾ in
102 - 120 mm

4⅛ in
10,5 cm
4⅜ in
11 cm
handle
glove

javelins

tip
metal head
shaft
cord grip

7 ft 2½ in - 7 ft 6½ in
220 - 230 cm

8 ft 6¼ in - 8 ft 10¼ in
260 - 270 cm

discus

rim
body
weight

8⅝ - 8⅜ in
219 - 221 mm

7⅛ - 7¼ in
180 - 182 mm

shots

4⅜ - 5⅛ in
110 - 130 mm

3¾ - 4⅜ in
95 - 110 mm

gymnastics

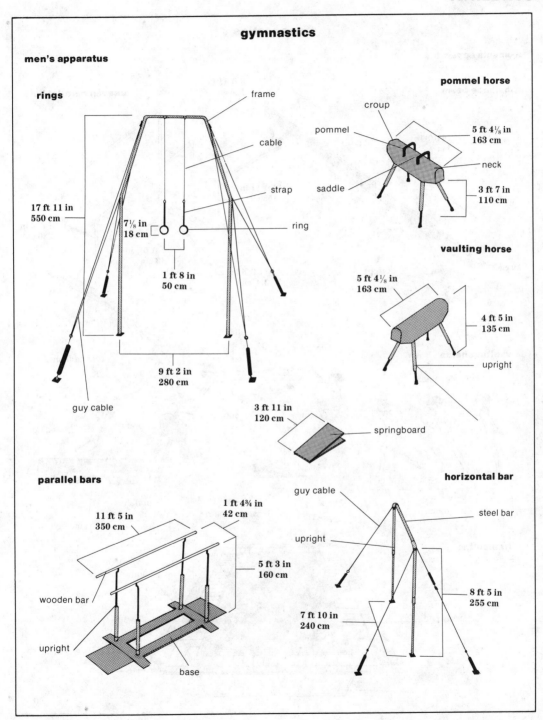

men's apparatus

rings

frame

cable

strap

17 ft 11 in
550 cm

7⅛ in
18 cm

ring

1 ft 8 in
50 cm

9 ft 2 in
280 cm

guy cable

pommel horse

croup

pommel

5 ft 4⅛ in
163 cm

neck

saddle

3 ft 7 in
110 cm

vaulting horse

5 ft 4⅛ in
163 cm

4 ft 5 in
135 cm

upright

3 ft 11 in
120 cm

springboard

parallel bars

1 ft 4¾ in
42 cm

11 ft 5 in
350 cm

5 ft 3 in
160 cm

wooden bar

upright

base

horizontal bar

guy cable

steel bar

upright

8 ft 5 in
255 cm

7 ft 10 in
240 cm

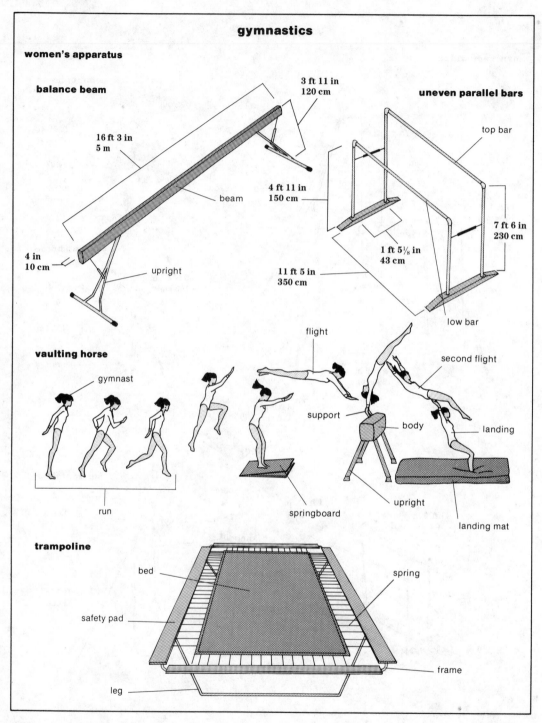

gymnastics

women's apparatus

balance beam

3 ft 11 in
120 cm

16 ft 3 in
5 m

beam

4 in
10 cm

upright

uneven parallel bars

top bar

4 ft 11 in
150 cm

7 ft 6 in
230 cm

1 ft 5⅛ in
43 cm

11 ft 5 in
350 cm

low bar

vaulting horse

gymnast

flight

second flight

support

body

landing

run

springboard

upright

landing mat

trampoline

bed

spring

safety pad

frame

leg

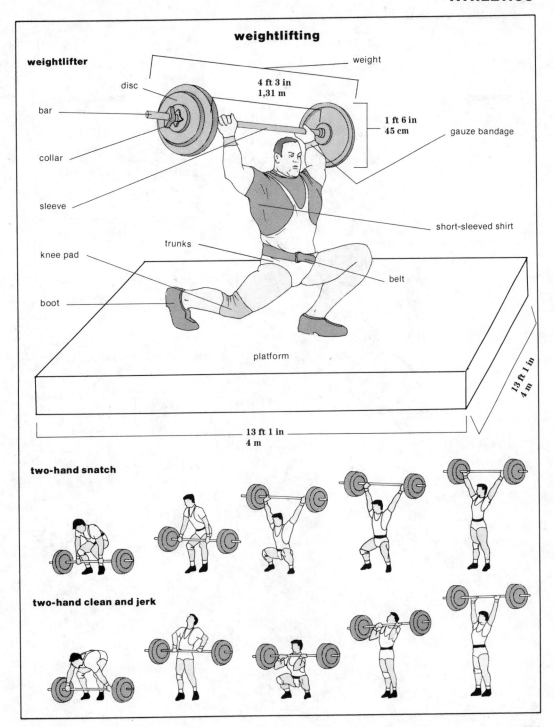

weightlifting

weightlifter

weight

disc

4 ft 3 in
1,31 m

bar

1 ft 6 in
45 cm

gauze bandage

collar

sleeve

short-sleeved shirt

trunks

knee pad

belt

boot

platform

13 ft 1 in
4 m

13 ft 1 in
4 m

two-hand snatch

two-hand clean and jerk

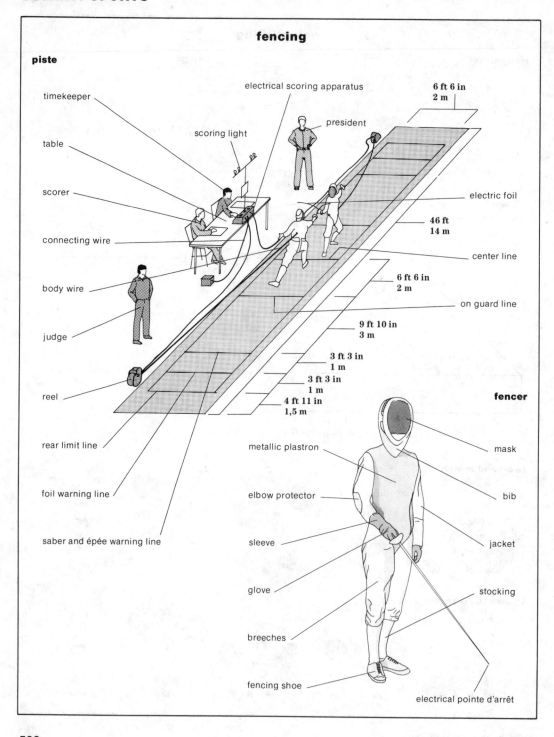

fencing

piste

timekeeper

electrical scoring apparatus

scoring light

president

6 ft 6 in
2 m

table

scorer

electric foil

46 ft
14 m

connecting wire

center line

body wire

6 ft 6 in
2 m

on guard line

judge

9 ft 10 in
3 m

3 ft 3 in
1 m

3 ft 3 in
1 m

4 ft 11 in
1,5 m

reel

fencer

rear limit line

metallic plastron

mask

foil warning line

elbow protector

bib

saber and épée warning line

jacket

sleeve

glove

stocking

breeches

fencing shoe

electrical pointe d'arrêt

fencing

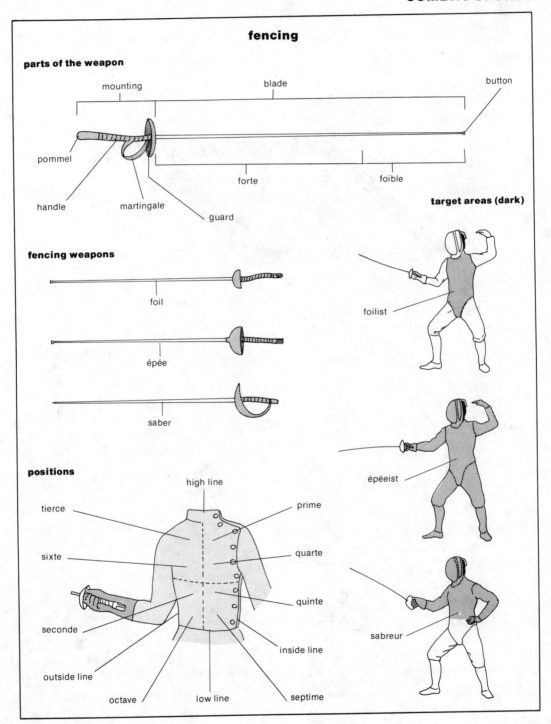

parts of the weapon

mounting — blade — button

pommel — handle — martingale — guard

forte — foible

fencing weapons

foil

épée

saber

positions

high line — tierce — prime

sixte — quarte

seconde — quinte

inside line

outside line

octave — low line — septime

target areas (dark)

foilist

épéeist

sabreur

COMBAT SPORTS

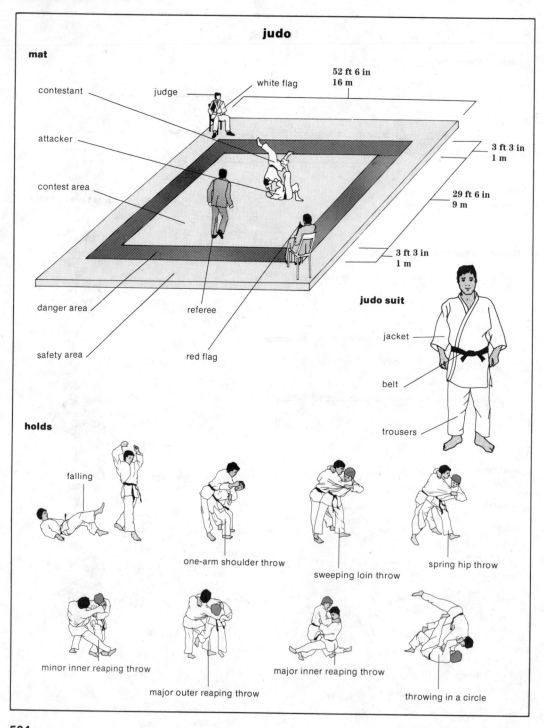

judo

mat

contestant

judge — white flag

52 ft 6 in
16 m

attacker

3 ft 3 in
1 m

contest area

29 ft 6 in
9 m

3 ft 3 in
1 m

danger area

referee

judo suit

jacket

belt

safety area

red flag

trousers

holds

falling

one-arm shoulder throw

sweeping loin throw

spring hip throw

minor inner reaping throw

major outer reaping throw

major inner reaping throw

throwing in a circle

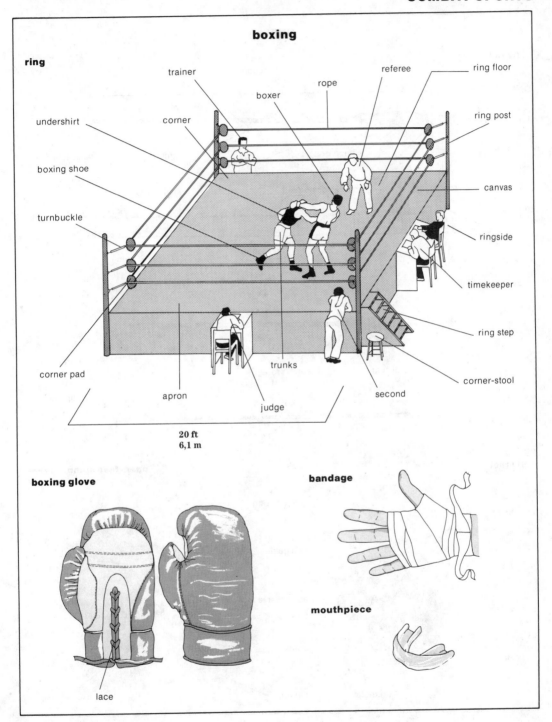

boxing

ring

trainer · referee · ring floor · rope · boxer · ring post · corner · undershirt · boxing shoe · canvas · turnbuckle · ringside · timekeeper · ring step · corner pad · apron · judge · trunks · second · corner-stool

20 ft
6,1 m

boxing glove

lace

bandage

mouthpiece

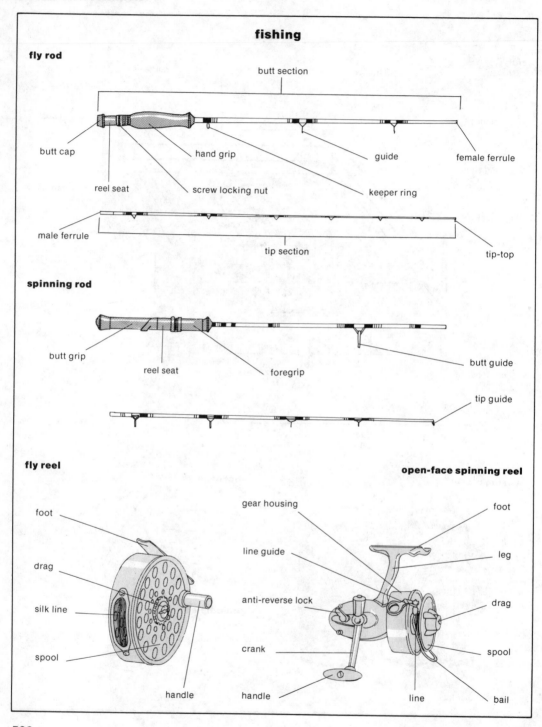

fishing

fly rod

butt section

butt cap

hand grip

guide

female ferrule

reel seat

screw locking nut

keeper ring

male ferrule

tip section

tip-top

spinning rod

butt grip

reel seat

foregrip

butt guide

tip guide

fly reel

open-face spinning reel

foot

gear housing

foot

drag

line guide

leg

silk line

anti-reverse lock

drag

spool

crank

spool

handle

handle

line

bail

566

fishing

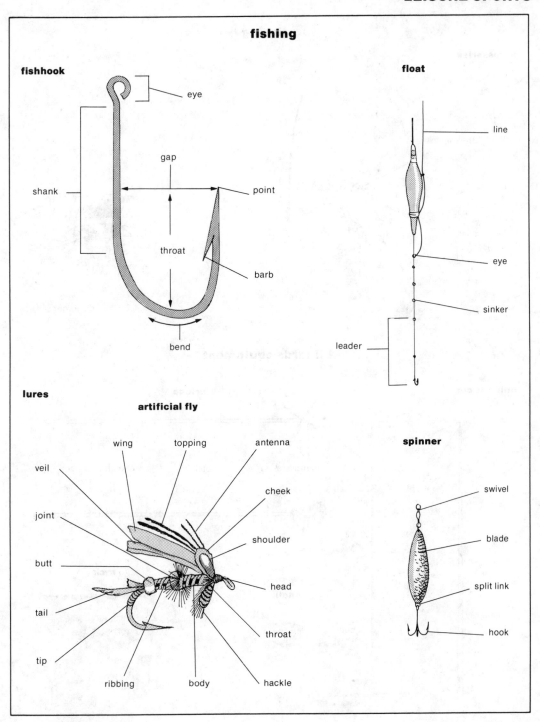

fishhook

eye

gap

shank

point

throat

barb

bend

float

line

eye

sinker

leader

lures

artificial fly

wing

topping

antenna

veil

cheek

joint

shoulder

butt

head

tail

throat

tip

ribbing

body

hackle

spinner

swivel

blade

split link

hook

LEISURE SPORTS

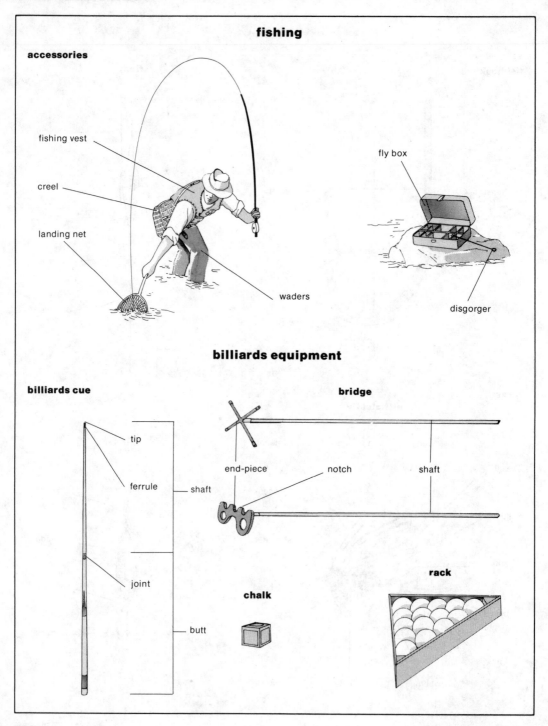

fishing

accessories

fishing vest

creel

landing net

waders

fly box

disgorger

billiards equipment

billiards cue

tip

ferrule

shaft

joint

butt

bridge

end-piece

notch

shaft

shaft

chalk

rack

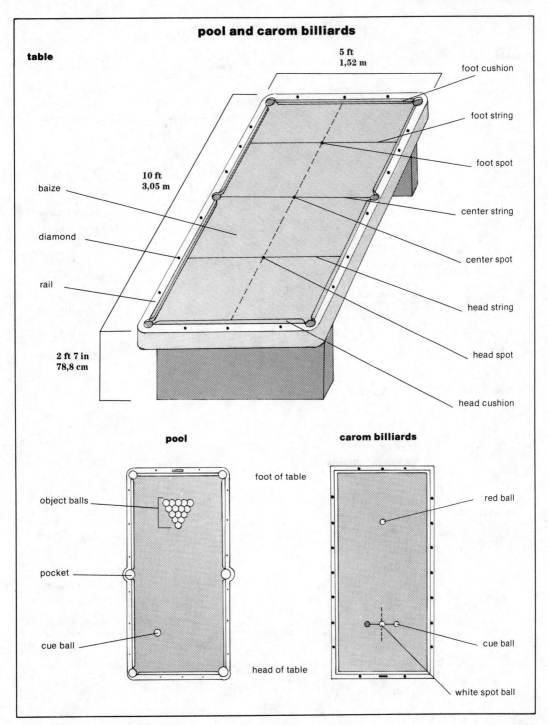

pool and carom billiards

table

5 ft
1,52 m

foot cushion

foot string

foot spot

10 ft
3,05 m

baize

center string

diamond

center spot

rail

head string

head spot

2 ft 7 in
78,8 cm

head cushion

pool

object balls

foot of table

pocket

cue ball

head of table

carom billiards

red ball

cue ball

white spot ball

English billiards and snooker

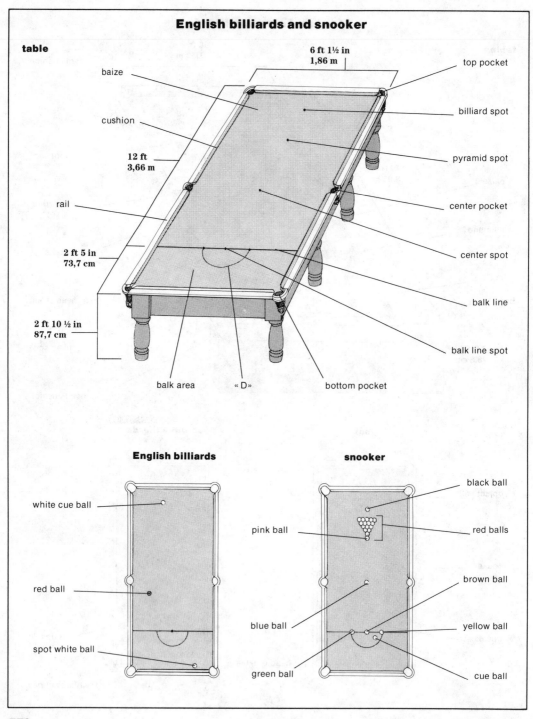

table

baize

cushion

6 ft 1½ in
1,86 m

top pocket

billiard spot

12 ft
3,66 m

pyramid spot

rail

center pocket

2 ft 5 in
73,7 cm

center spot

balk line

2 ft 10 ½ in
87,7 cm

balk line spot

balk area

« D »

bottom pocket

English billiards

white cue ball

red ball

spot white ball

snooker

black ball

pink ball

red balls

brown ball

blue ball

yellow ball

green ball

cue ball

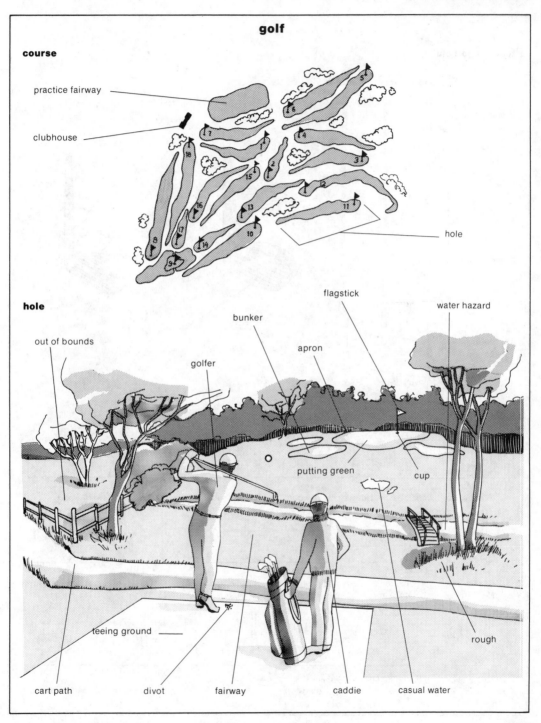

golf

course

practice fairway

clubhouse

hole

hole

flagstick

water hazard

bunker

apron

out of bounds

golfer

putting green

cup

teeing ground

rough

cart path

divot

fairway

caddie

casual water

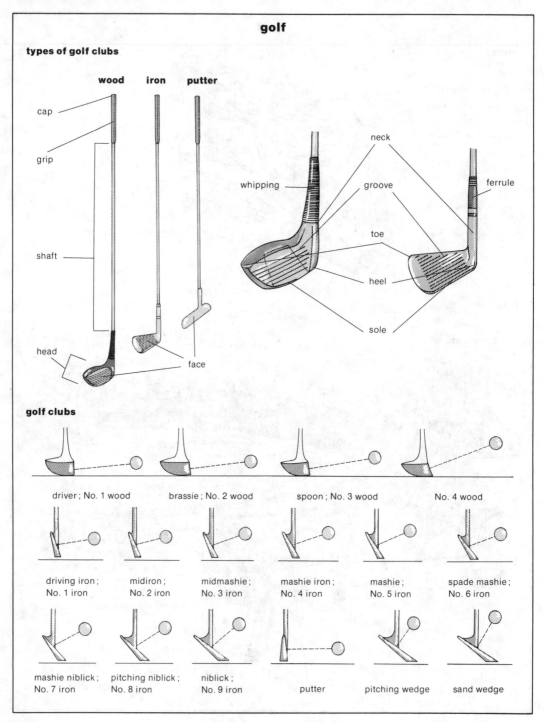

golf

types of golf clubs

wood   iron   putter

cap

grip

whipping

neck

groove

ferrule

toe

shaft

heel

sole

head

face

golf clubs

driver ; No. 1 wood   brassie ; No. 2 wood   spoon ; No. 3 wood   No. 4 wood

driving iron ;
No. 1 iron

midiron ;
No. 2 iron

midmashie ;
No. 3 iron

mashie iron ;
No. 4 iron

mashie ;
No. 5 iron

spade mashie ;
No. 6 iron

mashie niblick ;
No. 7 iron

pitching niblick ;
No. 8 iron

niblick ;
No. 9 iron

putter

pitching wedge

sand wedge

golf

golf bag

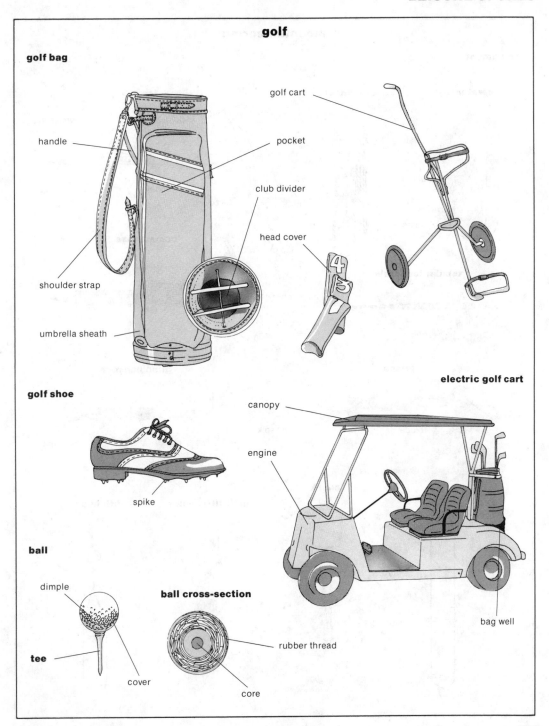

golf cart

handle

pocket

club divider

head cover

shoulder strap

umbrella sheath

electric golf cart

golf shoe

canopy

engine

spike

ball

dimple

ball cross-section

tee

cover

core

rubber thread

bag well

mountaineering

equipment

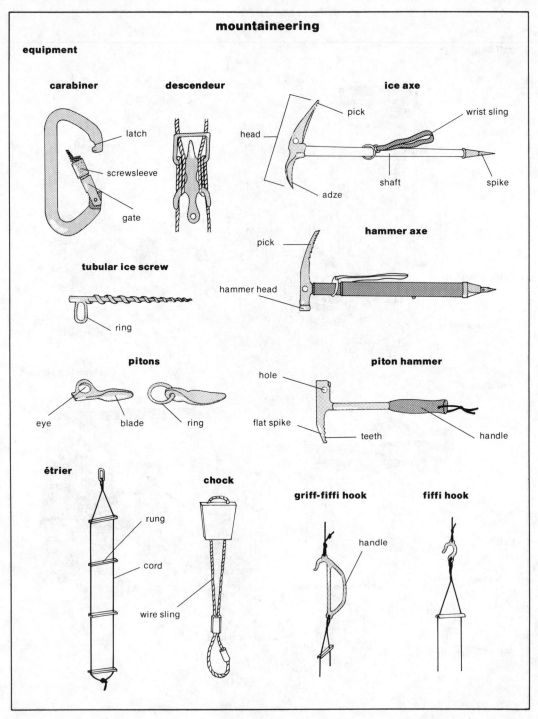

carabiner

latch

screwsleeve

gate

descendeur

ice axe

pick

head

adze

wrist sling

shaft

spike

hammer axe

pick

hammer head

tubular ice screw

ring

pitons

eye

blade

ring

piton hammer

hole

flat spike

teeth

handle

étrier

rung

cord

wire sling

chock

griff-fiffi hook

handle

fiffi hook

mountaineering

mountaineer

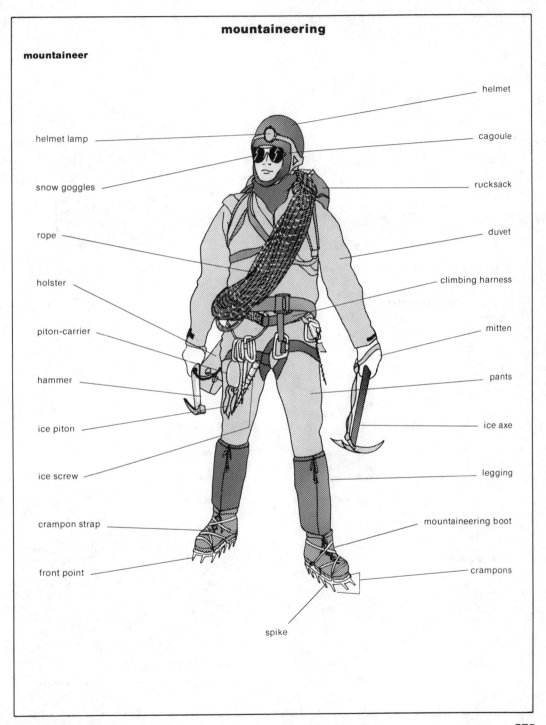

helmet

helmet lamp

cagoule

snow goggles

rucksack

rope

duvet

holster

climbing harness

piton-carrier

mitten

hammer

pants

ice piton

ice axe

ice screw

legging

crampon strap

mountaineering boot

front point

crampons

spike

LEISURE SPORTS

bowling

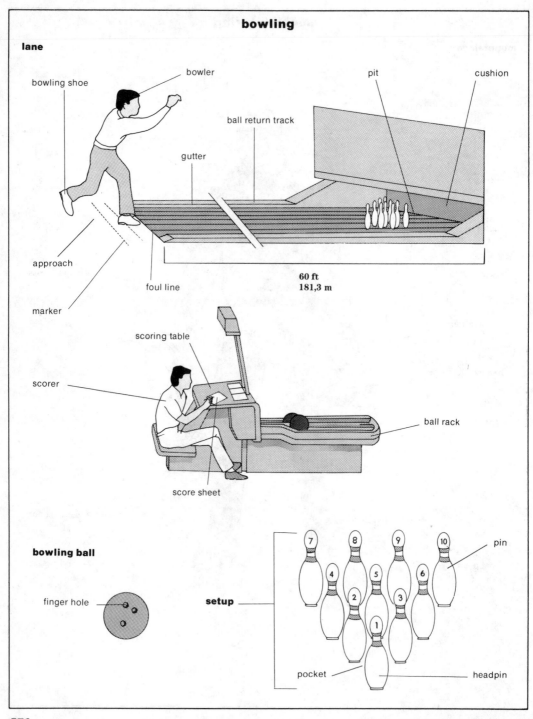

lane

bowler

pit

cushion

bowling shoe

ball return track

gutter

approach

foul line

marker

60 ft
181,3 m

scoring table

scorer

ball rack

score sheet

bowling ball

finger hole

setup

7

8

9

10

pin

4

5

6

2

3

1

pocket

headpin

chess

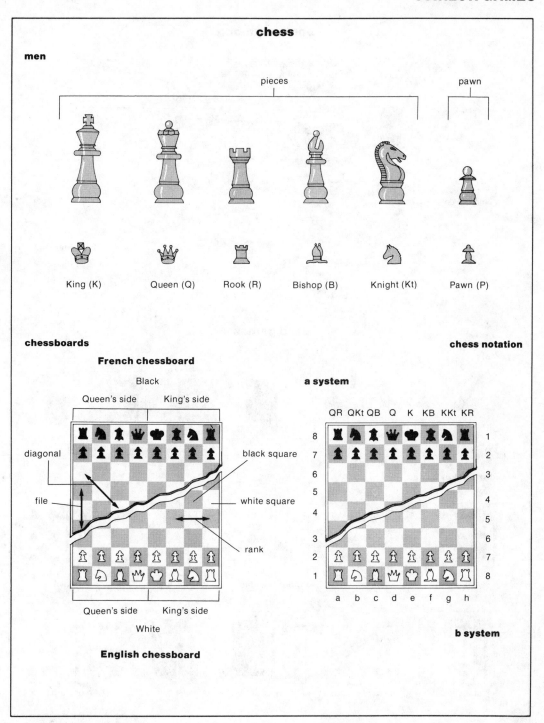

men

pieces

pawn

King (K) Queen (Q) Rook (R) Bishop (B) Knight (Kt) Pawn (P)

chessboards

chess notation

French chessboard

Black

Queen's side King's side

diagonal

file

black square

white square

rank

Queen's side King's side

White

English chessboard

a system

QR QKt QB Q K KB KKt KR

a b c d e f g h

b system

backgammon

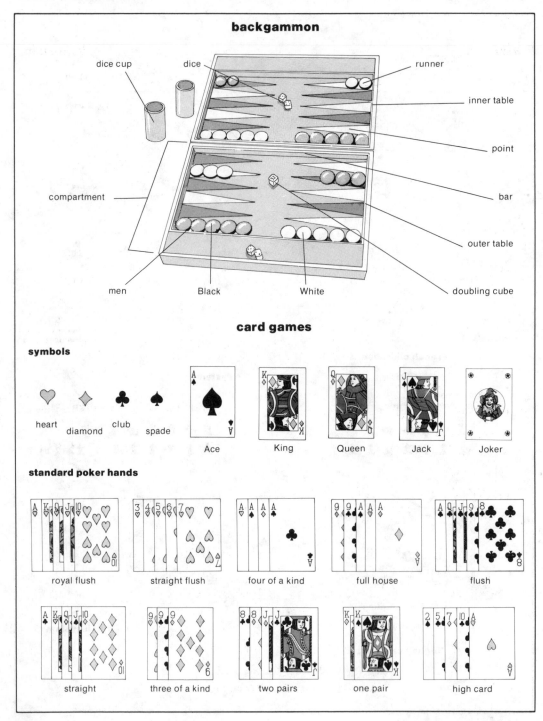

dice cup   dice   runner

inner table

point

bar

compartment

outer table

men   Black   White   doubling cube

card games

symbols

heart   diamond   club   spade

Ace   King   Queen   Jack   Joker

standard poker hands

royal flush   straight flush   four of a kind   full house   flush

straight   three of a kind   two pairs   one pair   high card

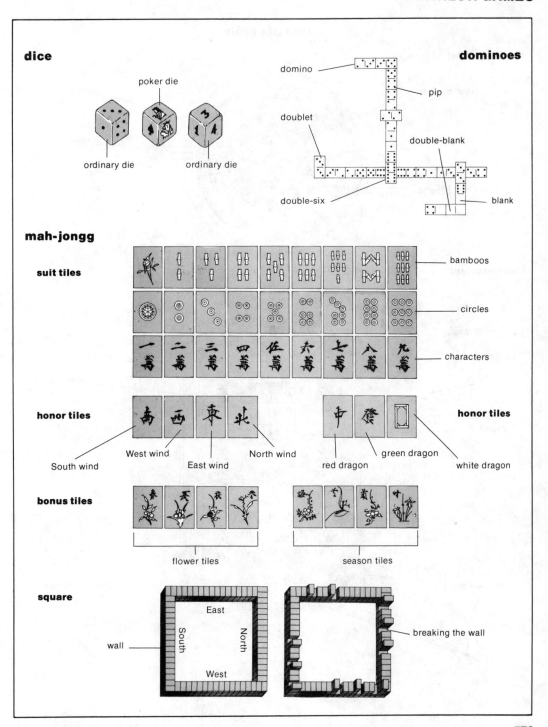

dice

poker die

ordinary die   ordinary die

dominoes

domino

pip

doublet

double-blank

double-six

blank

mah-jongg

suit tiles

bamboos

circles

characters

honor tiles

South wind

West wind   East wind   North wind

honor tiles

red dragon   green dragon

white dragon

bonus tiles

flower tiles   season tiles

square

East

wall   South   North

West

breaking the wall

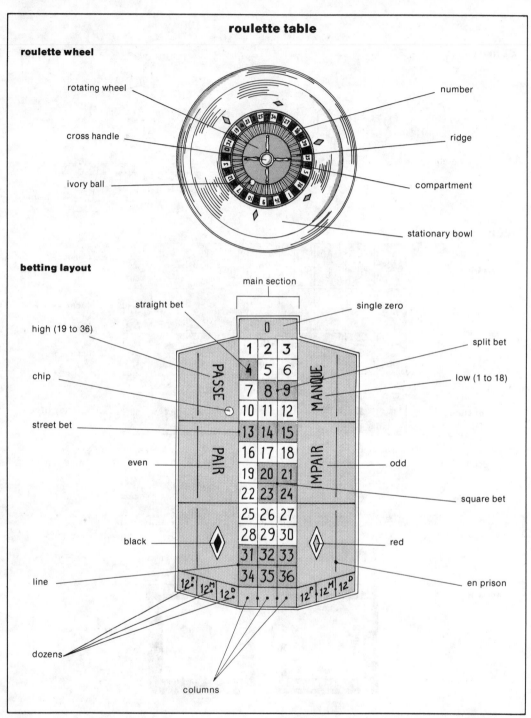

roulette table

roulette wheel

- rotating wheel
- number
- cross handle
- ridge
- ivory ball
- compartment
- stationary bowl

betting layout

- main section
- straight bet
- single zero
- high (19 to 36)
- split bet
- chip
- low (1 to 18)
- street bet
- even
- odd
- square bet
- black
- red
- line
- en prison
- dozens
- columns

PASSE · MANQUE · PAIR · IMPAIR

0
1 2 3
4 5 6
7 8 9
10 11 12
13 14 15
16 17 18
19 20 21
22 23 24
25 26 27
28 29 30
31 32 33
34 35 36

12ᴾ 12ᴹ 12ᴰ · 12ᴾ 12ᴹ 12ᴰ

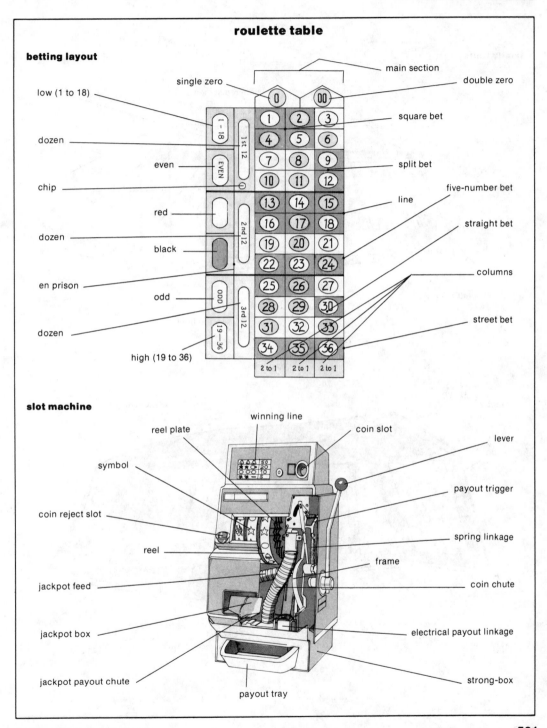

roulette table

betting layout

- single zero
- main section
- double zero
- low (1 to 18)
- square bet
- dozen
- even
- split bet
- chip
- five-number bet
- line
- red
- straight bet
- dozen
- black
- en prison
- columns
- odd
- dozen
- street bet
- high (19 to 36)

slot machine

- winning line
- reel plate
- coin slot
- lever
- symbol
- payout trigger
- coin reject slot
- spring linkage
- reel
- frame
- jackpot feed
- coin chute
- jackpot box
- electrical payout linkage
- jackpot payout chute
- strong-box
- payout tray

tents

family tents

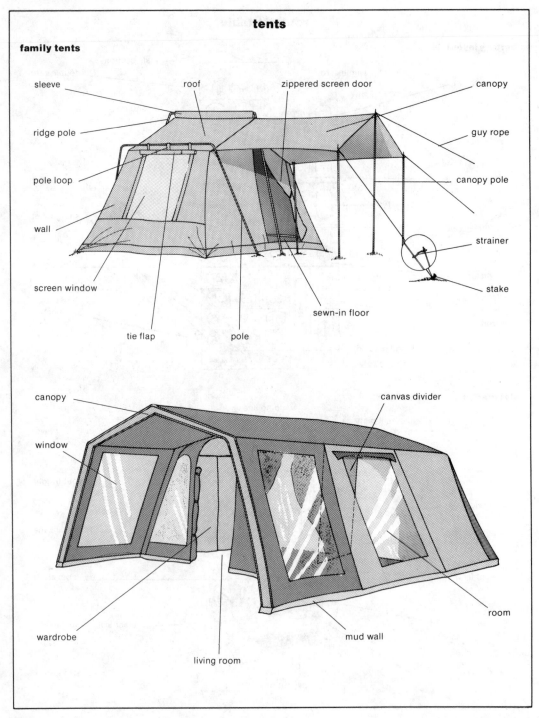

sleeve

roof

zippered screen door

canopy

ridge pole

guy rope

pole loop

canopy pole

wall

strainer

screen window

stake

sewn-in floor

tie flap

pole

canopy

canvas divider

window

wardrobe

living room

mud wall

room

tents

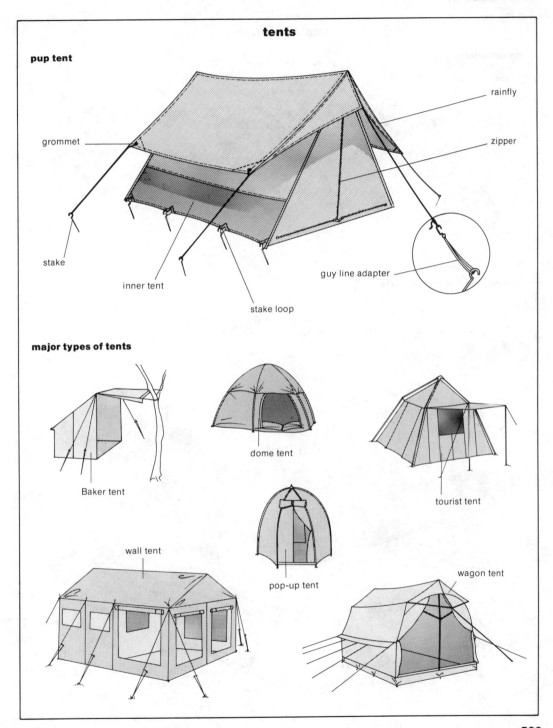

pup tent

- rainfly
- zipper
- grommet
- stake
- guy line adapter
- inner tent
- stake loop

major types of tents

- Baker tent
- dome tent
- tourist tent
- wall tent
- pop-up tent
- wagon tent

camping equipment

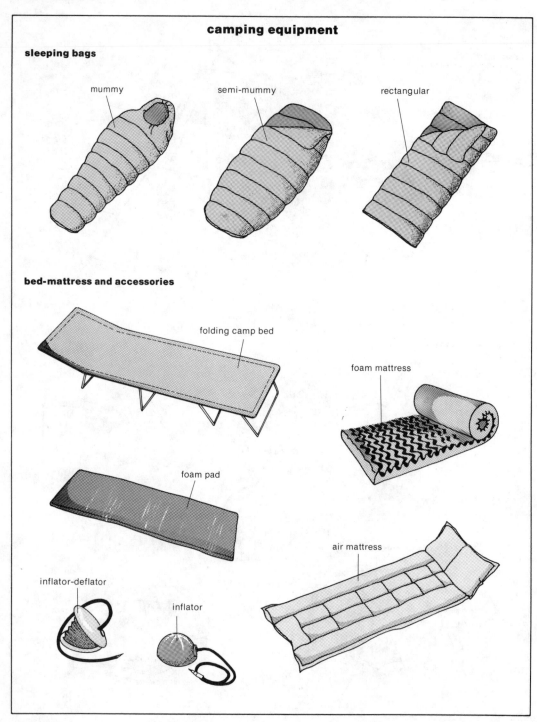

sleeping bags

mummy

semi-mummy

rectangular

bed-mattress and accessories

folding camp bed

foam mattress

foam pad

air mattress

inflator-deflator

inflator

camping equipment

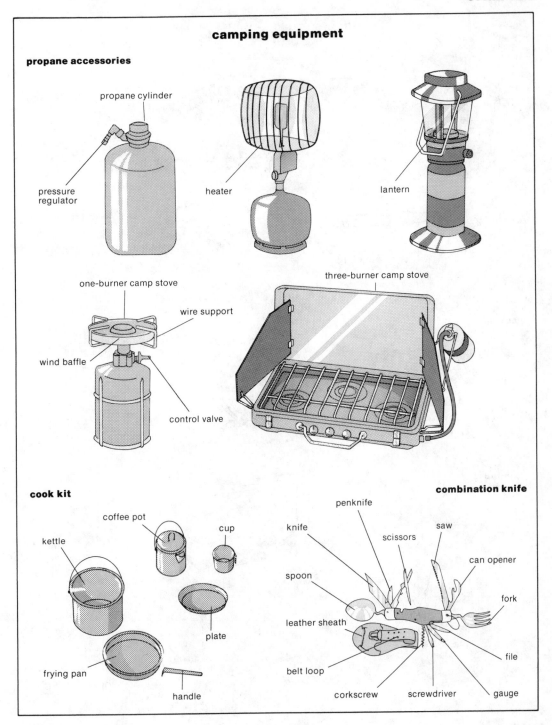

propane accessories

propane cylinder

pressure regulator

heater

lantern

one-burner camp stove

wire support

wind baffle

control valve

three-burner camp stove

cook kit

coffee pot

cup

kettle

plate

frying pan

handle

combination knife

penknife

knife

scissors

saw

can opener

spoon

fork

leather sheath

file

belt loop

corkscrew

screwdriver

gauge

camping equipment

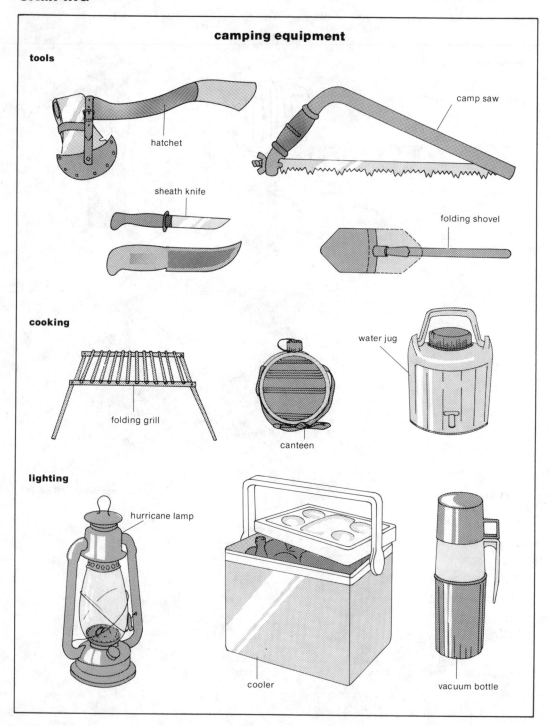

tools

hatchet

camp saw

sheath knife

folding shovel

cooking

water jug

folding grill

canteen

lighting

hurricane lamp

cooler

vacuum bottle

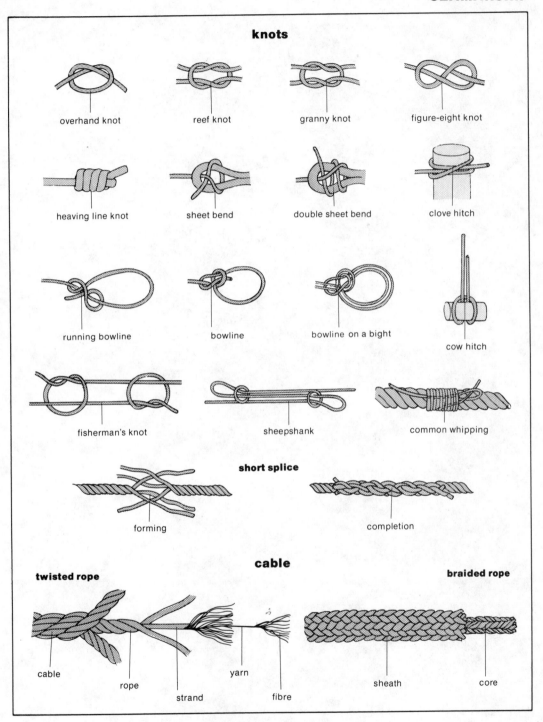

knots

overhand knot

reef knot

granny knot

figure-eight knot

heaving line knot

sheet bend

double sheet bend

clove hitch

running bowline

bowline

bowline on a bight

cow hitch

fisherman's knot

sheepshank

common whipping

short splice

forming

completion

cable

twisted rope

braided rope

cable

rope

strand

yarn

fibre

sheath

core

MEASURING DEVICES

measure of time

mechanical watch

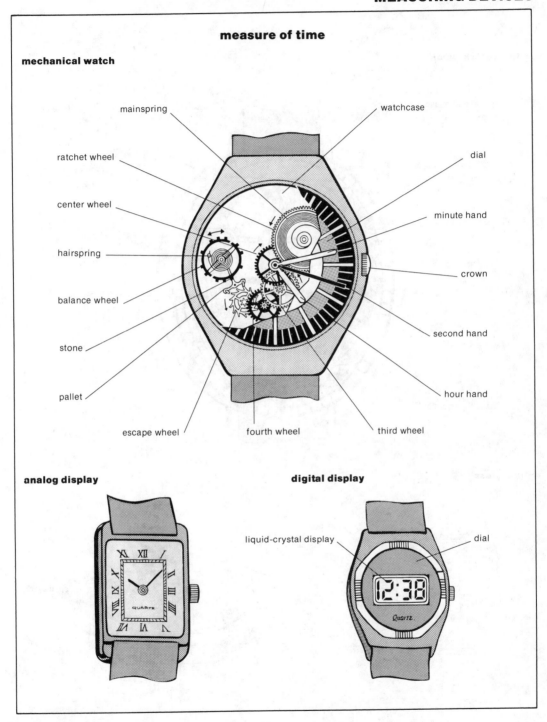

mainspring

watchcase

ratchet wheel

dial

center wheel

minute hand

hairspring

crown

balance wheel

stone

second hand

pallet

hour hand

escape wheel

fourth wheel

third wheel

analog display

digital display

liquid-crystal display

dial

MEASURING DEVICES

measure of time

tuning fork watch

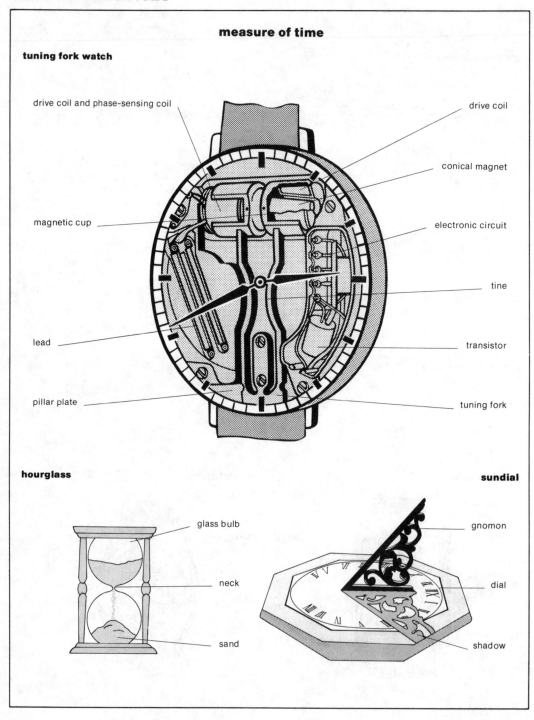

drive coil and phase-sensing coil

drive coil

conical magnet

magnetic cup

electronic circuit

tine

lead

transistor

pillar plate

tuning fork

hourglass

glass bulb

neck

sand

sundial

gnomon

dial

shadow

measure of time

weight-driven clock mechanism

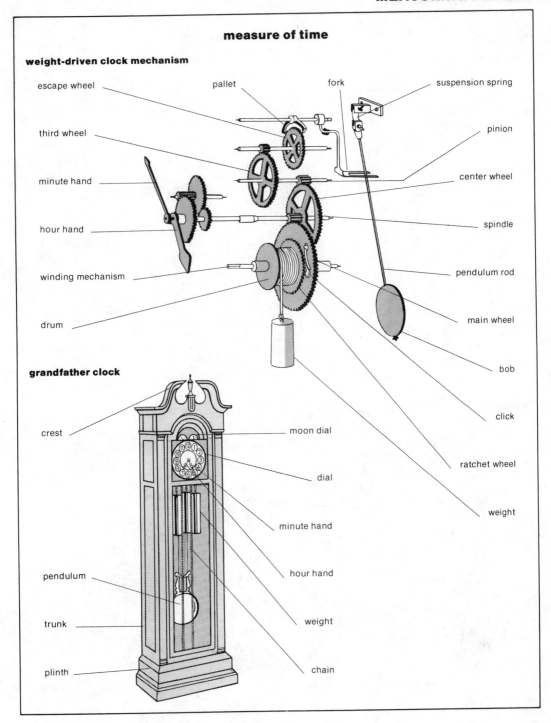

escape wheel

pallet

fork

suspension spring

third wheel

pinion

minute hand

center wheel

hour hand

spindle

winding mechanism

pendulum rod

drum

main wheel

bob

click

grandfather clock

ratchet wheel

crest

moon dial

weight

dial

minute hand

pendulum

hour hand

trunk

weight

plinth

chain

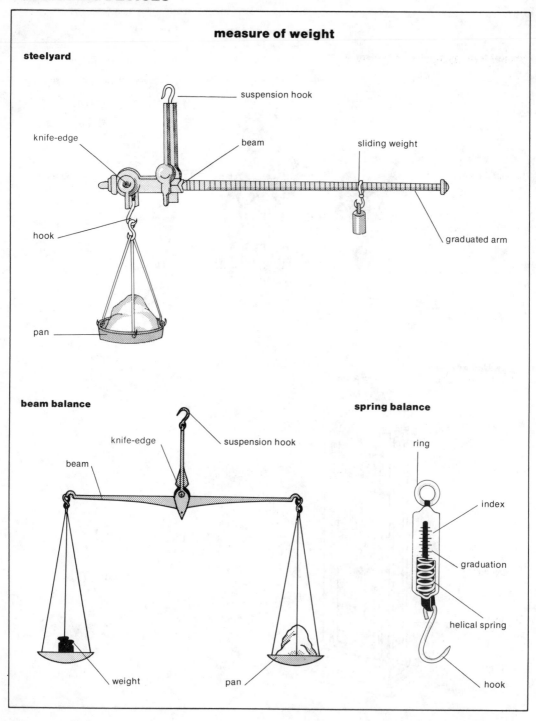

measure of weight

steelyard

suspension hook

knife-edge

beam

sliding weight

hook

graduated arm

pan

beam balance

spring balance

knife-edge

suspension hook

ring

beam

index

graduation

helical spring

weight

pan

hook

measure of weight

Roberval's balance

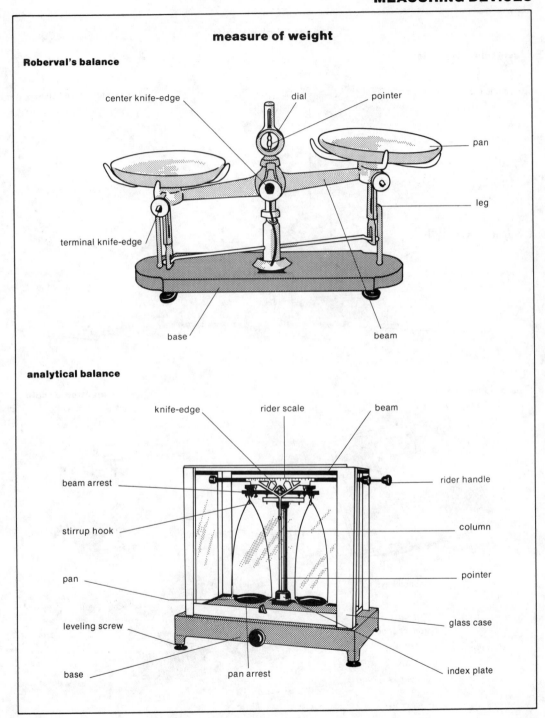

center knife-edge

dial

pointer

pan

leg

terminal knife-edge

base

beam

analytical balance

knife-edge

rider scale

beam

beam arrest

rider handle

stirrup hook

column

pan

pointer

leveling screw

glass case

base

pan arrest

index plate

MEASURING DEVICES

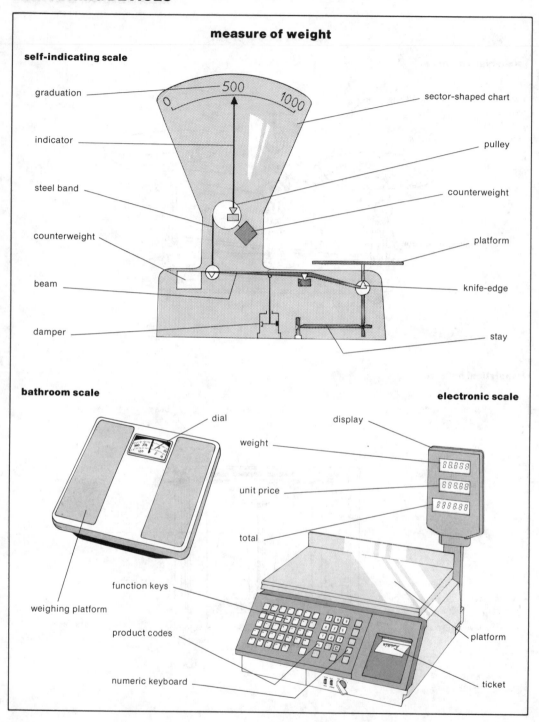

measure of weight

self-indicating scale

graduation — 500 1000 0

sector-shaped chart

indicator

pulley

steel band

counterweight

counterweight

platform

beam

knife-edge

damper

stay

bathroom scale

dial

weighing platform

electronic scale

display

weight

unit price

total

function keys

product codes

numeric keyboard

platform

ticket

measure of heat

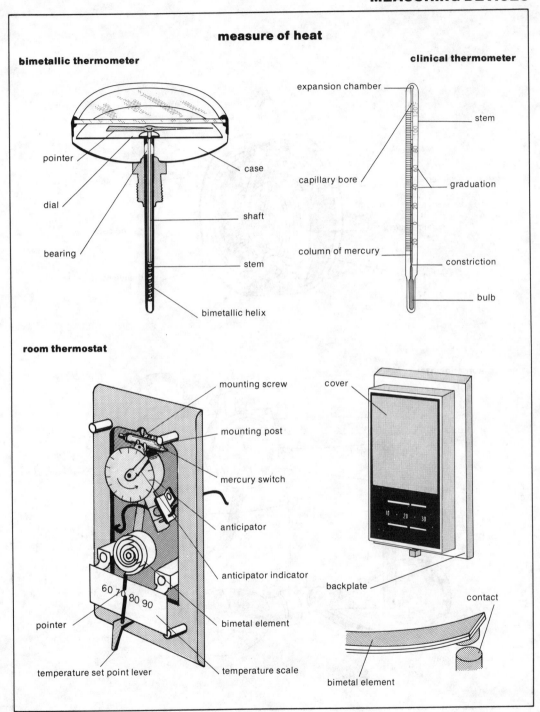

bimetallic thermometer

- pointer
- dial
- bearing
- case
- shaft
- stem
- bimetallic helix

clinical thermometer

- expansion chamber
- stem
- capillary bore
- graduation
- column of mercury
- constriction
- bulb

room thermostat

- mounting screw
- mounting post
- mercury switch
- anticipator
- anticipator indicator
- cover
- backplate
- contact
- pointer
- temperature set point lever
- bimetal element
- temperature scale
- bimetal element

60 70 80 90

10 · 20 · 30

MEASURING DEVICES

measure of pressure

aneroid barometer

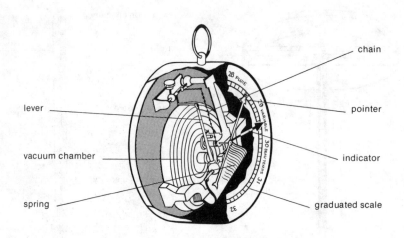

chain

lever

pointer

vacuum chamber

indicator

spring

graduated scale

sphygmomanometer

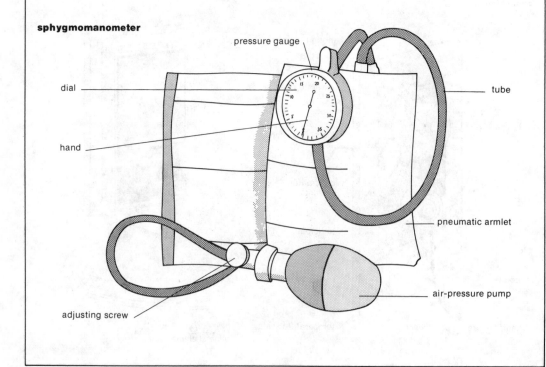

pressure gauge

dial

tube

hand

pneumatic armlet

air-pressure pump

adjusting screw

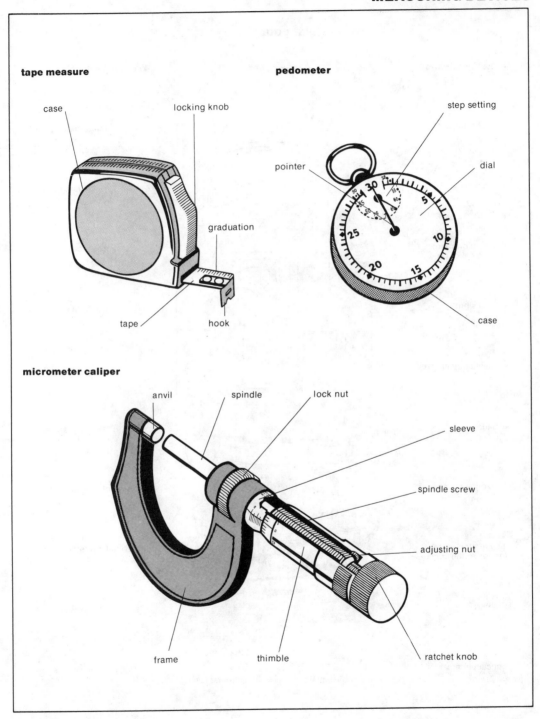

tape measure

case

locking knob

graduation

tape

hook

pedometer

step setting

pointer

dial

case

micrometer caliper

anvil

spindle

lock nut

sleeve

spindle screw

adjusting nut

frame

thimble

ratchet knob

MEASURING DEVICES

theodolite

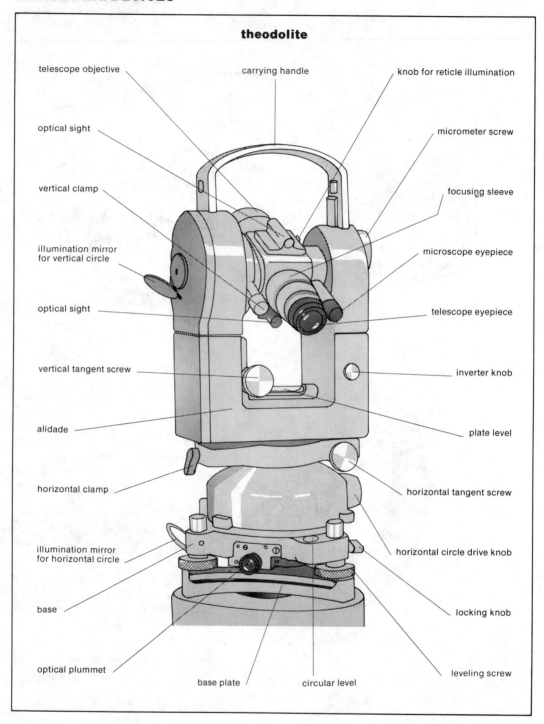

telescope objective

carrying handle

knob for reticle illumination

optical sight

micrometer screw

vertical clamp

focusing sleeve

illumination mirror for vertical circle

microscope eyepiece

optical sight

telescope eyepiece

vertical tangent screw

inverter knob

alidade

plate level

horizontal clamp

horizontal tangent screw

illumination mirror for horizontal circle

horizontal circle drive knob

base

locking knob

optical plummet

base plate

circular level

leveling screw

watt-hour meter

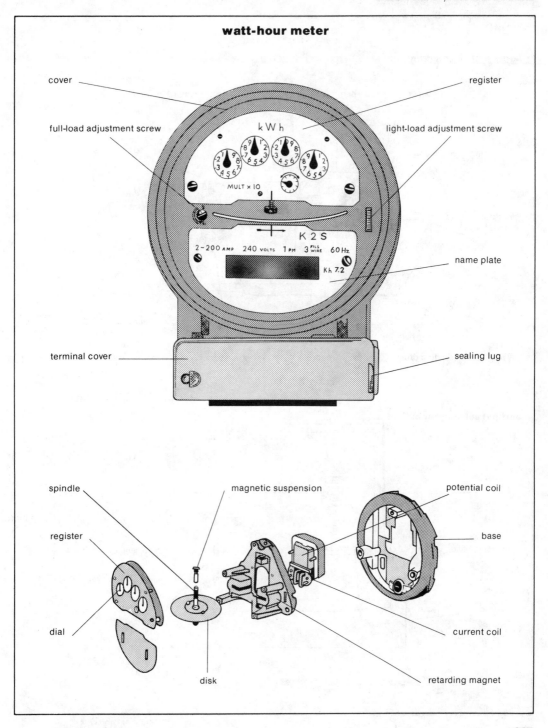

cover

register

full-load adjustment screw

light-load adjustment screw

kWh

MULT × 10

K 2 S

2–200 AMP 240 VOLTS 1 PH 3 FILS WIRE 60 Hz

Kh 7.2

name plate

terminal cover

sealing lug

spindle

magnetic suspension

potential coil

register

base

dial

current coil

disk

retarding magnet

MEASURING DEVICES

horizontal seismograph

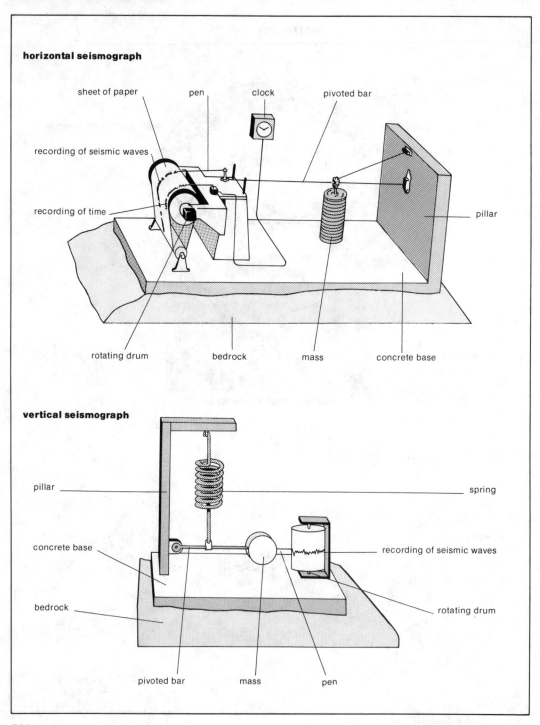

sheet of paper

pen

clock

pivoted bar

recording of seismic waves

recording of time

pillar

rotating drum

bedrock

mass

concrete base

vertical seismograph

pillar

spring

concrete base

recording of seismic waves

bedrock

rotating drum

pivoted bar

mass

pen

OPTICAL INSTRUMENTS

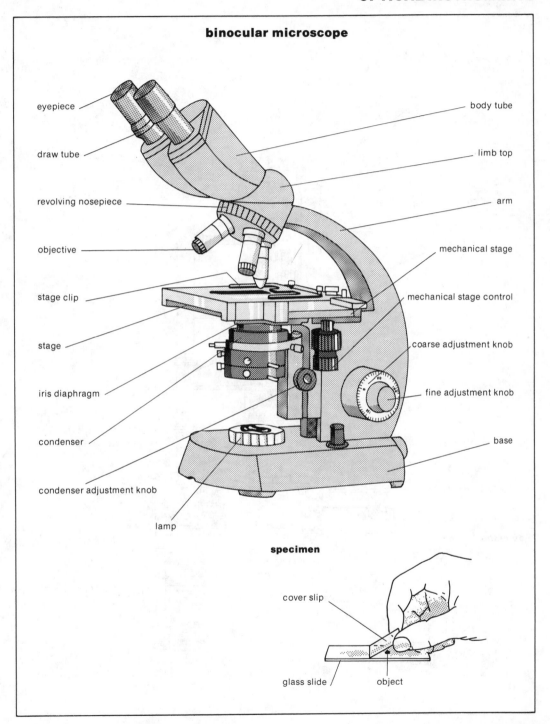

binocular microscope

eyepiece

body tube

draw tube

limb top

revolving nosepiece

arm

objective

mechanical stage

stage clip

mechanical stage control

stage

coarse adjustment knob

iris diaphragm

fine adjustment knob

condenser

base

condenser adjustment knob

lamp

specimen

cover slip

glass slide

object

electron microscope

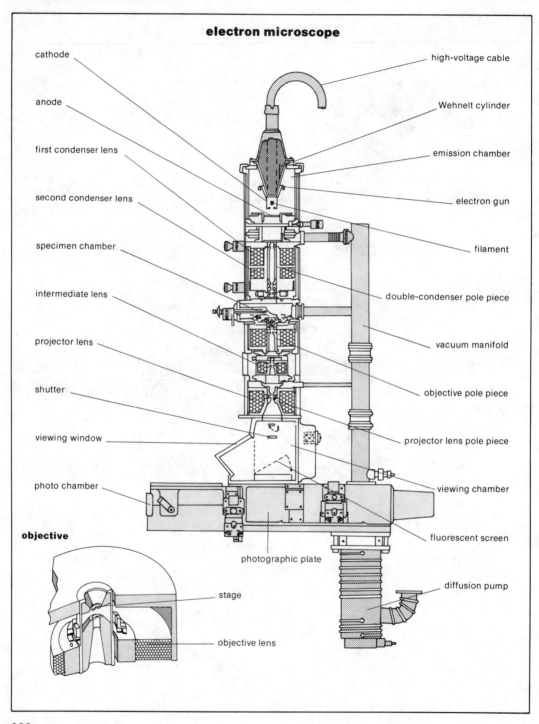

cathode

anode

first condenser lens

second condenser lens

specimen chamber

intermediate lens

projector lens

shutter

viewing window

photo chamber

objective

high-voltage cable

Wehnelt cylinder

emission chamber

electron gun

filament

double-condenser pole piece

vacuum manifold

objective pole piece

projector lens pole piece

viewing chamber

fluorescent screen

photographic plate

diffusion pump

stage

objective lens

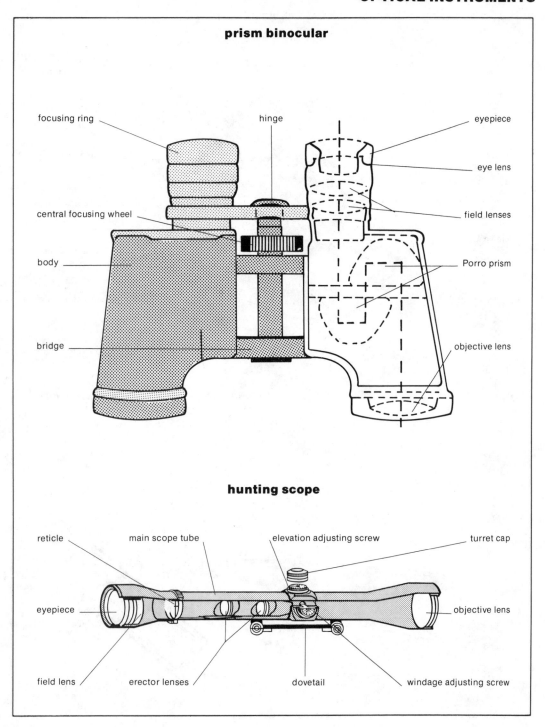

prism binocular

focusing ring

hinge

eyepiece

eye lens

central focusing wheel

field lenses

body

Porro prism

bridge

objective lens

hunting scope

reticle

main scope tube

elevation adjusting screw

turret cap

eyepiece

objective lens

field lens

erector lenses

dovetail

windage adjusting screw

reflector

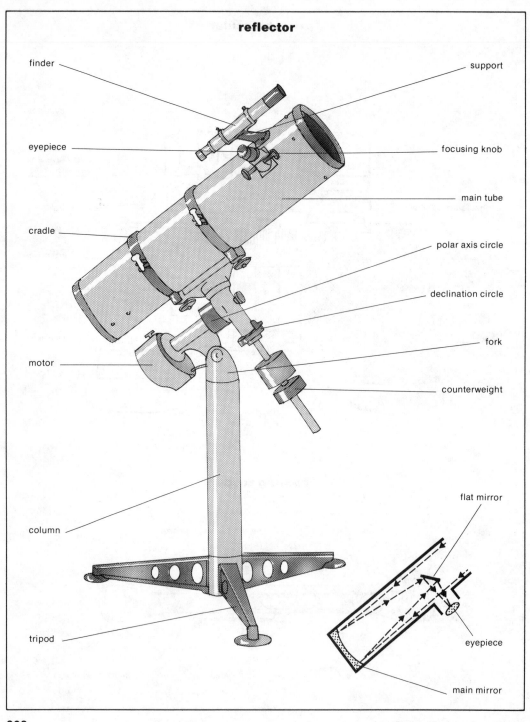

finder

support

eyepiece

focusing knob

main tube

cradle

polar axis circle

declination circle

motor

fork

counterweight

column

flat mirror

tripod

eyepiece

main mirror

refracting telescope

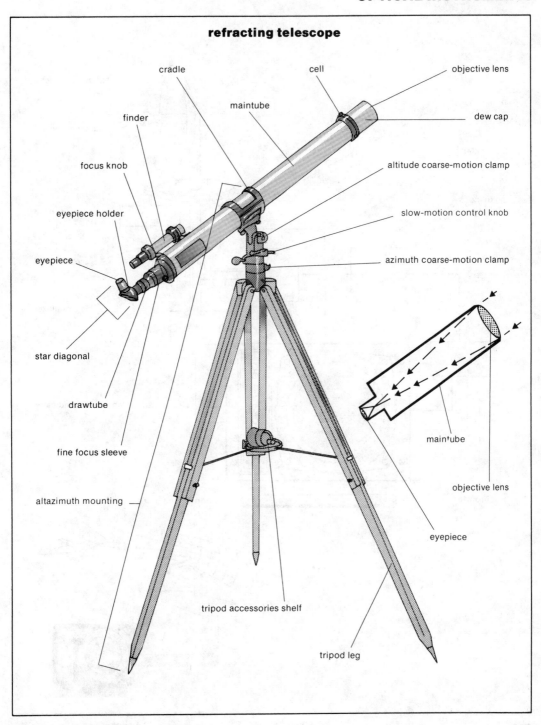

cradle

cell

objective lens

maintube

dew cap

finder

focus knob

altitude coarse-motion clamp

eyepiece holder

slow-motion control knob

azimuth coarse-motion clamp

eyepiece

star diagonal

drawtube

maintube

fine focus sleeve

objective lens

altazimuth mounting

eyepiece

tripod accessories shelf

tripod leg

DETECTION DEVICES

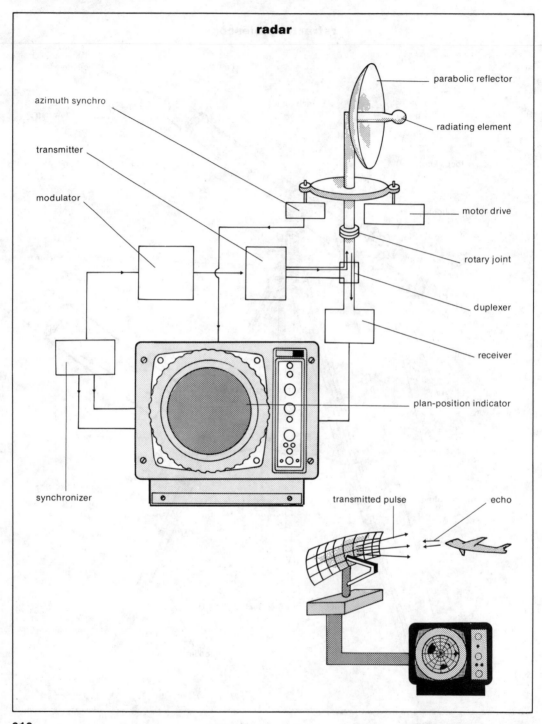

radar

parabolic reflector

radiating element

azimuth synchro

transmitter

modulator

motor drive

rotary joint

duplexer

receiver

plan-position indicator

synchronizer

transmitted pulse

echo

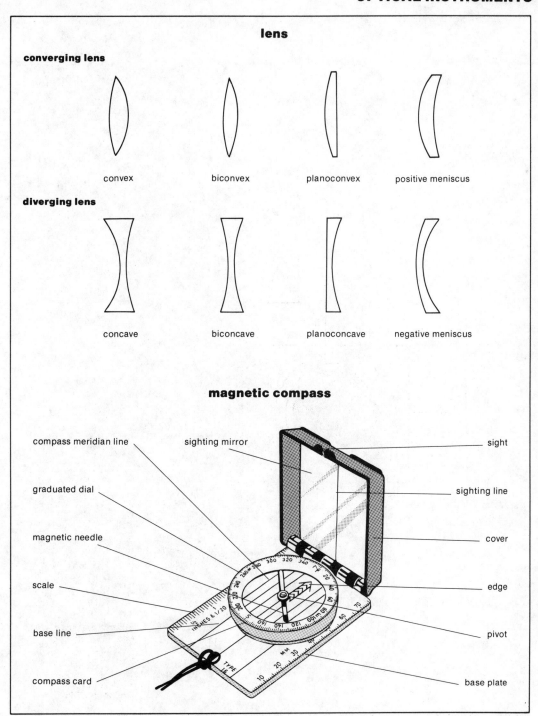

lens

converging lens

convex biconvex planoconvex positive meniscus

diverging lens

concave biconcave planoconcave negative meniscus

magnetic compass

compass meridian line
sighting mirror
sight

graduated dial
sighting line

magnetic needle
cover

scale
edge

base line
pivot

compass card
base plate

HEALTH

first aid kit

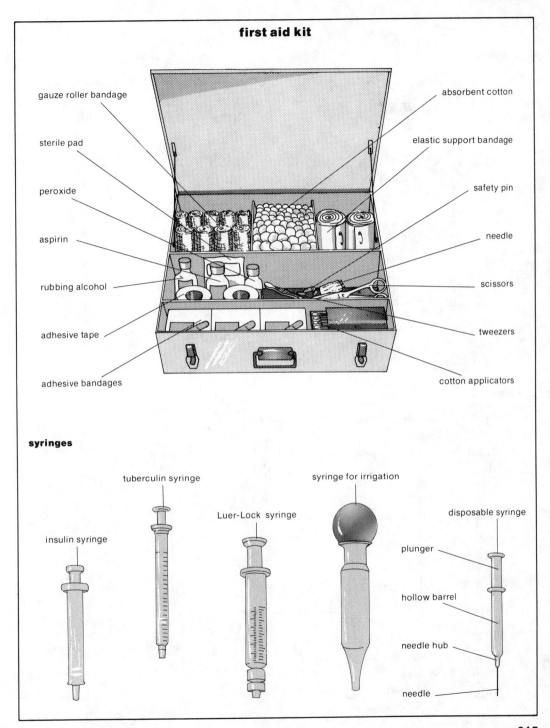

gauze roller bandage

sterile pad

peroxide

aspirin

rubbing alcohol

adhesive tape

adhesive bandages

absorbent cotton

elastic support bandage

safety pin

needle

scissors

tweezers

cotton applicators

syringes

insulin syringe

tuberculin syringe

Luer-Lock syringe

syringe for irrigation

disposable syringe

plunger

hollow barrel

needle hub

needle

walking aids

crutches

canes

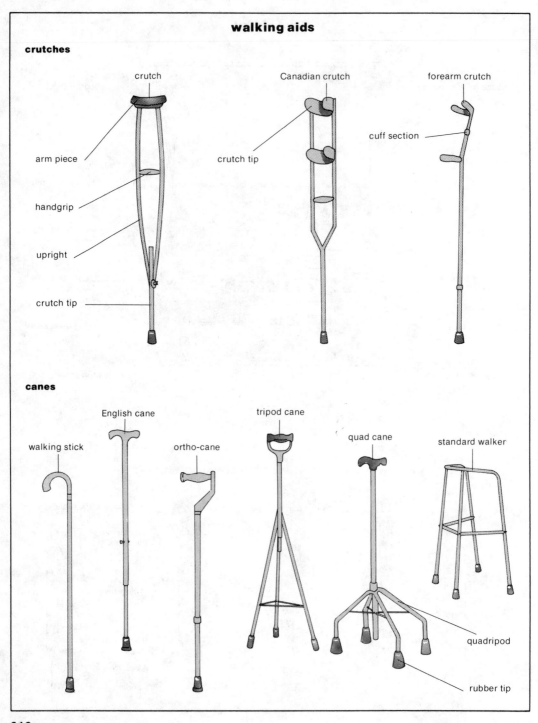

crutch

Canadian crutch

forearm crutch

cuff section

arm piece

crutch tip

handgrip

upright

crutch tip

walking stick

English cane

ortho-cane

tripod cane

quad cane

standard walker

quadripod

rubber tip

wheelchair

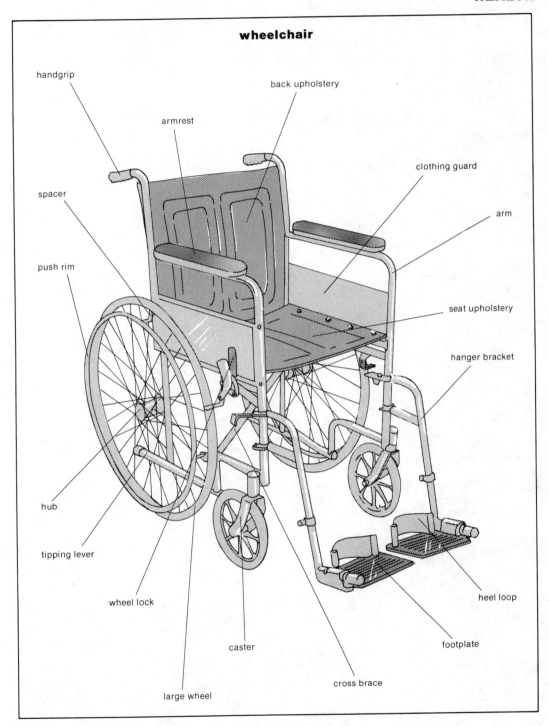

handgrip

back upholstery

armrest

clothing guard

spacer

arm

push rim

seat upholstery

hanger bracket

hub

tipping lever

wheel lock

heel loop

caster

footplate

large wheel

cross brace

ENERGY

coal mine

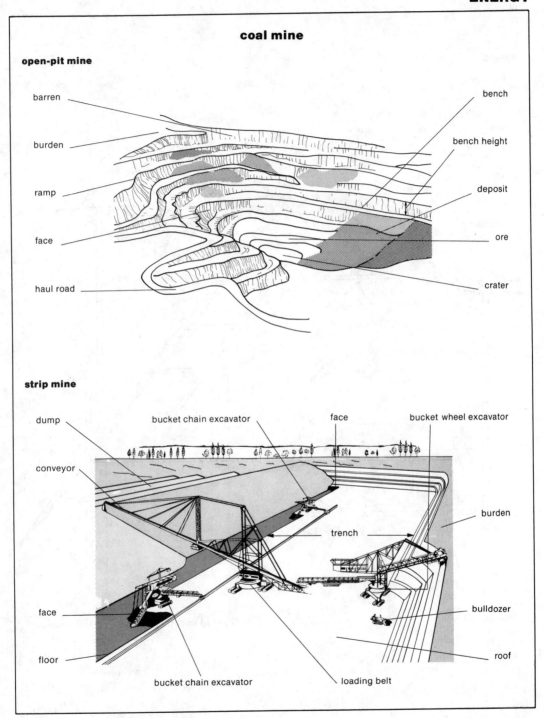

open-pit mine

- barren
- burden
- ramp
- face
- haul road
- bench
- bench height
- deposit
- ore
- crater

strip mine

- dump
- bucket chain excavator
- face
- bucket wheel excavator
- conveyor
- burden
- trench
- face
- floor
- bulldozer
- roof
- bucket chain excavator
- loading belt

coal mine

mining

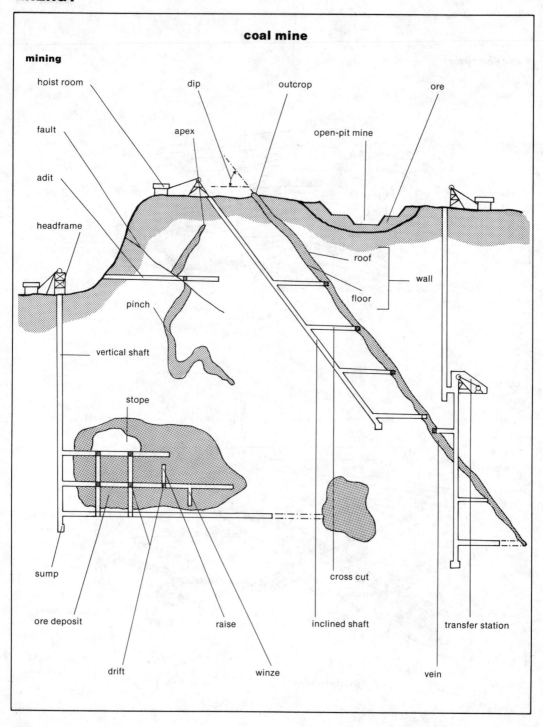

hoist room

dip

outcrop

ore

fault

apex

open-pit mine

adit

headframe

roof

wall

floor

pinch

vertical shaft

stope

sump

cross cut

ore deposit

raise

inclined shaft

transfer station

drift

winze

vein

coal mine

underground mine

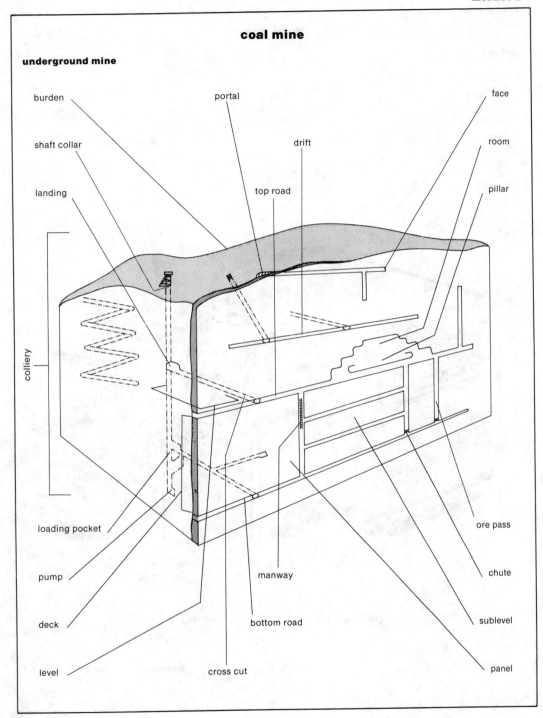

burden

portal

face

shaft collar

drift

room

landing

top road

pillar

colliery

loading pocket

ore pass

pump

manway

chute

deck

bottom road

sublevel

level

cross cut

panel

ENERGY

coal mine

pithead

dump

conveyor

washery

settling basin

water reservoir

gasometer

tower

power station

administration building

lamp room

day

bottom

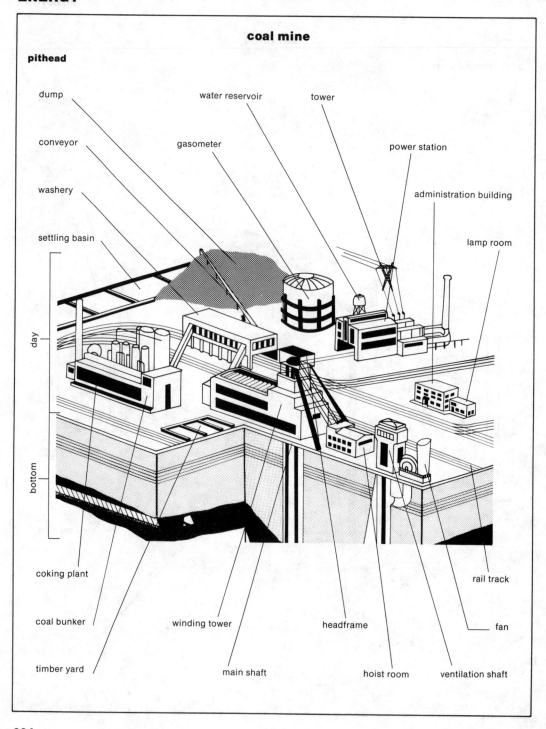

coking plant

coal bunker

timber yard

winding tower

main shaft

headframe

hoist room

ventilation shaft

rail track

fan

coal mine

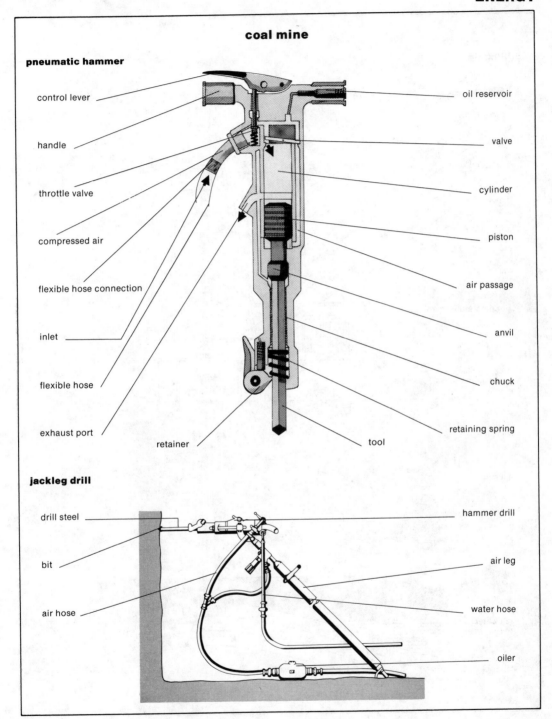

pneumatic hammer

control lever

handle

throttle valve

compressed air

flexible hose connection

inlet

flexible hose

exhaust port

retainer

oil reservoir

valve

cylinder

piston

air passage

anvil

chuck

retaining spring

tool

jackleg drill

drill steel

bit

air hose

hammer drill

air leg

water hose

oiler

oil

drilling rig

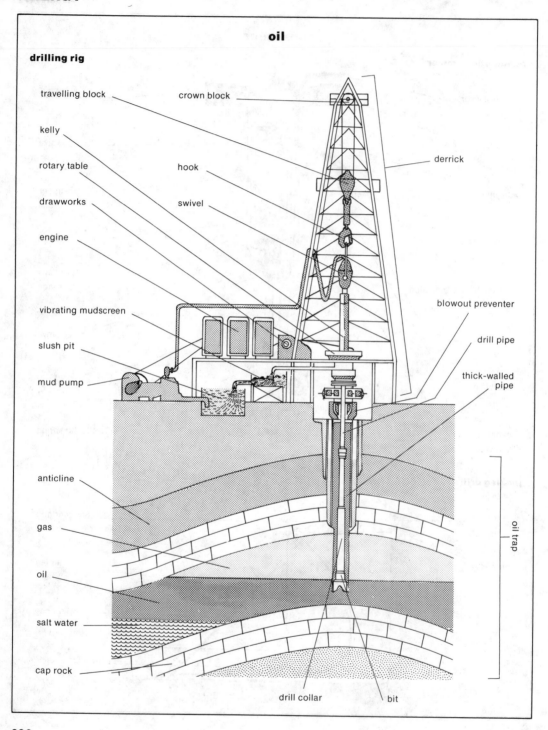

travelling block

crown block

kelly

rotary table

hook

drawworks

swivel

engine

derrick

vibrating mudscreen

slush pit

blowout preventer

mud pump

drill pipe

thick-walled pipe

anticline

gas

oil

salt water

cap rock

oil trap

drill collar

bit

oil

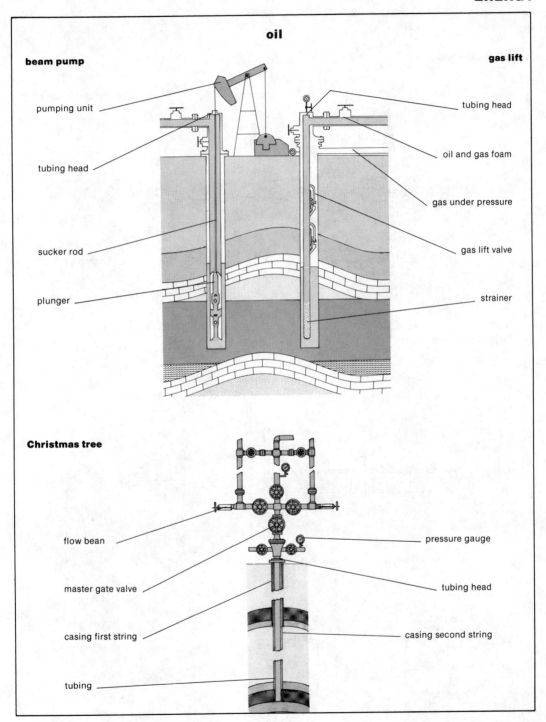

beam pump

- pumping unit
- tubing head
- sucker rod
- plunger

gas lift

- tubing head
- oil and gas foam
- gas under pressure
- gas lift valve
- strainer

Christmas tree

- flow bean
- master gate valve
- casing first string
- tubing
- pressure gauge
- tubing head
- casing second string

oil

offshore drilling

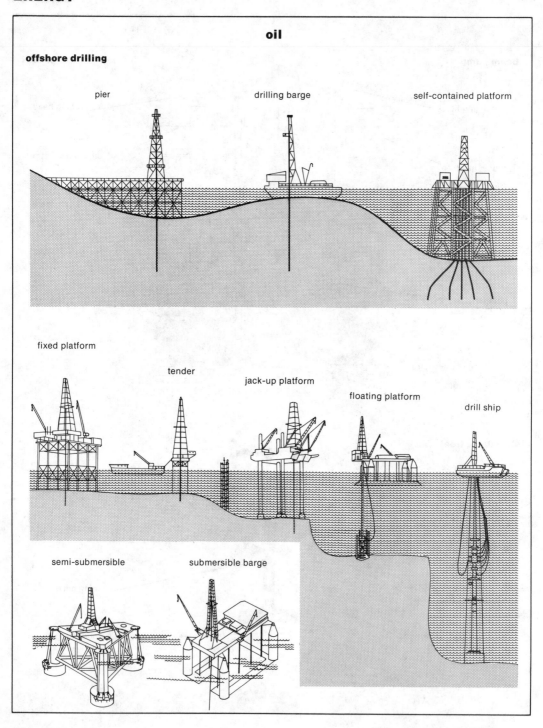

pier

drilling barge

self-contained platform

fixed platform

tender

jack-up platform

floating platform

drill ship

semi-submersible

submersible barge

oil

production platform

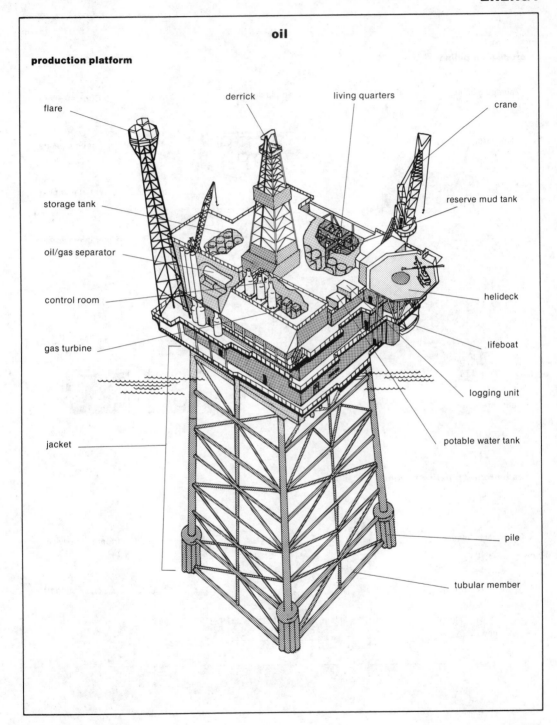

flare

derrick

living quarters

crane

storage tank

reserve mud tank

oil/gas separator

control room

helideck

gas turbine

lifeboat

logging unit

potable water tank

jacket

pile

tubular member

oil

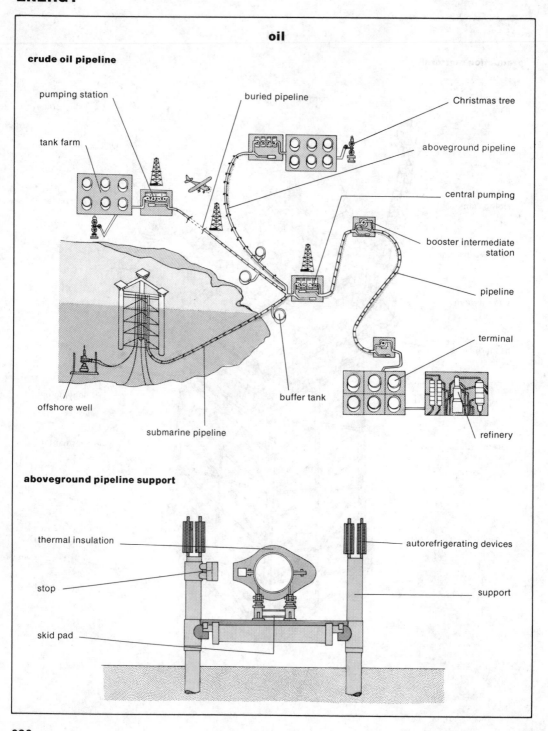

crude oil pipeline

pumping station

buried pipeline

Christmas tree

tank farm

aboveground pipeline

central pumping

booster intermediate station

pipeline

terminal

refinery

offshore well

buffer tank

submarine pipeline

aboveground pipeline support

thermal insulation

autorefrigerating devices

stop

support

skid pad

oil

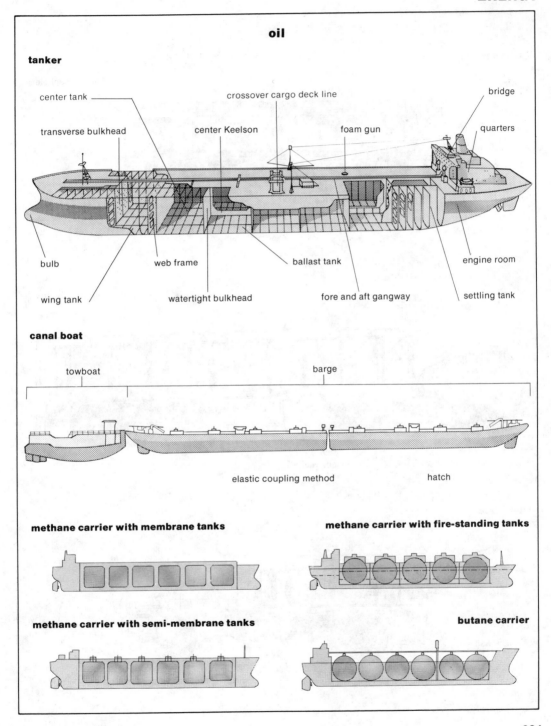

tanker

center tank

transverse bulkhead

crossover cargo deck line

center Keelson

foam gun

bridge

quarters

bulb

web frame

ballast tank

engine room

wing tank

watertight bulkhead

fore and aft gangway

settling tank

canal boat

towboat

barge

elastic coupling method

hatch

methane carrier with membrane tanks

methane carrier with fire-standing tanks

methane carrier with semi-membrane tanks

butane carrier

oil

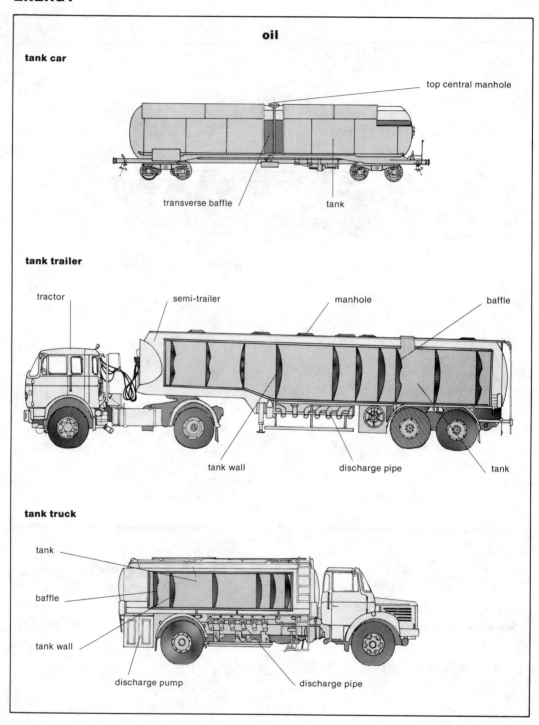

tank car

top central manhole

transverse baffle

tank

tank trailer

tractor

semi-trailer

manhole

baffle

tank wall

discharge pipe

tank

tank truck

tank

baffle

tank wall

discharge pump

discharge pipe

oil

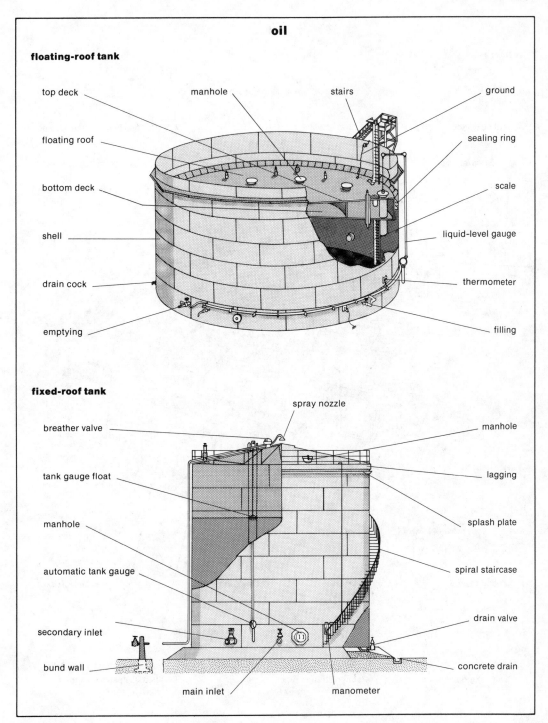

floating-roof tank

top deck · manhole · stairs · ground

floating roof · sealing ring

bottom deck · scale

shell · liquid-level gauge

drain cock · thermometer

emptying · filling

fixed-roof tank

spray nozzle

breather valve · manhole

tank gauge float · lagging

manhole · splash plate

automatic tank gauge · spiral staircase

secondary inlet · drain valve

bund wall · concrete drain

main inlet · manometer

oil

refinery

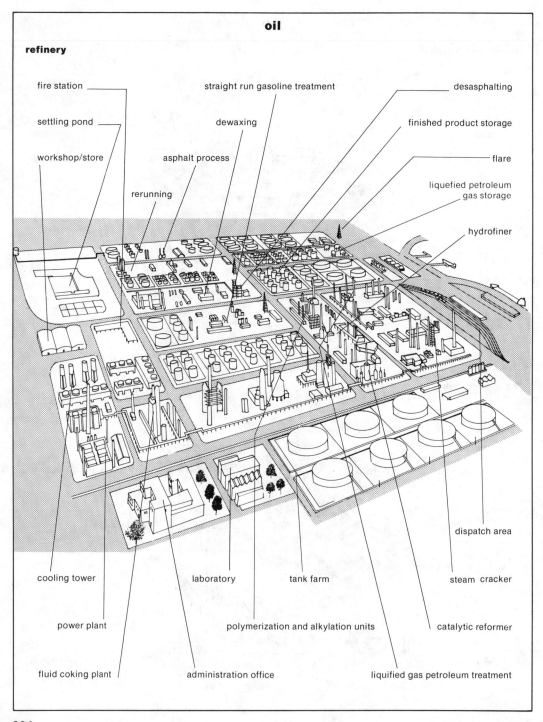

fire station

settling pond

workshop/store

rerunning

straight run gasoline treatment

dewaxing

asphalt process

desasphalting

finished product storage

flare

liquefied petroleum gas storage

hydrofiner

cooling tower

power plant

fluid coking plant

laboratory

administration office

tank farm

polymerization and alkylation units

liquified gas petroleum treatment

dispatch area

steam cracker

catalytic reformer

oil

refinery products

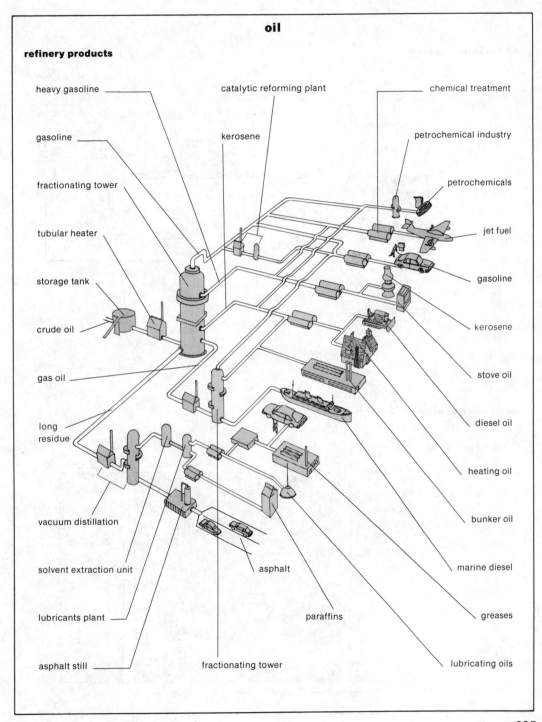

heavy gasoline

catalytic reforming plant

chemical treatment

gasoline

kerosene

petrochemical industry

fractionating tower

petrochemicals

tubular heater

jet fuel

storage tank

gasoline

crude oil

kerosene

gas oil

stove oil

long residue

diesel oil

heating oil

bunker oil

vacuum distillation

marine diesel

solvent extraction unit

asphalt

lubricants plant

paraffins

greases

asphalt still

fractionating tower

lubricating oils

oil

oil sands mining plant

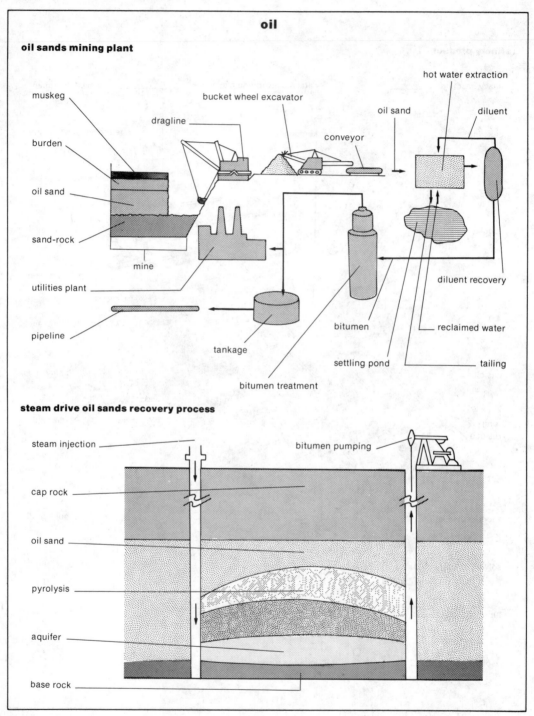

steam drive oil sands recovery process

electricity

hydroelectric complex

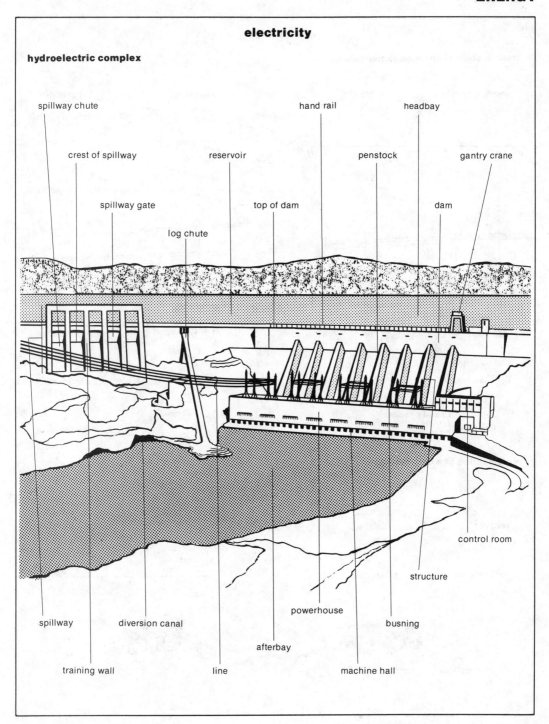

spillway chute

crest of spillway

spillway gate

log chute

hand rail

reservoir

top of dam

headbay

penstock

gantry crane

dam

spillway

training wall

diversion canal

line

afterbay

powerhouse

machine hall

busning

structure

control room

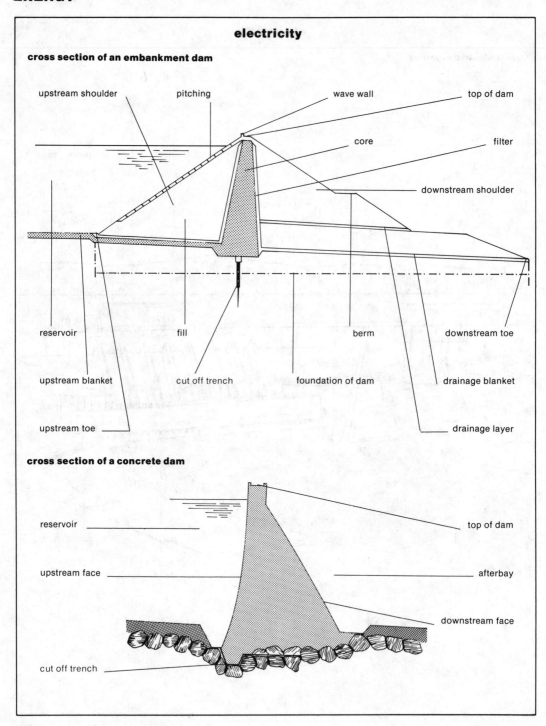

electricity

cross section of an embankment dam

upstream shoulder · pitching · wave wall · top of dam · core · filter · downstream shoulder · reservoir · fill · berm · downstream toe · upstream blanket · cut off trench · foundation of dam · drainage blanket · upstream toe · drainage layer

cross section of a concrete dam

reservoir · top of dam · upstream face · afterbay · downstream face · cut off trench

electricity

major types of dams

embankment dam

cross section of an embankment dam

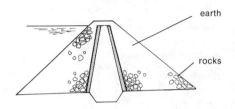

earth

rocks

gravity dam

cross section of a gravity dam

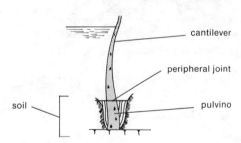

arch dam

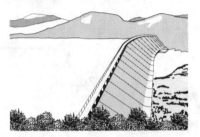

cross section of an arch dam

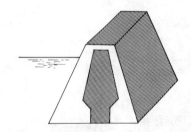

cantilever

peripheral joint

soil

pulvino

buttress dam

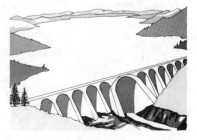

cross section of a buttress dam

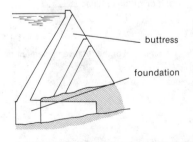

buttress

foundation

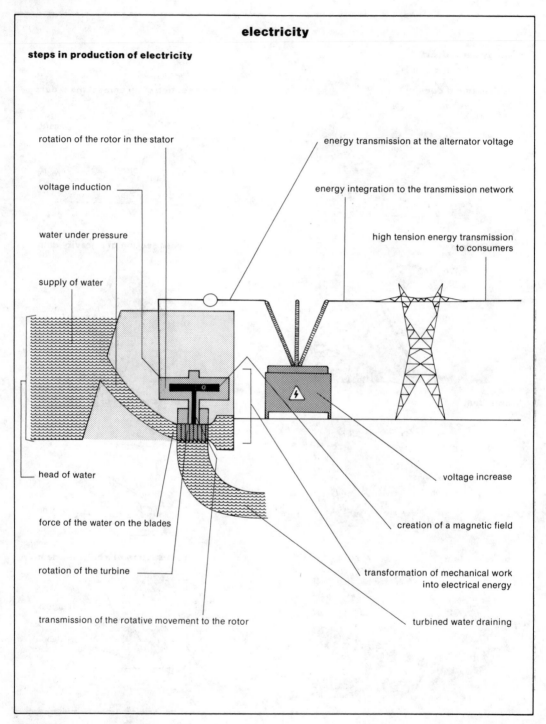

electricity

steps in production of electricity

rotation of the rotor in the stator

energy transmission at the alternator voltage

voltage induction

energy integration to the transmission network

water under pressure

high tension energy transmission to consumers

supply of water

head of water

force of the water on the blades

rotation of the turbine

transmission of the rotative movement to the rotor

voltage increase

creation of a magnetic field

transformation of mechanical work into electrical energy

turbined water draining

electricity

cross section of an hydroelectric power station

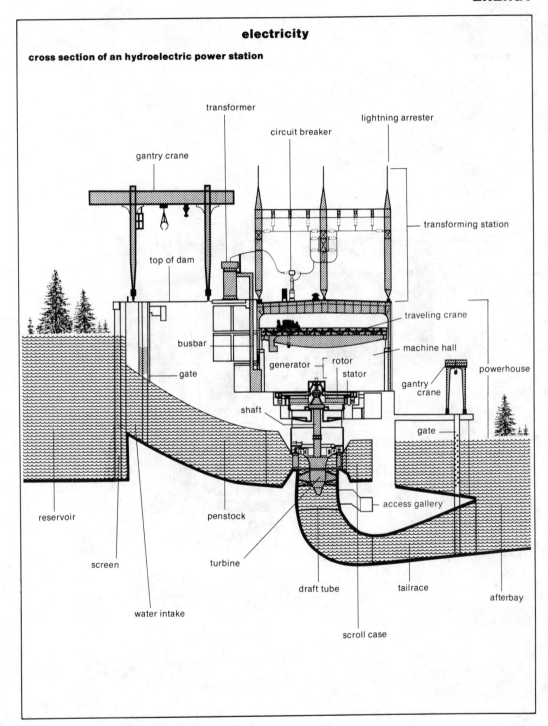

electricity

generator

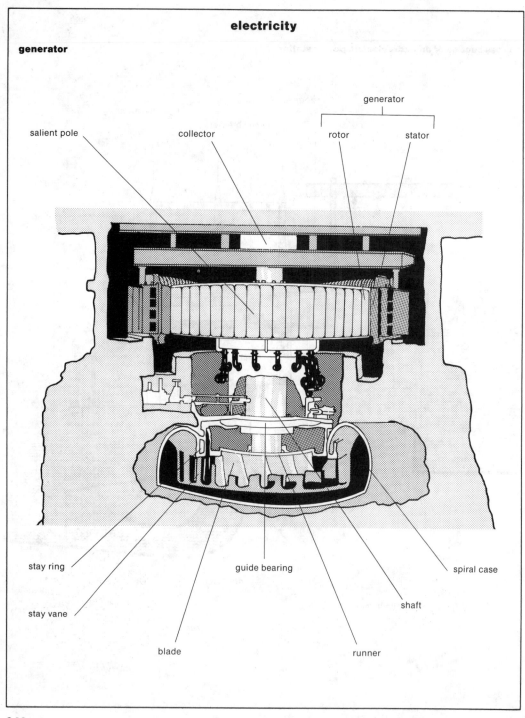

salient pole

collector

generator

rotor   stator

stay ring

stay vane

blade

guide bearing

runner

shaft

spiral case

electricity

cross section of an hydraulic turbine

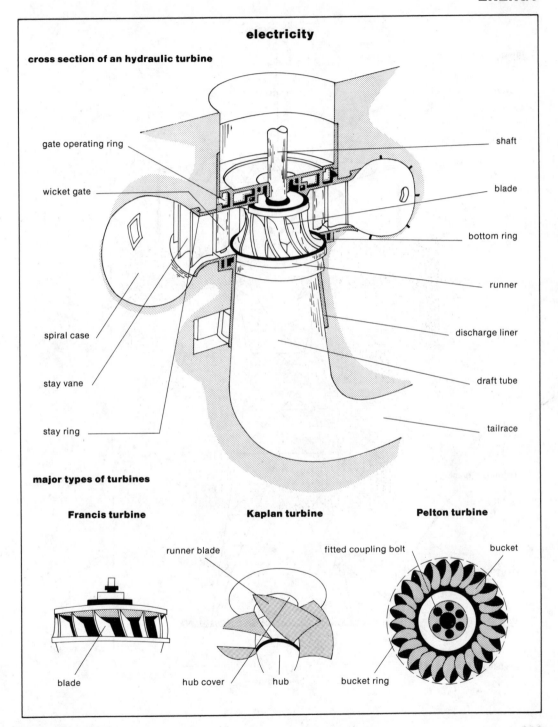

gate operating ring

wicket gate

spiral case

stay vane

stay ring

shaft

blade

bottom ring

runner

discharge liner

draft tube

tailrace

major types of turbines

Francis turbine

Kaplan turbine

Pelton turbine

runner blade

fitted coupling bolt

bucket

blade

hub cover

hub

bucket ring

electricity

tower

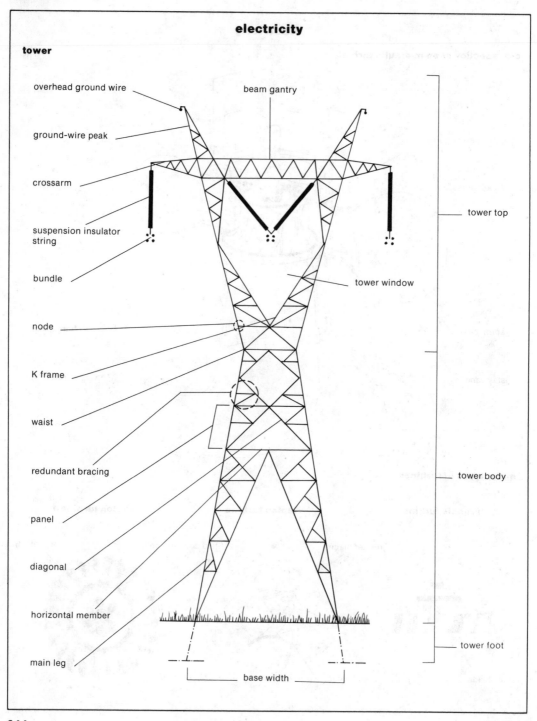

overhead ground wire

beam gantry

ground-wire peak

crossarm

suspension insulator string

bundle

tower window

node

K frame

waist

redundant bracing

panel

diagonal

horizontal member

main leg

tower top

tower body

tower foot

base width

electricity

overhead connection

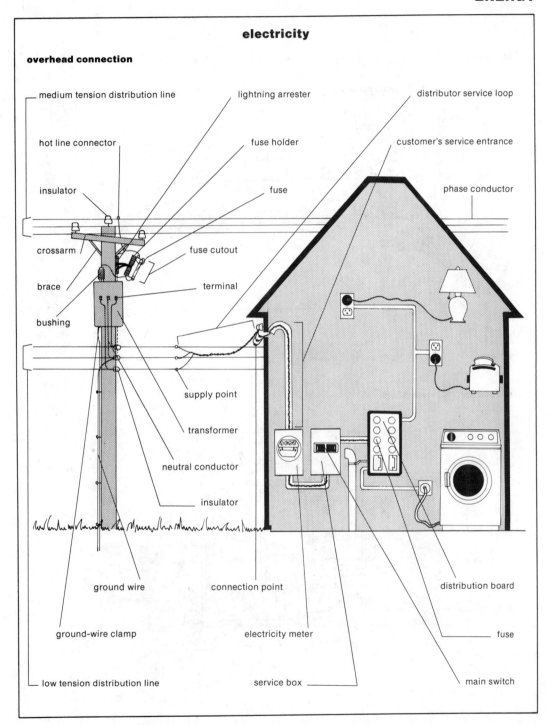

medium tension distribution line

lightning arrester

distributor service loop

hot line connector

fuse holder

customer's service entrance

insulator

fuse

phase conductor

crossarm

fuse cutout

brace

terminal

bushing

supply point

transformer

neutral conductor

insulator

ground wire

connection point

distribution board

ground-wire clamp

electricity meter

fuse

low tension distribution line

service box

main switch

electricity

tidal power plant

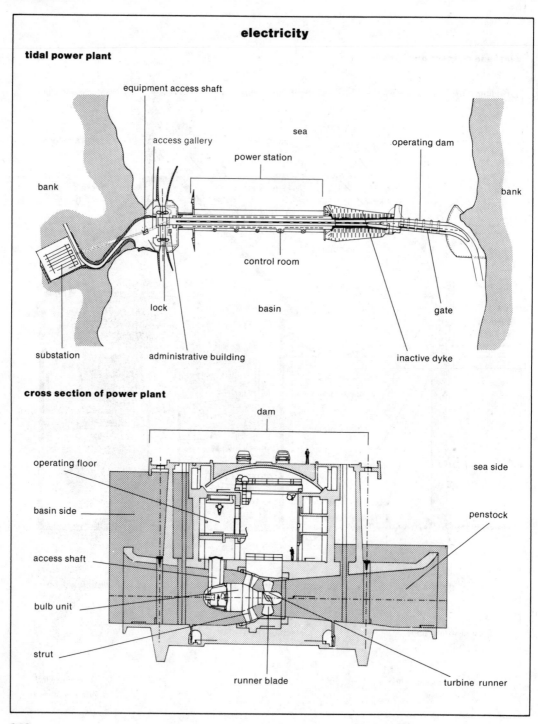

equipment access shaft

access gallery

sea

power station

operating dam

bank

bank

control room

lock

basin

gate

substation

administrative building

inactive dyke

cross section of power plant

dam

operating floor

sea side

basin side

penstock

access shaft

bulb unit

strut

runner blade

turbine runner

nuclear energy

CANDU nuclear generating station

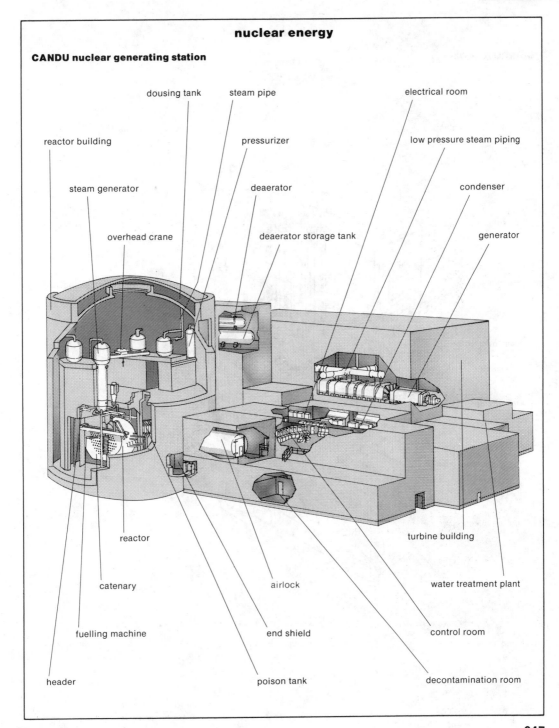

dousing tank

steam pipe

electrical room

reactor building

pressurizer

low pressure steam piping

steam generator

deaerator

condenser

overhead crane

deaerator storage tank

generator

reactor

turbine building

catenary

airlock

water treatment plant

fuelling machine

end shield

control room

header

poison tank

decontamination room

nuclear energy

CANDU reactor

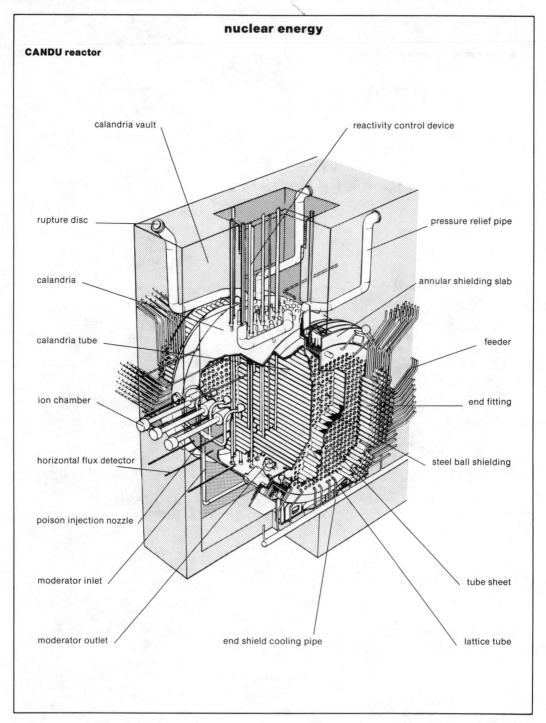

calandria vault

reactivity control device

rupture disc

pressure relief pipe

calandria

annular shielding slab

calandria tube

feeder

ion chamber

end fitting

horizontal flux detector

steel ball shielding

poison injection nozzle

moderator inlet

tube sheet

moderator outlet

end shield cooling pipe

lattice tube

nuclear energy

nuclear reactor

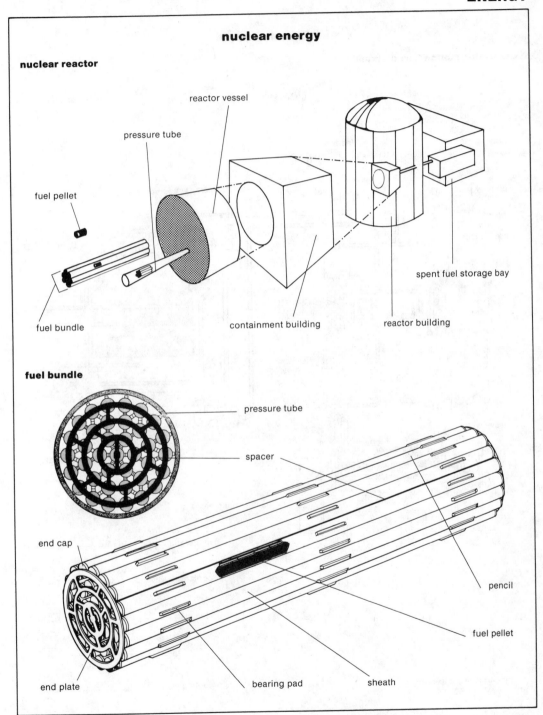

reactor vessel

pressure tube

fuel pellet

fuel bundle

containment building

reactor building

spent fuel storage bay

fuel bundle

pressure tube

spacer

pencil

fuel pellet

end cap

end plate

bearing pad

sheath

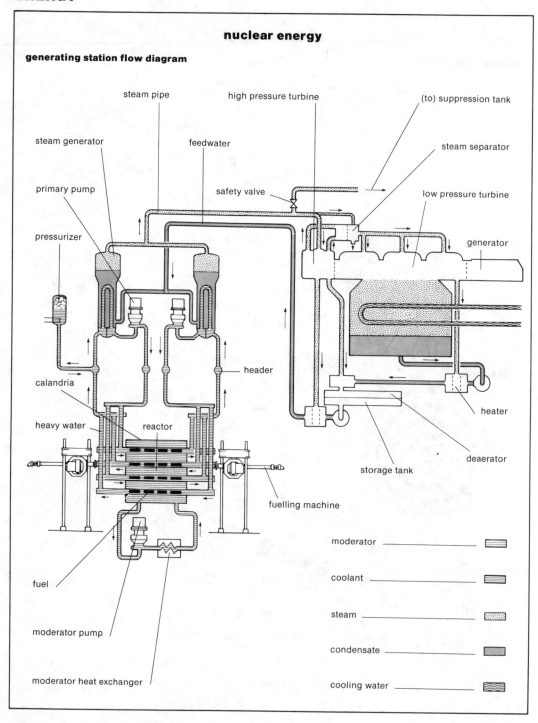

nuclear energy

generating station flow diagram

steam pipe

high pressure turbine

(to) suppression tank

steam generator

feedwater

steam separator

primary pump

safety valve

low pressure turbine

pressurizer

generator

calandria

header

heavy water   reactor

heater

fuelling machine

deaerator

storage tank

fuel

moderator pump

moderator heat exchanger

moderator ———— ▭

coolant ———— ▭

steam ———— ▭

condensate ———— ▭

cooling water ———— ▭

nuclear energy

fuel handling sequence

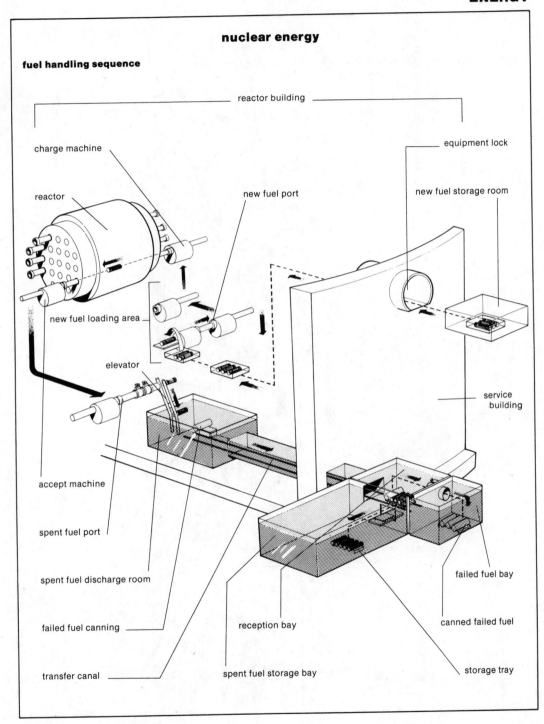

reactor building

charge machine

reactor

new fuel port

equipment lock

new fuel storage room

new fuel loading area

elevator

accept machine

spent fuel port

spent fuel discharge room

service building

failed fuel canning

reception bay

failed fuel bay

canned failed fuel

transfer canal

spent fuel storage bay

storage tray

nuclear energy

control room

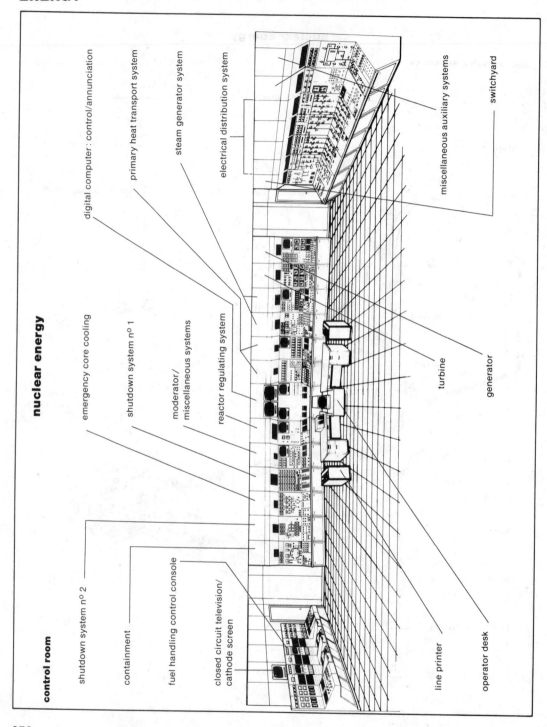

- digital computer : control/annunciation
- primary heat transport system
- steam generator system
- electrical distribution system
- miscellaneous auxiliary systems
- switchyard
- emergency core cooling
- shutdown system n° 1
- moderator/miscellaneous systems
- reactor regulating system
- turbine
- generator
- shutdown system n° 2
- containment
- fuel handling control console
- closed circuit television/cathode screen
- line printer
- operator desk

nuclear energy

production of electricity by nuclear energy

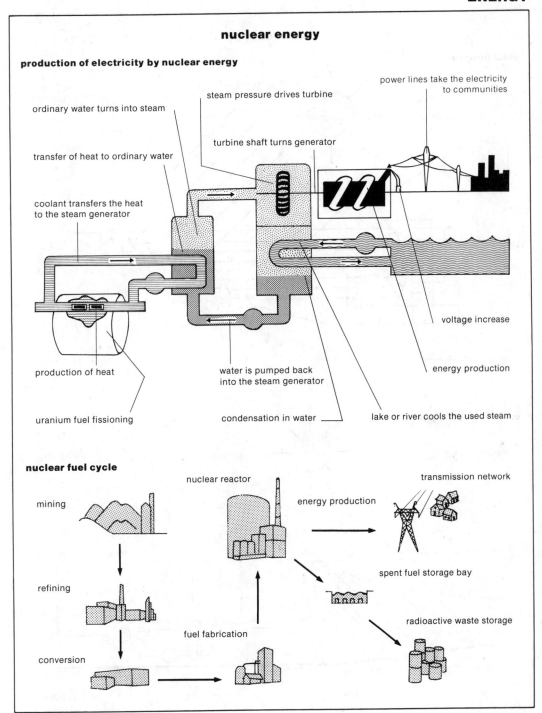

power lines take the electricity to communities

steam pressure drives turbine

ordinary water turns into steam

turbine shaft turns generator

transfer of heat to ordinary water

coolant transfers the heat to the steam generator

voltage increase

production of heat

water is pumped back into the steam generator

energy production

uranium fuel fissioning

condensation in water

lake or river cools the used steam

nuclear fuel cycle

nuclear reactor

transmission network

mining

energy production

refining

spent fuel storage bay

fuel fabrication

radioactive waste storage

conversion

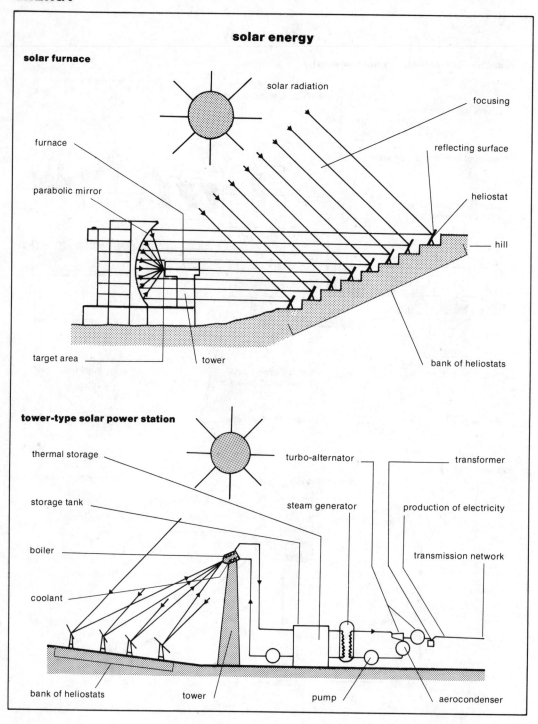

solar energy

solar furnace

solar radiation

focusing

reflecting surface

furnace

heliostat

parabolic mirror

hill

target area

tower

bank of heliostats

tower-type solar power station

thermal storage

turbo-alternator

transformer

storage tank

steam generator

production of electricity

boiler

transmission network

coolant

bank of heliostats

tower

pump

aerocondenser

solar energy

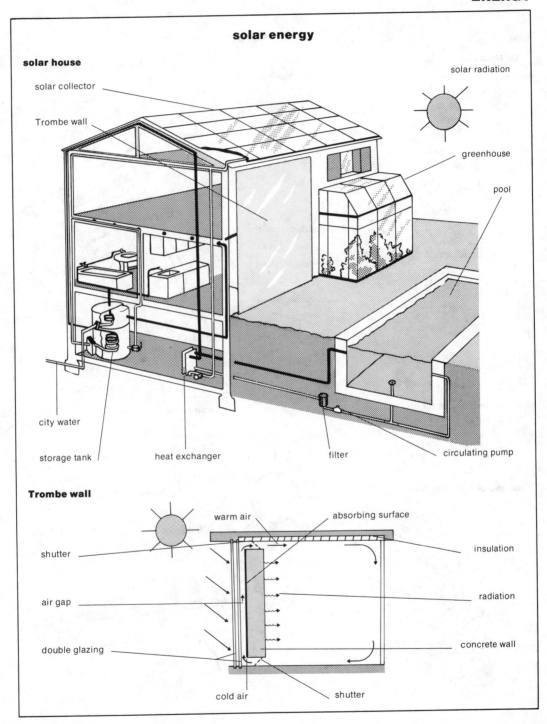

solar house

- solar collector
- Trombe wall
- solar radiation
- greenhouse
- pool
- city water
- storage tank
- heat exchanger
- filter
- circulating pump

Trombe wall

- warm air
- absorbing surface
- shutter
- insulation
- air gap
- radiation
- double glazing
- concrete wall
- cold air
- shutter

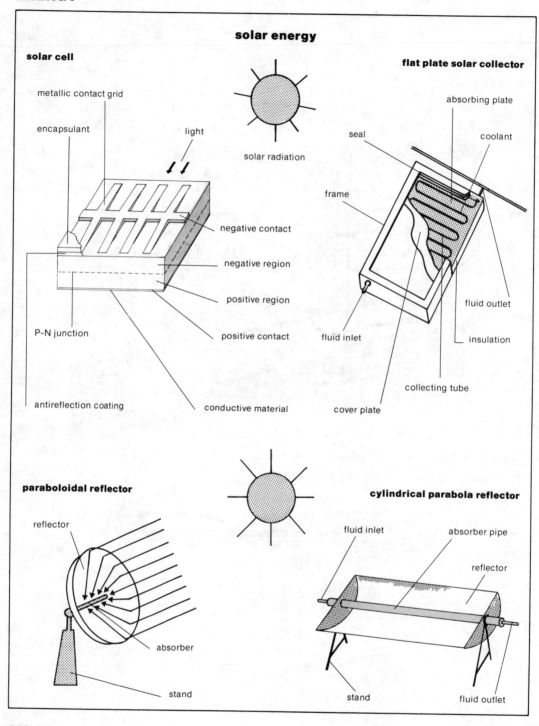

solar energy

solar cell

metallic contact grid

encapsulant

light

solar radiation

negative contact

negative region

positive region

P-N junction

positive contact

antireflection coating

conductive material

flat plate solar collector

absorbing plate

seal

coolant

frame

fluid outlet

fluid inlet

insulation

collecting tube

cover plate

paraboloidal reflector

reflector

absorber

stand

cylindrical parabola reflector

fluid inlet

absorber pipe

reflector

stand

fluid outlet

windmill

tower mill

post mill

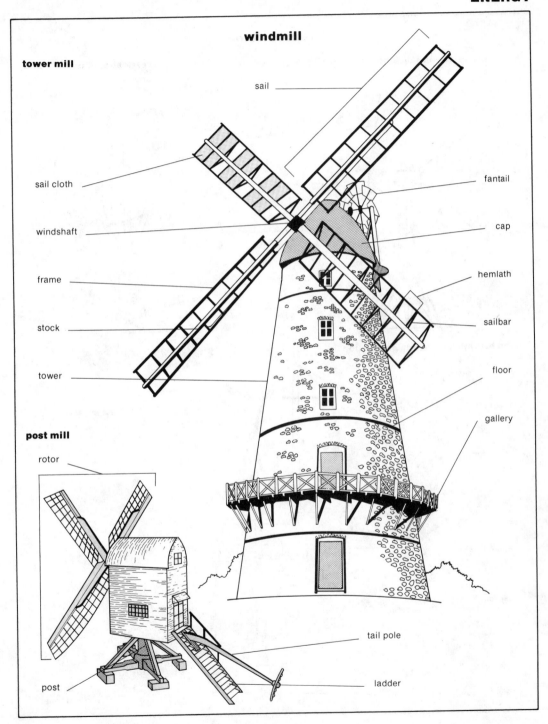

sail

sail cloth

windshaft

frame

stock

tower

rotor

post

fantail

cap

hemlath

sailbar

floor

gallery

tail pole

ladder

wind turbine

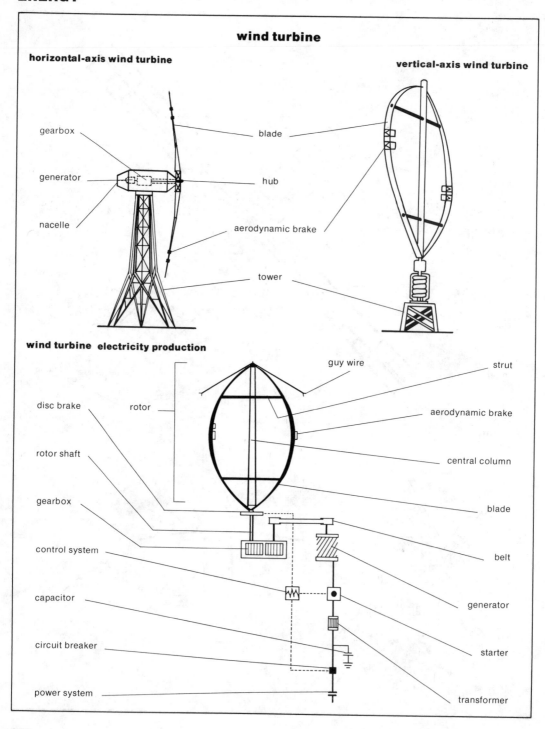

horizontal-axis wind turbine

gearbox

generator

nacelle

blade

hub

aerodynamic brake

tower

vertical-axis wind turbine

wind turbine electricity production

disc brake

rotor shaft

gearbox

control system

capacitor

circuit breaker

power system

rotor

guy wire

strut

aerodynamic brake

central column

blade

belt

generator

starter

transformer

HEAVY MACHINERY

dragline

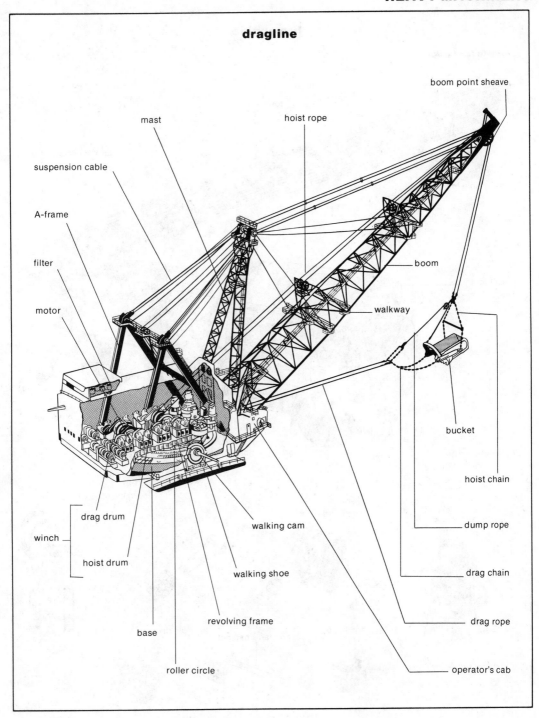

boom point sheave

mast

hoist rope

suspension cable

A-frame

filter

motor

boom

walkway

bucket

hoist chain

dump rope

drag drum

winch

hoist drum

walking cam

drag chain

walking shoe

drag rope

base

revolving frame

operator's cab

roller circle

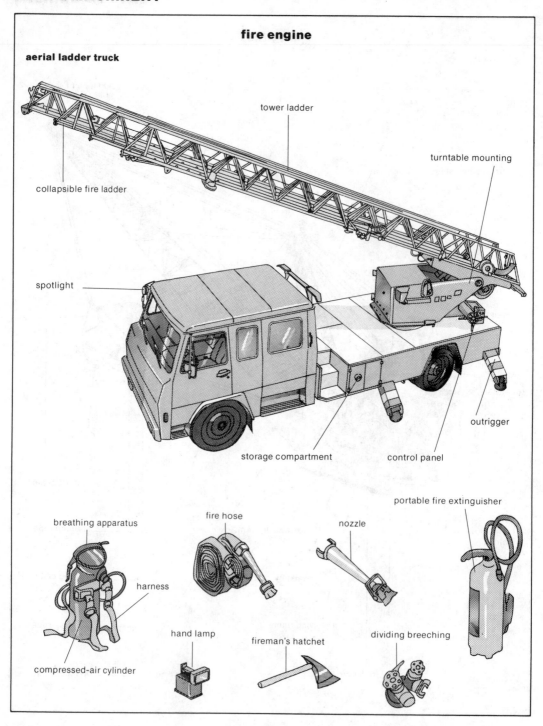

fire engine

aerial ladder truck

tower ladder

turntable mounting

collapsible fire ladder

spotlight

outrigger

storage compartment

control panel

portable fire extinguisher

breathing apparatus

fire hose

nozzle

harness

hand lamp

fireman's hatchet

dividing breeching

compressed-air cylinder

fire engine

pumper

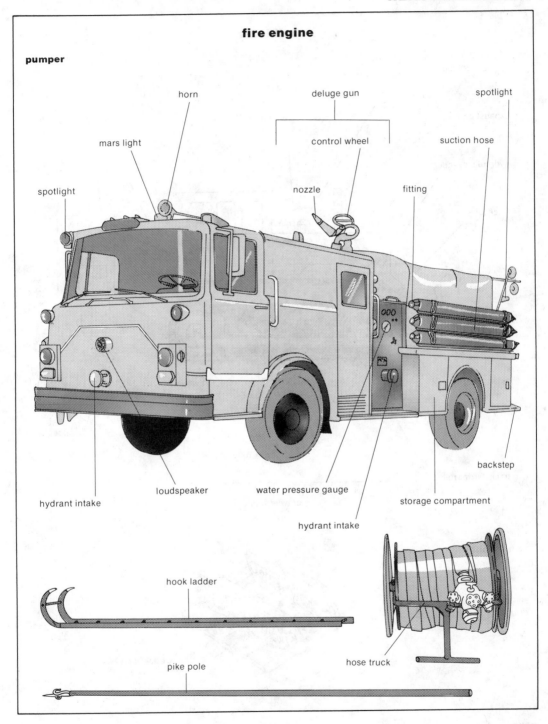

horn

deluge gun

spotlight

mars light

control wheel

suction hose

spotlight

nozzle

fitting

backstep

loudspeaker

water pressure gauge

storage compartment

hydrant intake

hydrant intake

hook ladder

hose truck

pike pole

bulldozer

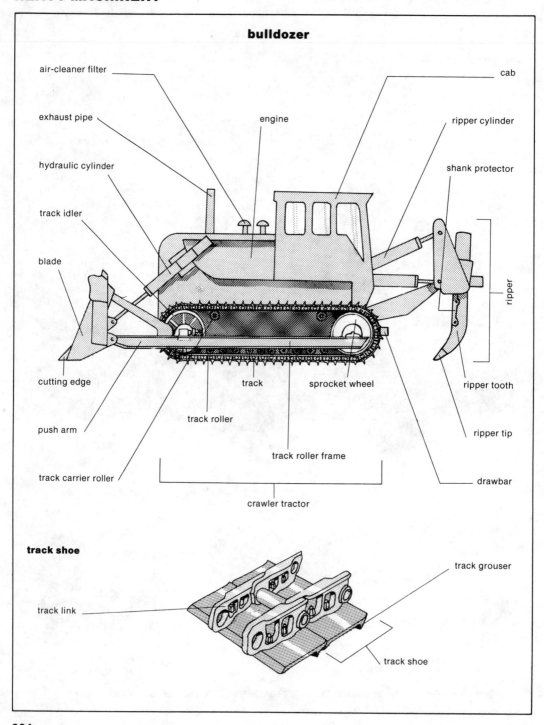

air-cleaner filter

cab

exhaust pipe

engine

ripper cylinder

hydraulic cylinder

shank protector

track idler

blade

ripper

cutting edge

track

sprocket wheel

ripper tooth

push arm

track roller

ripper tip

track carrier roller

track roller frame

drawbar

crawler tractor

track shoe

track grouser

track link

track shoe

backhoe loader

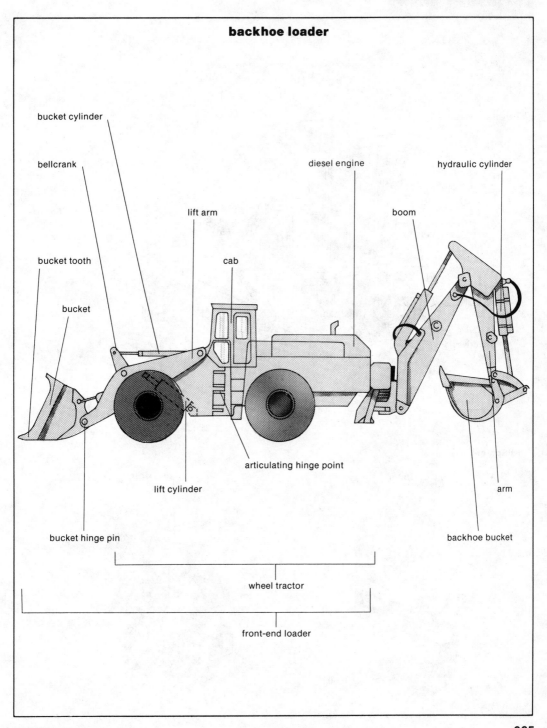

bucket cylinder

bellcrank

diesel engine

hydraulic cylinder

bucket tooth

lift arm

boom

bucket

cab

articulating hinge point

lift cylinder

arm

bucket hinge pin

backhoe bucket

wheel tractor

front-end loader

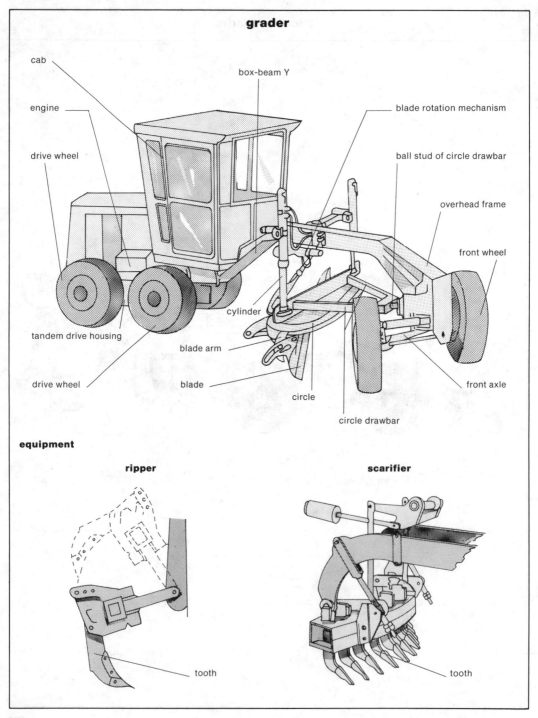

grader

cab

box-beam Y

blade rotation mechanism

engine

ball stud of circle drawbar

drive wheel

overhead frame

front wheel

cylinder

tandem drive housing

blade arm

drive wheel

blade

front axle

circle

circle drawbar

equipment

ripper

scarifier

tooth

tooth

hydraulic shovel

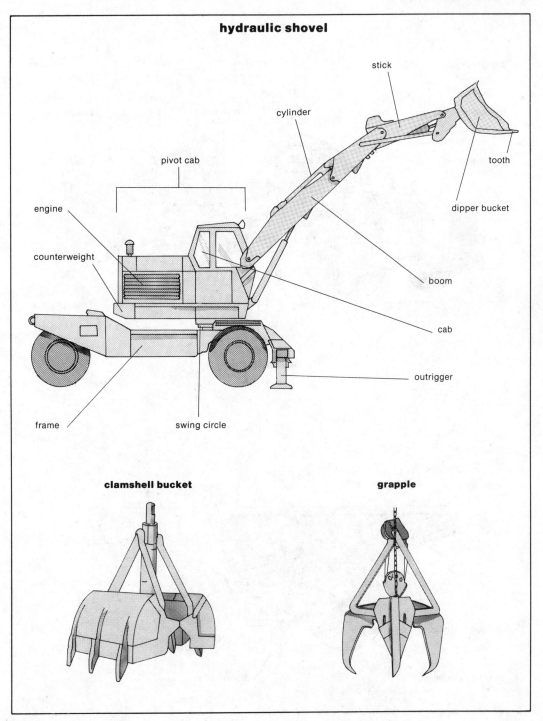

stick

cylinder

tooth

pivot cab

dipper bucket

engine

counterweight

boom

cab

outrigger

frame

swing circle

clamshell bucket

grapple

HEAVY MACHINERY

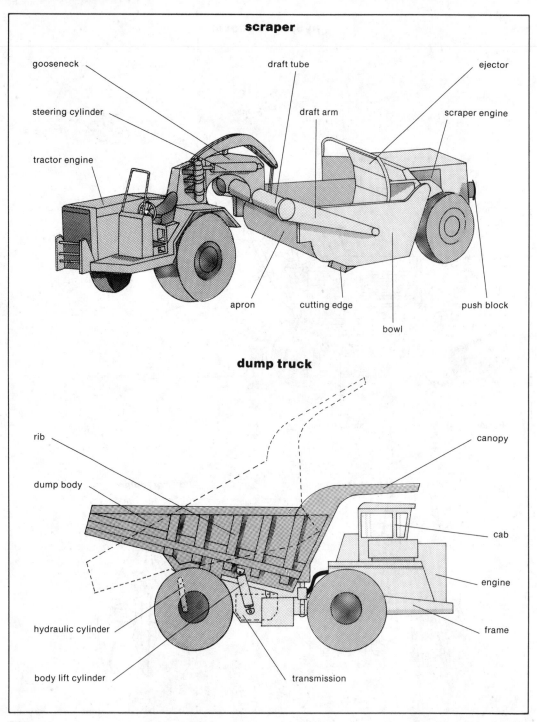

scraper

gooseneck

draft tube

ejector

steering cylinder

draft arm

scraper engine

tractor engine

apron

cutting edge

push block

bowl

dump truck

rib

canopy

dump body

cab

engine

frame

hydraulic cylinder

body lift cylinder

transmission

crane

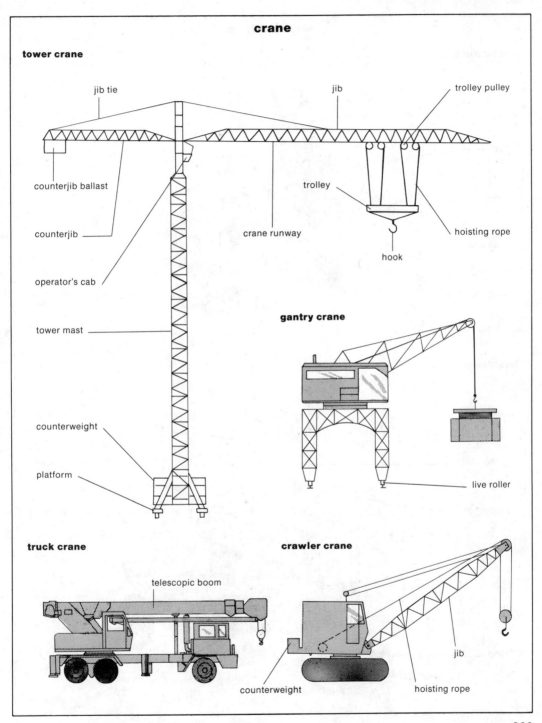

tower crane

jib tie

jib

trolley pulley

counterjib ballast

trolley

hoisting rope

counterjib

crane runway

hook

operator's cab

tower mast

gantry crane

counterweight

platform

live roller

truck crane

crawler crane

telescopic boom

jib

counterweight

hoisting rope

MATERIAL HANDLING

power lift truck

forklift truck

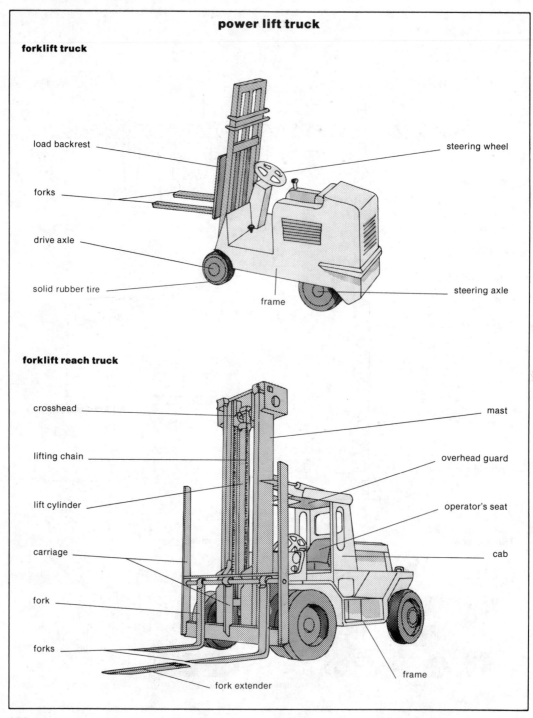

load backrest

steering wheel

forks

drive axle

solid rubber tire

frame

steering axle

forklift reach truck

crosshead

mast

lifting chain

overhead guard

lift cylinder

operator's seat

carriage

cab

fork

forks

frame

fork extender

handling engines

hand truck

platform truck

manual lift truck

hand pallet truck

pallets

double-decked pallet

single-decked pallet

top deckboard

stringer

top deckboard

bottom deckboard

entry

stringer board

block

wing pallet

box pallet

side

WEAPONS

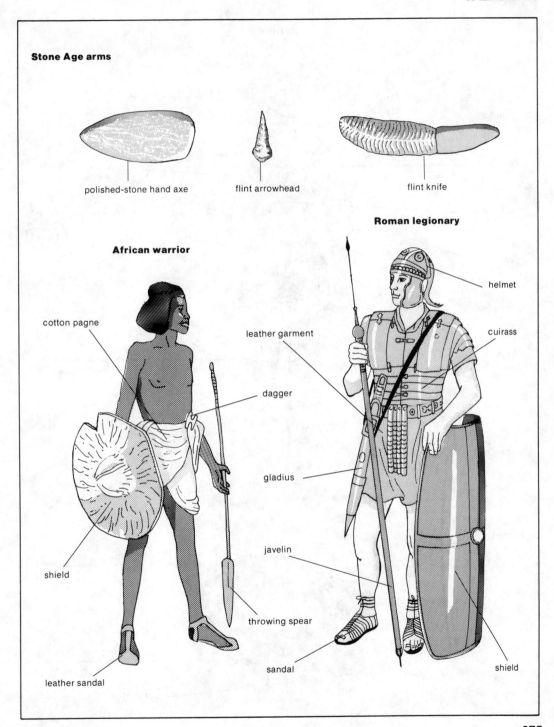

Stone Age arms

polished-stone hand axe

flint arrowhead

flint knife

Roman legionary

African warrior

cotton pagne

leather garment

dagger

helmet

cuirass

gladius

shield

javelin

throwing spear

sandal

shield

leather sandal

armor

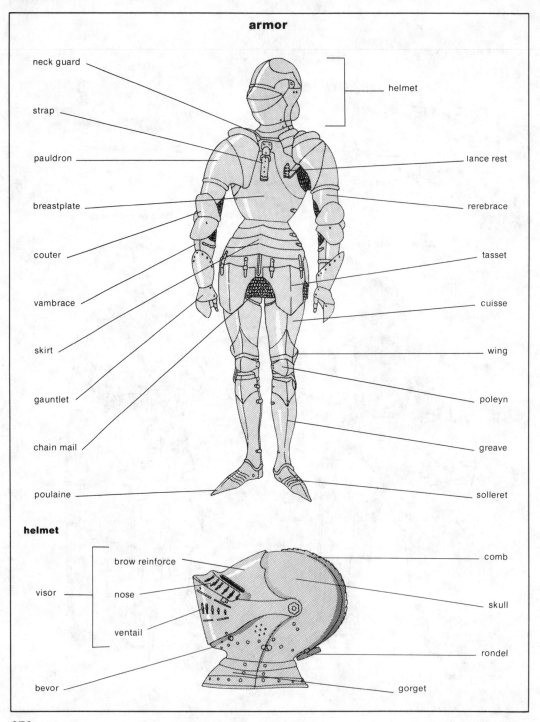

neck guard

strap

pauldron

breastplate

couter

vambrace

skirt

gauntlet

chain mail

poulaine

helmet

lance rest

rerebrace

tasset

cuisse

wing

poleyn

greave

solleret

helmet

brow reinforce

visor

nose

ventail

bevor

comb

skull

rondel

gorget

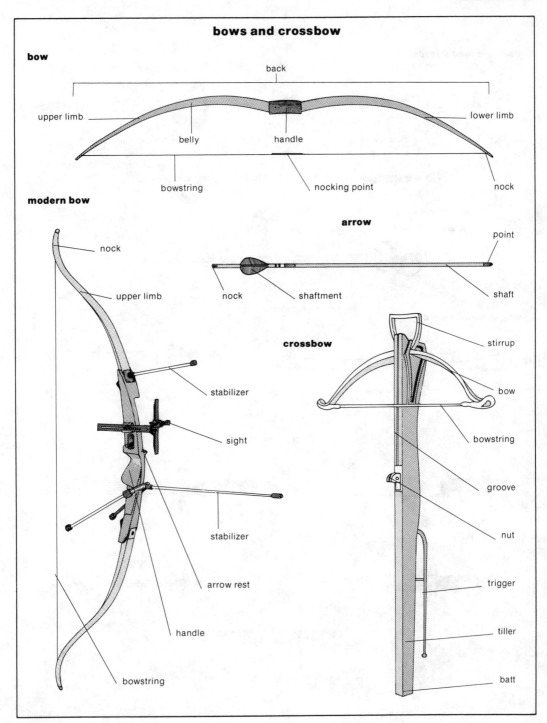

bows and crossbow

bow

back

upper limb · lower limb

belly · handle

bowstring · nocking point · nock

modern bow

nock

upper limb

stabilizer

sight

stabilizer

arrow rest

handle

bowstring

arrow

point

nock · shaftment · shaft

crossbow

stirrup

bow

bowstring

groove

nut

trigger

tiller

batt

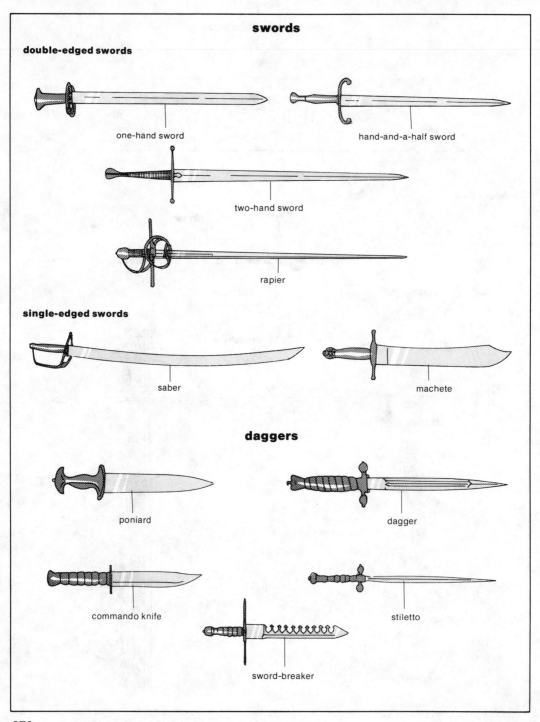

swords

double-edged swords

one-hand sword

hand-and-a-half sword

two-hand sword

rapier

single-edged swords

saber

machete

daggers

poniard

dagger

commando knife

stiletto

sword-breaker

bayonets

major types of bayonets

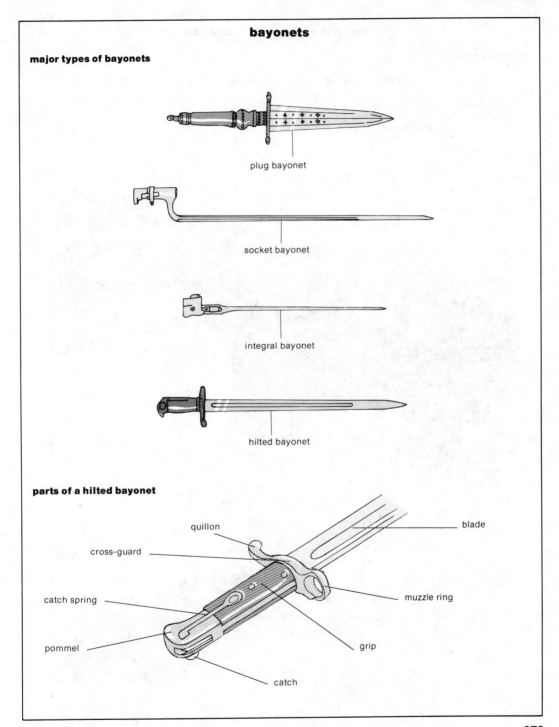

plug bayonet

socket bayonet

integral bayonet

hilted bayonet

parts of a hilted bayonet

quillon

cross-guard

catch spring

pommel

catch

blade

muzzle ring

grip

seventeenth century cannon

muzzle loading

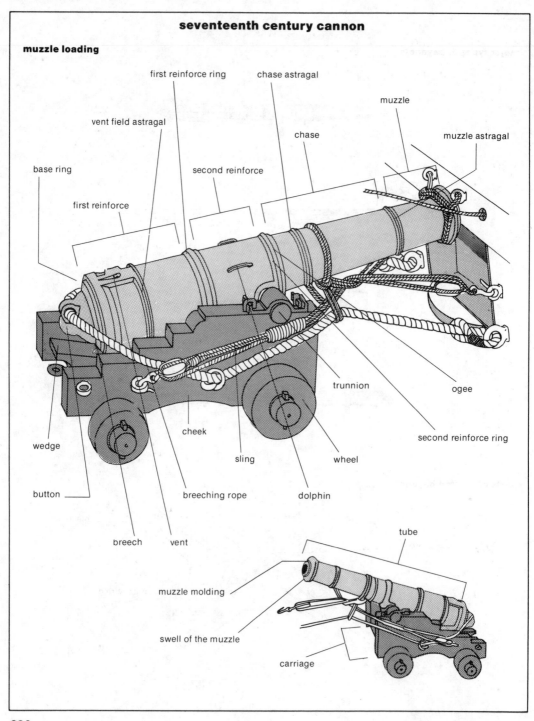

first reinforce ring

chase astragal

muzzle

vent field astragal

chase

muzzle astragal

base ring

second reinforce

first reinforce

trunnion

ogee

wedge

second reinforce ring

button

cheek

sling

wheel

breeching rope

dolphin

breech

vent

tube

muzzle molding

swell of the muzzle

carriage

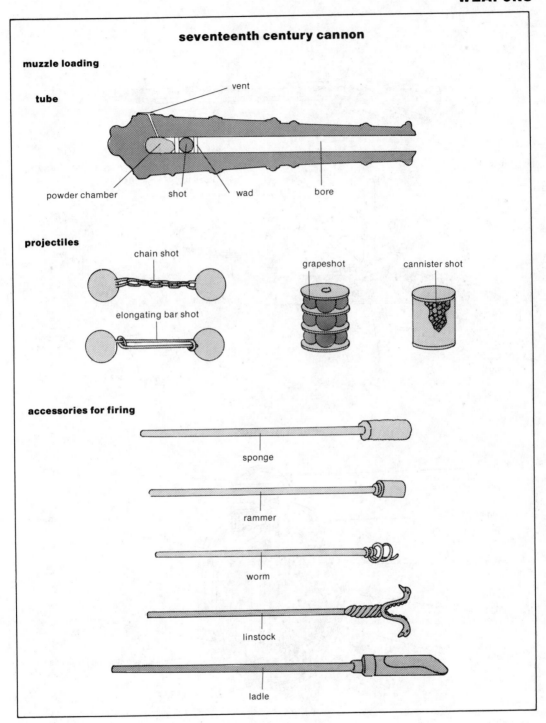

seventeenth century cannon

muzzle loading

tube

vent

powder chamber   shot   wad   bore

projectiles

chain shot

elongating bar shot

grapeshot

cannister shot

accessories for firing

sponge

rammer

worm

linstock

ladle

WEAPONS

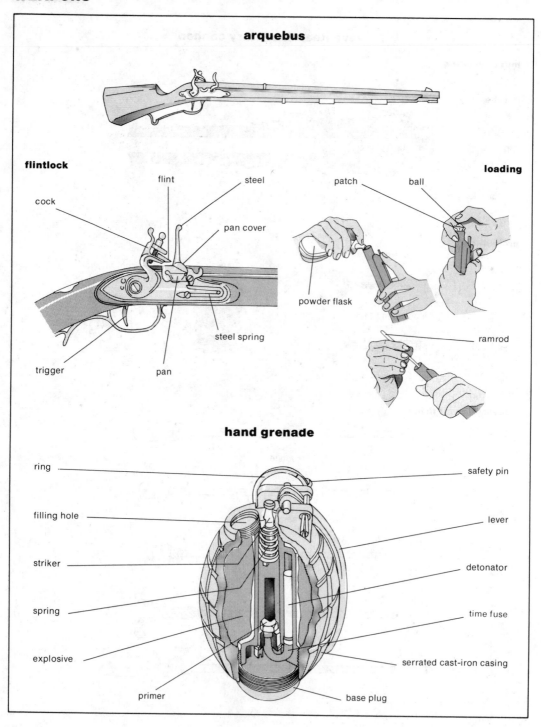

arquebus

flintlock

cock

flint

steel

pan cover

pan

trigger

steel spring

loading

patch

ball

powder flask

ramrod

hand grenade

ring

safety pin

filling hole

lever

striker

detonator

spring

time fuse

explosive

serrated cast-iron casing

primer

base plug

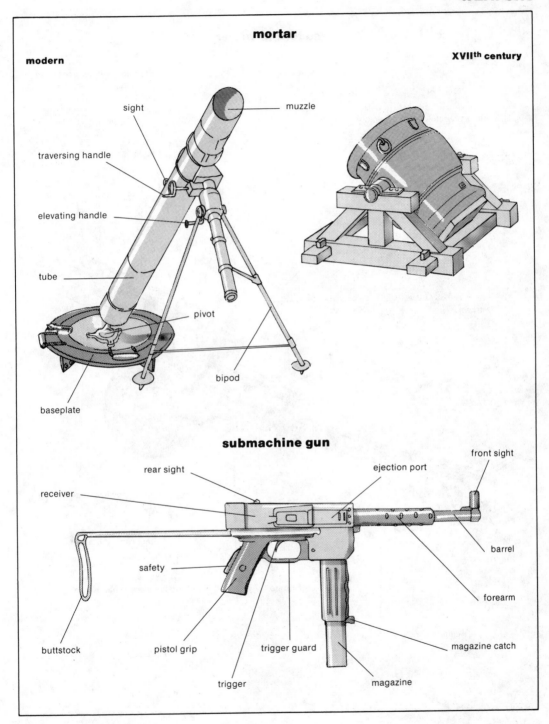

mortar

modern

XVIIth century

sight

muzzle

traversing handle

elevating handle

tube

pivot

bipod

baseplate

submachine gun

rear sight

ejection port

front sight

receiver

barrel

safety

forearm

buttstock

magazine catch

pistol grip

trigger guard

trigger

magazine

modern howitzer

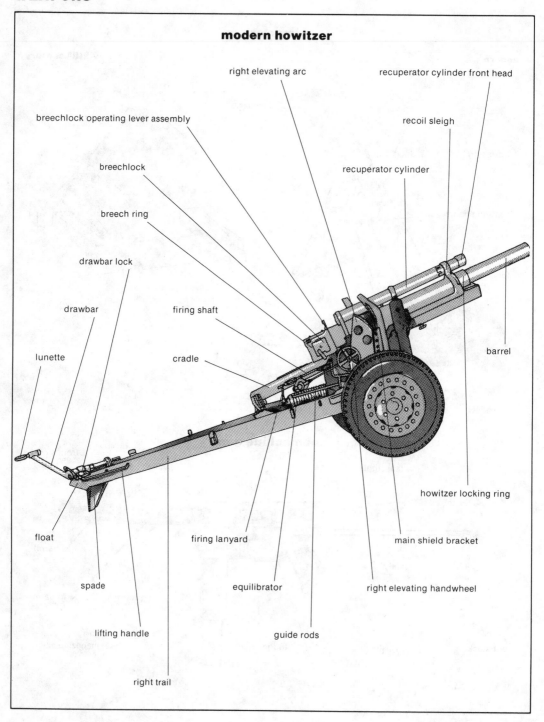

right elevating arc

recuperator cylinder front head

breechlock operating lever assembly

recoil sleigh

breechlock

recuperator cylinder

breech ring

drawbar lock

drawbar

firing shaft

lunette

cradle

barrel

float

firing lanyard

howitzer locking ring

spade

equilibrator

main shield bracket

lifting handle

guide rods

right elevating handwheel

right trail

automatic rifle

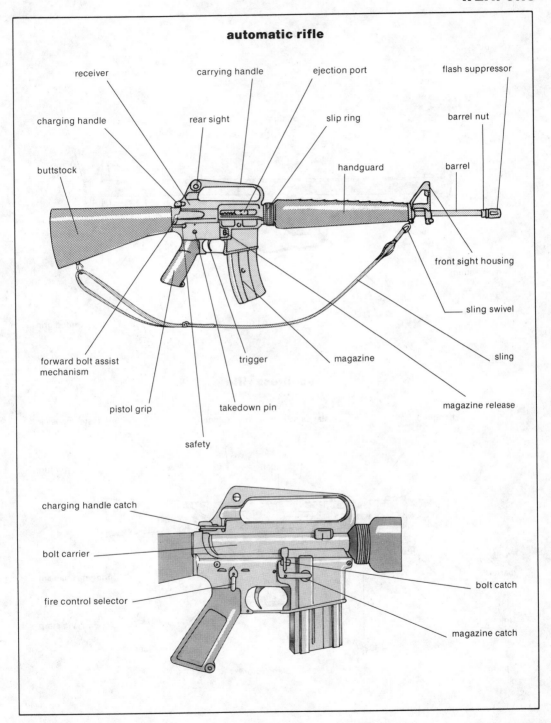

receiver

carrying handle

ejection port

flash suppressor

charging handle

rear sight

slip ring

barrel nut

buttstock

handguard

barrel

front sight housing

sling swivel

forward bolt assist mechanism

trigger

magazine

sling

pistol grip

takedown pin

magazine release

safety

charging handle catch

bolt carrier

fire control selector

bolt catch

magazine catch

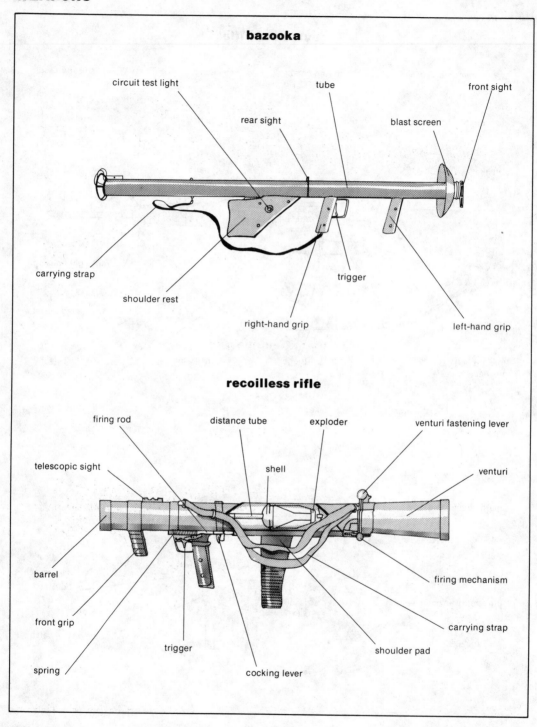

bazooka

circuit test light

tube

front sight

rear sight

blast screen

carrying strap

shoulder rest

trigger

left-hand grip

right-hand grip

recoilless rifle

firing rod

distance tube

exploder

venturi fastening lever

telescopic sight

shell

venturi

barrel

firing mechanism

front grip

carrying strap

spring

trigger

cocking lever

shoulder pad

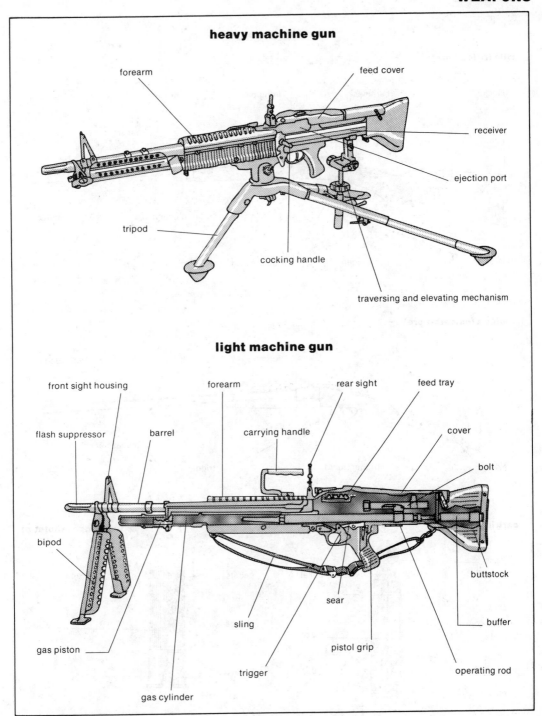

heavy machine gun

forearm

feed cover

receiver

ejection port

tripod

cocking handle

traversing and elevating mechanism

light machine gun

front sight housing

forearm

rear sight

feed tray

flash suppressor

barrel

carrying handle

cover

bolt

bipod

buttstock

gas piston

sear

buffer

sling

pistol grip

operating rod

trigger

gas cylinder

WEAPONS

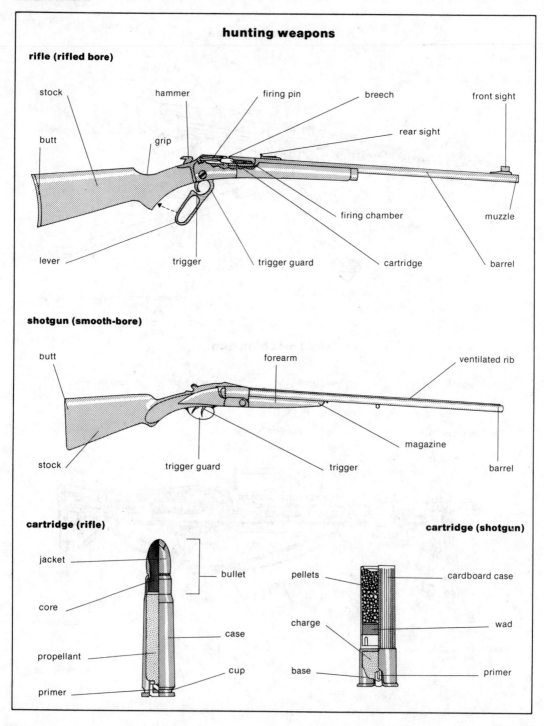

hunting weapons

rifle (rifled bore)

stock · hammer · firing pin · breech · front sight · butt · grip · rear sight · firing chamber · muzzle · lever · trigger · trigger guard · cartridge · barrel

shotgun (smooth-bore)

butt · forearm · ventilated rib · stock · trigger guard · trigger · magazine · barrel

cartridge (rifle)

jacket · bullet · core · case · propellant · cup · primer

cartridge (shotgun)

pellets · cardboard case · charge · wad · base · primer

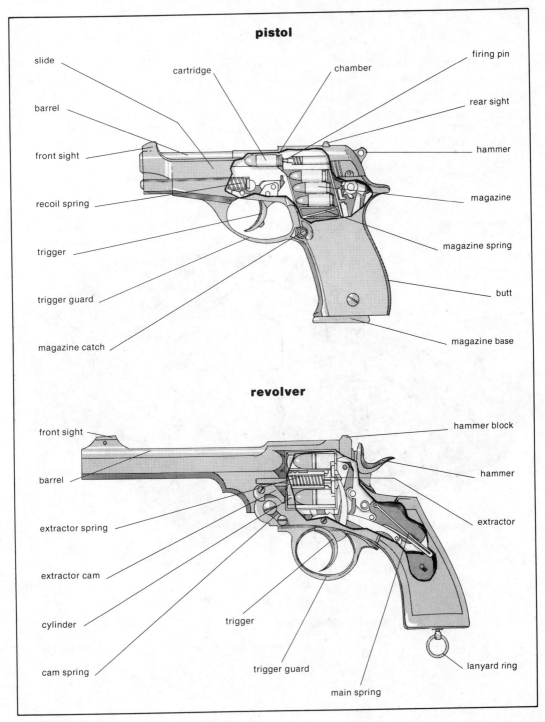

pistol

slide

cartridge

chamber

firing pin

barrel

rear sight

front sight

hammer

recoil spring

magazine

trigger

magazine spring

trigger guard

butt

magazine catch

magazine base

revolver

front sight

hammer block

barrel

hammer

extractor spring

extractor

extractor cam

cylinder

trigger

cam spring

trigger guard

lanyard ring

main spring

tank

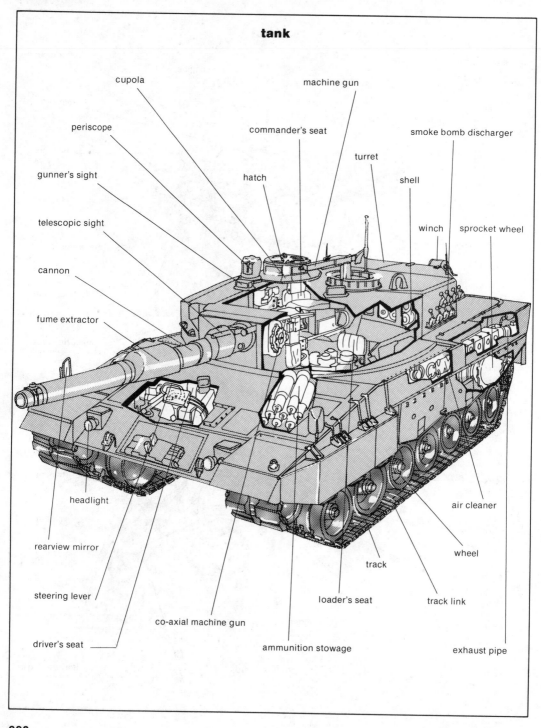

cupola

machine gun

periscope

commander's seat

smoke bomb discharger

turret

gunner's sight

hatch

shell

telescopic sight

winch

sprocket wheel

cannon

fume extractor

headlight

air cleaner

rearview mirror

wheel

track

steering lever

loader's seat

track link

co-axial machine gun

driver's seat

ammunition stowage

exhaust pipe

combat aircraft

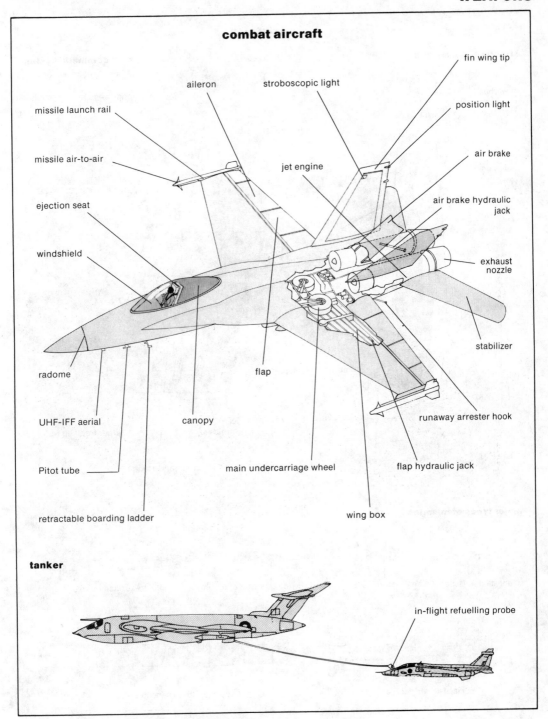

fin wing tip

aileron

stroboscopic light

position light

missile launch rail

air brake

missile air-to-air

jet engine

air brake hydraulic jack

ejection seat

exhaust nozzle

windshield

stabilizer

radome

flap

UHF-IFF aerial

canopy

runaway arrester hook

Pitot tube

main undercarriage wheel

flap hydraulic jack

retractable boarding ladder

wing box

tanker

in-flight refuelling probe

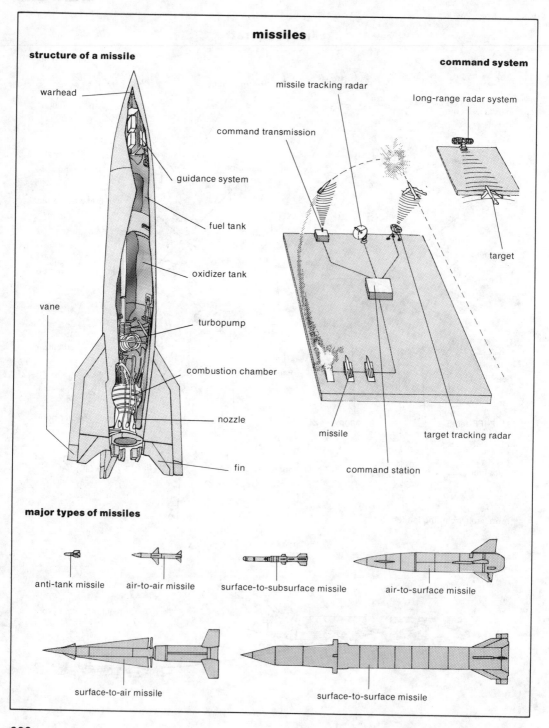

missiles

structure of a missile

warhead

guidance system

fuel tank

oxidizer tank

vane

turbopump

combustion chamber

nozzle

fin

command system

missile tracking radar

command transmission

long-range radar system

target

missile

target tracking radar

command station

major types of missiles

anti-tank missile

air-to-air missile

surface-to-subsurface missile

air-to-surface missile

surface-to-air missile

surface-to-surface missile

SYMBOLS

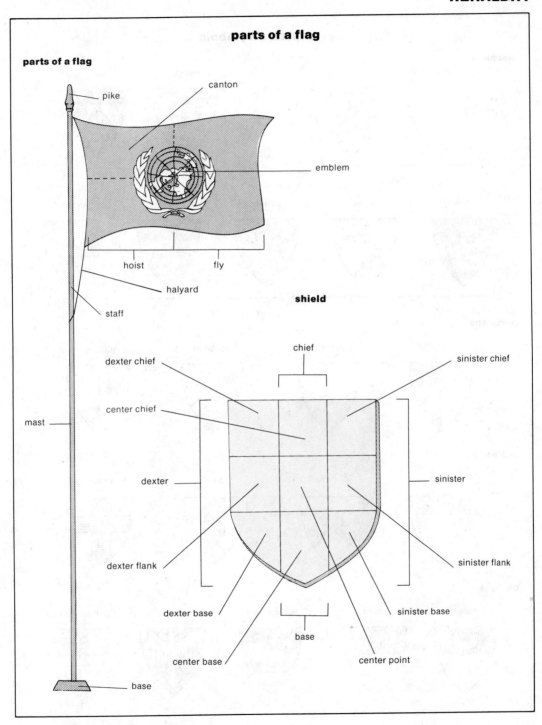

parts of a flag

parts of a flag

pike

canton

emblem

hoist

fly

halyard

staff

shield

chief

dexter chief

sinister chief

center chief

mast

dexter

sinister

dexter flank

sinister flank

dexter base

sinister base

base

center base

center point

base

HERALDRY

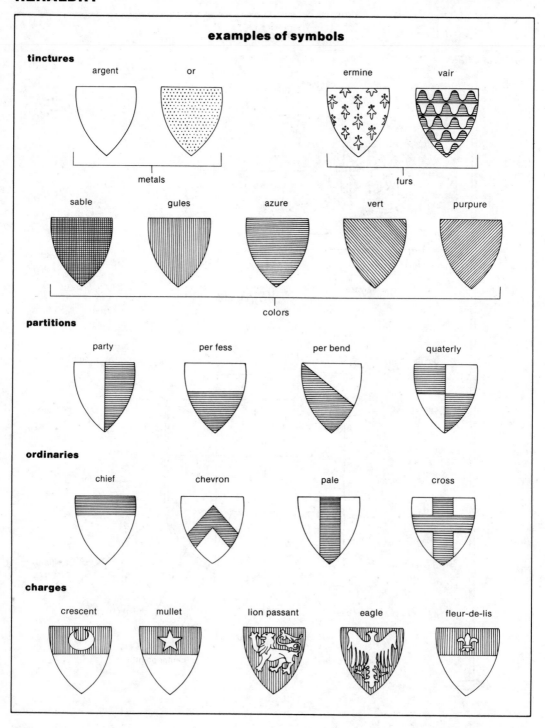

examples of symbols

tinctures

argent   or   ermine   vair

metals   furs

sable   gules   azure   vert   purpure

colors

partitions

party   per fess   per bend   quaterly

ordinaries

chief   chevron   pale   cross

charges

crescent   mullet   lion passant   eagle   fleur-de-lis

flag shapes

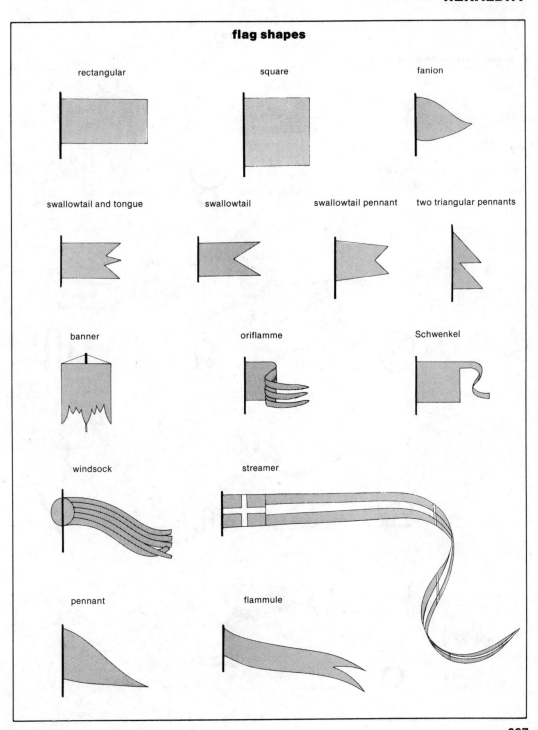

rectangular

square

fanion

swallowtail and tongue

swallowtail

swallowtail pennant

two triangular pennants

banner

oriflamme

Schwenkel

windsock

streamer

pennant

flammule

SIGNS OF THE ZODIAC

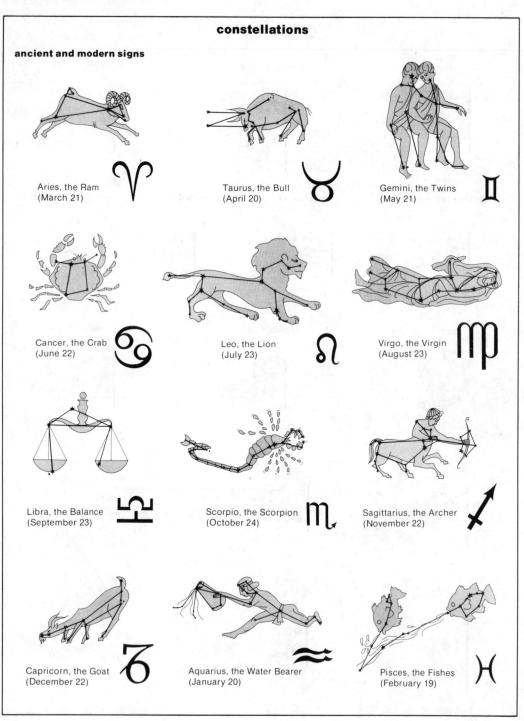

constellations

ancient and modern signs

Aries, the Ram
(March 21)

Taurus, the Bull
(April 20)

Gemini, the Twins
(May 21)

Cancer, the Crab
(June 22)

Leo, the Lion
(July 23)

Virgo, the Virgin
(August 23)

Libra, the Balance
(September 23)

Scorpio, the Scorpion
(October 24)

Sagittarius, the Archer
(November 22)

Capricorn, the Goat
(December 22)

Aquarius, the Water Bearer
(January 20)

Pisces, the Fishes
(February 19)

graphic elements for symbols

colors

red = danger, no... or do not...

examples

do not wash

no entry

blue = regulation, indication

examples

hospital

direction to be followed

yellow = be careful

examples

hand wash in lukerwarm water

priority road

green = permission, indication

example

50°C

machine wash in warm water
at a normal setting

graphic elements

or   = do not... no...

= danger, be careful

examples

do not dry clean

no entry for
power-driven vehicles

examples

flammable

pedestrian crossing

NOTICE SYMBOLS

international road signs

danger warning signs

right bend

double bend

dangerous bend

dangerous descent

steep hill

roadway narrows

bumps

ridge

slippery road

loose gravel

falling rocks

school zone

pedestrian crossing

international road signs

danger warning signs (cont.)

cyclists entering or crossing

cattle crossing

wild animals crossing

road works

light signals

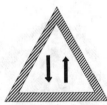
two-way traffic

other dangers

traffic circle

priority intersection

grade crossing

signs regulating priority at intersections

« give way » sign

stop at intersection

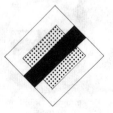
« priority road » sign

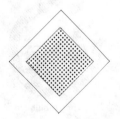
« end of priority » sign

NOTICE SYMBOLS

international road signs

prohibitory or regulatory signs

no entry

no entry for mopeds

no entry for bicycles

no entry for motorcycles

no entry for goods vehicles

no entry for pedestrians

no entry for
power-driven vehicles

width clearance

overhead clearance

weight limitation

no left turn

no U-turn

passing prohibited

end of prohibition
of passing

maximum speed limit

use of audible warning
devices prohibited

702

international road signs

mandatory signs

direction to be followed

direction to be followed

direction to be followed

direction to be followed

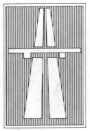

compulsory roundabout

informative signs

one-way traffic

superhighway

end of superhighway

standing and parking signs

parking prohibited or restricted

standing and parking
prohibited or restricted

parking

NOTICE SYMBOLS

common symbols

information

first aid

hospital

police

telephone

do not enter

no dogs

fire hose

fire extinguisher

caution,
pedestrian crossing

caution, slippery floor

caution

danger, electrical hazard

danger, poison

danger, flammable

common symbols

access for physically handicapped

do not use for wheelchairs

smoking permitted

smoking prohibited

toilet for men

toilet for women

toilet for men and women

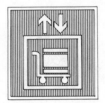
elevator for people

freight elevator

escalator, up

escalator, down

stairs

restaurant

coffee shop

NOTICE SYMBOLS

common symbols

lost and found articles

bar

duty-free

post office

currency exchange

telegrams

drug store

barber

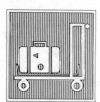

baggage carts

do not use
for baggage carts

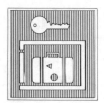

lockers

baggage claim

check-in

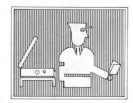

inspection services

common symbols

hotel information

car rental

taxi transportation

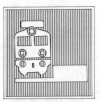
bus transportation

ground transportation

air transportation

helicopter transportation

rail transportation

breakdown service

service station

camping and caravan site

picnic area

picnics prohibited

camping area

camping prohibited

NOTICE SYMBOLS

fabric care

washing

machine wash
in lukewarm water at a gentle
setting-reduced agitation

machine wash
in warm water at a gentle
setting-reduced agitation

do not wash

hand wash
in lukewarm water

chlorine bleaching

machine wash
in warm water at a
normal setting

machine wash
in hot water at a
normal setting

do not use chlorine bleach

use chlorine bleach
as directed

drying

dry flat

tumble dry
at low temperature

tumble dry
at medium to high
temperature

hang to dry

drip dry

ironing

do not iron

iron at low setting

iron at medium setting

iron at high setting

dry cleaning

do not dry clean

dry clean

biology

♂   male

♀   female

†   death

✳   birth

mathematics

$+$ addition

$-$ subtraction

$\times$ multiplication

$\div$ division

$\pm$ plus or minus

$=$ is equal to

$\neq$ is not equal to

$\equiv$ is identical with

$\not\equiv$ is not identical with

$\approx$ is approximately equal to

$\simeq$ is equivalent to

$>$ is greater than

$\geq$ is equal to or greater than

$<$ is less than

$\leq$ is equal to or less than

$\sqrt[2]{\ }$ square root of

∞ infinity

$\%$ percent

$\cup$ union

$\cap$ intersection

$\subset$ is contained in

$\in$ is a member of

$\varnothing$ empty set

miscellaneous

℞   prescription

&   ampersand

©   copyright

®   registered trademark

$ dollar

¢   cent

£   pound

→   reaction direction

⇌   reversible reaction

$+$ positive charge

$-$ negative charge

GENERAL INDEX

1

10 yards line. 517.
120-volt circuit. 278.
15 yards line. 517.

2

240-volt circuit. 278.
240-volt feeder cable. 278.
25 yards line. 517.

5

5 yards line. 517.

A

A-frame. 661.
abacus. 160.
abdomen. 92, 95, 98, 106.
abdominal aorta. 117, 120.
abdominal rectus. 110.
abdominal segment. 92.
aboveground pipeline. 630.
abruptly pinnate. 62.
absorbent cotton. 615.
absorber. 656.
absorber pipe. 656.
absorbing plate. 656.
absorbing surface. 655.
abutment. 165, 400, 401, 402.
abyssal hill. 42.
abyssal plain. 42.
Ac cord. 363, 365.
acanthus leaf. 160, 200.
accelerator control. 243.
accent mark. 462.
accept machine. 651.
access for physically handicapped.
   705.
access gallery. 641, 646.
access panel. 195, 263.
access ramp. 177.
access shaft. 646.
accessories for firing. 681.
accidentals. 462.
accommodation ladder. 420.
accordion. 475.
accordion. 188, 189.
accordion bag. 338.
accordion door. 178.
accordion pleat. 294.
accordion windows. 341.
account book. 450.
Ace. 578.
acetylene cylinder. 271.
acetylene valve. 272.
achene. 66, 70.
acorn nut. 254.
acoustic baffle. 421.
acoustic ceiling. 169.
acoustic coupler. 457.
acoustic coupler. 455.

acoustic echo. 428.
acoustic resistance. 372.
acromion. 113.
acroterion. 161.
action. 465.
acute accent. 347.
Adam's apple. 106.
addition. 709.
adductor muscle. 94.
adhesive bandages. 615.
adhesive tape. 615.
adipose tissue. 109, 128.
adit. 622.
adjustable channel. 249.
adjustable foot. 368.
adjustable frame. 252.
adjustable lamp. 211.
adjustable pedestal. 195.
adjustable seat. 407.
adjustable spud wrench. 266.
adjustable waist tab. 283.
adjustable waistband. 307.
adjustable wrench. 248.
adjusting knob. 247.
adjusting lever. 478.
adjusting nut. 599.
adjusting ring. 250.
adjusting screw. 249, 272, 598.
adjustment slide. 284.
adjustment wheel. 277.
administration building. 624.
administration office. 634.
administrative building. 646.
advertising sign. 414.
adze. 574.
aerated filter. 267.
aerator. 261.
aerocondenser. 654.
aerodynamic brake. 658.
affricate consonants. 348.
Africa. 41.
African warrior. 675.
Afro. 321.
Afro comb. 328.
aft stabilizer fin. 419.
afterbay. 637, 638, 641.
afterfeather. 88.
aftermast. 416.
agitator. 230.
agnolotti. 137.
agricultural machinery. 152, 153,
   154.
aiguilette de gîte à la noix. 141.
aiguillette de romsteck. 141.
aileron. 434, 542, 691.
air bladder. 91.
air brake. 542, 691.
air brake handle. 542.
air brake hydraulic jack. 691.
air bulb release. 359.
air cap. 270.
air chamber. 257, 262.
air-circulating fan. 196.
air cleaner. 690.
air-cleaner filter. 664.
air concentrator. 330.

air conditioning. 196.
air conditioning. 407.
air fan. 155.
air filter. 243, 391.
air gap. 655.
air hole. 99, 335, 352.
air hose. 536, 625.
air impeller. 196.
air inlet. 436, 441.
air inlet control. 191.
air inlet grille. 330.
air intake. 34, 404, 422.
air leg. 625.
air lock. 423, 424.
air lock entrance hatch. 423.
air mattress. 584.
air outlet grille. 330.
air passage. 625.
air pressure adjusting screw. 270.
air-pressure pump. 598.
air scoop. 394.
air sealing gland. 468.
air space. 34, 89.
air tank. 423.
air temperature. 54, 55.
air-tight diaphragm. 391.
air-to-air missile. 692.
air-to-surface missile. 692.
air transportation. 707.
air tube. 195.
air valve. 270.
air vent. 232.
air warning radar. 425.
aircraft gate. 438.
airframe. 543.
airlock. 34, 647.
airport. 438, 439.
airspeed indicator. 542.
aisle. 164.
ala. 125.
Alaskan snowshoe. 549.
albumen. 89.
alidade. 600.
alighting board. 99.
align horizontally. 350.
align vertically. 350.
alkylation unit. 634.
alley. 523, 528.
almond. 67, 70.
alphabet. 371.
alphabet. 137.
alphanumeric keyboard. 456.
alpine skier. 545.
alpine skiing. 545, 546.
Alsace glass. 212.
Altar. 33.
altazimuth mounting. 609.
alteration line. 489.
alternator. 391, 404.
alternator indicator. 385.
altimeter. 541, 542.
altitude coarse-motion clamp. 609.
altitude control system. 57.
altitude scales. 39.
altocumulus. 44.
altostratus. 44.

alula. 88.
alveolar bone. 115.
amanita virosa. 65.
ambulatory. 164.
American bread. 138.
American Cheddar. 144.
American corn bread. 138.
American white bread. 138.
ammeter. 396.
ammunition stowage. 690.
ampersand. 709.
amplifier. 374.
amplifier-tuner. 364.
ampulla. 128.
ampulla of uterine tube. 109.
anal canal. 119.
anal fin. 90.
anal proleg. 92.
analog display. 591.
analog frequency meter. 364.
analytical balance. 595.
anchor. 433.
anchor cable. 433.
anchor-windlass room. 419.
anchorage block. 402.
anchors, types of. 433.
ancient writing instruments. 352.
ancitipator indicator. 597.
anconeus. 111.
andiron. 191.
Andromeda. 32.
anemometer. 55.
aneroid barometer. 598.
Anfrom. 144.
angle brace. 180.
angle scale. 253.
angle valve. 193.
Anik. 378.
animal cell. 105.
animal kingdom. 79.
ankle. 106.
ankle length. 287.
anklet. 301.
annular combustion chamber. 436.
annular eclipse. 29.
annular shielding slab. 648.
annulet. 160.
anode. 263, 606.
antarctic circle. 27.
Antarctic Ocean. 41.
Antarctica. 41.
antefix. 161.
antenna. 92, 95, 98, 383, 434,
   567.
antennule. 95.
anterior chamber. 123.
anterior commissure. 122.
anterior end. 93.
anterior notch. 124.
anterior pulmonary plexus. 118.
anterior root. 122.
anterior tibial. 110.
anther. 64.
anti-aircraft gun. 425.
anti-collision light. 434.
anti-friction pad. 546.

The terms in *italic* indicate the title of an illustration; those in **bold type** correspond to a chapter.

anti-reverse lock. 566.
anti-skating device. 365.
anti-slip shoe. 268.
anti-submarine mortar. 425.
anti-tank missile. 692.
anti-torque tail rotor. 441.
anticipator. 597.
anticline. 626.
antihelix. 124.
antireflection coating. 656.
antitragus. 124.
antivibration handle. 243.
anus. 91, 94, 108, 109, 119.
anvil. 599, 625.
aorta. 118.
aperture. 93.
aperture scale. 357.
apex. 93, 96, 115, 126, 622.
apical foramen. 115.
apocrine sweat gland. 128.
apostrophe. 347, 350.
apple. 68.
apple. 68.
appoggiatura. 462.
appointment book. 450.
approach. 576.
approach ramp. 402.
apricot. 67.
apron. 199, 200, 203, 438, 565,
    571, 668.
apse. 164.
apsidiole. 164.
Aquarius, the Water Bearer. 698.
aquastat. 194.
aquatic bird. 89.
aqueous humor. 123.
aquifer. 636.
Arabic writing system. 345.
arbor. 237.
arc tube. 274.
arc tube mount structure. 274.
arc welding. 271.
arc welding machine. 271.
arcade. 164.
arch. 34, 165, 401.
arch bridge. 401.
arch bridges, types of. 401.
arch dam. 639.
arch of the aorta. 116.
archboard. 450.
Archer. 33.
arches. 162.
arches, types of. 162, 401.
architectural styles. 160.
architecture. 157.
architrave. 160.
archivolt. 165.
Arctic. 41.
arctic circle. 27.
Arctic Ocean. 41.
area of ice. 530.
arena. 556, 557.
Arenberg parquet. 186.
areola. 109.
argent. 696.
Aries, the Ram. 698.
arm. 83, 107, 200, 211, 433, 473,
    485, 491, 492, 605, 617, 665.
arm elevator. 365.
arm guard. 516.
arm nut. 492.
arm pad. 520.
arm piece. 616.
arm position. 535.
arm rest. 365, 386.
arm slit. 291.
arm stump. 200.
armchair. 200.
armchairs. 201.
armchairs, principal types of. 200,
    201.
Armenian writing system. 345.
armhole. 287, 296.
armoire. 205.
armor. 676.
armored cord. 373.

armpit. 106.
armrest. 617.
armstand. 534.
armstand dive. 535.
arpeggio. 462.
arquebus. 682.
array elevation mechanism. 378.
arrivals concourse. 440.
arrivals schedule. 412.
Arrow. 32.
arrow rest. 677.
arteries. 117.
artichoke. 73.
articulating hinge point. 665.
articulation. 384.
artificial fly. 567.
artificial satellite. 39.
ASA exposure index. 357.
asbestos shingle. 185.
ascending aorta. 116.
ascending colon. 119.
ascot tie. 285.
ash. 334.
ash lid. 191.
ashtray. 334.
Asia. 41.
asparagus. 77.
asphalt. 635.
asphalt process. 634.
asphalt shingle. 185.
asphalt still. 635.
aspirin. 615.
assembly process. 507.
assistant timer. 531.
asterisk. 347.
asteroids. 28.
asthenosphere. 39.
astragal. 160, 431.
astronomical observatory. 34.
astronomy. 25.
athletic shirt. 287.
Atlantic Ocean. 41.
atlas. 113.
atrium. 163.
attaché case. 340.
attached curtain. 207.
attack knob. 481.
attack line. 522.
attack zone. 522.
attacker. 564.
attacking zone. 519.
attenna. 522.
attic. 197.
attitude acquisition. 379.
audio console. 374.
audio control room. 374.
audio input. 367.
audio operator. 374.
audio output. 367.
auditorium. 35.
auditory ossicles. 124.
auger bit. 250.
aunt-in-law. 130.
auricle. 98, 124.
auricular. 87.
Australia. 41.
auto answer indicator. 373.
auto/manual aperture control. 369.
auto-manual focusing switch. 369.
automatic air vent. 194.
automatic cable pulley. 544.
automatic circulating pump. 194.
automatic control system
    computer. 422.
automatic cord reel. 234.
automatic drip coffee maker. 224.
automatic face control. 369.
automatic gates. 410.
automatic relief valve. 194.
automatic rifle. 685.
automatic shutt-off. 196.
automatic tank gauge. 633.
automatic tweezers. 332.
automatically-controlled door. 440.
automobile. 383, 384, 385, 386.
automobile car. 406.

autopilot control. 437.
autorefrigerating devices. 630.
autumn. 27.
autumn squash. 73.
autumnal equinox. 27.
auxiliary handle. 251.
auxiliary projector. 35.
auxiliary tank. 388.
avocado. 72.
axial-flow compressor. 436.
axial rib. 93.
axillary artery. 117.
axillary bud. 61.
axillary nerve. 121.
axillary vein. 117.
axilliary bud. 62.
axis. 113.
axle. 404, 548.
axon. 127.
azimuth coarse-motion clamp. 609.
azimuth synchro. 610.
azure. 696.

B

baby doll. 301.
baby shells. 137.
back. 83, 87, 107, 203, 214, 215,
    216, 217, 252, 255, 283, 294,
    463, 677.
back beam. 494.
back belt. 290.
back binding. 540.
back board. 498.
back boundary line. 528.
back cornering. 498.
back court. 523, 527.
back crossbar. 549.
back judge. 514.
back pack. 312.
back pad. 520, 554.
back pocket. 284.
back score line. 530.
back stop. 466.
back strap. 554.
back upholstery. 617.
back wall. 526, 527.
back zone. 522.
backboard. 521.
backboard support. 521.
backdrop. 170.
backgammon. 578.
background. 359.
backguard. 228, 230, 231.
backhoe bucket. 665.
backhoe loader. 665.
backing. 500.
backing board. 500.
backing hammer. 500.
backing light. 152.
backing press. 500.
backplate. 597.
backrest. 386, 394.
backspace key. 453, 456.
backstay. 416, 548.
backstep. 663.
backstop. 511.
backstretch. 555.
backstroke. 533.
backstroke start. 533.
backstroke swimmer. 533.
backstroke turn indicator. 532.
backup light. 383.
backward. 534.
backward dive. 535.
badminton. 528.
badminton racket. 528.
badminton shoe. 528.
baffle. 191, 632.
bag. 337, 338, 339, 474, 511.
bag well. 573.
baggage cart. 440.
baggage carts. 706.
baggage check. 412.
baggage check-in counter. 440.

baggage claim. 706.
baggage claim area. 440.
baggage compartment. 441.
baggage conveyor. 439.
baggage lockers. 412.
baggage racks. 421.
baggage room. 412.
baggage trailer. 439.
bagpipe. 474.
bail. 566.
bailey. 167.
Bailey bridge. 403.
baize. 569, 570.
bake element. 228.
Baker tent. 583.
baking. 506.
baking utensils. 220.
balalaika. 473.
Balance. 33, 594, 595.
balance beam. 560.
balance control. 364.
balance wheel. 485, 591.
balance wheel locking screw. 485.
balcony. 178.
balde height adjustment. 252.
balk area. 570.
balk line. 570.
balk line spot. 570.
ball. 512, 573.
ball. 488, 496, 507, 529, 531, 682.
ball assembly. 261.
ball bearing. 352, 548.
ball boy. 523.
ball-cock supply valve. 258.
ball cross-section. 573.
ball of clay. 505.
ball peen. 247.
ball peen hammer. 247.
ball rack. 576.
ball return track. 576.
ball stud of circle drawbar. 666.
ball winder. 496.
ballast. 408.
ballast tank. 631.
ballerina. 311.
ballerina. 309.
balloon pants. 312.
ballpoint pen. 352.
baluster. 187.
balustrade. 172, 178.
bamboos. 579.
banana. 72.
band. 365.
band selectors. 364.
bandage. 565.
banding wheel. 505.
bands. 430.
bangs. 321.
banjo. 473.
bank. 646.
bank of heliostats. 654.
banner. 697.
Banon. 145.
banquette. 202.
bar. 85, 206, 471, 478, 561, 578,
    706.
bar frame. 211.
bar line. 462.
bar nose. 243.
barb. 53, 88, 567.
barber. 706.
barber comb. 328.
barbette. 166.
barbican. 167.
baren. 501.
barge. 631.
bark. 63.
barn. 151.
barn doors. 358.
barograph. 55, 542.
barometer. 598.
barometric pressure. 54.
barometric tendency. 54.
barred spiral galaxy. 31.
barrel. 338.

barrel. 330, 331, 352, 475, 683, 684, 685, 686, 687, 688, 689.
barrel cuff. 296.
barrel nut. 685.
barrel organ. 475.
barren. 621.
barrette. 333.
bartizan. 167.
basaltic layer. 40.
base. 160, 190, 210, 232, 233, 250, 251, 274, 330, 365, 377, 408, 409, 500, 559, 595, 600, 601, 605, 661, 688, 695.
base course. 399.
base elbow. 265.
base line. 611.
base of lamp. 357.
base of splat. 200.
base plate. 56, 253, 365, 546, 600, 611.
base plug. 682.
base ring. 680.
base rock. 636.
base width. 644.
baseball. 511, 512.
baseboard. 361.
baseboard radiator. 193.
baseboard register. 192.
baseline. 523.
basement. 179.
basement membrane. 127.
basement window. 177.
baseplate. 683.
basil. 133.
basilic vein. 117.
basin. 646.
basin side. 646.
basin wrench. 266.
basket. 521.
basket. 223, 224, 230, 521, 545, 547.
basket-handle. 162.
basket weave pattern. 186.
basketball. 521.
basketball shoe. 521.
bass bridge. 465.
bass drum. 472.
bass drum. 477, 479.
bass keyboard. 475.
bass pick-up. 480.
bass register. 475.
bass tone control. 364.
bassoon. 469, 476, 477.
bassoons. 479.
baster. 221.
bastion. 166.
bat. 100, 512.
bat. 512.
bateau neck. 299.
bathing trunks. 531.
bathing wrap. 305.
bathrobe. 301.
bathroom. 259.
bathroom. 179.
bathroom scale. 596.
bathtub. 259.
bathyscaphe. 423.
batrachian. 97.
batt. 677.
batt insulation. 185.
batten. 170, 537, 538, 543.
batten pocket. 537, 538.
batter. 511.
batter head. 472.
batter's box. 511.
batter's helmet. 512.
battery. 357, 392.
battery. 57, 356, 423.
battery box. 388.
battery case. 392.
battery check meter. 368.
battery cover. 392.
batting glove. 512.
battlement. 167.
batwing sleeve. 296.
bavette. 141.

bay. 30.
bay antler. 81.
bayonet mount. 353, 355.
bayonets. 679.
bazooka. 686.
beach. 40, 43.
beach bag. 338.
Beacon antenna. 57.
bead. 393.
beam. 81, 153, 560, 594, 595, 596.
beam arrest. 595.
beam balance. 594.
beam bridge. 400.
beam bridges, types of. 400.
beam gantry. 644.
beam pump. 627.
beam reach. 539.
bean bag chair. 202.
bean sprouts. 77.
bear away (to). 537.
bear paw. 549.
bearer. 468.
bearing. 597.
bearing pad. 649.
beater. 155, 225, 494.
beater ejector. 225.
beater handtree. 494.
beater sley. 494.
Beatle cut. 321.
Beaumont. 145.
beauty case. 337.
beaver. 82.
beaver tail. 549.
bed. 204.
bed. 499, 504, 560.
bed handle. 503.
bed lamp. 210.
bed-mattress. 584.
bedrock. 602.
bedroom. 179, 431.
bedside lamp. 210.
bedskirt. 204.
beef, North American cut. 140.
beef, Parisian cut. 141.
beehive. 151.
beer mug. 212.
beet. 76.
begin a new paragraph. 350.
belfry. 164.
bell. 469, 470.
bell brace. 469.
bell buoy. 430.
bell roof. 181.
bell tower. 165.
bellcrank. 665.
bellows. 361, 475.
bellows pocket. 294, 297.
bellows strap. 475.
bellowslike joint. 444.
belly. 83, 87, 142, 677.
below-stage. 170.
belt. 284.
belt. 251, 281, 393, 561, 564, 658.
belt buckle. 281.
belt loop. 281, 306, 585.
belted radial tire. 393.
bench. 202, 414, 621.
bench height. 621.
bench saw. 252.
bend. 318, 567.
Berenice's Hair. 32.
beret. 304.
bergère. 200.
bergschrund. 48.
Bering Sea. 41.
berm. 638.
Bermuda shorts. 300.
berries, major types of. 66.
berry, section of a. 66.
berry fruits. 66.
bertha collar. 298.
betting layout. 580, 581.
between-the-lens shutter. 356.
bevel. 524.
bevor. 676.
bezel. 315.

bezel facet. 317.
bi-fold. 188.
bias. 488.
bias-ply tire. 393.
bib. 305.
bib. 300, 306, 562.
bib necklace. 316.
biceps of arm. 110.
biceps of thigh. 111.
biconcave. 611.
biconvex. 611.
bicycle. 397, 398.
bicycle horn. 398.
bifocal. 318.
big bowtie. 312.
Big Dog. 33.
bikini. 303.
bikini briefs. 287.
bill. 433.
bill compartment. 341.
bill-file. 447.
billboard. 168.
billfold. 341.
billhook. 242.
billiard spot. 570.
billiards cue. 568.
billiards equipment. 568.
bills, principal types of. 89.
bimetal element. 597.
bimetallic helix. 597.
bimetallic thermometer. 597.
binding. 288, 540.
binocular microscope. 605.
biology. 709.
bipod. 683, 687.
bird. 87, 88, 89.
bird, morphology. 87.
Bird of Paradise. 33.
bird of prey. 89.
birth. 709.
biscuit. 147.
Bishop (B). 577.
bishop sleeve. 296.
bit. 250, 335, 554, 625, 626.
bitumen. 636.
bitumen pumping. 636.
bitumen treatment. 636.
Black. 577, 578, 580, 581.
black ball. 570.
black currant. 66.
black rye bread. 138.
black salsify. 76.
Black Sea. 41.
black square. 577.
blackhead remover. 333.
blade. 62, 140, 196, 214, 217, 224, 226, 242, 247, 248, 252, 253, 275, 277, 327, 328, 436, 486, 487, 520, 529, 536, 548, 563, 567, 574, 642, 643, 658, 664, 666, 679.
blade arm. 666.
blade close stop. 328.
blade guard. 252, 270.
blade injector. 327.
blade lever. 499.
blade lift fan. 421.
blade-locking bolt. 253.
blade rotation mechanism. 666.
blade tilt lock. 253.
blade tilting mechanism. 252.
blank. 579.
blanket. 204.
blanket insulation. 185.
blanket sleepers. 305.
blast screen. 686.
blastodisc. 89.
blazer. 297.
bleeder valve. 193.
blender. 225.
blending attachment. 225.
bleu de Bresse. 144.
blind. 209.
block. 468, 539, 671.
block bracket. 208.
blockboard. 255.

blood circulation. 116, 117.
blood vessel. 115, 128, 129.
blood vessels. 100.
bloomers. 307.
blouse. 524.
blouses. 295.
blow pipe. 474.
blower. 194, 195, 196, 467.
blower motor. 195.
blowing snow. 52.
blowout preventer. 626.
blucher oxford. 310.
blue ball. 570.
blue beam. 377.
blue cap. 531.
blue flag. 531.
blue line. 519.
blue mussel. 94.
blue outer circle. 530.
blueberry. 66.
blush brush. 322.
boa. 299.
board. 255.
board. 537.
board cutter. 499.
boarding joist. 186.
boarding step. 441.
boards. 519.
boater. 304.
bob. 321, 593.
bobbin. 492.
bobbin. 486, 495, 496.
bobbin case. 486.
bobbin lace. 492.
bobbin winder. 496.
bobbin winder. 485.
bobby pin. 333.
bobeche. 210.
bobsleigh. 550.
bobstay. 416.
bodies, types of. 384.
body. 126, 233, 250, 261, 349, 387, 407, 430, 468, 469, 549, 558, 560, 567, 607.
body lacing. 549.
body lift cylinder. 668.
body of nail. 129.
body pad. 520.
body shirt. 295.
body side molding. 383.
body stocking. 307.
body suit. 302.
body tube. 605.
body whorl. 93.
body wire. 562.
boiler. 194.
boiler. 193, 424, 654.
boiler room. 425.
boilers. 411.
boldface. 351.
boldface capitals. 351.
bole. 63.
bolero. 297.
bollard. 426.
bolster. 204, 214, 217.
bolt. 254.
bolt. 249, 256, 393, 530, 687.
bolt carrier. 685.
bolt catch. 685.
bonding jumper. 278.
bone folder. 498.
boning knife. 217.
bonnet. 261, 305.
bonus tiles. 579.
book end. 448.
bookbinding. 498, 499, 500.
bookbinding leather. 500.
booking hall. 412.
boom. 359, 538, 661, 665, 667.
boom operator. 375.
boom point sheave. 661.
boom truck. 439.
boom vang. 538.
booster intermediate station. 630.
booster parachute. 443.

boot. 468, 536, 541, 548, 551, 561.
boot jack. 310.
borage. 133.
bordeaux. 212.
bore. 681.
bottle cart. 271.
bottle opener. 219, 233.
bottom. 153, 540, 545, 624.
bottom bracket axle. 398.
bottom cylinder. 502, 504.
bottom deck. 633.
bottom deckboard. 671.
bottom-end transverse member. 411.
bottom of collar. 295.
bottom of the pool. 531, 534.
bottom pocket. 570.
bottom rail. 188, 205.
bottom retainer. 405.
bottom ring. 643.
bottom road. 623.
bottom side rail. 411.
bottom surface. 542.
bottomboard. 468.
bouffant. 320.
bound book. 498.
Boursault. 144.
bow. 464.
bow. 250, 288, 537.
bow collar. 298.
bow rudder. 420.
bow tie. 285.
bowl. 216, 226, 335, 429, 668.
bowl lid. 335.
bowl with serving spout. 226.
bowler. 576.
bowline. 587.
bowline on a bight. 587.
bowling. 576.
bowling ball. 576.
bowling shoe. 576.
bows. 677.
bows. 137.
bowsprit. 416.
bowstring. 677.
box. 169.
box and brush. 552.
box and gate. 552.
box bag. 338.
box-beam Y. 666.
box car. 405.
box end wrench. 248.
box front lights. 169.
box pallet. 671.
box pleat. 207, 294.
box spring. 204.
boxer. 565.
boxer shorts. 287.
boxing. 565.
boxing glove. 565.
boxing shoe. 565.
bra. 303.
brace. 250.
brace. 182, 269, 417, 645.
bracelet length. 289.
bracelets. 315.
brachial. 110.
brachial artery. 117.
brachial plexus. 121.
brachioradial. 110, 111.
bracket. 208, 209, 329, 428.
bracket base. 205.
bracket slot. 209.
brackets. 347.
bract. 70.
braided rope. 587.
braids. 320.
brail. 417.
braille alphabet. 346.
brain. 91.
brake cable. 397.
brake handle. 394.
brake line. 393.
brake lining. 393.
brake pad. 393.

brake pedal. 386, 396.
brake shoe. 393.
brakeman. 550.
brakes. 393.
branch. 63, 77, 85, 257, 553.
branch duct. 192.
branch return pipe. 193.
branch supply pipe. 193.
branches. 63.
brandy. 212.
brass ball faucet. 261.
brass family. 470.
brass floor frange. 258.
brassie. 572.
brassiere cup. 303.
brattice. 167.
brayer. 502.
Brazil nut. 70.
bread. 138.
bread and butter plate. 213.
bread guide. 227.
bread knife. 217.
break line. 298.
breakdown service. 707.
breake lever. 397.
breaker. 43.
breaking pliers. 507.
breaking the wall. 579.
breast. 109.
breast. 87, 106, 139, 143.
breast beam. 494.
breast collar. 554.
breast dart. 282.
breast pocket. 282, 285, 295.
breast welt pocket. 283.
breastplate. 676.
breastroke kick. 533.
breastroke swimmer. 533.
breastroke turn. 533.
breaststroke. 533.
breather valve. 633.
breathing apparatus. 662.
breathing in. 533.
breathing out. 533.
breech. 680, 688.
breech ring. 684.
breeches. 551, 562.
breeching rope. 680.
breechlock. 684.
breechlock operating lever assembly. 684.
Brick. 144, 183.
bridge. 568.
bridge. 208, 318, 400, 401, 402, 403, 424, 463, 475, 607, 631.
bridge and chart room. 420.
bridge unit. 480.
bridging. 182.
bridle. 553.
bridle. 554.
bridle tape. 466.
Brie. 145.
briefcase. 340.
briefelette. 302.
briefs. 287.
briefs. 303.
brig. 418.
brigantine. 418.
bright star projector. 35.
brightness control. 377.
brilliant cut facets. 317.
brilliant full cut. 317.
brim. 288, 304.
brioche. 146.
briolette cut. 317.
brisket. 140.
bristle. 327, 328, 329, 331.
bristles. 270.
broad beans. 77.
broad-leaved endive. 74.
broad ligament of uterus. 109.
broad reach. 539.
broad welt. 290.
broad welt side pocket. 281, 294.
broadest of back. 111.
broccoli. 73.

broil element. 228.
brooch. 315.
brood cell. 99.
brood chamber. 99.
broom. 191.
broom point downwards. 432.
broom point upwards. 432.
brother. 130.
brow brush. 323.
brow reinforce. 676.
brow tine. 81.
browband. 553.
brown ball. 570.
Brunn's membrane. 125.
brush. 270.
brush. 71, 329, 501.
brush and rails. 551, 552.
Brussels sprouts. 74.
buck shots. 137.
bucket. 643, 661, 665.
bucket chain excavator. 621.
bucket cylinder. 665.
bucket hinge pin. 665.
bucket ring. 643.
bucket seat. 386.
bucket tooth. 665.
bucket wheel excavator. 621, 636.
buckle. 488.
buckle. 284, 339, 386, 546.
bud. 75.
buffer. 687.
buffer tank. 630.
buffet. 206.
buffet and china cabinet. 206.
bugle. 470.
building. 168.
building materials. 183, 184, 185.
building sewer. 257.
built-in microphone. 369.
bulb. 77, 85, 274, 312, 597, 631.
bulb, section of a. 75.
bulb dibble. 239.
bulb unit. 646.
bulb vegetables. 75.
bulbil. 75.
bulk carrier. 427.
bulkhead. 388.
bulkhead deck. 420.
bulkhead flat car. 406.
Bull. 32.
bull's eye. 177.
bulldozer. 664.
bulldozer. 621.
bullet. 336, 688.
bullfighter. 311.
bullion stitch. 493.
bullseye. 432.
bulwark. 416.
bumper. 234, 383, 388, 389, 404, 410.
bumper guard. 383, 527.
bumps. 700.
bun. 320, 321.
bunch. 334.
bund wall. 633.
bundle. 77, 644.
bungalow. 173.
bunk. 424.
bunker. 571.
bunker oil. 635.
bunker silo. 151.
bunting bag. 306.
buoyancy compensator. 536.
buoys. 430.
burden. 621, 623, 636.
burgundy. 212.
buried pipeline. 630.
burin. 502.
burner. 223.
burner ring. 223.
burnisher. 501.
burr. 81.
bus stop. 168.
bus transportation. 707.
busbar. 641.
bush. 237.

bushing. 637, 645.
butane carrier. 631.
butane well. 334.
butt. 334, 492, 524, 567, 568, 688, 689.
butt cap. 566.
butt end. 520.
butt grip. 566.
butt guide. 566.
butt hinge. 199.
butt portion. 142, 143.
butt section. 566.
butt-strap. 318.
butt welding. 272.
butte. 47.
butter compartment. 229.
butter curler. 217.
butter dish. 213.
butter knife. 214.
butterfly. 92.
butterfly kick. 533.
butterfly stroke. 533.
butterfly swimmer. 533.
butterfly turn. 533.
buttock. 107.
button. 274, 285, 475, 488, 563, 680.
button loop. 284.
button notch. 233.
button straps. 306.
buttondown collar. 285.
buttoned placket. 285, 291, 295.
buttonhole. 281, 285, 286.
buttress. 85, 164, 165, 639.
buttress dam. 639.
buttsock. 683.
buttstock. 685, 687.
by-pass taxiway. 438.
bypass contact. 370.

C

C-clamp. 249.
c clef. 461.
cab. 394, 664, 665, 666, 667, 668, 670.
cabbage lettuce. 74.
cabin. 420, 434, 441, 544.
cabinet. 196, 230, 231, 232, 259, 363, 377.
cable. 587.
cable. 251, 312, 369, 428, 559, 587.
cable binding. 547.
cable car. 544.
cable release. 359.
cable ripper. 277.
cable sleeve. 251.
cable stay anchorage. 402.
cable-stayed bridge. 402.
cable stitch. 490.
cabochon cut. 317.
caboose. 406.
cabriole leg. 200.
cabriolet. 200.
cactus. 47.
caddie. 571.
café curtain. 207.
cage. 430.
cagoule. 575.
caisson. 427.
cake. 146.
cake mascara. 323.
cake pan. 220.
calamus. 88.
calandria. 648, 650.
calandria tube. 648.
calandria vault. 648.
calcaneus. 84, 113.
calcar. 100.
calculator. 341, 357.
calculator dial. 357.
calendar pad. 450.
calf. 107.
caliper. 393.

calipers. 503.
call director telephone. 373.
Callisto. 28.
calls indicator. 373.
callus. 93.
calm. 53.
calyx. 64, 66, 68, 71, 120.
cam. 492.
cam lever. 492.
cam ring. 250.
cam spring. 689.
camber. 547.
cambium. 63.
Camembert. 145.
camera. 353, 376.
camera battery. 368.
camera body. 353.
camera mount. 375.
camera platform. 359.
camera screw. 359.
cameraman. 375.
camisole. 302.
camp saw. 586.
camping, cooking equipment. 586.
camping, cooking equipment. 584.
camping, lighting equipment. 586.
camping, lighting equipment. 584.
camping, tools. 586.
camping area. 707.
camping equipment. 584, 585, 586.
camping prohibited. 707.
camping site. 707.
camshaft. 391, 503.
can. 432.
can buoy. 430.
can opener. 233.
can opener. 219, 585.
Canadian Cheddar. 144.
Canadian crutch. 616.
Canadian elk. 81.
canal bed. 426.
canal boat. 631.
canal lock. 426.
canal lock. 427.
Cancer, the Crab. 698.
cane. 336.
cane pen. 352.
canes. 616.
canine. 82, 115.
canned failed fuel. 651.
cannelloni. 137.
cannister shot. 681.
cannon. 83, 690.
canopy. 336, 434, 541, 573, 582, 668, 691.
canopy pole. 582.
Cantal. 145.
cantaloupe. 73.
canteen. 586.
cantilever. 639.
cantilever bridge. 400.
cantilever span. 400.
cantle. 553.
canton. 695.
canvas. 565.
canvas divider. 582.
cap. 65, 187, 265, 271, 275, 288, 304, 572, 657.
cap iron. 247.
cap rock. 626, 636.
cap sleeve. 296.
capacitor. 658.
cape. 291.
cape. 311.
capillary bore. 597.
capital. 160.
capitals. 351.
capitulum. 64.
capless wig. 321.
caponiere. 166.
capped column. 49.
capped tee. 192.
cappelletti. 137.
Caprice des Dieux. 144.
Capricorn, the Goat. 698.
capstan. 425.

capsule. 71.
capsule, section of a. 71.
captain. 550.
captain's quarters. 419.
captain's seat. 437.
car. 171, 411.
car buffer. 171.
car deck. 421.
car guide rail. 171.
car parking. 178.
car rental. 707.
car safety device. 171.
car wash. 387.
carabiner. 574.
carafe. 224.
carapace. 95, 101.
caravan site. 707.
caraway seeded rye bread. 138.
carbon. 507.
carbon copy. 349.
carbon granules. 372.
carburetor. 390, 391, 395.
card and photo case. 341.
card cabinet. 450.
card case. 341.
card games. 578.
card holder. 452.
card punch. 458.
card reader. 458.
card support. 56.
cardboard case. 688.
cardiac plexus. 118.
cardigan. 286, 297.
cardoon. 77.
cards. 450.
cards, symbols. 578.
cargo-bay access hatch. 443.
cargo-bay door. 443.
cargo boom. 420.
cargo hatch. 419.
cargo terminal. 438.
Caribbean Sea. 41.
caribou. 81.
carnassial. 82.
carnivore's jaw. 82.
carom billiards. 569.
carpal pad. 86.
carpenter: tools. 249.
carpenter's hammer. 247.
carpentry. 255.
carpentry: fasteners. 254.
carpentry: tools. 247, 248, 250, 251, 252, 253.
carpus. 84, 112.
carré. 142.
carré raccourci. 139.
carriage. 492.
carriage. 453, 491, 670, 680.
carriage release lever. 453.
carriage return. 453.
carriageway. 399.
carrier. 208, 397.
carrier bag. 338.
carrot. 76.
carrousel. 440.
carry handle. 331, 337.
carry-on bag. 337.
carrying handle. 600, 685, 687.
carrying strap. 686.
cars, types of. 406.
cart path. 571.
carton. 334.
cartoon. 507.
cartridge. 688.
cartridge. 352, 356, 688, 689.
cartridge fuse. 275.
cartridge stem. 261.
cartwheel hat. 304.
carving fork. 217.
carving knife. 217.
case. 327, 331, 332, 465, 475, 478, 597, 599, 688.
casement. 189.
casement window. 189.
cashew. 70.

casing first string. 627.
casing second string. 627.
Caspian Sea. 41.
cassette. 356, 455.
cassette holder. 366.
cassette loading slot. 367.
cassette recorder. 455.
Cassiopeia. 32.
cast-on stitches. 490.
castanets. 471.
castanets. 479.
caster. 196, 234, 617.
castle. 167.
castor. 472.
casual water. 571.
cat. 86.
cat, head. 86.
catadioptric ring. 432.
catalytic reformer. 634.
catalytic reforming plant. 635.
catch. 679.
catch glove. 520.
catch spring. 679.
catcher. 512.
catcher. 511.
catcher's box. 511.
catcher's glove. 512.
catenary. 647.
catering vehicle. 439.
caterpillar. 92.
cathedral. 164.
cathode. 606.
cathode screen. 652.
cattle crossing. 701.
catwalk. 375.
caudal fin. 90.
caudal vertebrae. 84.
cauliflower. 73.
caution. 704.
cave. 46.
cave. 43.
cavernous body. 108.
cecum. 119.
cedilla. 347.
ceiling. 526, 527.
ceiling collar. 192.
ceiling fan. 196.
ceiling fitting. 210.
ceiling joist. 182.
ceiling register. 192.
celeriac. 76.
celery. 77.
celesta. 479.
celestial coordinate system. 27.
celestial equator. 27.
celestial meridian. 27.
celestial sphere. 27.
celiac trunk. 116, 120.
cell. 105.
cell. 92, 541.
cell body. 127.
cell connector. 392.
cell membrane. 105.
cell wall. 105.
cement. 184.
cement screed. 186.
cementum. 115.
cent. 709.
Centaur. 33.
center. 350, 514, 515, 519, 521.
center-aisle. 407.
center back. 518, 522, 525.
center back vent. 283.
center base. 695.
center bearing. 436.
center chief. 695.
center circle. 518, 521.
center console. 385.
center court. 527.
center cut. 142.
center electrode. 392.
center face-off circle. 519.
center field. 511.
center fielder. 511.
center flag. 518.
center forward. 522, 525.

center foward. 518.
center hole. 365.
center Keelson. 631.
center knife-edge. 595.
center line. 513, 519, 521, 522, 525, 528, 529, 530, 562.
center mark. 523.
center pocket. 570.
center point. 695.
center post. 205, 383.
center service line. 523.
center span. 402.
center spot. 518, 569, 570.
center strap. 523.
center string. 569.
center tank. 631.
center wheel. 591, 593.
centerboard. 538.
Central America. 41.
central column. 658.
central compartment. 339.
central console. 437.
central focusing wheel. 607.
central incisor. 115.
central instrument panel. 437.
central nervous system. 122.
central ply. 255.
central processing unit. 454, 455.
central processsing unit. 458.
central pumping. 630.
central screw. 500.
centriole. 105.
cep. 65.
cephalic vein. 117.
cephalothorax. 95.
Cepheus. 32.
cerebellum. 122.
cerebrum. 122.
cervical plexus. 121.
cervical vertebra. 113.
cervical vertebrae. 84.
chad container bin. 371.
chaffer sieve. 155.
chain. 210, 398, 593, 598.
chain brake. 243.
chain guide. 398.
chain mail. 676.
chain of dunes. 47.
chain pipe wrench. 266.
chain shot. 681.
chain stay. 397.
chain stitch. 493.
chain wheel. 398.
chainsaw. 243.
chainsaw chain. 243.
chairs, types of. 203.
chaise longue. 203.
chalaza. 89.
chalet. 544.
chalk. 568.
chamber. 689.
Chameleon. 33.
champagne flute. 212.
champagne glass. 212.
chandelier. 210.
change dial. 491.
change machine. 412.
change purse. 341.
change purse. 341.
changer's booth. 414.
channel. 409, 507.
channel selector control. 367.
chanter. 474.
chanterelle. 65.
Chantilly parquet. 186.
chapel. 419.
character. 452.
characters. 579.
chard. 74.
charge. 688.
charge machine. 651.
charger. 327.
charges. 696.
charging handle. 685.
charging handle catch. 685.
charging light. 327.

Charioteer. 32.
charlotte. 146.
charm bracelet. 315.
charms. 315.
chase. 680.
chase astragal. 680.
cheater pocket. 341.
check. 466.
check-in. 706.
check nut. 56.
check-rail. 408.
check valve. 267, 272.
checkbook. 341.
checkbook holder. 341.
checkers. 430.
checkmate. 341.
cheek. 83, 106, 247, 567, 680.
cheek strap. 553.
cheese knife. 214.
cheeses, French. 144, 145.
cheeses, North American. 144.
chemical treatment. 635.
chemise. 167.
cherimoya. 72.
cherry. 67.
chervil. 133.
chess. 577.
chess notation. 577.
chessboards. 577.
chest. 83, 106, 206.
chest protector. 512, 516.
chesterfield. 201.
chestnut. 70, 83.
chevron. 696.
chevron stitch. 493.
chick peas. 77.
chicory. 74.
chief. 695, 696.
chief timekeeper. 532.
chiffonier. 206.
children. 130, 131.
children's clothing. 305, 306, 307.
chimney. 192.
chimney. 177, 190.
chimney connection. 191.
chimney flue. 190.
chimney pot. 177.
chimney stack. 177.
chin. 87, 106.
chin strap. 516.
China Sea. 41.
Chinese cabbage. 74.
Chinese writing system. 345.
chip. 580, 581.
chisel. 502.
chive. 75.
chlorine bleaching. 708.
chloroplast. 105.
chock. 574.
choir. 164.
choir organ manual. 467.
choker. 316.
chopsticks. 223.
chord. 462.
choroid. 123.
christening set. 305.
Christmas tree. 627.
Christmas tree. 630.
chromatin. 105.
chromosphere. 29.
chuck. 140, 248, 250, 251, 625.
chuck key. 251.
chuck short rib. 140.
chukka. 310.
chute. 623.
cigar. 334.
cigar band. 334.
cigar box. 334.
cigarette. 334.
cigarette holder. 334.
ciliary process. 123.
ciliate. 62.
cine scale. 357.
cinematography. 368.
circle. 666.
circle drawbar. 666.

circles. 579.
circuit breaker. 275.
circuit breaker. 641, 658.
circuit test light. 686.
circuit vent. 257.
circular level. 600.
circular needle. 490.
circular saw. 253.
circular saw blade. 253.
circulating pump. 193, 655.
circumflex accent. 347.
cirque. 30.
cirrocumulus. 44.
cirrostratus. 44.
cirrus. 44.
citrus fruit, section of a. 69.
citrus fruits, major types of. 69.
citrus juicer. 226.
citrus juicer. 218.
city houses. 173.
city water. 655.
clafoutis. 147.
clam. 94.
clam-cleat. 537, 539.
clamp. 211, 267, 275, 331, 491,
    496, 499, 547.
clamp binder. 449.
clamp lever. 331.
clamping handle. 226.
clamping nut. 226.
clamshell bucket. 667.
clapper. 372.
clarinet. 469, 476, 477.
clarinets. 479.
clasp. 339, 340.
class ring. 315.
classic. 295.
classification yard. 411.
clavicle. 112.
claw. 86.
claw. 87, 89, 92, 95, 98, 100, 247,
    315, 500.
claw weight. 491.
cleaning brush. 327.
cleaning tools. 234.
cleaning tools. 234.
cleanout. 260.
cleansing sponge. 323.
clear sky. 53.
clear space. 522.
clearance light. 388.
cleared ground. 55.
cleat. 538, 539.
cleated shoe. 516.
cleaver. 217.
clefs. 461.
clew. 537.
clew line. 417.
click. 593.
cliff. 30, 40, 43.
climates of the world. 51.
climbing harness. 575.
climbing iron. 310.
climbing plant. 237.
clinical thermometer. 597.
clip. 208, 284, 331, 352, 447.
clip earring. 315.
clipboard. 450.
clippers. 328.
clitoris. 109.
cloche. 304.
clock. 376, 385, 593, 602.
clock mechanism, weight-driven.
    593.
clock timer. 227, 228.
clog. 309.
close hauled. 539.
close reach. 539.
close up. 350.
close-up lens. 355.
closed circuit television. 652.
closed expansion tank. 194.
closed stringer. 187.
closeness setting. 327.
closet. 178, 179, 206.
closet bend. 257.

closing odds. 555.
closure rail. 408.
cloth beam. 494.
clothing. 279.
clothing guard. 617.
cloud of volcanic ash. 45.
clouds. 44.
clouds of vertical development. 44.
cloudy sky. 53.
clove hitch. 587.
clown. 312.
clown shoe. 312.
club. 578.
club chair. 201.
club divider. 573.
club house. 555.
club house turn. 555.
clubhouse. 571.
clump of flowers. 237.
clutch lever. 396.
clutch pedal. 386.
co-axial machine gun. 690.
coach car. 407.
coache's box. 511.
coal bunker. 624.
coal mine. 621, 622, 623, 624,
    625.
coarse adjustment knob. 605.
coast. 40.
coastal features, common. 43.
coat. 283.
coat dress. 292.
coat hook. 451.
coat rack. 451.
coat tree. 451.
coats. 290, 291.
cob. 77.
coccygeal nerve. 121.
coccyx. 112.
cochlea. 124.
cochlear nerve. 124.
cock. 682.
cocking handle. 687.
cocking lever. 686.
cockle. 94.
cockleshell. 200.
cockpit. 542.
cockpit. 538.
cockpit canopy. 542.
cocktail. 212.
coconut. 70.
coffee makers. 224.
coffee mill. 224.
coffee mug. 213.
coffee pot. 585.
coffee shop. 705.
coffee spoon. 216.
coil. 372.
coil spring. 209.
coiling. 505.
coin chute. 581.
coin reject slot. 581.
coin return bucket. 373.
coin return knob. 373.
coin slot. 373, 581.
coinbox telephone. 373.
coking plant. 624.
colander. 218.
Colby. 144.
cold air. 655.
cold room. 179.
cold-water line. 258, 263.
cold-water riser. 257.
cold-water shutoff valve. 263.
cold-water supply line. 262.
collagenous fiber. 128.
collapsible fire ladder. 662.
collar. 298.
collar. 35, 61, 281, 283, 285, 327,
    561.
collar bar. 316.
collar point. 285, 298.
collar stay. 285.
collaret. 298.
collars, types of. 298.
collateral. 127.

collecting funnel. 56.
collecting tube. 656.
collector. 642.
collector bow. 413.
collet. 139, 143, 250, 359.
collet nut. 250.
colliery. 623.
colon. 347.
color analyzer. 360.
color filter. 355.
color filter set. 358.
color selector. 227.
color temperature switch. 369.
colors. 696.
columella. 93.
columella fold. 93.
column. 46, 49, 193, 210, 251,
    359, 361, 401, 485, 595, 608.
column base. 160.
column crank. 359.
column lock. 359.
column of mercury. 597.
column radiator. 193.
columns. 580, 581.
coma. 31.
comb. 495.
comb. 676.
comb foundation. 99.
comb plate. 172.
combat aircraft. 691.
combination. 287.
combination box and open end
    wrench. 248.
combination knife. 585.
combination lock. 340.
combine harvester. 155.
combs. 328.
combustion chamber. 390, 436,
    692.
comet. 31.
comfort contoured handle. 331.
comforter. 204.
comma. 347, 350.
command antenna. 57, 378.
command module. 442.
command station. 692.
command system. 692.
command transmission. 692.
commander's seat. 690.
commando knife. 678.
commissure of lips of mouth. 126.
common carotid artery. 117.
common extensor of fingers. 111.
common hepatic artery. 117.
common iliac artery. 117, 120.
common iliac vein. 120.
common periwinkle. 96.
common peroneal nerve. 121.
common symbols. 704, 705, 706,
    707.
common whipping. 587.
communicating rami. 122.
communication device. 454.
communications. 343.
compartment. 340, 578, 580.
Compass. 33, 423, 536, 542.
compass card. 429, 611.
compass meridian line. 611.
compensating cables. 171.
competitive course. 532.
competitor. 532.
complex dune. 47.
complexus. 111.
complimentary close. 349.
compluvium. 163.
composite topmark. 432.
compound eye. 92, 98.
compound fleshy fruits. 66.
compound leaves. 62.
compressed air. 625.
compressed-air cylinder. 536, 662.
compression coupling. 260.
compression fitting. 264.
compressor. 194, 229, 390, 450.
compressor turbine. 390.
compulsory roundabout. 703.

computer room. 458.
Comté. 145.
concave. 155, 611.
concha. 124.
Concorde. 39.
concrete base. 602.
concrete block. 183.
concrete dam. 638.
concrete drain. 633.
concrete wall. 655.
condensate. 650.
condensation. 50.
condenser. 196, 361, 362, 605, 647.
condenser adjustment knob. 605.
condenser coil. 196, 229.
condensor. 194.
condominium. 173.
conductive material. 656.
conductor. 211.
conductor's podium. 479.
cone. 45, 363, 432.
configuration key. 457.
conical broach roof. 181.
conical buoy. 430.
conical magnet. 592.
conical snoot. 358.
conical washer. 258.
conjunctiva. 123.
connecting cable. 363.
connecting wire. 562.
connection cable. 457.
connection point. 645.
connective tissue. 127, 128.
connector. 278.
connector link. 541.
conning tower. 423, 424.
console. 467.
consonants. 348.
constellations. 698.
constellations of the northern hemisphere. 32.
constellations of the southern hemisphere. 33.
constriction. 597.
contact. 597.
contact printer. 360.
container. 411.
container. 56, 225, 270, 420.
container car. 406.
container hold. 420.
container-loading bridge. 427.
container ship. 420.
container ship. 427.
container terminal. 427.
containment. 652.
containment building. 649.
contest area. 564.
contestant. 564.
continental climates. 51.
continental margin. 42.
continental mass. 42.
continental rise. 42.
continental shelf. 40, 42.
continental slope. 40, 42.
continents, configuration of the. 41.
continuity tester. 276.
continuous beam. 400.
continuous drizzle. 52.
continuous rain. 52.
continuous snow. 52.
contour feather. 88.
contrabassoon. 479.
contral panel. 228.
contrast control. 377.
contre-filet. 141.
control bar. 543.
control cable. 398.
control column. 437.
control console. 35, 458.
control deck. 421, 424.
control key. 456.
control knob. 228, 457, 506.
control lever. 625.
control levers. 437.

control panel. 196, 227, 230, 231, 232, 374, 375, 457, 662.
control room. 652.
control room. 35, 431, 629, 637, 646, 647.
control rooms. 374.
control stand. 404.
control stick. 441, 542.
control system. 658.
control tower. 438.
control tower cab. 438.
control valve. 585.
control wheel. 663.
controller. 171, 172.
controls. 371.
convection zone. 29.
convector. 193.
conversion. 653.
converter. 358.
convertible. 384.
convex. 611.
conveyor. 621, 624, 636.
cook kit. 585.
cook's knife. 217.
cookie cutters. 220.
cookie press. 220.
cookie sheet. 220.
cooking surface. 227.
cooking utensils. 222, 223.
cooktop. 228.
cool tip. 331.
coolant. 650, 654, 656.
cooler. 586.
cooling air. 444.
cooling fan. 362, 390, 391, 392.
cooling/heating coils. 194.
cooling liquid pump. 444.
cooling tower. 634.
cooling water. 650.
copper foil. 507.
copper pipe. 264.
copper plate. 501.
copper to plastic. 265.
copper to steel. 265.
copy holder. 371.
copyright. 709.
corbel. 167.
corbel piece. 190.
cord. 233, 372, 499, 574.
cord grip. 558.
cord tieback. 207.
cordate. 62.
cordless shoe care kit. 310.
cordless telephone. 373.
core. 29, 68, 573, 587, 638, 688.
core plywood. 255.
corer. 221.
corinthian order. 160.
cork tip. 528.
corkscrew. 585.
corkscrew curls. 320.
corn. 77.
corn cutter. 332.
corn salad. 74.
cornea. 123.
corner. 498, 565.
corner arc. 518.
corner cap. 405.
corner cupboard. 206.
corner fitting. 411.
corner flag. 518.
corner lighting. 210.
corner pad. 565.
corner-stool. 565.
corner structure. 411.
corner stud. 182.
corner tower. 167.
cornet. 470, 477.
cornets. 479.
cornice. 161, 177, 188, 205, 207.
corolla. 64.
corona. 29.
coronal suture. 114.
coronal tine. 81.
coronet. 83.

corpus callosum. 122.
correct a letter. 350.
correct a word. 350.
correcting tape. 452.
correction fluid. 447.
correction paper. 447.
corrections of diacritic symbols. 350.
corrections of errors. 350.
corrections of punctuation marks. 350.
corrections of type. 350.
corrugation. 363.
corsage. 307.
corselet. 302.
corset. 303.
corssbar. 473.
cortex. 120, 129.
corymb. 64.
cosmetic sponge. 323.
cosmetic tray. 337.
costal shield. 101.
costumes. 311, 312.
côtelettes découvertes. 143.
côtelettes premières et secondes. 143.
côtes. 142.
côtes découvertes. 139.
cottage. 173.
cottage curtain. 207.
cotton applicators. 615.
cotton pagne. 675.
cotyledon. 61, 67, 71.
couched stitches. 493.
Coulommiers. 145.
coulter. 153.
counter. 308, 548.
counter memory button. 367.
counter reset button. 366.
counterguard. 166.
counterjib. 669.
counterjib ballast. 669.
counterscarp. 166.
countersink. 250.
counterweight. 171, 365, 403, 408, 409, 596, 608, 667, 669.
counterweight guide rail. 171.
coupler head. 405.
coupler knuckle. 405.
coupler knuckle pin. 405.
course, golf. 571.
course of obstacles. 552.
court, badminton. 528.
court, basketball. 521.
court, handball. 525.
court, racquetball. 527.
court, squash. 526.
court, tennis. 523.
court, volleyball. 522.
court referee. 525.
couscous kettle. 222.
cousins. 130.
couter. 676.
cover. 226, 259, 335, .512, 573, 597, 601, 611, 687.
cover plate. 656.
cover slip. 605.
covered parapet walk. 167.
covered postern. 166.
covered way. 166.
covering. 500.
covering. 529.
covering disk. 154.
cow hitch. 587.
cowl. 383.
cowl collar. 298.
Cowper's gland. 108.
cowshed. 151.
coxa. 92, 98.
Crab. 32, 95.
cradle. 209, 372, 608, 609, 684.
crak rye bread. 138.
crampon strap. 575.
crampons. 575.
cranberry. 66.
crane. 669.

Crane. 33, 34, 629.
crane runway. 669.
cranial nerves. 121.
crank. 398, 426, 566.
crank handle. 503.
crash helmet. 545, 550.
crater. 30, 45, 621.
crawl swimmer. 533.
crawler crane. 669.
crawler tractor. 664.
crayfish. 95.
cream blush. 322.
cream lipstick. 322.
creamer. 213.
crease. 284.
creative leisure activities. 483.
credenza. 451.
Cree snowshoe. 549.
creel. 568.
cremaster. 92.
crème de Gruyère. 145.
crenate. 62.
crenel. 167.
crenulate margin. 93.
crepidoma. 161.
crescent. 696.
crescentic dune. 47.
crest. 43, 46, 177, 593.
crest of spillway. 637.
crevasse. 48.
crevice tool. 234.
crew cut. 321.
crew neck. 305.
crew neck sweater. 286.
crew quarters. 419.
crew sweater. 297.
cribriform plate of ethmoid. 125.
crimper. 277.
crinoline stretcher. 203.
crisper. 229.
crisscross back straps overall. 306.
crisscross curtains. 207.
crochet hook. 490.
croissant. 138.
crook. 469, 474.
crop elevator. 155.
cross. 696.
cross brace. 617.
cross-country ski. 547.
cross-country ski. 547.
cross-country skier. 547.
cross-country skiing. 547.
cross cut. 622, 623.
cross-guard. 679.
cross handle. 580.
cross head (Phillips). 254.
cross poles. 552.
cross rail. 203.
cross rib. 140.
cross stitches group. 493.
crossarm. 644, 645.
crossbar. 152, 397, 495, 499, 517, 531, 543, 544, 556, 557.
crossbeam. 494.
crossbow. 677.
crossbuck sign. 409.
crosse. 139, 141, 142.
crosshead. 670.
crossing. 164, 413.
crossing gate mechanism. 409.
crossover cargo deck line. 631.
crosspiece. 199, 494.
crosstree. 538.
crosswise grain. 488.
crotch. 287.
crotch piece. 295.
croup. 83, 559.
Crow. 33.
crown. 63, 87, 115, 288, 304, 317, 433, 506, 591.
crown block. 626.
crownpiece. 553.
cruciform tail unit. 435.
crude oil. 635.
crude oil pipeline. 630.
crus of helix. 124.

crusader cap. 304.
crusader hood. 304.
crustacean. 95.
crutch. 616.
crutch tip. 616.
crutches. 616.
cubiculum. 163.
cubital vein. 117.
cucumber. 73.
cue ball. 569, 570.
cue screen. 376.
cuff. 284, 285, 308, 520.
cuff section. 616.
cuirass. 675.
cuisse. 676.
cuisseau. 139.
culet. 317.
culotte. 141, 293.
cultivated mushroom. 65.
cultivator. 153.
cumulonimbus. 44.
cumulus. 44.
Cup. 33, 213, 372, 571, 585, 688.
cup conveyor. 154.
cupola. 431, 690.
cupule. 70.
curb. 399.
curb bit. 553.
curb chain. 315, 553.
curb rein. 553.
curled endive. 74.
curled kale. 74.
curler. 530.
curling. 530.
curling broom. 530.
curling brush. 331.
curling iron. 331.
curling rink. 530.
curling stone. 530.
curly hair. 320.
curly lasagna. 136.
currant. 66.
currency exchange. 706.
currency exchange counter. 440.
currency exchange office. 412.
current coil. 601.
cursor. 457.
cursor movement key. 456.
curtain. 207.
curtain. 166, 337.
curtain pole. 208.
curtain track. 208.
curve. 520.
curved jaw. 249.
cushion. 548, 570, 576.
custard pie. 147.
customer's service entrance. 645.
customs control. 440.
cut. 170.
cut off trench. 638.
cut ribbed macaroni. 137.
cutaway armhole. 296.
cuticle. 129.
cuticle knife. 332.
cuticle nippers. 332.
cuticle pusher. 332.
cuticle scissors. 332.
cutlery basket. 232.
cutter bar. 155.
cutter link. 243.
cutting blade. 225, 499.
cutting cylinder. 242.
cutting edge. 214, 217, 328, 664, 668.
cutting guide. 499.
cutting line. 489.
cutting oxygen handle. 272.
cutting tip. 272.
cutting torch. 272.
cutting wheel. 233.
cutting wire. 505.
cyclists crossing. 701.
cyclists entering. 701.
cyclorama. 375.
cylinder. 256.

cylinder. 256, 390, 395, 504, 625, 666, 667, 689.
cylinder-head. 395.
cylinder head cover. 391.
cylinder hole. 256.
cylinder pressure gauge. 272.
cylindrical parabola reflector. 656.
cymbals. 471.
cymbals. 477, 479.
cytoplasm. 105.

D

["D['. 570.
dabber. 502.
dagger. 675, 678.
daggerboard. 537.
daggerboard well. 537.
daggers. 678.
dairy compartment. 229.
dam. 637, 638, 646.
damper. 190, 192, 466, 506, 596.
damper lever. 466.
damper rail. 466.
dams, major types of. 639.
dandelion. 74.
danger area. 564.
danger warning signs. 700, 701.
dangerous bend. 700.
dangerous descent. 700.
Danish rye bread. 138.
Danish writing system. 345.
darkroom. 360.
dart. 489.
dash. 347.
dashboard. 385.
dasher. 226.
data acquisition. 454.
data display. 454.
data processing. 454.
data processing devices. 454.
data recording on Ram memory. 454.
data storage. 454.
date. 67, 555.
date line. 349.
dater. 448.
dating nail. 408.
daughter. 130.
daughter-in-law. 131.
davit. 416.
day. 624.
daylight film tank. 360.
daylight filter control. 368.
dead ball line. 517.
dead bolt. 256.
deadly mushroom. 65.
deaerator. 647, 650.
deaerator storage tank. 647.
deaf-mute alphabet. 347.
death. 709.
decanter. 212.
deck. 388, 400, 401, 402, 623.
deck arch bridge. 401.
declination. 27.
declination axis. 34.
declination circle. 608.
décolleté bra. 303.
decontamination room. 647.
decorative sheet. 255.
deep fryer. 223.
deep peroneal nerve. 121.
deep-sea floor. 40.
deer, kinds of. 81.
deer antlers. 81.
deer family. 81.
defending zone. 519.
defensive. 514, 515.
deferent duct. 108.
deflexor. 543.
defrost heater. 229.
defrost timer. 229.
dehumidifier. 196.
dehumidifier. 444.
Deimos. 28.

delay indicator. 413.
delete. 350.
delicious lactarius. 65.
delta wing. 435.
deltoid. 110.
deluge gun. 663.
deluxe suite. 419.
demilune. 166.
demitasse. 213.
dendrite. 127.
dental alveolus. 115.
dental floss. 329.
dentate. 62.
dentil. 160.
dentin. 115.
department store. 168.
departure time indicator. 413.
departures concourse. 440.
departures room. 440.
departures schedule. 412.
deposit. 621.
depressed-center flat car. 406.
depth gauge. 536.
depth-of-field scale. 355.
depth of focus. 45.
depth stop. 251.
dermal papilla. 127, 128.
dermis. 128, 129.
derrick. 626, 629.
desasphalting. 634.
descendeur. 574.
descending aorta. 116.
descending colon. 119.
desert. 47.
desert. 51.
desk lamp. 211.
desk pad. 450.
desk tray. 448.
despin. 379.
dessert fork. 215.
dessert knife. 214.
dessert spoon. 216.
desserts. 146, 147.
dessus de côtes. 139, 141.
destination indicator. 413.
detachable control. 227.
detachable handle. 191.
detachable petrol tank. 423.
detergent dispenser. 232.
detonator. 682.
developer bath. 360.
developing film. 356.
dew cap. 609.
dew claw. 86.
dew pad. 86.
dewaxing. 634.
dexter. 695.
dexter base. 695.
dexter chief. 695.
dexter flank. 695.
diacritic symbols. 347.
diagonal. 577, 644.
diagonal buttress. 165.
dial. 371, 372, 591, 592, 593, 595, 596, 597, 598, 599, 601.
dial-type display. 428.
diamond. 432, 569, 578.
diamond head. 507.
diamond mesh metal lath. 184.
diamond point. 205.
diaper. 305.
diaphragm. 118, 119, 353, 363, 369, 372, 407.
diastema. 82.
dibble. 239.
dice. 579.
dice. 578.
dice cup. 578.
diesel-electric locomotive. 404.
diesel engine. 390.
diesel engine. 404, 422, 665.
diesel oil. 635.
diesel shop. 410.
diffuser. 358.
diffuser filter set. 358.
diffusion pump. 606.

digestive gland. 94.
digestive system. 119.
digit. 86, 97.
digital clock. 367.
digital computer. 652.
digital display. 591.
digital frequency display. 364.
digital nerve. 121.
digital pad. 86.
digital pulp. 129.
dike. 45.
dill. 133.
diluent. 636.
diluent recovery. 636.
dimmer control. 374.
dimmer switch. 275.
dimmer switch. 386.
dimple. 573.
dinghy. 538.
dinghy pack. 421.
dining car. 407.
dining room. 179, 419, 420.
dining section. 407.
dinner fork. 215.
dinner knife. 214.
dinner plate. 215.
dinnerware. 213.
dioptric ring. 432.
dip. 622.
dip switch. 396.
diphthongs. 348.
dipper bucket. 667.
direct-reading rain gauge. 56.
direction to be followed. 703.
directional sign. 414.
director's chair. 201.
disappearing handle. 340.
disc. 356, 393, 503, 544, 561.
disc brake. 658.
disc camera. 354.
disc seat. 261.
disc seat ring. 261.
discharge line. 267.
discharge liner. 643.
discharge pipe. 632.
discharge pump. 632.
discharge spout. 152, 153.
discs. 226.
discus. 558.
discus throw. 556.
disgorger. 568.
dishwasher. 232, 262.
disk. 458.
disk. 393, 601.
disk brake. 393.
disk brake. 395.
disk control unit. 458.
disk drive. 458.
disk storage. 458.
diskette. 455.
diskette drive. 455.
dispatch area. 634.
display. 455, 596.
display cabinet. 451.
disposable fuel cylinder. 271.
disposable razor. 327.
disposable syringe. 615.
distal phalanx. 86, 112, 113, 129.
distal sesamoid. 84.
distance. 318.
distance covered. 555.
distance scale. 355.
distance tube. 686.
distribution board. 278.
distribution board. 645.
distribution field. 267.
distributor. 391.
distributor service loop. 645.
ditali. 137.
ditch. 399.
ditch light. 413.
diver. 535, 536.
diverging lens. 611.
diversion canal. 637.
diverter valve. 259.
dives, groups of. 535.

divider. 155, 340, 449.
dividing breeching. 662.
diving. 534.
diving installations. 534.
diving suit. 312.
diving well. 534.
division. 709.
divot. 571.
do-it-yourself. 245.
do not enter. 704.
do not use for baggage carts. 706.
do not use for wheelchairs. 705.
dog collar. 316.
dog ear collar. 298.
dog tag. 315.
Dolby noise reduction switch. 366.
dollar. 709.
dolly. 530.
Dolphin. 32, 680.
dome fastener. 289.
dome roof. 181.
dome shoulder closure. 306.
dome shutter. 34.
dome tent. 583.
domed adjustable strap. 306.
domed front. 306.
domed inseam. 306.
domed snap side. 305.
domed waist. 305.
domestic appliances. 225, 226,
*   227, 228, 229, 230, 231, 232,*
*   233, 234.*
domino. 579.
door. 188, 386.
door. 177, 205, 227, 231, 383,
    526.
door handle. 383.
door hasp. 405.
door hasp fastener. 405.
door lock. 383.
door operator. 171.
door panel. 205, 415.
door shelf. 229.
door stop. 229, 405.
door switch. 231.
doorknob. 188.
doors, types of. 188.
doric order. 160.
dormant volcano. 45.
dormer. 177.
dorsal aorta. 91.
dorsum of nose. 125.
dot matrix printer. 457.
doubel breasted buttoning. 291.
double. 552.
double bass. 463, 477.
double basses. 479.
double bend. 700.
double-blank. 579.
double boiler. 222.
double-breasted buttoning. 281.
double-breasted jacket. 283.
double chair lift. 544.
double-condenser pole piece. 606
double curtain rod. 208.
double-decked pallet. 671.
double-edge blade. 327.
double-edge razor. 327.
double-edged swords. 678.
double flat. 462.
double fluked anchor. 433.
double glazing. 655.
double handles. 540.
double-hung. 189.
double kitchen sink. 257.
double-leaf bascule bridge. 403.
double plate. 182.
double pole breaker. 278.
double reed. 469, 474.
double seat. 415.
double sharp. 462.
double sheet bend. 587.
double-six. 579.
double-twist auger bit. 250.
double zero. 581.
doubles pole. 523.

doubles service court. 528.
doubles sideline. 523, 528.
doublet. 579.
doubling cube. 578.
doubly dentate. 62.
dough hook. 225.
doughnut. 146.
dousing tank. 647.
Doux de Montagne. 144.
Dove. 33.
dovetail. 607.
dowel hole. 318.
down. 178.
down tube. 397.
down wind. 539.
downhaul. 537.
downspout. 177.
downstream face. 638.
downstream shoulder. 638.
downstream toe. 638.
downtown. 168.
dozen. 581.
dozens. 580.
draft arm. 668.
draft tube. 641, 643, 668.
drag. 566.
drag chain. 661.
drag drum. 661.
drag rope. 661.
dragline. 661.
dragline. 636.
Dragon. 32.
drain. 257.
drain cock. 633.
drain elbow. 260.
drain hose. 230, 232, 262.
drain line. 194.
drain pan. 229.
drain tile. 182.
drain valve. 194, 263, 633.
drainage blanket. 638.
drainage layer. 638.
draining spoon. 219.
draped neck. 299.
draped neckline. 299.
draw drapery. 207.
draw tube. 605.
drawbar. 664, 684.
drawbar lock. 684.
drawbridge. 167.
drawer. 199, 206, 450.
drawers. 287.
drawstring. 311, 339.
drawstring hood. 307.
drawtube. 609.
drawworks. 626.
dredger. 221.
dress. 305.
dresser. 206.
dresses. 292.
dressmaker's model. 487.
drift. 622, 623.
drifting snow. 52.
drill. 250.
drill collar. 626.
drill pipe. 626.
drill press. 251.
drill ship. 628.
drill steel. 625.
drilling barge. 628.
drilling rig. 626.
drip bowl. 228.
drip molding. 383.
drip stone. 177.
drive. 485.
drive axle. 670.
drive belt. 230, 231, 365.
drive chain. 397.
drive coil. 592.
drive shaft. 441.
drive sheave. 171.
drive wheel. 233, 250, 666.
driver. 554, 555, 572.
driver's cab. 404.
driver's colors. 555.
driver's seat. 690.

driveway. 178.
driving iron. 572.
driving shaft. 420.
driving turbine. 390.
driving wheel. 496.
drone. 98.
drone. 474.
drop. 210.
drop earring. 315.
drop-leaf. 199.
drop-leaf table. 199.
drop light. 211.
drop waist dress. 292.
drug store. 706.
drum. 160, 209, 226, 231, 393,
    472, 593.
drum brake. 393.
drum kit. 477.
drupelet. 66.
dry cleaning. 708.
dry continental - arid. 51.
dry continental - semiarid. 51.
dry dock. 427.
dry fruits. 70.
dry fruits, various. 71.
dry gallery. 46.
dry mounting press. 360.
dry point. 501, 503.
dry snow. 49.
dry subtropical. 51.
dryer. 231.
drying. 708.
dual swivel mirror. 330.
dual voltage selector switch. 327,
    330.
duct. 128.
duffel bag. 339.
duffle coat. 282.
dump. 621, 624.
dump body. 668.
dump rope. 661.
dump truck. 668.
dune. 43.
duo. 476.
duodenum. 119.
duplex. 173.
duplexer. 610.
dura mater of spinal cord. 122.
dural cul-de-sac. 122.
dust cover. 365.
dust storm. 52.
dust tail. 31.
dusting brush. 234.
dutch oven. 222.
Dutch writing system. 345.
duty-free. 706.
duty-free shop. 440.
duvet. 575.
dynamics propeller. 421.

E

Eagle. 32, 33, 696.
ear. 100, 106, 107, 203, 468.
ear cushion. 363.
ear drum. 124.
ear flap. 288.
ear loaf. 138.
earphone jack. 377.
earpiece. 318, 372.
Earth. 28, 29, 30, 639.
Earth, strucutre of the. 39.
Earth coordinate system. 27.
Earth's atmosphere, profile of the.
*   39.*
Earth's crust. 39, 45.
Earth's crust, section of the. 40.
earth sensor. 378.
earthquake. 45.
easel. 361.
East. 579.
east-to-west axis. 35.
East wind. 579.
eccrine sweat gland. 128.
échine. 142.

echinus. 160.
echo. 610.
echo sounder. 428.
edge. 255, 487, 545, 547, 548,
    550, 611.
edger. 242.
edging. 237.
edible crustaceans, principal. 95.
edible gastropods, principal. 96.
edible gyromitra. 65.
edible mollusks, principal. 94.
edible mushrooms. 65.
egg. 89.
egg. 99.
egg beater. 220.
egg poacher. 223.
egg slicer. 221.
egg timer. 219.
egg tray. 229.
eggplant. 73.
eggs. 91, 97.
eight cut. 317.
eighth note. 461.
eighth rest. 461.
ejaculatory duct. 108.
eject. 367.
eject button. 366.
ejection port. 683, 685, 687.
ejection seat. 691.
ejector. 668.
elastic. 204.
elastic ankle. 307.
elastic coupling method. 631.
elastic leg opening. 305, 307.
elastic ligament. 86, 94.
elastic support bandage. 615.
elastic waistband. 305.
elastic webbing. 284.
elastic wristband. 307.
elasticized leg opening. 287.
elbow. 83, 100, 107, 191, 192,
    193, 265.
elbow macaroni. 137.
elbow pad. 516, 520, 550.
elbow protector. 562.
electric arc. 271.
electric current source. 370.
electric drill. 251.
electric foil. 562.
electric furnace. 195.
electric golf cart. 573.
electric guitar. 480.
electric instrument. 480.
electric kiln. 506.
electric motor. 172, 195, 356, 423.
electric range. 228.
electric razor. 327.
electric supply. 194, 263.
electric switch. 275.
electric water-heater tank. 263.
electrical box. 275.
electrical connection. 388.
electrical distribution system. 652.
electrical hazard danger. 704.
electrical payout linkage. 581.
electrical pointe d'arrêt. 562.
electrical power unit. 439.
electrical room. 647.
electrical scoring apparatus. 562.
electrical supplies. 275.
electricity. 274, 275, 637, 638,
*   639, 640, 641, 642, 643, 644,*
*   645, 646.*
electricity, tools. 276, 277.
electricity, tower. 644.
electricity cable. 399.
electricity meter. 645.
electrified fence. 151.
electrode. 271, 274, 372.
electrode assembly. 195.
electrode holder. 271.
electrode lead. 271.
electromagnet. 370.
electron beam. 377.
electron gun. 377, 606.
electron microscope. 606.

electronic circuit. 592.
electronic flash. 357.
electronic instrument. 481.
electronic scale. 596.
electronic viewfinder. 369.
electronic viewfinder display
 control. 369.
element. 392.
element release lever. 452.
elevating handle. 683.
elevating mechanism. 687.
elevation adjusting screw. 607.
elevator. 171.
elevator. 152, 434, 542, 651.
elevator for people. 705.
elevon. 443.
elk. 81.
ellipses. 347.
elliptical galaxy. 31.
elongating bar shot. 681.
embankment. 399.
embankment dam. 638, 639.
emblem. 383, 695.
embrasure. 166.
embroidery. 493.
emerald cut. 317.
emergency brake commutator.
 415.
emergency core cooling. 652.
emergency niche. 414.
emergency oxygen supply. 444.
emery board. 333.
emission chamber. 606.
empty set. 709.
emptying. 633.
en prison. 580, 581.
enamel. 115.
enameled hardboard. 184.
encapsulant. 656.
enclosure. 193, 196.
enclosure line. 349.
end bracket. 208.
end button. 463.
end cap. 208, 649.
end door. 411.
end fitting. 648.
end grain. 255.
end joist. 182.
end ladder. 405.
end line. 513, 521, 522, 529.
["end of priority[' sign. 701.
end of prohibition of passing. 702.
end of superhighway. 703.
end of the lap. 533.
end panel. 227.
end piece. 108, 568.
end plate. 649.
end shield. 647.
end shield cooling pipe. 648.
end stop. 208.
end wall. 532.
end zone. 513.
endocarp. 67, 68.
endoplasmic reticulum. 105.
endpaper. 498.
endpiece. 318.
energy. 619.
energy production. 653.
engagement ring. 315.
engine. 391.
engine. 436, 573, 626, 664, 666,
 667, 668.
engine air intake. 421.
engine block. 391.
engine housing. 243.
engine mounting pylon. 435.
engine room. 424, 425, 631.
engines. 390.
engines. 443.
Englis loaf. 138.
English billiards. 570.
English cane. 616.
English chessboard. 577.
English horn. 469, 479.
English writing system. 345.
enlarger. 361.

enlarger. 360.
enlarger timer. 360.
enlarging lens. 361.
entablature. 160, 188.
entame de romsteck. 141.
enter key. 456.
entire. 62.
entrance. 99.
entrance slide. 99.
entrance turnstile. 414.
entrecôtes couvertes. 141.
entrecôtes découvertes. 141.
entries. 534.
entry. 535, 671.
envelope bag. 338.
envelope shaper. 481.
EP adaptor. 365.
épaule. 139, 143.
epaulet. 281, 311.
epaulet sleeve. 296.
épée. 563.
épéeist. 563.
epicalyx. 66.
epicenter. 45.
epicondyle. 113.
epidermicula. 129.
epidermis. 127, 128, 129.
epiglottis. 118, 126.
epitrochlea. 113.
eponychium. 129.
equalizer. 363.
equalizing buckle. 209.
equator. 27.
equilateral. 162.
equilibrator. 684.
equipment access shaft. 646.
equipment lock. 651.
erase button. 373.
eraser. 447.
erector lenses. 607.
ermine. 696.
escalator. 172.
escalator. 414.
escalator, down. 705.
escalator, up. 705.
escape key. 456.
escape wheel. 591, 593.
escapement mechanism. 478.
escutcheon. 93, 256, 260.
esophagus. 91, 94, 119.
espadrille. 309.
espresso coffee maker. 224.
etching press. 502.
Eton jacket. 307.
Eton suit. 307.
étrier. 574.
Eurasia. 41.
Europa. 28.
Europe. 41.
European plug. 275.
Eustachian tube. 124, 125.
euthynteria. 161.
evaporation. 50.
evaporator. 196.
evaporator coil. 229.
even. 580, 581.
evaporator coils. 196.
examples of branching. 262.
exclamation point. 347.
excretory pore. 96.
executive desk. 451.
executive length. 287.
exhaust cone. 436.
exhaust duct. 231, 436.
exhaust gas admission. 390.
exhaust gas outflow. 390.
exhaust hose. 231.
exhaust manifold. 390, 391, 392.
exhaust nozzle. 436, 691.
exhaust pipe. 390, 392, 395, 436,
 441, 664, 690.
exhaust port. 625.
exhaust stock. 389.
exhaust system. 392.
exhaust tube. 274.
exhaust valve. 390.

exit turnstile. 414.
exocarp. 66, 67, 68.
exosphere. 39.
expandable file pouch. 340.
expanding file. 449.
expansion bolt. 254.
expansion chamber. 429, 597.
expansion space. 408.
expansion tank. 193.
exploder. 686.
explosive. 682.
exposure control. 356.
exposure counter. 353.
exposure meter. 357.
exposure-time scale. 357.
exposure value. 357.
exposure value scale. 357.
extended character. 456.
extendible solar array. 378.
extension ladder. 268.
extension table. 199.
extension wand. 234.
exterior dome shell. 34.
exterior door. 188.
exterior pocket. 337, 340.
exterior sign. 414.
external acoustic meatus. 124.
external auditory meatus. 114.
external conductive coating. 377.
external ear. 124.
external gills. 97.
external iliac artery. 117.
external oblique. 110, 111.
external tank. 443.
external tooth lock washer. 254.
extractor. 689.
extractor cam. 689.
extractor fan. 360.
extractor spring. 689.
extrados. 162.
eye. 123.
eye. 96, 101, 106, 247, 486, 487,
 495, 553, 567, 574.
eye cup. 368.
eye lens. 607.
eye liner. 322.
eye ring. 87.
eye shield protector. 507.
eye-socket. 83.
eyeball. 123.
eyeball. 97.
eyebrow. 123.
eyebrow pencil. 323.
eyebrow stripe. 87.
eyebrow tweezers. 332.
eyecup. 369.
eyecups. 355.
eyeglasses. 318, 319.
eyeglasses, principal types of. 319.
eyelash. 123.
eyelash curler. 323.
eyelashes. 86.
eyelet. 308, 491, 548.
eyelet tab. 308.
eyelid. 101.
eyepiece. 356, 357, 605, 607, 608,
 609.
eyepiece holder. 609.
eyepiece magnifier. 355.
eyeshadow. 322.
eyestalk. 96.

F

F-1 engine. 442.
f clef. 461.
fabric care. 708.
fabric guide. 233.
fabric structure. 488.
façade. 165.
face. 106, 166, 247, 341, 500, 507,
 529, 572, 621, 623.
face mask. 516, 520.
face-off circle. 519.
face-off spot. 519.

face pipes. 467.
face ply. 255.
face side. 255.
faceplate. 256, 377.
facial nerve. 124.
facing. 283.
faculae. 29.
failed fuel bay. 651.
failed fuel canning. 651.
fairlead. 539.
fairway. 571.
fall. 298.
falling. 564.
falling rocks. 700.
fallow. 151.
false rib. 113.
false strart rope. 532.
false tuck. 305.
family tents. 582.
family ties. 130, 131.
fan. 194, 195, 229, 231, 415, 436,
 624.
fan belt. 391, 392.
fan brush. 323.
fan cable stays. 402.
fan control. 196.
fan housing. 330.
fan motor. 196.
fang. 101.
fanion. 697.
fanny pack. 545.
fantail. 657.
far side. 30.
far turn. 555.
farm, buildings. 151.
farm, modern. 149.
farmhouse. 151.
farmyard. 151.
fascia. 160.
fast forward. 367.
fast-forward button. 366, 373.
fastener binder. 449.
fasteners. 488.
fastening screw. 357.
father. 130, 131.
father-in-law. 131.
faucet. 261.
faucet body. 261.
fault. 40, 45, 622.
feather crown. 528.
feather stitch. 493.
fedelini. 136.
feed cover. 687.
feed dog. 486.
feed lever. 251.
feed pin. 457.
feed tray. 687.
feed tube. 226, 352.
feeder. 648.
feeding dial. 491.
feedwater. 650.
feet. 464, 500.
feet, principal types of. 89.
feet-first entry. 534.
felt. 502, 504.
felt hat. 288.
felt hat. 304.
female. 709.
female ferrule. 566.
femoral artery. 117.
femoral nerve. 121.
femoral vein. 117.
femur. 84, 92, 97, 98, 100, 112.
fencer. 562.
fencing. 562, 563.
fencing shoe. 562.
fencing weapons. 563.
fender. 383, 389, 397.
ferrule. 214, 270, 328, 568, 572.
ferry. 420.
ferryboat. 427.
fertilizer distributor. 154.
fetlock. 83.
fetlock joint. 83.
fettling knife. 505.
fibre. 587.

fibula. 112.
field, baseball. 511.
field, rugby. 517.
field heap spreader. 154.
field lens. 607.
field lenses. 607.
fiffi hook. 574.
fifth. 462.
fifth wheel. 389.
fight information board. 440.
figure-eight knot. 587.
figure skate. 548.
figure ski. 540.
figure skiing handle. 540.
filament. 29, 64, 274, 606.
file. 577, 585.
file guides. 449.
filet. 142, 143.
filing box. 448.
fill. 638.
fill opening. 233.
filler. 334.
filler hole. 389, 391.
filler plug. 429.
filler rod. 272.
filler tube. 258.
fillet. 160, 177.
filleting knife. 217.
filling. 633.
filling hole. 682.
film advance lever. 353.
film drying cabinet. 360.
film footage counter. 368.
film leader. 356.
film-pack. 356.
film path. 368.
film speed indicator. 353.
film transport sprocket. 353.
filming trigger. 369.
films. 356.
filter. 194, 195, 223, 335, 429, 638, 655, 661.
filter basket. 224.
filter drawer. 361.
filter-oscillator. 481.
filter tip. 334.
fin. 421, 434, 441, 536, 537, 540, 692.
fin wing tip. 691.
final limit cam. 171.
final limit switch. 171.
final limit witch. 171.
finder. 608, 609.
fine bookbinding. 498, 499, 500.
fine focus sleeve. 609.
fine tuning knob. 377.
finger. 152, 512.
finger button. 470.
finger hole. 576.
finger stop. 372.
fingerboard. 463, 473, 480.
fingerwaves. 320.
fingerwheel. 154.
finish. 552.
finish line. 557.
finished product storage. 634.
finishing line. 555.
finishing post. 557.
finned tube. 193.
Finnish writing system. 345.
fire control selector. 685.
fire engine. 662, 663.
fire extinguisher. 704.
fire hose. 662, 704.
fire-standing tanks. 631.
fire station. 634.
firebox. 191.
firebrick. 195.
firebrick back. 190.
fireman's hatchet. 662.
fireplace. 190.
fireplace. 178.
firestopping. 182.
firetending tools. 191.
firing chamber. 688.
firing lanyard. 684.

firing mechanism. 686.
firing pin. 688.
firing pine. 689.
firing rod. 686.
firing shaft. 684.
firn. 48.
first aid. 704.
first aid kit. 615.
first base. 511.
first baseman. 511.
first-class swimming pool. 419.
first condenser lens. 606.
first dorsal fin. 90.
first molar. 115.
first officer's seat. 437.
first quarter. 30.
first reinforce. 680.
first reinforce ring. 680.
first space. 521.
first stage. 442.
first violins. 479.
fish. 90, 91.
fish, anatomy. 91.
fish, morphology. 90.
fish-eye lens. 35.
fish fork. 215.
fish knife. 214.
fish platter. 213.
fish poacher. 222.
fish wire. 277.
fishbone stitch. 493.
fisherman's knot. 587.
Fishes. 32.
fisheye lens. 355.
fishhook. 567.
fishing. 566, 567, 568.
fishing, accessories. 568.
fishing vest. 568.
fitted coupling bolt. 643.
fitted sheet. 204.
fitting. 264, 339, 663.
fittings. 265.
five-number bet. 581.
fixed arch. 401.
fixed blade. 499.
fixed bridges. 400, 401, 402.
fixed distance marking. 438.
fixed jaw. 248, 249.
fixed platform. 628.
fixed-roof tank. 633.
fixed stairs. 414.
fixed weight. 478.
fixing bath. 360.
fixture drain. 257.
flag. 695.
flag. 517, 522, 544.
flag shapes. 697.
flagstick. 571.
flagstone. 237.
flame adjustment wheel. 334.
flame spreader tip. 271.
flammable. 704.
flammule. 697.
flan pan. 220.
flanchet. 141.
flange bolt. 258.
flange nut. 264.
flank. 83, 87, 139, 140, 143, 166, 500.
flank forward. 517.
flanker. 515.
flanking tower. 167.
flap. 288, 339, 341, 553, 691.
flap guide rail. 435.
flap hydraulic jack. 691.
flap pocket. 282, 283, 294.
flap side pocket. 283.
flare. 29, 629, 634.
flare joint. 264.
flare nut. 264.
flare nut wrench. 248.
flash. 358.
flash bracket. 357.
flash lamp. 357.
flash meter. 358.
flash outlet. 357.

flash socket. 368.
flash suppressor. 685, 687.
flash synchronization terminal. 353.
flash unit. 357.
flashbar socket. 356.
flashcube. 357.
flashing. 192.
flashing light. 409.
flashlight. 211.
flat. 462.
flat-back brush. 328.
flat-bed. 485.
flat cake. 146.
flat car. 406.
flat end pin. 209.
flat head. 254.
flat mirror. 34, 608.
flat part. 490.
flat plate solar collector. 656.
flat pleat. 207.
flat roof. 180.
flat sheet. 204.
flat shuttle. 495.
flat side of the grip. 524.
flat spike. 574.
flat stitches group. 493.
flat tip. 248.
flat washer. 254.
flesh. 66, 67, 68.
fleshy fruits. 66, 69.
fleur-de-lis. 696.
flexible hose. 234, 259, 625.
flexible hose connection. 625.
flexible rubber hose. 262.
flexible skirt. 421.
flies. 170.
flight. 165, 535, 560.
flight deck. 437.
flight deck. 434, 441, 443.
flight engineer's panel. 437.
flight engineer's seat. 437.
flight instruments. 437, 543.
flight of stairs. 187.
flights. 534.
flint. 273, 682.
flint arrowhead. 675.
flint knife. 675.
flintlock. 682.
flip turn. 533.
float. 567.
float. 267, 429, 684.
float ball. 258.
float clamp. 267.
floating bridge. 403.
floating crane. 427.
floating dock. 427.
floating head. 327.
floating platform. 628.
floating rib. 112.
floating roof. 633.
floating-roof tank. 633.
floodlight. 375.
floor. 182, 526, 527, 621, 622, 657.
floor brush. 234.
floor crew. 375.
floor joist. 182.
floor lamp. 210.
floor manager. 375.
floor selector. 171.
floor tile. 185.
floorboard. 186.
Florence fennel. 77.
flow bean. 627.
flower. 61.
flower, structure of a. 64.
flower bed. 237.
flower bud. 61.
flower tiles. 579.
flue. 468.
flue collar. 191.
flue damper. 191.
flue pipe. 468.
flue pipe. 191.
fluid adjustment screw. 270.
fluid coking plant. 634.

fluid inlet. 656.
fluid outlet. 656.
fluke. 433.
fluorescent lamp. 274.
fluorescent screen. 606.
flush. 578.
flush bushing. 265.
flute. 250, 469, 476.
fluted land. 250.
fluted pole. 208.
fluted shaft. 384.
flutes. 479.
fluting. 160.
flux. 507.
flux brush. 507.
Fly. 33, 284, 287, 695.
fly amanita. 65.
fly box. 568.
fly front closing. 290, 307.
fly reel. 566.
fly rod. 566.
flying buttress. 164, 165.
Flying Fish. 33.
flying jib. 417.
flyleaf. 498.
flywheel. 390, 391, 502, 505.
FM mode selector. 364.
FM stereo indicator. 364.
foam. 43.
foam gun. 631.
foam insulation. 185.
foam mattress. 584.
foam pad. 584.
foam rubber insulation. 185.
foam windscreen. 369.
focus. 45.
focus knob. 609.
focus magnifier. 361.
focus setting ring. 369.
focusing. 654.
focusing control. 368.
focusing knob. 361, 362, 608.
focusing magnifier. 360.
focusing ring. 368, 607.
focusing sleeve. 600.
fodder corn. 151.
fog. 52.
fog light. 389.
foible. 563.
foil. 563.
foil warning line. 562.
foilist. 563.
fold line. 489.
fold-out table. 407.
foldaway ladder. 268.
folder. 449.
folding camera. 354.
folding camp bed. 584.
folding chair. 203.
folding grill. 586.
folding nail file. 333.
folding shovel. 586.
foliage. 63.
follicle. 71.
follicle, section of a. 71.
fondue fork. 215.
fondue pot. 223.
fondue set. 223.
food. 133.
food processor. 226.
foot. 87, 96, 100, 107, 142, 205, 305, 306, 468, 537, 566.
foot cushion. 569.
foot fault judge. 523.
foot hole. 468.
foot of table. 569.
foot pocket. 536.
foot rest. 505.
foot rope. 416.
foot score line. 530.
foot spot. 569.
foot string. 569.
football. 513, 514, 515, 516.
footboard. 204, 394.
footbridge. 410, 414.
footing. 182.

footlights. 170.
footpeg. 396.
footplate. 617.
footrest. 544.
footstrap. 300.
foramen cecum. 126.
foramen ovale. 114.
forced hot-water system. 193.
forced warm-air system. 192.
fore and aft gangway. 631.
fore court. 523.
fore edge. 498.
fore leg. 92, 98.
fore royal sail. 417.
fore wing. 92, 98.
forearm. 107, 683, 687, 688.
forearm crutch. 616.
foregrip. 566.
forehead. 87, 106.
foreleg. 86.
forelimb. 97.
forelock. 83.
foremast. 416.
foresail. 417.
forestay. 538.
fork. 215.
fork. 81, 397, 585, 593, 608.
fork extender. 670.
fork pocket. 411.
forked tongue. 101.
forklift reach truck. 670.
forklift truck. 670.
forks. 670.
forks, major types of. 215.
formeret. 165.
forte. 563.
fortification, Vauban. 166.
forward. 534.
forward bolt assist mechanism. 685.
forward car ramp. 421.
forward dive. 535.
forward/reverse switch. 368.
foul line. 511, 576.
foundation. 182, 639.
foundation of dam. 638.
foundation of tower. 402.
foundation slip. 302.
foundations. 182.
fountain pen. 352.
four-door sedan. 384.
four-four time. 462.
four-masted bark. 416, 417.
four of a kind. 578.
four pale beater. 225.
fourchette. 289.
fourth. 462.
fourth wheel. 591.
fovea. 123.
fractionating tower. 635.
frame. 182, 493.
frame. 99, 153, 249, 269, 284, 336, 337, 340, 395, 429, 471, 474, 494, 503, 524, 526, 549, 559, 560, 581, 599, 656, 657, 667, 668, 670.
frame rail. 389.
frame stile. 205.
framework. 432.
framing control. 368.
Francis turbine. 643.
free fall. 541.
free margin. 129.
free throw line. 521, 525.
freezer bucket. 226.
freezer compartment. 229.
freezer door. 229.
freezing rain. 52.
freight elevator. 705.
freight hold. 419.
freight station. 410.
French bread. 138.
French chessboard. 577.
French cuff. 296.
French cut. 317.
French horn. 470, 476, 477.

French horns. 479.
French knot stitch. 493.
French loaf. 138.
French twist. 321.
French window. 189.
French writing system. 345.
frequency automatic control. 364.
fresh air inlet. 190.
fret. 473, 480.
fricative consonants. 348.
friction strip. 335.
frieze. 160, 205.
frigate. 425.
fringe trimming. 207.
frog. 97.
frog. 85, 153, 282, 298, 311, 408, 464.
frog, life cycle of the. 97.
front. 139, 143, 283, 285.
front apron. 285.
front axle. 666.
front bearing. 436.
front binding. 540.
front board. 498.
front brake. 396, 397.
front court. 527.
front crawl stroke. 533.
front crossbar. 549.
front derailleur. 397, 398.
front-end loader. 665.
front fender. 395.
front flap. 335.
front foil. 422.
front foil control actuator. 422.
front footpeg. 395.
front grip. 686.
front hydraulic fork. 395.
front knob. 247.
front leg. 203.
front pipe. 392.
front point. 575.
front quarter. 140.
front runner. 550.
front sight. 683, 686, 688, 689.
front sight housing. 685, 687.
front spar. 435.
front tip. 233.
front top pocket. 300.
front wall. 526, 527.
front wheel. 666.
frontal. 110, 112.
frontal bone. 114.
frontal sinus. 125.
fronts. 53.
frontwall. 388.
fruit cake. 147.
fruit-picking ladder. 269.
frying pan. 223.
frying pan. 585.
fuel. 650.
fuel bundle. 649.
fuel fabrication. 653.
fuel handling control console. 652.
fuel handling sequence. 651.
fuel indicator. 385.
fuel pellet. 649.
fuel pump. 390.
fuel pump belt. 390.
fuel spray manifold. 436.
fuel tank. 243, 389, 395, 422, 431, 441, 692.
fuel transfer pipe. 442.
fuelling machine. 647, 650.
fulcrum. 534.
full and by. 539.
full back. 517.
full brisket. 140.
full house. 578.
full-load adjustment screw. 601.
full Moon. 30.
fullback. 514, 515.
fumarole. 45.
fume extractor. 690.
function key. 456.
function keys. 596.

function lever. 365.
function selector. 196.
funiculus. 66, 71.
funnel. 218, 377.
funnel aileron. 419.
furlong chute. 555.
Furnace. 33, 192, 194, 654.
furs. 696.
fuse. 645.
fuse block. 195.
fuse cutout. 645.
fuse holder. 645.
fuse pullers. 276.
fuselage. 434, 542.
fuses. 275.

G

g clef. 461.
G-meter. 542.
gable. 165.
gable roof. 180.
gaff. 416.
gaff sail boom. 416.
gaff topsail. 417.
gaiter. 545.
gaiting strap. 554.
galaxies, classification of. 31.
galaxy. 31.
gall bladder. 91.
gallbladder. 119.
gallery. 165, 169, 431, 657.
galley. 434.
game timekeeper. 519.
gantry crane. 637, 641.
Ganymede. 28.
gap. 567.
garage. 177, 179, 419, 420.
garbage disposal sink. 260.
garbage disposal unit. 260.
garden. 237.
garden. 163, 178.
garden hoe. 238.
garden hose. 240.
garden line. 239.
garden sorrel. 74.
gardening. 235.
gardening, tools and equipment. 238, 239, 240, 241, 242.
garlic. 75.
garlic press. 218.
garment bag. 337.
garment fabric. 488.
garment strap. 337.
garrison cap. 288.
garter. 302, 303.
garter belt. 303.
garter stitch. 490.
gas. 274, 626.
gas cylinder. 687.
gas inlet. 444.
gas lift. 627.
gas lift valve. 627.
gas main. 399.
gas oil. 635.
gas-oil line. 390.
gas outlet. 444.
gas pedal. 386.
gas piston. 687.
gas tail. 31.
gas tank cap. 396.
gas tank door. 383.
gas turbine. 421, 629.
gas under pressure. 627.
gasket. 228, 230, 232, 261, 264.
gaskin. 83.
gasoline. 635.
gasoline engine. 391.
gasoline pump. 387.
gasoline pump. 391.
gasoline pump hose. 387.
gasometer. 624.
gastrocnemius. 110, 111.
gastropod. 96.

gate. 544, 551, 552, 574, 641, 646.
gate arm. 409.
gate arm lamp. 409.
gate arm support. 409.
gate-leg. 199.
gate operating ring. 643.
gather. 295.
gather skirt. 293.
gathering. 498.
gauchos. 300.
gauge. 499, 585.
gauntlet. 273, 289, 676.
gauze bandage. 561.
gauze roller bandage. 615.
gear. 496.
gear housing. 566.
gear shift. 396.
gear train. 356.
gearbox. 422, 503, 658.
gearshift lever. 385, 395.
gemelli. 137.
Gemini, the Twins. 698.
gemstones, cuts for. 317.
generating station flow diagram. 650.
generator. 642.
generator. 397, 641, 642, 647, 650, 652, 658.
genital organs, female. 109.
genital organs, male. 108.
genital pore. 96.
geography. 37.
geostationary orbit. 379.
geostationary orbit injection. 379.
germ. 71.
German rye bread. 138.
German writing system. 345.
geyser. 45.
gigot. 143.
gill. 65.
gill cover. 90.
gill filament. 90.
gill raker. 90.
gills. 90.
gills. 91, 94.
gimbal ring. 429.
Giraffe. 32.
girder. 34, 182.
girdle. 317, 520.
girth. 553.
girth strap. 553.
gîte à la noix. 141.
gîte de derrière. 141.
gîte de devant. 141.
["give way["] sign. 701.
glacial cirque. 48.
glacier. 48.
glacier tongue. 48.
glacis. 166.
gladius. 675.
glans penis. 108.
glass. 519, 526.
glass bulb. 357, 592.
glass case. 595.
glass cover. 229.
glass curtain. 207.
glass cutter. 507.
glass cutting. 507.
glass dome. 429.
glass-fiber cloth. 444.
glass grinder. 507.
glass port. 312.
glass slide. 605.
glass sphere. 56.
glassware. 212.
glaze. 49.
glider. 542.
glides. 348.
gliding. 542.
globe. 210.
glove. 289.
glove. 444, 536, 541, 547, 550, 558, 562.
glove, baseball. 512.
glove, hockey. 520.

glove compartment. 385.
glove finger. 289.
gloves, types of. 289.
glue. 186.
glue stick. 447.
gluteal nerve. 121.
gnomon. 592.
goal. 531.
goal. 513, 517, 518, 519, 525.
goal area. 518, 525.
goal area line. 525.
goal crease. 519.
goal judge. 531.
goal judge's box. 519.
goal line. 513, 517, 518, 519, 525, 531.
goal line referee. 525.
goal post. 513, 517.
goalkeeper. 520.
goalkeeper. 518, 519, 525, 531.
goalkeeper's pad. 520.
goalkeeper's stick. 520.
gob hat. 304.
goggles. 273, 541, 550.
golf. 571, 572, 573.
golf bag. 573.
golf cart. 573.
golf clubs. 572.
golf clubs, types of. 572.
golf hose. 301.
golf shoe. 573.
golfer. 571.
Golgi apparatus. 105.
gondola car. 406.
gong. 471.
gong. 372, 479.
goose-neck. 187.
gooseberry. 66.
gooseneck. 668.
gored skirt. 293.
gorge. 46, 142, 166.
gorget. 676.
gothic cathedral. 164, 165.
gouge. 332.
gouged section. 504.
gour. 46.
Gournay. 145.
governor. 171.
grab handle. 389.
grade crossing. 701.
grade sloppe. 178.
grader. 666.
graduated arm. 594.
graduated dial. 611.
graduated scale. 598.
graduation. 594, 596, 597, 599.
grafting knife. 242.
grain. 255.
grain of wheat, section of a. 71.
grain pan. 155.
grain screw. 155.
grain sieve. 155.
grain tank. 155.
grain unloading auger. 155.
grandfather. 131.
grandfather clock. 593.
grandmother. 131.
grandson. 131.
grandstand. 555.
granitic layer. 40.
granivorous bird. 89.
granny knot. 587.
granulation. 29.
grape. 66.
grape. 66.
grapefruit. 69.
graperfruit knife. 217.
grapeshot. 681.
graphic elements for symbols. 699.
grapnel anchor. 433.
grapple. 667.
grass catcher. 242.
grater. 218.
grater disc. 226.
grave accent. 347.
gravel. 182, 267.

gravity band. 433.
gravity dam. 639.
gravy boat and stand. 213.
grease trap. 267.
grease well. 227.
greases. 635.
great adductor. 111.
Great Bear. 32.
great foramen. 114.
great-granddaughter. 131.
great-grandfather. 131.
great-grandmother. 131.
great organ manual. 467.
great saphenous vein. 117.
great scallop. 94.
greater alar cartilage. 125.
greater covert. 88.
greater lip. 109.
greater pectoral. 110.
greater trochanter. 113.
greatest gluteal. 111.
greave. 676.
Greek temple. 161.
Greek temple, basic plan of the. 161.
Greek writing system. 345.
green ball. 570.
green beam. 377.
green bean. 73.
green cabbage. 74.
green dragon. 579.
green peas. 77.
green russula. 65.
green walnut. 70.
greenhouse. 151, 655.
Greenland Sea. 41.
grid. 170.
griddle. 227.
griff-fiffi hook. 574.
grill. 161.
grill and waffle baker. 227.
grille. 196, 363, 383, 475.
grip. 357, 526, 572, 679, 688.
grips, types of. 529.
groin. 106.
grommet. 583.
groove. 227, 365, 486, 499, 545, 547, 572, 677.
grooved sleeve. 261.
gros bout de poitrine. 141.
ground. 370, 633.
ground airport equipment. 439.
ground bond. 278.
ground clamp. 271.
ground electrode. 392.
ground fault circuit interrupter. 278.
ground floor. 178, 179.
ground lead. 365.
ground moraine. 48.
ground/neutral bus bar. 278.
ground sill. 166.
ground transportation. 707.
ground wire. 278, 645.
ground-wire clamp. 645.
ground-wire peak. 644.
grounded receptacle. 267.
grounding prong. 275.
group retarders. 411.
grow sleepers. 305.
growth line. 93, 96.
grozzing teeth. 507.
guard. 187, 211, 217, 563.
guard rail. 177, 229, 400.
guardhouse. 167.
guava. 72.
guidance system. 692.
guide. 566.
guide bar. 243.
guide bearing. 642.
guide chain. 423.
guide post. 452.
guide rods. 684.
guiding and current bar. 415.
guiding tower. 403.
guillotine trimmer. 360.
gules. 696.

gully grate. 399.
gum. 115.
gun body. 270.
gun director. 425.
gun flap. 281.
gunner's sight. 690.
Gutenberg discontinuity. 39.
guttae. 160.
gutter. 81, 177, 399, 576.
guy cable. 559.
guy line adapter. 583.
guy rope. 582.
guy wire. 658.
guyot. 42.
gym rompers. 307.
gymnast. 560.
gymnastics. 559, 560.
gypsum block. 183.

H

H stretcher. 203.
hack. 530.
hackle. 567.
hacksaw. 252.
hacksaw. 266.
hail. 49.
hail shower. 52.
hair. 129.
hair. 107, 128, 464.
hair, kinds of. 320.
hair bulb. 129.
hair clip. 333.
hair dryer. 330.
hair follicle. 129.
hair roller. 333.
hair shaft. 129.
hair styles. 320, 321.
hair styles, components of. 320, 321.
hairbrushes. 328.
haircutting scissors. 328.
hairpieces. 321.
hairpin. 333.
hairsetter. 331.
hairspring. 591.
hairstyling implements. 333.
half barb. 53.
half court line. 526.
half-distance line. 531.
half-glasses. 319.
half handle. 217.
half note. 461.
half rest. 461.
half-slip. 303.
half-through arch bridge. 401.
half way line. 518.
halfback. 515.
halfway line. 517.
hall. 169.
hall. 179, 419.
hallway. 179.
halyard. 417, 695.
ham knife. 217.
hammer. 558.
hammer. 247, 277, 465, 466, 575, 688, 689.
hammer axe. 574.
hammer beam. 180.
hammer block. 689.
hammer butt. 466.
hammer drill. 625.
hammer head. 466, 574.
hammer rail. 466.
hammer shank. 466.
hammer throw. 556.
hampe. 141.
hand. 107, 598.
hand-and-a-half sword. 678.
hand blender. 225.
hand brake gear housing. 405.
hand brake wheel. 405.
hand brake winding chain. 405.
hand drill. 250.
hand fork. 239.

hand grenade. 682.
hand grip. 566.
hand guard. 516.
hand lamp. 662.
hand mixer. 225.
hand mower. 242.
hand pallet truck. 671.
hand rail. 637.
hand shield. 273.
hand truck. 413, 671.
hand vice. 501.
hand warmer pocket. 291.
hand warmer pouch. 294.
hand-wheel. 500.
handbags. 338, 339.
handball. 525.
handgrip. 368, 369, 616, 617.
handguard. 685.
handhold. 554.
handle. 540.
handle. 204, 211, 214, 215, 216, 225, 226, 227, 228, 229, 233, 234, 243, 247, 248, 249, 250, 252, 253, 261, 270, 272, 327, 328, 329, 330, 331, 336, 337, 339, 340, 370, 475, 487, 492, 494, 500, 503, 507, 512, 524, 529, 530, 545, 550, 558, 563, 566, 573, 574, 585, 625, 677.
handle post. 340.
handlebars. 394, 397.
handles, types of. 540.
handling engines. 671.
handrail. 172, 187, 415.
handrail drive. 172.
handsaw. 252.
handset. 372, 373, 457.
handset cord. 372.
handsfree telephone. 373.
hang glider. 543.
hang gliding. 543.
hang point. 543.
hang-up ring. 330.
hangar. 151.
hanger. 362.
hanger bracket. 617.
hanger loop. 286.
hanging basket. 237.
hanging folder. 449.
hanging glacier. 48.
hanging hook. 337.
hanging stile. 188, 189, 205.
hank. 538, 539.
harbor. 427.
harbor station. 427.
hard palate. 114, 126.
hard shell clam. 94.
hardboard. 255.
hardboards. 184.
hardtop. 384.
hardware. 337.
Hare. 33.
harmonica. 474.
harness. 494, 536, 541, 543, 549, 662.
harness racing. 554, 555.
harnesses. 494.
harp. 464.
Harp. 32, 479.
harp cable stays. 402.
harpsichord. 476.
harrow. 152.
hasp. 337.
hassock. 202.
hastate. 62.
hat. 311.
hat vell. 304.
hatband. 288.
hatch. 631, 690.
hatchet. 586.
hatching. 497.
haul road. 621.
haulage cable. 544.
haut de côtelettes. 143.
haut de côtes. 139.
hazelnut. 70.

hazelnut, section of a. 70.
head. 31, 77, 92, 96, 98, 107, 108, 116, 250, 254, 272, 327, 329, 334, 335, 408, 464, 472, 473, 480, 485, 490, 492, 500, 524, 558, 567, 572, 574.
head band. 304.
head cover. 573.
head cushion. 569.
head-first entry. 534.
head linesman. 514.
head number. 554.
head of femur. 113.
head of frame. 189.
head of humerus. 113.
head of sail. 537.
head of table. 569.
head pole. 554.
head roller. 494.
head rotation lock. 361.
head shell. 365.
head spot. 569.
head string. 569.
head tube. 397.
headband. 363, 498, 524, 547.
headbay. 637.
headboard. 204.
headbox. 209.
headcap. 498.
header. 188, 190, 647, 650.
headframe. 622, 624.
headgears. 288.
headgears, types of. 288.
headlamp bezel. 384.
headland. 43.
headlight. 384.
headlight. 383, 389, 394, 395, 413, 690.
headlight housing shell. 384.
headphone. 363.
headphone. 363.
headphone jack. 364, 366.
headpin. 576.
headrest. 386, 407.
heads. 247.
headwear. 304.
headwind. 539.
health. 613.
hearing. 124.
heart. 116.
heart. 91, 94, 507, 578.
hearth. 506.
heartwood. 63.
heat, measure of. 597.
heat comfort control. 331.
heat deflecting disc. 274.
heat exchanger. 655.
heat pipe radiator. 378.
heat ready indicator dot. 331.
heat shield. 443.
heat/speed selector switch. 330.
heater. 585, 650.
heater control. 385.
heating. 190, 191, 192, 193, 194, 195.
heating duct. 231.
heating element. 194, 195, 231, 232, 506.
heating elements indicator. 194.
heating oil. 635.
heating pump. 194.
heating room. 179.
heating unit. 193.
heaving line knot. 587.
heavy duty boot. 310.
heavy gasoline. 635.
heavy machine gun. 687.
heavy machinery. 659.
heavy thunderstorm. 52.
heavy water. 650.
Hebrew writing system. 345.
heddle. 494, 495.
heddle rod. 495.
heddles. 495.
hedge. 237.
hedge shears. 239.

hedge trimmer. 242.
heel. 85, 107, 153, 217, 247, 252, 287, 308, 464, 512, 520, 548, 572.
heel calk. 85.
heel flange. 546.
heel grip. 308.
heel lacing. 549.
heel loop. 617.
heel of round. 140.
heel piece. 540, 545, 546.
heel release setting indicator. 546.
heel rest. 225, 233.
heelplate. 547.
height. 534.
height adjustment screw. 546.
height control. 361.
height of the dive. 535.
height scale. 361.
height sensor. 422.
helical spring. 594.
helicopter. 441.
helicopter hangar. 425.
helicopter transportation. 707.
helideck. 629.
heliostat. 654.
helium sphere. 442.
helix. 124.
helm roof. 181.
helmet. 273, 312, 444, 516, 520, 541, 543, 575, 675, 676.
helmet lamp. 575.
hem. 209.
hemibranch. 90.
hemispherical dome. 35.
hemlath. 657.
hemline. 489.
hepatic vein. 116, 117.
heraldry. 695.
herbivore's jaw. 82.
herbs. 133.
Hercules. 32.
Herdsman. 32.
Hermes satellite. 378.
herringbone parquet. 186.
herringbone pattern. 186.
herringbone stitch. 493.
hex nut. 392.
hexagon bushing. 265.
high. 580, 581.
high-back overall. 306.
high beam warning light. 396.
high card. 578.
high clouds. 44.
high focal plane buoy. 430.
high jump. 557.
high line. 563.
high-power light bulb. 35.
high pressure center. 54.
high pressure turbine. 650.
high-rise apartment. 173.
high-speed exit taxiway. 438.
high-temperature cutoff. 263.
high-voltage cable. 606.
high-voltage tester. 276.
high warp loom. 495.
highball. 212.
highland climates. 51.
highway crossing. 409.
highway crossing bell. 409.
hill. 46, 654.
hilted bayonet. 679.
hilus of kidney. 120.
hind leg. 92, 100.
hind limb. 97.
hind quarter. 140.
hind toe. 87, 89.
hind wing. 92.
Hindi writing system. 345.
hindlimb, skeleton fo the. 97.
hing leg. 98.
hing wing. 98.
hinge. 188, 189, 205, 227, 228, 232, 337, 339, 365, 546, 607.
hinge tooth. 93.
hinged door. 178.

hinged presser foot. 485, 486.
hip. 107, 140.
hip-and-valley roof. 181.
hip pad. 516, 520.
hip roof. 180.
hitch pin. 465.
hitting area. 512.
hive. 99.
hive body. 99.
hoarding. 167.
hobble. 554.
hobble hanger. 554.
hock. 83, 142.
hockey. 509.
hockey skate. 548.
hoe. 238.
hoe-fork. 238.
hog score line. 530.
hoist. 170, 695.
hoist chain. 661.
hoist drum. 661.
hoist room. 622, 624.
hoist rope. 661.
hoist ropes. 171.
hoisting apparatus. 375.
hoisting ring. 433.
hoisting rope. 268, 669.
hold. 434.
hold yard. 411.
holdback. 207.
holder. 507.
holding area marking. 438.
holds. 564.
hole. 571.
hole. 503, 574.
hollow barrel. 615.
hollow-wood construction. 255.
holster. 575.
home key. 456.
home plate. 511.
homestretch. 555.
honey cell. 99.
honeybee. 98, 99.
honeycomb diffuser. 358.
honeycomb section. 99.
honor tiles. 579.
hood. 190, 234, 282, 383, 389, 536.
hood cover. 330.
hoof. 85.
hoof. 85.
hoof, plantar surface of the. 85.
hook. 189, 208, 211, 238, 341, 486, 488, 490, 492, 544, 548, 567, 594, 599, 626, 669.
hook and eyes. 488.
hook ladder. 268, 663.
hooker. 517.
hoop. 493.
hoop earring. 315.
hopper. 154.
hopper car. 406.
hopper ore car. 406.
horizon glass. 429.
horizon scanner. 57.
horizontal-axis wind turbine. 658.
horizontal bar. 559.
horizontal circle. 600.
horizontal circle drive knob. 600.
horizontal clamp. 600.
horizontal end handhold. 405.
horizontal flux detector. 648.
horizontal member. 644.
horizontal pivoting. 189.
horizontal seismograph. 602.
horizontal stabilizer. 434, 441, 542.
horizontal tangent screw. 600.
horn. 315, 385, 404, 663.
horn button. 396.
horns. 96.
horny beak. 101.
hors d'oeuvre dish. 213.
horse. 82, 83, 84, 85.
horse, morphology. 83.
horse, skeleton. 84.
horse-radish. 76.

horse's name. 555.
horse's number. 555.
horse's pedigree. 555.
horseshoe. 85.
horseshoe. 162, 315.
horseshoe mount. 34.
hose. 271, 301.
hose nozzle. 240.
hose reel. 240.
hose truck. 663.
hoses. 301.
hospital. 704.
host. 375.
hot-air register. 192.
hot bus bar. 278.
hot line connector. 645.
hot pepper. 73.
hot water extraction. 636.
hot-water heater. 257.
hot-water main. 194.
hot-water supply. 262.
hot-water supply line. 262, 263.
hotel information. 707.
hotel reservation desk. 440.
hour angle gear. 34.
hour hand. 591, 593.
hourglass. 592.
house. 175.
house. 178, 530.
house, exterior of a. 177.
house, plan reading. 178.
house, structure. 180, 182.
house drain. 262.
house furniture. 197.
housing. 251, 327, 329, 330, 369, 372, 395, 428.
hovercraft. 421.
howitzer. 684.
howitzer locking ring. 684.
hub. 256, 397, 617, 643, 658.
hub cover. 643.
hubcap. 383.
huckleberry. 66.
hull. 71.
human being. 103.
human body, anterior view. 106.
human body, posterior view. 107.
human denture. 115.
humerus. 84, 100, 112.
humid subtropical. 51.
humid temperate - long summer. 51.
humid temperate - short summer. 51.
humidifier. 194.
humidistat. 196.
humidity. 55.
hump. 411.
hump area. 411.
Hungarian writing system. 345.
Hunting Dogs. 32.
hunting scope. 607.
hunting weapons. 688.
hurdle. 556.
hurricane. 52.
hurricane deck. 420.
hurricane lamp. 586.
husband. 130, 131.
husk. 70, 77.
hut. 159.
hydrant intake. 663.
hydraulic cylinder. 664, 665, 668.
hydraulic shovel. 667.
hydraulic turbine. 643.
hydroelectric complex. 637.
hydroelectric power station. 641.
hydrofiner. 634.
hydrofoil boat. 422.
hydrologic cycle. 50.
hydrostatic pad. 34.
hygrograph. 55.
hypha. 65.
hyphen. 347, 350.
hypogastric artery. 120.
hyssop. 133.

I

ice. 50.
ice axe. 574.
ice axe. 575.
ice-cream can. 226.
ice-cream freezer. 226.
ice cream spoon. 221.
ice cube tray. 229.
ice hockey. 519, 520.
ice hockey player. 520.
ice piton. 575.
ice pudding. 147.
ice screw. 575.
icing syringe. 220.
identification of the track. 555.
identification tag. 337.
idler pulley. 231.
idler wheel. 394.
igloo. 159.
igneous rocks. 40.
ignition switch. 396.
ignition transformer. 195.
ileum. 119.
iliohypogastric nerve. 121.
ilioinguinal nerve. 121.
ilium. 112.
illumination mirror. 600.
image dissector camera. 57.
immigration control. 440.
impeller. 232.
imperial roof. 181.
implement bar. 152.
impluvium. 163.
impost. 162.
impression control. 452.
in-flight refuelling probe. 691.
in goal. 517.
inactive dyke. 646.
inbound line. 513.
incandescent lamp. 274.
incandescent lamp. 432.
incident-light measuring diffuser. 357.
incisor. 82.
inclined shaft. 622.
incoming message cassette. 373.
index. 594.
index arm. 429.
index mirror. 429.
index plate. 595.
Indian. 33.
Indian chapati bread. 138.
Indian fig. 72.
Indian naan bread. 138.
Indian Ocean. 41.
indication of types. 351.
indicator. 596, 598.
indicator board. 413.
indicator light. 457.
indicator needle. 357.
indifferent cells. 129.
indoor/outdoor position. 369.
inert gas. 274.
inferior dental arch. 126.
inferior mesenteric artery. 120.
inferior nasal concha. 125.
inferior umbilicus. 88.
inferior vena cava. 116, 117, 120.
infield. 511.
infiltration. 50.
infinity. 709.
inflated carrying tire. 415.
inflated guiding tire. 415.
inflator. 584.
inflator-deflator. 584.
inflorescence vegetables. 73.
inflorescences, types of. 64.
information. 704.
information counter. 440.
information office. 412.
informative signs. 703.
infraorbital foramen. 114.
infrared spectrometer. 57.
infrared transmitter. 358.
infrespinous. 111.

infundibulum of uterine tube. 109.
inhaul. 537.
injector. 390.
ink. 352, 502.
inked roller. 370.
inked surface. 504.
inking slab. 502.
inlaid parquet. 186.
inlet. 625.
inlet guide vanes. 436.
inlet hose. 230, 232.
inlet nozzle. 230.
inlet valve. 390, 391.
inner boot. 546.
inner core. 39.
inner edge. 85.
inner hearth. 190.
inner jib. 417.
inner lip. 93.
inner ply. 255.
inner rail. 172.
inner root sheath. 129.
inner table. 578.
inner tent. 583.
inner toe. 87.
input devices. 454.
input level control. 481.
input selectors. 364.
insectivorous bird. 89.
insert a letter. 350.
insert a word. 350.
insert here. 350.
insert space. 350.
inset pocket. 294.
inside. 216.
inside address. 349.
inside knob. 256.
inside left. 518.
inside line. 563.
inside linebacker. 514.
inside right. 518.
insole. 308, 310.
inspection chamber. 267.
inspection plug. 267.
inspection services. 706.
instep. 287.
instrument board. 385.
instrument board. 385.
instrument panel. 542.
instrument shelter. 55.
instrument unit. 442.
instrumental groups. 476, 477.
insulated blade. 276.
insulated handle. 276, 277.
insulating material. 186.
insulating sleeve. 275.
insulation. 263, 655, 656.
insulator. 392, 645.
insulin syringe. 615.
intaglio printing, diagram of. 504.
intaglio printing, equipment. 501.
intaglio printing process. 501.
integral bayonet. 679.
Intelsat. 378.
interchangeable end assembly. 34.
interchangeable lens. 353.
interconnecting truss. 57.
intercostal nerve. 121.
interface. 481.
interfacing. 285, 488.
interfemoral membrane. 100.
interior dome shell. 34.
interior door handle. 386.
interior door lock button. 386.
interior pocket. 337.
interlining. 488.
interloop. 497.
intermediate lens. 606.
intermittent drizzle. 52.
intermittent rain. 52.
intermittent snow. 52.
internal ear. 124.
internal iliac artery. 116, 117.
internal iliac vein. 116.
internal jufular vein. 117.
internal tooth lock washer. 254.

international phonetic alphabet. 348.
international road signs. 700, 701, 702, 703.
internode. 61.
interplanetary space. 39.
interrogation recording. 57.
intersection. 709.
intertragic notch. 124.
intervals. 462.
intervertebral foramen. 122.
intestine. 91, 94, 116.
intrados. 162.
intrusion rocks. 40.
invert. 415.
inverted pleat. 207, 294.
inverter knob. 600.
inward dive. 535.
Io. 28.
ion chamber. 648.
ionic order. 160.
ionosphere. 39.
Iranian writing system. 345.
iris. 123.
iris diaphragm. 605.
Irish bread. 138.
iron. 572.
iron curtain. 170.
iron shot silo. 423.
ironing. 708.
irregular crystal. 49.
irregular galaxy. 31.
is a member of. 709.
is approximately equal to. 709.
is contained in. 709.
is equal to. 709.
is equal to or less than. 709.
is equivalent to. 709.
is greater than. 709.
is identical with. 709.
is not equal to. 709.
is not identical with. 709.
isba. 159.
ischium. 113.
isobar. 54.
isoseismal line. 45.
isthmus of fauces. 126.
isthmus of uterine tube. 109.
ital. boldface capitals. 351.
Italian writing system. 345.
italic. 351.
italic capitals. 351.
ivory ball. 580.

J

J-2 engine. 442.
jabot. 298.
jack. 363, 466, 578.
jack spring. 466.
jack staff. 425.
jack-up platform. 628.
jacket. 283, 311, 562, 564, 629, 688.
jackled drill. 625.
jackpot box. 581.
jackpot feed. 581.
jackpot payout chute. 581.
jalousie. 189.
jamb. 188, 189, 190.
jambon. 142.
jambonneau arrière. 142.
jambonneau avant. 142.
Japan plum. 68.
Japanese persimmon. 72.
Japanese writing system. 345.
jar. 335.
jarret arrière. 139.
jarret avant. 139.
javelin. 675.
javelin throw. 557.
javelins. 558.
jaw. 248, 250, 251, 277, 333.

jaws, types of. 82.
jazz band. 477.
jeans. 300.
jejunum. 119.
jersey. 516.
Jerusalem artichoke. 76.
jet. 434.
jet deflector. 242.
jet engine. 691.
jet fuel. 635.
jet refueler. 439.
jet tip. 329.
Jew's harp. 474.
jewel cap. 429.
jewel neck. 299.
jewelry. 315, 316, 317.
jewelry, diversity of. 315.
jewelry, micellaneous. 316.
Jewish tchallaw. 138.
jib. 538, 669.
jib halyard. 538.
jib tie. 669.
jibsheet. 538.
jingle. 472.
jockey roller. 398.
joint. 352, 498, 567, 568.
joist. 186.
Joker. 578.
journal box. 404.
jowl. 142.
joystick. 457.
joystick. 455, 481.
judge. 562, 564, 565.
judge's stand. 555.
judo. 564.
judo suit. 564.
juice sac. 69.
juicer. 226.
jumeaux. 141.
jump ski. 540.
jumper. 307.
jumper. 292, 541.
jumpsuit. 306.
jumpsuit. 300.
junction box. 409.
Jupiter. 28.

K

K frame. 644.
Kaplan turbine. 643.
keel. 543.
keep. 167.
keeper. 281, 284.
keeper ring. 566.
kelly. 626.
kerchief. 304.
kernel. 70, 77.
kerosene. 442, 635.
ketch. 418.
kettle. 233.
kettle. 585.
kettledrum. 472.
key. 256, 370, 453, 465, 466, 469, 475, 478.
key case. 341.
key finger button. 469.
key lock. 340.
key signature. 462.
keybed. 465.
keyboard. 456.
keyboard. 371, 453, 455, 465, 481.
keyboard control. 481.
keyboard instruments. 465, 466.
keyhole. 256.
keystone. 162, 165.
khôl pencil. 322.
kick. 533.
kick pleat. 294.
kickplate. 229.
kidney. 91, 116.
kill button. 396.
kilt. 293.
kimono. 301.
kimono sleeve. 296.

King. 578.
King (K). 577.
king pin. 404.
king post. 543.
King's side. 577.
kingpin. 388, 548.
kiosk. 414.
kitchen. 163, 179, 407.
kitchen knife. 217.
kitchen knives, types of. 217.
kitchen scale. 219.
kitchen timer. 219.
kitchen utensil for straining. 218.
kitchen utensils. 217, 218, 219, 220.
kitchen utensils, miscellaneous. 221.
kitchen utensils for draining. 218.
kitchen utensils for grating. 218.
kitchen utensils for grinding. 218.
kitchen utensils for measuring. 219.
kitchen utensils for opening. 219.
kiwi. 72.
knee. 83, 100, 106.
knee boot. 554.
knee boot suspender. 554.
knee brace. 180.
knee pad. 512, 516, 520, 550, 561.
knee roll. 553.
knee sock. 547.
knickers. 300, 547.
knife. 214.
knife. 155, 502, 536, 585.
knife-blade cartridge fuse. 275.
knife-edge. 594, 595, 596.
knife pleat. 294.
Knight (Kt). 577.
knit shirt. 286.
knitting. 490.
knitting machine. 491, 492.
knitting measure. 490.
knitting needles. 490.
knives, major types of. 214.
knob. 199, 256, 512.
knob closure. 339, 341.
knob handle. 253.
knockout. 278.
knot. 497.
knot stitches group. 493.
knots. 587.
knurled bolt. 270.
knurled button. 428.
kohlrabi. 76.
kraft paper. 255.
kumquat. 69.

L

label. 334, 365.
label marker. 447.
labial palp. 92.
laboratory. 634.
laccolith. 45.
lace. 512, 548, 565.
lacrimal duct. 123.
lactiferous duct. 109.
ladder. 657.
ladder scaffold. 269.
ladder truck, aerial. 662.
ladders. 268, 269.
ladle. 219, 681.
Lady chapel. 164.
lagging. 633.
lagoon. 43.
lake. 30.
lam. 494.
lamb, North American cut. 143.
lamb, Parisian cut. 143.
lambdoid suture. 114.
laminate board. 255.
laminboard. 255.
lamp. 210, 274, 361, 368, 605.
lamp changer. 432.
lamp room. 624.

lamp socket. 275.
lamphouse. 361.
lance rest. 676.
lanceolate. 62.
lancet. 162.
land. 250.
landing. 179, 187, 560, 623.
landing area. 556, 557.
landing light. 441.
landing mat. 560.
landing net. 568.
landside. 153.
lane. 576.
lane. 557.
lane number. 532.
lane rope. 532.
lane timekeeper. 532.
languid. 468.
lantern. 237, 431, 585.
lantern of lighthouse. 432.
lantern pane. 431.
lanyard ring. 689.
lapel. 283, 298.
lapiaz. 46.
large intestine. 119.
large wheel. 617.
larger round. 111.
larva. 99.
larynx. 118.
lasagna. 136.
lash comb. 323.
LASH ship. 427.
last quarter. 30.
latch. 227, 228, 232, 492, 574.
latch bolt. 256.
latch lever. 256, 486.
latch needle. 492.
lateen sail. 418.
lateral adjusting lever. 247.
lateral condyle of femur. 113.
lateral cutaneous nerve of thigh. 121.
lateral filing cabinet. 451.
lateral furrow. 85.
lateral great. 110, 111.
lateral incisor. 115.
lateral line. 90, 530.
lateral moraine. 48.
lateral semicircular canal. 124.
latitude. 27.
latitude scale. 56.
lattice tube. 648.
launch escape system. 442.
launching orbit. 379.
laundry room. 179.
lava flow. 45.
lava plateau. 45.
lavaliere. 316.
lavatory. 179.
lavatory truck. 439.
lawn. 178, 237.
lawn aerator. 241.
lawn edger. 238.
lawn mowers. 242.
lawn rake. 238.
layout. 507.
lead. 530, 592.
lead came. 507.
lead-in wire. 274, 357.
lead knife. 507.
lead pencil. 352.
lead screw. 500.
lead shot ballast. 423.
lead stretcher. 507.
leader. 567.
leading edge. 294, 298, 434, 542, 543.
leading edge tube. 543.
leaf. 62.
leaf. 61, 77, 199, 426.
leaf axil. 61, 62.
leaf margin. 62.
leaf spring. 394.
leaf vegetables. 74.
lean-to roof. 180.
lease stick. 494, 495.

leather end. 284.
leather garment. 675.
leather goods. 340, 341.
leather sandal. 675.
leather sheath. 585.
leaves, types of. 62.
LED peak level meter. 366.
ledger. 182.
ledger line. 461.
leech. 537.
leek. 75.
left atrium. 116.
left back. 518, 522, 525.
left bronchus. 118.
left center. 517.
left cornerback. 514, 515.
left defense. 519.
left defensive end. 514, 515.
left defensive tackle. 514, 515.
left field. 511.
left fielder. 511.
left forward. 521, 522.
left guard. 514, 515, 521.
left half. 518.
left halfback. 514.
left-hand grip. 686.
left kidney. 120.
left lung. 116, 118.
left outside linebacker. 515.
left safety. 514.
left safety back. 515.
left service court. 523, 526.
left tackle. 514, 515.
left ventricle. 116.
left wing. 517, 519.
left winger. 525.
leg. 101, 107, 139, 142, 143, 153, 199, 204, 287, 472, 529, 560, 566, 595.
leg, butt portion. 139.
leg, shank portion. 139.
leg-of-mutton sleeve. 296.
leg position. 535.
legging. 575.
legume, section of a. 71.
lemon. 69.
lenghtwise grain. 489.
length. 534.
lengthwise grain. 488.
lens. 611.
lens. 123, 356, 357, 362.
lens aperture scale. 355.
lens cap. 355.
lens carriage. 432.
lens clock. 432.
lens hood. 355.
lens mount. 353.
lenses, interchangeable. 355.
lenticular galaxy. 31.
lentils. 77.
Leo, the Lion. 698.
leopard. 82.
lesser covert. 88.
lesser lip. 109.
let it stand. 350.
letter opener. 447.
letter scales. 447.
letterhead. 349.
letterpress printing, diagram of. 504.
leucoplast. 105.
level. 623.
level controls. 363.
level crossing. 410.
leveling foot. 362.
leveling screw. 56, 595, 600.
lever. 227, 249, 260, 261, 333, 370, 387, 457, 503, 581, 598, 682, 688.
lever corkscrew. 219.
lever cover. 261.
levigator. 503.
libial palp. 94.
Libra, the Balance. 698.
lid. 222, 223, 224, 226, 227, 230, 331.

lid latch. 331.
Liederkranz. 144.
life buoy. 422.
life raft. 425.
lifeboat. 416, 629.
lift. 416.
lift arm. 665.
lift bridge. 403.
lift cord. 209.
lift cord lock. 209.
lift cylinder. 665, 670.
lift-fan air intake. 421.
lift gate. 384.
lift span. 403.
lifting chain. 670.
lifting handle. 684.
lifting lever. 405.
ligature. 469.
light. 415, 430, 536.
light bar. 330.
light-load adjustment screw. 601.
light machine gun. 687.
light pen. 455.
light-reading scale. 357.
light sensor. 357.
light signals. 701.
lightbox. 360.
lighter, gas. 334.
lighthouse. 431.
lighting and vision control room. 374.
lighting arrester. 641.
lighting director. 374.
lighting switch. 396.
lightning arrester. 645.
lightning rod. 177.
lights. 210, 211.
lighttight box. 353.
limb. 63.
limb top. 605.
limousine. 384.
limpet. 96.
line. 370, 461, 566, 567, 580, 581, 637.
line guide. 371, 566.
line judge. 514.
line map. 414.
line of scrimmage. 514, 515.
line printer. 652.
line space regulator. 453.
linear. 62.
lineman's pliers. 277.
linen. 204.
lines. 370.
linesman. 517, 518, 519, 522, 523, 528.
lingual papillae. 126.
lingual tonsil. 126.
lining. 283, 308, 338, 340, 488, 548.
linstock. 681.
lint filter. 230.
lint trap. 231.
lintel. 165, 190.
Lion. 32.
lion passant. 696.
lip. 86, 256, 507.
lipbrush. 323.
lipid droplet. 105.
lipliner. 323.
lipstick. 323.
liquefied petroleum gas storage. 634.
liqueur. 212.
liquid compass. 429.
liquid consonants. 348.
liquid-cooled garment. 444.
liquid-crystal display. 591.
liquid foundation. 322.
liquid hydrogen (fuel). 442.
liquid-level gauge. 633.
liquid oxygen (lox). 442.
liquid oxygen (lox) transfer pipe. 442.
liquified gas petroleum treatment. 634.

listen button. 373.
litchi. 72.
litho crayon. 503.
litho pencil. 503.
lithographic press. 503.
lithographic stone. 504.
lithographic tusche. 503.
lithography. 503.
lithography, equipement. 503.
lithosphere. 39.
litre/gallon totalizer. 387.
litter basket. 168.
little finger hook. 470.
liver. 91, 116, 119.
livestock car. 406.
living quarters. 431, 443, 629.
living room. 179, 582.
Lizard. 32.
load backrest. 670.
loader's seat. 690.
loading. 682.
loading belt. 621.
loading door. 191.
loading pocket. 623.
loading tunnel. 438.
loafer. 310.
loam. 152.
lobate. 62.
lobate web. 89.
lobby. 440.
lobe. 89, 109.
lobster. 95.
lobule. 124.
location system antenna. 57.
lock. 256.
lock. 188, 205, 337, 398, 646.
lock-chamber. 426.
lock forward. 517.
lock keeper's building. 427.
lock nut. 56, 548, 599.
lock rail. 188.
lock ring. 362.
lock washer. 254.
locked groove. 365.
locker. 451.
lockers. 706.
locket. 316.
locking device. 268.
locking knob. 599, 600.
locking nut. 258.
locking pliers. 249.
lockling ring. 248.
locknut. 260.
locomotive. 404.
loculus. 68.
log carrier. 191.
log chute. 637.
log tongs. 191.
logging unit. 629.
loin. 83, 107, 139, 140, 142, 143.
long adductor. 110.
long and short stitch. 493.
long extensor of toes. 110.
long hub lever. 256.
long jump. 556.
long-nose pliers. 277.
long palmar. 110.
long peroneal. 110.
long radial extensor of wrist. 111.
long-range jet. 434.
long-range radar system. 692.
long residue. 635.
long service line. 528.
longe. 139.
longitude. 27.
longitudinal dunes. 47.
lookout tower. 167.
loom. 494, 495.
loop. 285.
loop stitches group. 493.
loophole. 167.
loose curtain. 207.
loose fill insulation. 185.
loose gravel. 700.
loose powder. 322.
loose powder brush. 322.

loosely tied bow. 299.
lopping shears. 239.
lore. 87.
lorgnette. 319.
lost and found articles. 706.
lot plan. 178.
loud pedal. 465.
loudness switch. 364.
loudspeaker. 363, 375, 457, 663.
lounge. 419.
louver. 196, 211.
louver-board. 168.
louvered window. 189.
lovage. 133.
love seat. 201.
low. 580, 581.
low bar. 560.
low clouds. 44.
low line. 563.
low pressure center. 54.
low pressure steam piping. 647.
low pressure turbine. 650.
low tension distribution line. 645.
low wrap loom. 494.
lower berth. 407.
lower blade guard. 253.
lower bowl. 224.
lower chord. 401.
lower eyelid. 86, 97, 123.
lower fore topgallant sail. 417.
lower fore topsail. 417.
lower gill arch. 90.
lower girdle facet. 317.
lower guard retracting lever. 253.
lower heating element. 263.
lower landing plate. 427.
lower level. 426.
lower limb. 677.
lower lip. 126, 468.
lower lobe. 118.
lower mandible. 87.
lower mantle. 39.
lower mast. 416.
lower pan-head mounting screw.
359.
lower rudder. 424.
lower shell. 546.
lower side-rail. 388.
lower sphere clamp. 56.
lower support screw. 56.
lower thermostat. 263.
lox tank baffles. 442.
lubber's line. 429.
lubber's-line disk. 429.
lubricants plant. 635.
lubricating oils. 635.
Luer-Lock syringe. 615.
luff. 537.
luff (to). 537.
lug. 472.
luggage. 337.
luggage carrier. 337.
luggage rack. 384.
lumache. 137.
lumbar plexus. 121.
lumbar vertebra. 122.
lumbar vertebra. 113.
lumbar vertebrae. 84.
lunar boot. 444.
lunar eclipse. 30.
lunar features. 30.
lunar module. 442.
lunette. 684.
lungs. 118.
lunula. 129.
lunule. 93.
lures. 567.
Lynx. 32.
lyre. 473.
lysosome. 105.

M

machete. 678.
machicolation. 167.

machine gun. 687, 690.
machine hall. 637, 641.
machinery. 155.
macreuse. 141.
macro focusing knob. 368.
mafalde. 136.
mafaldine. 136.
magazine. 683, 685, 688, 689.
magazine base. 689.
magazine catch. 683, 685, 689.
magazine release. 685.
magazine spring. 689.
magma. 45.
magma chamber. 45.
magnesium alloy. 312.
magnesium wire. 357.
magnet. 487.
magnet. 429.
magnetic compass. 611.
magnetic cup. 592.
magnetic gasket. 229.
magnetic lid holder. 233.
magnetic needle. 611.
magnetic suspension. 601.
magnetic tape controller. 458.
magnetic tape drive. 458.
magnetic tape storage. 458.
magnifying mirror. 330.
mah-jongg. 579.
main bevel drive gearbox. 421.
main breaker. 278.
main cable. 358.
main cleanout. 257.
main cord. 362.
main drive chain. 172.
main drive shaft. 172.
main duct. 192.
main electrode. 274.
main engines. 443.
main entrance. 178.
main gas tap. 396.
main generator. 404.
main halyard. 538.
main handle. 250.
main inlet. 633.
main landing gear. 434.
main leg. 644.
main line. 410.
main lower topgallant sail. 417.
main lower topsail. 417.
main mirror. 608.
main parachute. 541.
main power cable. 278.
main return pipe. 193.
main royal sail. 417.
main running track. 411.
main sail. 417.
main scope tube. 607.
main section. 580, 581.
main sewer. 399.
main shaft. 624.
main shield bracket. 684.
main spar. 435.
main spring. 689.
main stand. 395.
main street. 168.
main supply pipe. 193.
main switch. 645.
main tube. 608.
main undercarriage mounting
beam. 435.
main undercarriage wheel. 691.
main upper topgallant sail. 417.
main upper topsail. 417.
main wheel. 593.
mainmast. 416.
mainsail. 538.
mainsheet. 538.
mainspring. 591.
maintenance hangar. 438.
maintube. 609.
major inner reaping throw. 564.
major outer reaping throw. 564.
makeup. 322, 323.
makeup, accessories. 323.
makeup kit. 322.

make-up products. 322.
make-up sponges. 323.
malar bone. 112.
malar region. 87.
male. 709.
male ferrule. 566.
male urethra. 108.
mallet. 247.
mallet. 472, 502.
mallets. 471.
Malpighi's pyramid. 120.
mammary gland. 109.
mandarin. 69.
mandarin collar. 298.
mandatory signs. 703.
mandible. 84, 90, 92, 95, 98, 112,
114, 115.
mandolin. 473.
mane. 83.
maneuvering engine. 443.
mango. 67.
manhole. 399, 632, 633.
manicotti. 137.
manicure set. 332.
manicure stick. 332.
manicuring instruments. 333.
manometer. 194, 633.
mansard roof. 181.
mantel. 190.
mantel shelf. 190.
mantle. 96.
mantle edge. 94.
manual. 467.
manual aperture control. 368.
manual lift truck. 671.
manual release. 546.
manual zoom ring. 368, 369.
manuals. 467.
manure spreader. 153.
manure spreader box. 153.
manway. 623.
Marconi cutter. 418.
margin. 62.
margin stop. 453.
marginal shield. 101.
marine diesel. 635.
maritime signals. 430, 431, 432.
marjoram. 133.
marker. 352, 576.
marker light. 389.
marking, cardinal system of. 431.
marking, lateral system of. 432.
marking dot. 489.
Mars. 28.
mars light. 663.
martingale. 563.
mascara. 322.
mascara brush. 323.
mashie. 572.
mashie iron. 572.
mashie niblick. 572.
mask. 312, 512, 536, 562.
mass. 602.
masseter. 110.
mast. 409, 410, 441, 537, 538,
661, 670, 695.
mast foot. 537.
mast sleeve. 537.
master bedroom. 179.
master carrier. 208.
master cord. 549.
master gate valve. 627.
master retarders. 411.
masthead. 416, 537.
masthead light. 420.
masting. 416.
mastoid process. 114.
mat. 564.
matchbook. 335.
matchbox. 335.
matchstick. 335.
maternal aunt. 130.
maternal uncle. 130.
maternity dress. 292.
mathematics. 709.
matinee length necklace. 316.

matrix. 481.
mattock. 238.
mattress. 204.
mattress cover. 204.
maxilla. 90, 95, 112, 114, 115, 125.
maxilliped. 95.
maximum and minimum thermometers. 55.
maximum speed limit. 702.
measuring cap. 225.
measuring cup. 331.
measuring cups. 219.
measuring devices. 589.
measuring spoons. 219.
measuring tube. 56.
meat grinder. 218.
meat keeper. 229.
meat thermometer. 219.
mechanical connectors. 264.
mechanical pencil. 352.
mechanical stage. 605.
mechanical stage control. 605.
mechanical watch. 591.
mechanism of the organ. 468.
medial condyle of femur. 113.
medial great. 110.
medial moraine. 48.
median furrow. 85.
median lingual sulcus. 126.
median nerve. 121.
median vein of forearm. 117.
medical injection disk. 444.
Mediterranean Sea. 41.
Mediterranean subtropical. 51.
medium format SLR. 354.
medium tension distribution line. 645.
medulla. 120, 129.
medulla oblongata. 122.
Meissner's corpuscle. 128.
melanocyte. 128.
melody string. 473.
melting snow. 49.
meltwater. 48.
membrane tanks. 631.
memory button. 364.
men. 577.
men. 578.
men's apparatus. 559.
men's bag. 339.
men's clothing. 281, 282, 283, 284, 285, 286, 287, 288.
men's pompadour. 321.
mental foramen. 114.
Mercury. 28, 274.
mercury bath. 432.
Mercury capsule (USA). 39.
mercury switch. 597.
mercury-vapor lamp. 274.
meridian. 27.
méridienne. 201.
meringue. 146.
merlon. 167.
mesa. 47.
mesh. 529.
mesocarp. 66, 67, 68, 69.
mesosphere. 39.
mesothorax. 92.
metacarpal. 100.
metacarpus. 84, 86, 112.
metal. 272.
metal counterhoop. 472.
metal frame. 465.
metal head. 558.
metal heat reflector. 190.
metal plate. 318, 504.
metal rod. 471.
metal washer. 260.
metal water pipe. 278.
metallic contact grid. 656.
metallic plastron. 562.
metals. 696.
metamorphic rocks. 40.
metatarsus. 84, 97, 112.
metathorax. 92.

meteoralogical measuring instruments. 56.
meteorological ground. 55.
meteorological symbols of clouds. 44.
meteorology. 54, 55.
meteors. 52.
methane carrier. 631.
meteorological satellite. 57.
metope. 160.
metopic suture. 114.
metronome. 478.
mezzani. 136.
mezzanine. 169, 414.
Michigan snowshoe. 549.
micro-computer. 454, 455, 456, 457.
micrometer caliper. 599.
micrometer drum. 429.
micrometer screw. 600.
microphone. 363, 373, 457.
microphone, dynamic. 369.
microphone boom. 375.
microphone jack. 366.
microprocessor. 455.
microscope. 605.
microscope eyepiece. 600.
microwave oven. 227.
mid-calf length. 287.
mid range pick-up. 480.
middle clouds. 44.
middle covert. 88.
middle ear. 124.
middle jib. 417.
middle leg. 92, 98.
middle linebacker. 514, 515.
middle lobe. 118.
middle nasal concha. 125.
middle panel. 188.
middle phalanx. 86, 112, 113.
middle piece. 108.
middle primary covert. 88.
middle rail. 205.
middle sole. 308.
middle toe. 87.
middy. 295.
midiron. 572.
midmashie. 572.
midrange. 363.
midrib. 62.
midrid. 71.
midriff band. 303.
milieu de poitrine. 141.
milieu de sous-noix. 139.
milk bread. 138.
milk room. 151.
Milky Way. 32.
Milky Way projector. 35.
Mimolette. 145.
minaudiere. 339.
mine. 621, 622, 623, 624, 636.
mini shirtdress. 295.
mining. 622.
mining. 653.
minor inner reaping throw. 564.
mint. 133.
minute hand. 591, 593.
mirror. 330.
mirror. 322, 337, 353, 395.
miscellaneous auxiliary systems. 652.
missile. 424, 692.
missile air-to-air. 691.
missile director. 425.
missile launch rail. 691.
missile launcher. 425.
missile tracking radar. 692.
missile tube. 424.
missiles. 692.
mist. 52.
miter gate. 426.
miter gauge. 252.
miter gauge silot. 252.
mitochondrion. 105.
mitral valve. 116.
mitt. 273, 289.

mitten. 289, 307, 545, 575.
mixing bowl. 225.
mixing bowls. 220.
mixing chamber. 272.
mizzen sail. 417.
mizzenmast. 416.
moat. 166, 167.
mob-cap. 304.
mobile passenger escalator. 439.
mobile septum of nose. 125.
mocassin. 549.
moccasin. 309.
mock pocket. 291.
moderator. 650.
moderator heat exchanger. 650.
moderator inlet. 648.
moderator/miscellaneous systems. 652.
moderator outlet. 648.
moderator pump. 650.
modern bow. 677.
modern writing instruments. 352.
modesty. 298.
modillion. 160.
modulator. 610.
mogul base. 274.
Mohorovicic discontinuity. 39, 40.
moistener. 448.
molar. 82.
molar, cross section of a. 115.
moldboard. 153.
mollusk. 94.
money clip. 341.
money totalizer. 387.
monitor. 376.
monitor bank. 376.
monitor indicator. 364.
monitor pusher. 375.
monitor roof. 181.
monitor speaker. 376.
monkey wrench. 266.
mono-ski. 540.
monocle. 319.
mons pubis. 109.
monster. 515.
Monterey Jack. 144.
Moon. 30.
Moon. 28, 29, 30.
Moon, phases of the. 30.
moon dial. 593.
Moon's orbit. 30.
moose. 81.
mordent. 462.
morel. 65.
morning line. 555.
Morse code. 371.
mortar. 683.
mortar. 183, 218.
mortise. 335, 493.
mortise lock. 256.
mother. 130, 131.
mother-in-law. 131.
motor. 155, 196, 230, 231, 234, 250, 251, 253, 362, 485, 608, 661.
motor car. 415.
motor cell. 127.
motor-compressor unit. 196.
motor drive. 610.
motor end plate. 127.
motor generator. 171.
motor generator set. 171.
motor mower. 242.
motor neuron. 127.
motor pulley. 365.
motor unit. 225, 226.
motorcycle. 395, 396.
motro unit. 224.
moulded insulation. 185.
moulded plywood. 255.
mound. 511.
mount frame blinder. 362.
mountain. 46.
mountain range. 30, 40.
mountain slope. 46.
mountain torrent. 46.

mountaineer. 575.
mountaineering. 574, 575.
mountaineering, equipment. 574.
mountaineering boot. 575.
mounting. 563.
mounting post. 597.
mounting screw. 597.
mouse. 455.
mousse. 147.
mouth. 126.
mouth. 94, 96, 97, 106, 468.
mouthparts. 98.
mouthpiece. 565.
mouthpiece. 372, 469, 470, 536.
mouthpiece receiver. 470.
mouthpipe. 470.
movable bridges. 403.
movable condenser. 361.
movable jaw. 248, 249.
movable maxillary. 101.
move to left. 350.
move to right. 350.
moving coil. 369.
Mt Everest. 39.
mud flap. 388, 389.
mud pump. 626.
mud wall. 582.
muff. 339.
muffin pan. 220.
muffle. 506.
muffler. 243, 392.
mullet. 696.
multi-ply. 255.
multiple access station. 379.
multiple copy control. 453.
multiple-span beam bridge. 400.
multiplexing equipment. 379.
multiplication. 709.
multipurpose ladder. 268.
multipurpose tool. 277.
mummy. 584.
Munster. 145.
muntin. 188, 189.
murette. 431.
muscle arrector pili. 128, 129.
muscle fiber. 127.
muscle scar. 93.
muscle segment. 91.
muscles, anterior view. 110.
muscles, posterior view. 111.
musculocutaneous nerve. 121.
mushroom, structure of a. 65.
mushroom anchor. 433.
mushrooms. 65.
music. 459.
music rest. 478.
music stand. 478.
music stand. 465.
musical accessories. 478.
musical notation. 461, 462.
muskeg. 636.
muskmelon. 73.
mustard. 71.
mute. 470.
mutule. 160.
muzzle. 86, 680, 683, 688.
muzzle astragal. 680.
muzzle loading. 680, 681.
muzzle molding. 680.
muzzle ring. 679.
mycelium. 65.
myelin sheath. 127.

N

nacelle. 658.
nacreous cloud. 39.
nail. 129, 254.
nail. 95, 101.
nail bed. 129.
nail brush. 332.
nail buffer. 332.
nail cleaner. 333.
nail clippers. 333.
nail file. 332.

nail hole. 85.
nail matrix. 129.
nail nippers. 332.
nail scissors. 332.
nail shaper. 332.
nail whitener pencil. 333.
nails. 495.
name plate. 251, 601.
naos. 161.
nape. 87, 107.
naris. 97, 125.
narrow cuff. 296.
narthex. 164.
nasal bone. 114, 125.
nasal cavity. 118.
nasal fossa. 114.
nasal fossae. 125.
nasal vowels. 348.
nasopharynx. 125.
natural. 462.
natural arch. 43.
natural sponge. 323.
nave. 164.
navel. 106.
navette cut. 317.
navigating bridge. 420.
navigation devices. 428, 429.
navigation light. 434.
navigational radar. 425.
Neapolitan coffee maker. 224.
near side. 30.
neck. 83, 101, 106, 108, 115, 139, 140, 143, 215, 216, 377, 463, 464, 473, 480, 500, 572, 592.
neck guard. 676.
neck of femur. 113.
neck of uterus. 109.
neck ring. 444.
neckhole. 287.
necklaces. 316.
necklines. 299.
neckroll. 204.
necks. 299.
neckstrap lug. 353, 369.
necktie. 285.
nectarine. 67.
needle. 486.
needle. 49, 485, 487, 615.
needle bar. 486.
needle bed. 491.
needle bed. 491.
needle bed groove. 491.
needle clamp. 486.
needle clamp screw. 486.
needle hub. 615.
needle plate. 485.
needle threader. 487.
needle threader. 486.
needle tool. 505.
negative carrier. 361.
negative charge. 709.
negative contact. 656.
negative meniscus. 611.
negative plate. 392.
negative plate group. 392.
negative region. 656.
negative terminal. 392.
negligee. 301.
neon lamp. 276.
neon sign. 168.
neon tester. 276.
nephew. 130.
Neptune. 28.
nerve. 129.
nerve fiber. 127.
nerve termination. 127.
nerveux de gîte à la noix. 141.
nerveux de sous-noix. 139.
nervous system. 121, 122.
nest of tables. 199.
Net. 33, 519, 521, 522, 523, 525, 529.
net band. 523.
net judge. 523.
net stocking. 301.
network. 372.

network management center. 379.
neural spine. 91.
neuron. 127.
neutral conductor. 645.
neutral service wire. 278.
neutral wire. 278.
neutral zone. 515, 519.
new fuel loading area. 651.
new fuel port. 651.
new fuel storage room. 651.
new Moon. 30.
newel post. 187.
news dealer. 168.
nib. 352.
niblick. 572.
nictitating membrane. 86.
niece. 130.
nightgown. 301.
nightwear. 301.
nimbostratus. 44.
nipple. 106, 109, 265.
Nissl bodies. 127.
nitrogen. 274.
no. 8 forward. 517.
no dogs. 704.
no entry. 702.
no entry for bicycles. 702.
no entry for goods vehicles. 702.
no entry for mopeds. 702.
no entry for motorcycles. 702.
no entry for pedestrians. 702.
no entry for power-driven vehicules. 702.
no left turn. 702.
no U-turn. 702.
nock. 677.
nocking point. 677.
noctilucent cloud. 39.
node. 61, 644.
node of Ranvier. 127.
noise generator control. 481.
noix. 139.
noix de hachage. 142.
noix pâtissière. 139.
non-skid spaghetti. 136.
noodles. 136.
normal mode acquisition. 379.
normal mode satellite. 379.
normal tail unit. 435.
North. 579.
North America. 41.
North celestial pole. 27.
North pole. 27.
North Sea. 41.
North wind. 579.
Northern Crown. 32.
northern hemisphere. 27.
Norwegian writing system. 345.
nose. 83, 106, 434, 542, 543, 676.
nose, external. 125.
nose cone. 436.
nose landing gear. 434.
nose leaf. 100.
nose leather. 86.
nose of the quarter. 308.
nose pad. 318.
noseband. 553.
nosepad. 318.
nosing. 187.
nostril. 83, 87, 90, 101.
notch. 283, 489, 568.
notched lapel. 281, 291, 298.
note symbols. 461.
notepad. 341.
nozzle. 195, 270, 442, 662, 663, 692.
nuchal shield. 101.
nuclear energy. 647, 648, 649, 650, 651, 652, 653.
nuclear envelope. 105.
nuclear fuel cycle. 653.
nuclear generating station. 647.
nuclear reactor. 649.
nuclear reactor. 653.
nuclear whorl. 93.
nucleolus. 105.

nucleus. 31, 105, 127.
number. 580.
number of tracks sign. 409.
number three. 530.
number two. 530.
numbering machine. 448.
numerals. 371.
numeric keyboard. 596.
numeric keypad. 456.
nut. 254, 408, 428, 463, 480, 677.
nut and bolt. 249.
nutcracker. 218.
nuts, major types of. 70.
nylon rumba thights. 305.

O

o-ring. 261.
oasis. 47.
object. 605.
object balls. 569.
objective. 355, 606.
objective. 605.
objective lens. 357, 606, 607, 609.
objective pole piece. 606.
oboe. 469, 476.
oboes. 479.
obscured sky. 53.
observation deck. 440.
observation light. 423.
observation window. 443.
observer's seat. 437.
obstacles. 551.
obturator nerve. 121.
occipital. 111, 113.
occipital bone. 114.
occipital condyle. 114.
occluded front. 53.
ocean. 30, 50.
ocean floor. 42.
Oceania. 41.
ocelli. 92.
Octant. 33.
octave. 462, 563.
octave mechanism. 469.
odd. 580, 581.
odd pinnate. 62.
odometer. 385.
off-on knob. 377.
offensive. 514, 515.
office equipment. 445.
office furniture. 451.
office supplies. 445.
offset. 265.
offshore drilling. 628.
offshore well. 630.
ogee. 162, 680.
ogee roof. 181.
oil. 626, 627, 628, 629, 630, 631, 632, 633, 634, 635, 636.
oil. 626.
oil and gas foam. 627.
oil burner. 195.
oil drain hole. 391.
oil filter. 391.
oil/gas separator. 629.
oil indicator. 385.
oil-level stick. 391.
oil pan. 243, 391.
oil pressure warning light. 396.
oil pump. 195.
oil reservoir. 625.
oil sand. 636.
oil sands mining plant. 636.
oil sands recovery process, steam drive. 636.
oil supply line. 195.
oil tank cap. 396.
oil trap. 626.
oiler. 625.
oilstone. 501.
okra. 73.
old-fashioned. 212.
olecranon. 113.
olfactory bulb. 91, 125.

olfactory membrane. 125.
olfactory nerve. 91, 125.
olive. 67.
on-deck circle. 511.
on guard line. 562.
on light. 331.
on-off switch. 211, 327, 329, 330, 331, 369, 428.
on/off witch. 368.
on/play button. 373.
on the wind. 539.
one-arm shoulder throw. 564.
one-band sword. 678.
one-bar shoe. 309.
one-burner camp stove. 585.
one pair. 578.
one-piece coverall. 541.
one way head. 254.
one-way traffic. 703.
onglet. 139, 141.
open-air terrace. 419.
open compartment. 339.
open end wrench. 248.
open-face spinning reel. 566.
open-pit mine. 621.
open-pit mine. 622.
open string. 473.
open stringer. 187.
opening. 289.
opera glasses. 319.
opera length necklace. 316.
operating dam. 646.
operating floor. 646.
operating rod. 687.
operation cord. 208.
operator. 458.
operator desk. 652.
operator's cab. 661, 669.
operator's seat. 670.
operculum. 90, 97.
opisthodomos. 161.
opposite prompt side. 169.
optic chiasm. 122.
optic nerve. 123.
optical axis. 35.
optical instruments. 603.
optical plummet. 600.
optical sight. 600.
or. 696.
oral cavity. 118, 119.
oral hygiene center. 329.
orange. 69.
orange. 69.
orbicular of eye. 110.
orbiculate. 62.
orbital cavity. 114.
orbiter. 443.
orchard. 151.
orchestra pit. 170.
orchestra seat. 169.
order. 165.
order of finish. 555.
ordinaries. 696.
ordinary die. 579.
ore. 621, 622.
ore deposit. 622.
ore pass. 623.
oregano. 133.
organ. 467, 468.
organ pipes. 468.
Oriental couching stitch. 493.
oriflamme. 679.
Orion. 32, 33.
ornamental stitching. 339.
ornaments. 462.
ortho-cane. 616.
oscillating sprinkler. 240.
oscillators. 481.
ostium. 129.
other dangers. 701.
otolith. 91.
otter paw. 549.
ottoman. 202.
out of bounds. 571.
outbound. 411.
outcrop. 622.

outdoor condensing unit. 194.
outdoor sill cock. 257.
outer boundary line. 526.
outer core. 39.
outer edge. 85.
outer hearth. 190.
outer jib. 417.
outer lip. 93.
outer rail. 172.
outer root sheath. 129.
outer shell. 275.
outer table. 578.
outer toe. 87.
outfield. 511.
outgoing announcement cassette. 373.
outhaul. 537.
outlet. 275.
outlet grille. 193.
output controls. 481.
output devices. 454.
output filter. 481.
output jack. 480.
output lead. 365.
output monitor. 376.
outrigger. 662, 667.
outside counter. 308.
outside knob. 256.
outside left. 518.
outside line. 563.
outside linebacker. 514.
outside mirror. 383.
outside right. 518.
outside ticket pocket. 283.
outsole. 308.
oval cut. 317.
oval head. 254.
ovary. 64, 91, 109.
ovate. 62.
oven. 228.
oven lamp. 227, 228.
over-blouse. 295.
over-elbow length glove. 289.
overall. 306.
overalls. 300.
overcast sky. 53.
overcheck. 554.
overcoat. 282, 290.
overdrapery. 207.
overflow. 259.
overflow bend. 257.
overflow pipe. 263.
overflow protection switch. 232.
overflow tube. 258.
overhand knot. 587.
overhead clearance. 702.
overhead connection. 645.
overhead crane. 647.
overhead frame. 666.
overhead ground wire. 644.
overhead guard. 670.
overhead switch panel. 437.
overlap carrier. 208.
overlay flooring. 186.
overpass. 400.
overshoe. 310.
ovule. 64.
owner. 555.
oxer. 551, 552.
oxer wall. 552.
oxidizer tank. 692.
oxyacetylene welding. 271.
oxygen cylinder. 271.
oxygen supply pressure gauge. 444.
oxygen valve. 272.
oyster. 94.
oyster fork. 215.
oyster knife. 217.
oyster mushroom. 65.
ozone. 39.

P

["p[' trap. 257.

P-N junction. 656.
Pacific Ocean. 41.
Pacinian corpuscle. 128.
pack. 541.
packet, cellophane wrapped. 334.
packet of cigarette papers. 334.
packing. 261.
packing nut. 261.
packing retainer ring. 261.
pad. 318.
pad arm. 318.
paddle valve. 426.
paddock. 555.
padlock. 337.
page boy. 320.
pagoda sleeve. 296.
paint roller. 270.
painting upkeep. 268, 269, 270.
pajama. 301.
palate. 125.
palatine tonsil. 126.
palatoglossal arch. 126.
palatopharyngeal arch. 126.
palazzo pants. 300.
pale. 696.
paleron. 141.
palette. 142.
paling fence. 237.
pallet. 468, 475, 591, 593.
pallet and container transporter. 439.
pallet spring. 468.
pallets. 671.
pallial line. 93.
pallial sinus. 93.
palm. 81, 289, 433, 512.
palm grove. 47.
palmar pad. 86.
palmate. 62.
palmette. 200.
pan. 196, 594, 595, 682.
pan arrest. 595.
pan cover. 682.
pan handle. 359.
pancake. 147.
pancake pan. 223.
pancreas. 119.
pane. 189.
panel. 188, 207, 284, 303, 541, 553, 623, 644.
panoramic and tilting head. 359.
panoramic window. 407.
panpipe. 474.
pantry. 179.
pants. 284, 300.
pants. 305, 311, 512, 516, 520, 575.
panty girdle. 303.
panty hose. 301.
papaya. 72.
paper. 334, 504.
paper bail. 453.
paper centering scale. 453.
paper clips. 447.
paper easel. 360.
paper fasteners. 447.
paper guide. 453.
paper guide roller. 457.
paper punch. 448.
paper release lever. 453.
paper safe. 360.
paper tape. 370, 371.
paper tape start button. 371.
papilla. 123, 129.
papillary muscle. 116.
parabolic antenna. 379.
parabolic dune. 47.
parabolic mirror. 654.
parabolic reflector. 358, 610.
paraboloidal reflector. 656.
parachute. 541.
parachute. 543.
parachuting. 541.
parachutist. 541.
parade ground. 166.
paraffins. 635.

parallel bars. 559.
parapet walk. 167.
parcels office. 412.
parchment membrane. 473.
parentheses. 347, 350.
parents. 130, 131.
parents-in-law. 131.
parfait. 146.
parietal. 113.
parietal bone. 114.
parietal foramen. 114.
paring knife. 217.
parital pleura. 118.
parka. 282.
parka. 547.
parking area. 438.
parking brake lever. 385.
parking meter. 168.
parking signs. 703.
parsley. 133.
parsnip. 76.
parterre. 169.
partial eclipse. 29, 30.
particle board. 255.
particle board. 184.
partition. 70, 451.
partitions. 696.
partlow chart. 388.
party. 696.
pass. 46.
passageway. 407.
passenger cabin. 421.
passenger cars, types of. 407.
passenger liner. 419.
passenger platform. 413.
passenger seating. 422.
passenger station. 410.
passenger terminal. 440.
passenger terminal. 438.
passenger transfer vehicle. 439, 440.
passengers-conductor communications. 415.
passing prohibited. 702.
passport case. 341.
passport control. 440.
pasta. 136, 137.
pasta maker. 218.
pastern. 83.
pastry bag and nozzles. 220.
pastry brush. 220.
pastry cutting wheel. 220.
pasture. 151.
patch. 682.
patch pocket. 290, 294, 306.
patella. 84, 112.
patera. 200.
paternal aunt. 130.
paternal uncle. 130.
path. 237.
patio. 178.
patio door. 178.
pattern. 489.
pattern. 492, 507.
pattern reader. 491.
pattern scissors. 507.
pauldron. 676.
pause. 462.
pause button. 366.
pause/still. 367.
pavement. 399.
pavilion. 317.
pavilion facet. 317.
pavilion roof. 180.
pawl. 209, 250.
pawn. 577.
Pawn (P). 577.
payload. 442.
payout tray. 581.
payout trigger. 581.
pea. 71.
pea. 71.
pea jacket. 291.
peach. 67.
peach. 67.
Peacock. 33.

peak. 46, 288.
peaked lapel. 282, 283.
peanut. 70.
pear. 68.
pear-shaped cut. 317.
pearl. 81.
pearl screen. 362.
pecan nut. 70.
pecten. 98.
pectoral fin. 90.
pectoral limb. 116.
pedal. 397, 398, 464, 472.
pedal key. 467.
pedal keyboard. 467.
pedal pusher. 300.
pedal rod. 465.
pedestal. 387, 464.
pedestrian crossing. 168, 700, 704.
pedicel. 64, 66, 68.
pedicle. 81.
pediment. 161.
pedometer. 599.
peeled veneer. 255.
peeler. 217.
peep hole. 409.
peephole. 506.
peg. 205, 463, 464, 493, 496.
peg box. 463.
Pegasus. 32.
pelerine. 290.
pellets. 688.
peltate. 62.
Pelton turbine. 643.
pelvic fin. 90.
pelvic girdle. 97.
pelvic limb. 116.
pelvis. 84, 120.
pen. 370, 602.
pen holder. 341.
penalty arc. 518.
penalty area. 518.
penalty bench. 519.
penalty line. 525.
penalty spot. 518.
penalty timekeeper. 519.
pencil. 649.
pencil point tip. 271.
pencil sharpeners. 448.
pendant. 210.
pendulum. 593.
pendulum rod. 593.
penholder grip. 529.
penis. 106, 108.
penknife. 585.
pennant. 53, 697.
pennine. 137.
pens. 137.
penstock. 637, 641, 646.
pentaprism. 353.
penumbra. 30.
penumbra shadow. 29.
pepper shaker. 213.
per bend. 696.
per fess. 696.
percent. 709.
perching bird. 89.
percolator. 224.
percussion instruments. 471, 472.
perforated gypsum lath. 184.
perforated hardboard. 184.
perforated pipe. 267.
perforated toe cap. 308.
perforation. 289, 356.
perforator. 371.
performance. 555.
pergola. 237.
pericardium. 118.
pericarp. 69, 70.
period. 347, 350.
periodontal ligament. 115.
periople. 85.
peripheral equipment. 457.
peripheral joint. 639.
peripheral nervous system. 121.
periscope. 424, 690.
peristyle. 161, 163.

peritoneum. 108.
permanent magnet. 372.
peroxide. 615.
perron. 177.
Perseus. 32.
personal adornment. 313.
personal articles. 325.
pestle. 218.
petals. 64.
Peter Pan collar. 298.
petiole. 62.
Petit-Suisse. 145.
petits fours. 146.
petrochemical industry. 635.
petrochemicals. 635.
phalange. 84.
phalanxes. 97.
pharynx. 118, 119.
phase conductor. 645.
phase-sensing coil. 592.
Phillips tip. 248.
philtrum. 125.
phloem. 63.
Phobos. 28.
Phoenix. 33.
phosphor coating. 274.
phosphor dot. 377.
photo chamber. 606.
photoelectric cell. 356.
photographic accessories. 359.
photographic picture. 362.
photographic plate. 606.
photography. 353, 354, 355, 356,
357, 358, 359, 360, 361, 362.
photosphere. 29.
phrenic nerve. 118.
piano. 465, 476, 477, 479.
piccolo. 469, 479.
pick. 335, 574.
pick-up. 152.
pick-up selector. 480.
pickguard. 480.
pickling onion. 75.
pickup automatic baler. 152.
pickup loader. 152.
pickup reel. 155.
picnic area. 707.
picnic shoulder. 142.
picnics prohibited. 707.
picture tube. 377.
pie. 146.
pie pan. 220.
pieces. 577.
pied. 142.
piedmont glacier. 48.
pier. 162, 400, 401, 628.
pier foundation. 400.
pierce lever. 233.
pierced earring. 315.
piers. 165.
piggyback car. 406.
pigsty. 151.
pigtail. 311.
pigtails. 320.
pike. 695.
pike pole. 663.
pike position. 534.
pile. 629.
pillar. 165, 464, 602, 623.
pillar plate. 592.
pillbox hat. 304.
pillow. 492.
pillow. 204.
pillow protector. 204.
pillowcase. 204.
pilot. 466, 542, 543.
pilot light. 331.
pilot parachute. 541.
pilothouse. 422.
pin. 199, 256, 274, 475, 487, 576.
pin base. 274.
pin block. 465.
pin cushion. 487.
pinafore. 292.
pince-nez. 319.
pinch. 274, 622.

pinch pleat. 207.
pine seed. 70.
pineal body. 122.
pineapple. 72.
pinion. 250, 593.
pink ball. 570.
pink stocking. 311.
pinking shears. 487.
pinnacle. 164, 165, 409.
pinnatifid. 62.
pinocytotic vesicle. 105.
pinwheel passenger loading ramp.
438.
pip. 68, 69, 579.
pipe. 335.
pipe. 264, 468, 475.
pipe cleaner. 335.
pipe coupling. 265.
pipe cross section. 335.
pipe rack. 335.
pipe section. 192.
pipe threader. 266.
pipe tools. 335.
pipe-wrapping insulation. 185.
pipe wrench. 266.
pipeline. 630, 636.
pipeline support, aboveground.
630.
pipework. 467.
Pisces, the Fishes. 698.
pistachio nut. 70.
piste. 562.
pistil. 64.
pistol. 689.
pistol grip. 683, 685, 687.
pistol grip handle. 251, 252.
pistol nozzle. 240.
piston. 391, 393, 625.
pit. 576.
pita bread. 138.
pitch axis. 378.
pitch link. 441.
pitch nozzle. 57.
pitched-roof. 180.
pitcher. 511.
pitcher's plate. 511.
pitchfork comb. 328.
pitching. 638.
pitching niblick. 572.
pitching wedge. 572.
pith. 63.
pithead. 624.
piton-carrier. 575.
piton hammer. 574.
pitons. 574.
Pitot tube. 691.
pituitary gland. 122.
pivot. 277, 327, 328, 429, 478,
487, 548, 611, 683.
pivot cab. 667.
pivot point. 466.
pivoted bar. 602.
placard board. 405.
placing judge. 532.
placket. 298.
plain gypsum lath. 184.
plain pole. 208.
plain ring. 315.
plain weave. 497.
plan. 164.
plan-position indicator. 610.
plan symbols for doors. 188.
plane. 247.
planet projection system. 35.
planetarium. 35.
planetarium projector. 35.
planetarium projector. 35.
planets of the solar system. 28.
plank and pole. 552.
planoconcave. 611.
planoconvex. 611.
planographic printing, diagram of.
504.
plant, structure of a. 61, 62.
plant cell. 105.
plantar. 111.

plantar interosseous. 110.
plantar pad. 86.
planting box. 556.
plantlet. 67.
plasmodesma. 105.
plaster. 184.
plaster bat. 505.
plasterboard. 184.
plastic insulator. 278.
plastic-laminated hardboard. 184.
plastic pants. 305.
plasticine board. 556.
plastron. 101.
plat de côte couvert. 141.
plat de côte découvert. 141.
plate. 140, 227, 585.
plate crystal. 49.
plate grid. 392.
plate level. 600.
plate strap. 392.
plateau. 46.
platen. 453, 500.
platen knob. 453, 457.
platform. 388.
platform. 269, 403, 534, 561, 596,
669.
platform diver. 534.
platform edge. 413, 414.
platform entrance. 412.
platform ladder. 269.
platform number. 413.
platform roofing. 413.
platform shelter. 410.
platform truck. 413, 671.
platter. 213, 365.
play. 367.
play button. 366.
player. 512.
player. 531.
player's number. 516.
player's stick. 520.
players' bench. 511, 519, 521,
522.
players' rotation. 522.
playing area, water polo. 531.
playing field, soccer. 518.
playing field for American football.
513.
playing field for Canadian football.
513.
playing surface. 529.
playroom. 179, 419.
pleat skirts. 294.
pleated heading. 207.
plectrum. 473.
plenum. 192.
pleural cavity. 118.
pliers. 249.
plinth. 593.
plotter. 455.
plow anchor. 433.
plug. 275.
plug. 251, 369.
plug adapter. 331.
plug bayonet. 679.
plug fuse. 275.
plum. 67.
plumbing. 257, 258, 259, 260, 261,
262, 263, 264, 265, 266, 267.
plumbing system. 257.
plumbing tools. 266.
plunger. 224.
plunger. 266, 372, 615, 627.
plunging neckline. 299.
plus or minus. 709.
Pluto. 28.
ply. 393.
plywood. 184.
pneumatic armlet. 598.
pneumatic hammer. 625.
pneumostome. 96.
pocket. 338, 341, 569, 573, 576.
pocket handkerchief. 283.
pocket instamatic camera. 354.
pocket sliding door. 178.
pockets. 294.

pogo stick. 389.
point. 215, 217, 352, 464, 486,
490, 548, 567, 578.
point of sailing. 539.
point wire. 409.
pointed hat. 312.
pointed tab end. 285, 296.
pointer. 595, 597, 598, 599.
points motor. 409.
poison. 704.
poison injection nozzle. 648.
poison tank. 647.
poisonous mushroom. 65.
poitrine. 139, 142, 143.
poker. 191.
poker die. 579.
poker hands, standard. 578.
polar axis. 34.
polar axis circle. 608.
polar climates. 51.
polar ice cap. 51.
polar tundra. 51.
polarizing filter. 355.
Polaroid Land camera. 356.
pole. 208, 416, 544, 555, 556, 582.
pole beacon. 430.
pole grip. 547.
pole loop. 582.
pole over a bank. 552.
pole piece. 372.
pole shaft. 547.
Pole Star. 32.
pole tip. 547.
pole vault. 556.
poleyn. 676.
police. 704.
Polish writing system. 345.
polished-stone hand axe. 675.
pollen basket. 98.
pollen brush. 98.
pollen cell. 99.
pollen packer. 98.
polo collar. 298.
polo shirt. 295.
polojama. 307.
polymerization unit. 634.
poma lift. 544.
pome fleshy fruits. 68.
pome fruit, section of a. 68.
pome fruits, principal types of. 68.
pomegranate. 72.
pommel. 553, 559, 563, 679.
pommel horse. 559.
pompom. 304.
poncho. 291.
poniard. 678.
pons Varolii. 122.
Pont-l'évêque. 145.
pontoon. 403.
pony tail. 320.
poodle cut. 321.
pool. 569.
pool. 237, 655.
poop. 416.
pop-up tent. 583.
poppy. 71.
porch. 164, 177.
pore. 71, 105, 128.
pork, North American cut. 142.
pork, Parisian cut. 142.
Porro prism. 607.
port. 212.
port custom house. 427.
port sail plane. 424.
Port-Salut. 145.
port tack. 539.
portable fire extinguisher. 662.
portable life support system. 444.
portable life support system
control unit. 444.
portal. 165, 623.
portal bridge. 401.
portal frame. 401.
portal vein. 116, 117.
porterhouse. 140.
portfolio. 449.

portfolios. 340.
Portuguese writing system. 345.
position. 555.
position light. 691.
position marker. 480.
position of the ligament. 93.
positions. 563.
positive charge. 709.
positive contact. 656.
positive meniscus. 611.
positive plate. 392.
positive plate grou"p. 392.
positive region. 656.
positive terminal. 392.
post. 168, 494, 506, 522, 528, 531, 657.
post and plank. 551.
post and rail. 551.
post binder. 449.
post-hole digger. 238.
post lantern. 211.
post mill. 657.
post office. 706.
posterior chamber. 123.
posterior commissure. 122.
posterior cutaneous nerve of thigh. 121.
posterior end. 93.
posterior root. 122.
posterior ruga. 107.
posterior semicircular canal. 124.
postern. 167.
postscript. 349.
potable water tank. 629.
potable water truck. 439.
potato. 76.
potato masher. 219.
potato planter. 154.
potential coil. 601.
pothole lid. 191.
pottery. 505, 506.
pottery, tools. 505.
pouch. 339.
pouch of Douglas. 109.
poulaine. 676.
poultry house. 151.
poultry shears. 221.
pound. 709.
powder chamber. 681.
powder flask. 682.
powder puff. 322.
power cord. 327.
power generators. 431.
power indicator. 481.
power lift truck. 670.
power plant. 634.
power plant, cross section of. 646.
power plant instruments. 437.
power relay. 195.
power station. 624, 646.
power supply cord. 210, 211, 330.
power switch. 364, 366, 367, 481.
power system. 658.
power take off. 152.
power/timer off switch. 367.
power train. 398.
power zoom control. 369.
powerhouse. 637, 641.
practice fairway. 571.
pre-tuning control. 367.
preamplifier-amplifier. 363.
precipice. 46.
precipitation. 50.
precipitation, kinds of. 49.
precipitation area. 54.
premaxilla. 90.
premolar. 82.
prepuce. 108.
prescription. 709.
present state of weather. 54.
preset tuning button. 364.
president. 562.
press. 524.
press bed. 502, 503.
press-button. 338, 341.
press camera. 354.

pressed powder compact. 322.
presser bar. 486.
presser foot. 486.
presser foot lifter. 485.
pressing. 500.
pressing board. 500.
pressure. 55.
pressure, measure of. 598.
pressure bar. 465.
pressure change. 54.
pressure cooker. 222.
pressure gauge. 444, 598, 627.
pressure regulator. 272.
pressure regulator. 222, 271, 585.
pressure relief pipe. 648.
pressure relief valve. 263, 444.
pressure screw. 502, 503.
pressure suit. 444.
pressure tube. 649.
pressurizer. 647, 650.
preview monitor. 376.
price per litre/gallon. 387.
pricker. 492.
primaries. 88.
primary covert. 88.
primary heat transport system. 652.
primary mirror. 34.
primary pump. 650.
primary root. 61.
prime. 563.
prime focus. 34.
prime focus observing capsule. 34.
primer. 682, 688.
princess dress. 292.
princess seaming. 302.
principal rafter. 180.
print drying rack. 360.
print head. 457.
print washer. 360.
printed circuit. 356.
printer. 455, 458.
printing. 504.
priority intersection. 701.
["priority road[' sign. 701.
prism binocular. 607.
prismatic section. 432.
probe receptacle. 227.
proboscis. 92.
processing rollers. 356.
producer. 376.
product codes. 596.
production control room. 376.
production control room. 374.
production of electricity. 640.
production of electricity. 654.
production of sound. 467.
production platform. 629.
products for make-up. 323.
profiterole. 146.
programmable timer. 367.
programmer. 228, 230, 231, 232.
progressive wave. 43.
prohibitory signs. 702.
projectiles. 681.
projection gallery. 35.
projection lamp. 362.
projection room. 35.
projection screen. 362.
projector. 362.
projector lens. 606.
projector lens pole piece. 606.
projector zoom lens. 368.
proleg. 92.
prominence. 29.
prompt box. 170.
prompt side. 169.
pronaos. 161.
prong. 215.
proofreading. 350, 351.
prop forward. 517.
propane accessories. 585.
propane cylinder. 585.
propellant. 688.
propeller. 419, 422, 423, 424.

propeller gearbox. 421.
propeller shaft. 419, 422.
property line. 178.
propman. 375.
proscenium. 170.
prostate. 108.
protective clothing. 273.
protective cup. 516, 520.
protective equipment, football. 516.
protective relay. 195.
protective sheet. 255.
protective window. 377.
prothorax. 92.
protoneuron. 127.
proximal phalanx. 86, 112, 113.
proximal sesamoid. 84.
pruning hook. 239.
pruning knife. 242.
pruning saw. 242.
pruning shears. 239.
psychrometer. 55.
pubis. 106.
public water main. 257.
puck. 520.
puff. 147.
puff pastry. 147.
puff sleeve. 296.
pull bail. 362.
pull rod. 408.
pull strap. 337.
pulley. 251, 268, 391, 596.
pulley safety guard. 251.
pullman case. 337.
pullover. 297.
pullover sweater. 547.
pullovers. 286, 297.
pulmonary artery. 117, 118.
pulmonary trunk. 116.
pulmonary vein. 116, 117.
pulp. 69, 115.
pulp canal. 115.
pulp chamber. 115.
pulse button. 225.
pulse of sound. 428.
pulvino. 639.
pumice correcting pencil. 503.
pump. 230, 232, 309, 623, 627, 654.
pump attendant. 387.
pump island. 387.
pump motor. 267.
pump nozzle. 387.
pump suction head. 267.
pumper. 663.
pumpernickel bread. 138.
pumping station. 630.
pumping unit. 627.
pumpkin. 73.
punch card. 458.
punch card. 491.
punch card feeding dial. 491.
punch card feeding mechanism. 491.
punch card reader. 491.
punch hole. 284, 308.
punched paper tape reader. 371.
punctuation. 371.
punctuation marks. 347.
pup tent. 583.
pupa. 92.
pupil. 86, 123.
purfling. 463.
purge valve. 536.
purlin. 180.
purlin cleat. 180.
purpure. 696.
push arm. 664.
push block. 668.
push-button. 256, 336, 352, 362, 457.
push-button control board. 232.
push-button release. 327.
push-button telephone. 373.
push buttons. 373.
push rim. 617.
push up bra. 303.

pusher. 226.
putter. 572.
putter. 572.
putting green. 571.
pygal shield. 101.
pylon. 421, 544.
pyloric caecum. 91.
pylorus. 119.
pyramid spot. 570.
pyrolysis. 636.
pyrometer. 506.
pyrometric cone. 506.

Q

quad cane. 616.
quadriplex. 173.
quadripod. 616.
quarte. 563.
quarter. 85, 308.
quarter note. 461.
quarter rest. 461.
quarter window. 383.
quarterback. 514, 515.
quarters. 631.
quartet. 476.
quasi. 139.
quaterly. 696.
quay ramp. 427.
quayside crane. 427.
quayside railway. 427.
queen. 98.
Queen. 578.
Queen (Q). 577.
queen cell. 99.
queen excluder. 99.
Queen's side. 577.
question mark. 347.
quiche plate. 220.
quill. 250, 251, 352.
quill brush. 328.
quill lock. 251.
quillon. 679.
quince. 68.
quinte. 563.
quintet. 476.
quizzing glass. 319.
quotation marks. 347, 350.

R

raceme. 64.
racer glove. 289.
rachis. 88.
racing car. 384.
racing programm. 555.
rack. 568.
rack. 222, 228, 232, 432.
rackboard. 468.
racket. 529.
racks. 223.
racquetball. 527.
racquetball racquet. 527.
racquetballer. 527.
radar. 610.
radar antenna. 424.
radar scanner. 421.
radial artery. 117.
radial nerve. 121.
radial tire. 393.
radial vein. 117.
radiating element. 610.
radiation. 655.
radiation zone. 29.
radiator. 392.
radiator. 404.
radiator hose. 392.
radiator pressure cap. 392.
radicle. 61, 63.
radio antenna. 424, 444.
radioactive waste storage. 653.
radish. 76.
radius. 84, 100, 112.
radome. 691.
rafter. 180, 182.

raglan. 290.
raglan sleeve. 281, 290, 296, 306.
rail. 177, 408, 491, 536, 569, 570.
rail anchor. 408.
rail joint. 408.
rail track. 624.
rail transportation. 707.
railroad station. 410.
railroad track. 408, 409.
railway map. 412.
rain. 49.
rain cap. 192.
rain gauge. 55.
rain shower. 52.
raincoat. 281.
rainfall. 55.
rainfly. 583.
raise. 622.
raised band. 498.
rake. 238.
rake comb. 328.
Ram. 32.
Ram: Random Access Memory. 454.
ramekin. 213.
rammer. 681.
ramp. 161, 410, 621.
rampart. 166, 167.
ramrod. 682.
rangefinder. 354.
rank. 577.
rapier. 678.
raspberry, section of a. 66.
ratchet. 209, 248, 250, 494.
ratchet knob. 599.
ratchet wheel. 494, 591, 593.
ravioli. 137.
razor clam. 94.
razors. 327.
reaction control thruster. 378.
reaction direction. 709.
reactivity control device. 648.
reactor. 648.
reactor. 424, 647, 650, 651.
reactor building. 647, 649, 651.
reactor deck. 424.
reactor regulating system. 652.
reactor vessel. 649.
reading. 318.
reamer. 226.
rear apron. 285.
rear brake. 397.
rear bumper. 394.
rear derailleur. 397.
rear foil. 422.
rear foil control actuator. 422.
rear footpeg. 395.
rear leg. 203.
rear light. 397.
rear limit line. 562.
rear runner. 550.
rear seat. 386.
rear shock absorber. 395.
rear sight. 683, 685, 686, 687, 688, 689.
rear window. 383.
rear window frame. 383.
rearview mirror. 385, 690.
Reblochon. 144.
récamier. 201.
receiver. 370, 372.
receiver. 523, 526, 528, 529, 610, 683, 685, 687.
receiver-indicator. 428.
receiving line. 527.
receiving station. 370.
receiving yard. 411.
receptacle. 64, 66.
receptacle analyzer. 276.
reception bay. 651.
receptor. 127.
recessed cooktop. 228.
reciprocating knife mower. 152.
reclaimed water. 636.
recoil sleigh. 684.
recoil spring. 689.

recoilless rifle. 686.
record. 365.
record. 367.
record announcement button. 373.
record button. 366.
record muting button. 366.
recorder. 532.
recording level button. 366.
recording of seismic waves. 602.
recording of time. 602.
recording reproducing head. 368.
recording switch. 368.
rectangular. 584, 697.
rectum. 108, 119, 120.
recuperator cylinder. 684.
recuperator cylinder front head. 684.
red. 580, 581.
red ball. 569, 570.
red balls. 570.
red beam. 377.
red cap. 531.
red dragon. 579.
red flag. 531, 564.
red inner circle. 530.
red marker light. 388.
red ocher pencil. 503.
red safelight filter. 361.
Red Sea. 41.
redan. 166.
redcap. 413.
redingote. 290.
redoubt. 166.
reduce space. 350.
reducing coupling. 265.
redundant bracing. 644.
reed. 494.
reed hooks. 496.
reed panicle. 352.
reed pipe. 468.
reeds. 469.
reef band. 417.
reef knot. 587.
reef point. 417.
reel. 154, 360, 562, 581.
reel plate. 581.
reel seat. 566.
referee. 514, 517, 518, 519, 521, 522, 529, 531, 532, 564, 565.
referee initials. 349.
referee's stand. 528.
reference initials. 349.
reference station. 379.
refill. 352.
refill tube. 258.
refinery. 634.
refinery. 630.
refinery products. 635.
refining. 653.
reflecting screen. 358.
reflecting surface. 654.
reflector. 608.
reflector. 211, 274, 359, 388, 394, 656.
refracting telescope. 609.
refractory brick. 506.
refractory fire pot. 195.
refrigerant tubing. 194.
refrigeration unit. 388.
refrigerator. 229.
refrigerator car. 406.
refrigerator compartment. 229.
register. 492.
registered trademark. 709.
regulating button. 466.
regulatory signs. 702.
rein. 554.
reindeer. 81.
reinforced concrete. 183.
relay. 196.
release bar. 389.
release button. 353.
release handle. 386.
release lever. 249.
release setting screw. 546.
release treadle. 494.
relief printing, equipment. 502.

relief printing process. 502.
remote control. 362.
remote-control arm. 443.
remote control socket. 368.
removable blade. 270.
removable lid. 267.
renal artery. 117, 120.
renal papilla. 120.
renal vein. 117, 120.
reniform. 62.
repair shop. 387.
repeat mark. 462.
reptile. 101.
rerebrace. 676.
rerunning. 634.
reserve gas tap. 396.
reserve mud tank. 629.
reserve parachute. 541.
reservoir. 224, 467, 637, 638, 641.
reset button. 367.
reset key. 456.
resin-coated paper dryer. 360.
resonator. 392, 468, 471.
respiratory system. 118.
rest symbols. 461.
restaurant. 705.
restricted area. 521.
restricting circle. 521.
resurgence. 46.
retainer. 625.
retainer nut. 261.
retaining ring. 384.
retaining spring. 625.
retaining strap. 337.
retarding magnet. 601.
reticle. 607.
reticle illumination. 600.
retina. 123.
retractable boarding ladder. 691.
retractable cord. 234.
retrenchment. 166.
retriever. 522.
return. 451.
return air. 195.
return duct. 194.
return elevator. 155.
return key. 456.
return main. 194.
return spring. 370, 393.
reverb unit. 481.
reverse dive. 535.
reversible reaction. 709.
revolution counter. 385.
revolver. 689.
revolving cylinder. 492.
revolving frame. 661.
revolving nosepiece. 605.
revolving sprinkler. 240.
rewind. 367.
rewind button. 373.
rewing button. 366.
rewing lever. 353.
rhinencephalon. 125.
rhomboid. 111.
rhubarb. 77.
rib. 77, 139, 140, 143, 336, 463, 668.
rib eye. 140.
rib joint pliers. 249.
rib pad. 516.
rib portion. 142.
rib stitch. 490.
ribbing. 286, 291, 305, 306, 307, 567.
ribbing plow. 153.
ribbon. 311, 452, 453.
ribbon cartridge. 452.
ribbon end indicator. 452.
ribbon guide. 452.
ribbon load lever. 452.
ribosome. 105.
ribs. 84, 112, 505.
rider. 550.
rider handle. 595.
rider scale. 595.
ridge. 42, 294, 580, 700.

ridge beam. 180.
ridge pole. 582.
riding. 551, 552, 553.
riding coat. 551.
riding glove. 551.
riding helmet. 551.
riding whip. 551.
rifle. 688.
rift. 42.
rigging. 416.
rigging wire. 543.
right angle finder. 355.
right ascension. 27.
right atrium. 116.
right back. 518, 522, 525.
right bend. 700.
right bronchus. 118.
right center. 517.
right cornerback. 514, 515.
right defense. 519.
right defensive end. 514, 515.
right defensive tackle. 514, 515.
right elevating arc. 684.
right elevating handwheel. 684.
right field. 511.
right fielder. 511.
right forward. 521, 522.
right guard. 514, 515, 521.
right half. 518.
right halfback. 514.
right-hand grip. 686.
right kidney. 120.
right lung. 116, 118.
right outside linebacker. 515.
right safety. 514.
right safety back. 515.
right service court. 523, 526.
right side. 294.
right tackle. 514, 515.
right trail. 684.
right ventricle. 116.
right wing. 517, 519.
right winger. 525.
rigid board insulation. 185.
rigid frame. 35.
rigs, types of. 418.
rim. 318, 393, 395, 397, 521, 558.
rim flange. 393.
rim soup bowl. 213.
rinceau. 200.
rind. 69.
ring. 565.
ring. 63, 65, 208, 336, 433, 470, 488, 559, 574, 594, 682.
ring binder. 449.
ring floor. 565.
ring modulator. 481.
ring nut. 264.
ring post. 565.
ring step. 565.
ringer coil. 372.
rings. 315, 559.
rings. 137.
ringside. 565.
rink. 519.
rink. 530.
rink corner. 519.
rinse dispenser. 232.
rip fence. 252, 253.
rip fence adjustment. 252.
rip fence guide. 252.
rip fence lock. 252.
ripcord. 541.
ripper. 666.
ripper. 664.
ripper cylinder. 664.
ripper tip. 664.
ripper tooth. 664.
rise. 187.
riser. 35, 187, 541.
River Eridanus. 33.
rivet. 217, 249, 318.
road, cross section of a. 399.
road side sidewall. 388.
road train, articulated. 389.
road works. 701.

roadway narrows. 700.
Roamn legionary. 675.
roast sensor probe. 228.
roasting pans. 222.
Robertson tip. 248.
Roberval's balance. 595.
rock basin. 48.
rock garden. 237.
rock sample pocket. 444.
rock step. 48.
rocket. 442.
rocket. 39.
rocking chair. 201, 203.
rocking tool. 501.
rocks. 639.
rocky desert. 47.
rod. 196, 208, 478, 495.
rodent's jaw. 82.
roe deer. 81.
roll. 298.
roll axis. 378.
roll bag. 337.
roll line. 298.
roll nozzle. 57.
roll of paper. 371.
roll-up blind. 209.
roller. 208, 209, 232, 241, 331, 432, 452.
roller board and arms. 468.
roller circle. 661.
roller cover. 270.
roller frame. 270.
roller guides. 171.
roller picks. 333.
roller shade. 209.
roller skate. 548.
rolling ladder. 269.
rolling pin. 220.
ROM: Read Only Memory. 454.
Rom memory. 454.
romaine lettuce. 74.
Roman house. 163.
Roman metal pen. 352.
romsteck. 141.
rond de gîte à la noix. 141.
rondel. 676.
Rondele. 144.
roof. 99, 383, 388, 411, 582, 621, 622.
roof flashing. 257.
roof structure. 180.
roof vent. 177, 265.
roofs, types of. 180, 181.
Rook (R). 577.
room. 582, 623.
room air conditioner. 196.
room thermostat. 597.
rooms of the house. 179.
root. 61.
root. 61, 75, 115, 126, 215.
root cap. 61.
root-hair zone. 63.
root hairs. 61.
root of hair. 129.
root of nail. 129.
root of nose. 125.
root rib. 435.
root vegetables. 76.
rope. 316, 565, 575, 587.
rope belt. 306.
rope ladder. 268.
Roquefort. 144.
rose. 240, 256.
rose cut. 317.
rose window. 165.
rosemary. 133.
rosette. 160.
rostrum. 95.
rotary file. 450.
rotary hoe. 153.
rotary joint. 610.
rotary table. 626.
rotating auger. 155.
rotating dome. 34.
rotating dome truck. 34.
rotating drum. 602.

rotating wheel. 580.
rotisserie. 228.
rotor. 256, 641, 642, 657, 658.
rotor blade. 436, 441.
rotor head. 441.
rotor hub. 441.
rotor shaft. 658.
rotunda roof. 181.
rouelle. 139.
rough. 571.
roulette. 501.
roulette table. 580, 581.
roulette wheel. 580.
Roumanian couching stitch. 493.
round. 140.
round brush. 328.
round end pin. 209.
round eye. 488.
round head. 254.
round ligament of uterus. 109.
round loaf. 138.
round pronator. 110.
router. 250.
routing cardboard. 405.
row. 328, 329.
row indicator. 491.
royal antler. 81.
royal flush. 578.
royal mast. 416.
rub rail. 388.
rubber. 310.
rubber base. 328.
rubber gasket. 260.
rubber mat. 365.
rubber stamp. 448.
rubber thread. 573.
rubber tip. 616.
rubber washer. 260.
rubbing alcohol. 615.
ruching. 305.
rucksack. 547, 575.
rudder. 419, 421, 434, 443, 538, 542.
rudder pedal. 437, 542.
ruffle. 207.
ruffled rumba pants. 305.
ruffled skirt. 293.
rug and floor nozzle. 234.
rugby. 517.
ruler. 499.
Rumanian writing system. 345.
rump. 87, 140.
run. 187, 560.
run in. 350.
runaway arrester hook. 691.
rung. 268, 574.
runner. 199, 550, 578, 642, 643.
runner blade. 643, 646.
running. 556.
running bowline. 587.
running rail. 415.
running surface. 547.
running track. 411.
runway. 415, 438, 556, 557.
runway center line markings. 438.
runway designation marking. 438.
runway end lights. 438.
runway side stripe markings. 438.
runway threshold markings. 438.
runway touchdown zone marking. 438.
rupture disc. 648.
Russian pumpernickel. 138.
Russian writing system. 345.
rutabaga. 76.

S

s-band antenna. 57.
S-scroll. 200.
saber. 563, 678.
saber and épée warning line. 562.
sable. 696.
sabreur. 563.
sacral plexus. 121.

sacral vertebrae. 84.
sacrum. 112.
saddle. 553.
saddle. 335, 362, 395, 397, 559.
saddle bag. 339.
saddlecloth. 554.
safari. 297.
safe and arm device. 378.
safelight. 360.
safety. 683, 685.
safety area. 564.
safety bar. 544.
safety binding. 546.
safety binding. 545.
safety cage. 556.
safety glasses. 319.
safety goggles. 319.
safety line. 414.
safety match. 335.
safety pad. 560.
safety pin. 615, 682.
safety pins. 487.
safety rail. 269.
safety scissors. 333.
safety strap. 546.
safety thermostat. 231.
safety thong. 527.
safety valve. 222, 650.
sage. 133.
saggar. 506.
sagittal suture. 114.
Sagittarius, the Archer. 698.
sail. 537, 543, 657.
sail cloth. 657.
sail panel. 538.
sailbar. 657.
sailboard. 537.
sailor collar. 298.
sails. 417.
sails, types of. 418.
Saint-Marcelin. 145.
Saint-Nectaire. 145.
Sainte-maure. 144.
salad bowl. 213.
salad fork. 215.
salad plate. 213.
salad shaker. 218.
salad spinner. 218.
salient angle. 166.
salient pole. 642.
saline lake. 47.
salivary glands. 119.
salon-style hair dryer. 330.
salsify. 76.
salt marsh. 43.
salt shaker. 213.
salt water. 626.
saltire. 203.
salutation. 349.
sample. 490.
sand. 592.
sand bar. 43.
sand island. 43.
sand-rock. 636.
sand shoe. 388.
sand wedge. 572.
sandal. 309, 675.
sandstorm. 52.
sandy desert. 47.
saphenous nerve. 121.
sapwood. 63.
sarong. 293.
sartorius. 110.
sash. 311.
sash-frame. 189.
satellite, trajectory of a. 379.
satellite launcher separation. 379.
satellites, examples of. 378.
satin weave. 497.
saucepan. 222.
saucer. 213.
sauté pan. 223.
savarin. 146.
savory. 133.
saw. 585.
sawing-in. 499.

sawtooth roof. 181.
saxhorn. 470.
saxophone. 469.
saxophone. 469, 477.
scale. 461.
scale. 65, 89, 90, 101, 429, 596, 611, 633.
scale leaf. 75.
scale of speeds. 478.
scallion. 75.
scallop. 94.
scalper. 554.
scampi. 95.
Scandinavian crak bread. 138.
scapula. 84, 112.
scapular. 88.
scarf. 545.
scarifier. 666.
scarp. 166, 167.
scattered sky. 53.
schapska. 288.
schedules. 412.
school zone. 700.
schooner. 418.
Schwenkel. 697.
sciatic nerve. 121.
scientific symbols. 709.
scissors. 487.
scissors. 585, 615.
scissors crossing. 410.
scissors cut. 317.
scissors-glasses. 319.
sclera. 123.
scoop. 335.
score sheet. 576.
scorer. 519, 521, 522, 562, 576.
scoring light. 562.
scoring table. 576.
Scorpio, the Scorpion. 698.
Scorpion. 33.
scottia. 160.
scraper. 270, 668.
scraper. 501, 503.
scraper bar. 504.
scraper bar holder. 503.
scraper engine. 668.
scrath pad. 450.
screen. 261, 327, 369, 377, 641.
screen case. 362.
screen front. 305.
screen print. 306.
screen window. 582.
screw. 254.
screw. 256, 464, 548.
screw earring. 315.
screw eye. 494.
screw locking nut. 566.
screwdriver. 248.
screwdriver. 585.
screwsleeve. 574.
scrimmage in American football. 514.
scrimmage in Canadian football. 515.
script assistant. 376.
scroll. 463.
scroll case. 641.
scrotum. 106, 108.
scrum. 517.
scrum half. 517.
scuba diver. 536.
scuffle hoe. 238.
Sculptor. 33.
scum. 267.
scythe. 242.
sea. 30, 646.
sea anchor. 433.
Sea Goat. 33.
sea level. 40, 42.
sea-level pressure. 54.
sea side. 646.
seal. 263, 656.
seal ring. 315.
sealed-beam mounting ring. 384.
sealed cell. 99.
sealing lug. 601.

sealing ring. 633.
seam. 289, 334.
seam allowance. 489.
seam line. 489.
seam pocket. 290, 294.
seaming. 290.
seamount. 42.
sear. 687.
season tiles. 579.
seasons of the year. 27.
seat. 169, 200, 203, 259, 394, 505, 542, 544, 550, 553.
seat belt. 386.
seat post. 397.
seat stay. 397.
seat tube. 397.
seat upholstery. 617.
seats. 202, 386.
sebaceous gland. 128, 129.
second. 462, 565.
second balcony. 169.
second base. 511.
second baseman. 511.
second condenser lens. 606.
second dorsal fin. 90.
second flight. 560.
second hand. 591.
second molar. 115.
second premolar. 115.
second reinforce. 680.
second reinforce ring. 680.
second space. 521.
second stage. 442.
second violins. 479.
secondaries. 88.
secondary inlet. 633.
secondary root. 61.
secondary sheave. 171.
seconde. 563.
secretarial chair. 451.
secretarial desk. 451.
secretary. 206, 525, 531.
secretary clutch. 341.
section. 288.
sector. 458.
sector flag. 556.
sector-shaped chart. 596.
security check. 440.
sediment chamber. 392.
sedimentary rocks. 40.
seed. 66, 67, 68, 69, 70, 71.
seed coat. 67, 71.
seed drill. 154.
seed vegetables. 77.
seeder. 239, 241.
seeds. 137.
segment. 69.
seismic wave. 45.
seismograph. 602.
self-adhesive labels. 448.
self-contained platform. 628.
self-indicating scale. 596.
self timer. 353.
selle. 143.
selvage. 488.
semaphore. 410.
semi-circle. 521.
semi-detached cottage. 173.
semi-detached triplex. 173.
semi-fish-eye lens. 355.
semi-membrane tanks. 631.
semi-mummy. 584.
semi-submersible. 628.
semi-trailer. 632.
semicircular arch. 162.
semicolon. 347, 350.
semimembranous. 111.
seminal vesicle. 108.
semitendinous. 111.
semitrailer. 388.
semitrailer. 389.
sending station. 370.
sense organs. 123, 124, 125, 126, 127.
sense receptor. 127.
sensor probe. 227.

sensory impulse. 127.
sensory neuron. 127.
sepal. 66.
sepals. 64.
separator. 392.
separator wire. 452.
separators. 491.
septal cartilage of nose. 125.
septic tank. 267.
septic tank compartment. 267.
septime. 563.
septum. 71.
septum lucidum. 122.
septum of scrotum. 108.
sequence control. 481.
serac. 48.
serrated cast-iron casing. 682.
server. 522, 523, 526, 528, 529.
service area. 522.
service box. 526, 527, 645.
service box line. 527.
service building. 651.
service judge. 528.
service line. 523, 526, 527.
service main. 399.
service module. 442.
service room. 431.
service station. 387.
service station. 707.
service zone. 527.
serving bowl. 213.
serving table. 199.
sesame seeded pita. 138.
set in boldface. 350.
set in capitals. 350.
set in italic. 350.
set in lightface. 350.
set in lowercase. 350.
set in roman. 350.
set-in-sleeve. 281, 285, 286, 296.
set in small capitals. 350.
setting. 315.
setting ring. 355.
settling basin. 624.
settling pond. 634, 636.
settling tank. 631.
setup. 576.
seventeenth century cannon. 680.
seventeeth century cannon. 681.
seventh. 462.
sew-through buttons. 488.
sewing. 485, 486, 487, 488, 489.
sewing. 499.
sewing frame. 499.
sewing machine. 485, 486.
sewing spool. 485.
sewing supplies. 487.
sewn-in floor. 582.
sextant. 429.
sextet. 477.
shackle. 539.
shade. 209, 210, 211.
shade cloth. 209.
shadow. 592.
shadow mask. 377.
shadow roll. 554.
shaft. 53, 160, 318, 365, 496, 505, 520, 524, 526, 554, 558, 568, 572, 574, 597, 641, 642, 643.
shaft collar. 623.
shaft holder. 554.
shag. 321.
shag-vac-rake. 234.
shake-hands grip. 529.
shallot. 75, 468.
shallow root. 63.
sham. 204.
shank. 139, 140, 142, 143, 248, 250, 254, 308, 328, 335, 336, 433, 486, 487, 490, 492, 567.
shank button. 488.
shank portion. 142, 143.
shank protector. 664.
share. 153.
sharp. 462.
sharpener. 221.

sharpening steel. 217.
shaving brush. 327.
shaving mug. 327.
shawl collar. 298.
shawm. 474.
sheath. 62, 83, 587, 649.
sheath dress. 292.
sheath knife. 586.
sheath of Schwann. 127.
sheath skirt. 293.
shed. 237.
shed rod. 495.
sheep shelter. 151.
sheepshank. 587.
sheepskin jacket. 282.
sheer curtain. 207.
sheet. 417, 498.
sheet bend. 587.
sheet lead. 539.
sheet of paper. 602.
shelf. 206, 229, 269, 506.
shelf channel. 229.
shell. 70, 89, 94, 96, 101, 233, 337, 472, 633, 686, 690.
shell, bivalve. 93.
shell, univalve. 93.
shell membrane. 89.
shells. 137.
sherbet. 147.
SHF antenna. 378.
SHF beacon antenne. 378.
shield. 695.
Shield. 33, 318, 383, 675.
shift key. 453, 456.
shift lock key. 453, 456.
shifter. 397, 398.
shin boot. 554.
shin guard. 512, 516.
shingle. 185.
ship's anchor. 433.
Ship's Keel. 33.
ship's launch. 425.
Ship's Sails. 33.
Ship's Stern. 33.
shirred heading. 207.
shirt. 285.
shirt. 311, 524.
shirt collar. 295, 298.
shirt sleeve. 295.
shirttail. 285, 295.
shirtwaist dress. 292.
shirtwaist sleeve. 296.
shock absorber. 394.
shoe. 362.
shoe, parts of a. 308.
shoe bracket. 357.
shoe horn. 310.
shoe rack. 310.
shoe tree. 310.
shoelace. 308.
shoes. 308, 309, 310.
shoes, principal types of. 309, 310.
shoeshine kit. 310.
shoot. 61, 63.
shooting star. 39.
shop. 163.
shop window. 168.
shopping bag. 338.
shore. 43.
short extensor of toes. 110.
short line. 526, 527.
short palmar. 110.
short peroneal. 111.
short radial extensor of wrist. 111.
short ribs. 140.
short service line. 528.
short-sleeved shirt. 561.
shorts. 300, 524.
shortstop. 511.
shorty. 289.
shot. 681.
shot put. 557.
shot splice. 587.
shotgun. 688.
shots. 558.

shoulder. 46, 83, 106, 139, 140, 142, 143, 254, 399, 524, 567.
shoulder bag. 339.
shoulder blade. 107.
shoulder bolt. 254.
shoulder butt. 142.
shoulder of mutton sail. 418.
shoulder pad. 516, 520, 686.
shoulder rest. 686.
shoulder-strap. 303, 336, 337, 339, 573.
shovel. 191, 238, 545, 547.
showcase. 206.
shower and tub fixture. 257.
shower head. 259.
shrimp. 95.
shrink. 297.
shroud. 416, 538.
shutdown system. 652.
shutoff switch. 267.
shutoff valve. 257, 258, 260, 262.
shutter. 189, 353, 606, 655.
shutter button. 356.
shutter release. 353.
shutter speed selector. 353.
shutters. 209.
shutting stile. 188.
shuttle. 495.
shuttle. 486.
shuttlecock. 528.
sickle. 242.
side. 142, 214, 416, 671.
side back vent. 283.
side chair. 203.
side chapel. 164.
side door. 411.
side entrance. 178.
side handle. 250.
side handrail. 415.
side ladder. 405.
side ladder tread. 405.
side lever. 492.
side line. 529.
side-marker light. 383.
side mirror. 330.
side platform. 414.
side pocket. 281.
side post. 180.
side rail. 268.
side rib. 142.
side span. 402.
side stand. 395.
side-tilt lock. 359.
side wall. 85, 411, 426, 526, 527, 532.
side wall line. 526.
side window. 389.
sideline. 513, 521, 522, 525.
sidestroke. 533.
sidewalk. 399.
sieve. 218.
sifter. 220.
sight. 123.
sight. 611, 677, 683.
sight-glass tube. 233.
sighting line. 611.
sighting mirror. 611.
sigmoid colon. 119.
signal background plate. 409.
signal gantry. 410.
signal lamp. 228, 232, 506.
signal light. 395.
signals. 409.
signature. 349, 498.
signs of zodiac. 698.
signs regulating priority at intersections. 701.
silage harvester. 153.
silique, section of a. 71.
silk. 77.
silk line. 566.
sill. 45, 182.
sill of frame. 189.
sill plate. 182.
sill step. 405.
silverware. 214, 215, 216.

sima. 160.
simple leaves. 62.
simple-span beam bridge. 400.
simple topmarks. 432.
single-breasted coat. 283.
single curtain rod. 208.
single-decked pallet. 671.
single-edged swords. 678.
single-handle kitchen faucet. 261.
single-handle kitchen faucet. 260.
single-leaf bascule bridge. 403.
single-lens reflex camera. 353.
single pole breaker. 278.
single quotation marks. 347.
single reed. 469.
single seat. 415.
single twist. 250.
single zero. 580, 581.
singles pole. 523.
singles service court. 528.
singles sideline. 523, 528.
Sinhalese writing system. 345.
sinister. 695.
sinister base. 695.
sinister chief. 695.
sinister flank. 695.
sink. 260.
sink. 259, 360.
sink hole. 46.
sink strainer. 260.
sinker. 567.
sinus of kidney. 120.
siphon. 46.
siphonal canal. 93.
siren. 422.
sirloin. 140.
sirloin tip. 140.
sister. 130.
sixte. 563.
sixteenth note. 461.
sixteenth rest. 461.
sixth. 462.
sixty-fourth note. 461.
sixty-fourth rest. 461.
skate. 520.
skate guard. 548.
skates, types of. 548.
skating. 548.
skeleton, anterior view. 112.
skeleton, posterior view. 113.
sketch. 507.
ski. 394, 545.
ski boot. 546.
ski boot. 545.
ski cap. 288.
ski goggles. 319, 545, 547.
ski hat. 547.
ski instructor. 544.
ski jumper. 544.
ski jumping hill. 544.
ski pole. 545, 547.
ski resort. 544.
ski stop. 545, 546.
ski suit. 545.
ski tip. 547.
skid. 441.
skid pad. 630.
skid ramp. 389.
skiing. 544.
skimmer. 153, 219.
skin. 127, 128.
skin. 66, 67, 68, 97, 127.
skin diving. 536.
skin surface. 127, 128.
skip. 530.
skirt. 524, 553, 676.
skirt finger. 421.
skirt marker. 487.
skirts. 293.
skis, types of. 540.
skull. 84, 91, 106, 676.
skull, osteology of. 114.
skull cap. 288.
sky coverage. 53.
sky coverage. 54.
skylight. 177.

slab building. 505.
slalom course. 544.
slalomist. 544.
slash pocket. 284.
slat. 209, 493.
sleeper. 306.
sleeping bags. 584.
sleeping car. 407.
sleet. 49, 52.
sleeve. 336.
sleeve. 283, 561, 562, 582, 599.
sleeve protector. 473.
sleeve strap. 281.
sleeve strap loop. 281.
sleeves. 296.
slender. 111.
slide. 232, 362, 488, 689.
slide-bar. 491.
slide chair. 408.
slide changer. 362.
slide plate. 485.
slide projector. 362.
slide selector. 227, 233.
slide tray. 362.
slider. 468.
sliding. 188, 189.
sliding roof. 383.
sliding weight. 478, 594.
sliding window. 407.
slightly covered sky. 53.
slims. 300.
sling. 680, 685, 687.
sling swivel. 685.
slip. 170, 302.
slip joint. 249.
slip joint pliers. 249.
slip ring. 685.
slip-stitched seam. 285.
slippers. 311.
slippery floor. 704.
slippery road. 700.
slit. 497.
slope. 399.
sloped turret. 181.
sloping cornice. 161.
slot. 170, 215, 227, 254, 341, 499.
slot machine. 581.
slotback. 515.
slotted wall bracket. 259.
slow-motion control knob. 609.
sludge. 267.
slush pit. 626.
Small Bear. 32.
small bows. 137.
small capitals. 351.
Small Dog. 32.
small hand cultivator. 239.
Small Horse. 32.
small intestine. 119.
Small Lion. 32.
smaller round. 111.
smell. 125.
smock. 295.
smoke. 52.
smoke bomb discharger. 690.
smoke dome. 190.
smoke filter. 419.
smoking accessories. 334, 335.
smoking candle. 501.
smoking permitted. 705.
smoking prohibited. 705.
snaffle bit. 553.
snaffle rein. 553.
snail. 96.
snail dish. 221.
snail tongs. 221.
Snake. 32, 33.
Snake Bearer. 32, 33.
snap. 488.
s.nap shackle. 539.
snare. 472.
snare drum. 472.
snare drum. 477, 479.
snare head. 472.
snare strainer. 472.
sneaker. 309.

snooker. 570.
snorkel. 536.
snorkel exhaust. 424.
snorkel intake. 424.
snout. 97.
snow. 50.
snow crystals, classification of. 49.
snow goggles. 575.
snow guard. 394.
snow peas. 77.
snow pellet. 49.
snow shower. 52.
snow tire. 393.
snowmobile. 394.
snowshoe types. 549.
snowshoer. 549.
snowshoes. 549.
snowsuit. 307.
soap dish. 259.
soccer. 518.
soccer ball. 518.
sock. 287.
sock. 301, 516, 524.
sock lining. 308.
socket. 275, 488.
socket bayonet. 679.
socket head (Robertson). 254.
sofa. 201.
soft-drink dispenser. 387.
soft key. 456.
soft palate. 126.
soft pedal. 465.
soft ray. 90.
soft shell clam. 94.
softlight reflector. 358.
soil. 639.
soil-or-waste stack. 257.
solar cell. 656.
solar cell. 378.
solar collector. 655.
solar eclipse. 29.
solar energy. 654, 655, 656.
solar furnace. 654.
solar house. 655.
solar panel. 57.
solar panel deployment. 379.
solar power station. 654.
solar radiation. 654, 655, 656.
solder. 273, 507.
soldering. 271, 272, 273.
soldering gun. 271.
soldering iron. 271.
soldering iron. 507.
soldering process. 507.
soldering torch. 271.
sole. 85, 129, 287, 311, 546, 548, 572.
sole plate. 548.
soleplate. 233.
soleus. 110.
solid body. 480.
solid-rocket booster. 443.
solid rubber tire. 670.
solitaire ring. 315.
solleret. 676.
solvent extraction unit. 635.
something omitted. 350.
son. 130.
son-in-law. 131.
soufflé. 147.
sound-board. 463, 464, 465, 473.
sound box. 464.
sound camera. 368.
sound engineer. 374.
sound-hole. 463.
sound-on-sound control. 368.
sound-post. 464.
sound projector. 368.
sound reproducing system. 363, 364, 365, 366.
sounding balloon. 39, 55.
sounding gauge. 423.
soup bowl. 213.
soup spoon. 216.
soup tureen. 213.
South. 579.

South America. 41.
South celestial pole. 27.
South pole. 27.
South wind. 579.
Southern Cross. 33.
Southern Crown. 33.
Southern Fish. 33.
southern hemisphere. 27.
Southern Triangle. 33.
southwester. 304.
soybeans. 77.
space. 461.
space achievements. 39.
space bar. 453, 456.
space probe. 39.
space shuttle. 443.
space shuttle at takeoff. 443.
space shuttle in orbit. 443.
space suit. 444.
spacelab. 443.
spacer. 617, 649.
spade. 238, 578, 684.
spade mashie. 572.
spading fork. 238.
spadix. 64.
spaghetti. 136.
spaghetti tongs. 221.
spandrel. 162.
Spanish onion. 75.
Spanish writing system. 345.
spanker. 417.
spark plug. 392.
spark plug. 243.
spark plug body. 392.
spark plug cable. 391.
spark plug gap. 392.
spark plug gasket. 392.
spark plug terminal. 392.
spatial dendrite. 49.
spatula. 219, 502.
spatulate. 62.
speaker. 363.
speaker. 35, 368, 377.
speaker selector. 364.
speaking window membrane. 412.
spear. 77.
speargun. 536.
special effects. 376.
specific data processing program. 454.
specimen. 605.
specimen chamber. 606.
spectacles. 319.
speed control. 225.
speed selector. 226.
speed selector lever. 365.
speed skate. 548.
speedometer. 385, 396.
spencer. 297.
spent fuel discharge room. 651.
spent fuel port. 651.
spent fuel storage bay. 649, 651, 653.
spermatic cord. 108.
spermatozoon. 108.
sphenoid bone. 114.
sphenoidal sinus. 125.
sphere. 423, 432.
sphere support. 56.
sphincter muscle of anus. 119.
sphygmomanometer. 598.
spicule. 29.
spider. 153.
spike. 64, 408, 573, 574, 575.
spike-tooth. 152.
spiked shoe. 512.
spillway. 637.
spillway chute. 637.
spilway gate. 637.
spinach. 74.
spinach lasagna. 136.
spinach noodles. 136.
spinal cord. 91, 122, 127.
spinal ganglion. 127.
spinal nerve. 122, 127.

spindle. 203, 226, 256, 261, 593, 599, 601.
spindle screw. 599.
spine. 93, 498, 500.
spine of scapula. 113.
spine of the book. 500.
spinnaker boom. 538.
spinnaker sheet lead. 538.
spinner. 567.
spinning rod. 566.
spinous process of vertebra. 113.
spiny lobster. 95.
spiny ray. 90.
spiracle. 92.
spiral. 248, 365.
spiral arms. 31.
spiral beater. 225.
spiral binding. 449.
spiral case. 642, 643.
spiral galaxy. 31.
spiral-in groove. 365.
spiral ratchet screwdriver. 248.
spiral rib. 93.
spiral staircase. 633.
spire. 93, 96, 164.
spit. 43.
splash guard. 383.
splash plate. 633.
splat. 200.
splay. 165.
splayed leg. 199.
splaying. 190.
spleen. 91, 116.
spleeping compartment. 407.
splenic artery. 117.
splenic vein. 117.
splenius muscle of head. 111.
splice. 587.
splice bar. 408.
spline. 392.
split bet. 580, 581.
split end. 514, 515.
split link. 567.
spoiler. 434.
spoke. 397.
spoke wheel. 389.
spoked wheel. 554.
sponge. 681.
sponge-tipped applicator. 322.
spongy body. 108.
spool. 492, 566.
spool pin. 485.
spool rack. 496.
spoon. 216.
spoon. 572, 585.
spoons, major types of. 216.
spores. 65.
sports. 509.
spot. 211.
spot projector attachment. 358.
spot white ball. 570.
spotlight. 375, 422, 662, 663.
spotmeter. 357.
spouse. 130.
spout. 224, 233, 261.
spout assembly. 260.
spray. 233.
spray arm. 232.
spray button. 233.
spray head. 260.
spray hose. 260.
spray nozzle. 633.
spray paint gun. 270.
sprayer. 240.
spread collar. 285.
spreader. 241, 336.
spreader adjustment valve. 270.
spreading rotor. 153.
spring. 27, 211, 249, 256, 261, 352, 404, 560, 598, 602, 682, 686.
spring balance. 594.
spring binder. 449.
spring hip throw. 564.
spring linkage. 581.
spring washer. 408.

spring wing. 254.
springboard. 534, 559, 560.
springboard diver. 534.
springer. 162.
sprinkler hose. 240.
sprocket. 180, 394.
sprocket cluster. 398.
sprocket wheel. 664, 690.
spur. 46, 250, 472, 551.
squall. 52.
squamous suture. 114.
square. 579.
square. 498, 697.
square bet. 580, 581.
square cushion. 204.
square head plug. 265.
square neck. 299.
square root of. 709.
square sail. 418.
squash. 526.
squash ball. 526.
squash racket. 526.
St-George's cross. 432.
stabilizer. 420, 541, 677, 691.
stabilizer foot. 232.
stabilizing fin. 442.
stabilizing keel. 423.
stable. 555.
stack. 43, 420.
stack vent. 257.
stacking chairs. 203.
staff. 461.
staff. 695.
stage. 35, 170, 605, 606.
stage, cross section of a. 170.
stage clip. 605.
stage curtain. 170.
stage-house. 170.
stained glass. 507.
stairs. 187.
stairs. 178, 633, 705.
stairwell. 179.
stake. 237, 582, 583.
stake loop. 583.
stake pocket. 388.
stalactite. 46.
stalagmite. 46.
stalk. 66, 68, 77.
stalk vegetables. 77.
stalked eye. 95.
stamen. 64, 68.
stamp pad. 448.
stamp pocket. 341.
stamp rack. 448.
stanchion. 548.
stand. 555.
stand. 210, 223, 225, 298, 331, 337, 358, 359, 656.
stand off half. 517.
stand-up collar. 298.
standard hardboard. 184.
standard lens. 355.
standard walker. 616.
standardbred pacer. 554.
standing press. 500.
standing signs. 703.
standpipe. 262.
staple remover. 447.
stapler. 447.
staples. 447.
star anise. 71.
star diagonal. 609.
star facet. 317.
star projection condenser. 35.
star projection lens. 35.
star sphere. 35.
starboard diving plane. 424.
starch. 71.
starch granule. 105.
stars. 137.
start. 552.
start line. 556.
start switch. 231.
start wall. 532.
startboard tack. 539.
starter. 391, 532, 658.

starter handle. 243.
starter pedal. 396.
starting block. 532.
starting dive. 532.
starting electrode. 274.
starting grip. 532.
starting position. 532.
starting position. 535.
starting positions. 534.
starting resistor. 274.
starting signal. 413.
state of ground. 55.
station circle. 53, 54.
station hall. 412.
station model. 54.
station name. 414.
station platform. 413.
station platform. 410.
station sign. 413.
station wagon. 384.
station wagon, back of a. 384.
stationary bowl. 580.
stationary front. 53.
stationery. 447, 448, 449, 450.
stationery cabinet. 451.
stator. 256, 641, 642.
stator vane. 436.
statue. 161.
stay. 416, 596.
stay ring. 642, 643.
stay sail. 417.
stay vane. 642, 643.
staysail-stay. 416.
steak knife. 214.
steam. 650.
steam button. 233.
steam cracker. 634.
steam generator. 647, 650, 654.
steam generator system. 652.
steam injection. 636.
steam iron. 233.
steam pipe. 647, 650.
steam separator. 650.
steam turbine. 420.
steel. 183, 303, 682.
steel ball shielding. 648.
steel band. 596.
steel bar. 559.
steel hook. 312.
steel pen. 352.
steel safey wheel. 415.
steel spring. 682.
steel to plastic. 265.
steelyard. 594.
steep hill. 700.
steeplechase. 556.
steering. 386.
steering axle. 670.
steering cylinder. 668.
steering damper. 396.
steering lever. 690.
steering line. 541.
steering lock. 396.
steering track rod. 152.
steering wheel. 155, 385, 386, 670.
stellar crystal. 49.
stem. 61.
stem. 61, 65, 75, 224, 274, 335, 397, 416, 538, 597.
stem faucet. 261.
step. 172, 269, 389.
step chain. 172.
step chair. 202.
step cut. 317.
step groove. 187.
step setting. 599.
step stool. 269.
stepladder. 269.
stepladders. 268, 269.
steppe. 51.
stereo camera. 354.
sterile pad. 615.
stern. 537.
stern loading door. 420.
sternocleidomastoid. 110.

sternum. 84, 112.
sterring column. 386.
stick. 464, 667.
stick glove. 520.
stick umbrella. 336.
sticker. 475.
stickpin. 315.
sticks. 471.
stiffening girder. 402.
stiffle. 83.
stigma. 64, 70.
stile. 203.
stile groove of sash. 189.
stile tongue of sash. 189.
stiletto. 678.
still cameras. 354.
still water level. 43.
stilt. 506.
stilted. 162.
stimulator tip. 329.
sting. 98.
stipule. 62.
stirrup. 677.
stirrup hook. 595.
stirrup iron. 553.
stirrup leather. 553.
stirrup sock. 512.
stitch. 308.
stitch length regulator. 485.
stitch patterns. 490.
stitch selector. 485.
stitched pleat. 294.
stitches. 512.
stitches, groups of. 493.
stitching. 289.
stock. 433, 474, 657, 688.
stock pot. 222.
stockade. 167.
stocked anchor. 433.
stocking. 562.
stocking cap. 304.
stocking stitch. 490.
stockless anchor. 433.
stomach. 91, 94, 116, 119.
stone. 66, 67, 183, 591.
Stone Age arms. 675.
stone fleshy fruits. 67.
stone fruit, section of a. 67.
stone fruits, major types of. 67.
stoner. 221.
stool. 202.
stop. 367, 488, 630.
stop at intersection. 701.
stop bath. 360.
stop button. 243, 366, 373, 478.
stop consonants. 348.
stop knob. 467, 468.
stop nod. 468.
stopboard. 557.
stope. 622.
storage compartment. 662, 663.
storage door. 229.
storage furniture. 205, 206.
storage space. 179.
storage tank. 629, 635, 650, 654, 655.
storage tray. 651.
storm collar. 192.
storm sewer. 399.
stove oil. 635.
straight. 552, 578.
straight bet. 580, 581.
straight eye. 488.
straight flush. 578.
straight hair. 320.
straight jaw. 249.
straight ladder. 268.
straight muscle of thigh. 110.
straight position. 534.
straight razor. 327.
straight run gasoline treatment. 634.
straight skirt. 293.
straight-up ribbed top. 287.
straight wing. 435.
strainer. 226, 261, 582, 627.

strainer body. 260.
strainer coupling. 260.
strainer plug. 261.
strainer sleeve. 260.
strand. 587.
strap. 341, 512, 550, 559, 676.
strap handle. 336.
strap wrench. 266.
strapless brassiere. 303.
stratocumulus. 44.
stratosphere. 39.
stratum basale. 128.
stratum corneum. 128.
stratum granulosum. 128.
stratum lucidum. 128.
stratum spinosum. 128.
stratus. 44.
straw walker. 155.
strawberry, section of a. 66.
streamer. 697.
street, cross section of a. 399.
street bet. 580, 581.
street café. 168.
street light. 168.
street sign. 168.
stretcher. 199.
stretcher bar. 409.
stretchers. 203.
strike. 256.
striker. 273, 682.
striker wheel. 334.
string. 77, 282, 304, 463, 464, 465, 466.
stringed instruments. 463, 464.
stringer. 435, 671.
stringer board. 671.
stringing. 524.
strings. 526.
strip fixture. 211.
strip flooring with alternate joints. 186.
strip light. 375.
strip loin. 140.
strip mine. 621.
striped trousers. 307.
stripes. 430.
stripper beater. 155.
strirrer cover. 227.
stroboscopic light. 691.
stroke judge. 532.
strokes, types of. 533.
strong-box. 581.
structure. 637.
strut. 180, 422, 550, 646, 658.
stub out. 258.
stud. 182, 428.
studio. 374.
studio. 374.
studio accessories. 359.
studio crane. 375.
studio floor. 375.
studio lighting. 358.
study. 179.
stummel. 335.
stump. 63.
style. 64, 66, 67, 68, 71.
stylobate. 161.
stylus. 352.
sub-base. 56.
subarctic climates. 51.
subbase. 399.
subclavian artery. 117.
subclavian vein. 117.
subcutaneous tissue. 128.
subfloor. 182.
subgrade. 399.
subject line. 349.
sublevel. 623.
sublimation. 50.
submachine gun. 683.
submarine. 424.
submarine canyon. 42.
submarine pipeline. 630.
submerged foils. 422.
submersible barge. 628.
submersible watch. 536.

subminiature camera. 354.
subpapillary network. 128.
subscript. 350.
subsidiary track. 410.
subsoil plow. 154.
substation. 646.
substitute. 522, 525, 531.
substitutes' bench. 525.
subterranean stream. 46.
subtraction. 709.
subtropical climates. 51.
suburban commuter railroad. 410.
subway entrance. 168.
subway map. 414, 415.
subway station. 414.
subway train. 415.
sucker rod. 627.
suction hose. 663.
suction regulator. 234.
sugar bowl. 213.
sugar spoon. 216.
suit tiles. 579.
sulcus terminalis. 126.
sulky. 554.
summer. 27.
summer solstice. 27.
summer squash. 73.
summit. 46.
sump. 267, 622.
sump pump. 267.
Sun. 29.
Sun. 27, 28, 29, 30.
Sun, structure of the. 29.
sun sensor. 57, 378.
sun visor. 385.
sundae spoon. 216.
sundeck. 419.
sundial. 592.
sundress. 292.
sunshine. 55.
sunshine recorder. 56.
sunshine recorder. 55.
sunspot. 29.
super. 99.
superciliary arch. 114.
superficial peroneal nerve. 121.
superhighway. 703.
superior dental arch. 126.
superior longitudinal sinus. 122.
superior mesenteric artery. 117, 120.
superior nasal concha. 125.
superior semicircular canal. 124.
superior umbilicus. 88.
superior vena cava. 116, 117.
superscript. 350.
supertweeter. 363.
supply duct. 194.
supply line. 257.
supply point. 645.
supply reel. 368.
supply riser. 257.
supply spool. 452.
supply tube. 260.
support. 56, 203, 208, 274, 495, 529, 560, 608, 630.
support leg. 388.
support leg crank. 388.
support wheel. 231.
suppression tank. 650.
supraorbital foramen. 114.
suprarenal gland. 120.
suprascapular nerve. 121.
sural nerve. 121.
surcingle. 554.
surface cold front. 53.
surface course. 399.
surface element. 228.
surface of the water. 534.
surface-piercing foils. 422.
surface runoff. 50.
surface-to-air missile. 692.
surface-to-subsurface missile. 692.
surface-to-surface missile. 692.
surface warm front. 53.
surlonge. 141.

surroyal antler. 81.
suspended span. 400.
suspender. 402.
suspender clip. 284.
suspenders. 284.
suspension bridge. 402.
suspension cable. 402, 661.
suspension hook. 594.
suspension insulator string. 644.
suspension line. 541.
suspension spring. 593.
suspensory ligament. 123.
sustaining pedal. 465.
suture. 71, 93.
swag lamp. 210.
swagger bag. 339.
swagger stick. 336.
swallow-hole. 46.
swallowtail. 697.
swallowtail and tongue. 697.
swallowtail pennant. 697.
Swan. 32.
sweater. 297.
Swedish writing system. 345.
sweeper. 530.
sweeping loin throw. 564.
sweeping score line. 530.
sweet bay. 133.
sweet pepper. 73.
sweet potato. 76.
sweetheart neckline. 299.
swell of the muzzle. 680.
swell organ manual. 467.
swell pedal. 467.
sweptback wing. 435.
swift. 496.
swimmer. 532.
swimmeret. 95.
swimming. 532.
swimming competition. 532.
swimming pool. 531.
swing. 188.
swing bridge. 403.
swing circle. 667.
swinger wall lamp. 210.
Swiss chard. 77.
Swiss roll. 147.
switch. 228, 229, 234, 250, 251, 275, 357, 410, 453, 457.
switch, manually-operated. 408.
switch, remote-controlled. 409.
switch engine. 411.
switch point. 408.
switch point lock. 409.
switch signal. 408, 409.
switch stand. 408.
switch tower. 410.
switchboard. 379.
switcher. 376.
switchhook. 372.
switchyard. 652.
swivel. 558, 567, 626.
swivel base. 249.
swivel head. 249.
swivel lock. 249.
swivel-tilter armchair. 451.
swiveling power supply cord. 331.
sword-breaker. 678.
Swordfish. 33.
swords. 678.
symbol. 581.
symbols. 693.
symbols, heraldry. 696.
symbols of the planets. 28.
Symphony. 378.
symphony orchestra. 479.
symphysis pubis. 108, 109.
synapse. 127.
sync cable. 358.
synchro cord. 357.
synchronizer. 610.
synthesizer. 481.
synthetic sponge. 323.
syringe for irrigation. 615.
syringes. 615.

system, configuration of a. 455.
system, functions in a. 454.
system elements. 363.

T

T. 432.
T-bar lift. 544.
T-bone. 140.
T-shirt dress. 292.
T-strap shoe. 309.
T-tail unit. 435.
tab. 336, 339, 340, 341, 449, 488, 553.
tab-key. 456.
table. 199, 529.
table. 251, 252, 317, 468, 499, 562.
table, English billiards. 570.
table, pool. 569.
table cut. 317.
table extension. 252.
table lamp. 210.
table-locking clamp. 251.
table mixer. 225.
table tennis. 529.
table tennis player. 529.
table tennis shoe. 529.
tables, major types of. 199.
tablespoon. 216.
tablinum. 163.
tabulator. 453.
tabulator clear key. 453.
tabulator set key. 453.
tachometer. 396.
tack. 537.
tag. 308.
tail. 95, 100, 101, 108, 434, 500, 540, 542, 543, 545, 547, 549, 567.
tail assembly. 434.
tail boom. 441.
tail comb. 328.
tail edge. 498.
tail feather. 87.
tail of helix. 124.
tail-out groove. 365.
tail parachute. 542.
tail pipe. 392.
tail pipe extension. 392.
tail pole. 657.
tail shape. 435.
tailing. 636.
taillight. 383, 388, 395.
tailored collar. 291, 298.
tailored sleeve. 296.
tailpiece. 260, 463.
tailrace. 641, 643.
take back to previous line. 350.
take-off board. 556, 557.
take-off line. 556.
take over to next line. 350.
take-up handle. 494.
take-up knob. 452.
take-up reel. 368.
take-up spool. 353, 452.
takedown pin. 685.
taking mirror. 356.
talus. 113.
tam o'shanter. 304.
tambourine. 472.
tamper. 335.
tandem disk harrow. 154.
tandem drive housing. 666.
tang. 214, 217.
tank. 690.
tank. 632, 633.
tank ball. 258.
tank car. 632.
tank car. 406.
tank farm. 630, 634.
tank gauge float. 633.
tank lid. 259.
tank sprayer. 240.
tank trailer. 632.

tank truck. *632.*
tank wall. 632.
tankage. 636.
tanker. 631, 691.
tanks. 443.
tape. 209, 447, 488, 493, 512, 522, 599.
tape counter. 366, 367.
tape deck. 366.
tape deck. 363.
tape dispenser. 447.
tape load lever. 452.
tape measure. 487, 599.
tape monitor switch. 364.
tape selector. 366.
tape speed selector. 367.
tape-type indicator. 366.
tapered wing. 435.
tapestry bobbin. 495.
taproot. 63.
target. 692.
target area. 654.
target areas. 563.
target tracking radar. 692.
tarlatan. 501.
tarpaulin covered gondola. 406.
tarragon. 133.
tarsus. 84, 87, 92, 97, 98, 112.
tart. 146.
tassel. 207, 311.
tasset. 676.
taste. 126.
taste, sense of. 125.
Taurus, the Bull. 698.
taxi stand. 168.
taxi telephone. 168.
taxi transportation. 707.
taxiway. 438.
tea ball. 221.
team. 517.
team bench. 531.
team shirt. 512.
teapot. 213.
tear-off calendar. 450.
tear tape. 334.
teaser comb. 328.
teaspoon. 216.
technical director. 376.
tee. 573.
tee. 262, 265, 530.
teeing ground. 571.
teeth. 115.
teeth. 252, 488, 574.
tele-converter. 355.
Telecom 1 satellite. 379.
telecommunication satellites. 378, 379.
telecommunications network. 379.
telecomputer. 379.
teleconference. 379.
telecopy. 379.
telegrams. 706.
telegraph. 370, 371.
Teleme. 144.
telemetry antenna. 378.
telephone. 704.
telephone answering machine. 373.
telephone booth. 168.
telephone cable. 399.
telephone cord. 373.
telephone index. 450.
telephone line. 312.
telephone set. 372.
telephone shower head. 259.
telephones, types of. 373.
telephoto lens. 355.
teleprinter. 371.
teleprompter. 375.
Telescope. 33, 429, 609.
telescope base. 34.
telescope control room. 34.
telescope eyepiece. 600.
telescope objective. 600.
telescopic antenna. 377.
telescopic boom. 669.

telescopic corridor. 438.
telescopic sight. 686, 690.
telescopic umbrella. 336.
telescoping leg. 359.
telescoping uncoupling rod. 405.
teletex. 379.
television. 374, 375, 376, 377.
television set. 377.
telex. 371.
telltale. 526, 538.
telson. 95.
temperate climates. 51.
temperate marine. 51.
temperature. 555.
temperature control. 331.
temperature dial. 233.
temperature indicator. 385.
temperature of dew point. 54.
temperature of the soil surface. 55.
temperature scale. 597.
temperature selector. 230, 231.
temperature sensing bulb. 228.
temperature set point lever. 597.
template. 457.
temple. 318, 496.
temple. 106, 499.
temporal. 112.
temporal bone. 114.
temporal fossa. 114.
tenaille. 166.
tender. 628.
tenderloin. 140.
tenderloin portion. 142.
tendon. 86.
tendon guard. 548.
tendron. 139, 141.
tennis. 523, 524.
tennis ball. 524.
tennis players. 524.
tennis racket. 524.
tennis shoe. 309, 524.
tenon. 335.
tenon saw. 499.
tenor drum. 472.
tenor drum. 477.
tension block. 486, 491.
tension block. 485.
tension check spring. 486.
tension controller. 491.
tension dial. 486, 491, 492.
tension disc. 486, 491.
tension guide. 491.
tension pulley set. 208.
tension pulley wheel. 208.
tension rod. 472.
tension roller. 398.
tension screw. 472.
tension spring. 384, 491.
tensor of fascia lata. 110.
tentacle. 96.
tents. 582, 583.
tents, major types of. 583.
tepee. 159.
terminal. 228, 275, 458, 630, 645.
terminal arborization. 127.
terminal bronchiole. 118.
terminal bud. 61.
terminal connections. 194.
terminal cover. 601.
terminal filament. 122.
terminal knife-edge. 595.
terminal moraine. 48.
terminal stopping switch cam. 171.
terminal stopping witch. 171.
terrace. 168, 177, 237.
terreplein. 166.
terrestrial sphere. 27.
tertial. 88.
test pattern. 376.
tester probe. 276.
testicle. 108.
theater. 169, 170.
theater. 168, 419.
theodolite. 600.
theodolite. 55.
thermal control shutter. 57.

thermal insulation. 630.
thermal storage. 654.
thermometer. 597, 633.
thermosphere. 39.
thermostat. 194, 195, 196, 597.
thermostat control. 229.
thick-walled pipe. 626.
thigh. 83, 87, 107.
thigh-high stocking. 301.
thigh pad. 516.
thimble. 487.
thimble. 599.
thin macaroni. 136.
thin spaghetti. 136.
thin spring-metal insulation. 185.
thinning razor. 328.
thinning scissors. 328.
third. 462.
third base. 511.
third baseman. 511.
third molar. 115.
third stage. 442.
third wheel. 591, 593.
thirty-second clock operator. 521.
thirty-second note. 461.
thirty-second rest. 461.
thong. 309.
thoracic leg. 92.
thoracic vertebra. 113.
thoracic vertebrae. 84.
thorax. 92, 98, 106.
thread. 254, 261.
thread guide. 485, 486, 496.
thread take-up. 485.
thread trimmer. 486.
threaded cap. 265.
threaded rod. 254.
three-branched air tube. 312.
three-burner camp stove. 585.
three-four time. 462.
three-hinged arch. 401.
three of a kind. 578.
three-quarter coat. 282.
three-quarter sleeve. 296.
threequarter backs. 517.
threshold. 177, 188.
throat. 87, 190, 249, 433, 524, 567.
throat latch. 553.
throat protector. 512, 520.
throttle valve. 625.
through arch bridge. 401.
throwing arc. 557.
throwing circle. 556, 557.
throwing in a circle. 564.
throwing spear. 675.
throwings. 558.
thrust. 401.
thrust device. 352.
thrust tube. 352.
thumb. 100, 289, 512.
thumb hook. 469, 470.
thumb piston. 467.
thumb rest. 233.
thumb string. 473.
thumb string peg. 473.
thumbscrew. 248.
thunderstorm. 52.
thyme. 133.
tibia. 84, 92, 98, 100, 112.
tibial nerve. 121.
tibiofibula. 97.
ticket. 596.
ticket counter. 412, 440.
ticket office. 412.
ticket pocket. 341.
tidal basin. 427.
tidal power plant. 646.
tie. 285, 311, 336, 408, 462.
tie bar. 316.
tie beam. 180.
tie closure. 336.
tie flap. 582.
tie plate. 408.
tie tack. 316.
tieback. 207.

tieback hook. 207.
tierce. 563.
tight end. 514, 515.
tightening band. 56.
tights. 305, 311.
tile. 161, 185.
tiller. 241, 538, 677.
tilt-back head. 225.
tilt cord. 209.
tilt tube. 209.
timber. 161.
timber yard. 624.
time, measure of. 591, 592, 593.
time fuse. 682.
time signatures. 462.
timed outlet. 228.
timekeeper. 521, 525, 531, 562, 565.
timer. 360.
timer on switch. 367.
timing. 555.
timpani. 479.
tinctures. 696.
tine. 592.
tip. 62, 77, 214, 216, 248, 253, 254, 272, 284, 333, 336, 507, 540, 543, 545, 549, 558, 567, 568.
tip cleaner. 507.
tip cleaners. 273.
tip guard. 548.
tip guide. 566.
tip of nose. 125.
tip section. 566.
tip-top. 566.
tipping lever. 617.
tipping valve faucet. 261.
tire. 389, 397.
tire dolly. 387.
tire inflator. 387.
tire pump. 397.
tires. 393.
tissue holder. 259.
Titan. 28.
title. 349.
toaster. 227.
tobacco. 334.
tobacco hole. 335.
tobacco pouch. 335.
toboggan. 550.
toe. 85, 89, 106, 247, 252, 287, 311, 572.
toe binding. 547.
toe box. 548.
toe clip. 85, 397.
toe hole. 549.
toe lacing. 549.
toe pick. 548.
toe piece. 540, 545, 546.
toe-piece release setting indicator. 546.
toe piston. 467.
toe rubber. 309.
toe stop. 548.
toe strap. 540.
toenail scissors. 333.
toeplate. 547.
toggle bolt. 254.
toggle fastening. 282.
toilet. 258.
toilet. 259, 407.
toilet bowl. 258, 259.
toilet for men and women. 705.
toilet for women. 705.
toilet tank. 259.
tomato. 73.
tombolo. 43.
Tomme aux raisins. 144.
tone arm. 365.
tone control. 368, 480.
tongs. 221.
tongue. 91, 119, 125, 126, 284, 308, 339, 468, 474, 488, 546, 548.
tongue, dorsum of. 126.
tongue sheath. 101.

tool. 625.
tool tray. 269.
tooth. 101, 154, 253, 328, 666, 667.
toothbrush. 329.
toothbrush shaft. 329.
toothbrush well. 329.
toothed jaw. 249.
toothed rotor. 154.
toothing stone. 177.
toothpaste. 329.
top. 63, 416, 524.
top bar. 560.
top central manhole. 632.
top collar. 283.
top cylinder. 502, 504.
top deck. 633.
top deckboard. 671.
top edge. 498.
top-end transverse member. 411.
top hat. 288.
top lift. 308.
top of dam. 637, 638, 641.
top plate. 180, 453.
top pocket. 570.
top rail. 188, 203, 205.
top rail of sash. 189.
top road. 623.
top stitched pleat. 294.
top stitching. 284, 306.
top surface. 542.
top-work surface. 232.
topgallant mast. 416.
topmark. 430.
topmast. 416.
topping. 567.
topping lift. 416.
toque. 304.
torch. 266.
torpedo. 424.
torpedo room. 424.
tortellini. 137.
torus. 160.
total. 596.
total eclipse. 29, 30.
tote bag. 337, 338.
tote board. 555.
Toucan. 33.
touch. 127.
touch in goal line. 517.
touch line. 517, 518.
toupee. 321.
touring boot. 547.
tourist-class cabin. 419.
tourist tent. 583.
tow bar. 540.
tow hook. 542.
tow release knob. 542.
tow tractor. 439.
towboat. 631.
towel bar set. 259.
tower. 164, 402, 624, 644, 654, 657, 658.
tower crane. 669.
tower crane. 427.
tower foot. 644.
tower ladder. 662.
tower mast. 669.
tower mill. 657.
tower top. 644.
tower window. 644.
towing fairlead. 423.
towing hook. 152.
towing truck. 387.
town house. 173.
towrope. 540.
tracery. 165.
trachea. 118.
tracing wheel. 487.
track. 415, 555.
track. 208, 394, 413, 414, 458, 544, 557, 664, 690.
track and field athletics. 556, 557, 558.
track bolt. 408.

track carrier roller. 664.
track grouser. 664.
track idler. 664.
track lighting. 211.
track link. 664, 690.
track roller. 664.
track roller frame. 664.
track shoe. 664.
track shoe. 664.
tracker. 468.
tracking control. 367.
traction motor. 404.
traction motor ventilator. 404.
tractor. 152.
tractor. 632.
tractor engine. 668.
trade sign. 168.
traditional houses. 159.
traditional musical instruments. 473, 474, 475.
traffic circle. 701.
traffic island. 168.
traffic light. 168.
tragus. 100, 124.
trailer car. 415.
trailer car interior. 415.
trailing edge. 434, 542, 543.
trailing edge flap. 434.
train delays notice board. 412.
train set. 410.
trainer. 555, 565.
training shoe. 309.
training wall. 637.
trampoline. 560.
tranche grasse. 141.
transceiver. 444.
transducer. 428.
transept. 164.
transfer. 379.
transfer canal. 651.
transfer dispensing machine. 414.
transfer orbit satellite. 379.
transfer orbit solar cell. 378.
transfer scale. 357.
transfer station. 622.
transform fault. 42.
transformer. 195, 641, 645, 654, 658.
transforming station. 641.
transistor. 592.
transit shed. 427.
transition fittings. 265.
translation wave. 43.
transmission. 230, 668.
transmission-line contact. 370.
transmission network. 653, 654.
transmission of telegraph signals. 370.
transmitted pulse. 610.
transmitter. 370, 372.
transmitter. 610.
transmitter-receiver. 379.
transmitter-receiver terminal. 379.
transparency slide. 362.
transparent line indicator. 453.
transpiration. 50.
transportation. 381.
transporter bridge. 403.
transpose lines. 350.
transpose two letters. 350.
transpose two words. 350.
transverse baffle. 632.
transverse bulkhead. 631.
transverse colon. 119.
transverse dunes. 47.
transverse process of vertebra. 113.
trap. 260, 265.
trap and drain auger. 266.
trap coupling. 260.
trapezius. 110.
traveler. 539.
traveling cables. 171.
traveling crane. 641.
travelling block. 626.
traverse arch. 165.

traverse rod. 208.
traversing handle. 683.
traversing mechanism. 687.
tray. 270.
tray. 223, 337.
tread. 187, 553.
tread design. 393.
treadle. 494.
treadle cord. 494.
treble. 552.
treble bridge. 465.
treble keyboard. 475.
treble pick-up. 480.
treble register. 475.
treble tone control. 364.
tree. 63.
tree. 553.
tree, structure of a. 63.
tree pruner. 239.
trefoil. 162, 165.
trellis. 237.
trench. 42, 621.
trench coat. 281.
triangle. 471.
Triangle. 32, 479.
triangular body. 473.
triangular fossa. 124.
triceps of arm. 111.
triclinium. 163.
tricuspid valve. 116.
trifoliolate. 62.
triforium. 164, 165.
trigger. 243, 270, 368, 677, 682, 683, 685, 686, 687, 688, 689.
trigger guard. 683, 688, 689.
trigger switch. 253.
triglyph. 160.
trill. 462.
trim. 337.
trim collar. 191.
trim ring. 228.
trimmer. 327.
trimming. 499.
trimming. 341.
trimming tool. 505.
trio. 476.
trip handle. 259.
trip lever. 258.
triple bar. 551, 552.
triple jump. 557.
triple tail unit. 435.
triplex. 173.
tripod. 359.
tripod. 362, 478, 608, 687.
tripod accessories shelf. 609.
tripod cane. 616.
tripod leg. 609.
tripod stand. 472.
Triton. 28.
trochanter. 92, 98.
trolley. 403, 669.
trolley pulley. 669.
trolley wire. 413.
Trombe wall. 655.
trombone. 470, 477.
trombones. 479.
tropic of Cancer. 27.
tropic of Capricorn. 27.
tropical climates. 51.
tropical fruits. 72.
tropical rain forest. 51.
tropical savanna. 51.
tropical storm. 52.
troposphere. 39.
trough. 43, 54, 409.
trousers. 564.
trowel. 239.
truck. 415.
truck. 404, 407, 548.
truck crane. 669.
truck frame. 404.
truck level floor. 439.
truck tractor. 389.
truck trailer. 389.
truck trailer. 389.
true skin. 127.

truffle. 65.
trumpet. 470.
trumpet. 470, 477.
trumpets. 479.
trunk. 337.
trunk. 63, 107, 383, 593.
trunk, cross section of a. 63.
trunk floor. 384.
trunks. 561, 565.
trunnion. 680.
truss. 172, 180.
truss rod adjustment. 480.
trussed arch. 401.
TT & C belt antenna. 378.
tub. 230, 232, 237.
tuba. 470, 479.
tube. 681.
tube. 362, 598, 680, 683, 686.
tube bangle. 315.
tube cutter. 266.
tube end. 264.
tube flaring tool. 266.
tube sheet. 648.
tuber vegetables. 76.
tubercles. 93.
tuberculin syringe. 615.
tubing. 627.
tubing head. 627.
tubular bells. 471.
tubular bells. 479.
tubular element. 228.
tubular heater. 635.
tubular ice screw. 574.
tubular lock. 256.
tubular member. 629.
tuck. 334.
tuck brush. 492.
tuck position. 534.
Tudor. 162.
tumbler holder. 259.
tuner. 363.
tunic. 292, 295.
tuning buttons. 364.
tuning control. 428.
tuning fork. 478.
tuning fork. 592.
tuning fork watch. 592.
tuning hammer. 478.
tuning machine. 480.
tuning pin. 465.
tuning screw. 472.
tuning slide. 470.
tuning wire. 468.
tunnel belt loop. 284.
turban. 304.
turbine. 424, 436, 641, 652.
turbine blade. 436.
turbine building. 647.
turbine-compressor shaft. 436.
turbine guide vane. 436.
turbine runner. 646.
turbines, major types of. 643.
turbo-alternator. 654.
turbo-compressor engine. 390.
turbo-jet engine. 436.
turbo-jet engine. 434.
turbocharger. 404.
turbofan engine. 436.
turbopump. 692.
turn. 462.
turn and slip indicator. 542.
turn-down flap. 290.
turn knob hub. 256.
turn signal. 388.
turn signal lever. 386.
turn-up. 300.
turnbuckle. 409, 539, 565.
turner. 219.
turning handle. 250.
turning judge. 532.
turning wheel. 505.
turnip. 76.
turntable. 365.
turntable. 225, 363, 403.
turntable mounting. 662.
turret. 167, 690.

turret cap. 607.
turrets. 137.
turtle. 101.
turtleneck. 286, 297, 298, 545.
tutu. 311.
tweeter. 363.
tweezers. 333, 615.
twig. 61, 63.
twill weave. 497.
twin-lens reflex camera. 354.
twin-set. 297.
twin skis. 540.
twin turret. 425.
Twins. 32.
twist dive. 535.
twist drill. 250.
twist grip throttle. 396.
twisted macaroni. 136.
twisted rope. 587.
two cones base to base. 431.
two cones point downwards. 431.
two cones point to point. 431.
two cones point upwards. 431.
two-door sedan. 384.
two-hand clean and jerk. 561.
two-hand snatch. 561.
two-hand sword. 678.
two-hinged arch. 401.
two pairs. 578.
two triangular pennants. 697.
two-two time. 462.
two-way collar. 281.
two-way traffic. 701.
tympan. 504.
tympanum. 97, 101, 161, 165.
type of fuel. 387.
type of high cloud. 54.
type of low cloud. 54.
type of middle cloud. 54.
type of the air mass. 54.
typed name. 349.
typestyle. 452.
typewriter. 452, 453.
typical letter. 349.
typing element. 452.

U

U-bend. 265.
U-shaped gouge. 502.
UHF channel selector. 377.
UHF-IFF aerial. 691.
Ukrainian writing system. 345.
ulna. 112.
ulnar artery. 117.
ulnar extensor of wrist. 111.
ulnar flexor of wrist. 110, 111.
ulnar nerve. 121.
umbel. 64.
umbilicus. 93.
umbo. 93.
umbra. 30.
umbra shadow. 29.
umbrella. 336.
umbrella diffuser. 358.
umbrella sheath. 573.
umbrella stand. 336.
umlaut. 347.
umpire. 514, 521, 522, 523, 528, 529.
umpire-in-chief. 511.
uncle-in-law. 130.
under tail covert. 87.
underground flow. 50.
underground mine. 623.
underground railway. 415.
underlining. 488.
underlying fabrics. 488.
underpass. 400.
undershirt. 512, 565.
underwear. 287, 302, 303.
underwiring. 303.
uneven parallel bars. 560.
Unicorn. 33.
uniform, football. 516.

union. 264.
union. 709.
union nut. 264.
unison. 462.
unit price. 596.
universal step. 439.
unleavened bread. 138.
unmounted sleeve. 296.
uphaul. 537.
upholstery nozzle. 234.
upper. 546.
upper berth. 407.
upper blade guard. 253.
upper bowl. 224.
upper chord. 401.
upper cold front. 53.
upper cuff. 546.
upper deck. 420.
upper edge. 529.
upper eyelid. 86, 97, 123.
upper floor. 178, 179.
upper fore topgallant sail. 417.
upper fore topsail. 417.
upper gill arch. 90.
upper girdle facet. 317.
upper heating element. 263.
upper level. 426.
upper limb. 677.
upper lip. 126, 468.
upper lobe. 118.
upper mandible. 87.
upper mantle. 39.
upper rudder. 424.
upper shell. 546.
upper side-rail. 388.
upper sphere clamp. 56.
upper support screw. 56.
upper tail covert. 87.
upper thermostat. 263.
upper warm front. 53.
upperboard. 468.
upperworks. 539.
upright. 494, 495, 499, 500, 556, 557, 559, 560, 616.
upright piano. 465.
upright piano action. 466.
upstage. 169, 170.
upstream blanket. 638.
upstream face. 638.
upstream gate. 426.
upstream level. 426.
upstream shoulder. 638.
upstream toe. 638.
uranary system. 120.
Uranus. 28.
ureter. 120.
urethra. 109, 120.
urinary bladder. 91, 108, 109, 120.
urinary meatus. 108.
urine transfer fitting. 444.
urogenital aperture. 91.
uropod. 95.
urostyle. 97.
use of audible warning devices prohibited. 702.
user station. 379.
uterine tube. 109.
uterovesical pouch. 109.
uterus. 109.
utilities plant. 636.
utility case. 337.
utility speaker. 376.
uvula. 125, 126.

V

V-neck. 283, 286.
V-neck cardigan. 286.
V-shaped gouge. 502.
V-shaped neck. 299.
V-shaped row. 126.
vaccuum cleaner. 234.
vacherin. 146.
vacuole. 105.

vacuum bottle. 586.
vacuum chamber. 598.
vacuum coffee maker. 224.
vacuum distillation. 635.
vacuum manifold. 606.
vagina. 109.
vagus nerve. 118.
vair. 696.
valance. 207.
valance lighting. 210.
Valençay. 144.
valley. 46, 177.
valley gutter. 177.
valve. 71, 93, 334, 426, 470, 625.
valve casing. 470.
valve seat. 261.
valve seat shaft. 258.
valve seat wrench. 266.
valve slide. 470.
valve spring. 390, 391.
vambrace. 676.
vamp. 308.
vane. 88, 177, 231, 692.
vanity mirror. 385.
variable depth sonar. 425.
variable spacer. 453.
variable sweep wing. 435.
variometer. 542.
varistor. 372.
varnish-roller. 501.
vault. 165.
vaulting horse. 559, 560.
VCR pause switch. 369.
veal, North American cut. 139.
veal, Parisian cut. 139.
vegetable bowl. 213.
vegetable brush. 221.
vegetable garden. 151, 178.
vegetable kingdom. 59.
vegetable steamer. 222.
vegetables. 73, 74, 75, 76, 77.
veil. 567.
vein. 62, 622.
veins. 117.
velum. 98.
Venetian blind. 209.
venom canal. 101.
venom-conducting tube. 101.
venom gland. 101.
venomous snake's head. 101.
vent. 45, 196, 385, 680, 681.
vent brush. 328.
vent cap. 392.
vent door. 388.
vent field astragal. 680.
vent hole. 270, 541.
vent line. 265.
ventail. 676.
ventilated rib. 688.
ventilating fan. 404.
ventilation shaft. 624.
ventral aorta. 91.
ventricular septum. 116.
venturi. 686.
venturi fastening lever. 686.
Venus. 28.
vermicelli. 136.
vermiform appendix. 119.
vernal equinox. 27.
Versailles parquet. 186.
vert. 696.
vertebral column. 91, 97, 112.
vertebral shield. 101.
vertical-axis wind turbine. 658.
vertical circle. 600.
vertical clamp. 600.
vertical cord lift. 233.
vertical frame. 495.
vertical pivoting. 189.
vertical pupil. 101.
vertical seismograph. 602.
vertical shaft. 622.
vertical side band. 522.
vertical silo. 151.
vertical speed indicator. 423.
vertical stabilizer. 542.

vertical tangent screw. 600.
very cloudy sky. 53.
very large elbows. 137.
vest. 283, 305.
vest. 286, 306, 307, 311.
vest pocket. 297.
vestibular nerve. 124.
vestibule. 124, 163, 407.
vestibule door. 407.
vests. 297.
VHF aerial. 435.
VHF channel selector. 377.
viaduct. 400.
vibrating mudscreen. 626.
vibrato arm. 480.
video camera. 369.
video input. 367.
video output. 367.
video tape recorder. 367.
video technician. 374.
video/TV selector. 367.
videotape recorder. 374.
Vienna bread. 138.
Vietnamese writing system. 345.
view camera. 354.
viewfinder. 353, 368.
viewing chamber. 606.
viewing window. 606.
viewtop tab. 449.
vine leaf. 74.
vinyl grip sole. 305, 306.
vinyl insulation. 185.
viola. 463, 476.
violas. 479.
violin. 463, 464.
violin. 463, 476.
violin family. 463.
violoncello. 463, 476.
violoncellos. 479.
Virgin. 32, 33.
Virgo, the Virgin. 698.
virgule. 347.
vise. 249.
visor. 409, 444, 676.
vitelline membrane. 89.
vitreous body. 123.
vocal cord. 118.
volcanic island. 42.
volcano. 45.
volcano. 40.
volleyball. 522.
voltage stabilizer. 361.
voltage tester. 276.
voltmeter. 276.
volume control. 363, 364, 368, 373, 480.
volute. 160, 200.
volva. 65.
voussoir. 162.
vowels. 348.
VU meter. 481.
VU meter switch. 481.
vulva. 109.

W

wad. 681, 688.
waders. 568.
wading bird. 89.
waffle. 147.
wagon tent. 583.
waist. 107, 463, 644.
waistband. 284, 287, 291.
waistband extension. 284.
waiting room. 412.
walking aids. 616.
walking cam. 661.
walking leg. 95.
walking shoe. 661.
walking stick. 616.
walkway. 661.
wall. 30, 69, 85, 393, 551, 552, 579, 582, 622.
wall and rails. 551, 552.
wall fitting. 210.

wall lantern. 211.
wall register. 192.
wall stack section. 192.
wall stud. 182.
wall tent. 583.
wallet. 341.
walnut. 70.
walnut, section of a. 70.
wand. 234.
waning crescent. 30.
waning gibbous. 30.
wapiti. 81.
wardrobe. 206, 582.
warhead. 692.
warm air. 655.
warm-air comb. 328.
warming plate. 224.
warning plate. 251.
warp. 494, 495.
warp beam. 494.
warp thread. 497.
warping reel. 496.
wash tower. 232.
washer. 230, 262.
washer. 254, 261.
washery. 624.
washing. 708.
WASP helicopter. 425.
Wassily chair. 200.
waste pipe. 258.
waste stack. 257.
waste tee. 262.
watch. 591, 592.
watch pocket. 283.
watchcase. 591.
Water Bearer. 33.
water bottle. 397.
water bottle clip. 397.
water cress. 74.
water ditch. 556.
water forms. 49.
water goblet. 212.
water hazard. 571.
water hose. 625.
water intake. 641.
water jug. 586.
water jump. 551, 552.
water key. 470.
water level selector. 230.
water meter. 257.
Water Monster. 32, 33.
water pitcher. 213.
water polo. 531.
water pressure gauge. 663.
water pump. 392.
water reservoir. 624.
water service pipe. 257.
water skiing. 540.
Water Snake. 33.
water table. 46.
water tank. 404, 407.
water treatment plant. 647.
waterfall. 46.
watering can. 240.
waterline. 425.
watermelon. 73.
waterproof pants. 305.
watertight bulkhead. 631.
watt-hour meter. 601.
wave. 43.
wave base. 43.
wave clip. 333.
wave height. 43.
wave lenght. 43.
wave wall. 638.
wavy hair. 320.
wax plate. 98.
wax seal. 258.
waxing crescent. 30.
waxing gibbous. 30.
weapon, parts of the. 563.
weapons. 673.
weather map. 54.
weather radar. 434.
weather symbols, international. 52, 53.

weatherboard. 188, 189.
weaves, basic. 497.
weaving. 494, 495, 496, 497.
weaving accessories. 495.
weaving brush. 492.
weaving principle, diagram of. 497.
web. 89, 408, 512.
web frame. 631.
web member. 180.
webbed toe. 97.
webbing. 493.
wedding band. 315.
wedge. 468, 680.
wedge iron. 247.
wedge lever. 247.
weeder. 239.
weeding hoe. 238.
weekender. 337.
weft. 494.
weft thread. 497.
Wehnelt cylinder. 606.
weighing platform. 596.
weight. 558, 561, 593, 594, 596.
weight, measure of. 594, 595, 596.
weight belt. 536.
weight limitation. 702.
weightlifter. 561.
weightlifting. 561.
weld bead. 271, 272.
welding. 271, 272, 273.
welding curtain. 273.
welding torch. 272.
welding torch. 271.
well. 151.
Welsh writing system. 345.
welt. 308.
welt pocket. 286, 294.
weskit. 297.
West. 579.
West Coast mirror. 389.
West wind. 579.
wet dock. 427.
wet snow. 49.
wet suit. 536.
Whale. 32, 33.
whale boat. 418.
wheel. 393.
wheel. 337, 383, 487, 507, 548, 680, 690.
wheel chock. 439.
wheel cylinder. 393.
wheel head. 505.
wheel lock. 617.
wheel tractor. 665.
wheelbarrow. 241.
wheelchair. 617.
wheels. 137.
whelk. 96.
whipping. 572.
whisk. 220.
whiskers. 86.
whistle buoy. 430.
White. 577, 578.
white balance control. 369.
white cabbage. 74.
white cap. 531.
white cue ball. 570.
white dragon. 579.
white flag. 531, 564.
white line. 85.
white spot ball. 569.
white square. 531.
white-tailed deer. 81.
white tape. 528, 529.
white wine. 212.
whiteface. 312.
whole loin. 139, 143.
whole note. 461.
whole rest. 461.
whole wheat bread. 138.
wholemeal bread. 138.
whorl. 93.
wicket gate. 643.
wide angle adapter. 357.
wide-angle lens. 355.
width. 534.

width clearance. 702.
wife. 130, 131.
wigs. 321.
wigwam. 159.
wild animals crossing. 701.
wild blackberry, section of a. 66.
winch. 420, 425, 539, 661, 690.
wind. 53.
wind. 47, 539.
wind abeam. 539.
wind arrow. 53.
wind baffle. 585.
wind chest. 467.
wind deflector. 389.
wind direction. 54.
wind direction and speed. 54.
wind duct. 467.
wind indicator. 538.
wind instruments. 469, 470.
wind scale. 53.
wind speed. 53, 54, 55.
wind trunk. 467, 468.
wind turbine. 658.
wind turbine electricity production. 658.
wind vane. 55.
windage adjusting screw. 607.
windbreaker. 291.
winder. 496.
winding mechanism. 209.
winding mechanism. 593.
winding tower. 624.
windlass. 422.
windmill. 657.
window. 189.
window. 177, 178, 227, 228, 341, 383, 415, 434, 537, 582.
window accessories. 207, 208, 209.
window regulator handle. 386.
windows, types of. 189.
windscreen. 34.
windshaft. 657.
windshield. 383, 389, 394, 437, 691.
windshield wiper. 384.
windshield wiper blade. 384.
windsock. 697.
wine cellar. 419.
wine waiter corkscrew. 219.
wing. 88.
wing. 87, 100, 140, 434, 443, 542, 543, 567, 676.
wing box. 691.
wing covert. 87.
wing membrane. 100.
wing nut. 254.
wing nut. 252.
wing pallet. 671.
wing rib. 435.
wing shape. 435.
wing slat. 434.
wing structure. 435.
wing tank. 631.
wing tip. 435, 542.
wing vein. 92.
wing wire. 543.
wings. 169.
winning line. 581.
winter. 27.
winter solstice. 27.
winze. 622.
wiper. 384.
wiper arm. 384.
wiper switch. 386.
wippen. 466.
wire. 393, 546, 558.
wire beater. 225.
wire brushes. 471.
wire cutter. 249, 277.
wire sling. 574.
wire stripper. 277.
wire support. 585.
wishbone boom. 537.
withers. 83.
wok. 223.

wok set. 223.
Wolf. 33.
women's apparatus. 560.
women's clothing. 290, 291, 292, 293, 294, 295, 296, 297, 298, 299, 300, 301, 302, 303, 304.
women's pompadour. 321.
wood. 572.
wood. 184.
wood-based panel. 255.
wood block. 504.
wood chip car. 406.
wood engraving. 502.
wood flooring. 186.
wood flooring arrangements. 186.
wood ray. 63.
wood stove. 191.
woodcut. 502.
wooden bar. 559.
wooden modeling tools. 505.
woodwind family. 469.
woofer. 363.
word processing key. 456.
work drawing. 507.
work lead. 271.
worker. 98.
worker, hind legs of the. 98.
working area. 35.
working pressure gauge. 272.
workshop. 179.
workshop store. 634.
worm. 475, 496, 681.
worm gear. 209.
wrap dress. 292.
wrap over top. 295.
wraparound diaper shirt. 305.
wraparound skirt. 293.
wrapper. 334.
wrenches. 248.
wrist. 100, 107.
wrist pad. 516.
wrist sling. 574.
wrist strap. 339, 340, 369, 547.
wristband. 524.
writing brush. 352.
writing case. 340.
writing instruments. 352.
writing systems. 345.
wye branch. 265.

X

X-15 (USA). 39.
xylophone. 471.
xylophone. 479.

Y

yard. 411.
yard. 416.
yard line. 513.
yard office. 411.
yarn. 587.
yarn clip. 491.
yarn feeder. 492.
yarn rod. 491.
yaw axis. 378.
yaw nozzle. 57.
yellow ball. 570.
yoke. 208, 285, 295.
yoke skirt. 293.
yolk. 89.
yurt. 159.

Z

zenith. 35.
zest. 69.
zester. 217.
zipper. 488.
zipper. 305, 306, 307, 332, 336, 337, 338, 583.
zipper line. 489.
zipper pocket. 340.

THEMATIC INDEXES

ANIMAL KINGDOM

abdomen. 92, 95, 98.
abdominal segment. 92.
adductor muscle. 94.
afterfeather. 88.
air bladder. 91.
air hole. 99.
air space. 89.
albumen. 89.
alighting board. 99.
alula. 88.
anal fin. 90.
anal proleg. 92.
animal kingdom. 79.
antenna. 92, 95, 98.
antennule. 95.
anterior end. 93.
anus. 91, 94.
aperture. 93.
apex. 93, 96.
aquatic bird. 89.
arm. 83.
auricle. 98.
auricular. 87.
axial rib. 93.
back. 83, 87.
bar. 85.
barb. 88.
bat. 100.
batrachian. 97.
bay antler. 81.
beam. 81.
beaver. 82.
belly. 83, 87.
bills, principal types of. 89.
bird. 87, 88, 89.
bird, morphology. 87.
bird of prey. 89.
blastodisc. 89.
blood vessels. 100.
blue mussel. 94.
body whorl. 93.
brain. 91.
branch. 85.
breast. 87.
brood cell. 99.
brood chamber. 99.
brow tine. 81.
bulb. 85.
burr. 81.
butterfly. 92.
buttress. 85.
calamus. 88.
calcaneus. 84.
calcar. 100.
callus. 93.
Canadian elk. 81.
canine. 82.
cannon. 83.
carapace. 95, 101.
caribou. 81.
carnassial. 82.
carnivore's jaw. 82.
carpal pad. 86.
carpus. 84.

cat. 86.
cat, head. 86.
caterpillar. 92.
caudal fin. 90.
caudal vertebrae. 84.
cell. 92.
cephalothorax. 95.
cervical vertebrae. 84.
chalaza. 89.
cheek. 83.
chest. 83.
chestnut. 83.
chin. 87.
clam. 94.
claw. 86.
claw. 87, 89, 92, 95, 98, 100.
cockle. 94.
columella. 93.
columella fold. 93.
comb foundation. 99.
common periwinkle. 96.
compound eye. 92, 98.
contour feather. 88.
coronal tine. 81.
coronet. 83.
costal shield. 101.
coxa. 92, 98.
crab. 95.
crayfish. 95.
cremaster. 92.
crenulate margin. 93.
croup. 83.
crown. 87.
crustacean. 95.
deer, kinds of. 81.
deer antlers. 81.
deer family. 81.
dew claw. 86.
dew pad. 86.
diastema. 82.
digestive gland. 94.
digit. 86, 97.
digital pad. 86.
distal phalanx. 86.
distal sesamoid. 84.
dorsal aorta. 91.
drone. 98.
ear. 100.
edible crustaceans, principal. 95.
edible gastropods, principal. 96.
edible mollusks, principal. 94.
egg. 89.
egg. 99.
eggs. 91, 97.
elastic ligament. 86, 94.
elbow. 83, 100.
elk. 81.
entrance. 99.
entrance slide. 99.
escutcheon. 93.
esophagus. 91, 94.
excretory pore. 96.
external gills. 97.
eye. 96, 101.
eye ring. 87.
eye-socket. 83.

eyeball. 97.
eyebrow stripe. 87.
eyelashes. 86.
eyelid. 101.
eyestalk. 96.
fang. 101.
feet, principal types of. 89.
femur. 84, 92, 97, 98, 100.
fetlock. 83.
fetlock joint. 83.
first dorsal fin. 90.
fish. 90, 91.
fish, anatomy. 91.
fish, morphology. 90.
flank. 83, 87.
foot. 87, 96, 100.
fore leg. 92, 98.
fore wing. 92, 98.
forehead. 87.
foreleg. 86.
forelimb. 97.
forelock. 83.
fork. 81.
forked tongue. 101.
frame. 99.
frog. 97.
frog. 85.
frog, life cycle of the. 97.
gall bladder. 91.
gaskin. 83.
gastropod. 96.
genital pore. 96.
gill cover. 90.
gill filament. 90.
gill raker. 90.
gills. 90.
gills. 91, 94.
granivorous bird. 89.
great scallop. 94.
greater covert. 88.
growth line. 93, 96.
gutter. 81.
hard shell clam. 94.
head. 92, 96, 98.
heart. 91, 94.
heel. 85.
heel calk. 85.
hemibranch. 90.
herbivore's jaw. 82.
hind leg. 92, 100.
hind limb. 97.
hind toe. 87, 89.
hind wing. 92.
hindlimb, skeleton fo the. 97.
hing leg. 98.
hing wing. 98.
hinge tooth. 93.
hive. 99.
hive body. 99.
hock. 83.
honey cell. 99.
honeybee. 98, 99.
honeycomb section. 99.
hoof. 85.
hoof. 83.
hoof, plantar surface of the. 85.

horns. 96.
horny beak. 101.
horse. 82, 83, 84, 85.
horse, morphology. 83.
horse, skeleton. 84.
horseshoe. 85.
humerus. 84, 100.
incisor. 82.
inferior umbilicus. 88.
inner edge. 85.
inner lip. 93.
inner toe. 87.
insectivorous bird. 89.
interfemoral membrane. 100.
intestine. 91, 94.
jaws, types of. 82.
kidney. 91.
knee. 83, 100.
labial palp. 92.
larva. 99.
lateral furrow. 85.
lateral line. 90.
leg. 101.
leopard. 82.
lesser covert. 88.
libial palp. 94.
limpet. 96.
lip. 86.
liver. 91.
lobate web. 89.
lobe. 89.
lobster. 95.
loin. 83.
lore. 87.
lower eyelid. 86, 97.
lower gill arch. 90.
lower mandible. 87.
lumbar vertebrae. 84.
lunule. 93.
malar region. 87.
mandible. 84, 90, 92, 95, 98.
mane. 83.
mantle. 96.
mantle edge. 94.
marginal shield. 101.
maxilla. 90, 95.
maxilliped. 95.
median furrow. 85.
mesothorax. 92.
metacarpal. 100.
metacarpus. 84, 86.
metatarsus. 84, 97.
metathorax. 92.
middle covert. 88.
middle leg. 92, 98.
middle phalanx. 86.
middle primary covert. 88.
middle toe. 87.
molar. 82.
mollusk. 94.
moose. 81.
mouth. 94, 96, 97.
mouthparts. 98.
movable maxillary. 101.
muscle scar. 93.
muscle segment. 91.

The terms in *italic* indicate the title of an illustration; those in **bold type** correspond to a chapter.

muzzle. 86.
nail. 95, 101.
nail hole. 85.
nape. 87.
naris. 97.
neck. 83, 101.
neural spine. 91.
nictitating membrane. 86.
nose. 83.
nose leaf. 100.
nose leather. 86.
nostril. 83, 87, 90, 101.
nuchal shield. 101.
nuclear whorl. 93.
ocelli. 92.
olfactory bulb. 91.
olfactory nerve. 91.
operculum. 90, 97.
otolith. 91.
outer edge. 85.
outer lip. 93.
outer toe. 87.
ovary. 91.
oyster. 94.
pallial line. 93.
pallial sinus. 93.
palm. 81.
palmar pad. 86.
pastern. 83.
patella. 84.
pearl. 81.
pecten. 98.
pectoral fin. 90.
pedicle. 81.
pelvic fin. 90.
pelvic girdle. 97.
pelvis. 84.
perching bird. 89.
periople. 85.
phalange. 84.
phalanxes. 97.
plantar pad. 86.
plastron. 101.
pneumostome. 96.
pollen basket. 98.
pollen brush. 98.
pollen cell. 99.
pollen packer. 98.
position of the ligament. 93.
posterior end. 93.
premaxilla. 90.
premolar. 82.
primaries. 88.
primary covert. 88.
proboscis. 92.
proleg. 92.
prothorax. 92.
proximal phalanx. 86.
proximal sesamoid. 84.
pupa. 92.
pupil. 86.
pygal shield. 101.
pyloric caecum. 91.
quarter. 85.
queen. 98.
queen cell. 99.
queen excluder. 99.
rachis. 88.
radius. 84, 100.
razor clam. 94.
reindeer. 81.
reptile. 101.
ribs. 84.
rodent's jaw. 82.
roe deer. 81.
roof. 99.
rostrum. 95.
royal antler. 81.
rump. 87.
sacral vertebrae. 84.
scale. 89, 90, 101.
scallop. 94.
scampi. 95.
scapula. 84.
scapular. 88.
sealed cell. 99.

second dorsal fin. 90.
secondaries. 88.
sheath. 83.
shell. 89, 94, 96, 101.
shell, bivalve. 93.
shell, univalve. 93.
shell membrane. 89.
shoulder. 83.
shrimp. 95.
side wall. 85.
siphonal canal. 93.
skin. 97.
skull. 84, 91.
snail. 96.
snout. 97.
soft ray. 90.
soft shell clam. 94.
sole. 85.
spinal cord. 91.
spine. 93.
spiny lobster. 95.
spiny ray. 90.
spiracle. 92.
spiral rib. 93.
spire. 93, 96.
spleen. 91.
stalked eye. 95.
sternum. 84.
stiffle. 83.
sting. 98.
stomach. 91, 94.
super. 99.
superior umbilicus. 88.
surroyal antler. 81.
suture. 93.
swimmeret. 95.
tail. 95, 100, 101.
tail feather. 87.
tarsus. 84, 87, 92, 97, 98.
telson. 95.
tendon. 86.
tentacle. 96.
tertial. 88.
thigh. 83, 87.
thoracic leg. 92.
thoracic vertebrae. 84.
thorax. 92, 98.
throat. 87.
thumb. 100.
tibia. 84, 92, 98, 100.
tibiofibula. 97.
toe. 85, 89.
toe clip. 85.
tongue. 91.
tongue sheath. 101.
tooth. 101.
tragus. 100.
trochanter. 92, 98.
tubercles. 93.
turtle. 101.
tympanum. 97, 101.
umbilicus. 93.
umbo. 93.
under tail covert. 87.
upper eyelid. 86, 97.
upper gill arch. 90.
upper mandible. 87.
upper tail covert. 87.
urinary bladder. 91.
urogenital aperture. 91.
uropod. 95.
urostyle. 97.
valve. 93.
vane. 88.
velum. 98.
venom canal. 101.
venom-conducting tube. 101.
venom gland. 101.
venomous snake's head. 101.
ventral aorta. 91.
vertebral column. 91, 97.
vertebral shield. 101.
vertical pupil. 101.
vitelline membrane. 89.
wading bird. 89.
walking leg. 95.

wall. 85.
wapiti. 81.
wax plate. 98.
web. 89.
webbed toe. 97.
whelk. 96.
whiskers. 86.
white line. 85.
white-tailed deer. 81.
whorl. 93.
wing. 88.
wing. 87, 100.
wing covert. 87.
wing membrane. 100.
wing vein. 92.
withers. 83.
worker. 98.
worker, hind legs of the. 98.
wrist. 100.
yolk. 89.

ARCHITECTURE

abacus. 160.
abutment. 165.
acanthus leaf. 160.
acoustic ceiling. 169.
acroterion. 161.
aisle. 164.
ambulatory. 164.
annulet. 160.
antefix. 161.
apse. 164.
apsidiole. 164.
arcade. 164.
arch. 165.
arches. 162.
arches, types of. 162.
architectural styles. 160.
architecture. 157.
architrave. 160.
archivolt. 165.
astragal. 160.
atrium. 163.
backdrop. 170.
bailey. 167.
balustrade. 172.
barbette. 166.
barbican. 167.
bartizan. 167.
base. 160.
basket-handle. 162.
bastion. 166.
batten. 170.
battlement. 167.
belfry. 164.
bell tower. 165.
below-stage. 170.
billboard. 168.
box. 169.
box front lights. 169.
brattice. 167.
building. 168.
bungalow. 173.
bus stop. 168.
buttress. 164, 165.
capital. 160.
caponiere. 166.
car. 171.
car buffer. 171.
car guide rail. 171.
car safety device. 171.
castle. 167.
cathedral. 164.
chemise. 167.
choir. 164.
city houses. 173.
column base. 160.
comb plate. 172.
compensating cables. 171.
compluvium. 163.
condominium. 173.
controller. 171, 172.
corbel. 167.
corinthian order. 160.

corner tower. 167.
cornice. 161.
cottage. 173.
counterguard. 166.
counterscarp. 166.
counterweight. 171.
counterweight guide rail. 171.
covered parapet walk. 167.
covered postern. 166.
covered way. 166.
crenel. 167.
crepidoma. 161.
crossing. 164.
cubiculum. 163.
curtain. 166.
cut. 170.
demilune. 166.
dentil. 160.
department store. 168.
diagonal buttress. 165.
door operator. 171.
doric order. 160.
downtown. 168.
drawbridge. 167.
drive sheave. 171.
drum. 160.
duplex. 173.
echinus. 160.
electric motor. 172.
elevator. 171.
embrasure. 166.
entablature. 160.
equilateral. 162.
escalator. 172.
euthynteria. 161.
extrados. 162.
façade. 165.
face. 166.
fascia. 160.
fillet. 160.
final limit cam. 171.
final limit switch. 171.
final limit witch. 171.
flank. 166.
flanking tower. 167.
flies. 170.
flight. 165.
floor selector. 171.
fluting. 160.
flying buttress. 164, 165.
footlights. 170.
formeret. 165.
fortification, Vauban. 166.
frieze. 160.
gable. 165.
gallery. 165, 169.
garden. 163.
glacis. 166.
gorge. 166.
gothic cathedral. 164, 165.
governor. 171.
Greek temple. 161.
Greek temple, basic plan of the.
161.
grid. 170.
grill. 161.
ground sill. 166.
guardhouse. 167.
guttae. 160.
hall. 169.
handrail. 172.
handrail drive. 172.
high-rise apartment. 173.
hoarding. 167.
hoist. 170.
hoist ropes. 171.
horseshoe. 162.
hut. 159.
igloo. 159.
impluvium. 163.
impost. 162.
inner rail. 172.
intrados. 162.
ionic order. 160.
iron curtain. 170.
isba. 159.

keep. 167.
keystone. 162, 165.
kitchen. 163.
Lady chapel. 164.
lancet. 162.
lintel. 165.
litter basket. 168.
lookout tower. 167.
loophole. 167.
louver-board. 165.
lower landing plate. 172.
machicolation. 167.
main drive chain. 172.
main drive shaft. 172.
main street. 168.
merlon. 167.
metope. 160.
mezzanine. 169.
moat. 166, 167.
modillion. 160.
motor generator. 171.
motor generator set. 171.
mutule. 160.
naos. 161.
narthex. 164.
nave. 164.
neon sign. 168.
news dealer. 168.
ogee. 162.
opisthodomos. 161.
opposite prompt side. 169.
orchestra pit. 170.
orchestra seat. 169.
order. 165.
outer rail. 172.
parade ground. 166.
parapet walk. 167.
parking meter. 168.
parterre. 169.
pedestrian crossing. 168.
pediment. 161.
peristyle. 161, 163.
pier. 162.
piers. 165.
pillar. 165.
pinnacle. 164, 165.
plan. 164.
porch. 164.
portal. 165.
post. 168.
postern. 167.
prompt box. 170.
prompt side. 169.
pronaos. 161.
proscenium. 170.
quadriplex. 173.
ramp. 161.
rampart. 166, 167.
redan. 166.
redoubt. 166.
retrenchment. 166.
roller guides. 171.
Roman house. 163.
rose window. 165.
rosette. 160.
salient angle. 166.
scarp. 166, 167.
scottia. 160.
seat. 169.
second balcony. 169.
secondary sheave. 171.
semi-detached cottage. 173.
semi-detached triplex. 173.
semicircular arch. 162.
shaft. 160.
shop. 163.
shop window. 168.
side chapel. 164.
sima. 160.
slip. 170.
sloping cornice. 161.
slot. 170.
spandrel. 162.
spire. 164.
splay. 165.
springer. 162.

stage. 170.
stage, cross section of a. 170.
stage curtain. 170.
stage-house. 170.
statue. 161.
step. 172.
step chain. 172.
stilted. 162.
stockade. 167.
street café. 168.
street light. 168.
street sign. 168.
stylobate. 161.
subway entrance. 168.
tablinum. 163.
taxi stand. 168.
taxi telephone. 168.
telephone booth. 168.
tenaille. 166.
tepee. 159.
terminal stopping switch cam. 171.
terminal stopping witch. 171.
terrace. 168.
terreplein. 166.
theater. 169, 170.
theater. 168.
tile. 161.
timber. 161.
torus. 160.
tower. 164.
town house. 173.
tracery. 165.
trade sign. 168.
traditional houses. 159.
traffic island. 168.
traffic light. 168.
transept. 164.
traveling cabies. 171.
traverse arch. 165.
trefoil. 162, 165.
triclinium. 163.
triforium. 164, 165.
triglyph. 160.
triplex. 173.
truss. 172.
Tudor. 162.
turret. 167.
tympanum. 161, 165.
upstage. 169, 170.
vault. 165.
vestibule. 163.
volute. 160.
voussoir. 162.
wigwam. 159.
wings. 169.
yurt. 159.

ASTRONOMY

air intake. 34.
air space. 34.
airlock. 34.
Altar. 33.
Andromeda. 32.
annular eclipse. 29.
antarctic circle. 27.
arch. 34.
Archer. 33.
arctic circle. 27.
Arrow. 32.
asteroids. 28.
astronomical observatory. 34.
astronomy. 25.
auditorium. 35.
autumn. 27.
autumnal equinox. 27.
auxiliary projector. 35.
Balance. 33.
barred spiral galaxy. 31.
bay. 30.
Berenice's Hair. 32.
Big Dog. 33.
Bird of Paradise. 33.
bright star projector. 35.
Bull. 32.

Callisto. 28.
Cassiopeia. 32.
celestial coordinate system. 27.
celestial equator. 27.
celestial meridian. 27.
celestial sphere. 27.
Centaur. 33.
Cepheus. 32.
Chameleon. 33.
Charioteer. 32.
chromosphere. 29.
cirque. 30.
cliff. 30.
collar. 35.
coma. 31.
comet. 31.
Compass. 33.
constellations of the northern
  hemisphere. 32.
constellations of the southern
  hemisphere. 33.
control console. 35.
control room. 35.
convection zone. 29.
core. 29.
corona. 29.
Crab. 32.
Crane. 33, 34.
crater. 30.
Crow. 33.
Cup. 33.
declination. 27.
declination axis. 34.
Deimos. 28.
Dolphin. 32.
dome shutter. 34.
Dove. 33.
Dragon. 32.
dust tail. 31.
Eagle. 32, 33.
Earth. 28, 29, 30.
Earth coordinate system. 27.
east-to-west axis. 35.
elliptical galaxy. 31.
equator. 27.
Europa. 28.
exterior dome shell. 34.
faculae. 29.
far side. 30.
filament. 29.
first quarter. 30.
fish-eye lens. 35.
Fishes. 32.
flare. 29.
flat mirror. 34.
Fly. 33.
Flying Fish. 33.
full Moon. 30.
Furnace. 33.
galaxies, classification of. 31.
galaxy. 31.
Ganymede. 28.
gas tail. 31.
Giraffe. 32.
girder. 34.
granulation. 29.
Great Bear. 32.
Hare. 32.
Harp. 32.
head. 31.
hemispherical dome. 35.
Hercules. 32.
Herdsman. 32.
high-power light bulb. 35.
horseshoe mount. 34.
hour angle gear. 34.
Hunting Dogs. 32.
hydrostatic pad. 34.
Indian. 33.
interchangeable end assembly. 34.
interior dome shell. 34.
Io. 28.
irregular galaxy. 31.
Jupiter. 28.
lake. 30.
last quarter. 30.

latitude. 27.
lenticular galaxy. 31.
Lion. 32.
Lizard. 32.
longitude. 27.
lunar eclipse. 30.
lunar features. 30.
Lynx. 32.
Mars. 28.
Mercury. 28.
meridian. 27.
Milky Way. 32.
Milky Way projector. 35.
Moon. 30.
Moon. 28, 29, 30.
Moon, phases of the. 30.
Moon's orbit. 30.
mountain range. 30.
near side. 30.
Neptune. 28.
Net. 33.
new Moon. 30.
North celestial pole. 27.
North pole. 27.
Northern Crown. 32.
northern hemisphere. 27.
nucleus. 31.
ocean. 30.
Octant. 33.
optical axis. 35.
Orion. 32, 33.
partial eclipse. 29, 30.
Peacock. 33.
Pegasus. 32.
penumbra. 30.
penumbra shadow. 29.
Perseus. 32.
Phobos. 28.
Phoenix. 33.
photosphere. 29.
planet projection system. 35.
planetarium. 35.
planetarium projector. 35.
planetarium projector. 35.
planets of the solar system. 28.
Pluto. 28.
polar axis. 34.
Pole Star. 32.
primary mirror. 34.
prime focus. 34.
prime focus observing capsule. 34.
projection gallery. 35.
projection room. 35.
prominence. 29.
radiation zone. 29.
Ram. 32.
right ascension. 27.
rigid frame. 35.
riser. 35.
River Eridanus. 33.
rotating dome. 34.
rotating dome truck. 34.
Scorpion. 33.
Sculptor. 33.
sea. 30.
Sea Goat. 33.
seasons of the year. 27.
Shield. 33.
Ship's Keel. 33.
Ship's Sails. 33.
Ship's Stern. 33.
Small Bear. 32.
Small Dog. 32.
Small Horse. 32.
Small Lion. 32.
Snake. 32, 33.
Snake Bearer. 32, 33.
solar eclipse. 29.
South celestial pole. 27.
South pole. 27.
Southern Cross. 33.
Southern Crown. 33.
Southern Fish. 33.
southern hemisphere. 27.
Southern Triangle. 33.
speaker. 35.

spicule. 29.
spiral arms. 31.
spiral galaxy. 31.
spring. 27.
stage. 35.
star projection condenser. 35.
star projection lens. 35.
star sphere. 35.
summer. 27.
summer solstice. 27.
Sun. 29.
Sun. 27, 28, 29, 30.
Sun, structure of the. 29.
sunspot. 29.
Swan. 32.
Swordfish. 33.
symbols of the planets. 28.
Telescope. 33.
telescope base. 34.
telescope control room. 34.
terrestrial sphere. 27.
Titan. 28.
total eclipse. 29, 30.
Toucan. 33.
Triangle. 32.
Triton. 28.
tropic of Cancer. 27.
tropic of Capricorn. 27.
Twins. 32.
umbra. 30.
umbra shadow. 29.
Unicorn. 33.
Uranus. 28.
Venus. 28.
vernal equinox. 27.
Virgin. 32, 33.
wall. 30.
waning crescent. 30.
waning gibbous. 30.
Water Bearer. 33.
Water Monster. 32, 33.
Water Snake. 33.
waxing crescent. 30.
waxing gibbous. 30.
Whale. 32, 33.
windscreen. 34.
winter. 27.
winter solstice. 27.
Wolf. 33.
working area. 35.
zenith. 35.

CLOTHING

accordion pleat. 294.
adjustable waist tab. 283.
adjustable waistband. 307.
adjustment slide. 284.
ankle length. 287.
anklet. 301.
arm slit. 291.
armhole. 287, 296.
ascot tie. 285.
athletic shirt. 287.
baby doll. 301.
back. 283, 294.
back belt. 290.
back pack. 312.
back pocket. 284.
ballerina. 311.
ballerina. 287.
balloon pants. 312.
barrel cuff. 296.
bateau neck. 299.
bathing wrap. 305.
bathrobe. 301.
batwing sleeve. 296.
bellows pocket. 294, 297.
belt. 284.
belt. 281.
belt buckle. 281.
belt loop. 281, 306.
beret. 304.
Bermuda shorts. 300.
bertha collar. 298.

bib. 305.
bib. 300, 306.
big bowtie. 312.
bikini. 303.
bikini briefs. 287.
binding. 288.
bishop sleeve. 296.
blanket sleepers. 305.
blazer. 297.
bloomers. 307.
blouses. 295.
blucher oxford. 310.
boa. 299.
boater. 304.
body shirt. 295.
body stocking. 307.
body suit. 302.
bolero. 297.
bonnet. 305.
boot jack. 310.
bottom of collar. 295.
bow. 288.
bow collar. 298.
bow tie. 285.
box pleat. 294.
boxer shorts. 287.
bra. 303.
bracelet length. 289.
brassiere cup. 303.
break line. 298.
breast dart. 282.
breast pocket. 282, 285, 295.
breast welt pocket. 283.
briefelette. 302.
briefs. 287.
briefs. 303.
brim. 288, 304.
broad welt. 290.
broad welt side pocket. 281, 294.
buckle. 284.
bulb. 312.
bullfighter. 311.
bunting bag. 306.
button. 285.
button loop. 284.
button straps. 306.
buttondown collar. 285.
buttoned placket. 285, 291, 295.
buttonhole. 281, 285, 286.
cable. 312.
camisole. 302.
cap. 288, 304.
cap sleeve. 296.
cape. 291.
cape. 311.
cardigan. 286, 297.
cartwheel hat. 304.
center back vent. 283.
children's clothing. 305, 306, 307.
christening set. 305.
chukka. 310.
classic. 295.
climbing iron. 310.
clip. 284.
cloche. 304.
clog. 309.
clothing. 279.
clown. 312.
clown shoe. 312.
coat. 283.
coat dress. 292.
coats. 290, 291.
collar. 298.
collar. 281, 283, 285.
collar point. 285, 298.
collar stay. 285.
collaret. 298.
collars, types of. 298.
combination. 287.
cordless shoe care kit. 310.
corsage. 307.
corselet. 302.
corset. 303.
costumes. 311, 312.
counter. 308.
cowl collar. 298.

crease. 284.
crew neck. 305.
crew neck sweater. 286.
crew sweater. 297.
crisscross back straps overall. 306.
crotch. 287.
crotch piece. 295.
crown. 288, 304.
crusader cap. 304.
crusader hood. 304.
cuff. 284, 285, 308.
culotte. 293.
cutaway armhole. 296.
décolleté bra. 303.
diaper. 305.
diving suit. 312.
dog ear collar. 298.
dome fastener. 289.
dome shoulder closure. 306.
domed adjustable strap. 306.
domed front. 306.
domed inseam. 306.
domed snap side. 305.
domed waist. 305.
doubel breasted buttoning. 291.
double-breasted buttoning. 281.
double-breasted jacket. 283.
draped neck. 299.
draped neckline. 299.
drawers. 287.
drawstring. 311.
drawstring hood. 307.
dress. 305.
dresses. 292.
drop waist dress. 292.
duffle coat. 282.
ear flap. 288.
elastic ankle. 307.
elastic leg opening. 305, 307.
elastic waistband. 305.
elastic webbing. 284.
elastic wristband. 307.
elasticized leg opening. 287.
epaulet. 283, 311.
epaulet sleeve. 296.
espadrille. 309.
Eton jacket. 307.
Eton suit. 307.
executive length. 287.
eyelet. 308.
eyelet tab. 308.
facing. 283.
fall. 305.
false tuck. 305.
felt hat. 288.
felt hat. 304.
flap. 288.
flap pocket. 282, 283, 294.
flap side pocket. 283.
fly. 284, 287.
fly front closing. 290, 307.
foot. 305, 306.
footstrap. 300.
foundation slip. 302.
fourchette. 289.
frame. 284.
French cuff. 296.
frog. 282, 298, 311.
front. 283, 285.
front apron. 285.
front top pocket. 300.
garrison cap. 288.
garter. 302, 303.
garter belt. 303.
gather. 295.
gather skirt. 293.
gauchos. 300.
gauntlet. 289.
glass port. 312.
glove. 289.
glove finger. 289.
gloves, types of. 289.
gob hat. 304.
golf shoe. 310.
gored skirt. 293.
grow sleepers. 305.

gun flap. 281.
gym rompers. 307.
half-slip. 303.
hand warmer pocket. 291.
hand warmer pouch. 294.
hanger loop. 286.
hat. 311.
hat vell. 304.
hatband. 288.
head band. 304.
headgears. 288.
headgears, types of. 288.
headwear. 304.
heavy duty boot. 310.
heel. 287, 308.
heel grip. 308.
helmet. 312.
high-back overall. 306.
hood. 282.
hose. 301.
hoses. 301.
inset pocket. 294.
insole. 308, 310.
instep. 287.
interfacing. 285.
inverness cape. 282.
inverted pleat. 294.
jabot. 298.
jacket. 283, 311.
jeans. 300.
jewel neck. 299.
jumper. 307.
jumper. 292.
jumpsuit. 306.
jumpsuit. 306.
keeper. 281, 284.
kerchief. 304.
kick pleat. 294.
kilt. 293.
kimono. 301.
kimono sleeve. 296.
knickers. 300.
knife pleat. 294.
knit shirt. 286.
lapel. 283, 298.
leading edge. 294, 298.
leather end. 284.
leg. 287.
leg-of-mutton sleeve. 296.
lining. 283, 308.
loafer. 310.
loop. 285.
loosely tied bow. 299.
magnesium alloy. 312.
mandarin collar. 298.
mask. 312.
maternity dress. 292.
men's clothing. 281, 282, 283, 284, 285, 286, 287, 288.
mid-calf length. 287.
middle sole. 308.
middy. 295.
midriff band. 303.
mini shirtdress. 295.
mitt. 289.
mitten. 289, 307.
mob-cap. 304.
moccasin. 309.
mock pocket. 291.
modesty. 298.
narrow cuff. 296.
neckhole. 287.
necklines. 299.
necks. 299.
necktie. 285.
negligee. 301.
net stocking. 301.
nightgown. 301.
nightwear. 301.
nose of the quarter. 308.
notch. 283.
notched lapel. 281, 291, 298.
nylon rumba thights. 305.
one-bar shoe. 309.
opening. 289.
outside counter. 308.

outside ticket pocket. 283.
outsole. 308.
over-blouse. 295.
over-elbow length glove. 289.
overall. 306.
overalls. 300.
overcoat. 282, 290.
overshoe. 310.
pagoda sleeve. 296.
pajama. 301.
palazzo pants. 300.
palm. 289.
panel. 284, 303.
pants. 284, 300.
pants. 305, 311.
panty girdle. 303.
panty hose. 301.
parka. 282.
patch pocket. 290, 294, 306.
pea jacket. 291.
peak. 288.
peaked lapel. 282, 283.
pedal pusher. 300.
pelerine. 290.
perforated toe cap. 308.
perforation. 289.
Peter Pan collar. 298.
pigtail. 311.
pillbox hat. 304.
pinafore. 292.
pink stocking. 311.
placket. 298.
plastic pants. 305.
pleat skirts. 294.
plunging neckline. 299.
pocket handkerchief. 283.
pockets. 294.
pointed hat. 312.
pointed tab end. 285, 296.
polo collar. 298.
polo shirt. 295.
polojama. 307.
pompom. 304.
poncho. 291.
princess dress. 292.
princess seaming. 302.
puff sleeve. 296.
pullover. 297.
pullovers. 286, 297.
pump. 309.
punch hole. 284, 308.
push up bra. 303.
quarter. 308.
racer glove. 289.
raglan. 290.
raglan sleeve. 281, 290, 296, 306.
raincoat. 281.
rear apron. 285.
redingote. 290.
ribbing. 286, 291, 305, 306, 307.
ribbon. 311.
ridge. 294.
right side. 294.
roll. 298.
roll line. 298.
rope belt. 306.
rubber. 310.
ruching. 305.
ruffled rumba pants. 305.
ruffled skirt. 293.
safari. 297.
sailor collar. 298.
sandal. 309.
sarong. 293.
sash. 311.
schapska. 288.
screen front. 305.
screen print. 306.
seam. 289.
seam pocket. 290, 294.
seaming. 290.
section. 288.
set-in-sleeve. 281, 285, 286, 296.
shank. 308.
shawl collar. 298.
sheath dress. 292.

sheath skirt. 293.
sheepskin jacket. 282.
shirt. 285.
shirt. 311.
shirt collar. 295, 298.
shirt sleeve. 295.
shirttail. 285, 295.
shirtwaist dress. 292.
shirtwaist sleeve. 296.
shoe, parts of a. 308.
shoe horn. 310.
shoe rack. 310.
shoe tree. 310.
shoelace. 308.
shoes. 308, 309, 310.
shoes, principal types of. 309, 310.
shoeshine kit. 310.
shorts. 300.
shorty. 289.
shoulder-strap. 303.
shrink. 297.
side back vent. 283.
side pocket. 281.
single-breasted coat. 283.
ski cap. 288.
skirts. 293.
skull cap. 288.
slash pocket. 284.
sleeper. 306.
sleeve. 283.
sleeve strap. 281.
sleeve strap loop. 281.
sleeves. 296.
slims. 300.
slip. 302.
slip-stitched seam. 285.
slippers. 311.
smock. 295.
sneaker. 309.
snowsuit. 307.
sock. 287.
sock. 301.
sock lining. 308.
sole. 287, 311.
southwester. 304.
spencer. 297.
spread collar. 285.
square neck. 299.
stand. 298.
stand-up collar. 298.
steel. 303.
steel hook. 312.
stitch. 308.
stitched pleat. 294.
stitching. 289.
stocking cap. 304.
straight skirt. 293.
straight-up ribbed top. 287.
strapless brassiere. 303.
string. 282, 304.
striped trousers. 307.
sundress. 292.
suspender clip. 284.
suspenders. 284.
sweater. 297.
sweetheart neckline. 299.
T-shirt dress. 292.
T-strap shoe. 309.
tag. 308.
tailored collar. 291, 298.
tailored sleeve. 296.
tam o'shanter. 304.
tassel. 311.
telephone line. 312.
tennis shoe. 309.
thigh-high stocking. 301.
thong. 309.
three-branched air tube. 312.
three-quarter coat. 282.
three-quarter sleeve. 296.
thumb. 289.
tie. 285, 311.
tights. 305, 311.
tip. 284.
toe. 287, 311.
toe rubber. 309.

toggle fastening. 282.
tongue. 284, 308.
top collar. 283.
top hat. 288.
top lift. 308.
top stitched pleat. 294.
top stitching. 284, 306.
toque. 304.
training shoe. 309.
trench coat. 281.
tunic. 292, 295.
tunnel belt loop. 284.
turban. 304.
turn-down flap. 290.
turn-up. 300.
turtleneck. 286, 297, 298.
tutu. 311.
twin-set. 297.
two-way collar. 281.
underwear. 287, 302, 303.
underwiring. 303.
unmounted sleeve. 296.
V-neck. 283, 286.
V-neck cardigan. 286.
V-shaped neck. 299.
vamp. 308.
vest. 283, 305.
vest. 286, 306, 307, 311.
vest pocket. 297.
vests. 297.
vinyl grip sole. 305, 306.
waistband. 284, 287, 291.
waistband extension. 284.
watch pocket. 283.
waterproof pants. 305.
welt. 308.
welt pocket. 286, 294.
weskit. 297.
whiteface. 312.
windbreaker. 291.
women's clothing. 290, 291, 292,
293, 294, 295, 296, 297, 298,
299, 300, 301, 302, 303, 304.
wrap dress. 292.
wrap over top. 295.
wraparound diaper shirt. 305.
wraparound skirt. 293.
yoke. 285, 295.
yoke skirt. 293.
zipper. 305, 306, 307.

COMMUNICATIONS

Ac cord. 363, 365.
acoustic resistance. 372.
acute accent. 347.
adjustable foot. 368.
affricate consonants. 348.
air bulb release. 359.
air hole. 352.
align horizontally. 350.
align vertically. 350.
alphabet. 371.
amplifier. 374.
amplifier-tuner. 364.
analog frequency meter. 364.
ancient writing instruments. 352.
Anik. 378.
anti-skating device. 365.
aperture scale. 357.
apostrophe. 347, 350.
Arabic writing system. 345.
arm elevator. 365.
arm rest. 365.
Armenian writing system. 345.
armored cord. 373.
array elevation mechanism. 378.
ASA exposure index. 357.
asterisk. 347.
attitude acquisition. 379.
audio console. 374.
audio control room. 374.
audio input. 367.
audio operator. 374.
audio output. 367.

auto answer indicator. 373.
auto/manual aperture control. 369.
auto-manual focusing switch. 369.
automatic face control. 369.
background. 359.
balance control. 364.
ball bearing. 352.
ballpoint pen. 352.
band. 365.
band selectors. 364.
barn doors. 358.
barrel. 352.
base. 365, 377.
base of lamp. 357.
base plate. 365.
baseboard. 361.
bass tone control. 364.
battery. 357.
battery. 356.
battery check meter. 368.
bayonet mount. 353, 355.
begin a new paragraph. 350.
bellows. 361.
between-the-lens shutter. 356.
blue beam. 377.
body. 349.
boldface. 351.
boldface capitals. 351.
boom. 359.
boom operator. 375.
brackets. 347.
braille alphabet. 346.
brightness control. 377.
built-in microphone. 369.
bypass contact. 370.
cabinet. 363, 377.
cable. 369.
cable release. 359.
calculator. 357.
calculator dial. 357.
call director telephone. 373.
calls indicator. 373.
camera. 353, 376.
camera battery. 368.
camera body. 353.
camera mount. 375.
camera platform. 359.
camera screw. 359.
cameraman. 375.
cane pen. 352.
capitals. 351.
carbon copy. 349.
carbon granules. 372.
cartridge. 352, 356.
cassette. 356.
cassette holder. 366.
cassette loading slot. 367.
catwalk. 375.
cedilla. 347.
center. 350.
center hole. 365.
chad container bin. 371.
channel selector control. 367.
Chinese writing system. 345.
cine scale. 357.
cinematography. 368.
circumflex accent. 347.
clapper. 372.
clip. 352.
clock. 376.
close up. 350.
close-up lens. 355.
coil. 372.
coin return bucket. 373.
coin return knob. 373.
coin slot. 373.
coinbox telephone. 373.
collet. 359.
colon. 347.
color analyzer. 360.
color filter. 355.
color filter set. 358.
color temperature switch. 369.
column. 359, 361.
column crank. 359.
column lock. 359.

comma. 347, 350.
command antenna. 378.
communications. 343.
complimentary close. 349.
condenser. 361, 362.
cone. 363.
conical snoot. 358.
connecting cable. 363.
consonants. 348.
contact printer. 360.
contrast control. 377.
control panel. 374, 375.
control rooms. 374.
controls. 371.
converter. 358.
cooling fan. 362.
copy holder. 371.
cord. 372.
cordless telephone. 373.
correct a letter. 350.
correct a word. 350.
corrections of diacritic symbols. 350.
corrections of errors. 350.
corrections of punctuation marks. 350.
corrections of type. 350.
corrugation. 363.
counter memory button. 367.
counter reset button. 366.
counterweight. 365.
cradle. 372.
cue screen. 376.
cup. 372.
cyclorama. 375.
Danish writing system. 345.
darkroom. 360.
dash. 347.
date line. 349.
daylight film tank. 360.
daylight filter control. 368.
deaf-mute alphabet. 347.
delete. 350.
depth-of-field scale. 355.
despin. 379.
developer bath. 360.
developing film. 356.
diacritic symbols. 347.
dial. 371, 372.
diaphragm. 353, 363, 369, 372.
diffuser. 358.
diffuser filter set. 358.
digital clock. 367.
digital frequency display. 364.
dimmer control. 374.
diphthongs. 348.
disc. 356.
disc camera. 354.
distance scale. 355.
Dolby noise reduction switch. 366.
drive belt. 365.
dry mounting press. 360.
dust cover. 365.
Dutch writing system. 345.
ear cushion. 363.
earphone jack. 377.
earpiece. 372.
earth sensor. 378.
easel. 361.
eject. 367.
eject button. 366.
electric current source. 370.
electric motor. 356.
electrode. 377.
electromagnet. 370.
electron beam. 377.
electron gun. 377.
electronic flash. 357.
electronic viewfinder. 369.
electronic viewfinder display control. 369.
ellipses. 347.
enclosure line. 349.
English writing system. 345.
enlarger. 361.
enlarger. 360.

enlarger timer. 360.
enlarging lens. 361.
EP adaptor. 365.
equalizer. 363.
erase button. 373.
exclamation point. 347.
exposure control. 356.
exposure counter. 353.
exposure meter. 357.
exposure-time scale. 357.
exposure value. 357.
exposure value scale. 357.
extendible solar array. 378.
external conductive coating. 377.
extractor fan. 360.
eye cup. 368.
eyecup. 369.
eyecups. 355.
eyepiece. 356, 357.
eyepiece magnifier. 355.
faceplate. 377.
fast forward. 367.
fast-forward button. 366, 373.
fastening screw. 357.
feed tube. 352.
film advance lever. 353.
film drying cabinet. 360.
film footage counter. 368.
film leader. 356.
film-pack. 356.
film path. 368.
film speed indicator. 353.
film transport sprocket. 353.
filming trigger. 369.
films. 356.
filter drawer. 361.
fine tuning knob. 377.
finger stop. 372.
Finnish writing system. 345.
fisheye lens. 355.
fixing bath. 360.
flash. 358.
flash bracket. 357.
flash lamp. 357.
flash meter. 358.
flash outlet. 357.
flash socket. 368.
flash synchronization terminal. 353.
flash unit. 357.
flashbar socket. 356.
flashcube. 357.
floodight. 375.
floor crew. 375.
floor manager. 375.
FM mode selector. 364.
FM stereo indicator. 364.
foam windscreen. 369.
focus magnifier. 361.
focus setting ring. 369.
focusing control. 368.
focusing knob. 361, 362.
focusing magnifier. 360.
focusing ring. 368.
folding camera. 354.
forward/reverse switch. 368.
fountain pen. 352.
framing control. 368.
French writing system. 345.
frequency automatic control. 364.
fricative consonants. 348.
function lever. 365.
funnel. 377.
gear train. 356.
geostationary orbit. 379.
geostationary orbit injection. 379.
German writing system. 345.
glass bulb. 357.
glides. 348.
gong. 372.
grave accent. 347.
Greek writing system. 345.
green beam. 377.
grille. 363.
grip. 357.
groove. 365.
ground. 370.

ground lead. 365.
guillotine trimmer. 360.
handgrip. 368, 369.
handle. 370.
handset. 372, 373.
handset cord. 372.
handsfree telephone. 373.
hanger. 362.
head rotation lock. 361.
head shell. 365.
headband. 363.
headphone. 363.
headphone. 363.
headphone jack. 364, 366.
heat pipe radiator. 378.
Hebrew writing system. 345.
height control. 361.
height scale. 361.
Hermes satellite. 378.
Hindi writing system. 345.
hinge. 362.
hoisting apparatus. 375.
honeycomb diffuser. 358.
host. 375.
housing. 369, 372.
Hungarian writing system. 345.
hyphen. 347, 350.
incident-light measuring diffuser. 357.
incoming message cassette. 373.
indication of types. 351.
indicator needle. 357.
indoor/outdoor position. 369.
infrared transmitter. 358.
ink. 352.
inked roller. 370.
input selectors. 364.
insert a letter. 350.
insert a word. 350.
insert here. 350.
insert space. 350.
inside address. 349.
Intelsat. 378.
interchangeable lens. 353.
international phonetic alphabet. 348.
Inuktitut writing system. 345.
Iranian writing system. 345.
ital. boldface capitals. 351.
Italian writing system. 345.
italic. 351.
italic capitals. 351.
jack. 363.
Japanese writing system. 345.
joint. 352.
key. 370.
keyboard. 371.
label. 365.
lamp. 361, 368.
lamphouse. 361.
launching orbit. 379.
lead-in wire. 357.
lead pencil. 352.
LED peak level meter. 366.
lens. 356, 357, 362.
lens aperture scale. 355.
lens cap. 355.
lens hood. 355.
lens mount. 353.
lenses, interchangeable. 355.
let it stand. 350.
letterhead. 349.
level controls. 363.
leveling foot. 362.
lever. 370.
light-reading scale. 357.
light sensor. 357.
lightbox. 360.
lighting and vision control room. 374.
lighting director. 374.
lighttight box. 353.
line. 370.
line guide. 371.
lines. 370.
liquid consonants. 348.

listen button. 373.
lock ring. 362.
locked groove. 365.
loudness switch. 364.
loudspeaker. 363, 375.
lower pan-head mounting screw. 359.
macro focusing knob. 368.
magnesium wire. 357.
main cable. 358.
main cord. 362.
manual aperture control. 368.
manual zoom ring. 368, 369.
marker. 352.
mechanical pencil. 352.
medium format SLR. 354.
memory button. 364.
microphone. 363, 373.
microphone, dynamic. 369.
microphone boom. 375.
microphone jack. 366.
midrange. 363.
mirror. 353.
modern writing instruments. 352.
monitor. 376.
monitor bank. 376.
monitor indicator. 364.
monitor pusher. 375.
monitor speaker. 376.
Morse code. 371.
motor. 362.
motor pulley. 365.
mount frame blinder. 362.
mouthpiece. 372.
movable condenser. 361.
move to left. 350.
move to right. 350.
moving coil. 369.
multiple access station. 379.
multiplexing equipment. 379.
nasal vowels. 348.
neck. 377.
neckstrap lug. 353, 369.
negative carrier. 361.
network. 372.
network management center. 379.
nib. 352.
normal mode acquisition. 379.
normal mode satellite. 379.
Norwegian writing system. 345.
numerals. 371.
objective. 355.
objective lens. 357.
off-on knob. 377.
on/off switch. 369.
on/off witch. 368.
on/play button. 373.
outgoing announcement cassette. 373.
output lead. 365.
output monitor. 376.
pan handle. 359.
panoramic and tilting head. 359.
paper easel. 360.
paper safe. 360.
paper tape. 370, 371.
paper tape start button. 371.
parabolic antenna. 379.
parabolic reflector. 358.
parentheses. 347, 350.
pause button. 366.
pause/still. 367.
pearl screen. 362.
pen. 370.
pentaprism. 353.
perforation. 356.
perforator. 371.
period. 347, 350.
permanent magnet. 372.
phosphor dot. 377.
photoelectric cell. 356.
photographic accessories. 359.
photographic picture. 362.
photography. 353, 354, 355, 356, 357, 358, 359, 360, 361, 362.
picture tube. 377.

pitch axis. 378.
platter. 365.
play. 367.
play button. 366.
plug. 369.
plunger. 372.
pocket instamatic camera. 354.
point. 352.
polarizing filter. 355.
Polaroid Land camera. 356.
pole piece. 372.
Polish writing system. 345.
Portuguese writing system. 345.
postscript. 349.
power switch. 364, 366, 367.
power/timer off switch. 367.
power zoom control. 369.
pre-tuning control. 367.
preamplifier-amplifier. 363.
preset tuning button. 364.
press camera. 354.
preview monitor. 376.
print drying rack. 360.
print washer. 360.
printed circuit. 356.
processing rollers. 356.
producer. 376.
production control room. 376.
production control room. 374.
programmable timer. 367.
projection lamp. 362.
projection screen. 362.
projector. 362.
projector zoom lens. 368.
proofreading. 350, 351.
propman. 375.
protective window. 377.
pull bail. 362.
punched paper tape reader. 371.
punctuation. 371.
punctuation marks. 347.
push-button. 352, 362.
push-button telephone. 373.
push buttons. 373.
question mark. 347.
quill. 352.
quotation marks. 347, 350.
rangefinder. 354.
reaction control thruster. 378.
receiver. 370, 372.
receiving station. 370.
record. 365.
record. 367.
record announcement button. 373.
record button. 366.
record muting button. 366.
recording level button. 366.
recording reproducing head. 368.
recording switch. 368.
red beam. 377.
red safelight filter. 361.
reduce space. 350.
reed panicle. 352.
reel. 360.
reference initials. 349.
reference station. 379.
refill. 352.
reflecting screen. 358.
reflector. 359.
release button. 353.
remote control. 362.
remote control socket. 368.
reset button. 367.
resin-coated paper dryer. 360.
return spring. 370.
rewind. 367.
rewind button. 373.
rewing button. 366.
rewing lever. 353.
right angle finder. 355.
ringer coil. 372.
roll axis. 378.
roll of paper. 371.
Roman metal pen. 352.
rubber mat. 365.
Rumanian writing system. 345.

run in. 350.
Russian writing system. 345.
saddle. 362.
safe and arm device. 378.
safelight. 360.
salutation. 349.
satellite, trajectory of a. 379.
satellite launcher separation. 379.
satellites, examples of. 378.
screen. 369, 377.
screen case. 362.
script assistant. 376.
self timer. 353.
semi-fish-eye lens. 355.
semicolon. 347, 350.
sending station. 370.
set in boldface. 350.
set in capitals. 350.
set in italic. 350.
set in lightface. 350.
set in lowercase. 350.
set in roman. 350.
set in small capitals. 350.
setting ring. 355.
shadow mask. 377.
shaft. 365.
SHF antenna. 378.
SHF beacon antenne. 378.
shoe. 362.
shoe bracket. 357.
shutter. 353.
shutter button. 356.
shutter release. 353.
shutter speed selector. 353.
side-tilt lock. 359.
signature. 349.
single-lens reflex camera. 353.
single quotation marks. 347.
Sinhalese writing system. 345.
sink. 360.
slide. 362.
slide changer. 362.
slide projector. 362.
slide tray. 362.
small capitals. 351.
softlight reflector. 358.
solar cell. 378.
solar panel deployment. 379.
something omitted. 350.
sound camera. 368.
sound engineer. 374.
sound-on-sound control. 368.
sound projector. 368.
sound reproducing system. 363,
* 364, 365, 366.*
Spanish writing system. 345.
speaker. 363.
speaker. 368, 377.
speaker selector. 364.
special effects. 364.
speed selector lever. 365.
spiral. 365.
spiral-in groove. 365.
spot projector attachment. 358.
spotlight. 375.
spotmeter. 357.
spring. 352.
stand. 358, 359.
standard lens. 355.
steel pen. 352.
stereo camera. 354.
still cameras. 354.
stop. 367.
stop bath. 360.
stop button. 366, 373.
stop consonants. 348.
strip light. 375.
studio. 374.
studio. 374.
studio accessories. 359.
studio crane. 375.
studio floor. 375.
studio lighting. 358.
stylus. 352.
subject line. 349.
subminiature camera. 354.

subscript. 350.
sun sensor. 378.
superscript. 350.
supertweeter. 363.
supply reel. 368.
Swedish writing system. 345.
switch. 357.
switchboard. 379.
switcher. 376.
switchhook. 372.
Symphony. 378.
sync cable. 358.
synchro cord. 357.
system elements. 363.
tail-out groove. 365.
take back to previous line. 350.
take over to next line. 350.
take-up reel. 368.
take-up spool. 353.
taking mirror. 356.
tape counter. 366, 367.
tape deck. 366.
tape deck. 363.
tape monitor switch. 364.
tape selector. 366.
tape speed selector. 367.
tape-type indicator. 366.
technical director. 376.
tele-converter. 355.
Telecom 1 satellite. 379.
telecommunication satellites. 378,
* 379.*
telecommunications network. 379.
telecomputer. 379.
teleconference. 379.
telecopy. 379.
telegraph. 370, 371.
telemetry antenna. 378.
telephone answering machine.
* 373.*
telephone cord. 373.
telephone set. 372.
telephones, types of. 373.
telephoto lens. 355.
teleprinter. 371.
teleprompter. 375.
telescopic antenna. 377.
telescoping leg. 359.
teletex. 379.
television. 374, 375, 376, 377.
television set. 377.
telex. 371.
test pattern. 376.
thrust device. 352.
thrust tube. 352.
timer. 360.
timer on switch. 367.
title. 349.
tone arm. 365.
tone control. 368.
tracking control. 367.
transfer. 379.
transfer orbit satellite. 379.
transfer orbit solar cell. 378.
transfer scale. 357.
transmission-line contact. 370.
transmission of telegraph signals.
  370.
transmitter. 370, 372.
transmitter-receiver. 379.
transmitter-receiver terminal. 379.
transparency slide. 362.
transpose lines. 350.
transpose two letters. 350.
transpose two words. 350.
treble tone control. 364.
trigger. 368.
tripod. 359.
tripod. 362.
TT & C belt antenna. 378.
tube. 362.
tuner. 363.
tuning buttons. 364.
turntable. 365.
turntable. 363.
tweeter. 363.

twin-lens reflex camera. 354.
typed name. 349.
typical letter. 349.
UHF channel selector. 377.
Ukrainian writing system. 345.
umbrella diffuser. 358.
umlaut. 347.
user station. 379.
utility speaker. 376.
varistor. 372.
VCR pause switch. 369.
VHF channel selector. 377.
video camera. 369.
video input. 367.
video output. 367.
video tape recorder. 367.
video technician. 374.
video/TV selector. 367.
videotape recorder. 374.
Vietnamese writing system. 345.
view camera. 354.
viewfinder. 353, 368.
virgule. 347.
voltage stabilizer. 361.
volume control. 363, 364, 368,
  373.
vowels. 348.
Welsh writing system. 345.
white balance control. 369.
wide angle adapter. 357.
wide-angle lens. 355.
woofer. 363.
wrist strap. 369.
writing brush. 352.
writing instruments. 352.
writing systems. 345.
yaw axis. 378.
zoom lens. 355, 369.
zoom-speed selector. 369.

CREATIVE LEISURE ACTIVITIES

alteration line. 489.
arm. 485, 491, 492.
arm nut. 492.
assembly process. 507.
back beam. 494.
back board. 498.
back cornering. 498.
backing. 500.
backing board. 500.
backing hammer. 500.
backing press. 500.
baking. 506.
balance wheel. 485.
balance wheel locking screw. 485.
ball. 488, 496, 507.
ball of clay. 505.
ball winder. 496.
banding wheel. 505.
baren. 501.
base. 500.
beater. 494.
beater handtree. 494.
beater sley. 494.
bed. 499, 504.
bed handle. 503.
bias. 488.
blade. 486, 487.
blade lever. 499.
board cutter. 499.
bobbin. 492.
bobbin. 486, 495, 496.
bobbin case. 486.
bobbin lace. 492.
bobbin winder. 496.
bobbin winder. 485.
bone folder. 498.
bookbinding. 498, 499, 500.
bookbinding leather. 500.
bottom cylinder. 502, 504.
bound book. 498.
brayer. 502.
breaking pliers. 507.

breast beam. 494.
brush. 501.
buckle. 488.
bullion stitch. 493.
burin. 502.
burnisher. 501.
butt. 492.
button. 488.
cable stitch. 490.
calipers. 503.
cam. 492.
cam lever. 492.
camshaft. 503.
carbon. 507.
carriage. 492.
carriage. 491.
cartoon. 507.
cast-on stitches. 490.
central screw. 500.
chain stitch. 493.
change dial. 491.
channel. 507.
chevron stitch. 493.
chisel. 502.
circular needle. 490.
clamp. 491, 496, 499.
claw. 500.
claw weight. 491.
cloth beam. 494.
coiling. 505.
column. 485.
comb. 495.
control knob. 506.
copper foil. 507.
copper plate. 501.
cord. 499.
corner. 498.
couched stitches. 493.
covering. 500.
crank handle. 503.
creative leisure activities. 483.
crochet hook. 490.
cross stitches group. 493.
crossbar. 495, 499.
crossbeam. 494.
crosspiece. 494.
crosswise grain. 488.
crown. 506.
cutting blade. 499.
cutting guide. 499.
cutting line. 489.
cutting wire. 505.
cylinder. 504.
dabber. 502.
damper. 506.
dart. 489.
diamond head. 507.
disc. 503.
dressmaker's model. 487.
drive. 485.
driving wheel. 496.
dry point. 501, 503.
edge. 487.
electric kiln. 506.
embroidery. 493.
endpaper. 498.
etching press. 502.
eye. 486, 487, 495.
eye shield protector. 507.
eyelet. 491.
fabric structure. 488.
face. 500, 507.
fasteners. 488.
feather stitch. 493.
feed dog. 486.
feeding dial. 491.
feet. 500.
felt. 502, 504.
fettling knife. 505.
fine bookbinding. 498, 499, 500.
fishbone stitch. 493.
fixed blade. 499.
flank. 500.
flat-bed. 485.
flat part. 490.
flat shuttle. 495.

flat stitches group. 493.
flux. 507.
flux brush. 507.
flyleaf. 498.
flywheel. 502, 505.
fold line. 489.
foot rest. 505.
fore edge. 498.
frame. 493.
frame. 494, 503.
French knot stitch. 493.
front board. 498.
garment fabric. 488.
garter stitch. 490.
gathering. 498.
gauge. 499.
gear. 496.
gearbox. 503.
glass cutter. 507.
glass cutting. 507.
glass grinder. 507.
gouged section. 504.
groove. 486, 499.
grozzing teeth. 507.
hand vice. 501.
hand-wheel. 500.
handle. 487, 492, 494, 500, 503, 507.
harness. 494.
harnesses. 494.
hatching. 497.
head. 485, 490, 492, 500.
head roller. 494.
headband. 498.
headcap. 498.
heart. 507.
hearth. 506.
heating element. 506.
heddle. 494, 495.
heddle rod. 495.
heddles. 495.
hemline. 489.
herringbone stitch. 493.
high warp loom. 495.
hinged presser foot. 485, 486.
holder. 507.
hole. 503.
hook. 486, 488, 490, 492.
hook and eyes. 488.
hoop. 493.
ink. 502.
inked surface. 504.
inking slab. 502.
intaglio printing, diagram of. 504.
intaglio printing, equipment. 501.
intaglio printing process. 501.
interfacing. 488.
interlining. 488.
interloop. 497.
joint. 498.
knife. 502.
knitting. 490.
knitting machine. 491, 492.
knitting measure. 490.
knitting needles. 490.
knot. 497.
knot stitches group. 493.
lam. 494.
latch. 492.
latch lever. 486.
latch needle. 492.
layout. 507.
lead came. 507.
lead knife. 507.
lead stretcher. 507.
lease stick. 494, 495.
lenghtwise grain. 489.
lengthwise grain. 488.
letterpress printing, diagram of. 504.
lever. 503.
levigator. 503.
lining. 488.
lip. 507.
litho crayon. 503.
litho pencil. 503.

lithographic press. 503.
lithographic stone. 504.
lithographic tusche. 503.
lithography. 503.
lithography, equipement. 503.
long and short stitch. 493.
loom. 494, 495.
loop stitches group. 493.
low wrap loom. 494.
magnet. 487.
mallet. 502.
marking dot. 489.
metal plate. 504.
mortise. 493.
motor. 485.
muffle. 506.
nails. 495.
neck. 500.
needle. 486.
needle. 485, 487.
needle bar. 486.
needle bed. 491.
needle bed. 491.
needle bed groove. 491.
needle clamp. 486.
needle clamp screw. 486.
needle plate. 485.
needle threader. 487.
needle threader. 486.
needle tool. 505.
notch. 489.
oilstone. 501.
Oriental couching stitch. 493.
paper. 504.
pattern. 489.
pattern. 492, 507.
pattern reader. 491.
pattern scissors. 507.
peephole. 506.
peg. 493, 496.
pillow. 492.
pin. 487.
pin cushion. 487.
pinking shears. 487.
pivot. 487.
plain weave. 497.
planographic printing, diagram of. 504.
plaster bat. 505.
platen. 500.
point. 486, 490.
post. 494, 506.
pottery. 505, 506.
pottery, tools. 505.
press bed. 502, 503.
presser bar. 486.
presser foot. 486.
presser foot lifter. 485.
pressing. 500.
pressing board. 500.
pressure screw. 502, 503.
pricker. 492.
printing. 504.
pumice correcting pencil. 503.
punch card. 491.
punch card feeding dial. 491.
punch card feeding mechanism. 491.
punch card reader. 491.
pyrometer. 506.
pyrometric cone. 506.
rail. 491.
raised band. 498.
ratchet. 494.
ratchet wheel. 494.
red ocher pencil. 503.
reed. 494.
reed hooks. 496.
refractory brick. 506.
release treadle. 494.
relief printing, equipment. 502.
relief printing process. 502.
revolving cylinder. 492.
rib stitch. 490.
ribs. 505.
ring. 488.

rocking tool. 501.
rod. 495.
roulette. 501.
Roumanian couching stitch. 493.
round eye. 488.
row indicator. 491.
ruler. 499.
safety pins. 487.
saggar. 506.
sample. 490.
satin weave. 497.
sawing-in. 499.
scissors. 487.
scraper. 501, 503.
scraper bar. 504.
scraper bar holder. 503.
screw eye. 494.
seam allowance. 489.
seam line. 489.
seat. 505.
selvage. 488.
separators. 491.
sew-through buttons. 488.
sewing. 485, 486, 487, 488, 489.
sewing. 499.
sewing frame. 499.
sewing machine. 485, 486.
sewing spool. 485.
sewing supplies. 487.
shaft. 496, 505.
shank. 486, 487, 490, 492.
shank button. 488.
shed rod. 495.
sheet. 498.
shelf. 506.
shuttle. 495.
shuttle. 486.
side lever. 492.
signal lamp. 506.
signature. 498.
sketch. 507.
skirt marker. 487.
slab building. 505.
slat. 493.
slide. 488.
slide-bar. 491.
slide plate. 485.
slit. 497.
slot. 499.
smoking candle. 501.
snap. 488.
socket. 488.
solder. 507.
soldering iron. 507.
soldering process. 507.
spatula. 502.
spine. 498, 500.
spine of the book. 500.
spool. 492.
spool pin. 485.
spool rack. 496.
square. 498.
stained glass. 507.
standing press. 500.
stilt. 506.
stitch length regulator. 485.
stitch patterns. 490.
stitch selector. 485.
stitches, groups of. 493.
stocking stitch. 490.
stop. 488.
straight eye. 488.
support. 495.
swift. 496.
tab. 488.
table. 499.
tail. 500.
tail edge. 498.
take-up handle. 494.
tape. 488, 493.
tape measure. 487.
tapestry bobbin. 495.
tarlatan. 501.
teeth. 488.
temple. 496.
temple. 499.

tenon saw. 499.
tension block. 486, 491.
tension block. 485.
tension check spring. 486.
tension controller. 491.
tension dial. 486, 491, 492.
tension disc. 486, 491.
tension guide. 491.
tension spring. 491.
thimble. 487.
thread guide. 485, 486, 496.
thread take-up. 485.
thread trimmer. 486.
tip. 507.
tip cleaner. 507.
tongue. 488.
top cylinder. 502, 504.
top edge. 498.
tracing wheel. 487.
treadle. 494.
treadle cord. 494.
trimming. 499.
trimming tool. 505.
tuck brush. 492.
turning wheel. 505.
twill weave. 497.
tympan. 504.
U-shaped gouge. 502.
underlining. 488.
underlying fabrics. 488.
upright. 494, 495, 499, 500.
V-shaped gouge. 502.
varnish-roller. 501.
vertical frame. 495.
warp. 494, 495.
warp beam. 494.
warp thread. 497.
warping reel. 496.
weaves, basic. 497.
weaving. 494, 495, 496, 497.
weaving accessories. 495.
weaving brush. 492.
weaving principle, diagram of. 497.
webbing. 493.
weft. 494.
weft thread. 497.
wheel. 487, 507.
wheel head. 505.
winder. 496.
wood block. 504.
wood engraving. 502.
woodcut. 502.
wooden modeling tools. 505.
work drawing. 507.
worm. 496.
yarn clip. 491.
yarn feeder. 492.
yarn rod. 491.
zipper. 488.
zipper line. 489.

DO-IT-YOURSELF

120-volt circuit. 278.
240-volt circuit. 278.
240-volt feeder cable. 278.
access panel. 263.
acetylene cylinder. 271.
acetylene valve. 272.
acorn nut. 254.
adjustable channel. 249.
adjustable frame. 252.
adjustable spud wrench. 266.
adjustable wrench. 248.
adjusting knob. 247.
adjusting ring. 250.
adjusting screw. 249, 272.
adjustment wheel. 277.
aerated filter. 267.
aerator. 261.
air cap. 270.
air chamber. 257, 262.
air pressure adjusting screw. 270.
air valve. 270.
angle scale. 253.

anode. 263.
anti-slip shoe. 268.
arc tube. 274.
arc tube mount structure. 274.
arc welding. 271.
arc welding machine. 271.
auger bit. 250.
auxiliary handle. 251.
back. 252, 255.
balde height adjustment. 252.
ball assembly. 261.
ball-cock supply valve. 258.
ball peen. 247.
ball peen hammer. 247.
base. 250, 251, 274.
base elbow. 265.
base plate. 253.
basin wrench. 266.
bathroom. 259.
bathtub. 259.
belt. 251.
bench saw. 252.
bit. 250.
blade. 247, 248, 252, 253, 275, 277.
blade guard. 252, 270.
blade-locking bolt. 253.
blade tilt lock. 253.
blade tilting mechanism. 252.
blockboard. 255.
board. 255.
body. 250, 261.
bolt. 254.
bolt. 249, 256.
bonding jumper. 278.
bonnet. 261.
bottle cart. 271.
bow. 250.
box end wrench. 248.
brace. 250.
brace. 269.
branch. 257.
brass ball faucet. 261.
brass floor frange. 258.
bristles. 270.
brush. 270.
building sewer. 257.
bulb. 274.
butt welding. 272.
button. 274.
C-clamp. 249.
cabinet. 259.
cable. 251.
cable ripper. 277.
cable sleeve. 251.
cam ring. 250.
cap. 265, 271, 275.
cap iron. 247.
carpenter: tools. 249.
carpenter's hammer. 247.
carpentry. 255.
carpentry: fasteners. 254.
carpentry: tools. 247, 248, 250, 251, 252, 253.
cartridge fuse. 275.
cartridge stem. 261.
central ply. 255.
chain pipe wrench. 266.
check valve. 267, 272.
cheek. 247.
chuck. 248, 250, 251.
chuck key. 251.
circuit breaker. 275.
circuit vent. 257.
circular saw. 253.
circular saw blade. 253.
clamp. 267, 275.
claw. 247.
cleanout. 260.
closet bend. 257.
cold-water line. 258, 263.
cold-water riser. 257.
cold-water shutoff valve. 263.
cold-water supply line. 262.
collet. 250.
collet nut. 250.

column. 251.
combination box and open end wrench. 248.
compression coupling. 260.
compression fitting. 264.
conical washer. 258.
connector. 278.
container. 270.
continuity tester. 276.
copper pipe. 264.
copper to plastic. 265.
copper to steel. 265.
core plywood. 255.
countersink. 250.
cover. 259.
crimper. 277.
cross head (Phillips). 254.
curved jaw. 249.
cutting oxygen handle. 272.
cutting tip. 272.
cutting torch. 272.
cylinder. 256.
cylinder. 256.
cylinder hole. 256.
cylinder pressure gauge. 272.
dead bolt. 256.
decorative sheet. 255.
depth stop. 251.
dimmer switch. 275.
disc seat. 261.
disc seat ring. 261.
discharge line. 267.
dishwasher. 262.
distribution board. 278.
distribution field. 267.
diverter valve. 259.
do-it-yourself. 245.
double kitchen sink. 257.
double pole breaker. 278.
double-twist auger bit. 250.
drain. 257.
drain elbow. 260.
drain hose. 262.
drain valve. 263.
drill. 250.
drill press. 251.
drive wheel. 250.
edge. 255.
elbow. 265.
electric arc. 271.
electric drill. 251.
electric supply. 263.
electric switch. 275.
electric water-heater tank. 263.
electrical box. 275.
electrical supplies. 275.
electricity. 274, 275, 278.
electricity, tools. 276, 277.
electrode. 271, 274.
electrode holder. 271.
electrode lead. 271.
end grain. 255.
escutcheon. 256, 260.
European plug. 275.
examples of branching. 262.
exhaust tube. 274.
expansion bolt. 254.
extension ladder. 268.
external tooth lock washer. 254.
eye. 247.
face. 247.
face ply. 255.
face side. 255.
faceplate. 256.
faucet. 261.
faucet body. 261.
feed lever. 251.
ferrule. 270.
filament. 274.
filler rod. 272.
filler tube. 258.
fish wire. 277.
fitting. 264.
fittings. 265.
fixed jaw. 248, 249.

fixture drain. 257.
flame spreader tip. 271.
flange bolt. 258.
flange nut. 264.
flare joint. 264.
flare nut. 264.
flare nut wrench. 248.
flat head. 254.
flat tip. 248.
flat washer. 254.
flexible hose. 259.
flexible rubber hose. 262.
flint. 273.
float. 267.
float ball. 258.
float clamp. 267.
fluid adjustment screw. 270.
fluorescent lamp. 274.
flush bushing. 265.
flute. 250.
fluted land. 250.
foldaway ladder. 268.
frame. 249, 269.
front knob. 247.
fruit-picking ladder. 269.
fuse pullers. 276.
fuses. 275.
garbage disposal sink. 260.
garbage disposal unit. 260.
gas. 274.
gasket. 261, 264.
gauntlet. 273.
goggles. 273.
grain. 255.
gravel. 267.
grease trap. 267.
grooved sleeve. 261.
ground bond. 278.
ground clamp. 271.
ground fault circuit interrupter. 278.
ground/neutral bus bar. 278.
ground wire. 278.
grounded receptacle. 267.
grounding prong. 275.
gun body. 270.
hacksaw. 252.
hacksaw. 266.
hammer. 247, 277.
hand drill. 250.
hand shield. 273.
handle. 247, 248, 249, 250, 252, 253, 261, 270, 272.
handsaw. 252.
hardboard. 255.
head. 250, 254, 272.
heads. 247.
heat deflecting disc. 274.
heel. 247, 252.
helmet. 273.
hexagon bushing. 265.
high-temperature cutoff. 263.
high-voltage tester. 276.
hoisting rope. 268.
hollow-wood construction. 255.
hook ladder. 268.
hose. 271.
hot bus bar. 278.
hot-water heater. 257.
hot-water supply. 262.
hot-water supply line. 262, 263.
house drain. 262.
housing. 251.
hub. 256.
incandescent lamp. 274.
inert gas. 274.
inner ply. 255.
inside knob. 256.
inspection chamber. 267.
inspection plug. 267.
insulated blade. 276, 277.
insulated handle. 276, 277.
insulating sleeve. 275.
insulation. 263.
internal tooth lock washer. 254.
jaw. 248, 250, 251, 277.
key. 256.

keyhole. 256.
knife-blade cartridge fuse. 275.
knob. 256.
knob handle. 253.
knockout. 278.
knurled bolt. 270.
kraft paper. 255.
ladder scaffold. 269.
ladders. 268, 269.
laminate board. 255.
laminboard. 255.
lamp. 274.
lamp socket. 275.
land. 250.
latch bolt. 256.
latch lever. 256.
lateral adjusting lever. 247.
lead-in wire. 274.
lead screw. 250.
lever. 249, 260, 261.
lever cover. 261.
lineman's pliers. 277.
lip. 256.
lock. 256.
lock washer. 254.
locking device. 268.
locking nut. 258.
locking pliers. 249.
lockling ring. 248.
locknut. 260.
long hub lever. 256.
long-nose pliers. 277.
lower blade guard. 253.
lower guard retracting lever. 253.
lower heating element. 263.
lower thermostat. 263.
main breaker. 278.
main cleanout. 257.
main electrode. 274.
main handle. 250.
main power cable. 278.
mallet. 247.
mechanical connectors. 264.
mercury. 274.
mercury-vapor lamp. 274.
metal. 272.
metal washer. 260.
metal water pipe. 278.
miter gauge. 252.
miter gauge silot. 252.
mitt. 273.
mixing chamber. 272.
mogul base. 274.
monkey wrench. 266.
mortise lock. 256.
motor. 250, 251, 253.
moulded plywood. 255.
movable jaw. 248, 249.
multi-ply. 255.
multipurpose ladder. 268.
multipurpose tool. 277.
nail. 254.
name plate. 251.
neon lamp. 276.
neon tester. 276.
neutral service wire. 278.
neutral wire. 278.
nipple. 265.
nitrogen. 274.
nozzle. 270.
nut. 254.
nut and bolt. 249.
o-ring. 261.
offset. 265.
one way head. 254.
open end wrench. 248.
outdoor sill cock. 257.
outer shell. 275.
outlet. 275.
outside knob. 256.
oval head. 254.
overflow. 259.
overflow bend. 257.
overflow pipe. 263.
overflow tube. 258.
oxyacetylene welding. 271.

oxygen cylinder. 271.
oxygen valve. 272.
["p[" trap. 257.
packing. 261.
packing nut. 261.
packing retainer ring. 261.
paint roller. 270.
painting upkeep. 268, 269, 270.
particle board. 255.
pawl. 250.
peeled veneer. 255.
pencil point tip. 271.
perforated pipe. 267.
Phillips tip. 248.
phosphor coating. 274.
pin. 256, 274.
pin base. 274.
pinch. 274.
pinion. 250.
pipe. 264.
pipe coupling. 265.
pipe threader. 266.
pipe wrench. 266.
pistol grip handle. 251, 252.
pivot. 277.
plane. 247.
plastic insulator. 278.
platform. 269.
platform ladder. 269.
pliers. 249.
plug. 275.
plug. 251.
plug fuse. 275.
plumbing. 257, 258, 259, 260, 261, 262, 263, 264, 265, 266, 267.
plumbing system. 257.
plumbing tools. 266.
plunger. 266.
pressure regulator. 272.
pressure regulator. 271.
pressure relief valve. 263.
protective clothing. 273.
protective sheet. 255.
public water main. 257.
pulley. 251, 268.
pulley safety guard. 251.
pump motor. 267.
pump suction head. 267.
push-button. 256.
quill. 250, 251.
quill lock. 251.
ratchet. 248, 250.
receptacle analyzer. 276.
reducing coupling. 265.
refill tube. 258.
reflector. 274.
release lever. 249.
removable blade. 270.
removable lid. 267.
retainer nut. 261.
rib joint pliers. 249.
ring nut. 264.
rip fence. 252, 253.
rip fence adjustment. 252.
rip fence guide. 252.
rip fence lock. 252.
rivet. 249.
Robertson tip. 248.
roller cover. 270.
roller frame. 270.
rolling ladder. 269.
roof flashing. 257.
roof vent. 265.
rope ladder. 268.
rose. 256.
rotor. 256.
round head. 254.
router. 250.
rubber gasket. 260.
rubber washer. 260.
rung. 268.
safety rail. 269.
scraper. 270.
screen. 261.
screw. 254.
screw. 256.

screwdriver. 248.
scum. 267.
seal. 263.
seat. 259.
septic tank. 267.
septic tank compartment. 267.
shank. 248, 250, 254.
shelf. 269.
shoulder. 254.
shoulder bolt. 254.
shower and tub fixture. 257.
shower head. 259.
shutoff switch. 267.
shutoff valve. 257, 258, 260, 262.
side handle. 250.
side rail. 268.
single-handle kitchen faucet. 261.
single-handle kitchen faucet. 260.
single pole breaker. 278.
single twist. 250.
sink. 260.
sink. 259.
sink strainer. 260.
slip joint. 249.
slip joint pliers. 249.
slot. 254.
slotted wall bracket. 259.
sludge. 267.
soap dish. 259.
socket. 275.
socket head (Robertson). 254.
soil-or-waste stack. 257.
solder. 273.
soldering. 271, 272, 273.
soldering gun. 271.
soldering iron. 271.
soldering torch. 271.
spindle. 256, 261.
spiral. 248.
spiral ratchet screwdriver. 248.
spout. 261.
spout assembly. 260.
spray head. 260.
spray hose. 260.
spray paint gun. 270.
spreader adjustment valve. 270.
spring. 249, 256, 261.
spring wing. 254.
spur. 250.
square head plug. 265.
stack vent. 257.
standpipe. 262.
starting electrode. 274.
starting resistor. 274.
stator. 250.
steel to plastic. 265.
stem. 274.
stem faucet. 261.
step. 269.
step stool. 269.
stepladder. 269.
stepladders. 268, 269.
straight jaw. 249.
straight ladder. 268.
strainer. 261.
strainer body. 260.
strainer coupling. 260.
strainer plug. 261.
strainer sleeve. 260.
strap wrench. 266.
strike. 256.
striker. 273.
stub out. 258.
sump. 267.
sump pump. 267.
supply line. 257.
supply riser. 257.
supply tube. 260.
support. 274.
switch. 250, 251, 275.
switch plate. 275.
swivel base. 249.
swivel head. 249.
swivel lock. 249.
table. 251, 252.
table extension. 252.

table-locking clamp. 251.
tailpiece. 260.
tank ball. 258.
tank lid. 259.
tee. 262, 265.
teeth. 252.
telephone shower head. 259.
terminal. 275.
tester probe. 276.
thread. 254, 261.
threaded cap. 265.
threaded rod. 254.
throat. 249.
thumbscrew. 248.
tip. 248, 253, 254, 272.
tip cleaners. 273.
tipping valve faucet. 261.
tissue holder. 259.
toe. 247, 252.
toggle bolt. 254.
toilet. 258.
toilet. 259.
toilet bowl. 258, 259.
toilet tank. 259.
tool tray. 269.
tooth. 253.
toothed jaw. 249.
torch. 266.
towel bar set. 259.
transition fittings. 265.
trap. 260, 265.
trap and drain auger. 266.
trap coupling. 260.
tray. 270.
trigger. 270.
trigger switch. 253.
trip handle. 259.
trip lever. 258.
tube cutter. 266.
tube end. 264.
tube flaring tool. 266.
tubular lock. 256.
tumbler holder. 259.
turn knob hub. 256.
turning handle. 250.
twist drill. 250.
U-bend. 265.
union. 264.
union nut. 264.
upper blade guard. 253.
upper heating element. 263.
upper thermostat. 263.
valve seat. 261.
valve seat shaft. 258.
valve seat wrench. 266.
vent hole. 270.
vent line. 265.
vise. 249.
voltage tester. 276.
voltmeter. 276.
warning plate. 251.
washer. 262.
washer. 254, 261.
waste pipe. 258.
waste stack. 257.
waste tee. 262.
water meter. 257.
water service pipe. 257.
wax seal. 258.
wedge iron. 247.
wedge lever. 247.
weld bead. 271, 272.
welding. 271, 272, 273.
welding curtain. 273.
welding torch. 272.
welding torch. 271.
wing nut. 254.
wing nut. 252.
wire cutter. 249, 277.
wire stripper. 277.
wood-based panel. 255.
work lead. 271.
working pressure gauge. 272.
wrenches. 248.
wye branch. 265.

ENERGY

aboveground pipeline. 630.
absorber. 656.
absorber pipe. 656.
absorbing plate. 656.
absorbing surface. 655.
accept machine. 651.
access gallery. 641, 646.
access shaft. 646.
adit. 622.
administration building. 624.
administration office. 634.
administrative building. 646.
aerocondenser. 654.
aerodynamic brake. 658.
afterbay. 637, 638, 641.
air gap. 655.
air hose. 625.
air leg. 625.
air passage. 625.
airlock. 647.
alkylation unit. 634.
annular shielding slab. 648.
anticline. 626.
antireflection coating. 656.
anvil. 625.
apex. 622.
aquifer. 636.
arch dam. 639.
asphalt. 635.
asphalt process. 634.
asphalt still. 635.
automatic tank gauge. 633.
autorefrigerating devices. 630.
baffle. 632.
ballast tank. 631.
bank. 646.
bank of heliostats. 654.
barge. 631.
barren. 621.
base rock. 636.
base width. 644.
basin. 646.
basin side. 646.
beam gantry. 644.
beam pump. 627.
bearing pad. 649.
belt. 658.
bench. 621.
bench height. 621.
berm. 638.
bit. 625, 626.
bitumen. 636.
bitumen pumping. 636.
bitumen treatment. 636.
blade. 642, 643, 658.
blowout preventer. 626.
boiler. 654.
booster intermediate station. 630.
bottom. 624.
bottom deck. 633.
bottom ring. 643.
bottom road. 623.
brace. 645.
breather valve. 633.
bridge. 631.
bucket. 643.
bucket chain excavator. 621.
bucket ring. 643.
bucket wheel excavator. 621, 636.
buffer tank. 630.
bulb. 631.
bulb unit. 646.
bulldozer. 621.
bund wall. 633.
bundle. 644.
bunker oil. 635.
burden. 621, 623, 636.
buried pipeline. 630.
busbar. 641.
bushing. 637, 645.
butane carrier. 631.
buttress. 639.
buttress dam. 639.
calandria. 648, 650.

calandria tube. 648.
calandria vault. 648.
canal boat. 631.
canned failed fuel. 651.
cantilever. 639.
cap. 657.
cap rock. 626, 636.
capacitor. 658.
casing first string. 627.
casing second string. 627.
catalytic reformer. 634.
catalytic reforming plant. 635.
catenary. 647.
cathode screen. 652.
center Keelson. 631.
center tank. 631.
central column. 658.
central pumping. 630.
charge machine. 651.
chemical treatment. 635.
Christmas tree. 627.
Christmas tree. 630.
chuck. 625.
chute. 623.
circuit breaker. 641, 658.
circulating pump. 655.
city water. 655.
closed circuit television. 652.
coal bunker. 624.
coal mine. 621, 622, 623, 624,
625.
coking plant. 624.
cold air. 655.
collecting tube. 656.
collector. 642.
colliery. 623.
compressed air. 625.
concrete dam. 638.
concrete drain. 633.
concrete wall. 655.
condensate. 650.
condenser. 647.
conductive material. 656.
connection point. 645.
containment. 652.
containment building. 649.
control lever. 625.
control room. 652.
control room. 629, 637, 646, 647.
control system. 658.
conversion. 653.
conveyor. 621, 624, 636.
coolant. 650, 654, 656.
cooling tower. 634.
cooling water. 650.
core. 638.
cover plate. 656.
crane. 629.
crater. 621.
crest of spillway. 637.
cross cut. 622, 623.
crossarm. 644, 645.
crossover cargo deck line. 631.
crown block. 626.
crude oil. 635.
crude oil pipeline. 630.
customer's service entrance. 645.
cut off trench. 638.
cylinder. 625.
cylindrical parabola reflector. 656.
dam. 637, 638, 646.
dams, major types of. 639.
day. 624.
deaerator. 647, 650.
deaerator storage tank. 647.
deck. 623.
decontamination room. 647.
deposit. 621.
derrick. 626, 629.
desasphalting. 634.
dewaxing. 634.
diagonal. 644.
diesel oil. 635.
digital computer. 652.
diluent. 636.
diluent recovery. 636.

dip. 622.
disc brake. 658.
discharge liner. 643.
discharge pipe. 632.
discharge pump. 632.
dispatch area. 634.
distribution board. 645.
distributor service loop. 645.
diversion canal. 637.
double glazing. 655.
dousing tank. 647.
downstream face. 638.
downstream shoulder. 638.
downstream toe. 638.
draft tube. 641, 643.
dragline. 636.
drain cock. 633.
drain valve. 633.
drainage blanket. 638.
drainage layer. 638.
drawworks. 626.
drift. 622, 623.
drill collar. 626.
drill pipe. 626.
drill ship. 628.
drill steel. 625.
drilling barge. 628.
drilling rig. 626.
dump. 621, 624.
earth. 639.
elastic coupling method. 631.
electrical distribution system. 652.
electrical room. 647.
electricity. 637, 638, 639, 640, 641,
642, 643, 644, 645, 646.
electricity, tower. 644.
electricity meter. 645.
elevator. 651.
embankment dam. 638, 639.
emergency core cooling. 652.
emptying. 633.
encapsulant. 656.
end cap. 649.
end fitting. 648.
end plate. 649.
end shield. 647.
end shield cooling pipe. 648.
energy. 619.
energy production. 653.
engine. 626.
engine room. 631.
equipment access shaft. 646.
equipment lock. 651.
exhaust port. 625.
face. 621, 623.
failed fuel bay. 651.
failed fuel canning. 651.
fan. 624.
fantail. 657.
fault. 622.
feeder. 648.
feedwater. 650.
fill. 638.
filling. 633.
filter. 638, 655.
finished product storage. 634.
fire-standing tanks. 631.
fire station. 634.
fitted coupling bolt. 643.
fixed platform. 628.
fixed-roof tank. 633.
flare. 629, 634.
flat plate solar collector. 656.
flexible hose. 625.
flexible hose connection. 625.
floating platform. 628.
floating roof. 633.
floating-roof tank. 633.
floor. 621, 622, 657.
flow bean. 627.
fluid coking plant. 634.
fluid inlet. 656.
fluid outlet. 656.
foam gun. 631.
focusing. 654.
fore and aft gangway. 631.

foundation. 639.
foundation of dam. 638.
fractionating tower. 635.
frame. 656, 657.
Francis turbine. 643.
fuel. 650.
fuel bundle. 649.
fuel fabrication. 653.
fuel handling control console. 652.
fuel handling sequence. 651.
fuel pellet. 649.
fuelling machine. 647, 650.
furnace. 654.
fuse. 645.
fuse cutout. 645.
fuse holder. 645.
gallery. 657.
gantry crane. 637, 641.
gas. 626.
gas lift. 627.
gas lift valve. 627.
gas oil. 635.
gas turbine. 629.
gas under pressure. 627.
gasoline. 635.
gasometer. 624.
gate. 641, 646.
gate operating ring. 643.
gearbox. 658.
generating station flow diagram.
650.
generator. 642.
generator. 641, 642, 647, 650,
652, 658.
gravity dam. 639.
greases. 635.
greenhouse. 655.
ground. 633.
ground wire. 645.
ground-wire clamp. 645.
ground-wire peak. 644.
guide bearing. 642.
guy wire. 658.
hammer drill. 625.
hand rail. 637.
handle. 625.
hatch. 631.
haul road. 621.
headbay. 637.
header. 647, 650.
headframe. 622, 624.
heat exchanger. 655.
heater. 655.
heating oil. 635.
heavy gasoline. 635.
heavy water. 650.
helideck. 629.
heliostat. 654.
hemlath. 657.
high pressure turbine. 650.
hill. 654.
hoist room. 622, 624.
hook. 626.
horizontal-axis wind turbine. 658.
horizontal flux detector. 648.
horizontal member. 644.
hot line connector. 645.
hot water extraction. 636.
hub. 643, 658.
hub cover. 643.
hydraulic turbine. 643.
hydroelectric complex. 637.
hydroelectric power station. 641.
hydrofiner. 634.
inactive dyke. 646.
inclined shaft. 622.
inlet. 625.
insulation. 655, 656.
insulator. 645.
ion chamber. 648.
jack-up platform. 628.
jacket. 629.
jackled drill. 625.
jet fuel. 635.
K frame. 644.
Kaplan turbine. 643.

kelly. 626.
kerosene. 635.
laboratory. 634.
ladder. 657.
lagging. 633.
lamp room. 624.
landing. 623.
lattice tube. 648.
level. 623.
lifeboat. 629.
lighting arrester. 641.
lightning arrester. 645.
line. 637.
line printer. 652.
liquefied petroleum gas storage. 634.
liquid-level gauge. 633.
liquified gas petroleum treatment. 634.
living quarters. 629.
loading belt. 621.
loading pocket. 623.
lock. 646.
log chute. 637.
logging unit. 629.
long residue. 635.
low pressure steam piping. 647.
low pressure turbine. 650.
low tension distribution line. 645.
lubricants plant. 635.
lubricating oils. 635.
machine hall. 637, 641.
main inlet. 633.
main leg. 644.
main shaft. 624.
main switch. 645.
manhole. 632, 633.
manometer. 633.
manway. 623.
marine diesel. 635.
master gate valve. 627.
medium tension distribution line. 645.
membrane tanks. 631.
metallic contact grid. 656.
methane carrier. 631.
mine. 621, 622, 623, 624, 636.
mining. 622.
mining. 653.
miscellaneous auxiliary systems. 652.
moderator. 650.
moderator heat exchanger. 650.
moderator inlet. 648.
moderator/miscellaneous systems. 652.
moderator outlet. 648.
moderator pump. 650.
mud pump. 626.
muskeg. 636.
nacelle. 658.
negative contact. 656.
negative region. 656.
neutral conductor. 645.
new fuel loading area. 651.
new fuel port. 651.
new fuel storage room. 651.
node. 644.
nuclear energy. 647, 648, 649, 650, 651, 652, 653.
nuclear fuel cycle. 653.
nuclear generating station. 647.
nuclear reactor. 649.
nuclear reactor. 653.
offshore drilling. 628.
offshore well. 630.
oil. 626, 627, 628, 629, 630, 631, 632, 633, 634, 635, 636.
oil. 626.
oil and gas foam. 627.
oil/gas separator. 629.
oil reservoir. 625.
oil sand. 636.
oil sands mining plant. 636.
oil sands recovery process, steam drive. 636.

oil trap. 626.
oiler. 625.
open-pit mine. 621.
open-pit mine. 622.
operating dam. 646.
operating floor. 646.
operator desk. 652.
ore. 621, 622.
ore deposit. 622.
ore pass. 623.
outcrop. 622.
overhead connection. 645.
overhead crane. 647.
overhead ground wire. 644.
P-N junction. 656.
panel. 623, 644.
parabolic mirror. 654.
paraboloidal reflector. 656.
paraffins. 635.
Pelton turbine. 643.
pencil. 649.
penstock. 637, 641, 646.
peripheral joint. 639.
petrochemical industry. 635.
petrochemicals. 635.
phase conductor. 645.
pier. 628.
pile. 629.
pillar. 623.
pinch. 622.
pipeline. 630, 636.
pipeline support, aboveground. 630.
piston. 625.
pitching. 638.
pithead. 624.
plunger. 627.
pneumatic hammer. 625.
poison injection nozzle. 648.
poison tank. 647.
polymerization unit. 634.
pool. 655.
portal. 623.
positive contact. 656.
positive region. 656.
post. 657.
post mill. 657.
potable water tank. 629.
power plant. 634.
power plant, cross section of. 646.
power station. 624, 646.
power system. 658.
powerhouse. 637, 641.
pressure gauge. 627.
pressure relief pipe. 648.
pressure tube. 649.
pressurizer. 647, 650.
primary heat transport system. 652.
primary pump. 650.
production of electricity. 640.
production of electricity. 654.
production platform. 629.
pulvino. 639.
pump. 623, 627, 654.
pumping station. 630.
pumping unit. 627.
pyrolysis. 636.
quarters. 631.
radiation. 655.
radioactive waste storage. 653.
rail track. 624.
raise. 622.
ramp. 621.
reactivity control device. 648.
reactor. 648.
reactor. 647, 650, 651.
reactor building. 647, 649, 651.
reactor regulating system. 652.
reactor vessel. 649.
reception bay. 651.
reclaimed water. 636.
redundant bracing. 644.
refinery. 634.
refinery. 630.
refinery products. 635.

refining. 653.
reflecting surface. 654.
reflector. 656.
rerunning. 634.
reserve mud tank. 629.
reservoir. 637, 638, 641.
retainer. 625.
retaining spring. 625.
rocks. 639.
roof. 621, 622.
room. 623.
rotary table. 626.
rotor. 641, 642, 657, 658.
rotor shaft. 658.
runner. 642, 643.
runner blade. 643, 646.
rupture disc. 648.
safety valve. 650.
sail. 657.
sail cloth. 657.
sailbar. 657.
salient pole. 642.
salt water. 626.
sand-rock. 636.
scale. 633.
screen. 641.
scroll case. 641.
sea. 646.
sea side. 646.
seal. 656.
sealing ring. 633.
secondary inlet. 633.
self-contained platform. 628.
semi-membrane tanks. 631.
semi-submersible. 628.
semi-trailer. 632.
service box. 645.
service building. 651.
settling basin. 624.
settling pond. 634, 636.
settling tank. 631.
shaft. 641, 642, 643.
shaft collar. 623.
sheath. 649.
shell. 633.
shutdown system. 652.
shutter. 655.
skid pad. 630.
slush pit. 626.
soil. 639.
solar cell. 656.
solar collector. 655.
solar energy. 654, 655, 656.
solar furnace. 654.
solar house. 655.
solar power station. 654.
solar radiation. 654, 655, 656.
solvent extraction unit. 635.
spacer. 649.
spent fuel discharge room. 651.
spent fuel port. 651.
spent fuel storage bay. 649, 651, 653.
spillway. 637.
spillway chute. 637.
spilway gate. 637.
spiral case. 642, 643.
spiral staircase. 633.
splash plate. 633.
spray nozzle. 633.
stairs. 633.
stand. 656.
starter. 658.
stator. 641, 642.
stay ring. 642, 643.
stay vane. 642, 643.
steam. 650.
steam cracker. 634.
steam generator. 647, 650, 652.
steam generator system. 652.
steam injection. 636.
steam pipe. 647, 650.
steam separator. 650.
steel ball shielding. 648.
stock. 657.
stop. 630.

stope. 622.
storage tank. 629, 635, 650, 654, 655.
storage tray. 651.
stove oil. 635.
straight run gasoline treatment. 634.
strainer. 627.
strip mine. 621.
structure. 637.
strut. 646, 658.
sublevel. 623.
submarine pipeline. 630.
submersible barge. 628.
substation. 646.
sucker rod. 627.
sump. 622.
supply point. 645.
support. 630.
suppression tank. 650.
suspension insulator string. 644.
switchyard. 652.
swivel. 626.
tail pole. 657.
tailing. 636.
tailrace. 641, 643.
tank. 632, 633.
tank car. 632.
tank farm. 630, 634.
tank gauge float. 633.
tank trailer. 632.
tank truck. 632.
tank wall. 632.
tankage. 636.
tanker. 631.
target area. 654.
tender. 628.
terminal. 630, 645.
thermal insulation. 630.
thermal storage. 654.
thermometer. 633.
thick-walled pipe. 626.
throttle valve. 625.
tidal power plant. 646.
timber yard. 624.
tool. 625.
top central manhole. 632.
top deck. 633.
top of dam. 637, 638, 641.
top road. 623.
towboat. 631.
tower. 624, 644, 654, 657, 658.
tower body. 644.
tower foot. 644.
tower mill. 657.
tower top. 644.
tower window. 644.
tractor. 632.
training wall. 637.
transfer canal. 651.
transfer station. 622.
transformer. 641, 645, 654, 658.
transforming station. 641.
transmission network. 653, 654.
transverse baffle. 632.
transverse bulkhead. 631.
traveling crane. 641.
travelling block. 626.
trench. 621.
Trombe wall. 655.
tube sheet. 648.
tubing. 627.
tubing head. 627.
tubular heater. 635.
tubular member. 629.
turbine. 641, 652.
turbine building. 647.
turbine runner. 646.
turbines, major types of. 643.
turbo-alternator. 654.
underground mine. 623.
upstream blanket. 638.
upstream face. 638.
upstream shoulder. 638.
upstream toe. 638.
utilities plant. 636.

vacuum distillation. 635.
valve. 625.
vein. 622.
ventilation shaft. 624.
vertical-axis wind turbine. 658.
vertical shaft. 622.
vibrating mudscreen. 626.
waist. 644.
wall. 622.
warm air. 655.
washery. 624.
water hose. 625.
water intake. 641.
water reservoir. 624.
water treatment plant. 647.
watertight bulkhead. 631.
wave wall. 638.
web frame. 631.
wicket gate. 643.
wind turbine. 658.
wind turbine electricity production.
658.
winding tower. 624.
windmill. 657.
windshaft. 657.
wing tank. 631.
winze. 622.
workshop store. 634.

FARM

A-frame. 661.
agricultural machinery. 152, 153,
154.
air fan. 155.
backing light. 152.
barn. 151.
base. 661.
beam. 153.
beater. 155.
beehive. 151.
boom. 661.
boom point sheave. 661.
bottom. 153.
bucket. 661.
bunker silo. 151.
cardan shaft. 152.
chaffer sieve. 155.
combine harvester. 155.
concave. 155.
coulter. 153.
covering disk. 154.
cowshed. 151.
crop elevator. 155.
crossbar. 152.
cultivator. 153.
cup conveyor. 154.
cutter bar. 155.
discharge spout. 152, 153.
divider. 155.
drag chain. 661.
drag drum. 661.
drag rope. 661.
dragline. 661.
dump rope. 661.
electrified fence. 151.
elevator. 152.
fallow. 151.
farm, buildings. 151.
farm, modern. 149.
farmhouse. 151.
farmyard. 151.
fertilizer distributor. 154.
field heap spreader. 154.
filter. 661.
finger. 152.
fingerwheel. 154.
fodder corn. 151.
frame. 153.
frog. 153.
grain pan. 155.
grain screw. 155.
grain sieve. 155.
grain tank. 155.
grain unloading auger. 155.

greenhouse. 151.
hangar. 151.
harrow. 152.
heel. 153.
hoist chain. 661.
hoist drum. 661.
hoist rope. 661.
hopper. 154.
implement bar. 152.
knife. 155.
landside. 153.
leg. 153.
loam. 152.
machinery. 155.
manure spreader. 153.
manure spreader box. 153.
mast. 661.
milk room. 151.
moldboard. 153.
motor. 155, 661.
operator's cab. 661.
orchard. 151.
pasture. 151.
pick-up. 152.
pickup automatic baler. 152.
pickup loader. 152.
pickup reel. 155.
pigsty. 151.
potato planter. 154.
poultry house. 151.
power take off. 152.
reciprocating knife mower. 152.
reel. 154.
return elevator. 155.
revolving frame. 661.
ribbing plow. 153.
roller circle. 661.
rotary hoe. 153.
rotating auger. 155.
seed drill. 154.
share. 153.
sheep shelter. 151.
silage harvester. 153.
skimmer. 153.
spider. 153.
spike-tooth. 152.
spreading rotor. 153.
steering track rod. 152.
steering wheel. 155.
straw walker. 155.
stripper beater. 155.
subsoil plow. 154.
suspension cable. 661.
tandem disk harrow. 154.
tooth. 154.
toothed rotor. 154.
towing hook. 152.
tractor. 152.
vegetable garden. 151.
vertical silo. 151.
walking cam. 661.
walking shoe. 661.
walkway. 661.
well. 151.
winch. 661.

FOOD

agnolotti. 137.
aiguillette de gîte à la noix. 141.
aiguillette de romsteck. 141.
alphabet. 137.
American bread. 138.
American Cheddar. 144.
American corn bread. 138.
American white bread. 138.
Anfrom. 144.
baby shells. 137.
Banon. 145.
basil. 133.
bavette. 141.
Beaumont. 145.
beef, North American cut. 140.

beef, Parisian cut. 141.
belly. 142.
biscuit. 147.
black rye bread. 138.
blade. 140.
bleu de Bresse. 144.
borage. 133.
Boursault. 144.
bows. 137.
bread. 138.
breast. 139, 143.
Brick. 144.
Brie. 145.
brioche. 146.
brisket. 140.
buck shots. 137.
butt portion. 142, 143.
cake. 146.
Camembert. 145.
Canadian Cheddar. 144.
cannelloni. 137.
Cantal. 145.
cappelletti. 137.
Caprice des Dieux. 144.
caraway seeded rye bread. 138.
carré. 142.
carré raccourci. 139.
center cut. 142.
charlotte. 146.
cheeses, French. 144, 145.
cheeses, North American. 144.
chervil. 133.
chuck. 140.
chuck short rib. 140.
clafoutis. 147.
Colby. 144.
collet. 139, 143.
Comté. 145.
contre-filet. 141.
côtelettes découvertes. 143.
côtelettes premières et secondes.
143.
côtes. 142.
côtes découvertes. 139.
Coulommiers. 145.
crak rye bread. 138.
crème de Gruyère. 145.
croissant. 138.
cross rib. 140.
crosse. 139, 141, 142.
cuisseau. 139.
culotte. 141.
curly lasagna. 136.
custard pie. 147.
cut ribbed macaroni. 137.
Danish rye bread. 138.
desserts. 146, 147.
dessus de côtes. 139, 141.
dill. 133.
ditali. 137.
doughnut. 146.
Doux de Montagne. 144.
ear loaf. 138.
échine. 142.
elbow macaroni. 137.
Englis loaf. 138.
entame de romsteck. 141.
entrecôtes couvertes. 141.
entrecôtes découvertes. 141.
épaule. 139, 143.
fedelini. 136.
filet. 142, 143.
flanchet. 141.
flank. 139, 140, 143.
flat cake. 146.
food. 133.
foot. 142.
French bread. 138.
French loaf. 138.
front. 139, 143.
front quarter. 140.
fruit cake. 147.
full brisket. 140.
gemelli. 137.
German rye bread. 138.
gigot. 143.

gîte à la noix. 141.
gîte de derrière. 141.
gîte de devant. 141.
gorge. 142.
Gournay. 145.
gros bout de poitrine. 141.
hampe. 141.
haut de côtelettes. 143.
haut de côtes. 139.
heel of round. 140.
herbs. 133.
hind quarter. 140.
hip. 140.
hock. 142.
hyssop. 133.
ice pudding. 147.
Indian chapati bread. 138.
Indian naan bread. 138.
Irish bread. 138.
jambon. 142.
jambonneau arrière. 142.
jambonneau avant. 142.
jarret arrière. 139.
jarret avant. 139.
Jewish tchallaw. 138.
jowl. 142.
jumeaux. 141.
lamb, North American cut. 143.
lamb, Parasian cut. 143.
lasagna. 136.
leg. 139, 142, 143.
leg, butt portion. 139.
leg, shank portion. 139.
Liederkranz. 144.
loin. 139, 140, 142, 143.
longe. 139.
lovage. 133.
lumache. 137.
macreuse. 141.
mafalde. 136.
mafaldine. 136.
manicotti. 137.
marjoram. 133.
meringue. 146.
mezzani. 136.
milieu de poitrine. 141.
milieu de sous-noix. 139.
milk bread. 138.
Mimolette. 145.
mint. 133.
Monterey Jack. 144.
mousse. 147.
Munster. 145.
neck. 139, 140, 143.
nerveux de gîte à la noix. 141.
nerveux de sous-noix. 139.
noix. 139.
noix de hachage. 142.
noix pâtissière. 139.
non-skid spaghetti. 136.
noodles. 136.
onglet. 139, 141.
oregano. 133.
paleron. 141.
palette. 142.
pancake. 147.
parfait. 146.
parsley. 133.
pasta. 136, 137.
pennine. 137.
pens. 137.
Petit-Suisse. 145.
petits fours. 146.
picnic shoulder. 142.
pie. 146.
pied. 142.
pita bread. 138.
plat de côte couvert. 141.
plat de côte découvert. 141.
plate. 140.
poitrine. 139, 142, 143.
Pont-l'évêque. 145.
pork, North American cut. 142.
pork, Parasian cut. 142.
Port-Salut. 145.
porterhouse. 140.

profiterole. 146.
puff. 147.
puff pastry. 147.
pumpernickel bread. 138.
quasi. 139.
ravioli. 137.
Reblochon. 144.
rib. 139, 140, 143.
rib eye. 140.
rib portion. 142.
rings. 137.
romsteck. 141.
rond de gîte à la noix. 141.
Rondele. 144.
Roquefort. 144.
rosemary. 133.
rouelle. 139.
round. 140.
round loaf. 138.
rump. 140.
Russian pumpernickel. 138.
sage. 133.
Saint-Marcelin. 145.
Saint-Nectaire. 145.
Sainte-maure. 144.
savarin. 146.
savory. 133.
Scandinavian crak bread. 138.
seeds. 137.
selle. 143.
sesame seeded pita. 138.
shank. 139, 140, 142, 143.
shank portion. 142, 143.
shells. 137.
sherbet. 147.
short ribs. 140.
shoulder. 139, 140, 142, 143.
shoulder butt. 142.
side. 142.
side rib. 142.
sirloin. 140.
sirloin tip. 140.
small bows. 137.
soufflé. 147.
spaghetti. 136.
spinach lasagna. 136.
spinach noodles. 136.
stars. 137.
strip loin. 140.
surlonge. 141.
sweet bay. 133.
Swiss roll. 147.
T-bone. 140.
tarragon. 133.
tart. 146.
Teleme. 144.
tenderloin. 140.
tenderloin portion. 142.
tendron. 139, 141.
thin macaroni. 136.
thin spaghetti. 136.
thyme. 133.
Tomme aux raisins. 144.
tortellini. 137.
tranche grasse. 141.
turrets. 137.
twisted macaroni. 136.
unleavened bread. 138.
vacherin. 146.
Valençay. 144.
veal, North American cut. 139.
veal, Parisian cut. 139.
vermicelli. 136.
very large elbows. 137.
Vienna bread. 138.
waffle. 147.
wheels. 137.
whole loin. 139, 143.
whole wheat bread. 138.
wholemeal bread. 138.
wing. 140.
ziti. 136.

GARDENING

accelerator control. 243.

air filter. 243.
antivibration handle. 243.
arbor. 237.
bar nose. 243.
billhook. 242.
blade. 242.
bulb dibble. 239.
bush. 237.
chain brake. 243.
chainsaw. 243.
chainsaw chain. 243.
climbing plant. 237.
clump of flowers. 237.
cutter link. 243.
cutting cylinder. 242.
dibble. 239.
edger. 242.
edging. 237.
engine housing. 243.
flagstone. 237.
flower bed. 237.
fuel tank. 243.
garden. 237.
garden hoe. 238.
garden shoe. 240.
garden line. 239.
gardening. 235.
gardening, tools and equipment.
    238, 239, 240, 241, 242.
grafting knife. 242.
grass catcher. 242.
guide bar. 243.
hand fork. 239.
hand mower. 242.
handle. 243.
hanging basket. 237.
hedge. 237.
hedge shears. 239.
hedge trimmer. 242.
hoe. 238.
hoe-fork. 238.
hook. 238.
hose nozzle. 240.
hose reel. 240.
jet deflector. 242.
lantern. 237.
lawn. 237.
lawn aerator. 241.
lawn edger. 238.
lawn mowers. 242.
lawn rake. 238.
lopping shears. 239.
mattock. 238.
motor mower. 242.
muffler. 243.
oil pan. 243.
oscillating sprinkler. 240.
paling fence. 237.
path. 237.
pergola. 237.
pistol nozzle. 240.
pool. 237.
post-hole digger. 238.
pruning hook. 239.
pruning knife. 242.
pruning saw. 242.
pruning shears. 239.
rake. 238.
revolving sprinkler. 240.
rock garden. 237.
roller. 241.
rose. 240.
scuffle hoe. 238.
scythe. 242.
seeder. 239, 241.
shed. 237.
shovel. 238.
sickle. 242.
small hand cultivator. 239.
spade. 238.
spading fork. 238.
spark plug. 243.
sprayer. 240.
spreader. 241.
sprinkler hose. 240.
stake. 237.

starter handle. 243.
stop button. 243.
tank sprayer. 240.
terrace. 237.
tiller. 241.
tree pruner. 239.
trellis. 237.
trigger. 243.
trowel. 239.
tub. 237.
watering can. 240.
weeder. 239.
weeding hoe. 238.
wheelbarrow. 241.

GEOGRAPHY

abyssal hill. 42.
abyssal plain. 42.
Africa. 41.
air temperature. 54, 55.
altitude control system. 57.
altitude scales. 39.
altocumulus. 44.
altostratus. 44.
anemometer. 55.
Antarctic Ocean. 41.
Antarctica. 41.
Arctic. 41.
Arctic Ocean. 41.
artificial satellite. 39.
Asia. 41.
asthenosphere. 39.
Atlantic Ocean. 41.
Australia. 41.
barb. 53.
barograph. 55.
barometric pressure. 54.
barometric tendency. 54.
basaltic layer. 40.
base plate. 56.
battery. 57.
beach. 40, 43.
Beacon antenna. 57.
bergschrund. 48.
Bering Sea. 41.
Black Sea. 41.
blowing snow. 52.
breaker. 43.
butte. 47.
cactus. 47.
calm. 53.
capped column. 49.
card support. 56.
Caribbean Sea. 41.
Caspian Sea. 41.
cave. 46.
cave. 43.
Central America. 41.
chain of dunes. 47.
check nut. 56.
China Sea. 41.
cirrocumulus. 44.
cirrostratus. 44.
cirrus. 44.
clear sky. 53.
cleared ground. 55.
cliff. 40, 43.
climates of the world. 51.
cloud of volcanic ash. 45.
clouds. 44.
clouds of vertical development. 44.
cloudy sky. 53.
coast. 40.
coastal features, common. 43.
collecting funnel. 56.
column. 46, 49.
command antenna. 57.
complex dune. 47.
Concorde. 39.
condensation. 50.
cone. 45.
container. 56.
continental climates. 51.
continental margin. 42.
continental mass. 42.

continental rise. 42.
continental shelf. 40, 42.
continental slope. 40, 42.
continents, configuration of the.
    41.
continuous drizzle. 52.
continuous rain. 52.
continuous snow. 52.
crater. 45.
crescentic dune. 47.
crest. 43, 46.
crevasse. 48.
cumulonimbus. 44.
cumulus. 44.
deep-sea floor. 40.
depth of focus. 45.
desert. 47.
desert. 51.
dike. 45.
direct-reading rain gauge. 56.
dormant volcano. 45.
drifting snow. 52.
dry continental - arid. 51.
dry continental - semiarid. 51.
dry gallery. 46.
dry snow. 49.
dry subtropical. 51.
dune. 43.
dust storm. 52.
Earth, strucutre of the. 39.
Earth's atmosphere, profile of the.
    39.
Earth's crust. 39, 45.
Earth's crust, section of the. 40.
earthquake. 45.
epicenter. 45.
Eurasia. 41.
Europe. 41.
evaporation. 50.
exosphere. 39.
fault. 40, 45.
firn. 48.
foam. 43.
focus. 45.
fog. 52.
freezing rain. 52.
fronts. 53.
fumarole. 45.
geography. 37.
geyser. 45.
glacial cirque. 48.
glacier. 48.
glacier tongue. 48.
glass sphere. 56.
glaze. 49.
gorge. 46.
gour. 46.
granitic layer. 40.
Greenland Sea. 41.
ground moraine. 48.
Gutenberg discontinuity. 39.
guyot. 42.
hail. 49.
hail shower. 52.
half barb. 53.
hanging glacier. 48.
headland. 43.
heavy thunderstorm. 52.
high clouds. 44.
high pressure center. 54.
highland climates. 51.
hill. 46.
horizon scanner. 57.
humid subtropical. 51.
humid temperate - long summer.
    51.
humid temperate - short summer.
    51.
humidity. 55.
hurricane. 52.
hydrologic cycle. 50.
hygrograph. 55.
ice. 50.
igneous rocks. 40.
image dissector camera. 57.
Indian Ocean. 41.

infiltration. 50.
infrared spectrometer. 57.
inner core. 39.
instrument shelter. 55.
interconnecting truss. 57.
intermittent drizzle. 52.
intermittent rain. 52.
intermittent snow. 52.
interplanetary space. 39.
interrogation recording. 57.
intrusion rocks. 40.
ionosphere. 39.
irregular crystal. 49.
isobar. 54.
isoseismal line. 45.
laccolith. 45.
lagoon. 43.
lapiaz. 46.
lateral moraine. 48.
latitude scale. 56.
lava flow. 45.
lava plateau. 45.
leveling screw. 56.
lithosphere. 39.
location system antenna. 57.
lock nut. 56.
longitudinal dunes. 47.
low clouds. 44.
low pressure center. 54.
lower mantle. 39.
lower sphere clamp. 56.
lower support screw. 56.
magma. 45.
magma chamber. 45.
maximum and minimum
  thermometers. 55.
measuring tube. 56.
medial moraine. 48.
Mediterranean Sea. 41.
Mediterranean subtropical. 51.
melting snow. 49.
meltwater. 49.
Mercury capsule (USA). 39.
mesa. 47.
mesosphere. 39.
metamorphic rocks. 40.
*meteoralogical measuring
  instruments. 56.*
meteorological ground. 55.
meteorological symbols of clouds.
  44.
meteorology. 54, 55.
meteors. 52.
meteorological satellite. 57.
middle clouds. 44.
mist. 52.
Mohorovicic discontinuity. 39, 40.
mountain. 46.
mountain range. 40.
mountain slope. 46.
mountain torrent. 46.
Mt Everest. 39.
nacreous cloud. 39.
natural arch. 43.
needle. 49.
nimbostratus. 44.
noctilucent cloud. 39.
North America. 41.
North Sea. 41.
oasis. 47.
obscured sky. 53.
occluded front. 53.
ocean. 50.
ocean floor. 42.
Oceania. 41.
outer core. 39.
overcast sky. 53.
ozone. 39.
Pacific Ocean. 41.
palm grove. 47.
parabolic dune. 47.
pass. 46.
peak. 46.
pennant. 53.
piedmont glacier. 48.
pitch nozzle. 57.

plate crystal. 49.
plateau. 46.
polar climates. 51.
polar ice cap. 51.
polar tundra. 51.
precipice. 46.
precipitation. 50.
precipitation, kinds of. 49.
precipitation area. 54.
present state of weather. 54.
pressure. 55.
pressure change. 54.
progressive wave. 43.
psychrometer. 55.
rain. 49.
rain gauge. 55.
rain shower. 52.
rainfall. 55.
Red Sea. 41.
resurgence. 46.
ridge. 42.
rift. 42.
rock basin. 48.
rock step. 48.
rocket. 39.
rocky desert. 47.
roll nozzle. 57.
s-band antenna. 57.
saline lake. 47.
salt marsh. 43.
sand bar. 43.
sand island. 43.
sandstorm. 52.
sandy desert. 47.
scattered sky. 53.
sea level. 40, 42.
sea-level pressure. 54.
seamount. 42.
sedimentary rocks. 40.
seismic wave. 45.
serac. 48.
shaft. 53.
shooting star. 39.
shore. 43.
shoulder. 46.
sill. 45.
sink hole. 46.
siphon. 46.
sky coverage. 53.
sky coverage. 54.
sleet. 49, 52.
slightly covered sky. 53.
smoke. 52.
snow. 50.
snow crystals, classification of. 49.
snow pellet. 49.
snow shower. 52.
solar panel. 57.
sounding balloon. 39, 55.
South America. 41.
space achievements. 39.
space probe. 39.
spatial dendrite. 49.
sphere support. 56.
spit. 43.
spur. 46.
squall. 52.
stack. 43.
stalactite. 46.
stalagmite. 46.
state of ground. 55.
station circle. 53, 54.
station model. 54.
stationary front. 53.
stellar crystal. 49.
steppe. 51.
still water level. 43.
stratocumulus. 44.
stratosphere. 39.
stratus. 44.
sub-base. 56.
subarctic climates. 51.
sublimation. 50.
submarine canyon. 42.
subterranean stream. 46.
subtropical climates. 51.

summit. 46.
sun sensor. 57.
sunshine. 55.
sunshine recorder. 56.
sunshine recorder. 55.
support. 56.
surface cold front. 53.
surface runoff. 50.
surface warm front. 53.
swallow-hole. 46.
temperate climates. 51.
temperate marine. 51.
temperature of dew point. 54.
temperature of the soil surface. 55.
terminal moraine. 48.
theodolite. 55.
thermal control shutter. 57.
thermosphere. 39.
thunderstorm. 52.
tightening band. 56.
tombolo. 43.
transform fault. 42.
translation wave. 43.
transpiration. 50.
transverse dunes. 47.
trench. 42.
tropical climates. 51.
tropical rain forest. 51.
tropical savanna. 51.
tropical storm. 52.
troposphere. 39.
trough. 43, 54.
type of high cloud. 54.
type of low cloud. 54.
type of middle cloud. 54.
type of the air mass. 54.
underground flow. 50.
upper cold front. 53.
upper mantle. 39.
upper sphere clamp. 56.
upper support screw. 56.
upper warm front. 53.
valley. 46.
vent. 45.
very cloudy sky. 53.
volcanic island. 42.
volcano. 45.
volcano. 40.
water forms. 49.
water table. 46.
waterfall. 46.
wave. 43.
wave base. 43.
wave height. 43.
wave lenght. 43.
weather map. 53.
*weather symbols, international. 52,
  53.*
wet snow. 49.
wind. 53.
wind. 47.
wind arrow. 53.
wind direction. 54.
wind direction and speed. 54.
wind scale. 53.
wind speed. 53, 54, 55.
wind vane. 55.
X-15 (USA). 39.
yaw nozzle. 57.

HEALTH

absorbent cotton. 615.
adhesive bandages. 615.
adhesive tape. 615.
arm. 617.
arm piece. 616.
armrest. 617.
aspirin. 615.
back upholstery. 617.
Canadian crutch. 616.
canes. 616.
caster. 617.
clothing guard. 617.
cotton applicators. 615.

cross brace. 617.
crutch. 616.
crutch tip. 616.
crutches. 616.
cuff section. 616.
disposable syringe. 615.
elastic support bandage. 615.
English cane. 616.
first aid kit. 615.
footplate. 617.
forearm crutch. 616.
gauze roller bandage. 615.
handgrip. 616, 617.
hanger bracket. 617.
health. 613.
heel loop. 617.
hollow barrel. 615.
hub. 617.
insulin syringe. 615.
large wheel. 617.
Luer-Lock syringe. 615.
needle. 615.
needle hub. 615.
ortho-cane. 616.
peroxide. 615.
plunger. 615.
push rim. 617.
quad cane. 616.
quadripod. 616.
rubber tip. 616.
rubbing alcohol. 615.
safety pin. 615.
scissors. 615.
seat upholstery. 617.
spacer. 617.
standard walker. 616.
sterile pad. 615.
syringe for irrigation. 615.
syringes. 615.
tipping lever. 617.
tripod cane. 616.
tuberculin syringe. 615.
tweezers. 615.
upright. 616.
walking aids. 616.
walking stick. 616.
wheel lock. 617.
wheelchair. 617.

HEAVY MACHINERY

A-frame. 661.
*agricultural machinery. 152, 153,
  154.*
air-cleaner filter. 664.
air fan. 155.
apron. 668.
arm. 665.
articulating hinge point. 665.
backhoe bucket. 665.
backhoe loader. 665.
backing light. 152.
backstep. 663.
ball stud of circle drawbar. 666.
barn. 151.
base. 661.
beam. 153.
beater. 155.
beehive. 151.
bellcrank. 665.
blade. 664, 666.
blade arm. 666.
blade rotation mechanism. 666.
block. 671.
body lift cylinder. 668.
boom. 661, 665, 667.
boom point sheave. 661.
bottom. 153.
bottom deckboard. 671.
bowl. 668.
box-beam Y. 666.
box pallet. 671.
breathing apparatus. 662.
bucket. 661, 665.
bucket cylinder. 665.

bucket hinge pin. 665.
bucket tooth. 665.
bulldozer. 664.
bunker silo. 151.
cab. 664, 665, 666, 667, 668, 670.
canopy. 668.
cardan shaft. 152.
carriage. 670.
chaffer sieve. 155.
circle. 666.
circle drawbar. 666.
clamshell bucket. 667.
collapsible fire ladder. 662.
combine harvester. 155.
compressed-air cylinder. 662.
concave. 155.
control panel. 662.
control wheel. 663.
coulter. 153.
counterjib. 669.
counterjib ballast. 669.
counterweight. 667, 669.
covering disk. 154.
cowshed. 151.
crane. 669.
crane runway. 669.
crawler crane. 669.
crawler tractor. 664.
crop elevator. 155.
crossbar. 152.
crosshead. 670.
cultivator. 153.
cup conveyor. 154.
cutter bar. 155.
cutting edge. 664, 668.
cylinder. 666, 667.
deluge gun. 663.
diesel engine. 665.
dipper bucket. 667.
discharge spout. 152, 153.
divider. 155.
dividing breeching. 662.
double-decked pallet. 671.
draft arm. 668.
draft tube. 668.
drag chain. 661.
drag drum. 661.
drag rope. 661.
dragline. 661.
drawbar. 664.
drive axle. 670.
drive wheel. 666.
dump body. 668.
dump rope. 661.
dump truck. 668.
ejector. 668.
electrified fence. 151.
elevator. 152.
engine. 664, 666, 667, 668.
entry. 671.
exhaust pipe. 664.
fallow. 151.
farm, buildings. 151.
farm, modern. 149.
farmhouse. 151.
farmyard. 151.
fertilizer distributor. 154.
field heap spreader. 154.
filter. 661.
finger. 152.
fingerwheel. 154.
fire engine. 662, 663.
fire hose. 662.
fireman's hatchet. 662.
fitting. 663.
fodder corn. 151.
fork extender. 670.
forklift reach truck. 670.
forklift truck. 670.
forks. 670.
frame. 153, 667, 668, 670.
frog. 153.
front axle. 666.
front-end loader. 665.
front wheel. 666.
gooseneck. 668.

grader. 666.
grain pan. 155.
grain screw. 155.
grain sieve. 155.
grain tank. 155.
grain unloading auger. 155.
grapple. 667.
greenhouse. 151.
hand lamp. 662.
hand pallet truck. 671.
hand truck. 671.
handling engines. 671.
hangar. 151.
harness. 662.
harrow. 152.
heavy machinery. 659.
heel. 153.
hoist chain. 661.
hoist drum. 661.
hoist rope. 661.
hoisting rope. 669.
hook. 669.
hook ladder. 663.
hopper. 154.
horn. 663.
hose truck. 663.
hydrant intake. 663.
hydraulic cylinder. 664, 665, 668.
hydraulic shovel. 667.
implement bar. 152.
jib. 669.
jib tie. 669.
knife. 155.
ladder truck, aerial. 662.
landside. 153.
leg. 153.
lift arm. 665.
lift cylinder. 665, 670.
lifting chain. 670.
load backrest. 670.
loam. 152.
loudspeaker. 663.
machinery. 155.
manual lift truck. 671.
manure spreader. 153.
manure spreader box. 153.
mars light. 663.
mast. 661, 670.
milk room. 151.
moldboard. 153.
motor. 155, 661.
nozzle. 662, 663.
operator's cab. 661, 669.
operator's seat. 670.
orchard. 151.
outrigger. 662, 667.
overhead frame. 666.
overhead guard. 670.
pallets. 671.
pasture. 151.
pick-up. 152.
pickup automatic baler. 152.
pickup loader. 152.
pickup reel. 155.
pigsty. 151.
pike pole. 663.
pivot cab. 667.
platform. 669.
platform truck. 671.
portable fire extinguisher. 662.
potato planter. 154.
poultry house. 151.
power lift truck. 670.
power take off. 152.
pumper. 663.
push arm. 664.
push block. 664.
reciprocating knife mower. 152.
reel. 154.
return elevator. 155.
revolving frame. 661.
rib. 668.
ribbing plow. 153.
ripper. 666.
ripper. 664.
ripper cylinder. 664.

ripper tip. 664.
ripper tooth. 664.
roller circle. 661.
rotary hoe. 153.
rotating auger. 155.
scarifier. 666.
scraper. 668.
scraper engine. 668.
seed drill. 154.
shank protector. 664.
share. 153.
sheep shelter. 151.
side. 671.
silage harvester. 153.
single-decked pallet. 671.
skimmer. 153.
solid rubber tire. 670.
spider. 153.
spike-tooth. 152.
spotlight. 662, 663.
spreading rotor. 153.
sprocket wheel. 664.
steering axle. 670.
steering cylinder. 668.
steering track rod. 152.
steering wheel. 155, 670.
stick. 667.
storage compartment. 662, 663.
straw walker. 155.
stringer. 671.
stringer board. 671.
stripper beater. 155.
subsoil plow. 154.
suction hose. 663.
suspension cable. 661.
swing circle. 667.
tandem disk harrow. 154.
tandem drive housing. 666.
telescopic boom. 669.
tooth. 154, 666, 667.
toothed rotor. 154.
top deckboard. 671.
tower crane. 669.
tower ladder. 662.
tower mast. 669.
towing hook. 152.
track. 664.
track carrier roller. 664.
track grouser. 664.
track idler. 664.
track link. 664.
track roller. 664.
track roller frame. 664.
track shoe. 664.
track shoe. 664.
tractor. 152.
tractor engine. 668.
transmission. 668.
trolley. 669.
trolley pulley. 669.
truck crane. 669.
turntable mounting. 662.
vegetable garden. 151.
vertical silo. 151.
walking cam. 661.
walking shoe. 661.
walkway. 661.
water pressure gauge. 663.
well. 151.
wheel tractor. 665.
winch. 661.
wing pallet. 671.

HOUSE

access panel. 195.
access ramp. 177.
accordion. 188, 189.
accordion door. 178.
adjustable pedestal. 195.
air-circulating fan. 196.
air conditioning. 196.
air impeller. 196.
air inlet control. 191.
air tube. 195.

andiron. 191.
angle brace. 180.
angle valve. 193.
aquastat. 194.
Arenberg parquet. 186.
asbestos shingle. 185.
ash lid. 191.
asphalt shingle. 185.
attic. 177.
automatic air vent. 194.
automatic circulating pump. 194.
automatic relief valve. 194.
automatic shutt-off. 196.
baffle. 191.
balcony. 178.
baluster. 187.
balustrade. 178.
base. 190.
baseboard radiator. 193.
baseboard register. 192.
basement. 179.
basement window. 177.
basket weave pattern. 186.
bathroom. 179.
batt insulation. 185.
bedroom. 179.
bell roof. 181.
bi-fold. 188.
blade. 196.
blanket insulation. 185.
bleeder valve. 193.
blower. 194, 195, 196.
blower motor. 195.
boarding joist. 186.
boiler. 194.
boiler. 193.
bottom rail. 188.
brace. 182.
branch duct. 192.
branch return pipe. 193.
branch supply pipe. 193.
brick. 183.
bridging. 182.
broom. 191.
building materials. 183, 184, 185.
bull's eye. 177.
cabinet. 196.
cap. 187.
capped tee. 192.
car parking. 178.
casement. 189.
casement window. 189.
caster. 196.
ceiling collar. 192.
ceiling fan. 196.
ceiling joist. 182.
ceiling register. 192.
cement. 184.
cement screed. 186.
Chantilly parquet. 186.
chimney. 192.
chimney. 177, 190.
chimney connection. 191.
chimney flue. 190.
chimney pot. 177.
chimney stack. 177.
circulating pump. 193.
closed expansion tank. 194.
closed stringer. 187.
closet. 178, 179.
cold room. 179.
column. 193.
column radiator. 193.
compressor. 194.
concrete block. 183.
condenser. 196.
condenser coil. 196.
condensor. 196.
conical broach roof. 181.
control panel. 196.
convector. 193.
cooling/heating coils. 194.
corbel piece. 190.
corner stud. 182.
cornice. 177, 188.
crest. 177.

damper. 190, 192.
dehumidifier. 196.
detachable handle. 191.
diamond mesh metal lath. 184.
dining room. 179.
dome roof. 181.
door. 188.
door. 177.
doorknob. 188.
doors, types of. 188.
dormer. 177.
double-hung. 189.
double plate. 182.
down. 178.
downspout. 177.
drain line. 194.
drain tile. 182.
drain valve. 194.
drip stone. 177.
driveway. 178.
elbow. 191, 192, 193.
electric furnace. 195.
electric motor. 195.
electric supply. 194.
electrode assembly. 195.
enameled hardboard. 184.
enclosure. 193, 196.
end joist. 182.
entablature. 188.
evaporator. 196.
eveporator coils. 196.
expansion tank. 193.
exterior door. 188.
fan. 194, 195.
fan control. 196.
fan motor. 196.
fillet. 177.
filter. 194, 195.
finned tube. 193.
firebox. 191.
firebrick. 195.
firebrick back. 190.
fireplace. 190.
fireplace. 178.
firestopping. 182.
firetending tools. 191.
flashing. 192.
flat roof. 180.
flight of stairs. 187.
floor. 182.
floor joist. 182.
floor tile. 185.
floorboard. 186.
flue collar. 191.
flue damper. 191.
flue pipe. 191.
foam insulation. 185.
foam rubber insulation. 185.
footing. 182.
forced hot-water system. 193.
forced warm-air system. 192.
foundation. 182.
foundations. 182.
frame. 182.
French window. 189.
fresh air inlet. 190.
function selector. 196.
furnace. 192, 194.
fuse block. 195.
gable roof. 180.
garage. 177, 179.
garden. 178.
girder. 182.
glue. 186.
goose-neck. 187.
grade sloppe. 178.
gravel. 182.
grille. 196.
ground floor. 178, 179.
guard. 187.
guard rail. 177.
gutter. 177.
gypsum block. 183.
hall. 179.
hallway. 179.
hammer beam. 180.

handrail. 187.
hanging stile. 188, 189.
hardboards. 184.
head of frame. 189.
header. 188, 190.
heating. 190, 191, 192, 193, 194, 195.
heating element. 194, 195.
heating elements indicator. 194.
heating pump. 194.
heating room. 179.
heating unit. 193.
helm roof. 181.
herringbone parquet. 186.
herringbone pattern. 186.
hinge. 188, 189.
hinged door. 178.
hip-and-valley roof. 181.
hip roof. 180.
hood. 190.
hook. 189.
horizontal pivoting. 189.
hot-air register. 192.
hot-water main. 194.
house. 175.
house. 178.
house, exterior of a. 177.
house, plan reading. 178.
house, structure. 180, 182.
humidifier. 194.
humidistat. 196.
ignition transformer. 195.
imperial roof. 181.
inlaid parquet. 186.
inner hearth. 190.
insulating material. 186.
jalousie. 189.
jamb. 188, 189, 190.
joist. 186.
kitchen. 179.
knee brace. 180.
landing. 179, 187.
laundry room. 179.
lavatory. 179.
lawn. 178.
lean-to roof. 180.
ledger. 182.
lightning rod. 177.
lintel. 190.
living room. 179.
loading door. 191.
lock. 188.
lock rail. 188.
log carrier. 191.
lot plan. 178.
log tongs. 191.
loose fill insulation. 185.
louver. 196.
louvered window. 189.
main duct. 192.
main entrance. 178.
main return pipe. 193.
main supply pipe. 193.
manometer. 194.
mansard roof. 181.
mantel. 190.
mantel shelf. 190.
master bedroom. 179.
metal heat reflector. 190.
middle rail. 188.
monitor roof. 181.
mortar. 183.
motor. 196.
motor-compressor unit. 196.
moulded insulation. 185.
muntin. 188, 189.
newel post. 187.
nosing. 187.
nozzle. 195.
ogee roof. 181.
oil burner. 195.
oil pump. 195.
oil supply line. 195.
open stringer. 187.
outdoor condensing unit. 194.
outer hearth. 190.

outlet grille. 193.
overlay flooring. 186.
pan. 196.
pane. 189.
panel. 188.
pantry. 179.
particle board. 184.
patio. 178.
patio door. 178.
pavilion roof. 180.
perforated gypsum lath. 184.
perforated hardboard. 184.
perron. 177.
pipe section. 192.
pipe-wrapping insulation. 185.
pitched-roof. 180.
plain gypsum lath. 184.
plan symbols for doors. 188.
plaster. 184.
plasterboard. 184.
plastic-laminated hardboard. 184.
playroom. 179.
plenum. 192.
plywood. 184.
pocket sliding door. 178.
poker. 191.
porch. 177.
pothole lid. 191.
power relay. 195.
prestressed concrete. 183.
principal rafter. 180.
property line. 178.
protective relay. 195.
purlin. 180.
purlin cleat. 180.
rafter. 180, 182.
rail. 177.
rain cap. 192.
refractory fire pot. 195.
refrigerant tubing. 194.
reinforced concrete. 183.
relay. 196.
return air. 195.
return duct. 194.
return main. 194.
ridge beam. 180.
rigid board insulation. 185.
rise. 187.
riser. 187.
rod. 196.
roof structure. 180.
roof vent. 177.
roofs, types of. 180, 181.
room air conditioner. 196.
rooms of the house. 179.
rotunda roof. 181.
run. 187.
sash-frame. 189.
sawtooth roof. 181.
shingle. 185.
shovel. 191.
shutter. 188.
shutting stile. 188.
side entrance. 178.
side post. 180.
sill. 182.
sill of frame. 189.
sill plate. 182.
skylight. 177.
sliding. 188, 189.
sloped turret. 181.
smoke dome. 190.
splaying. 190.
sprocket. 180.
stairs. 187.
stairs. 178.
stairwell. 179.
standard hardboard. 184.
steel. 183.
step groove. 187.
stile groove of sash. 189.
stile tongue of sash. 189.
stone. 183.
storage space. 179.
storm collar. 192.

strip flooring with alternate joints. 186.
strut. 180.
stud. 182.
study. 179.
subfloor. 182.
supply duct. 194.
swing. 188.
terminal connections. 194.
terrace. 177.
thermostat. 194, 195, 196.
thin spring-metal insulation. 185.
threshold. 177, 188.
throat. 190.
tie beam. 180.
tile. 185.
toothing stone. 177.
top plate. 180.
top rail. 188.
top rail of sash. 189.
transformer. 195.
tread. 187.
trim collar. 191.
truss. 180.
upper floor. 178, 179.
valley. 177.
valley gutter. 177.
vane. 177.
vegetable garden. 178.
vent. 196.
Versailles parquet. 186.
vertical pivoting. 189.
vinyl insulation. 185.
wall register. 192.
wall stack section. 192.
wall stud. 182.
weatherboard. 188, 189.
web member. 180.
window. 189.
window. 177, 178.
windows, types of. 189.
wood. 184.
wood flooring. 186.
wood flooring arrangements. 186.
wood stove. 191.
workshop. 179.

HOUSE FURNITURE

acanthus leaf. 200.
adjustable lamp. 211.
agitator. 230.
air vent. 232.
Alsace glass. 212.
apron. 199, 200, 203.
arm. 200, 211.
arm stump. 200.
armchair. 200.
armchairs. 201.
armchairs, principal types of. 200, 201.
armoire. 205.
attached curtain. 207.
automatic cord reel. 234.
automatic drip coffee maker. 224.
back. 203, 214, 215, 216, 217.
backguard. 228, 230, 231.
bake element. 228.
baking utensils. 220.
banquette. 202.
bar. 206.
bar frame. 211.
base. 210, 232, 233.
base of splat. 200.
basket. 223, 224, 230.
baster. 221.
bean bag chair. 202.
beater. 225.
beater ejector. 225.
bed. 204.
bed lamp. 210.
bedside lamp. 210.
bedskirt. 204.
beer mug. 212.
bench. 202.

Thematic Indexes

bergère. 200.
blade. 214, 217, 224, 226.
blanket. 204.
blender. 225.
blending attachment. 225.
blind. 209.
block bracket. 208.
bobeche. 210.
body. 233.
bolster. 204, 214, 217.
boning knife. 217.
bordeaux. 212.
bottle opener. 219, 233.
bottom rail. 205.
bowl. 216, 226.
bowl with serving spout. 226.
box pleat. 207.
box spring. 204.
bracket. 208, 209.
bracket base. 205.
bracket slot. 209.
brandy. 212.
bread and butter plate. 213.
bread guide. 227.
bread knife. 217.
bridge. 208.
broil element. 228.
buffet. 206.
buffet and china cabinet. 206.
bumper. 234.
burgundy. 212.
burner. 223.
burner ring. 223.
butt hinge. 199.
butter compartment. 229.
butter curler. 217.
butter dish. 213.
butter knife. 214.
button notch. 233.
cabinet. 231, 232.
cabriole leg. 200.
cabriolet. 200.
café curtain. 207.
cake pan. 220.
can opener. 233.
can opener. 219.
carafe. 224.
carrier. 208.
carving fork. 215.
carving knife. 217.
caster. 234.
ceiling fitting. 210.
center post. 205.
chain. 210.
chairs, types of. 203.
chaise longue. 201.
champagne flute. 212.
champagne glass. 212.
chandelier. 210.
cheese knife. 214.
chest. 206.
chesterfield. 201.
chiffonier. 206.
chopsticks. 223.
citrus juicer. 226.
citrus juicer. 218.
clamp. 211.
clamping handle. 226.
clamping nut. 226.
cleaning tools. 234.
cleaning tools. 234.
cleaver. 217.
clip. 208.
clock timer. 227, 228.
closet. 206.
club chair. 201.
cockleshell. 200.
cocktail. 212.
coffee makers. 224.
coffee mill. 224.
coffee mug. 213.
coffee spoon. 216.
coil spring. 209.
colander. 218.
color selector. 227.
column. 210.

comforter. 204.
compressor. 229.
condenser coil. 229.
conductor. 211.
container. 225.
contral panel. 228.
control knob. 228.
control panel. 227, 230, 231, 232.
cook's knife. 217.
cookie cutters. 220.
cookie press. 220.
cookie sheet. 220.
cooking surface. 227.
cooking utensils. 222, 223.
cooktop. 228.
cord. 233.
cord tieback. 207.
corer. 221.
corner cupboard. 206.
corner lighting. 210.
cornice. 205, 207.
cottage curtain. 207.
couscous kettle. 222.
cover. 226.
cradle. 209.
creamer. 213.
crevice tool. 234.
crinoline stretcher. 203.
crisper. 229.
crisscross curtains. 207.
cross rail. 203.
crosspiece. 199.
cup. 213.
curtain. 207.
curtain pole. 208.
curtain track. 208.
cutlery basket. 232.
cutting blade. 225.
cutting edge. 214, 217.
cutting wheel. 233.
dairy compartment. 229.
dasher. 226.
decanter. 212.
deep fryer. 223.
defrost heater. 229.
defrost timer. 229.
demitasse. 213.
desk lamp. 211.
dessert fork. 215.
dessert knife. 214.
dessert spoon. 216.
detachable control. 227.
detergent dispenser. 232.
diamond point. 205.
dinner fork. 215.
dinner knife. 214.
dinner plate. 213.
dinnerware. 213.
director's chair. 201.
discs. 226.
dishwasher. 232.
domestic appliances. 225, 226, 227, 228, 229, 230, 231, 232, 233, 234.
door. 205, 227, 231.
door panel. 205.
door shelf. 229.
door stop. 229.
door switch. 231.
double boiler. 222.
double curtain rod. 208.
dough hook. 225.
drain hose. 230, 232.
drain pan. 229.
draining spoon. 219.
draw drapery. 207.
drawer. 199, 206.
dredger. 221.
dresser. 206.
drip bowl. 228.
drive belt. 230, 231.
drive wheel. 233.
drop. 210.
drop-leaf. 199.
drop-leaf table. 199.
drop light. 211.

drum. 209, 226, 231.
dryer. 231.
dusting brush. 234.
dutch oven. 222.
ear. 203.
egg beater. 220.
egg poacher. 223.
egg slicer. 221.
egg timer. 219.
egg tray. 229.
elastic. 204.
electric range. 228.
end bracket. 208.
end cap. 208.
end panel. 227.
end stop. 208.
equalizing buckle. 209.
espresso coffee maker. 224.
evaporator coil. 229.
exhaust duct. 231.
exhaust hose. 231.
extension table. 199.
extension wand. 234.
fabric guide. 233.
fan. 229, 231.
feed tube. 226.
ferrule. 214.
fill opening. 233.
filleting knife. 217.
filter. 223.
filter basket. 224.
fish fork. 215.
fish knife. 214.
fish platter. 213.
fish poacher. 222.
fitted sheet. 204.
flan pan. 220.
flashlight. 211.
flat end pin. 209.
flat pleat. 207.
flat sheet. 204.
flexible hose. 234.
floor brush. 234.
floor lamp. 210.
fluted pole. 208.
folding chair. 203.
fondue fork. 215.
fondue pot. 223.
fondue set. 223.
food processor. 226.
foot. 205.
footboard. 204.
fork. 215.
forks, major types of. 215.
four pale beater. 225.
frame stile. 205.
freezer bucket. 226.
freezer compartment. 229.
freezer door. 229.
frieze. 205.
fringe trimming. 207.
front leg. 203.
front tip. 233.
frying pan. 223.
funnel. 218.
garlic press. 218.
gasket. 228, 230, 232.
gate-leg. 199.
glass cover. 229.
glass curtain. 207.
glassware. 212.
globe. 210.
graperfruit knife. 217.
grater. 218.
grater disc. 226.
gravy boat and stand. 213.
grease well. 227.
griddle. 227.
grill and waffle baker. 227.
groove. 227.
guard. 211, 217.
guard rail. 229.
H stretcher. 203.
half handle. 217.
ham knife. 217.
hand blender. 225.

hand mixer. 225.
handle. 204, 211, 214, 215, 216, 225, 226, 227, 228, 229, 233, 234.
hanging stile. 205.
hassock. 202.
headboard. 204.
headbox. 209.
heating duct. 231.
heating element. 231, 232.
heel. 217.
heel rest. 225, 233.
hem. 209.
highball. 212.
hinge. 205, 227, 228, 232.
holdback. 207.
hood. 234.
hook. 208, 211.
hors d'oeuvre dish. 213.
house furniture. 197.
ice-cream can. 226.
ice-cream freezer. 226.
ice cream spoon. 221.
ice cube tray. 229.
icing syringe. 220.
idler pulley. 231.
impeller. 232.
inlet hose. 230, 232.
inlet nozzle. 230.
inside. 216.
inverted pleat. 207.
juicer. 226.
kettle. 233.
kickplate. 229.
kitchen knife. 217.
kitchen knives, types of. 217.
kitchen scale. 219.
kitchen timer. 219.
kitchen utensil for straining. 218.
kitchen utensils. 217, 218, 219, 220.
kitchen utensils, miscellaneous. 221.
kitchen utensils for draining. 218.
kitchen utensils for grating. 218.
kitchen utensils for grinding. 218.
kitchen utensils for measuring. 219.
kitchen utensils for opening. 219.
knife. 214.
knives, major types of. 214.
knob. 199.
ladle. 219.
lamp. 210.
latch. 227, 228, 232.
leaf. 199.
leg. 199, 204.
lever. 227.
lever corkscrew. 219.
lid. 222, 223, 224, 226, 227, 230.
lift cord. 209.
lift cord lock. 209.
lights. 210, 211.
linen. 204.
lint filter. 230.
lint trap. 231.
liqueur. 212.
lock. 205.
loose curtain. 207.
louver. 211.
love seat. 201.
lower bowl. 224.
magnetic gasket. 229.
magnetic lid holder. 233.
master carrier. 208.
mattress. 204.
mattress cover. 204.
measuring cap. 225.
measuring cups. 219.
measuring spoons. 219.
meat grinder. 218.
meat keeper. 229.
meat thermometer. 219.
méridienne. 201.
microwave oven. 227.
middle rail. 205.

mixing bowl. 225.
mixing bowls. 220.
mortar. 218.
motor. 230, 231, 234.
motor unit. 225, 226.
motro unit. 224.
muffin pan. 220.
Neapolitan coffee maker. 224.
neck. 215, 216.
neckroll. 204.
nest of tables. 199.
nutcracker. 218.
old-fashioned. 212.
on-off switch. 211.
operation cord. 208.
ottoman. 202.
oven. 228.
oven lamp. 227, 228.
overdrapery. 207.
overflow protection switch. 232.
overlap carrier. 208.
oyster fork. 215.
oyster knife. 217.
palmette. 200.
pancake pan. 223.
panel. 207.
paring knife. 217.
pasta maker. 218.
pastry bag and nozzles. 220.
pastry brush. 220.
pastry cutting wheel. 220.
patera. 200.
pawl. 209.
peeler. 217.
peg. 205.
pendant. 210.
pepper shaker. 213.
percolator. 224.
pestle. 218.
pie pan. 220.
pierce lever. 233.
pillow. 204.
pillow protector. 204.
pillowcase. 204.
pin. 199.
pinch pleat. 207.
plain pole. 208.
plate. 227.
platter. 213.
pleated heading. 207.
plunger. 226.
point. 215, 217.
pole. 208.
port. 212.
post lantern. 211.
potato masher. 219.
poultry shears. 221.
power supply cord. 210, 211.
pressure cooker. 222.
pressure regulator. 222.
probe receptacle. 227.
programmer. 228, 230, 231, 232.
prong. 215.
pulse button. 225.
pump. 230, 232.
push-button control board. 232.
pusher. 226.
quiche plate. 220.
rack. 222, 228, 232.
racks. 223.
ramekin. 213.
ratchet. 209.
reamer. 226.
rear leg. 203.
récamier. 201.
recessed cooktop. 228.
reflector. 211.
refrigerator. 229.
refrigerator compartment. 229.
reservoir. 224.
retractable cord. 234.
rim soup bowl. 213.
rinceau. 200.
ring. 208.
rinse dispenser. 232.
rivet. 217.

roast sensor probe. 228.
roasting pans. 222.
rocking chair. 201, 203.
rod. 208.
roll-up blind. 209.
roller. 208, 209, 232.
roller shade. 209.
rolling pin. 220.
root. 215.
rotisserie. 228.
round end pin. 209.
ruffle. 207.
rug and floor nozzle. 234.
runner. 199.
S-scroll. 200.
safety thermostat. 231.
safety valve. 222.
salad bowl. 213.
salad fork. 215.
salad plate. 213.
salad shaker. 218.
salad spinner. 218.
salt shaker. 213.
saltire. 203.
saucepan. 222.
saucer. 213.
sauté pan. 223.
seat. 200, 203.
seats. 202.
secretary. 206.
sensor probe. 227.
serving bowl. 213.
serving table. 199.
shade. 209, 210, 211.
shade cloth. 209.
shag-vac-rake. 234.
sham. 204.
sharpener. 221.
sharpening steel. 217.
sheer curtain. 207.
shelf. 206, 229.
shelf channel. 229.
shell. 233.
shirred heading. 207.
showcase. 206.
shutters. 209.
side. 214.
side chair. 203.
sieve. 218.
sifter. 220.
sight-glass tube. 233.
signal lamp. 228, 232.
silverware. 214, 215, 216.
single curtain rod. 208.
skimmer. 219.
slat. 209.
slide. 232.
slide selector. 227, 233.
slot. 215, 227.
snail dish. 221.
snail tongs. 221.
sofa. 201.
soleplate. 233.
soup bowl. 213.
soup spoon. 216.
soup tureen. 213.
spaghetti tongs. 221.
spatula. 219.
speed control. 225.
speed selector. 226.
spindle. 203, 226.
spiral beater. 225.
splat. 200.
splayed leg. 199.
spoon. 216.
spoons, major types of. 216.
spot. 211.
spout. 224, 233.
spray. 233.
spray arm. 232.
spray button. 233.
spring. 211.
square cushion. 204.
stabilizer foot. 232.
stacking chairs. 203.
stand. 210, 223, 225.

start switch. 231.
steak knife. 214.
steam button. 233.
steam iron. 233.
stem. 224.
step chair. 202.
stile. 203.
stock pot. 222.
stoner. 221.
stool. 202.
storage door. 229.
storage furniture. 205, 206.
strainer. 226.
stretcher. 199.
stretchers. 203.
strip fixture. 211.
strirrer cover. 227.
suction regulator. 234.
sugar bowl. 213.
sugar spoon. 216.
sundae spoon. 216.
support. 203, 208.
support wheel. 231.
surface element. 228.
swag lamp. 210.
swinger wall lamp. 210.
switch. 228, 229, 234.
table. 199.
table lamp. 210.
table mixer. 225.
tables, major types of. 199.
tablespoon. 216.
tang. 214, 217.
tape. 209.
tassel. 207.
tea ball. 221.
teapot. 213.
teaspoon. 216.
temperature dial. 233.
temperature selector. 230, 231.
temperature sensing bulb. 228.
tension pulley set. 208.
tension pulley wheel. 208.
terminal. 228.
thermostat control. 229.
thumb rest. 233.
tieback. 207.
tieback hook. 207.
tilt-back head. 225.
tilt cord. 209.
tilt tube. 209.
timed outlet. 228.
tip. 214, 216.
toaster. 227.
tongs. 221.
top rail. 203, 205.
top-work surface. 232.
track. 208.
track lighting. 211.
transmission. 230.
traverse rod. 208.
tray. 223.
trim ring. 228.
tub. 230, 232.
tubular element. 228.
turner. 219.
turntable. 225.
upholstery nozzle. 234.
upper bowl. 224.
utensils, set of. 219.
vaccuum cleaner. 234.
vacuum coffee maker. 224.
valance. 207.
valance lighting. 210.
vane. 231.
vegetable bowl. 213.
vegetable brush. 221.
vegetable steamer. 222.
Venetian blind. 209.
vertical cord lift. 233.
volute. 200.
wall fitting. 210.
wall lantern. 211.
wand. 234.
wardrobe. 206.

warming plate. 224.
wash tower. 232.
washer. 230.
Wassily chair. 200.
water goblet. 212.
water level selector. 230.
water pitcher. 213.
whisk. 220.
white wine. 212.
winding mechanism. 209.
window. 227, 228.
window accessories. 207, 208, 209.
wine waiter corkscrew. 219.
wire beater. 225.
wok. 223.
wok set. 223.
worm gear. 209.
yoke. 208.
zester. 217.

HUMAN BEING

abdomen. 106.
abdominal aorta. 117, 120.
abdominal rectus. 110.
acromion. 113.
Adam's apple. 106.
adipose tissue. 109, 128.
ala. 125.
alveolar bone. 115.
ampulla. 128.
ampulla of uterine tube. 109.
anal canal. 119.
anconeus. 111.
ankle. 106.
anterior chamber. 123.
anterior commissure. 122.
anterior notch. 124.
anterior pulmonary plexus. 118.
anterior root. 122.
anterior tibial. 110.
antihelix. 124.
antitragus. 124.
anus. 108, 109, 119.
aorta. 118.
apex. 115, 126.
apical foramen. 115.
apocrine sweat gland. 128.
aqueous humor. 123.
arch of the aorta. 116.
areola. 109.
arm. 106.
armpit. 106.
arteries. 117.
ascending aorta. 116.
ascending colon. 119.
atlas. 113.
auditory ossicles. 124.
auricle. 124.
axillary artery. 117.
axillary nerve. 121.
axillary vein. 117.
axis. 113.
axon. 127.
back. 107.
basement membrane. 127.
basilic vein. 117.
biceps of arm. 110.
biceps of thigh. 111.
blood circulation. 116, 117.
blood vessel. 115, 128, 129.
body. 107.
body of nail. 129.
brachial. 110.
brachial artery. 117.
brachial plexus. 121.
brachioradial. 110, 111.
breast. 109.
breast. 106.
broad ligament of uterus. 109.
broadest of back. 111.
Brunn's membrane. 125.
buttock. 107.
calcaneus. 113.

calf. 107.
calyx. 120.
canine. 115.
cardiac plexus. 118.
carpus. 112.
cavernous body. 108.
cecum. 119.
celiac trunk. 116, 120.
cell body. 127.
cementum. 115.
central incisor. 115.
central nervous system. 122.
cephalic vein. 117.
cerebellum. 122.
cerebrum. 122.
cervical plexus. 121.
cervical vertebra. 113.
cheek. 106.
chest. 106.
chin. 106.
choroid. 123.
ciliary process. 123.
clavicle. 112.
clitoris. 109.
coccygeal nerve. 121.
coccyx. 112.
cochlea. 124.
cochlear nerve. 124.
collagenous fiber. 128.
collateral. 127.
commissure of lips of mouth. 126.
common carotid artery. 117.
common extensor of fingers. 111.
common hepatic artery. 117.
common iliac artery. 117, 120.
common iliac vein. 120.
common peroneal nerve. 121.
communicating rami. 122.
complexus. 111.
concha. 124.
conjunctiva. 123.
connective tissue. 127, 128.
cornea. 123.
coronal suture. 114.
corpus callosum. 122.
cortex. 120, 129.
Cowper's gland. 108.
cranial nerves. 121.
cribriform plate of ethmoid. 125.
crown. 115.
crus of helix. 124.
cubital vein. 117.
cuticle. 129.
deep peroneal nerve. 121.
deferent duct. 108.
deltoid. 110.
dendrite. 127.
dental alveolus. 115.
dentin. 115.
dermal papilla. 127, 128.
dermis. 128, 129.
descending aorta. 116.
descending colon. 119.
diaphragm. 118, 119.
digestive system. 119.
digital nerve. 121.
digital pulp. 129.
distal phalanx. 112, 113, 129.
dorsum of nose. 125.
duct. 128.
duodenum. 119.
dura mater of spinal cord. 122.
dural cul-de-sac. 122.
ear. 106, 107.
ear drum. 124.
eccrine sweat gland. 128.
ejaculatory duct. 108.
elbow. 107.
enamel. 115.
end piece. 108.
epicondyle. 113.
epidermicula. 129.
epidermis. 127, 128, 129.
epiglottis. 118, 126.
epitrochlea. 113.
eponychium. 129.

esophagus. 119.
Eustachian tube. 124, 125.
external acoustic meatus. 124.
external auditory meatus. 114.
external ear. 124.
external iliac artery. 117.
external oblique. 110, 111.
eye. 123.
eye. 106.
eyeball. 123.
eyebrow. 123.
eyelash. 123.
face. 106.
facial nerve. 124.
false rib. 113.
femoral artery. 117.
femoral nerve. 121.
femoral vein. 117.
femur. 112.
fibula. 112.
first molar. 115.
floating rib. 112.
foot. 107.
foramen cecum. 126.
foramen ovale. 114.
forearm. 107.
forehead. 106.
fovea. 123.
free margin. 129.
frontal. 110, 112.
frontal bone. 114.
frontal sinus. 125.
gallbladder. 119.
gastrocnemius. 110, 111.
genital organs, female. 109.
genital organs, male. 108.
glans penis. 108.
gluteal nerve. 121.
great adductor. 111.
great foramen. 114.
great saphenous vein. 117.
greater alar cartilage. 125.
greater lip. 109.
greater pectoral. 110.
greater trochanter. 113.
greatest gluteal. 111.
groin. 107.
gum. 115.
hair. 129.
hair. 107, 128.
hair bulb. 129.
hair follicle. 129.
hair shaft. 129.
hand. 107.
hard palate. 114, 126.
head. 107, 108, 116.
head of femur. 113.
head of humerus. 113.
hearing. 124.
heart. 116.
heel. 107.
helix. 124.
hepatic vein. 116, 117.
hilus of kidney. 120.
hip. 107.
human being. 103.
human body, anterior view. 106.
human body, posterior view. 107.
human denture. 115.
humerus. 112.
hypogastric artery. 120.
ileum. 119.
iliohypogastric nerve. 121.
ilioinguinal nerve. 121.
ilium. 112.
indifferent cells. 129.
inferior dental arch. 126.
inferior mesenteric artery. 120.
inferior nasal concha. 125.
inferior vena cava. 116, 117, 120.
infraorbital foramen. 114.
infrespinous. 111.
infundibulum of uterine tube. 109.
inner root sheath. 129.
intercostal nerve. 121.
internal ear. 124.

internal iliac artery. 116, 117.
internal iliac vein. 116.
internal jufular vein. 117.
intertragic notch. 124.
intervertebral foramen. 122.
intestine. 116.
iris. 123.
ischium. 113.
isthmus of fauces. 126.
isthmus of uterine tube. 109.
jejunum. 119.
kidney. 116.
knee. 106.
lacrimal duct. 123.
lactiferous duct. 109.
lambdoid suture. 114.
large intestine. 119.
larger round. 111.
larynx. 118.
lateral condyle of femur. 113.
lateral cutaneous nerve of thigh. 121.
lateral great. 110, 111.
lateral incisor. 115.
lateral semicircular canal. 124.
left atrium. 116.
left bronchus. 118.
left kidney. 120.
left lung. 116, 118.
left ventricle. 116.
leg. 107.
lens. 123.
lesser lip. 109.
lingual papillae. 126.
lingual tonsil. 126.
liver. 116, 119.
lobe. 109.
lobule. 124.
loin. 107.
long adductor. 110.
long extensor of toes. 110.
long palmar. 110.
long peroneal. 110.
long radial extensor of wrist. 111.
lower eyelid. 123.
lower lip. 126.
lower lobe. 118.
lumbar plexus. 121.
lumbar vertebra. 122.
lumbar vertebra. 113.
lungs. 118.
lunula. 129.
malar bone. 112.
male urethra. 108.
Malpighi's pyramid. 120.
mammary gland. 109.
mandible. 112, 114, 115.
masseter. 110.
mastoid process. 114.
maxilla. 112, 114, 115, 125.
medial condyle of femur. 113.
medial great. 110.
median lingual sulcus. 126.
median nerve. 121.
median vein of forearm. 117.
medulla. 120, 129.
medulla oblongata. 122.
Meissner's corpuscle. 128.
melanocyte. 128.
mental foramen. 114.
metacarpus. 112.
metatarsus. 112.
metopic suture. 114.
middle ear. 124.
middle lobe. 118.
middle nasal concha. 125.
middle phalanx. 112, 113.
middle piece. 108.
mitral valve. 116.
mobile septum of nose. 125.
molar, cross section of a. 115.
mons pubis. 109.
motor cell. 127.
motor end plate. 127.
motor neuron. 127.
mouth. 126.

mouth. 106.
muscle arrector pili. 128, 129.
muscle fiber. 127.
muscles, anterior view. 110.
muscles, posterior view. 111.
musculocutaneous nerve. 121.
myelin sheath. 127.
nail. 129.
nail bed. 129.
nail matrix. 129.
nape. 107.
naris. 125.
nasal bone. 114, 125.
nasal cavity. 118.
nasal fossa. 114.
nasal fossae. 125.
nasopharynx. 125.
navel. 106.
neck. 106, 108, 115.
neck of femur. 113.
neck of uterus. 109.
nerve. 129.
nerve fiber. 127.
nerve termination. 127.
nervous system. 121, 122.
neuron. 127.
nipple. 106, 109.
Nissl bodies. 127.
node of Ranvier. 127.
nose. 106.
nose, external. 125.
nucleus. 127.
obturator nerve. 121.
occipital. 111, 113.
occipital bone. 114.
occipital condyle. 114.
olecranon. 113.
olfactory bulb. 125.
olfactory membrane. 125.
olfactory nerve. 125.
optic chiasm. 122.
optic nerve. 123.
oral cavity. 118, 119.
orbicular of eye. 110.
orbital cavity. 114.
ostium. 129.
outer root sheath. 129.
ovary. 109.
Pacinian corpuscle. 128.
palate. 125.
palatine tonsil. 126.
palatoglossal arch. 126.
palatopharyngeal arch. 126.
pancreas. 119.
papilla. 123, 129.
papillary muscle. 116.
parietal. 113.
parietal bone. 114.
parietal foramen. 114.
parital pleura. 118.
patella. 112.
pectoral limb. 116.
pelvic limb. 116.
pelvis. 120.
penis. 106, 108.
pericardium. 118.
periodontal ligament. 115.
peripheral nervous system. 121.
peritoneum. 108.
pharynx. 118, 119.
philtrum. 125.
phrenic nerve. 118.
pineal body. 122.
pituitary gland. 122.
plantar. 111.
plantar interosseous. 110.
pleural cavity. 118.
pons Varolii. 122.
pore. 129.
portal vein. 116, 117.
posterior chamber. 123.
posterior commissure. 122.
posterior cutaneous nerve of thigh. 121.
posterior root. 122.
posterior ruga. 107.

posterior semicircular canal. 124.
pouch of Douglas. 109.
prepuce. 108.
prostate. 108.
protoneuron. 127.
proximal phalanx. 112, 113.
pubis. 106.
pulmonary artery. 117, 118.
pulmonary trunk. 116.
pulmonary vein. 116, 117.
pulp. 115.
pulp canal. 115.
pulp chamber. 115.
pupil. 123.
pylorus. 119.
radial artery. 117.
radial nerve. 121.
radial vein. 117.
radius. 112.
receptor. 127.
rectum. 108, 119, 120.
renal artery. 117, 120.
renal papilla. 120.
renal vein. 117, 120.
respiratory system. 118.
retina. 123.
rhinencephalon. 125.
rhomboid. 111.
ribs. 112.
right atrium. 116.
right bronchus. 118.
right kidney. 120.
right lung. 116, 118.
right ventricle. 116.
root. 115, 126.
root of hair. 129.
root of nail. 129.
root of nose. 125.
round ligament of uterus. 109.
round pronator. 110.
sacral plexus. 121.
sacrum. 112.
sagittal suture. 114.
salivary glands. 119.
saphenous nerve. 121.
sartorius. 110.
scapula. 112.
sciatic nerve. 121.
sclera. 123.
scrotum. 106, 108.
sebaceous gland. 128, 129.
second molar. 115.
second premolar. 115.
semimembranous. 111.
seminal vesicle. 108.
semitendinous. 111.
sense organs. 123, 124, 125, 126, 127.
sense receptor. 127.
sensory impulse. 127.
sensory neuron. 127.
septal cartilage of nose. 125.
septum lucidum. 122.
septum of scrotum. 108.
sheath of Schwann. 127.
short extensor of toes. 110.
short palmar. 110.
short peroneal. 111.
short radial extensor of wrist. 111.
shoulder. 106.
shoulder blade. 107.
sight. 123.
sigmoid colon. 119.
sinus of kidney. 120.
skeleton, anterior view. 112.
skeleton, posterior view. 113.
skin. 127, 128.
skin. 127.
skin surface. 127, 128.
skull. 106.
skull, osteology of. 114.
slender. 111.
small intestine. 119.
smaller round. 111.
smell. 125.
soft palate. 126.

sole. 129.
soleus. 110.
spermatic cord. 108.
spermatozoon. 108.
sphenoid bone. 114.
sphenoidal sinus. 125.
sphincter muscle of anus. 119.
spinal cord. 122, 127.
spinal ganglion. 127.
spinal nerve. 122, 127.
spine of scapula. 113.
spinous process of vertebra. 113.
spleen. 116.
splenic artery. 117.
splenic vein. 117.
splenius muscle of head. 111.
spongy body. 108.
squamous suture. 114.
sternocleidomastoid. 110.
sternum. 112.
stomach. 116, 119.
straight muscle of thigh. 110.
stratum basale. 128.
stratum corneum. 128.
stratum granulosum. 128.
stratum lucidum. 128.
stratum spinosum. 128.
subclavian artery. 117.
subclavian vein. 117.
subcutaneous tissue. 128.
subpapillary network. 128.
sulcus terminalis. 126.
superciliary arch. 114.
superficial peroneal nerve. 121.
superior dental arch. 126.
superior longitudinal sinus. 122.
superior mesenteric artery. 117, 120.
superior nasal concha. 125.
superior semicircular canal. 124.
superior vena cava. 116, 117.
supraorbital foramen. 114.
suprarenal gland. 120.
suprascapular nerve. 121.
sural nerve. 121.
suspensory ligament. 123.
symphysis pubis. 108, 109.
synapse. 127.
tail. 108.
tail of helix. 124.
talus. 113.
tarsus. 112.
taste. 126.
taste, sense of. 125.
teeth. 115.
temple. 106.
temporal. 112.
temporal bone. 114.
temporal fossa. 114.
tensor of fascia lata. 110.
terminal arborization. 127.
terminal bronchiole. 118.
terminal filament. 122.
testicle. 108.
thigh. 107.
third molar. 115.
thoracic vertebra. 113.
thorax. 106.
tibia. 112.
tibial nerve. 121.
tip of nose. 125.
toe. 106.
tongue. 119, 125, 126.
tongue, dorsum of. 126.
touch. 127.
trachea. 118.
tragus. 124.
transverse colon. 119.
transverse process of vertebra. 113.
trapezius. 110.
triangular fossa. 124.
triceps of arm. 111.
tricuspid valve. 116.
true skin. 127.

trunk. 107.
ulna. 112.
ulnar artery. 117.
ulnar extensor of wrist. 111.
ulnar flexor of wrist. 110, 111.
ulnar nerve. 121.
upper eyelid. 123.
upper lip. 126.
upper lobe. 118.
uranary system. 120.
ureter. 120.
urethra. 109, 120.
urinary bladder. 108, 109, 120.
urinary meatus. 108.
uterine tube. 109.
uterovesical pouch. 109.
uterus. 109.
uvula. 125, 126.
V-shaped row. 126.
vagina. 109.
vagus nerve. 118.
veins. 117.
ventricular septum. 116.
vermiform appendix. 119.
vertebral column. 112.
vestibular nerve. 124.
vestibule. 124.
vitreous body. 123.
vocal cord. 118.
vulva. 109.
waist. 107.
wrist. 107.
zygomatic arch. 114.
zygomatic bone. 114.
zygomaticofacial foramen. 114.

MEASURING DEVICES

adjusting nut. 599.
adjusting screw. 598.
air-pressure pump. 598.
alidade. 600.
analog display. 591.
analytical balance. 595.
ancitipator indicator. 597.
aneroid barometer. 598.
anticipator. 597.
anvil. 599.
backplate. 597.
balance. 594, 595.
balance wheel. 591.
barometer. 598.
base. 595, 600, 601.
base plate. 600.
bathroom scale. 596.
beam. 594, 595, 596.
beam arrest. 595.
beam balance. 594.
bearing. 597.
bedrock. 602.
bimetal element. 597.
bimetallic helix. 597.
bimetallic thermometer. 597.
bob. 593.
bulb. 597.
capillary bore. 597.
carrying handle. 600.
case. 597, 599.
center knife-edge. 595.
center wheel. 591, 593.
chain. 593, 598.
circular level. 600.
click. 593.
clinical thermometer. 597.
clock. 593, 602.
clock mechanism, weight-driven. 593.
column. 595.
column of mercury. 597.
concrete base. 602.
conical magnet. 592.
constriction. 597.
contact. 597.
counterweight. 596.
cover. 597, 601.

crest. 593.
crown. 591.
current coil. 601.
damper. 596.
dial. 591, 592, 593, 595, 596, 597, 598, 599, 601.
digital display. 591.
disk. 601.
display. 596.
drive coil. 592.
drum. 593.
electronic circuit. 592.
electronic scale. 596.
escape wheel. 591, 593.
expansion chamber. 597.
focusing sleeve. 600.
fork. 593.
fourth wheel. 591.
frame. 599.
full-load adjustment screw. 601.
function keys. 596.
glass bulb. 592.
glass case. 595.
gnomon. 592.
graduated arm. 594.
graduated scale. 598.
graduation. 594, 596, 597, 599.
grandfather clock. 593.
hairspring. 591.
hand. 598.
heat, measure of. 597.
helical spring. 594.
hook. 594, 599.
horizontal circle. 600.
horizontal circle drive knob. 600.
horizontal clamp. 600.
horizontal seismograph. 602.
horizontal tangent screw. 600.
hour hand. 591, 593.
hourglass. 592.
illumination mirror. 600.
index. 594.
index plate. 595.
indicator. 596, 598.
inverter knob. 600.
knife-edge. 594, 595, 596.
lead. 592.
leg. 595.
leveling screw. 595, 600.
lever. 598.
light-load adjustment screw. 601.
liquid-crystal display. 591.
lock nut. 599.
locking knob. 599, 600.
magnetic cup. 592.
magnetic suspension. 601.
main wheel. 593.
mainspring. 591.
mass. 602.
measuring devices. 589.
mechanical watch. 591.
mercury switch. 597.
micrometer caliper. 599.
micrometer screw. 600.
microscope eyepiece. 600.
minute hand. 591, 593.
moon dial. 593.
mounting post. 597.
mounting screw. 597.
name plate. 601.
neck. 592.
numeric keyboard. 596.
optical plummet. 600.
optical sight. 600.
pallet. 591, 593.
pan. 594, 595.
pan arrest. 595.
pedometer. 599.
pen. 602.
pendulum. 593.
pendulum rod. 593.
phase-sensing coil. 592.
pillar. 602.
pillar plate. 592.
pinion. 593.
pivoted bar. 602.

plate level. 600.
platform. 596.
plinth. 593.
pneumatic armlet. 598.
pointer. 595, 597, 598, 599.
potential coil. 601.
pressure, measure of. 598.
pressure gauge. 598.
product codes. 596.
pulley. 596.
ratchet knob. 599.
ratchet wheel. 591, 593.
recording of seismic waves. 602.
recording of time. 602.
register. 601.
retarding magnet. 601.
reticle illumination. 600.
rider handle. 595.
rider scale. 595.
ring. 594.
Roberval's balance. 595.
room thermostat. 597.
rotating drum. 602.
sand. 592.
scale. 596.
sealing lug. 601.
second hand. 591.
sector-shaped chart. 596.
seismograph. 602.
self-indicating scale. 596.
shadow. 592.
shaft. 597.
sheet of paper. 602.
sleeve. 599.
sliding weight. 594.
sphygmomanometer. 598.
spindle. 593, 599, 601.
spindle screw. 599.
spring. 598, 602.
spring balance. 594.
stay. 596.
steel band. 596.
steelyard. 594.
stem. 597.
step setting. 599.
stirrup hook. 595.
stone. 591.
sundial. 592.
suspension hook. 594.
suspension spring. 593.
tape. 599.
tape measure. 599.
telescope eyepiece. 600.
telescope objective. 600.
temperature scale. 597.
temperature set point lever. 597.
terminal cover. 601.
terminal knife-edge. 595.
theodolite. 600.
thermometer. 597.
thermostat. 597.
thimble. 599.
third wheel. 591, 593.
ticket. 596.
time, measure of. 591, 592, 593.
tine. 592.
total. 596.
transistor. 592.
trunk. 593.
tube. 598.
tuning fork. 592.
tuning fork watch. 592.
unit price. 596.
vacuum chamber. 598.
vertical circle. 600.
vertical clamp. 600.
vertical seismograph. 602.
vertical tangent screw. 600.
watch. 591, 592.
watchcase. 591.
watt-hour meter. 601.
weighing platform. 596.
weight. 593, 594, 596.
weight, measure of. 594, 595, 596.
winding mechanism. 593.

MUSIC

accent mark. 462.
accidentals. 462.
accordion. 475.
action. 465.
adjusting lever. 478.
air sealing gland. 468.
appoggiatura. 462.
arm. 473.
arpeggio. 462.
attack knob. 481.
back. 463.
back stop. 466.
bag. 474.
bagpipe. 474.
balalaika. 473.
banjo. 473.
bar. 471, 478.
bar line. 462.
barrel. 475.
barrel organ. 475.
bass bridge. 465.
bass drum. 472.
bass drum. 477, 479.
bass keyboard. 475.
bass pick-up. 480.
bass register. 475.
bassoon. 469, 476, 477.
bassoons. 479.
batter head. 472.
bearer. 468.
bell. 469, 470.
bell brace. 469.
bellows. 475.
bellows strap. 475.
block. 468.
blow pipe. 474.
blower. 467.
body. 468, 469.
boot. 468.
bottomboard. 468.
bow. 464.
brass family. 470.
bridge. 463, 475.
bridge unit. 480.
bridle tape. 466.
bugle. 470.
button. 475.
c clef. 461.
case. 465, 475, 478.
castanets. 471.
castanets. 479.
castor. 472.
celesta. 479.
chanter. 474.
check. 466.
choir organ manual. 467.
chord. 462.
clarinet. 469, 476, 477.
clarinets. 479.
clefs. 461.
conductor's podium. 479.
console. 467.
contrabassoon. 479.
cornet. 470, 477.
cornets. 479.
corssbar. 473.
crook. 469, 474.
cymbals. 471.
cymbals. 477, 479.
damper. 466.
damper lever. 466.
damper rail. 466.
double bass. 463, 477.
double basses. 479.
double flat. 462.
double reed. 469, 474.
double sharp. 462.
drone. 474.
drum. 472.
drum kit. 477.
duo. 476.
ear. 468.
eighth note. 461.
eighth rest. 461.

electric guitar. 480.
electric instrument. 480.
electronic instrument. 481.
end button. 463.
English horn. 469, 479.
envelope shaper. 481.
escapement mechanism. 478.
f clef. 461.
face pipes. 467.
feet. 464.
fifth. 462.
filter-oscillator. 481.
finger button. 470.
fingerboard. 463, 473, 480.
first violins. 479.
fixed weight. 478.
flat. 462.
flue. 468.
flue pipe. 468.
flute. 469, 476.
flutes. 479.
foot. 468.
foot hole. 468.
four-four time. 462.
fourth. 462.
frame. 471, 474.
French horn. 470, 476, 477.
French horns. 479.
fret. 473, 480.
frog. 464.
g clef. 461.
gong. 471.
gong. 479.
great organ manual. 467.
grille. 475.
hair. 464.
half note. 461.
half rest. 461.
hammer. 465, 466.
hammer butt. 466.
hammer head. 466.
hammer rail. 466.
hammer shank. 466.
handle. 475.
harmonica. 474.
harp. 464.
harp. 479.
harpsichord. 476.
head. 464, 472, 473, 480.
heel. 464.
hitch pin. 465.
input level control. 481.
instrumental groups. 476, 477.
interface. 481.
intervals. 462.
jack. 466.
jack spring. 466.
jazz band. 477.
Jew's harp. 474.
jingle. 472.
joystick. 481.
kettledrum. 472.
key. 465, 466, 469, 475, 478.
key finger button. 469.
key signature. 462.
keybed. 465.
keyboard. 465, 481.
keyboard control. 481.
keyboard instruments. 465, 466.
languid. 468.
ledger line. 461.
leg. 472.
ligature. 469.
line. 461.
little finger hook. 470.
loud pedal. 465.
lower lip. 468.
lug. 472.
lyre. 473.
mallet. 472.
mallets. 471.
mandolin. 473.
manual. 468.
manuals. 467.
matrix. 481.
mechanism of the organ. 468.

melody string. 473.
metal counterhoop. 472.
metal frame. 465.
metal rod. 471.
metronome. 478.
mid range pick-up. 480.
mordent. 462.
mouth. 468.
mouthpiece. 469, 470.
mouthpiece receiver. 470.
mouthpipe. 470.
music. 459.
music rest. 478.
music stand. 478.
music stand. 465.
musical accessories. 478.
musical notation. 461, 462.
mute. 470.
natural. 462.
neck. 463, 464, 473, 480.
noise generator control. 481.
note symbols. 461.
nut. 463, 480.
oboe. 469, 476.
oboes. 479.
octave. 462.
octave mechanism. 469.
open string. 473.
organ. 467, 468.
organ pipes. 468.
ornaments. 462.
oscillators. 481.
output controls. 481.
output filter. 481.
output jack. 480.
pallet. 468, 475.
pallet spring. 468.
panpipe. 474.
parchment membrane. 473.
pause. 462.
pedal. 464, 472.
pedal key. 467.
pedal keyboard. 467.
pedal rod. 465.
pedestal. 464.
peg. 463, 464.
peg box. 463.
percussion instruments. 471, 472.
piano. 465, 476, 477, 479.
piccolo. 469, 479.
pick-up selector. 480.
pickguard. 480.
pillar. 464.
pilot. 466.
pin. 475.
pin block. 465.
pipe. 468, 475.
pipework. 467.
pivot. 478.
pivot point. 466.
plectrum. 473.
point. 464.
position marker. 480.
power indicator. 481.
power switch. 481.
pressure bar. 465.
production of sound. 467.
purfling. 463.
quarter note. 461.
quarter rest. 461.
quartet. 476.
quintet. 476.
rackboard. 468.
reed pipe. 468.
reeds. 469.
regulating button. 466.
repeat mark. 462.
reservoir. 467.
resonator. 468, 471.
rest symbols. 461.
reverb unit. 481.
rib. 463.
ring. 470.
ring modulator. 481.
rod. 471.
roller board and arms. 468.

saxhorn. 470.
saxophone. 469.
saxophone. 469, 477.
scale. 461.
scale of speeds. 478.
screw. 464.
scroll. 463.
second. 462.
second violins. 479.
sequence control. 481.
seventh. 462.
sextet. 477.
shallot. 468.
sharp. 462.
shawm. 474.
shell. 472.
single reed. 469.
sixteenth note. 461.
sixteenth rest. 461.
sixth. 462.
sixty-fourth note. 461.
sixty-fourth rest. 461.
sleeve protector. 473.
slider. 468.
sliding weight. 478.
snare. 472.
snare drum. 472.
snare drum. 477, 479.
snare head. 472.
snare strainer. 472.
soft pedal. 465.
solid body. 480.
sound-board. 463, 464, 465, 473.
sound box. 464.
sound-hole. 463.
sound-post. 464.
space. 461.
spur. 472.
staff. 461.
stick. 464.
sticker. 475.
sticks. 471.
stock. 474.
stop button. 478.
stop knob. 467, 468.
stop rod. 468.
string. 463, 464, 465, 466.
stringed instruments. 463, 464.
sustaining pedal. 465.
swell organ manual. 467.
swell pedal. 467.
symphony orchestra. 479.
synthesizer. 481.
table. 468.
tailpiece. 463.
tambourine. 472.
tenor drum. 472.
tenor drum. 477.
tension rod. 472.
tension screw. 472.
third. 462.
thirty-second note. 461.
thirty-second rest. 461.
three-four time. 462.
thumb hook. 469, 470.
thumb piston. 467.
thumb string. 473.
thumb string peg. 473.
tie. 462.
time signatures. 462.
timpani. 479.
toe piston. 467.
tone control. 480.
tongue. 468, 474.
tracker. 468.
traditional musical instruments.
473, 474, 475.
treble bridge. 465.
treble keyboard. 475.
treble pick-up. 480.
treble register. 475.
triangle. 471.
triangle. 479.
triangular body. 473.
trill. 462.
trio. 476.

tripod. 478.
tripod stand. 472.
trombone. 470, 477.
trombones. 479.
trumpet. 470.
trumpet. 470, 477.
trumpets. 479.
truss rod adjustment. 480.
tuba. 470, 479.
tubular bells. 471.
tubular bells. 479.
tuning fork. 478.
tuning hammer. 478.
tuning machine. 480.
tuning pin. 465.
tuning screw. 472.
tuning slide. 470.
tuning wire. 468.
turn. 462.
two-two time. 462.
unison. 462.
upper lip. 468.
upperboard. 468.
upright piano. 465.
upright piano action. 466.
valve. 470.
valve casing. 470.
valve slide. 470.
vibrato arm. 480.
viola. 463, 476.
violas. 479.
violin. 463, 464.
violin. 463, 476.
violin family. 463.
violoncello. 463, 476.
violoncellos. 479.
volume control. 480.
VU meter. 481.
VU meter switch. 481.
waist. 463.
water key. 470.
wedge. 468.
whole note. 461.
whole rest. 461.
wind chest. 467.
wind duct. 467.
wind instruments. 469, 470.
wind trunk. 467, 468.
wippen. 466.
wire brushes. 471.
woodwind family. 469.
worm. 475.
xylophone. 471.
xylophone. 479.
zither. 473.

OFFICE SUPPLIES AND EQUIPMENT

account book. 450.
appointment book. 450.
archboard. 450.
backspace key. 453.
bill-file. 447.
book end. 448.
calendar pad. 450.
card cabinet. 450.
card holder. 452.
cards. 450.
carriage. 453.
carriage release lever. 453.
carriage return. 453.
character. 452.
clamp binder. 449.
clip. 447.
clipboard. 450.
coat hook. 451.
coat rack. 451.
coat tree. 451.
compressor. 450.
correcting tape. 452.
correction fluid. 447.
correction paper. 447.
credenza. 451.
dater. 448.

desk pad. 450.
desk tray. 448.
display cabinet. 451.
divider. 449.
drawer. 450.
element release lever. 452.
eraser. 447.
executive desk. 451.
expanding file. 449.
fastener binder. 449.
file guides. 449.
filing box. 448.
folder. 449.
glue stick. 447.
guide post. 452.
hanging folder. 449.
impression control. 452.
key. 453.
keyboard. 453.
label marker. 447.
lateral filing cabinet. 451.
letter opener. 447.
letter scales. 447.
line space regulator. 453.
locker. 451.
margin stop. 453.
moistener. 448.
multiple copy control. 453.
numbering machine. 448.
office equipment. 445.
office furniture. 451.
office supplies. 445.
paper bail. 453.
paper centering scale. 453.
paper clips. 447.
paper fasteners. 447.
paper guide. 453.
paper punch. 448.
paper release lever. 453.
partition. 451.
pencil sharpeners. 448.
platen. 453.
platen knob. 453.
portfolio. 449.
post binder. 449.
return. 451.
ribbon. 452, 453.
ribbon cartridge. 452.
ribbon end indicator. 452.
ribbon guide. 452.
ribbon load lever. 452.
ring binder. 449.
roller. 452.
rotary file. 450.
rubber stamp. 448.
scrath pad. 450.
secretarial chair. 451.
secretarial desk. 451.
self-adhesive labels. 448.
separator wire. 452.
shift key. 453.
shift lock key. 453.
space bar. 453.
spiral binding. 449.
spring binder. 449.
stamp pad. 448.
stamp rack. 448.
staple remover. 447.
stapler. 447.
staples. 447.
stationery. 447, 448, 449, 450.
stationery cabinet. 451.
supply spool. 452.
switch. 453.
swivel-tilter armchair. 451.
tab. 449.
tabulator. 453.
tabulator clear key. 453.
tabulator set key. 453.
take-up knob. 452.
take-up spool. 452.
tape. 447.
tape dispenser. 447.
tape load lever. 452.
tear-off calendar. 450.
telephone index. 450.

top plate. 453.
transparent line indicator. 453.
typestyle. 452.
typewriter. 452, 453.
typing element. 452.
variable spacer. 453.
viewtop tab. 449.

OPTICAL INSTRUMENTS

altazimuth mounting. 609.
altitude coarse-motion clamp. 609.
anode. 606.
arm. 605.
azimuth coarse-motion clamp. 609.
azimuth synchro. 610.
base. 605.
base line. 611.
base plate. 611.
biconcave. 611.
biconvex. 611.
binocular microscope. 605.
body. 607.
body tube. 605.
bridge. 607.
cathode. 606.
central focusing wheel. 607.
coarse adjustment knob. 605.
column. 608.
compass card. 611.
compass meridian line. 611.
concave. 611.
condenser. 605.
condenser adjustment knob. 605.
converging lens. 611.
convex. 611.
counterweight. 608.
cover. 611.
cover slip. 605.
cradle. 608, 609.
declination circle. 608.
dew cap. 609.
diffusion pump. 606.
diverging lens. 611.
double-condenser pole piece. 606.
dovetail. 607.
draw tube. 605.
drawtube. 609.
duplexer. 610.
echo. 610.
edge. 611.
electron gun. 606.
electron microscope. 606.
elevation adjusting screw. 607.
emission chamber. 606.
erector lenses. 607.
eye lens. 607.
eyepiece. 605, 607, 608, 609.
eyepiece holder. 609.
field lens. 607.
field lenses. 607.
filament. 606.
finder. 608, 609.
fine focus sleeve. 609.
first condenser lens. 606.
flat mirror. 608.
fluorescent screen. 606.
focus knob. 609.
focusing knob. 608.
focusing ring. 607.
fork. 608.
glass slide. 605.
graduated dial. 611.
high-voltage cable. 606.
hinge. 607.
hunting scope. 607.
intermediate lens. 606.
iris diaphragm. 605.
lamp. 605.
lens. 605.
limb top. 605.
magnetic compass. 611.
magnetic needle. 611.
main mirror. 608.
main scope tube. 607.

main tube. 608.
maintube. 609.
mechanical stage. 605.
mechanical stage control. 605.
microscope. 605.
modulator. 610.
motor. 608.
motor drive. 610.
negative meniscus. 611.
object. 605.
objective. 606.
objective. 605.
objective lens. 606, 607, 609.
objective pole piece. 606.
optical instruments. 603.
parabolic reflector. 610.
photo chamber. 606.
photographic plate. 606.
pivot. 611.
plan-position indicator. 610.
planoconcave. 611.
planoconvex. 611.
polar axis circle. 608.
Porro prism. 607.
positive meniscus. 611.
prism binocular. 607.
projector lens. 606.
projector lens pole piece. 606.
radar. 610.
radiating element. 610.
receiver. 610.
reflector. 608.
refracting telescope. 609.
reticle. 607.
revolving nosepiece. 605.
rotary joint. 610.
scale. 611.
second condenser lens. 606.
shutter. 606.
sight. 611.
sighting line. 611.
sighting mirror. 611.
slow-motion control knob. 609.
specimen. 605.
specimen chamber. 606.
stage. 605, 606.
stage clip. 605.
star diagonal. 609.
support. 608.
synchronizer. 610.
telescope. 609.
transmitted pulse. 610.
transmitter. 610.
tripod. 608.
tripod accessories shelf. 609.
tripod leg. 609.
turret cap. 607.
vacuum manifold. 606.
viewing chamber. 606.
viewing window. 606.
Wehnelt cylinder. 606.
windage adjusting screw. 607.

PERSONAL
ADORNMENT

Afro. 321.
baguette cut. 317.
bangs. 321.
Beatle cut. 321.
bend. 318.
bezel. 315.
bezel facet. 317.
bib necklace. 316.
bifocal. 318.
blush brush. 322.
bob. 321.
bouffant. 320.
bracelets. 315.
braids. 320.
bridge. 318.
brilliant cut facets. 317.
brilliant full cut. 317.
briolette cut. 317.
brooch. 315.

brow brush. 323.
bun. 320, 321.
butt-strap. 318.
cabochon cut. 317.
cake mascara. 323.
capless wig. 321.
charm bracelet. 315.
charms. 315.
choker. 316.
class ring. 315.
claw. 315.
cleansing sponge. 323.
clip earring. 315.
collar bar. 316.
corkscrew curls. 320.
cosmetic sponge. 323.
cream blush. 322.
cream lipstick. 322.
crew cut. 321.
crown. 317.
culet. 317.
curb chain. 315.
curly hair. 320.
distance. 318.
dog collar. 316.
dog tag. 315.
dowel hole. 318.
drop earring. 315.
earpiece. 318.
eight cut. 317.
emerald cut. 317.
endpiece. 318.
engagement ring. 315.
eye liner. 322.
eyebrow pencil. 323.
eyeglasses. 318, 319.
eyeglasses, principal types of. 319.
eyelash curler. 323.
eyeshadow. 322.
fan brush. 323.
fingerwaves. 320.
French cut. 317.
French twist. 321.
gemstones, cuts for. 317.
girdle. 317.
hair, kinds of. 320.
hair styles. 320, 321.
hair styles, components of. 320, 321.
hairpieces. 321.
half-glasses. 319.
hoop earring. 315.
horn. 315.
horseshoe. 315.
jewelry. 315, 316, 317.
jewelry, diversity of. 315.
jewelry, miscellaneous. 316.
khôl pencil. 322.
lash comb. 323.
lavaliere. 316.
lipbrush. 323.
lipliner. 323.
lipstick. 323.
liquid foundation. 322.
locket. 316.
loose powder. 322.
loose powder brush. 322.
lorgnette. 319.
lower girdle facet. 317.
make-up. 322, 323.
make-up, accessories. 323.
make-up kit. 323.
make-up products. 322.
make-up sponges. 323.
mascara. 322.
mascara brush. 323.
matinee length necklace. 316.
men's pompadour. 321.
metal plate. 318.
mirror. 322.
monocle. 319.
natural sponge. 323.
navette cut. 317.
necklaces. 316.
nose pad. 318.
nosepad. 318.

opera glasses. 319.
opera length necklace. 316.
oval cut. 317.
pad. 318.
pad arm. 318.
page boy. 320.
pavilion. 317.
pavilion facet. 317.
pear-shaped cut. 317.
personal adornment. 313.
pierced earring. 315.
pigtails. 320.
pince-nez. 319.
plain ring. 315.
pony tail. 320.
poodle cut. 321.
powder puff. 322.
pressed powder compact. 322.
products for make-up. 323.
quizzing glass. 319.
reading. 318.
rim. 318.
rings. 315.
rivet. 318.
rope. 316.
rose cut. 317.
safety glasses. 319.
safety goggles. 319.
scissors cut. 317.
scissors-glasses. 319.
screw earring. 315.
seal ring. 315.
setting. 315.
shaft. 318.
shag. 321.
shield. 318.
ski goggles. 319.
solitaire ring. 315.
spectacles. 319.
sponge-tipped applicator. 322.
star facet. 317.
step cut. 317.
stickpin. 315.
straight hair. 320.
synthetic sponge. 323.
table. 317.
table cut. 317.
temple. 318.
tie bar. 316.
tie tack. 316.
toupee. 321.
tube bangle. 315.
upper girdle facet. 317.
wavy hair. 320.
wedding band. 315.
wigs. 321.
women's pompadour. 321.

PERSONAL ARTICLES

accordion bag. 338.
accordion windows. 341.
Afro comb. 328.
air concentrator. 330.
air hole. 335.
air inlet grille. 330.
air outlet grille. 330.
ash. 334.
ashtray. 334.
attaché case. 340.
automatic tweezers. 332.
bag. 337, 338, 339.
barber comb. 328.
barrel. 338.
barrel. 330, 331.
barrette. 333.
base. 330.
beach bag. 338.
beauty case. 337.
bill compartment. 341.
billfold. 341.
bit. 335.
blackhead remover. 333.
blade. 327, 328.
blade close stop. 328.

blade injector. 327.
bobby pin. 333.
bowl. 335.
bowl lid. 335.
box bag. 338.
bracket. 329.
briefcase. 340.
bristle. 327, 328, 329, 331.
brush. 329.
buckle. 339.
bullet. 336.
bunch. 334.
butane well. 334.
butt. 334.
calculator. 341.
cane. 336.
canopy. 336.
card and photo case. 341.
card case. 341.
carrier bag. 338.
carry handle. 331, 337.
carry-on bag. 337.
carton. 334.
case. 327, 331, 332.
central compartment. 339.
change purse. 341.
change purse. 341.
charger. 327.
charging light. 327.
cheater pocket. 341.
checkbook. 341.
checkbook holder. 341.
checkmate. 341.
cigar. 334.
cigar band. 334.
cigar box. 334.
cigarette. 334.
cigarette holder. 334.
clamp. 331.
clamp lever. 331.
clasp. 339, 340.
cleaning brush. 327.
clip. 331.
clippers. 328.
closeness setting. 327.
collar. 327.
combination lock. 340.
combs. 328.
comfort contoured handle. 331.
compartment. 340.
cool tip. 331.
corn cutter. 332.
cosmetic tray. 337.
cover. 335.
curling brush. 331.
curling iron. 331.
curtain. 337.
cuticle knife. 332.
cuticle nippers. 332.
cuticle pusher. 332.
cuticle scissors. 332.
cutting edge. 328.
dental floss. 329.
disappearing handle. 340.
disposable razor. 327.
divider. 340.
double-edge blade. 327.
double-edge razor. 327.
drawstring. 339.
dual swivel mirror. 330.
dual voltage selector switch. 327, 330.
duffel bag. 339.
electric razor. 327.
emery board. 333.
envelope bag. 338.
expandable file pouch. 340.
exterior pocket. 337, 340.
eyebrow tweezers. 332.
face. 341.
fan housing. 330.
ferrule. 328.
filler. 335.
filter. 335.
filter tip. 334.
fitting. 339.

flame adjustment wheel. 334.
flap. 339, 341.
flat-back brush. 328.
floating head. 327.
folding nail file. 333.
frame. 336, 337, 340.
friction strip. 335.
front flap. 335.
garment bag. 337.
garment strap. 337.
gouge. 332.
hair clip. 333.
hair dryer. 330.
hair roller. 333.
hairbrushes. 328.
haircutting scissors. 328.
hairpin. 333.
hairsetter. 331.
hairstyling implements. 333.
handbags. 338, 339.
handle. 327, 328, 329, 330, 331, 336, 337, 339, 340.
handle post. 340.
hang-up ring. 330.
hanging hook. 337.
hardware. 337.
hasp. 337.
head. 327, 329, 334, 335.
heat comfort control. 331.
heat ready indicator dot. 331.
heat/speed selector switch. 330.
hinge. 337, 339.
hood cover. 330.
hook. 341.
housing. 327, 329, 330.
identification tag. 337.
interior pocket. 337.
jar. 335.
jaw. 333.
jet tip. 329.
key case. 341.
key lock. 340.
knob closure. 339, 341.
label. 334.
leather goods. 340, 341.
lever. 333.
lid. 331.
lid latch. 331.
light bar. 330.
lighter, gas. 334.
lining. 338, 340.
lock. 337.
luggage. 337.
luggage carrier. 337.
magnifying mirror. 330.
manicure set. 332.
manicure stick. 332.
manicuring instruments. 333.
matchbook. 335.
matchbox. 335.
matchstick. 335.
measuring cup. 331.
men's bag. 339.
minaudiere. 339.
mirror. 330.
mirror. 337.
money clip. 341.
mortise. 335.
muff. 339.
nail brush. 332.
nail buffer. 332.
nail cleaner. 333.
nail clippers. 333.
nail file. 332.
nail nippers. 332.
nail scissors. 332.
nail shaper. 332.
nail whitener pencil. 333.
notepad. 341.
on light. 331.
on-off switch. 327, 329, 330, 331.
open compartment. 339.
oral hygiene center. 329.
ornamental stitching. 339.
packet, cellophane wrapped. 334.
packet of cigarette papers. 334.

padlock. 337.
paper. 334.
passport case. 341.
pen holder. 341.
personal articles. 325.
pick. 335.
pilot light. 331.
pipe. 335.
pipe cleaner. 335.
pipe cross section. 335.
pipe rack. 335.
pipe tools. 335.
pitchfork comb. 328.
pivot. 327, 328.
plug adapter. 331.
pocket. 338, 341.
portfolios. 340.
pouch. 339.
power cord. 327.
power supply cord. 330.
press-button. 338, 341.
pull strap. 337.
pullman case. 337.
push button. 336.
push-button release. 327.
quill brush. 328.
rake comb. 328.
razors. 327.
retaining strap. 337.
rib. 336.
ring. 336.
roll bag. 337.
roller. 331.
roller picks. 333.
round brush. 328.
row. 328, 329.
rubber base. 328.
saddle. 335.
saddle bag. 339.
safety match. 335.
safety scissors. 333.
salon-style hair dryer. 330.
scoop. 335.
screen. 327.
seam. 334.
secretary clutch. 341.
shank. 328, 335, 336.
shaving brush. 327.
shaving mug. 327.
shell. 337.
shopping bag. 338.
shoulder bag. 339.
shoulder strap. 336, 337, 339.
side mirror. 330.
sleeve. 336.
slot. 341.
smoking accessories. 334, 335.
spreader. 336.
stamp pocket. 341.
stand. 331, 337.
stem. 335.
stick umbrella. 336.
stimulator tip. 329.
straight razor. 327.
strap. 341.
strap handle. 336.
striker wheel. 334.
stummel. 335.
swagger bag. 339.
swagger stick. 336.
swiveling power supply cord. 331.
tab. 336, 339, 340, 341.
tail comb. 328.
tamper. 335.
tear tape. 334.
teaser comb. 328.
telescopic umbrella. 336.
temperature control. 331.
tenon. 335.
thinning razor. 328.
thinning scissors. 328.
ticket pocket. 341.
tie. 336.
tie closure. 336.
tip. 333, 336.
tobacco. 334.

tobacco hole. 335.
tobacco pouch. 335.
toenail scissors. 333.
tongue. 339.
tooth. 328.
toothbrush. 329.
toothbrush shaft. 329.
toothbrush well. 329.
toothpaste. 329.
tote bag. 337, 338.
tray. 337.
trim. 337.
trimmer. 327.
trimming. 341.
trunk. 337.
tuck. 337.
tweezers. 333.
umbrella. 336.
umbrella stand. 336.
utility case. 337.
valve. 334.
vent brush. 328.
wallet. 341.
warm-air comb. 328.
wave clip. 333.
weekender. 337.
wheel. 337.
window. 341.
wrapper. 334.
wrist strap. 339, 340.
writing case. 340.
zipper. 332, 336, 337, 338.
zipper pocket. 340.
zippered inside section. 341.

SPORTS

10 yards line. 517.
15 yards line. 517.
25 yards line. 517.
5 yards line. 517.
Ace. 578.
adze. 574.
aileron. 542.
air brake. 542.
air brake handle. 542.
air hose. 536.
air mattress. 584.
airframe. 543.
airspeed indicator. 542.
Alaskan snowshoe. 549.
alley. 523, 528.
alpine skier. 545.
alpine skiing. 545, 546.
altimeter. 541, 542.
antenna. 567.
anti-friction pad. 546.
anti-reverse lock. 566.
approach. 576.
apron. 565, 571.
area of ice. 530.
arena. 556, 557.
arm guard. 516.
arm pad. 520.
arm position. 535.
armstand. 534.
armstand dive. 535.
artificial fly. 567.
assistant timer. 531.
attack line. 522.
attack zone. 522.
attacker. 564.
attacking zone. 519.
attenna. 522.
automatic cable pulley. 544.
axle. 548.
back binding. 540.
back boundary line. 528.
back court. 523, 527.
back crossbar. 549.
back judge. 514.
back pad. 520, 544.
back score line. 530.
back strap. 554.
back wall. 526, 527.

back zone. 522.
backboard. 521.
backboard support. 521.
backgammon. 578.
backstay. 548.
backstop. 511.
backstretch. 555.
backstroke. 533.
backstroke start. 533.
backstroke swimmer. 533.
backstroke turn indicator. 532.
backward. 534.
backward dive. 535.
badminton. 528.
badminton racket. 528.
badminton shoe. 528.
bag. 511.
bag well. 573.
bail. 566.
baize. 569, 570.
Baker tent. 583.
balance beam. 560.
balk area. 570.
balk line. 570.
balk line spot. 570.
ball. 512, 573.
ball. 529, 531.
ball bearing. 548.
ball boy. 523.
ball cross-section. 573.
ball rack. 576.
ball return track. 576.
bamboos. 579.
bandage. 565.
bar. 561, 578.
barb. 567.
barograph. 542.
base. 559.
base plate. 546.
baseball. 511, 512.
baseline. 523.
basket. 521.
basket. 521, 545, 547.
basketball. 521.
bat. 512.
bat. 512.
bathing trunks. 531.
batten. 537, 538, 543.
batten pocket. 537, 538.
batter. 511.
batter's box. 511.
batter's helmet. 512.
batting glove. 512.
beam. 560.
beam reach. 539.
bear away (to). 537.
bear paw. 549.
beaver tail. 549.
bed. 560.
bed-mattress. 584.
belt. 561, 564.
belt loop. 585.
bend. 567.
betting layout. 580, 581.
bevel. 524.
bib. 562.
billiard spot. 570.
billiards cue. 568.
billiards equipment. 568.
binding. 540.
Bishop (B). 577.
bit. 554.
Black. 577, 578, 580, 581.
black ball. 570.
black square. 577.
blade. 520, 529, 536, 548, 563, 567, 574.
blank. 579.
block. 539.
blouse. 524.
blue ball. 570.
blue cap. 531.
blue flag. 531.
blue line. 519.
blue outer circle. 530.

board. 537.
boards. 519.
bobsleigh. 550.
body. 549, 558, 560, 567.
body lacing. 549.
body pad. 520.
body wire. 562.
bolt. 530.
bonus tiles. 579.
boom. 538.
boom vang. 538.
boot. 536, 541, 548, 551, 561.
bottom. 540, 545.
bottom of the pool. 531, 534.
bottom pocket. 570.
bottom surface. 542.
bow. 537.
bowler. 576.
bowline. 587.
bowline on a bight. 587.
bowling. 576.
bowling ball. 576.
bowling shoe. 576.
box and brush. 552.
box and gate. 552.
boxer. 565.
boxing. 565.
boxing glove. 565.
boxing shoe. 565.
braided rope. 587.
brakeman. 550.
branch. 553.
brassie. 572.
breaking the wall. 579.
breast collar. 554.
breaststroke kick. 533.
breaststroke swimmer. 533.
breaststroke turn. 533.
breaststroke. 533.
breathing in. 533.
breathing out. 533.
breeches. 551, 562.
bridge. 568.
bridle. 553.
bridle. 554.
broad reach. 539.
browband. 553.
brown ball. 570.
brush and rails. 551, 552.
buckle. 546.
bumper guard. 527.
bunker. 571.
buoyancy compensator. 536.
butt. 524, 567, 568.
butt cap. 566.
butt end. 520.
butt grip. 566.
butt guide. 566.
butt section. 566.
butterfly kick. 533.
butterfly stroke. 533.
butterfly swimmer. 533.
butterfly turn. 533.
button. 563.
cabin. 544.
cable. 587.
cable. 559, 587.
cable binding. 547.
cable car. 544.
caddie. 571.
cagoule. 575.
camber. 547.
camp saw. 586.
camping, cooking equipment. 586.
camping, cooking equipment. 584.
camping, lighting equipment. 586.
camping, lighting equipment. 584.
camping, tools. 586.
camping equipment. 584, 585, 586.
can opener. 585.
canopy. 541, 573, 582.
canopy pole. 582.
canteen. 586.
cantle. 553.
canvas. 565.
canvas divider. 582.

cap. 572.
captain. 550.
carabiner. 574.
card games. 578.
cards, symbols. 578.
carom billiards. 569.
cart path. 571.
casual water. 571.
catch glove. 520.
catcher. 512.
catcher. 511.
catcher's box. 511.
catcher's glove. 512.
ceiling. 526, 527.
cell. 541.
center. 514, 515, 519, 521.
center back. 518, 522, 525.
center circle. 518, 521.
center court. 527.
center face-off circle. 519.
center field. 511.
center fielder. 511.
center flag. 518.
center forward. 522, 525.
center foward. 518.
center line. 513, 519, 521, 522, 525, 528, 529, 530, 562.
center mark. 523.
center pocket. 570.
center service line. 523.
center spot. 518, 569, 570.
center strap. 523.
center string. 569.
centerboard. 538.
chalet. 544.
chalk. 568.
characters. 579.
cheek. 567.
cheek strap. 553.
chess. 577.
chess notation. 577.
chessboards. 577.
chest protector. 512, 516.
chief timekeeper. 532.
chin strap. 516.
chip. 580, 581.
chock. 574.
circles. 579.
clam-cleat. 537, 539.
clamp. 547.
clear space. 522.
cleat. 538, 539.
cleated shoe. 516.
clew. 537.
climbing harness. 575.
close hauled. 539.
close reach. 539.
closing odds. 555.
clove hitch. 587.
club. 568.
club divider. 573.
club house. 555.
club house turn. 555.
clubhouse. 571.
coache's box. 511.
cockpit. 542.
cockpit. 538.
cockpit canopy. 542.
coffee pot. 585.
coin chute. 581.
coin reject slot. 581.
coin slot. 581.
collar. 561.
columns. 580, 581.
combination knife. 585.
common whipping. 587.
compartment. 578, 580.
compass. 536, 542.
competitive course. 532.
competitor. 532.
compressed-air cylinder. 536.
connecting wire. 562.
connector link. 541.
contest area. 564.
contestant. 564.
control bar. 543.

control stick. 542.
control valve. 585.
cook kit. 585.
cooler. 586.
cord. 574.
cord grip. 558.
core. 573, 587.
cork tip. 528.
corkscrew. 585.
corner. 565.
corner arc. 518.
corner flag. 518.
corner pad. 565.
corner-stool. 565.
counter. 548.
course, golf. 571.
course of obstacles. 552.
court, badminton. 528.
court, basketball. 521.
court, handball. 525.
court, racquetball. 527.
court, squash. 526.
court, tennis. 523.
court, volleyball. 522.
court referee. 525.
cover. 512, 573.
covering. 529.
cow hitch. 587.
crampon strap. 575.
crampons. 575.
crank. 566.
crash helmet. 545, 550.
crawl swimmer. 533.
Cree snowshoe. 549.
creel. 568.
cross-country ski. 547.
cross-country ski. 547.
cross-country skier. 547.
cross-country skiing. 547.
cross handle. 580.
cross poles. 552.
crossbar. 517, 531, 543, 544, 556, 557.
crosstree. 538.
croup. 559.
crownpiece. 553.
cue ball. 569, 570.
cuff. 520.
cup. 571, 585.
curb bit. 553.
curb chain. 553.
curb rein. 553.
curler. 530.
curling. 530.
curling broom. 530.
curling rink. 530.
curling stone. 530.
curve. 520.
cushion. 548, 570, 576.
["D['. 570.
daggerboard. 537.
daggerboard well. 537.
danger area. 564.
date. 555.
dead ball line. 517.
defending zone. 519.
defensive. 514, 515.
deflexor. 543.
depth gauge. 536.
descendeur. 574.
diagonal. 577.
diamond. 569, 578.
dice. 579.
dice. 578.
dice cup. 578.
dimple. 573.
dinghy. 538.
disc. 544, 561.
discus. 558.
discus throw. 556.
disgorger. 568.
distance covered. 555.
diver. 535, 536.
dives, groups of. 535.
diving. 534.
diving installations. 534.

diving well. 534.
divot. 571.
dolly. 530.
dome tent. 583.
domino. 579.
door. 526.
double. 552.
double-blank. 579.
double chair lift. 544.
double handles. 540.
double sheet bend. 587.
double-six. 579.
double zero. 581.
doubles pole. 523.
doubles service court. 528.
doubles sideline. 523, 528.
doublet. 579.
doubling cube. 578.
down wind. 539.
downhaul. 537.
dozen. 581.
dozens. 580.
drag. 566.
driver. 554, 555, 572.
driver's colors. 555.
driving iron. 572.
duvet. 575.
East. 579.
East wind. 579.
edge. 545, 547, 548, 550.
elbow pad. 516, 520, 550.
elbow protector. 562.
electric foil. 562.
electric golf cart. 573.
electrical payout linkage. 581.
electrical pointe d'arrêt. 562.
electrical scoring apparatus. 562.
elevator. 542.
en prison. 580, 581.
end line. 513, 521, 522, 529.
end of the lap. 533.
end-piece. 568.
end wall. 532.
end zone. 513.
engine. 573.
English billiards. 570.
English chessboard. 577.
entries. 534.
entry. 535.
épée. 563.
épéeist. 563.
étrier. 574.
even. 580, 581.
eye. 553, 567, 574.
eyelet. 548.
face. 529, 572.
face mask. 516, 520.
face-off circle. 519.
face-off spot. 519.
fairlead. 539.
fairway. 571.
falling. 564.
false strart rope. 532.
family tents. 582.
fanny pack. 545.
far turn. 555.
feather crown. 528.
feet-first entry. 534.
female ferrule. 566.
fencer. 562.
fencing. 562, 563.
fencing shoe. 562.
fencing weapons. 563.
ferrule. 568, 572.
fibre. 587.
field, baseball. 511.
field, rugby. 517.
fiffi hook. 574.
figure-eight knot. 587.
figure skate. 548.
figure ski. 540.
figure skiing handle. 540.
file. 577, 585.
fin. 536, 537, 540.
finger. 512.
finger hole. 576.

finish. 552.
finish line. 557.
finishing line. 555.
finishing post. 557.
first base. 511.
first baseman. 511.
first space. 521.
fisherman's knot. 587.
fishhook. 567.
fishing. 566, 567, 568.
fishing, accessories. 568.
fishing vest. 568.
five-number bet. 581.
flag. 517, 522, 544.
flagstick. 571.
flank forward. 517.
flanker. 515.
flap. 553.
flat side of the grip. 524.
flat spike. 574.
flight. 535, 560.
flight instruments. 543.
flights. 534.
flip turn. 533.
float. 567.
floor. 526, 527.
flower tiles. 579.
flush. 578.
fly box. 568.
fly reel. 566.
fly rod. 566.
foam mattress. 584.
foam pad. 584.
foible. 563.
foil. 563.
foil warning line. 562.
foilist. 563.
folding camp bed. 584.
folding grill. 586.
folding shovel. 586.
foot. 537, 566.
foot cushion. 569.
foot fault judge. 523.
foot of table. 569.
foot pocket. 536.
foot score line. 530.
foot spot. 569.
foot string. 569.
football. 513, 514, 515, 516.
footrest. 544.
fore court. 523.
foregrip. 566.
forestay. 538.
fork. 585.
forte. 563.
forward. 534.
forward dive. 535.
foul line. 511, 576.
four of a kind. 578.
frame. 524, 526, 549, 559, 560,
    581.
free fall. 541.
free throw line. 521, 525.
French chessboard. 577.
front binding. 540.
front court. 527.
front crawl stroke. 533.
front crossbar. 549.
front point. 575.
front runner. 550.
front wall. 526, 527.
frying pan. 585.
fulcrum. 534.
full and by. 539.
full back. 517.
full house. 578.
fullback. 514, 515.
furlong chute. 555.
fuselage. 542.
G-meter. 542.
gaiter. 545.
gaiting strap. 554.
game timekeeper. 519.
gap. 567.
gate. 544, 551, 552, 574.
gauge. 585.

gauze bandage. 561.
gear housing. 566.
girdle. 520.
girth. 553.
girth strap. 553.
glass. 519, 526.
glider. 542.
gliding. 542.
glove. 536, 541, 547, 550, 558,
    562.
glove, baseball. 512.
glove, hockey. 520.
goal. 531.
goal. 513, 517, 518, 519, 525.
goal area. 518, 525.
goal area line. 525.
goal crease. 519.
goal judge. 531.
goal judge's box. 519.
goal line. 513, 517, 518, 519, 525,
    531.
goal line referee. 525.
goal post. 513, 517.
goalkeeper. 520.
goalkeeper. 518, 519, 525, 531.
goalkeeper's pad. 520.
goalkeeper's stick. 520.
goggles. 541, 550.
golf. 571, 572, 573.
golf bag. 573.
golf cart. 573.
golf clubs. 572.
golf clubs, types of. 572.
golf shoe. 573.
golfer. 571.
grandstand. 555.
granny knot. 587.
green ball. 570.
green dragon. 579.
griff-fiffi hook. 574.
grip. 526, 572.
grips, types of. 529.
grommet. 583.
groove. 545, 547, 572.
guard. 563.
guide. 566.
gutter. 576.
guy cable. 559.
guy line adapter. 583.
guy rope. 582.
gymnast. 560.
gymnastics. 559, 560.
hack. 530.
hackle. 567.
half court line. 526.
half-distance line. 531.
half way line. 518.
halfback. 515.
halfway line. 517.
hammer. 558.
hammer. 575.
hammer axe. 574.
hammer head. 574.
hammer throw. 556.
hand grip. 566.
hand guard. 516.
handball. 525.
handhold. 554.
handle. 540.
handle. 512, 524, 529, 530, 545,
    550, 558, 563, 566, 573, 574,
    585.
handles, types of. 540.
hang glider. 543.
hang gliding. 543.
hang point. 543.
hank. 538, 539.
harness. 536, 541, 543, 549.
harness racing. 554, 555.
hatchet. 586.
haulage cable. 544.
head. 524, 558, 567, 572, 574.
head cover. 573.
head cushion. 569.
head-first entry. 534.
head linesman. 514.

head number. 554.
head of sail. 537.
head of table. 569.
head pole. 554.
head spot. 569.
head string. 569.
headband. 524, 547.
headpin. 576.
headwind. 539.
heart. 578.
heater. 585.
heaving line knot. 587.
heel. 512, 520, 548, 572.
heel flange. 546.
heel lacing. 549.
heel piece. 540, 545, 546.
heel release setting indicator. 546.
heelplate. 547.
height. 534.
height adjustment screw. 546.
height of the dive. 535.
helmet. 516, 520, 541, 543, 575.
helmet lamp. 575.
high. 580, 581.
high card. 578.
high jump. 557.
high line. 563.
hinge. 546.
hip pad. 516, 520.
hitting area. 512.
hobble. 554.
hobble hanger. 554.
hockey. 519.
hockey skate. 548.
hog score line. 530.
holds. 564.
hole. 571.
hole. 574.
holster. 575.
home plate. 511.
homestretch. 555.
honor tiles. 579.
hood. 536.
hook. 544, 548, 567.
hooker. 517.
horizontal bar. 559.
horizontal stabilizer. 542.
horse's name. 555.
horse's number. 555.
horse's pedigree. 555.
house. 530.
hurdle. 556.
hurricane lamp. 586.
ice axe. 574.
ice axe. 575.
ice hockey. 519, 520.
ice hockey player. 520.
ice piton. 575.
ice screw. 575.
identification of the track. 555.
in goal. 517.
inbound line. 513.
infield. 511.
inflator. 584.
inflator-deflator. 584.
inhaul. 537.
inner boot. 546.
inner table. 578.
inner tent. 583.
inside left. 518.
inside line. 563.
inside linebacker. 514.
inside right. 518.
instrument panel. 542.
inward dive. 535.
iron. 572.
ivory ball. 580.
Jack. 578.
jacket. 562, 564.
jackpot box. 581.
jackpot feed. 581.
jackpot payout chute. 581.
javelin throw. 557.
javelins. 558.
jersey. 516.
jib. 538.

jib halyard. 538.
jibsheet. 538.
joint. 567, 568.
Joker. 578.
judge. 562, 564, 565.
judge's stand. 555.
judo. 564.
judo suit. 564.
jump ski. 540.
jumper. 541.
keel. 543.
keeper ring. 566.
kettle. 585.
kick. 533.
King. 578.
King (K). 577.
king post. 543.
King's side. 577.
kingpin. 548.
knee boot. 554.
knee boot suspender. 554.
knee pad. 512, 516, 520, 550, 561.
knee roll. 553.
knee sock. 547.
knickers. 547.
knife. 536, 585.
Knight (Kt). 577.
knob. 512.
knots. 587.
lace. 512, 548, 565.
landing. 560.
landing area. 556, 557.
landing mat. 560.
landing net. 568.
lane. 576.
lane. 557.
lane number. 532.
lane rope. 532.
lane timekeeper. 532.
lantern. 585.
latch. 574.
lateral line. 530.
lead. 530.
leader. 567.
leading edge. 542, 543.
leading edge tube. 543.
leather sheath. 585.
leech. 537.
left back. 518, 522, 525.
left center. 517.
left cornerback. 514, 515.
left defense. 519.
left defensive end. 514, 515.
left defensive tackle. 514, 515.
left field. 511.
left fielder. 511.
left forward. 521, 522.
left guard. 514, 515, 521.
left half. 518.
left halfback. 514.
left outside linebacker. 515.
left safety. 514.
left safety back. 515.
left service court. 523, 526.
left tackle. 514, 515.
left wing. 517, 519.
left winger. 525.
leg. 529, 560, 566.
leg position. 535.
legging. 575.
length. 534.
lever. 581.
light. 536.
line. 566, 567, 580, 581.
line guide. 566.
line judge. 514.
line of scrimmage. 514, 515.
linesman. 517, 518, 519, 522, 523,
    528.
lining. 548.
living room. 582.
lock forward. 517.
lock nut. 548.
long jump. 556.
long service line. 528.
low. 580, 581.

Thematic Indexes

low bar. 560.
low line. 563.
lower shell. 546.
luff. 537.
luff (to). 537.
lures. 567.
mah-jongg. 579.
main halyard. 538.
main parachute. 541.
main section. 580, 581.
mainsail. 538.
mainsheet. 538.
major inner reaping throw. 564.
major outer reaping throw. 564.
male ferrule. 566.
manual release. 546.
marker. 576.
martingale. 563.
mashie. 572.
mashie iron. 572.
mashie niblick. 572.
mask. 512, 536, 562.
mast. 537, 538.
mast foot. 537.
mast sleeve. 537.
master cord. 549.
masthead. 537.
mat. 564.
men. 577.
men. 578.
men's apparatus. 559.
mesh. 529.
metal head. 558.
metallic plastron. 562.
Michigan snowshoe. 549.
middle linebacker. 514, 515.
midiron. 572.
midmashie. 572.
minor inner reaping throw. 564.
mitten. 545, 575.
mocassin. 549.
mono-ski. 540.
monster. 515.
morning line. 555.
mound. 511.
mountaineer. 575.
mountaineering. 574, 575.
mountaineering, equipment. 574.
mountaineering boot. 575.
mounting. 563.
mouthpiece. 565.
mouthpiece. 536.
mud wall. 582.
mummy. 584.
neck. 572.
net. 519, 521, 522, 523, 525, 529.
net band. 523.
net judge. 523.
neutral zone. 515, 519.
niblick. 572.
no. 8 forward. 517.
North. 579.
North wind. 579.
nose. 542, 543.
noseband. 553.
notch. 568.
number. 580.
number three. 530.
number two. 530.
object balls. 569.
obstacles. 551.
octave. 563.
odd. 580, 581.
offensive. 514, 515.
on-deck circle. 511.
on guard line. 562.
on the wind. 539.
one-arm shoulder throw. 564.
one-burner camp stove. 585.
one pair. 578.
one-piece coverall. 541.
open-face spinning reel. 566.
order of finish. 555.
ordinary die. 579.
otter paw. 549.
out of bounds. 571.

outer boundary line. 526.
outer table. 578.
outfield. 511.
outhaul. 537.
outside left. 518.
outside line. 563.
outside linebacker. 514.
outside right. 518.
overcheck. 554.
overhand knot. 587.
owner. 555.
oxer. 551, 552.
oxer wall. 552.
pack. 541.
paddock. 555.
palm. 512.
panel. 541, 553.
pants. 512, 516, 520, 575.
parachute. 541.
parachute. 543.
parachuting. 541.
parachutist. 541.
parallel bars. 559.
parka. 547.
pawn. 577.
Pawn (P). 577.
payout tray. 581.
payout trigger. 581.
penalty arc. 518.
penalty area. 518.
penalty bench. 519.
penalty line. 525.
penalty spot. 518.
penalty timekeeper. 519.
penholder grip. 529.
penknife. 585.
performance. 555.
pick. 574.
pieces. 577.
pike position. 534.
pilot. 542, 543.
pilot parachute. 541.
pin. 576.
pink ball. 570.
pip. 579.
piste. 562.
pit. 576.
pitcher. 511.
pitcher's plate. 511.
pitching niblick. 572.
pitching wedge. 572.
piton-carrier. 575.
piton hammer. 574.
pitons. 574.
pivot. 548.
placing judge. 532.
plank and pole. 552.
planting box. 556.
plasticine board. 556.
plate. 585.
platform. 534, 561.
platform diver. 534.
player. 512.
player. 531.
player's number. 516.
player's stick. 520.
players' bench. 511, 519, 521, 522.
players' rotation. 522.
playing area, water polo. 531.
playing field, soccer. 518.
playing field for American football. 513.
playing field for Canadian football. 513.
playing surface. 529.
pocket. 569, 573, 576.
point. 548, 567, 578.
point of sailing. 539.
poker die. 579.
poker hands, standard. 578.
pole. 544, 555, 556, 582.
pole grip. 547.
pole loop. 582.
pole over a bank. 552.
pole shaft. 547.

pole tip. 547.
pole vault. 556.
poma lift. 544.
pommel. 553, 559, 563.
pommel horse. 559.
pool. 569.
pop-up tent. 583.
port tack. 539.
position. 555.
positions. 563.
post. 522, 528, 531.
post and plank. 551.
post and rail. 551.
practice fairway. 571.
president. 562.
press. 524.
pressure regulator. 585.
prime. 563.
prop forward. 517.
propane accessories. 585.
propane cylinder. 585.
protective cup. 516, 520.
protective equipment, football. 516.
puck. 520.
pullover sweater. 547.
pup tent. 583.
purge valve. 536.
putter. 572.
putter. 572.
putting green. 571.
pylon. 544.
pyramid spot. 570.
quarte. 563.
quarterback. 514, 515.
Queen. 578.
Queen (Q). 577.
Queen's side. 577.
quinte. 563.
racing programm. 555.
rack. 568.
racket. 529.
racquetball. 527.
racquetball racquet. 527.
racquetballer. 527.
rail. 536, 569, 570.
rainfly. 583.
rank. 577.
rear limit line. 562.
rear runner. 550.
receiver. 523, 526, 528, 529.
receiving line. 527.
recorder. 532.
rectangular. 584.
red. 580, 581.
red ball. 569, 570.
red balls. 570.
red cap. 531.
red dragon. 579.
red flag. 531, 564.
red inner circle. 530.
reef knot. 587.
reel. 562, 581.
reel plate. 581.
reel seat. 566.
referee. 514, 517, 518, 519, 521, 522, 529, 531, 532, 564, 565.
referee's stand. 528.
rein. 554.
release setting screw. 546.
reserve parachute. 541.
restricted area. 521.
restricting circle. 521.
retriever. 522.
reverse dive. 535.
rib pad. 516.
ribbing. 567.
rider. 550.
ridge. 580.
ridge pole. 582.
riding. 551, 552, 553.
riding coat. 551.
riding glove. 551.
riding helmet. 551.
riding whip. 551.
rigging wire. 543.
right back. 518, 522, 525.

right center. 517.
right cornerback. 514, 515.
right defense. 519.
right defensive end. 514, 515.
right defensive tackle. 514, 515.
right field. 511.
right fielder. 511.
right forward. 521, 522.
right guard. 514, 515, 521.
right half. 518.
right halfback. 514.
right outside linebacker. 515.
right safety. 514.
right safety back. 515.
right service court. 523, 526.
right tackle. 514, 515.
right wing. 517, 519.
right winger. 525.
rim. 521, 558.
ring. 565.
ring. 559, 574.
ring floor. 565.
ring post. 565.
ring step. 565.
rings. 559.
ringside. 565.
rink. 519.
rink. 530.
rink corner. 519.
ripcord. 541.
riser. 541.
roller skate. 548.
roof. 582.
Rook (R). 577.
room. 582.
rope. 565, 575, 587.
rotating wheel. 580.
rough. 571.
roulette table. 580, 581.
roulette wheel. 580.
royal flush. 578.
rubber thread. 573.
rucksack. 547, 575.
rudder. 538, 542.
rudder pedal. 542.
rugby. 517.
run. 560.
rung. 574.
runner. 550, 578.
running. 556.
running bowline. 587.
running surface. 547.
runway. 556, 557.
saber. 563.
saber and épée warning line. 562.
sabreur. 563.
saddle. 553.
saddle. 559.
saddlecloth. 554.
safety area. 564.
safety bar. 544.
safety binding. 546.
safety binding. 545.
safety cage. 556.
safety pad. 560.
safety strap. 546.
safety thong. 527.
sail. 537, 543.
sail panel. 538.
sailboard. 537.
sand wedge. 572.
saw. 585.
scalper. 554.
scarf. 545.
scissors. 585.
score sheet. 576.
scorer. 519, 521, 522, 562, 576.
scoring light. 562.
scoring table. 576.
screen window. 582.
screw. 548.
screw locking nut. 566.
screwdriver. 585.
screwsleeve. 574.
scrimmage in American football. 514.

scrimmage in Canadian football. 515.
scrum. 517.
scrum half. 517.
scuba diver. 536.
season tiles. 579.
seat. 542, 544, 550, 553.
second. 565.
second base. 511.
second baseman. 511.
second flight. 560.
second space. 521.
seconde. 563.
secretary. 525, 531.
sector flag. 556.
semi-circle. 521.
semi-mummy. 584.
septime. 563.
server. 522, 523, 526, 528, 529.
service area. 522.
service box. 526, 527.
service box line. 527.
service judge. 528.
service line. 523, 526, 527.
service zone. 527.
setup. 576.
sewn-in floor. 582.
shackle. 539.
shadow roll. 554.
shaft. 520, 524, 526, 554, 558, 568, 572, 574.
shaft holder. 554.
shake-hands grip. 529.
shank. 567.
sheath. 587.
sheath knife. 586.
sheepshank. 587.
sheet bend. 587.
sheet lead. 539.
shin boot. 554.
shin guard. 512, 516.
shirt. 524.
short line. 526, 527.
short service line. 528.
short-sleeved shirt. 561.
shorts. 524.
shortstop. 511.
shot put. 557.
shot splice. 587.
shots. 558.
shoulder. 524, 567.
shoulder pad. 516, 520.
shoulder strap. 573.
shovel. 545, 547.
shroud. 538.
shuttlecock. 528.
side line. 529.
side wall. 526, 527, 532.
side wall line. 526.
sideline. 513, 521, 522, 525.
sidestroke. 533.
silk line. 566.
single zero. 580, 581.
singles pole. 523.
singles service court. 528.
singles sideline. 523, 528.
sinker. 567.
sixte. 563.
skate. 520.
skate guard. 548.
skates, types of. 548.
skating. 548.
ski. 545.
ski boot. 546.
ski boot. 545.
ski goggles. 545, 547.
ski hat. 547.
ski instructor. 544.
ski jumper. 544.
ski jumping hill. 544.
ski pole. 545, 547.
ski resort. 544.
ski stop. 545, 546.
ski suit. 545.
ski tip. 547.
skiing. 544.

skin diving. 536.
skip. 530.
skirt. 524, 553.
skis, types of. 540.
slalom course. 544.
slalomist. 544.
sleeping bags. 584.
sleeve. 561, 562, 582.
slot machine. 581.
slotback. 515.
snaffle bit. 553.
snaffle rein. 553.
snap shackle. 539.
snooker. 570.
snorkel. 536.
snow goggles. 575.
snowshoe types. 549.
snowshoer. 549.
snowshoes. 549.
soccer. 518.
soccer ball. 518.
sock. 516, 524.
sole. 546, 548, 572.
sole plate. 548.
South. 579.
South wind. 579.
spade. 578.
spade mashie. 572.
speargun. 536.
speed skate. 548.
spike. 573, 574, 575.
spiked shoe. 512.
spinnaker boom. 538.
spinnaker sheet lead. 538.
spinner. 567.
spinning rod. 566.
splice. 587.
split bet. 580, 581.
split end. 514, 515.
split link. 567.
spoked wheel. 554.
spool. 566.
spoon. 572, 585.
sports. 509.
spot white ball. 570.
spring. 560.
spring hip throw. 564.
spring linkage. 581.
springboard. 534, 559, 560.
springboard diver. 534.
spur. 551.
square. 579.
square bet. 580, 581.
squash. 526.
squash ball. 526.
squash racket. 526.
stabilizer. 541.
stable. 555.
stake. 582, 583.
stake loop. 583.
stanchion. 548.
stand. 555.
stand off half. 517.
standardbred pacer. 554.
start. 552.
start line. 556.
start wall. 532.
startboard tack. 539.
starter. 532.
starting block. 532.
starting dive. 532.
starting grip. 532.
starting position. 532.
starting position. 535.
starting positions. 534.
stationary bowl. 580.
steel bar. 559.
steeplechase. 556.
steering line. 541.
stem. 538.
stern. 537.
stick glove. 520.
stirrup iron. 553.
stirrup leather. 553.
stirrup sock. 512.
stitches. 512.

stocking. 562.
stopboard. 557.
straight. 552, 578.
straight bet. 580, 581.
straight flush. 578.
straight position. 534.
strainer. 582.
strand. 587.
strap. 512, 550, 559.
street bet. 580, 581.
stringing. 524.
strings. 526.
stroke judge. 532.
strokes, types of. 533.
strong-box. 581.
strut. 550.
submersible watch. 536.
substitute. 522, 525, 531.
substitutes' bench. 525.
suit tiles. 579.
sulky. 554.
support. 529, 560.
surcingle. 554.
surface of the water. 534.
suspension line. 541.
sweeper. 530.
sweeping loin throw. 564.
sweeping score line. 530.
swimmer. 532.
swimming. 532.
swimming competition. 532.
swimming pool. 531.
swivel. 558, 567.
symbol. 581.
T-bar lift. 544.
tab. 553.
table. 529.
table. 562.
table, English billiards. 570.
table, pool. 569.
table tennis. 529.
table tennis player. 529.
table tennis shoe. 529.
tack. 537.
tail. 540, 542, 543, 545, 547, 549, 524.
tail parachute. 542.
take-off board. 556, 557.
take-off line. 556.
tape. 512, 522.
target areas. 563.
team. 517.
team bench. 531.
team shirt. 512.
tee. 573.
tee. 530.
teeing ground. 571.
teeth. 574.
telltale. 526, 538.
temperature. 555.
tendon guard. 548.
tennis. 523, 524.
tennis ball. 524.
tennis players. 524.
tennis racket. 524.
tennis shoe. 524.
tents. 582, 583.
tents, major types of. 583.
thigh pad. 516.
third base. 511.
third baseman. 511.
thirty-second clock operator. 521.
three-burner camp stove. 585.
three of a kind. 578.
threequarter backs. 517.
throat. 524, 567.
throat latch. 553.
throat protector. 512, 520.
throwing arc. 557.
throwing circle. 556, 557.
throwing in a circle. 564.
throwings. 558.
thumb. 512.
tie flap. 582.
tierce. 563.
tight end. 514, 515.

tiller. 538.
timekeeper. 521, 525, 531, 562, 565.
timing. 555.
tip. 540, 543, 545, 549, 558, 567, 568.
tip guard. 548.
tip guide. 566.
tip section. 566.
tip-top. 566.
toboggan. 550.
toe. 572.
toe binding. 547.
toe box. 548.
toe hole. 549.
toe lacing. 549.
toe pick. 548.
toe piece. 540, 545, 546.
toe-piece release setting indicator. 546.
toe stop. 548.
toe strap. 540.
toeplate. 547.
tongue. 546, 548.
top. 524.
top bar. 560.
top pocket. 570.
top surface. 542.
topping. 567.
tote board. 555.
touch in goal line. 517.
touch line. 517, 518.
touring boot. 547.
tourist tent. 583.
tow bar. 540.
tow hook. 542.
tow release knob. 542.
towrope. 540.
track. 555.
track. 544, 557.
track and field athletics. 556, 557, 558.
trailing edge. 542, 543.
trainer. 555, 565.
trampoline. 560.
traveler. 539.
tread. 553.
treble. 553.
tree. 553.
triple bar. 551, 552.
triple jump. 557.
trousers. 564.
truck. 548.
trunks. 561, 565.
tubular ice screw. 574.
tuck position. 534.
turn and slip indicator. 542.
turnbuckle. 539, 565.
turning judge. 532.
turtleneck. 545.
twin skis. 540.
twist dive. 535.
twisted rope. 587.
two-hand clean and jerk. 561.
two-hand snatch. 561.
two pairs. 578.
umbrella sheath. 573.
umpire. 514, 521, 522, 523, 528, 529.
umpire-in-chief. 511.
undershirt. 512, 565.
uneven parallel bars. 560.
uniform, football. 516.
uphaul. 537.
upper. 546.
upper cuff. 546.
upper edge. 529.
upper shell. 546.
upperworks. 539.
upright. 556, 557, 559, 560.
vacuum bottle. 586.
variometer. 542.
vaulting horse. 559, 560.
veil. 567.
vent hole. 541.
vertical side band. 522.

vertical stabilizer. 542.
volleyball. 522.
waders. 568.
wagon tent. 583.
wall. 551, 552, 579, 582.
wall and rails. 551, 552.
wall tent. 583.
wardrobe. 582.
water ditch. 556.
water hazard. 571.
water jug. 586.
water jump. 551, 552.
water polo. 531.
water skiing. 540.
weapon, parts of the. 563.
web. 512.
weight. 558, 561.
weight belt. 536.
weightlifter. 561.
weightlifting. 561.
West. 579.
West wind. 579.
wet suit. 536.
wheel. 548.
whipping. 572.
White. 577, 578.
white cap. 531.
white cue ball. 570.
white dragon. 579.
white flag. 531, 564.
white spot ball. 569.
white square. 577.
white tape. 528, 529.
width. 534.
winch. 539.
wind. 539.
wind abeam. 539.
wind baffle. 585.
wind indicator. 538.
window. 537, 582.
wing. 542, 543, 567.
wing tip. 542.
wing wire. 543.
winning line. 581.
wire. 546, 558.
wire sling. 574.
wire support. 585.
wishbone boom. 537.
women's apparatus. 560.
wood. 572.
wooden bar. 559.
wrist pad. 516.
wrist sling. 574.
wrist strap. 547.
wristband. 524.
yard line. 513.
yarn. 587.
yellow ball. 570.
zipper. 583.
zippered screen door. 582.

SYMBOLS

access for physically handicapped. 705.
addition. 709.
air transportation. 707.
ampersand. 709.
Aquarius, the Water Bearer. 698.
argent. 696.
Aries, the Ram. 698.
azure. 696.
baggage carts. 706.
baggage claim. 706.
banner. 697.
bar. 706.
barber. 706.
base. 695.
biology. 709.
birth. 709.
breakdown service. 707.
bumps. 700.
bus transportation. 707.
camping area. 707.
camping prohibited. 707.
camping site. 707.
Cancer, the Crab. 698.
canton. 695.
Capricorn, the Goat. 698.
car rental. 707.
caravan site. 707.
cattle crossing. 701.
caution. 704.
cent. 709.
center base. 695.
center chief. 695.
center point. 695.
charges. 696.
check-in. 706.
chevron. 696.
chief. 695, 696.
chlorine bleaching. 708.
coffee shop. 705.
colors. 696.
common symbols. 704, 705, 706, 707.
compulsory roundabout. 703.
constellations. 698.
copyright. 709.
crescent. 696.
cross. 696.
currency exchange. 706.
cyclists crossing. 701.
cyclists entering. 701.
danger warning signs. 700, 701.
dangerous bend. 700.
dangerous descent. 700.
death. 709.
dexter. 695.
dexter base. 695.
dexter chief. 695.
dexter flank. 695.
direction to be followed. 703.
division. 709.
do not enter. 704.
do not use for baggage carts. 706.
do not use for wheelchairs. 705.
dollar. 709.
double bend. 700.
drug store. 706.
dry cleaning. 708.
drying. 708.
duty-free. 706.
eagle. 696.
electrical hazard danger. 704.
elevator for people. 705.
emblem. 695.
empty set. 709.
["end of priority[' sign. 701.
end of prohibition of passing. 702.
end of superhighway. 703.
ermine. 696.
escalator, down. 705.
escalator, up. 705.
fabric care. 708.
falling rocks. 700.
fanion. 697.
female. 709.
fire extinguisher. 704.
fire hose. 704.
first aid. 704.
flag. 695.
flag shapes. 697.
flammable. 704.
flammule. 697.
fleur-de-lis. 696.
fly. 695.
freight elevator. 705.
furs. 696.
Gemini, the Twins. 698.
["give way[' sign. 701.
grade crossing. 701.
graphic elements for symbols. 699.
ground transportation. 707.
gules. 696.
halyard. 695.
helicopter transportation. 707.
heraldry. 695.
hoist. 695.
hospital. 704.
hotel information. 707.
infinity. 709.
information. 704.
informative signs. 703.
inspection services. 706.
international road signs. 700, 701, 702, 703.
intersection. 709.
ironing. 708.
is a member of. 709.
is approximately equal to. 709.
is contained in. 709.
is equal to. 709.
is equal to or less than. 709.
is equivalent to. 709.
is greater than. 709.
is identical with. 709.
is not equal to. 709.
is not identical with. 709.
Leo, the Lion. 698.
Libra, the Balance. 698.
light signals. 701.
lion passant. 696.
lockers. 705.
loose gravel. 700.
lost and found articles. 706.
male. 709.
mandatory signs. 703.
mast. 695.
mathematics. 709.
maximum speed limit. 702.
metals. 696.
mullet. 696.
multiplication. 709.
negative charge. 709.
no dogs. 704.
no entry. 702.
no entry for bicycles. 702.
no entry for goods vehicles. 702.
no entry for mopeds. 702.
no entry for motorcycles. 702.
no entry for pedestrians. 702.
no entry for power-driven vehicules. 702.
no left turn. 702.
no U-turn. 702.
one-way traffic. 703.
or. 696.
ordinaries. 696.
oriflamme. 697.
other dangers. 701.
overhead clearance. 702.
pale. 696.
parking signs. 703.
partitions. 696.
party. 696.
passing prohibited. 702.
pedestrian crossing. 700, 704.
pennant. 697.
per bend. 696.
per fess. 696.
percent. 709.
picnic area. 707.
picnics prohibited. 707.
pike. 695.
Pisces, the Fishes. 698.
plus or minus. 709.
poison. 704.
police. 704.
positive charge. 709.
post office. 706.
pound. 709.
prescription. 709.
priority intersection. 701.
["priority road[' sign. 701.
prohibitory signs. 702.
purpure. 696.
quaterly. 696.
rail transportation. 707.
reaction direction. 709.
rectangular. 697.
registered trademark. 709.
regulatory signs. 702.
restaurant. 705.
reversible reaction. 709.
ridge. 700.
right bend. 700.
road works. 701.
roadway narrows. 700.
sable. 696.
Sagittarius, the Archer. 698.
school zone. 700.
Schwenkel. 697.
scientific symbols. 709.
Scorpio, the Scorpion. 698.
service station. 707.
shield. 695.
signs of zodiac. 698.
signs regulating priority at intersections. 701.
sinister. 695.
sinister base. 695.
sinister chief. 695.
sinister flank. 695.
slippery floor. 704.
slippery road. 700.
smoking permitted. 705.
smoking prohibited. 705.
square. 697.
square root of. 709.
staff. 695.
stairs. 705.
standing signs. 703.
steep hill. 700.
stop at intersection. 701.
streamer. 697.
subtraction. 709.
superhighway. 703.
swallowtail. 697.
swallowtail and tongue. 697.
swallowtail pennant. 697.
symbols. 693.
symbols, heraldry. 696.
Taurus, the Bull. 698.
taxi transportation. 707.
telegrams. 706.
telephone. 706.
tinctures. 696.
toilet for men and women. 705.
toilet for women. 705.
traffic circle. 701.
two triangular pennants. 697.
two-way traffic. 701.
union. 709.
use of audible warning devices prohibited. 702.
vair. 696.
vert. 696.
Virgo, the Virgin. 698.
washing. 708.
weight limitation. 702.
width clearance. 702.
wild animals crossing. 701.
windsock. 697.

TRANSPORTATION

abutment. 400, 401, 402.
accommodation ladder. 420.
acoustic baffle. 421.
acoustic echo. 428.
adjustable seat. 407.
advertising sign. 414.
aft stabilizer fin. 419.
aftermast. 416.
aileron. 434.
air conditioning. 407.
air filter. 391.
air inlet. 436, 441.
air intake. 404, 422.
air lock. 423, 424.
air lock entrance hatch. 423.
air scoop. 394.
air tank. 423.
air-tight diaphragm. 391.
air warning radar. 425.
aircraft gate. 438.
airport. 438, 439.
alternator. 391, 404.
alternator indicator. 385.
ammeter. 396.
anchor. 433.

anchor cable. 433.
anchor-windlass room. 419.
anchorage block. 402.
anchors, types of. 433.
annular combustion chamber. 436.
antenna. 383, 434.
anti-aircraft gun. 425.
anti-collision light. 434.
anti-submarine mortar. 425.
anti-torque tail rotor. 441.
approach ramp. 402.
apron. 438.
arch. 401.
arch bridge. 401.
arch bridges, types of. 401.
arches, types of. 401.
arm. 433.
arm rest. 386.
arrivals concourse. 440.
arrivals schedule. 412.
articulation. 384.
astragal. 431.
automatic control system
    computer. 422.
automatic gates. 410.
automatically-controlled door. 440.
automobile. 383, 384, 385, 386.
automobile car. 406.
autopilot control. 437.
auxiliary tank. 388.
axial-flow compressor. 436.
axle. 404.
backrest. 386, 394.
backstay. 416.
backup light. 383.
baggage cart. 440.
baggage check. 412.
baggage check-in counter. 440.
baggage claim area. 440.
baggage compartment. 441.
baggage conveyor. 439.
baggage lockers. 412.
baggage racks. 421.
baggage room. 412.
baggage trailer. 439.
Bailey bridge. 403.
ballast. 408.
bands. 430.
base. 408, 409.
base course. 399.
bathyscaphe. 423.
battery. 392.
battery. 423.
battery box. 388.
battery case. 392.
battery cover. 392.
bead. 393.
beam bridge. 400.
beam bridges, types of. 400.
bedroom. 431.
bell buoy. 430.
bellowslike joint. 444.
belt. 393.
belted radial tire. 393.
bench. 414.
bias-ply tire. 393.
bicycle. 397, 398.
bicycle horn. 398.
bill. 433.
blade. 436.
blade lift fan. 421.
boarding step. 441.
bobstay. 416.
bodies, types of. 384.
body. 387, 407, 430.
body side molding. 383.
boiler. 424.
boiler room. 425.
boilers. 419.
bollard. 426.
bolt. 393.
booking hall. 412.
boom truck. 439.
booster parachute. 443.
bottom bracket axle. 398.

bottom-end transverse member.
    411.
bottom retainer. 405.
bottom side rail. 411.
bow rudder. 420.
bowl. 429.
bowsprit. 416.
box car. 405.
brace. 417.
bracket. 428.
brail. 417.
brake cable. 397.
brake handle. 394.
brake line. 393.
brake lining. 393.
brake pad. 393.
brake pedal. 386, 396.
brake shoe. 393.
brakes. 393.
breake lever. 397.
bridge. 400, 401, 402, 403, 424.
bridge and chart room. 420.
brig. 418.
brigantine. 418.
broom point downwards. 432.
broom point upwards. 432.
bucket seat. 386.
buckle. 386.
bulk carrier. 427.
bulkhead. 388.
bulkhead deck. 420.
bulkhead flat car. 406.
bullseye. 432.
bulwark. 416.
bumper. 383, 388, 389, 404, 410.
bumper guard. 383.
bunk. 424.
buoys. 430.
by-pass taxiway. 438.
cab. 394.
cabin. 420, 434, 441.
cable. 428.
cable stay anchorage. 402.
cable-stayed bridge. 402.
caboose. 406.
cage. 430.
caisson. 427.
caliper. 393.
camshaft. 391.
can. 432.
can buoy. 430.
canal bed. 426.
canal lock. 426.
canal lock. 427.
canopy. 434.
cantilever bridge. 400.
cantilever span. 400.
capstan. 425.
captain's quarters. 419.
captain's seat. 437.
car. 411.
car deck. 421.
car wash. 387.
carburetor. 390, 391, 395.
cargo-bay access hatch. 443.
cargo-bay door. 443.
cargo boom. 420.
cargo hatch. 419.
cargo terminal. 438.
carriageway. 399.
carrier. 397.
carrousel. 440.
cars, types of. 406.
catadioptric ring. 432.
catering vehicle. 439.
cell connector. 392.
center-aisle. 407.
center bearing. 436.
center console. 385.
center electrode. 392.
center post. 383.
center span. 402.
central console. 437.
central instrument panel. 437.
chain. 398.
chain guide. 398.

chain stay. 397.
chain wheel. 398.
change machine. 412.
changer's booth. 414.
channel. 409.
chapel. 419.
check-rail. 408.
checkers. 430.
classification yard. 411.
clearance light. 388.
clew line. 417.
clock. 385.
closure rail. 408.
clutch lever. 396.
clutch pedal. 386.
coach car. 407.
collector bow. 413.
column. 401.
combustion chamber. 390, 436.
command module. 442.
compass. 423.
compass card. 429.
composite topmark. 432.
compressor. 390.
compressor turbine. 390.
cone. 432.
conical buoy. 430.
conning tower. 423, 424.
container. 411.
container. 420.
container car. 406.
container hold. 420.
container-loading bridge. 427.
container ship. 420.
container ship. 427.
container terminal. 427.
continuous beam. 400.
control cable. 398.
control column. 437.
control deck. 421, 424.
control levers. 437.
control room. 431.
control stand. 404.
control stick. 441.
control tower. 438.
control tower cab. 438.
convertible. 384.
cooling air. 444.
cooling fan. 390, 391, 392.
cooling liquid pump. 444.
corner cap. 405.
corner fitting. 411.
corner structure. 411.
counterweight. 403, 408, 409.
coupler head. 405.
coupler knuckle. 405.
coupler knuckle pin. 405.
cowl. 383.
crank. 398, 426.
crew quarters. 419.
crossbar. 397.
crossbuck sign. 409.
crossing. 413.
crossing gate mechanism. 409.
crown. 433.
cruciform tail unit. 435.
cupola. 431.
curb. 399.
currency exchange counter. 440.
currency exchange office. 412.
customs control. 440.
cylinder. 390, 395.
cylinder-head. 395.
cylinder head cover. 391.
dashboard. 385.
dating nail. 408.
davit. 416.
deck. 388, 400, 401, 402.
deck arch bridge. 401.
dehumidifier. 444.
delay indicator. 413.
delta wing. 435.
deluxe suite. 419.
departure time indicator. 413.
departures concourse. 440.
departures room. 440.

departures schedule. 412.
depressed-center flat car. 406.
destination indicator. 413.
detachable petrol tank. 423.
dial-type display. 428.
diamond. 432.
diaphragm. 407.
diesel-electric locomotive. 404.
diesel engine. 390.
diesel engine. 404, 422.
diesel shop. 410.
dimmer switch. 386.
dinghy pack. 421.
dining car. 407.
dining room. 419, 420.
dining section. 407.
dioptric ring. 432.
dip switch. 396.
directional sign. 414.
disc. 393.
disk. 393.
disk brake. 393.
disk brake. 395.
distributor. 391.
ditch. 399.
ditch light. 413.
door. 386.
door. 383.
door handle. 383.
door hasp. 405.
door hasp fastener. 405.
door lock. 383.
door panel. 415.
door stop. 405.
double fluked anchor. 433.
double-leaf bascule bridge. 403.
double seat. 415.
down tube. 397.
drip molding. 383.
drive chain. 397.
drive shaft. 441.
driver's cab. 404.
driving shaft. 420.
driving turbine. 390.
drum. 393.
drum brake. 393.
dry dock. 427.
duty-free shop. 440.
dynamics propeller. 421.
echo sounder. 428.
electric motor. 423.
electrical connection. 388.
electrical power unit. 439.
electricity cable. 399.
element. 392.
elevator. 434.
elevon. 443.
embankment. 399.
emblem. 383.
emergency brake commutator.
    415.
emergency niche. 414.
emergency oxygen supply. 444.
end door. 411.
end ladder. 405.
engine. 391.
engine. 436.
engine air intake. 421.
engine block. 391.
engine mounting pylon. 435.
engine room. 424, 425.
engines. 390.
engines. 443.
entrance turnstile. 414.
escalator. 414.
exhaust cone. 436.
exhaust duct. 436.
exhaust gas admission. 390.
exhaust gas outflow. 390.
exhaust manifold. 390, 391, 392.
exhaust nozzle. 436.
exhaust pipe. 390, 392, 395, 436,
    441.
exhaust stock. 389.
exhaust system. 392.
exhaust valve. 390.

exit turnstile. 414.
expansion chamber. 429.
expansion space. 408.
exterior sign. 414.
external tank. 443.
F-1 engine. 442.
fan. 415, 436.
fan belt. 391, 392.
fan cable stays. 402.
fender. 383, 389, 397.
ferry. 420.
ferryboat. 427.
fifth wheel. 389.
fight information board. 440.
filler hole. 389, 391.
filler plug. 429.
filter. 429.
fin. 421, 434, 441.
first-class swimming pool. 419.
first officer's seat. 437.
first stage. 442.
fixed arch. 401.
fixed bridges. 400, 401, 402.
fixed distance marking. 438.
fixed stairs. 414.
flap guide rail. 435.
flashing light. 409.
flat car. 406.
flexible skirt. 421.
flight deck. 437.
flight deck. 434, 441, 443.
flight engineer's panel. 437.
flight engineer's seat. 437.
flight instruments. 437.
float. 429.
floating bridge. 403.
floating crane. 427.
floating dock. 427.
fluke. 433.
fluted shaft. 384.
flying jib. 417.
flywheel. 390, 391.
fog light. 389.
fold-out table. 407.
foot rope. 416.
footboard. 394.
footbridge. 410, 414.
footpeg. 396.
fore royal sail. 417.
foremast. 416.
foresail. 417.
fork. 397.
fork pocket. 411.
forward car ramp. 421.
foundation of tower. 402.
four-door sedan. 384.
four-masted bark. 416, 417.
frame. 395, 429.
frame rail. 389.
framework. 432.
freight hold. 419.
freight station. 410.
frigate. 425.
frog. 408.
front bearing. 436.
front brake. 396, 397.
front derailleur. 397, 398.
front fender. 395.
front foil. 422.
front foil control actuator. 422.
front footpeg. 395.
front hydraulic fork. 395.
front pipe. 392.
front spar. 435.
frontwall. 388.
fuel indicator. 385.
fuel pump. 390.
fuel pump belt. 390.
fuel spray manifold. 436.
fuel tank. 389, 395, 422, 431, 441.
fuel transfer pipe. 442.
funnel aileron. 419.
fuselage. 434.
gaff. 416.
gaff sail boom. 416.
gaff topsail. 417.

gallery. 431.
galley. 434.
garage. 419, 420.
gas inlet. 444.
gas main. 399.
gas-oil line. 390.
gas outlet. 444.
gas pedal. 386.
gas tank cap. 396.
gas tank door. 383.
gas turbine. 421.
gasoline engine. 391.
gasoline pump. 387.
gasoline pump. 391.
gasoline pump hose. 387.
gate arm. 409.
gate arm lamp. 409.
gate arm support. 409.
gear shift. 396.
gearbox. 422.
gearshift lever. 385, 395.
generator. 397.
gimbal ring. 429.
glass dome. 429.
glass-fiber cloth. 444.
glove. 444.
glove compartment. 385.
gondola car. 406.
grab handle. 389.
grapnel anchor. 433.
gravity band. 433.
grille. 383.
ground airport equipment. 439.
ground electrode. 392.
group retarders. 411.
guard rail. 400.
guide chain. 423.
guiding and current bar. 415.
guiding tower. 403.
gully grate. 399.
gun director. 425.
gutter. 399.
half-through arch bridge. 401.
hall. 419.
halyard. 417.
hand brake gear housing. 405.
hand brake wheel. 405.
hand brake winding chain. 405.
hand truck. 413.
handlebars. 394, 397.
handrail. 415.
harbor. 427.
harbor station. 427.
hardtop. 384.
harp cable stays. 402.
head. 408.
head tube. 397.
headlamp bezel. 384.
headlight. 384.
headlight. 383, 389, 394, 395, 413.
headlight housing shell. 384.
headrest. 386, 407.
heat shield. 443.
heater control. 385.
height sensor. 422.
helicopter. 441.
helicopter hangar. 425.
helium sphere. 442.
helmet. 444.
hex nut. 392.
high beam warning light. 396.
high focal plane buoy. 430.
high-speed exit taxiway. 438.
highway crossing. 409.
highway crossing bell. 409.
hoisting ring. 433.
hold. 434.
hold yard. 411.
holding area marking. 438.
hood. 383, 389.
hopper car. 406.
hopper ore car. 406.
horizon glass. 429.
horizontal end handhold. 405.
horizontal stabilizer. 434, 441.
horn. 385, 404.

horn button. 396.
hotel reservation desk. 440.
housing. 395, 428.
hovercraft. 421.
hub. 397.
hubcap. 383.
hump. 411.
hump area. 411.
hurricane deck. 420.
hydrofoil boat. 422.
idler wheel. 394.
ignition switch. 396.
immigration control. 440.
incandescent lamp. 432.
index arm. 429.
index mirror. 429.
indicator board. 413.
inflated carrying tire. 415.
inflated guiding tire. 415.
information counter. 440.
information office. 412.
injector. 390.
inlet guide vanes. 436.
inlet valve. 390, 391.
inner jib. 417.
instrument board. 385.
instrument board. 385.
instrument unit. 442.
insulator. 392.
interior door handle. 386.
interior door lock button. 386.
invert. 415.
iron shot silo. 423.
J-2 engine. 442.
jack staff. 425.
jet. 434.
jet refueler. 439.
jewel cap. 429.
jockey roller. 398.
journal box. 404.
junction box. 409.
kerosene. 442.
ketch. 418.
kill button. 396.
king pin. 404.
kingpin. 388.
kiosk. 414.
kitchen. 407.
knurled button. 428.
lamp changer. 432.
landing light. 441.
lantern. 431.
lantern of lighthouse. 432.
lantern pane. 431.
LASH ship. 427.
lateen sail. 418.
launch escape system. 442.
lavatory truck. 439.
lead shot ballast. 423.
leading edge. 434.
leaf. 426.
leaf spring. 394.
lens carriage. 432.
lens clock. 432.
level crossing. 410.
lever. 387.
life buoy. 422.
life raft. 425.
lifeboat. 416.
lift. 416.
lift bridge. 403.
lift-fan air intake. 421.
lift gate. 384.
lift span. 403.
lifting lever. 405.
light. 415, 430.
lighthouse. 431.
lighting switch. 396.
limousine. 384.
line map. 414.
liquid compass. 429.
liquid-cooled garment. 444.
liquid hydrogen (fuel). 442.
liquid oxygen (lox). 442.
liquid oxygen (lox) transfer pipe.
   442.

litre/gallon totalizer. 387.
livestock car. 406.
living quarters. 431, 443.
loading tunnel. 438.
lobby. 440.
lock. 398.
lock-chamber. 426.
lock keeper's building. 427.
locomotive. 404.
long-range jet. 434.
lounge. 419.
lower berth. 407.
lower chord. 401.
lower fore topgallant sail. 417.
lower fore topsail. 417.
lower level. 426.
lower mast. 416.
lower rudder. 424.
lower side-rail. 388.
lox tank baffles. 442.
lubber's line. 429.
lubber's-line disk. 429.
luggage rack. 384.
lunar boot. 444.
lunar module. 442.
magnet. 429.
main bevel drive gearbox. 421.
main engines. 443.
main gas tap. 396.
main generator. 404.
main landing gear. 434.
main line. 410.
main lower topgallant sail. 417.
main lower topsail. 417.
main royal sail. 417.
main running track. 411.
main sail. 417.
main sewer. 399.
main spar. 435.
main stand. 395.
main undercarriage mounting
   beam. 435.
main upper topgallant sail. 417.
main upper topsail. 417.
mainmast. 416.
maintenance hangar. 438.
maneuvering engine. 443.
manhole. 399.
Marconi cutter. 418.
marker light. 389.
maritime signals. 430, 431, 432.
marking, cardinal system of. 431.
marking, late.al system of. 432.
mast. 409, 410, 441.
master retarders. 411.
masthead. 416.
masthead light. 420.
masting. 416.
medical injection disk. 444.
mercury bath. 432.
mezzanine. 414.
micrometer drum. 429.
middle jib. 417.
mirror. 395.
missile. 424.
missile director. 425.
missile launcher. 425.
missile tube. 424.
miter gate. 426.
mizzen sail. 417.
mizzenmast. 416.
mobile passenger escalator. 439.
money totalizer. 387.
motor car. 415.
motorcycle. 395, 396.
movable bridges. 403.
mud flap. 388, 389.
muffler. 392.
multiple-span beam bridge. 400.
murette. 431.
mushroom anchor. 433.
navigating bridge. 420.
navigation devices. 428, 429.
navigation light. 434.
navigational radar. 425.
neck ring. 444.

negative plate. 392.
negative plate group. 392.
negative terminal. 392.
normal tail unit. 435.
nose. 434.
nose cone. 436.
nose landing gear. 434.
nozzle. 442.
number of tracks sign. 409.
nut. 408, 428.
observation deck. 440.
observation light. 423.
observation window. 443.
observer's seat. 437.
odometer. 385.
oil drain hole. 391.
oil filter. 391.
oil indicator. 385.
oil-level stick. 391.
oil pan. 391.
oil pressure warning light. 396.
oil tank cap. 396.
on-off switch. 428.
open-air terrace. 419.
orbiter. 443.
outbound. 411.
outer jib. 417.
outside mirror. 383.
overhead switch panel. 437.
overpass. 400.
oxygen supply pressure gauge. 444.
paddle valve. 426.
pallet and container transporter. 439.
palm. 433.
panoramic window. 407.
parcels office. 412.
parking area. 438.
parking brake lever. 385.
partlow chart. 388.
passageway. 407.
passenger cabin. 421.
passenger cars, types of. 407.
passenger liner. 419.
passenger platform. 413.
passenger seating. 422.
passenger station. 410.
passenger terminal. 440.
passenger terminal. 438.
passenger transfer vehicle. 439, 440.
passengers-conductor communications. 415.
passport control. 440.
pavement. 399.
payload. 442.
pedal. 397, 398.
pedestal. 387.
peep hole. 409.
periscope. 424.
pier. 400, 401.
pier foundation. 400.
piggyback car. 406.
pilothouse. 422.
pinnacle. 401.
pinwheel passenger loading ramp. 438.
piston. 391, 393.
pitch link. 441.
pivot. 429.
placard board. 405.
plate grid. 392.
plate strap. 392.
platform. 388.
platform. 403.
platform edge. 413, 414.
platform entrance. 412.
platform number. 413.
platform roofing. 413.
platform shelter. 410.
platform truck. 413.
playroom. 419.
plow anchor. 433.
ply. 393.
pogo stick. 389.

point wire. 409.
points motor. 409.
pole. 416.
pole beacon. 430.
pontoon. 403.
poop. 416.
port custom house. 427.
port sail plane. 424.
portable life support system. 444.
portable life support system control unit. 444.
portal bridge. 401.
portal frame. 401.
positive plate. 392.
positive plate grou"p. 392.
positive terminal. 392.
potable water truck. 439.
power generators. 431.
power plant instruments. 437.
power train. 398.
pressure gauge. 444.
pressure relief valve. 444.
pressure suit. 444.
price per litre/gallon. 387.
prismatic section. 432.
propeller. 419, 422, 423, 424.
propeller gearbox. 421.
propeller shaft. 419, 422.
pull rod. 408.
pulley. 391.
pulse of sound. 428.
pump attendant. 387.
pump island. 387.
pump nozzle. 387.
pylon. 421.
quarter window. 383.
quay ramp. 427.
quayside crane. 427.
quayside railway. 427.
racing car. 384.
rack. 432.
radar antenna. 424.
radar scanner. 421.
radial tire. 393.
radiator. 392.
radiator. 404.
radiator hose. 392.
radiator pressure cap. 392.
radio antenna. 424, 444.
rail. 408.
rail anchor. 408.
rail joint. 408.
railroad station. 410.
railroad track. 408, 409.
railway map. 412.
ramp. 410.
reactor. 424.
reactor deck. 424.
rear brake. 397.
rear bumper. 394.
rear derailleur. 397.
rear foil. 422.
rear foil control actuator. 422.
rear footpeg. 395.
rear light. 397.
rear seat. 386.
rear shock absorber. 395.
rear window. 383.
rear window frame. 383.
rearview mirror. 385.
receiver-indicator. 428.
receiving yard. 411.
red marker light. 388.
redcap. 413.
reef band. 417.
reef point. 417.
reflector. 388, 394.
refrigeration unit. 388.
refrigerator car. 406.
release bar. 389.
release handle. 386.
remote-control arm. 443.
repair shop. 387.
reserve gas tap. 396.
resonator. 392.
retaining ring. 384.

return spring. 393.
revolution counter. 385.
rigging. 416.
rigs, types of. 418.
rim. 393, 395, 397.
rim flange. 393.
ring. 433.
road, cross section of a. 399.
road side sidewall. 388.
road train, articulated. 389.
rock sample pocket. 444.
rocket. 442.
roller. 432.
roof. 383, 388, 411.
root rib. 435.
rotor blade. 436, 441.
rotor head. 441.
rotor hub. 441.
routing cardboard. 405.
royal mast. 416.
rub rail. 388.
rudder. 419, 421, 434, 443.
rudder pedal. 437.
running rail. 415.
running track. 411.
runway. 415, 438.
runway center line markings. 438.
runway designation marking. 438.
runway end lights. 438.
runway side stripe markings. 438.
runway threshold markings. 438.
runway touchdown zone marking. 438.
saddle. 395, 397.
safety line. 414.
sails. 417.
scils, types of. 418.
sand shoe. 388.
scale. 429.
schedules. 412.
schooner. 418.
scissors crossing. 410.
sea anchor. 433.
sealed-beam mounting ring. 384.
seat. 394.
seat belt. 386.
seat post. 397.
seat stay. 397.
seat tube. 397.
seats. 386.
second stage. 442.
security check. 440.
sediment chamber. 392.
semaphore. 410.
semitrailer. 388.
semitrailer. 389.
separator. 392.
service main. 399.
service module. 442.
service room. 431.
service station. 387.
sextant. 429.
shank. 433.
sheet. 417.
shield. 383.
shifter. 397, 398.
ship's anchor. 433.
ship's launch. 425.
shock absorber. 394.
shoulder. 399.
shoulder of mutton sail. 418.
shroud. 416.
side. 416.
side door. 411.
side handrail. 415.
side ladder. 405.
side ladder tread. 405.
side-marker light. 383.
side platform. 414.
side span. 402.
side stand. 395.
side wall. 411, 426.
side window. 389.
sidewalk. 399.
signal background plate. 409.
signal gantry. 410.

signal light. 395.
signals. 409.
sill step. 405.
simple-span beam bridge. 400.
simple topmarks. 432.
single-leaf bascule bridge. 403.
single seat. 415.
siren. 422.
ski. 394.
skid. 441.
skid ramp. 389.
skirt finger. 421.
sleeping car. 407.
slide chair. 408.
sliding roof. 383.
sliding window. 407.
slope. 399.
smoke filter. 419.
snorkel exhaust. 424.
snorkel intake. 424.
snow guard. 394.
snow tire. 393.
snowmobile. 394.
soft-drink dispenser. 387.
solid-rocket booster. 443.
sounding gauge. 423.
space shuttle. 443.
space shuttle at takeoff. 443.
space shuttle in orbit. 443.
space suit. 444.
spacelab. 443.
spanker. 417.
spark plug. 392.
spark plug body. 392.
spark plug cable. 391.
spark plug gap. 392.
spark plug gasket. 392.
spark plug terminal. 392.
speaking window membrane. 412.
speedometer. 385, 396.
sphere. 423, 432.
spike. 408.
splash guard. 383.
spleeping compartment. 407.
splice bar. 408.
spline. 392.
spoiler. 434.
spoke. 397.
spoke wheel. 389.
spotlight. 422.
spring. 404.
spring washer. 408.
sprocket. 397.
sprocket cluster. 398.
square sail. 418.
St-George's cross. 432.
stabilizer. 420.
stabilizing fin. 442.
stabilizing keel. 423.
stack. 420.
stake pocket. 388.
starboard diving plane. 424.
starter. 391.
starter pedal. 396.
starting signal. 413.
station hall. 412.
station name. 414.
station platform. 413.
station platform. 410.
station sign. 411.
station wagon. 384.
station wagon, back of a. 384.
stator vane. 436.
stay. 416.
stay sail. 417.
staysail-stay. 416.
steam turbine. 420.
steel safey wheel. 415.
steering. 386.
steering damper. 396.
steering lock. 396.
steering wheel. 385, 386.
stem. 397, 416.
step. 405.
stern loading door. 420.
sterring column. 386.

Thematic Indexes

stiffening girder. 402.
stock. 433.
stocked anchor. 433.
stockless anchor. 433.
storm sewer. 399.
straight wing. 435.
street, cross section of a. 399.
stretcher bar. 409.
stringer. 435.
stripes. 430.
strut. 422.
stud. 428.
subbase. 399.
subgrade. 399.
submarine. 424.
submerged foils. 422.
subsidiary track. 410.
suburban commuter railroad. 410.
subway map. 414, 415.
subway station. 414.
subway train. 415.
sun visor. 385.
sundeck. 419.
support leg. 388.
support leg crank. 388.
surface course. 399.
surface-piercing foils. 422.
suspended span. 400.
suspender. 402.
suspension bridge. 402.
suspension cable. 402.
sweptback wing. 435.
swing bridge. 403.
switch. 410.
switch, manually-operated. 408.
switch, remote-controlled. 409.
switch engine. 411.
switch point. 408.
switch point lock. 409.
switch signal. 408, 409.
switch stand. 408.
switch tower. 410.
T. 432.
T-tail unit. 435.
tachometer. 396.
tail. 434.
tail assembly. 434.
tail boom. 441.
tail pipe. 392.
tail pipe extension. 392.
tail shape. 435.
taillight. 383, 388, 395.
tank car. 406.
tanks. 443.
tapered wing. 435.
tarpaulin covered gondola. 406.
taxiway. 438.
telephone cable. 399.
telescope. 429.
telescopic corridor. 438.
telescoping uncoupling rod. 405.
temperature indicator. 385.
tension roller. 398.
tension spring. 384.
theater. 419.
third stage. 442.
three-hinged arch. 401.
throat. 433.
through arch bridge. 401.
thrust. 401.
ticket counter. 412, 440.
ticket office. 412.
tidal basin. 427.
tie. 408.
tie plate. 408.
tire. 389, 397.
tire dolly. 387.
tire inflator. 387.
tire pump. 397.
tires. 393.
toe clip. 397.
toilet. 428.
top. 416.
top-end transverse member. 411.
topgallant mast. 416.
topmark. 430.

topmast. 416.
topping lift. 416.
torpedo. 424.
torpedo room. 424.
tourist-class cabin. 419.
tow tractor. 439.
tower. 402.
tower crane. 427.
towing fairlead. 423.
towing truck. 387.
track. 415.
track. 394, 413, 414.
track bolt. 408.
traction motor. 404.
traction motor ventilator. 404.
trailer car. 415.
trailer car interior. 415.
trailing edge. 434.
trailing edge flap. 434.
train delays notice board. 412.
train set. 410.
transceiver. 444.
transducer. 428.
transfer dispensing machine. 414.
transit shed. 427.
transportation. 381.
transporter bridge. 403.
tread design. 393.
triple tail unit. 435.
trolley. 403.
trolley wire. 413.
trough. 409.
truck. 415.
truck. 404, 407.
truck frame. 404.
truck level floor. 439.
truck tractor. 389.
truck trailer. 389.
truck trailer. 389.
trunk. 383.
trunk floor. 384.
trussed arch. 401.
tuning control. 428.
turbine. 424, 436.
turbine blade. 436.
turbine-compressor shaft. 436.
turbine guide vane. 436.
turbo-compressor engine. 390.
turbo-jet engine. 436.
turbo-jet engine. 434.
turbocharger. 404.
turbofan engine. 436.
turn signal. 388.
turn signal lever. 386.
turnbuckle. 409.
turntable. 403.
twin turret. 425.
twist grip throttle. 396.
two cones base to base. 431.
two cones point downwards. 431.
two cones point to point. 431.
two cones point upwards. 431.
two-door sedan. 384.
two-hinged arch. 401.
type of fuel. 387.
underground railway. 415.
underpass. 400.
universal step. 439.
upper berth. 407.
upper chord. 401.
upper deck. 420.
upper fore topgallant sail. 417.
upper fore topsail. 417.
upper level. 426.
upper rudder. 422.
upper side-rail. 388.
upstream gate. 426.
upstream level. 426.
urine transfer fitting. 444.
valve. 426.
valve spring. 390, 391.
vanity mirror. 385.
variable depth sonar. 425.
variable sweep wing. 435.
vent. 385.
vent cap. 392.

vent door. 388.
ventilating fan. 404.
vertical speed indicator. 423.
vestibule. 407.
vestibule door. 407.
VHF aerial. 435.
viaduct. 400.
visor. 409, 444.
waiting room. 412.
wall. 393.
WASP helicopter. 425.
water bottle. 397.
water bottle clip. 397.
water pump. 392.
water tank. 404, 407.
waterline. 425.
weather radar. 434.
web. 408.
West Coast mirror. 389.
wet dock. 427.
whale boat. 418.
wheel. 393.
wheel. 383.
wheel chock. 439.
wheel cylinder. 393.
whistle buoy. 430.
winch. 420, 425.
wind deflector. 389.
windlass. 422.
window. 383, 415, 434.
window regulator handle. 386.
windshield. 383, 389, 394, 437.
windshield wiper. 384.
windshield wiper blade. 384.
wine cellar. 419.
wing. 434, 443.
wing rib. 435.
wing shape. 435.
wing slat. 434.
wing structure. 435.
wing tip. 435.
wiper. 384.
wiper arm. 384.
wiper switch. 386.
wire. 393.
wood chip car. 406.
yard. 411.
yard. 416.
yard office. 411.

VEGETABLE KINGDOM

abruptly pinnate. 62.
achene. 66, 70.
almond. 67, 70.
amanita virosa. 65.
animal cell. 105.
anther. 64.
apple. 68.
apple. 68.
apricot. 67.
artichoke. 73.
asparagus. 77.
autumn squash. 73.
avocado. 72.
axillary bud. 61.
axilliary bud. 62.
banana. 72.
bark. 63.
bean sprouts. 77.
beet. 76.
berries, major types of. 66.
berry, section of a. 66.
berry fruits. 66.
black currant. 66.
black salsify. 76.
blade. 62.
blueberry. 66.
bole. 63.
bract. 70.
branch. 63, 77.
branches. 63.
Brazil nut. 70.
broad beans. 77.
broad-leaved endive. 74.

broccoli. 73.
brush. 71.
Brussels sprouts. 74.
bud. 75.
bulb. 77.
bulb, section of a. 75.
bulb vegetables. 75.
bulbil. 75.
bundle. 77.
cabbage lettuce. 74.
calyx. 64, 66, 68, 71.
cambium. 63.
cantaloupe. 73.
cap. 65.
capitulum. 64.
capsule. 71.
capsule, section of a. 71.
cardoon. 77.
carrot. 76.
cashew. 70.
cauliflower. 73.
celeriac. 76.
celery. 77.
cell. 105.
cell membrane. 105.
cell wall. 105.
centriole. 105.
cep. 65.
chanterelle. 65.
chard. 74.
cherimoya. 72.
cherry. 67.
chestnut. 70.
chick peas. 77.
chicory. 74.
Chinese cabbage. 74.
chive. 75.
chloroplast. 105.
chromatin. 105.
ciliate. 62.
citrus fruit, section of a. 69.
citrus fruits, major types of. 69.
cob. 77.
coconut. 70.
collar. 61.
compound fleshy fruits. 66.
compound leaves. 62.
cordate. 62.
core. 68.
corn. 77.
corn salad. 74.
corolla. 64.
corymb. 64.
cotyledon. 61, 67, 71.
cranberry. 66.
crenate. 62.
crown. 63.
cucumber. 73.
cultivated mushroom. 65.
cupule. 70.
curled endive. 74.
curled kale. 74.
currant. 66.
cytoplasm. 105.
dandelion. 74.
date. 67.
deadly mushroom. 65.
delicious lactarius. 65.
dentate. 62.
doubly dentate. 62.
drupelet. 66.
dry fruits. 70.
dry fruits, various. 71.
edible gyromitra. 65.
edible mushrooms. 65.
eggplant. 73.
endocarp. 67, 68.
endoplasmic reticulum. 105.
entire. 62.
epicalyx. 66.
exocarp. 66, 67, 68.
filament. 64.
flesh. 66, 67, 68.
fleshy fruits. 66, 69.
Florence fennel. 77.
flower. 61.

flower, structure of a. 64.
flower bud. 61.
fly amanita. 65.
foliage. 63.
follicle. 71.
follicle, section of a. 71.
fruit vegetables. 73.
funiculus. 66, 71.
garden sorrel. 74.
garlic. 75.
germ. 71.
gill. 65.
Golgi apparatus. 105.
gooseberry. 66.
grain of wheat, section of a. 71.
grape. 66.
grape. 66.
grapefruit. 69.
green bean. 73.
green cabbage. 74.
green peas. 77.
green russula. 65.
green walnut. 70.
guava. 72.
hastate. 62.
hazelnut. 70.
hazelnut, section of a. 70.
head. 77.
heartwood. 63.
horse-radish. 76.
hot pepper. 73.
huckleberry. 66.
hull. 71.
husk. 70, 77.
hypha. 65.
Indian fig. 72.
inflorescence vegetables. 73.
inflorescences, types of. 64.
internode. 61.
Japan plum. 68.
Japanese persimmon. 72.
Jerusalem artichoke. 76.
juice sac. 69.
kernel. 70, 77.
kiwi. 72.
kohlrabi. 76.
kumquat. 69.
lanceolate. 62.
leaf. 62.
leaf. 61, 77.
leaf axil. 61, 62.
leaf margin. 62.
leaf vegetables. 74.
leaves, types of. 62.
leek. 75.
legume, section of a. 71.
lemon. 69.
lentils. 77.
leucoplast. 105.
limb. 63.
linear. 62.
lipid droplet. 105.
litchi. 72.
lobate. 62.
loculus. 68.
lysosome. 105.
mandarin. 69.
mango. 67.
margin. 62.
mesocarp. 66, 67, 68, 69.
midrib. 62.
midrid. 71.
mitochondrion. 105.
morel. 65.
mushroom, structure of a. 65.
mushrooms. 65.
muskmelon. 73.
mustard. 71.
mycelium. 65.
nectarine. 67.
node. 61.
nuclear envelope. 105.
nucleolus. 105.
nucleus. 105.
nuts, major types of. 70.
odd pinnate. 62.

okra. 73.
olive. 67.
orange. 69.
orange. 69.
orbiculate. 62.
ovary. 64.
ovate. 62.
ovule. 64.
oyster mushroom. 65.
palmate. 64.
papaya. 72.
parsnip. 76.
partition. 70.
pea. 71.
pea. 71.
peach. 67.
peach. 67.
peanut. 70.
pear. 68.
pecan nut. 70.
pedicel. 64, 66, 68.
peltate. 62.
pericarp. 69, 70.
petals. 64.
petiole. 62.
phloem. 63.
pickling onion. 75.
pine seed. 70.
pineapple. 72.
pinnatifid. 62.
pinocytotic vesicle. 105.
pip. 68, 69.
pistachio nut. 70.
pistil. 64.
pith. 63.
plant, structure of a. 61, 62.
plant cell. 105.
plantlet. 67.
plasmodesma. 105.
plum. 67.
poisonous mushroom. 65.
pome fleshy fruits. 68.
pome fruit, section of a. 68.
pome fruits, principal types of. 68.
pomegranate. 72.
poppy. 71.
pore. 71, 105.
potato. 76.
primary root. 61.
pulp. 69.
pumpkin. 73.
quince. 68.
raceme. 64.
radicel. 61, 63.
radish. 76.
raspberry, section of a. 66.
receptacle. 64, 66.
reniform. 62.
rhubarb. 77.
rib. 77.
ribosome. 105.
rind. 69.
ring. 63, 65.
romaine lettuce. 74.
root. 61.
root. 61, 75.
root cap. 61.
root-hair zone. 63.
root hairs. 61.
root vegetables. 76.
rutabaga. 76.
salsify. 76.
sapwood. 63.
scale. 65.
scale leaf. 75.
scallion. 75.
secondary root. 61.
seed. 66, 67, 68, 69, 70, 71.
seed coat. 67, 71.
seed vegetables. 77.
segment. 69.
sepal. 64.
sepals. 64.
septum. 71.
shallot. 75.
shallow root. 63.

sheath. 62.
shell. 70.
shoot. 61, 63.
silique, section of a. 71.
silk. 77.
simple leaves. 62.
skin. 66, 67, 68.
snow peas. 77.
soybeans. 77.
Spanish onion. 75.
spadix. 64.
spatulate. 62.
spear. 77.
spike. 64.
spinach. 74.
spores. 65.
stalk. 66, 68, 77.
stalk vegetables. 77.
stamen. 64, 68.
star anise. 71.
starch. 71.
starch granule. 105.
stem. 61.
stem. 61, 65, 75.
stigma. 64, 70.
stipule. 62.
stone. 66, 67.
stone fleshy fruits. 67.
stone fruit, section of a. 67.
stone fruits, major types of. 67.
strawberry, section of a. 66.
string. 77.
stump. 63.
style. 64, 66, 67, 68, 71.
summer squash. 73.
suture. 71.
sweet pepper. 73.
sweet potato. 76.
Swiss chard. 77.
taproot. 63.
terminal bud. 61.
tip. 62, 77.
tomato. 73.
top. 63.
tree. 63.
tree, structure of a. 63.
trifoliolate. 62.
tropical fruits. 72.
truffle. 65.
trunk. 63.
trunk, cross section of a. 63.
tuber vegetables. 76.
turnip. 76.
twig. 61, 63.
umbel. 64.
vacuole. 105.
valve. 71.
vegetable kingdom. 59.
vegetables. 73, 74, 75, 76, 77.
vein. 62.
vine leaf. 74.
volva. 65.
wall. 69.
walnut. 70.
walnut, section of a. 70.
water cress. 74.
watermelon. 73.
white cabbage. 74.
wild blackberry, section of a. 66.
wood ray. 63.
zest. 69.
zucchini. 73.

WEAPONS

accessories for firing. 681.
African warrior. 675.
aileron. 691.
air brake. 691.
air brake hydraulic jack. 691.
air cleaner. 690.
air-to-air missile. 692.
air-to-surface missile. 692.
ammunition stowage. 690.
anti-tank missile. 692.

armor. 676.
arquebus. 682.
arrow rest. 677.
automatic rifle. 685.
back. 677.
ball. 682.
barrel. 683, 684, 685, 686, 687, 688, 689.
barrel nut. 685.
base. 688.
base plug. 682.
base ring. 680.
baseplate. 683.
batt. 677.
bayonets. 679.
bazooka. 686.
belly. 677.
bevor. 676.
bipod. 683, 687.
blade. 679.
blast screen. 686.
bolt. 687.
bolt carrier. 685.
bolt catch. 685.
bore. 681.
bows. 677.
bowstring. 677.
breastplate. 676.
breech. 680, 688.
breech ring. 684.
breeching rope. 680.
breechlock. 684.
breechlock operating lever assembly. 684.
brow reinforce. 676.
buffer. 687.
bullet. 688.
butt. 688, 689.
button. 680.
buttsock. 683.
buttstock. 685, 687.
cam spring. 688.
cannister shot. 681.
cannon. 690.
canopy. 691.
cardboard case. 688.
carriage. 680.
carrying handle. 685, 687.
carrying strap. 686.
cartridge. 688.
cartridge. 688, 689.
case. 688.
catch. 679.
catch spring. 679.
chain mail. 676.
chain shot. 681.
chamber. 689.
charge. 688.
charging handle. 685.
charging handle catch. 685.
chase. 680.
chase astragal. 680.
cheek. 680.
circuit test light. 686.
co-axial machine gun. 690.
cock. 682.
cocking handle. 687.
cocking lever. 686.
comb. 676.
combat aircraft. 691.
combustion chamber. 692.
command station. 692.
command system. 692.
command transmission. 692.
commander's seat. 690.
commando knife. 678.
core. 688.
cotton pagne. 675.
couter. 676.
cover. 687.
cradle. 684.
cross-guard. 679.
crossbow. 677.
cuirass. 675.
cuisse. 676.
cup. 688.

cupola. 690.
cylinder. 689.
dagger. 675, 678.
daggers. 678.
detonator. 682.
distance tube. 686.
dolphin. 680.
double-edged swords. 678.
drawbar. 684.
drawbar lock. 684.
driver's seat. 690.
ejection port. 683, 685, 687.
ejection seat. 691.
elevating handle. 683.
elevating mechanism. 687.
elongating bar shot. 681.
equilibrator. 684.
exhaust nozzle. 691.
exhaust pipe. 690.
exploder. 686.
explosive. 682.
extractor. 689.
extractor cam. 689.
extractor spring. 689.
feed cover. 687.
feed tray. 687.
filling hole. 682.
fin. 692.
fin wing tip. 691.
fire control selector. 685.
firing chamber. 688.
firing lanyard. 684.
firing mechanism. 686.
firing pin. 688.
firing pine. 689.
firing rod. 686.
firing shaft. 684.
first reinforce. 680.
first reinforce ring. 680.
flap. 691.
flap hydraulic jack. 691.
flash suppressor. 685, 687.
flint. 682.
flint arrowhead. 675.
flint knife. 675.
flintlock. 682.
float. 684.
forearm. 683, 687, 688.
forward bolt assist mechanism. 685.
front grip. 686.
front sight. 683, 686, 688, 689.
front sight housing. 685, 687.
fuel tank. 692.
fume extractor. 690.
gas cylinder. 687.
gas piston. 687.
gauntlet. 676.
gladius. 675.
gorget. 676.
grapeshot. 681.
greave. 676.
grip. 679, 688.
groove. 677.
guidance system. 692.
guide rods. 684.
gunner's sight. 690.
hammer. 688, 689.
hammer block. 689.
hand-and-a-half sword. 678.
hand grenade. 682.
handguard. 685.
handle. 677.
hatch. 690.
headlight. 690.
heavy machine gun. 687.
helmet. 675, 676.
hilted bayonet. 679.
howitzer. 684.
howitzer locking ring. 684.
hunting weapons. 688.
in-flight refuelling probe. 691.
integral bayonet. 679.
jacket. 688.
javelin. 675.
jet engine. 691.

ladle. 681.
lance rest. 676.
lanyard ring. 689.
leather garment. 675.
leather sandal. 675.
left-hand grip. 686.
lever. 682, 688.
lifting handle. 684.
light machine gun. 687.
linstock. 681.
loader's seat. 690.
loading. 682.
long-range radar system. 692.
lower limb. 677.
lunette. 684.
machete. 678.
machine gun. 687, 690.
magazine. 683, 685, 688, 689.
magazine base. 689.
magazine catch. 683, 685, 689.
magazine release. 685.
magazine spring. 689.
main shield bracket. 684.
main spring. 689.
main undercarriage wheel. 691.
missile. 692.
missile air-to-air. 691.
missile launch rail. 691.
missile tracking radar. 692.
missiles. 692.
modern bow. 677.
mortar. 683.
muzzle. 680, 683, 688.
muzzle astragal. 680.
muzzle loading. 680, 681.
muzzle molding. 680.
muzzle ring. 679.
neck guard. 676.
nock. 677.
nocking point. 677.
nose. 676.
nozzle. 692.
nut. 677.
ogee. 680.
one-band sword. 678.
operating rod. 687.
oxidizer tank. 692.
pan. 682.
pan cover. 682.
patch. 682.
pauldron. 676.
pellets. 688.
periscope. 690.
pistol. 689.
pistol grip. 683, 685, 687.
Pitot tube. 691.
pivot. 683.
plug bayonet. 679.
poleyn. 676.
polished-stone hand axe. 675.
pommel. 679.
poniard. 678.
position light. 691.
poulaine. 676.
powder chamber. 681.
powder flask. 682.
primer. 682, 688.
projectiles. 681.
propellant. 688.
quillon. 679.
radome. 691.
rammer. 681.
ramrod. 682.
rapier. 678.
rear sight. 683, 685, 686, 687, 688, 689.
rearview mirror. 690.
receiver. 683, 685, 687.
recoil sleigh. 684.
recoil spring. 689.
recoilless rifle. 686.
recuperator cylinder. 684.
recuperator cylinder front head. 684.
rerebrace. 676.
retractable boarding ladder. 691.

revolver. 689.
rifle. 688.
right elevating arc. 684.
right elevating handwheel. 684.
right-hand grip. 686.
right trail. 684.
ring. 682.
Roamn legionarv. 375.
rondel. 676.
runaway arreste hook. 691.
saber. 678.
safety. 683, 685.
safety pin. 682.
sandal. 675.
sear. 687.
second reinforce. 680.
second reinforce ring. 680.
serrated cast-iron casing. 682.
seventeenth century cannon. 680.
seventeeth century cannon. 681.
shell. 686, 690.
shield. 675.
shot. 681.
shotgun. 688.
shoulder pad. 686.
shoulder rest. 686.
sight. 677, 683.
single-edged swords. 678.
skirt. 676.
skull. 676.
slide. 689.
sling. 680, 685, 687.
sling swivel. 685.
slip ring. 685.
smoke bomb discharger. 690.
socket bayonet. 679.
solleret. 676.
spade. 684.
sponge. 681.
spring. 682, 686.
sprocket wheel. 690.
stabilizer. 677, 691.
steel. 682.
steel spring. 682.
steering lever. 690.
stiletto. 678.
stirrup. 677.
stock. 688.
Stone Age arms. 675.
strap. 676.
striker. 682.
stroboscopic light. 691.
submachine gun. 683.
surface-to-air missile. 692.
surface-to-subsurface missile. 692.
surface-to-surface missile. 692.
swell of the muzzle. 680.
sword-breaker. 678.
swords. 678.
takedown pin. 685.
tank. 690.
tanker. 691.
target. 692.
target tracking radar. 692.
tasset. 676.
telescopic sight. 686, 690.
throwing spear. 675.
tiller. 677.
time fuse. 682.
track. 690.
track link. 690.
traversing handle. 683.
traversing mechanism. 687.
trigger. 677, 682, 683, 685, 686, 687, 688, 689.
trigger guard. 683, 688, 689.
tripod. 687.
trunnion. 680.
tube. 681.
tube. 680, 683, 686.
turbopump. 692.
turret. 690.
two-hand sword. 678.
UHF-IFF aerial. 691.
upper limb. 677.
vambrace. 676.

vane. 692.
vent. 680, 681.
vent field astragal. 680.
ventail. 676.
ventilated rib. 688.
venturi. 686.
venturi fastening lever. 686.
visor. 676.
wad. 681, 688.
warhead. 692.
weapons. 673.
wedge. 680.
wheel. 680, 690.
winch. 690.
windshield. 691.
wing. 676.
wing box. 691.
worm. 681.

SPECIALIZED INDEXES

ATHLETICS

arena. *556, 557.*
balance beam. *560.*
bar. 561.
base. 559.
beam. 560.
bed. 560.
belt. 561.
body. 558, 560.
boot. 561.
cable. 559.
collar. 561.
cord grip. 558.
crossbar. 556, 557.
croup. 559.
disc. 561.
discus. *558.*
discus throw. *556.*
finish line. 557.
finishing post. 557.
flight. 560.
frame. 559, 560.
gauze bandage. 561.
glove. 558.
guy cable. 559.
gymnast. 558.
gymnastics. *559, 560.*
hammer. *558.*
hammer throw. *556.*
handle. 558.
head. 558.
high jump. *557.*
horizontal bar. *559.*
hurdle. 556.
javelin throw. *557.*
javelins. *558.*
knee pad. 561.
landing. 560.
landing area. 556, 557.
landing mat. 560.
lane. 557.
leg. 560.
long jump. *556.*
low bar. 560.
men's apparatus. *559.*
metal head. 558.
parallel bars. *559.*
planting box. 556.
plasticine board. 556.
platform. 561.
pole. 559.
pole vault. *556.*
pommel. 559.
pommel horse. *559.*
rim. 558.
ring. 559.
rings. *559.*
run. 560.
running. *556.*
runway. 556, 557.
saddle. 559.
safety cage. 556.
safety pad. 560.
second flight. 560.
sector flag. 556.

shaft. 558.
short-sleeved shirt. 561.
shot put. *557.*
shots. 558.
sleeve. 561.
spring. 560.
springboard. 559, 560.
start line. 556.
steel bar. 559.
steeplechase. *556.*
stopboard. 557.
strap. 559.
support. 560.
swivel. 558.
take-off board. 556, 557.
take-off line. 556.
throwing arc. 557.
throwing circle. 556, 557.
throwings. *558.*
tip. 558.
top bar. 560.
track. 557.
track and field athletics. *556, 557, 558.*
trampoline. *560.*
triple jump. *557.*
trunks. 561.
two-hand clean and jerk. *561.*
two-hand snatch. *561.*
uneven parallel bars. *560.*
upright. 556, 557, 559, 560.
vaulting horse. *559, 560.*
water ditch. 556.
weight. 558, 561.
weightlifter. *561.*
weightlifting. *561.*
wire. 558.
women's apparatus. *560.*
wooden bar. 559.

AUTOMOBILE

abutment. 400, 401, 402.
air filter. 391.
air-tight diaphragm. 391.
alternator. 391.
alternator indicator. 385.
anchorage block. 402.
antenna. 383.
approach ramp. 402.
arch. 401.
arch bridge. *401.*
arch bridges, types of. *401.*
arches, types of. *401.*
arm rest. 386.
articulation. 384.
automobile. *383, 384, 385, 386.*
backrest. 386.
backup light. 383.
Bailey bridge. *403.*
base course. 399.
battery. *392.*
battery case. 392.
battery cover. 392.
bead. 393.

beam bridge. *400.*
beam bridges, types of. *400.*
belt. 393.
belted radial tire. *393.*
bias-ply tire. *393.*
bodies, types of. *384.*
body. 387.
body side molding. 383.
bolt. 393.
brake line. 393.
brake lining. 393.
brake pad. 393.
brake pedal. 386.
brake shoe. 393.
brakes. *393.*
bridge. 400, 401, 402, 403.
bucket seat. 386.
buckle. 386.
bumper. 383.
bumper guard. 383.
cable stay anchorage. 402.
cable-stayed bridge. *402.*
caliper. 393.
camshaft. 391.
cantilever bridge. *400.*
cantilever span. 400.
car wash. 387.
carburetor. 390, 391.
carriageway. 399.
cell connector. 392.
center console. 385.
center electrode. 392.
center post. 383.
center span. 402.
clock. 385.
clutch pedal. 386.
column. 401.
combustion chamber. 390.
compressor. 390.
compressor turbine. 390.
continuous beam. 400.
convertible. 384.
cooling fan. 390, 391, 392.
counterweight. 403.
cowl. 383.
curb. 399.
cylinder. 390.
cylinder head cover. 391.
dashboard. *385.*
deck. 400, 401, 402.
deck arch bridge. 401.
diesel engine. *390.*
dimmer switch. 386.
disc. 393.
disk. 393.
disk brake. *393.*
distributor. 391.
ditch. 399.
door. *386.*
door. 383.
door handle. 383.
door lock. 383.
double-leaf bascule bridge. *403.*
drip molding. 383.
driving turbine. 390.
drum. 393.

drum brake. *393.*
electricity cable. 399.
element. 392.
embankment. 399.
emblem. 383.
engine. *391.*
engine block. 391.
engines. *390.*
exhaust gas admission. 390.
exhaust gas outflow. 390.
exhaust manifold. 390, 391, 392.
exhaust pipe. 390, 392.
exhaust system. *392.*
exhaust valve. 390.
fan belt. 391, 392.
fan cable stays. *402.*
fender. 383.
filler hole. 391.
fixed arch. 401.
fixed bridges. *400, 401, 402.*
floating bridge. *403.*
fluted shaft. 384.
flywheel. 390, 391.
foundation of tower. 402.
four-door sedan. 384.
front pipe. 392.
fuel indicator. 385.
fuel pump. 390.
fuel pump belt. 390.
gas main. 399.
gas-oil line. 390.
gas pedal. 386.
gas tank door. 383.
gasoline engine. *391.*
gasoline pump. *387.*
gasoline pump. 391.
gasoline pump hose. 387.
gearshift lever. 385.
glove compartment. 385.
grille. 383.
ground electrode. 392.
guard rail. 400.
guiding tower. 403.
gully grate. 399.
gutter. 399.
half-through arch bridge. 401.
hardtop. 384.
harp cable stays. *402.*
headlamp bezel. 384.
headlight. *384.*
headlight. 383.
headlight housing shell. 384.
headrest. 386.
heater control. 385.
hex nut. 392.
hood. 383.
horn. 385.
hubcap. 383.
injector. 390.
inlet valve. 390, 391.
instrument board. *385.*
instrument board. 385.
insulator. 392.
interior door handle. 386.
interior door lock button. 386.
lever. 387.

lift bridge. 403.
lift gate. 384.
lift span. 403.
limousine. 384.
litre/gallon totalizer. 387.
lower chord. 401.
luggage rack. 384.
main sewer. 399.
manhole. 399.
money totalizer. 387.
movable bridges. 403.
muffler. 392.
multiple-span beam bridge. 400.
negative plate. 392.
negative plate group. 392.
negative terminal. 392.
odometer. 385.
oil drain hole. 391.
oil filter. 391.
oil indicator. 385.
oil-level stick. 391.
oil pan. 391.
outside mirror. 383.
overpass. 400.
parking brake lever. 385.
pavement. 399.
pedestal. 387.
pier. 400, 401.
pier foundation. 400.
piston. 391, 393.
plate grid. 392.
plate strap. 392.
platform. 403.
ply. 393.
pontoon. 403.
portal bridge. 401.
portal frame. 401.
positive plate. 392.
positive plate grou"p. 392.
positive terminal. 392.
price per litre/gallon. 387.
pulley. 391.
pump attendant. 387.
pump island. 387.
pump nozzle. 387.
quarter window. 383.
racing car. 384.
radial tire. 393.
radiator. 392.
radiator hose. 392.
radiator pressure cap. 392.
rear seat. 386.
rear window. 383.
rear window frame. 383.
rearview mirror. 385.
release handle. 386.
repair shop. 387.
resonator. 392.
retaining ring. 384.
return spring. 393.
revolution counter. 385.
rim. 393.
rim flange. 393.
road, cross section of a. 399.
roof. 383.
sealed-beam mounting ring. 384.
seat belt. 386.
seats. 386.
sediment chamber. 392.
separator. 392.
service main. 399.
service station. 387.
shield. 383.
shoulder. 399.
side-marker light. 383.
side span. 402.
sidewalk. 399.
simple-span beam bridge. 400.
single-leaf bascule bridge. 403.
sliding roof. 383.
slope. 399.
snow tire. 393.
soft-drink dispenser. 387.
spark plug. 392.
spark plug body. 392.
spark plug cable. 391.

spark plug gap. 392.
spark plug gasket. 392.
spark plug terminal. 392.
speedometer. 385.
splash guard. 383.
spline. 392.
starter. 391.
station wagon. 384.
station wagon, back of a. 384.
steering. 386.
steering wheel. 385, 386.
sterring column. 386.
stiffening girder. 402.
storm sewer. 399.
street, cross section of a. 399.
subbase. 399.
subgrade. 399.
sun visor. 385.
surface course. 399.
suspended span. 400.
suspender. 402.
suspension bridge. 402.
suspension cable. 402.
swing bridge. 403.
tail pipe. 392.
tail pipe extension. 392.
taillight. 383.
telephone cable. 399.
temperature indicator. 385.
tension spring. 384.
three-hinged arch. 401.
through arch bridge. 401.
thrust. 401.
tire dolly. 387.
tire inflator. 387.
tires. 393.
tower. 402.
towing truck. 387.
transporter bridge. 403.
tread design. 393.
trolley. 403.
trunk. 383.
trunk floor. 384.
trussed arch. 401.
turbo-compressor engine. 390.
turn signal lever. 386.
turntable. 403.
two-door sedan. 384.
two-hinged arch. 401.
type of fuel. 387.
underpass. 400.
upper chord. 401.
valve spring. 390, 391.
vanity mirror. 385.
vent. 385.
vent cap. 392.
viaduct. 400.
wall. 393.
water pump. 392.
wheel. 393.
wheel. 383.
wheel cylinder. 393.
window. 383.
window regulator handle. 386.
windshield. 383.
windshield wiper. 384.
windshield wiper blade. 384.
wiper. 384.
wiper arm. 384.
wiper switch. 386.
wire. 393.

BASEBALL

backstop. 511.
bag. 511.
ball. 512.
baseball. 511, 512.
bat. 512.
bat. 512.
batter. 511.
batter's box. 511.
batter's helmet. 512.
batting glove. 512.
catcher. 512.

catcher. 511.
catcher's box. 511.
catcher's glove. 512.
center field. 511.
center fielder. 511.
chest protector. 512.
coache's bo::. 511.
cover. 512.
field, basel ll. 511.
finger. 512.
first base. 511.
first baseman. 511.
foul line. 511.
glove, baseball. 512.
handle. 512.
heel. 512.
hitting area. 512.
home plate. 511.
infield. 511.
knee pad. 512.
knob. 512.
lace. 512.
left field. 511.
left fielder. 511.
mask. 512.
mound. 511.
on-deck circle. 511.
outfield. 511.
palm. 512.
pants. 512.
pitcher. 511.
pitcher's plate. 511.
player. 512.
players' bench. 511.
right field. 511.
right fielder. 511.
second base. 511.
second baseman. 511.
shin guard. 512.
shortstop. 511.
spiked shoe. 512.
stirrup sock. 512.
stitches. 512.
strap. 512.
tape. 512.
team shirt. 512.
third base. 511.
third baseman. 511.
throat protector. 512.
thumb. 512.
umpire-in-chief. 511.
undershirt. 512.
web. 512.

BICYCLE

bicycle. 397, 398.
bicycle horn. 398.
bottom bracket axle. 398.
brake cable. 397.
breake lever. 397.
carrier. 397.
chain. 398.
chain guide. 398.
chain stay. 397.
chain wheel. 398.
control cable. 398.
crank. 398.
crossbar. 397.
down tube. 397.
drive chain. 397.
fender. 397.
fork. 397.
front brake. 397.
front derailleur. 397, 398.
generator. 397.
handlebars. 397.
head tube. 397.
hub. 397.
jockey roller. 398.
lock. 398.
pedal. 397, 398.
power train. 398.
rear brake. 397.
rear derailleur. 397.

rear light. 397.
rim. 397.
saddle. 397.
seat post. 397.
seat stay. 397.
seat tube. 397.
shifter. 397, 398.
spoke. 397.
sprocket cluster. 398.
stem. 397.
tension roller. 398.
tire. 397.
tire pump. 397.
toe clip. 397.
water bottle. 397.
water bottle clip. 397.

CAMPING

air mattress. 584.
Baker tent. 583.
bed-mattress. 584.
belt loop. 585.
bowline. 587.
bowline on a bight. 587.
braided rope. 587.
cable. 587.
cable. 587.
camp saw. 586.
camping, cooking equipment. 586.
camping, cooking equipment. 584.
camping, lighting equipment. 586.
camping, lighting equipment. 584.
camping, tools. 586.
camping equipment. 584, 585, 586.
can opener. 585.
canopy. 582.
canopy pole. 582.
canteen. 586.
canvas divider. 582.
clove hitch. 587.
coffee pot. 585.
combination knife. 585.
common whipping. 587.
control valve. 585.
cook kit. 585.
cooler. 586.
core. 587.
corkscrew. 585.
cow hitch. 587.
cup. 585.
dome tent. 583.
double sheet bend. 587.
family tents. 582.
fibre. 587.
figure-eight knot. 587.
file. 585.
fisherman's knot. 587.
foam mattress. 584.
foam pad. 584.
folding camp bed. 584.
folding grill. 586.
folding shovel. 586.
fork. 585.
frying pan. 585.
gauge. 585.
granny knot. 587.
grommet. 583.
guy line adapter. 583.
guy rope. 582.
handle. 585.
hatchet. 586.
heater. 585.
heaving line knot. 587.
hurricane lamp. 586.
inflator. 584.
inflator-deflator. 584.
inner tent. 583.
kettle. 585.
knife. 585.
knots. 587.
lantern. 585.
leather sheath. 585.
living room. 582.
mud wall. 582.

mummy. 584.
one-burner camp stove. 585.
overhand knot. 587.
penknife. 585.
plate. 585.
pole. 582.
pole loop. 582.
pop-up tent. 583.
pressure regulator. 585.
propane accessories. 585.
propane cylinder. 585.
pup tent. 583.
rainfly. 583.
rectangular. 584.
reef knot. 587.
ridge pole. 582.
roof. 582.
room. 582.
rope. 587.
running bowline. 587.
saw. 585.
scissors. 585.
screen window. 582.
screwdriver. 585.
semi-mummy. 584.
sewn-in floor. 582.
sheath. 587.
sheath knife. 586.
sheepshank. 587.
sheet bend. 587.
shot splice. 587.
sleeping bags. 584.
sleeve. 582.
splice. 587.
spoon. 585.
stake. 582, 583.
stake loop. 583.
strainer. 582.
strand. 587.
tents. 582, 583.
tents, major types of. 583.
three-burner camp stove. 585.
tie flap. 582.
tourist tent. 583.
twisted rope. 587.
vacuum bottle. 586.
wagon tent. 583.
wall. 582.
wall tent. 583.
wardrobe. 582.
water jug. 586.
wind baffle. 585.
window. 582.
wire support. 585.
yarn. 587.
zipper. 583.
zippered screen door. 582.

CARPENTRY

acorn nut. 254.
adjustable channel. 249.
adjustable frame. 252.
adjustable wrench. 248.
adjusting knob. 247.
adjusting ring. 250.
adjusting screw. 249.
angle scale. 253.
auger bit. 250.
auxiliary handle. 251.
back. 252, 255.
balde height adjustment. 252.
ball peen. 247.
ball peen hammer. 247.
base. 250, 251.
base plate. 253.
belt. 251.
bench saw. 252.
bit. 250.
blade. 247, 248, 252, 253.
blade guard. 252.
blade-locking bolt. 253.
blade tilt lock. 253.
blade tilting mechanism. 252.
blockboard. 255.

board. 255.
body. 250.
bolt. 254.
bolt. 249.
bow. 250.
box end wrench. 248.
brace. 250.
C-clamp. 249.
cable. 251.
cable sleeve. 251.
cam ring. 250.
cap iron. 247.
carpenter: tools. 249.
carpenter's hammer. 247.
carpentry. 255.
carpentry: fasteners. 254.
carpentry: tools. 247, 248, 250, 251, 252, 253.
central ply. 255.
cheek. 247.
chuck. 248, 250, 251.
chuck key. 251.
circular saw. 253.
circular saw blade. 253.
claw. 247.
collet. 250.
collet nut. 250.
column. 251.
combination box and open end wrench. 248.
core plywood. 255.
countersink. 250.
cross head (Phillips). 254.
curved jaw. 249.
decorative sheet. 255.
depth stop. 251.
double-twist auger bit. 250.
drill. 250.
drill press. 251.
drive wheel. 250.
edge. 255.
electric drill. 251.
end grain. 255.
expansion bolt. 254.
external tooth lock washer. 254.
eye. 247.
face. 247.
face ply. 255.
face side. 255.
feed lever. 251.
fixed jaw. 248, 249.
flare nut wrench. 248.
flat head. 254.
flat tip. 248.
flat washer. 254.
flute. 250.
fluted land. 250.
frame. 249.
front knob. 247.
grain. 255.
hacksaw. 252.
hammer. 247.
hand drill. 250.
handle. 247, 248, 249, 250, 252, 253.
handsaw. 252.
hardboard. 255.
head. 250, 254.
heads. 247.
heel. 247, 252.
hollow-wood construction. 255.
housing. 251.
inner ply. 255.
internal tooth lock washer. 254.
jaw. 248, 250, 251.
knob handle. 253.
kraft paper. 255.
laminate board. 255.
laminboard. 255.
land. 250.
lateral adjusting lever. 247.
lead screw. 250.
lever. 249.
lock washer. 254.
locking pliers. 249.
lockling ring. 248.

lower blade guard. 253.
lower guard retracting lever. 253.
main handle. 250.
mallet. 247.
miter gauge. 252.
miter gauge silot. 252.
motor. 250, 251, 253.
moulded plywood. 255.
movable jaw. 248, 249.
multi-ply. 255.
nail. 254.
name plate. 251.
nut. 254.
nut and bolt. 249.
one way head. 254.
open end wrench. 248.
oval head. 254.
particle board. 255.
pawl. 250.
peeled veneer. 255.
Phillips tip. 248.
pinion. 250.
pistol grip handle. 251, 252.
plane. 247.
pliers. 249.
plug. 251.
protective sheet. 255.
pulley. 251.
pulley safety guard. 251.
quill. 250, 251.
quill lock. 251.
ratchet. 248, 250.
release lever. 249.
rib joint pliers. 249.
rip fence. 252, 253.
rip fence adjustment. 252.
rip fence guide. 252.
rip fence lock. 252.
rivet. 249.
Robertson tip. 248.
round head. 254.
router. 250.
screw. 254.
screwdriver. 248.
shank. 248, 250, 254.
shoulder. 254.
shoulder bolt. 254.
side handle. 250.
single twist. 250.
slip joint. 249.
slip joint pliers. 249.
slot. 254.
socket head (Robertson). 254.
spiral. 248.
spiral ratchet screwdriver. 248.
spring. 249.
spring wing. 254.
spur. 250.
straight jaw. 249.
switch. 250, 251.
swivel base. 249.
swivel head. 249.
swivel lock. 249.
table. 251, 252.
table extension. 252.
table-locking clamp. 251.
teeth. 252.
thread. 254.
threaded rod. 254.
throat. 250.
thumbscrew. 248.
tip. 248, 253, 254.
toe. 247, 252.
toggle bolt. 254.
tooth. 253.
toothed jaw. 249.
trigger switch. 253.
turning handle. 250.
twist drill. 250.
upper blade guard. 253.
vise. 249.
warning plate. 251.
washer. 254.
wedge iron. 247.
wedge lever. 247.
wing nut. 254.

wing nut. 252.
wire cutter. 249.
wood-based panel. 255.
wrenches. 248.

DOMESTIC APPLIANCES

agitator. 230.
air vent. 232.
automatic cord reel. 234.
automatic drip coffee maker. 224.
backguard. 228, 230, 231.
bake element. 228.
base. 232, 233.
basket. 224, 230.
beater. 225.
beater ejector. 225.
blade. 224, 226.
blender. 225.
blending attachment. 225.
body. 233.
bottle opener. 233.
bowl. 226.
bowl with serving spout. 226.
bread guide. 227.
broil element. 228.
bumper. 234.
butter compartment. 229.
button notch. 233.
cabinet. 230, 231, 232.
can opener. 233.
carafe. 224.
caster. 234.
citrus juicer. 226.
clamping handle. 226.
clamping nut. 226.
cleaning tools. 234.
cleaning tools. 234.
clock timer. 227, 228.
coffee makers. 224.
coffee mill. 224.
color selector. 227.
compressor. 229.
condenser coil. 229.
container. 225.
contral panel. 228.
control knob. 228.
control panel. 227, 230, 231, 232.
cooking surface. 227.
cooktop. 228.
cord. 233.
cover. 226.
crevice tool. 234.
crisper. 229.
cutlery basket. 232.
cutting blade. 225.
cutting wheel. 233.
dairy compartment. 229.
dasher. 226.
defrost heater. 229.
defrost timer. 229.
detachable control. 227.
detergent dispenser. 232.
discs. 226.
dishwasher. 232.
domestic appliances. 225, 226, 227, 228, 229, 230, 231, 232, 233, 234.
door. 227, 231.
door shelf. 229.
door stop. 229.
door switch. 231.
dough hook. 225.
drain hose. 230, 232.
drain pan. 229.
drip bowl. 228.
drive belt. 230, 231.
drive wheel. 233.
drum. 226, 231.
dryer. 231.
dusting brush. 234.
egg tray. 229.
electric range. 228.
end panel. 227.
espresso coffee maker. 224.

Specialized Indexes

evaporator coil. 229.
exhaust duct. 231.
exhaust hose. 231.
extension wand. 234.
fabric guide. 233.
fan. 229, 231.
feed tube. 226.
fill opening. 233.
filter basket. 224.
flexible hose. 234.
floor brush. 234.
food processor. 226.
four pale beater. 225.
freezer bucket. 226.
freezer compartment. 229.
freezer door. 229.
front tip. 233.
gasket. 228, 230, 232.
glass cover. 229.
grater disc. 226.
grease well. 227.
griddle. 227.
grill and waffle baker. 227.
groove. 227.
guard rail. 229.
hand blender. 225.
hand mixer. 225.
handle. 225, 226, 227, 228, 229,
    233, 234.
heating bail. 231.
heating element. 231, 232.
heel rest. 225, 233.
hinge. 227, 228, 232.
hood. 234.
ice-cream can. 226.
ice-cream freezer. 226.
ice cube tray. 229.
idler pulley. 231.
impeller. 232.
inlet hose. 230, 232.
inlet nozzle. 230.
juicer. 226.
kettle. 233.
kickplate. 229.
latch. 227, 228, 232.
lever. 227.
lid. 224, 226, 227, 230.
lint filter. 230.
lint trap. 231.
lower bowl. 224.
magnetic gasket. 229.
magnetic lid holder. 233.
measuring cap. 225.
meat keeper. 229.
microwave oven. 227.
mixing bowl. 225.
motor. 230, 231, 234.
motor unit. 225, 226.
motro unit. 224.
Neapolitan coffee maker. 224.
oven. 228.
oven lamp. 227, 228.
overflow protection switch. 232.
percolator. 224.
pierce lever. 233.
plate. 227.
plunger. 224.
probe receptable. 227.
programmer. 228, 230, 231, 232.
pulse button. 225.
pump. 230, 232.
push-button control board. 232.
pusher. 226.
rack. 228, 232.
reamer. 226.
recessed cooktop. 228.
refrigerator. 229.
refrigerator compartment. 229.
reservoir. 224.
retractable cord. 234.
rinse dispenser. 232.
roast sensor probe. 228.
roller. 232.
rotisserie. 228.
rug and floor nozzle. 234.
safety thermostat. 231.

sensor probe. 227.
shag-vac-rake. 234.
shelf. 229.
shelf channel. 229.
shell. 233.
sight-glass tube. 233.
signal lamp. 228, 232.
slide. 232.
slide selector. 227, 233.
slot. 227.
soleplate. 233.
speed control. 225.
speed selector. 226.
spindle. 226.
spiral beater. 225.
spout. 224, 233.
spray. 233.
spray arm. 232.
spray button. 233.
stabilizer foot. 232.
stand. 225.
start switch. 231.
steam button. 233.
steam iron. 233.
stem. 224.
storage door. 229.
strainer. 226.
stirrer cover. 226.
suction regulator. 234.
support wheel. 231.
surface element. 228.
switch. 228, 229, 234.
table mixer. 225.
temperature dial. 233.
temperature selector. 230, 231.
temperature sensing bulb. 228.
terminal. 228.
thermostat control. 229.
thumb rest. 233.
tilt-back head. 225.
timed outlet. 228.
toaster. 227.
top-work surface. 232.
transmission. 230.
trim ring. 228.
tub. 230, 232.
tubular element. 228.
turntable. 225.
upholstery nozzle. 234.
upper bowl. 224.
vacuum cleaner. 234.
vacuum coffee maker. 224.
vane. 231.
vertical cord lift. 233.
wand. 234.
warming plate. 224.
wash tower. 232.
washer. 230.
water level selector. 230.
window. 227, 228.
wire beater. 225.

ELECTRICITY

access gallery. 641, 646.
access shaft. 646.
administrative building. 646.
afterbay. 637, 638, 641.
arch dam. 639.
bank. 646.
base width. 644.
basin. 646.
basin side. 646.
beam gantry. 644.
berm. 638.
blade. 642, 643.
bottom ring. 643.
brace. 645.
bucket. 643.
bucket ring. 643.
bulb unit. 646.
bundle. 644.
busbar. 641.
bushing. 637, 645.
buttress. 639.

buttress dam. 639.
cantilever. 639.
circuit breaker. 641.
collector. 642.
concrete dam. 638.
connection point. 645.
control room. 637, 646.
core. 638.
crest of spillway. 637.
crossarm. 644, 645.
customer's service entrance. 645.
cut off trench. 638.
dam. 637, 638, 646.
dams, major types of. 639.
diagonal. 644.
discharge liner. 643.
distribution board. 645.
distributor service loop. 645.
diversion canal. 637.
downstream face. 638.
downstream shoulder. 638.
downstream toe. 638.
draft tube. 641, 643.
drainage blanket. 638.
drainage layer. 638.
earth. 639.
*electricity. 637, 638, 639, 640, 641,
    642, 643, 644, 645, 646.*
electricity, tower. 644.
electricity meter. 645.
embankment dam. 638, 639.
equipment access shaft. 646.
fill. 638.
filter. 638.
fitted coupling bolt. 643.
foundation. 639.
foundation of dam. 638.
Francis turbine. 643.
fuse. 645.
fuse cutout. 645.
fuse holder. 645.
gantry crane. 637, 641.
gate. 641, 646.
gate operating ring. 643.
generator. 642.
generator. 641, 642.
gravity dam. 639.
ground wire. 645.
ground-wire clamp. 645.
ground-wire peak. 644.
guide bearing. 642.
hand rail. 637.
headbay. 637.
horizontal member. 644.
hot line connector. 645.
hub. 643.
hub cover. 643.
hydraulic turbine. 643.
hydroelectric complex. 637.
hydroelectric power station. 641.
inactive dyke. 646.
insulator. 645.
K frame. 644.
Kaplan turbine. 643.
lighting arrester. 641.
lightning arrester. 645.
line. 637.
lock. 646.
log chute. 637.
low tension distribution line. 645.
machine hall. 637, 641.
main leg. 644.
main switch. 645.
medium tension distribution line.
    645.
neutral conductor. 645.
node. 644.
operating dam. 646.
operating floor. 646.
overhead connection. 645.
overhead ground wire. 644.
panel. 644.
Pelton turbine. 643.
penstock. 637, 641, 646.
peripheral joint. 639.
phase conductor. 645.

pitching. 638.
power plant, cross section of. 646.
power station. 646.
powerhouse. 637, 641.
production of electricity. 640.
pulvino. 639.
redundant bracing. 644.
reservoir. 637, 638, 641.
rocks. 639.
rotor. 641, 642.
runner. 642, 643.
runner blade. 643, 646.
salient pole. 642.
screen. 641.
scroll case. 641.
sea. 646.
sea side. 646.
service box. 645.
shaft. 641, 642, 643.
soil. 639.
spillway. 637.
spillway chute. 637.
spilway gate. 637.
spiral case. 642, 643.
stator. 641, 642.
stay ring. 642, 643.
stay vane. 642, 643.
structure. 637.
strut. 646.
substation. 646.
supply point. 645.
suspension insulator string. 644.
tailrace. 641, 643.
terminal. 645.
tidal power plant. 646.
top of dam. 637, 638, 641.
tower. 644.
tower body. 644.
tower foot. 644.
tower top. 644.
tower window. 644.
training wall. 637.
transformer. 641, 645.
transforming station. 641.
traveling crane. 641.
turbine. 641.
turbine runner. 646.
turbines, major types of. 643.
upstream blanket. 638.
upstream face. 638.
upstream shoulder. 638.
upstream toe. 638.
waist. 644.
water intake. 641.
wave wall. 638.
wicket gate. 643.

ELECTRICITY (DO-IT-YOURSELF)

120-volt circuit. 278.
240-volt circuit. 278.
240-volt feeder cable. 278.
adjustment wheel. 277.
arc tube. 274.
arc tube mount structure. 274.
base. 274.
blade. 275, 277.
bonding jumper. 278.
bulb. 274.
button. 274.
cable ripper. 277.
cap. 275.
cartridge fuse. 275.
circuit breaker. 275.
clamp. 275.
connector. 278.
continuity tester. 276.
crimper. 277.
dimmer switch. 275.
distribution board. 278.
double pole breaker. 278.
electric switch. 275.
electrical box. 275.
electrical supplies. 275.

electricity. *274, 275, 278.*
electricity, tools. *276, 277.*
electrode. *274.*
European plug. *275.*
exhaust tube. *274.*
filament. *274.*
fish wire. *277.*
fluorescent lamp. *274.*
fuse pullers. *276.*
fuses. *275.*
gas. *274.*
ground bond. *278.*
ground fault circuit interrupter. *278.*
ground/neutral bus bar. *278.*
ground wire. *278.*
grounding prong. *275.*
hammer. *277.*
heat deflecting disc. *274.*
high-voltage tester. *276.*
hot bus bar. *278.*
incandescent lamp. *274.*
inert gas. *274.*
insulated blade. *276.*
insulated handle. *276, 277.*
insulating sleeve. *275.*
jaw. *277.*
knife-blade cartridge fuse. *275.*
knockout. *278.*
lamp. *274.*
lamp socket. *275.*
lead-in wire. *274.*
lineman's pliers. *277.*
long-nose pliers. *277.*
main breaker. *278.*
main electrode. *274.*
main power cable. *278.*
mercury. *274.*
mercury-vapor lamp. *274.*
metal water pipe. *278.*
mogul base. *274.*
multipurpose tool. *277.*
neon lamp. *276.*
neon tester. *276.*
neutral service wire. *278.*
neutral wire. *278.*
nitrogen. *274.*
outer shell. *275.*
outlet. *275.*
phosphor coating. *274.*
pin. *274.*
pin base. *274.*
pinch. *274.*
pivot. *277.*
plastic insulator. *278.*
plug. *275.*
plug fuse. *275.*
receptacle analyzer. *276.*
reflector. *274.*
single pole breaker. *278.*
socket. *275.*
starting electrode. *274.*
starting resistor. *274.*
stem. *274.*
support. *274.*
switch. *275.*
switch plate. *275.*
terminal. *275.*
tester probe. *276.*
voltage tester. *276.*
voltmeter. *276.*
wire cutter. *277.*
wire stripper. *277.*

FISHING

antenna. *567.*
anti-reverse lock. *566.*
artificial fly. *567.*
bail. *566.*
barb. *567.*
bend. *567.*
blade. *567.*
body. *567.*
butt. *567.*
butt cap. *566.*

butt grip. *566.*
butt guide. *566.*
butt section. *566.*
cheek. *567.*
crank. *566.*
drag. *566.*
eye. *567.*
female ferrule. *566.*
fishhook. *567.*
fishing. *566, 567.*
float. *567.*
fly reel. *566.*
fly rod. *566.*
foot. *566.*
foregrip. *566.*
gap. *567.*
gear housing. *566.*
guide. *566.*
hackle. *567.*
hand grip. *566.*
handle. *566.*
head. *567.*
hook. *567.*
joint. *567.*
keeper ring. *566.*
leader. *567.*
leg. *566.*
line. *566, 567.*
line guide. *566.*
lures. *567.*
male ferrule. *566.*
open-face spinning reel. *566.*
point. *567.*
reel seat. *566.*
ribbing. *567.*
screw locking nut. *566.*
shank. *567.*
shoulder. *567.*
silk line. *566.*
sinker. *567.*
spinner. *567.*
spinning rod. *566.*
split link. *567.*
spool. *566.*
swivel. *567.*
tail. *567.*
throat. *567.*
tip. *567.*
tip guide. *566.*
tip section. *566.*
tip-top. *566.*
topping. *567.*
veil. *567.*
wing. *567.*

FOOTBALL

arm guard. *516.*
back judge. *514.*
center. *514, 515.*
center line. *513.*
chest protector. *516.*
chin strap. *516.*
cleated shoe. *516.*
defensive. *514, 515.*
elbow pad. *516.*
end line. *513.*
end zone. *513.*
face mask. *516.*
flanker. *515.*
football. *513, 514, 515, 516.*
fullback. *514, 515.*
goal. *513.*
goal line. *513.*
goal post. *513.*
halfback. *515.*
hand guard. *516.*
head linesman. *514.*
helmet. *516.*
hip pad. *516.*
inbound line. *513.*
inside linebacker. *514.*
jersey. *516.*
knee pad. *516.*
left cornerback. *514, 515.*

left defensive end. *514, 515.*
left defensive tackle. *514, 515.*
left guard. *514, 515.*
left halfback. *514.*
left outside linebacker. *515.*
left safety. *514.*
left safety back. *515.*
left tackle. *514, 515.*
line judge. *514.*
line of scrimmage. *514, 515.*
middle linebacker. *514, 515.*
monster. *515.*
neutral zone. *515.*
offensive. *514, 515.*
outside linebacker. *514.*
pants. *516.*
player's number. *516.*
playing field for American football. *513.*
playing field for Canadian football. *513.*
protective cup. *516.*
protective equipment, football. *516.*
quarterback. *514, 515.*
referee. *514.*
rib pad. *516.*
right cornerback. *514, 515.*
right defensive end. *514, 515.*
right defensive tackle. *514, 515.*
right guard. *514, 515.*
right halfback. *514.*
right outside linebacker. *515.*
right safety. *514.*
right safety back. *515.*
right tackle. *514, 515.*
scrimmage in American football. *514.*
scrimmage in Canadian football. *515.*
shin guard. *516.*
shoulder pad. *516.*
sideline. *513.*
slotback. *515.*
sock. *516.*
split end. *514, 515.*
thigh pad. *516.*
tight end. *514, 515.*
umpire. *514.*
uniform, football. *516.*
wrist pad. *516.*
yard line. *513.*

FRUITS

achene. *66, 70.*
almond. *67, 70.*
apple. *68.*
apple. *68.*
apricot. *67.*
avocado. *72.*
banana. *72.*
berries, major types of. *66.*
berry, section of a. *66.*
berry fruits. *66.*
black currant. *66.*
blueberry. *66.*
bract. *70.*
Brazil nut. *70.*
brush. *71.*
calyx. *66, 68, 71.*
capsule. *71.*
capsule, section of a. *71.*
cashew. *70.*
cherimoya. *72.*
cherry. *67.*
chestnut. *70.*
citrus fruit, section of a. *69.*
citrus fruits, major types of. *69.*
coconut. *70.*
compound fleshy fruits. *66.*
core. *68.*
cotyledon. *67, 71.*
cranberry. *66.*
cupule. *70.*
currant. *66.*

date. *67.*
drupelet. *66.*
dry fruits. *70.*
dry fruits, various. *71.*
endocarp. *67, 68.*
epicalyx. *66.*
exocarp. *66, 67, 68.*
flesh. *66, 67, 68.*
fleshy fruits. *66, 69.*
follicle. *71.*
follicle, section of a. *71.*
funiculus. *66, 71.*
germ. *71.*
gooseberry. *66.*
grain of wheat, section of a. *71.*
grape. *66.*
grape. *66.*
grapefruit. *69.*
green walnut. *70.*
guava. *72.*
hazelnut. *70.*
hazelnut, section of a. *70.*
huckleberry. *66.*
hull. *71.*
husk. *70.*
Indian fig. *72.*
Japan plum. *68.*
Japanese persimmon. *72.*
juice sac. *69.*
kernel. *71.*
kiwi. *72.*
kumquat. *69.*
legume, section of a. *71.*
lemon. *69.*
litchi. *72.*
loculus. *68.*
mandarin. *69.*
mango. *67.*
mesocarp. *66, 67, 68, 69.*
midrib. *71.*
mustard. *71.*
nectarine. *67.*
nuts, major types of. *70.*
olive. *67.*
orange. *69.*
orange. *69.*
papaya. *72.*
partition. *70.*
pea. *71.*
pea. *71.*
peach. *67.*
peach. *67.*
peanut. *70.*
pear. *68.*
pecan nut. *70.*
pedicel. *66, 68.*
pericarp. *69, 70.*
pine seed. *70.*
pineapple. *72.*
pip. *68, 69.*
pistachio nut. *70.*
plantlet. *67.*
plum. *67.*
pome fleshy fruits. *68.*
pome fruit, section of a. *68.*
pome fruits, principal types of. *68.*
pomegranate. *72.*
poppy. *71.*
pore. *71.*
pulp. *69.*
quince. *68.*
raspberry, section of a. *66.*
receptacle. *66.*
rind. *69.*
seed. *66, 67, 68, 69, 70, 71.*
seed coat. *67, 71.*
segment. *69.*
sepal. *66.*
septum. *71.*
shell. *70.*
silique, section of a. *71.*
skin. *66, 67, 68.*
stalk. *66, 68.*
stamen. *68.*
star anise. *71.*
starch. *71.*

Specialized Indexes

stigma. 70.
stone. 66, 67.
stone fleshy fruits. 67.
stone fruit, section of a. 67.
stone fruits, major types of. 67.
strawberry, section of a. 66.
style. 66, 67, 68, 71.
suture. 71.
tropical fruits. 72.
valve. 71.
wall. 69.
walnut. 70.
walnut, section of a. 70.
wild blackberry, section of a. 66.
zest. 69.

GOLF

apron. 571.
bag well. 573.
ball. 573.
ball cross-section. 573.
brassie. 572.
bunker. 571.
caddie. 571.
canopy. 573.
cap. 572.
cart path. 571.
casual water. 571.
club divider. 573.
clubhouse. 571.
core. 573.
course, golf. 571.
cover. 573.
cup. 571.
dimple. 573.
divot. 571.
driver. 572.
driving iron. 572.
electric golf cart. 573.
engine. 573.
face. 572.
fairway. 571.
ferrule. 572.
flagstick. 571.
golf. 571, 572, 573.
golf bag. 573.
golf cart. 573.
golf clubs. 572.
golf clubs, types of. 572.
golf shoe. 573.
golfer. 571.
grip. 572.
groove. 572.
handle. 573.
head. 572.
head cover. 573.
heel. 572.
hole. 571.
iron. 572.
mashie. 572.
mashie iron. 572.
mashie niblick. 572.
midiron. 572.
midmashie. 572.
neck. 572.
niblick. 572.
out of bounds. 571.
pitching niblick. 572.
pitching wedge. 572.
pocket. 573.
practice fairway. 571.
putter. 572.
putter. 572.
putting green. 571.
rough. 571.
rubber thread. 573.
sand wedge. 572.
shaft. 572.
shoulder strap. 573.
sole. 572.
spade mashie. 572.
spike. 573.
spoon. 572.
tee. 573.

teeing ground. 571.
toe. 572.
umbrella sheath. 573.
water hazard. 571.
whipping. 572.
wood. 572.

HOCKEY

arm pad. 520.
attacking zone. 519.
back pad. 520.
blade. 520.
blue line. 519.
boards. 519.
body pad. 520.
butt end. 520.
catch glove. 520.
center. 519.
center face-off circle. 519.
center line. 519.
cuff. 520.
curve. 520.
defending zone. 519.
elbow pad. 520.
face mask. 520.
face-off circle. 519.
face-off spot. 519.
game timekeeper. 519.
girdle. 520.
glass. 519.
glove, hockey. 520.
goal. 519.
goal crease. 519.
goal judge's box. 519.
goal line. 519.
goalkeeper. 520.
goalkeeper. 519.
goalkeeper's pad. 520.
goalkeeper's stick. 520.
heel. 520.
helmet. 520.
hip pad. 520.
hockey. 519.
ice hockey. 519, 520.
ice hockey player. 520.
knee pad. 520.
left defense. 519.
left wing. 519.
linesman. 519.
net. 519.
neutral zone. 519.
pants. 520.
penalty bench. 519.
penalty timekeeper. 519.
player's stick. 520.
players' bench. 519.
protective cup. 520.
puck. 520.
referee. 519.
right defense. 519.
right wing. 519.
rink. 519.
rink corner. 519.
scorer. 519.
shaft. 520.
shoulder pad. 520.
skate. 520.
stick glove. 520.
throat protector. 520.

JET AND HELICOPTER

aileron. 434.
air inlet. 436, 441.
aircraft gate. 438.
airport. 438, 439.
annular combustion chamber. 436.
antenna. 434.
anti-collision light. 434.
anti-torque tail rotor. 441.
apron. 438.
arrivals concourse. 440.
automatically-controlled door. 440.
autopilot control. 437.

axial-flow compressor. 436.
baggage cart. 440.
baggage check-in counter. 440.
baggage claim area. 440.
baggage compartment. 441.
baggage conveyor. 439.
baggage trailer. 439.
blade. 436.
boarding step. 441.
boom truck. 439.
by-pass taxiway. 438.
cabin. 434, 441.
canopy. 434.
captain's seat. 437.
cargo terminal. 438.
carrousel. 440.
catering vehicle. 439.
center bearing. 436.
central console. 437.
central instrument panel. 437.
combustion chamber. 436.
control column. 437.
control levers. 437.
control stick. 441.
control tower. 438.
control tower cab. 438.
cruciform tail unit. 435.
currency exchange counter. 440.
customs control. 440.
delta wing. 435.
departures concourse. 440.
departures room. 440.
drive shaft. 441.
duty-free shop. 440.
electrical power unit. 439.
elevator. 434.
engine. 436.
engine mounting pylon. 435.
exhaust cone. 436.
exhaust duct. 436.
exhaust nozzle. 436.
exhaust pipe. 436, 441.
fan. 436.
fight information board. 440.
fin. 434, 441.
first officer's seat. 437.
fixed distance marking. 438.
flap guide rail. 435.
flight deck. 437.
flight deck. 434, 441.
flight engineer's panel. 437.
flight engineer's seat. 437.
flight instruments. 437.
front bearing. 436.
front spar. 435.
fuel spray manifold. 436.
fuel tank. 441.
fuselage. 434.
galley. 434.
ground airport equipment. 439.
helicopter. 441.
high-speed exit taxiway. 438.
hold. 434.
holding area marking. 438.
horizontal stabilizer. 434, 441.
hotel reservation desk. 440.
immigration control. 440.
information counter. 440.
inlet guide vanes. 436.
jet. 434.
jet refueler. 439.
landing light. 441.
lavatory truck. 439.
leading edge. 434.
loading tunnel. 438.
lobby. 440.
long-range jet. 434.
main landing gear. 434.
main spar. 435.
main undercarriage mounting beam. 435.
maintenance hangar. 438.
mast. 441.
mobile passenger escalator. 439.
navigation light. 434.
normal tail unit. 435.

nose. 434.
nose cone. 436.
nose landing gear. 434.
observation deck. 440.
observer's seat. 437.
overhead switch panel. 437.
pallet and container transporter. 439.
parking area. 438.
passenger terminal. 440.
passenger terminal. 438.
passenger transfer vehicle. 439, 440.
passport control. 440.
pinwheel passenger loading ramp. 438.
pitch link. 441.
potable water truck. 439.
power plant instruments. 437.
root rib. 435.
rotor blade. 436, 441.
rotor head. 441.
rotor hub. 441.
rudder. 434.
rudder pedal. 437.
runway. 438.
runway center line markings. 438.
runway designation marking. 438.
runway end lights. 438.
runway side stripe markings. 438.
runway threshold markings. 438.
runway touchdown zone marking. 438.
security check. 440.
skid. 441.
spoiler. 436.
stator vane. 436.
straight wing. 435.
stringer. 435.
sweptback wing. 435.
T-tail unit. 435.
tail. 434.
tail assembly. 434.
tail boom. 441.
tail shape. 435.
tapered wing. 435.
taxiway. 438.
telescopic corridor. 438.
ticket counter. 440.
tow tractor. 439.
trailing edge. 434.
trailing edge flap. 434.
triple tail unit. 435.
truck level floor. 439.
turbine. 436.
turbine blade. 436.
turbine-compressor shaft. 436.
turbine guide vane. 436.
turbo-jet engine. 436.
turbo-jet engine. 434.
turbofan engine. 436.
universal step. 439.
variable sweep wing. 435.
VHF aerial. 435.
weather radar. 434.
wheel chock. 439.
window. 434.
windshield. 437.
wing. 434.
wing rib. 435.
wing shape. 435.
wing slat. 434.
wing structure. 435.
wing tip. 435.

KITCHEN UTENSILS

back. 217.
baking utensils. 220.
baster. 221.
blade. 217.
bolster. 217.
boning knife. 217.
bottle opener. 219.
bread knife. 217.

butter curler. 217.
cake pan. 220.
can opener. 219.
carving fork. 217.
carving knife. 217.
citrus juicer. 218.
cleaver. 217.
colander. 218.
cook's knife. 217.
cookie cutters. 220.
cookie press. 220.
cookie sheet. 220.
corer. 221.
cutting edge. 217.
draining spoon. 219.
dredger. 221.
egg beater. 220.
egg slicer. 221.
egg timer. 219.
filleting knife. 217.
flan pan. 220.
funnel. 218.
garlic press. 218.
graperfruit knife. 217.
grater. 218.
guard. 217.
half handle. 217.
ham knife. 217.
heel. 217.
ice cream spoon. 221.
icing syringe. 220.
kitchen knife. 217.
kitchen knives, types of. 217.
kitchen scale. 219.
kitchen timer. 219.
kitchen utensil for straining. 218.
kitchen utensils. 217, 218, 219, 220.
kitchen utensils, miscellaneous. 221.
kitchen utensils for draining. 218.
kitchen utensils for grating. 218.
kitchen utensils for grinding. 218.
kitchen utensils for measuring. 219.
kitchen utensils for opening. 219.
ladle. 219.
lever corkscrew. 219.
measuring cups. 219.
measuring spoons. 219.
meat grinder. 218.
meat thermometer. 219.
mixing bowls. 220.
mortar. 219.
muffin pan. 220.
nutcracker. 218.
oyster knife. 217.
paring knife. 217.
pasta maker. 218.
pastry bag and nozzles. 220.
pastry brush. 220.
pastry cutting wheel. 220.
peeler. 217.
pestle. 218.
pie pan. 220.
point. 217.
potato masher. 219.
poultry shears. 221.
quiche plate. 220.
rivet. 217.
rolling pin. 220.
salad shaker. 218.
salad spinner. 218.
sharpener. 221.
sharpening steel. 217.
sieve. 218.
sifter. 220.
skimmer. 219.
snail dish. 221.
snail tongs. 221.
spaghetti tongs. 221.
spatula. 219.
stoner. 221.
tang. 217.
tea ball. 221.
tongs. 221.

turner. 219.
utensils, set of. 219.
vegetable brush. 221.
whisk. 220.
wine waiter corkscrew. 219.
zester. 217.

MEN'S CLOTHING

adjustable waist tab. 283.
adjustment slide. 284.
ankle length. 287.
armhole. 287.
ascot tie. 285.
athletic shirt. 287.
back. 283.
back pocket. 284.
belt. 284.
belt. 281.
belt buckle. 281.
belt loop. 281.
bikini briefs. 287.
binding. 288.
bow. 288.
bow tie. 285.
boxer shorts. 287.
bracelet length. 289.
breast dart. 282.
breast pocket. 282, 285.
breast welt pocket. 283.
briefs. 287.
brim. 288.
broad welt side pocket. 281.
buckle. 284.
button. 285.
button loop. 284.
buttondown collar. 285.
buttoned placket. 285.
buttonhole. 281, 285, 286.
cap. 288.
cardigan. 286.
center back vent. 283.
clip. 284.
coat. 283.
collar. 281, 283, 285.
collar point. 285.
collar stay. 285.
combination. 287.
crease. 284.
crew neck sweater. 286.
crotch. 287.
crown. 288.
cuff. 284, 285.
dome fastener. 289.
double-breasted buttoning. 281.
double-breasted jacket. 283.
drawers. 287.
duffle coat. 282.
ear flap. 288.
elastic webbing. 284.
elasticized leg opening. 287.
epaulet. 281.
executive length. 287.
facing. 283.
felt hat. 288.
flap. 288.
flap pocket. 282, 283.
flap side pocket. 283.
fly. 284, 287.
fourchette. 289.
frame. 284.
frog. 282.
front. 283, 285.
front apron. 285.
garrison cap. 288.
gauntlet. 289.
glove. 289.
glove finger. 289.
gloves, types of. 289.
gun flap. 281.
hanger loop. 286.
hatband. 288.
headgear. 288.
headgears, types of. 288.
heel. 287.

hood. 282.
instep. 287.
interfacing. 285.
inverness cape. 282.
jacket. 283.
keeper. 281, 284.
knit shirt. 286.
lapel. 283.
leather end. 284.
leg. 287.
lining. 283.
loop. 285.
men's clothing. 281, 282, 283, 284, 285, 286, 287, 288.
mid-calf length. 287.
mitt. 289.
mitten. 289.
neckhole. 287.
necktie. 285.
notch. 283.
notched lapel. 281.
opening. 289.
outside ticket pocket. 283.
over-elbow length glove. 289.
overcoat. 282.
palm. 289.
panel. 284.
pants. 284.
parka. 282.
peak. 288.
peaked lapel. 282, 283.
perforation. 289.
pocket handkerchief. 283.
pointed tab end. 285.
pullovers. 286.
punch hole. 284.
racer glove. 289.
raglan sleeve. 281.
raincoat. 281.
rear apron. 285.
ribbing. 286.
schapska. 288.
seam. 289.
section. 288.
set-in-sleeve. 281, 285, 286.
sheepskin jacket. 282.
shirt. 285.
shirttail. 285.
shorty. 289.
side back vent. 283.
side pocket. 281.
single-breasted coat. 283.
ski cap. 288.
skull cap. 288.
slash pocket. 284.
sleeve. 283.
sleeve strap. 281.
sleeve strap loop. 281.
slip-stitched seam. 285.
sock. 287.
sole. 287.
spread collar. 285.
stitching. 289.
straight-up ribbed top. 287.
string. 282.
suspender clip. 284.
suspenders. 284.
three-quarter coat. 282.
thumb. 289.
tie. 284.
tip. 284.
toe. 287.
toggle fastening. 282.
tongue. 284.
top collar. 283.
top hat. 288.
top stitching. 284.
trench coat. 281.
tunnel belt loop. 284.
turtleneck. 286.
two-way collar. 281.
underwear. 287.
V-neck. 283, 286.
V-neck cardigan. 286.
vest. 283.
vest. 286.

waistband. 284, 287.
waistband extension. 284.
watch pocket. 283.
welt pocket. 286.
yoke. 285.

MICRO COMPUTER

acoustic coupler. 457.
acoustic coupler. 455.
alphanumeric keyboard. 456.
backspace key. 456.
card punch. 458.
card reader. 458.
cassette. 455.
cassette recorder. 455.
central processing unit. 454, 455.
central processsing unit. 458.
communication device. 454.
computer room. 458.
configuration key. 457.
connection cable. 457.
control console. 458.
control key. 456.
control knob. 457.
control panel. 457.
cursor. 457.
cursor movement key. 456.
data acquisition. 454.
data display. 454.
data processing. 454.
data processing devices. 454.
data recording on Ram memory. 454.
data storage. 454.
disk. 458.
disk control unit. 458.
disk drive. 458.
disk storage. 458.
diskette. 455.
diskette drive. 455.
display. 455.
dot matrix printer. 457.
enter key. 456.
escape key. 456.
extended character. 456.
feed pin. 457.
function key. 456.
handset. 457.
home key. 456.
indicator light. 457.
input devices. 454.
joystick. 457.
joystick. 455.
keyboard. 456.
keyboard. 455.
lever. 457.
light pen. 455.
loudspeaker. 457.
magnetic tape controller. 458.
magnetic tape drive. 458.
magnetic tape storage. 458.
micro-computer. 454, 455, 456, 457.
microphone. 457.
microprocessor. 455.
mouse. 455.
numeric keypad. 456.
operator. 458.
output devices. 454.
paper guide roller. 457.
peripheral equipment. 457.
platen knob. 457.
plotter. 455.
print head. 457.
printer. 455, 458.
punch card. 458.
push button. 457.
Ram: Random Access Memory. 454.
reset key. 456.
return key. 456.
ROM: Read Only Memory. 454.
Rom memory. 454.
sector. 458.

shift key. 456.
shift lock key. 456.
soft key. 456.
space bar. 456.
specific data processing program. 454.
switch. 457.
system, configuration of a. 455.
system, functions in a. 454.
tab-key. 456.
template. 457.
terminal. 458.
track. 458.
word processing key. 456.

MOTORCYCLE

ammeter. 396.
brake pedal. 396.
carburetor. 395.
clutch lever. 396.
cylinder. 395.
cylinder-head. 395.
dip switch. 396.
disk brake. 395.
exhaust pipe. 395.
footpeg. 396.
frame. 395.
front brake. 396.
front fender. 395.
front footpeg. 395.
front hydraulic fork. 395.
fuel tank. 395.
gas tank cap. 396.
gear shift. 396.
gearshift lever. 395.
headlight. 395.
high beam warning light. 396.
horn button. 396.
housing. 395.
ignition switch. 396.
kill button. 396.
lighting switch. 396.
main gas tap. 396.
main stand. 396.
mirror. 395.
motorcycle. 395, 396.
oil pressure warning light. 396.
oil tank cap. 396.
rear footpeg. 395.
rear shock absorber. 395.
reserve gas tap. 396.
rim. 395.
saddle. 395.
side stand. 395.
signal light. 395.
speedometer. 396.
starter pedal. 396.
steering damper. 396.
steering lock. 396.
tachometer. 396.
taillight. 395.
twist grip throttle. 396.

NUCLEAR ENERGY

accept machine. 651.
airlock. 647.
annular shielding slab. 648.
bearing pad. 649.
calandria. 648, 650.
calandria tube. 648.
calandria vault. 648.
canned failed fuel. 651.
catenary. 647.
cathode screen. 652.
charge machine. 651.
closed circuit television. 652.
condensate. 650.
condenser. 647.
containment. 652.
containment building. 649.
control room. 652.
control room. 647.
conversion. 653.

coolant. 650.
cooling water. 650.
deaerator. 647, 650.
deaerator storage tank. 647.
decontamination room. 647.
digital computer. 652.
dousing tank. 647.
electrical distribution system. 652.
electrical room. 647.
elevator. 651.
emergency core cooling. 652.
end cap. 649.
end fitting. 648.
end plate. 649.
end shield. 647.
end shield cooling pipe. 648.
energy production. 653.
equipment lock. 651.
failed fuel bay. 651.
failed fuel canning. 651.
feeder. 648.
feedwater. 650.
fuel. 650.
fuel bundle. 649.
fuel fabrication. 653.
fuel handling control console. 652.
fuel handling sequence. 651.
fuel pellet. 649.
fuelling machine. 647, 650.
generating station flow diagram. 650.
generator. 647, 650, 652.
header. 647, 650.
heater. 650.
heavy water. 650.
high pressure turbine. 650.
horizontal flux detector. 648.
ion chamber. 648.
lattice tube. 648.
line printer. 652.
low pressure steam piping. 647.
low pressure turbine. 650.
mining. 653.
miscellaneous auxiliary systems. 652.
moderator. 650.
moderator heat exchanger. 650.
moderator inlet. 648.
moderator/miscellaneous systems. 652.
moderator outlet. 648.
moderator pump. 650.
new fuel loading area. 651.
new fuel port. 651.
new fuel storage room. 651.
nuclear energy. 647, 648, 649, 650, 651, 652, 653.
nuclear fuel cycle. 653.
nuclear generating station. 647.
nuclear reactor. 649.
nuclear reactor. 653.
operator desk. 652.
overhead crane. 647.
pencil. 649.
poison injection nozzle. 648.
poison tank. 647.
pressure relief pipe. 648.
pressure tube. 649.
pressurizer. 647, 650.
primary heat transport system. 652.
primary pump. 650.
radioactive waste storage. 653.
reactivity control device. 648.
reactor. 648.
reactor. 647, 650, 651.
reactor building. 647, 649, 651.
reactor regulating system. 652.
reactor vessel. 649.
reception bay. 651.
refining. 653.
rupture disc. 648.
safety valve. 650.
service building. 651.
sheath. 649.
shutdown system. 652.

spacer. 649.
spent fuel discharge room. 651.
spent fuel port. 651.
spent fuel storage bay. 649, 651, 653.
steam. 650.
steam generator. 647, 650.
steam generator system. 652.
steam pipe. 647, 650.
steam separator. 650.
steel ball shielding. 648.
storage tank. 650.
storage tray. 651.
suppression tank. 650.
switchyard. 652.
transfer canal. 651.
transmission network. 653.
tube sheet. 648.
turbine. 652.
turbine building. 647.
water treatment plant. 647.

OIL

aboveground pipeline. 630.
administration office. 634.
alkylation unit. 634.
anticline. 626.
aquifer. 636.
asphalt. 635.
asphalt process. 634.
asphalt still. 635.
automatic tank gauge. 633.
autorefrigerating devices. 630.
baffle. 632.
ballast tank. 631.
barge. 631.
base rock. 636.
beam pump. 627.
bit. 626.
bitumen. 636.
bitumen pumping. 636.
bitumen treatment. 636.
blowout preventer. 626.
booster intermediate station. 630.
bottom deck. 633.
breather valve. 633.
bridge. 631.
bucket wheel excavator. 636.
buffer tank. 630.
bulb. 631.
bund wall. 633.
bunker oil. 635.
burden. 636.
buried pipeline. 630.
butane carrier. 631.
canal boat. 631.
cap rock. 626, 636.
casing first string. 627.
casing second string. 627.
catalytic reformer. 634.
catalytic reforming plant. 635.
center Keelson. 631.
center tank. 631.
central pumping. 630.
chemical treatment. 635.
Christmas tree. 627.
Christmas tree. 630.
concrete drain. 633.
control room. 629.
conveyor. 631.
cooling tower. 634.
crane. 629.
crossover cargo deck line. 631.
crown block. 626.
crude oil. 635.
crude oil pipeline. 630.
derrick. 626, 629.
desasphalting. 634.
dewaxing. 634.
diesel oil. 635.
diluent. 636.
diluent recovery. 636.
discharge pipe. 632.
discharge pump. 632.

dispatch area. 634.
dragline. 636.
drain cock. 633.
drain valve. 633.
drawworks. 626.
drill collar. 626.
drill pipe. 626.
drill ship. 628.
drilling barge. 628.
drilling rig. 626.
elastic coupling method. 631.
emptying. 633.
engine. 626.
engine room. 631.
filling. 633.
finished product storage. 634.
fire-standing tanks. 631.
fire station. 634.
fixed platform. 628.
fixed-roof tank. 633.
flare. 629, 634.
floating platform. 628.
floating roof. 633.
floating-roof tank. 633
flow bean. 627.
fluid coking plant. 634.
foam gun. 631.
fore and aft gangway. 631.
fractionating tower. 635.
gas. 626.
gas lift. 627.
gas lift valve. 627.
gas oil. 635.
gas turbine. 629.
gas under pressure. 627.
gasoline. 635.
greases. 635.
ground. 633.
hatch. 631.
heating oil. 635.
heavy gasoline. 635.
helideck. 629.
hook. 626.
hot water extraction. 636.
hydrofiner. 634.
jack-up platform. 628.
jacket. 629.
jet fuel. 635.
kelly. 626.
kerosene. 635.
laboratory. 634.
lagging. 633.
lifeboat. 629.
liquefied petroleum gas storage. 634.
liquid-level gauge. 633.
liquified gas petroleum treatment. 634.
living quarters. 629.
logging unit. 629.
long residue. 635.
lubricants plant. 635.
lubricating oils. 635.
main inlet. 633.
manhole. 632, 633.
manometer. 633.
marine diesel. 635.
master gate valve. 627.
membrane tanks. 631.
methane carrier. 631.
mine. 636.
mud pump. 626.
muskeg. 636.
offshore drilling. 628.
offshore well. 630.
oil. 626, 627, 628, 629, 630, 631, 632, 633, 634, 635, 636.
oil. 626.
oil and gas foam. 627.
oil/gas separator. 629.
oil sand. 636.
oil sands mining plant. 636.
oil sands recovery process, steam drive. 636.
oil trap. 626.
paraffins. 635.

petrochemical industry. 635.
petrochemicals. 635.
pier. 628.
pile. 629.
pipeline. 630, 636.
pipeline support, aboveground.
630.
plunger. 627.
polymerization unit. 634.
potable water tank. 629.
power plant. 634.
pressure gauge. 627.
production platform. 629.
pump. 627.
pumping station. 630.
pumping unit. 627.
pyrolysis. 636.
quarters. 631.
reclaimed water. 636.
refinery. 634.
refinery. 630.
refinery products. 635.
rerunning. 634.
reserve mud tank. 629.
rotary table. 626.
salt water. 626.
sand-rock. 636.
scale. 633.
sealing ring. 633.
secondary inlet. 633.
self-contained platform. 628.
semi-membrane tanks. 631.
semi-submersible. 628.
semi-trailer. 632.
settling pond. 634, 636.
settling tank. 631.
shell. 633.
skid pad. 630.
slush pit. 626.
solvent extraction unit. 635.
spiral staircase. 633.
splash plate. 633.
spray nozzle. 633.
stairs. 633.
steam cracker. 634.
steam injection. 636.
stop. 630.
storage tank. 629, 635.
stove oil. 635.
straight run gasoline treatment.
634.
strainer. 627.
submarine pipeline. 630.
submersible barge. 628.
sucker rod. 627.
support. 630.
swivel. 626.
tailing. 636.
tank. 632, 633.
tank car. 632.
tank farm. 630, 634.
tank gauge float. 633.
tank trailer. 632.
tank truck. 632.
tank wall. 632.
tankage. 636.
tanker. 631.
tender. 628.
terminal. 630.
thermal insulation. 630.
thermometer. 633.
thick-walled pipe. 626.
top central manhole. 632.
top deck. 633.
towboat. 631.
tractor. 632.
transverse baffle. 632.
transverse bulkhead. 631.
travelling block. 626.
tubing. 627.
tubing head. 627.
tubular heater. 635.
tubular member. 629.
utilities plant. 636.
vacuum distillation. 635.
vibrating mudscreen. 626.

watertight bulkhead. 631.
web frame. 631.
wing tank. 631.
workshop store. 634.

PAINTING UPKEEP

air cap. 270.
air pressure adjusting screw. 270.
air valve. 270.
anti-slip shoe. 268.
blade guard. 270.
brace. 269.
bristles. 270.
brush. 270.
container. 270.
extension ladder. 268.
ferrule. 270.
fluid adjustment screw. 270.
foldaway ladder. 268.
frame. 269.
fruit-picking ladder. 269.
gun body. 270.
handle. 270.
hoisting rope. 268.
hook ladder. 268.
knurled bolt. 270.
ladder scaffold. 269.
ladders. 268, 269.
locking device. 268.
multipurpose ladder. 268.
nozzle. 270.
paint roller. 270.
painting upkeep. 268, 269, 270.
platform. 269.
platform ladder. 269.
pulley. 268.
removable blade. 270.
roller cover. 270.
roller frame. 270.
rolling ladder. 269.
rope ladder. 268.
rung. 269.
safety rail. 269.
scraper. 270.
shelf. 269.
side rail. 268.
spray paint gun. 270.
spreader adjustment valve. 270.
step. 269.
step stool. 269.
stepladder. 269.
stepladders. 268, 269.
straight ladder. 268.
tool tray. 269.
tray. 270.
trigger. 270.
vent hole. 270.

PHOTOGRAPHY

adjustable foot. 368.
air bulb release. 359.
aperture scale. 357.
ASA exposure index. 357.
background. 359.
barn doors. 358.
base of lamp. 357.
baseboard. 361.
battery. 357.
battery. 357.
battery check meter. 368.
bayonet mount. 353, 355.
bellows. 361.
between-the-lens shutter. 356.
boom. 359.
cable release. 359.
calculator. 357.
calculator dial. 357.
camera. 353.
camera battery. 368.
camera body. 353.
camera platform. 359.
camera screw. 359.
cartridge. 356.

cassette. 356.
cine scale. 357.
cinematography. 368.
close-up lens. 355.
collet. 359.
color analyzer. 360.
color filter. 355.
color filter set. 358.
column. 359, 361.
column crank. 359.
column lock. 359.
condenser. 361, 362.
conical snoot. 358.
contact printer. 360.
converter. 358.
cooling fan. 362.
darkroom. 360.
daylight film tank. 360.
daylight filter control. 368.
depth-of-field scale. 355.
developer bath. 360.
developing film. 356.
diaphragm. 353.
diffuser. 358.
diffuser filter set. 358.
disc. 356.
disc camera. 354.
distance scale. 355.
dry mounting press. 360.
easel. 361.
electric motor. 356.
electronic flash. 357.
enlarger. 361.
enlarger. 360.
enlarger timer. 360.
enlarging lens. 361.
exposure control. 356.
exposure counter. 353.
exposure meter. 357.
exposure-time scale. 357.
exposure value. 357.
exposure value scale. 357.
extractor fan. 360.
eye cup. 368.
eyecups. 355.
eyepiece. 356, 357.
eyepiece magnifier. 355.
fastening screw. 357.
film advance lever. 353.
film drying cabinet. 360.
film footage counter. 368.
film leader. 356.
film-pack. 356.
film path. 368.
film speed indicator. 353.
film transport sprocket. 353.
films. 356.
filter drawer. 361.
fisheye lens. 355.
fixing bath. 360.
flash. 358.
flash bracket. 357.
flash lamp. 357.
flash meter. 358.
flash outlet. 357.
flash socket. 368.
flash synchronization terminal. 353.
flash unit. 357.
flashbar socket. 356.
flashcube. 357.
focus magnifier. 361.
focusing control. 368.
focusing knob. 361, 362.
focusing magnifier. 360.
focusing ring. 368.
folding camera. 354.
forward/reverse switch. 368.
framing control. 368.
gear train. 356.
glass bulb. 357.
grip. 357.
guillotine trimmer. 360.
handgrip. 368.
hanger. 362.
head rotation lock. 361.
height control. 361.

height scale. 361.
honeycomb diffuser. 358.
incident-light measuring diffuser.
357.
indicator needle. 357.
infrared transmitter. 358.
interchangeable lens. 353.
lamp. 361, 368.
lamphouse. 361.
lead-in wire. 357.
lens. 356, 357, 362.
lens aperture scale. 355.
lens cap. 355.
lens hood. 355.
lens mount. 353.
lenses, interchangeable. 355.
leveling foot. 362.
light-reading scale. 357.
light sensor. 357.
lightbox. 360.
lighttight box. 353.
lock ring. 362.
lower pan-head mounting screw.
359.
macro focusing knob. 368.
magnesium wire. 357.
main cable. 358.
main cord. 362.
manual aperture control. 368.
manual zoom ring. 368.
medium format SLR. 354.
mirror. 353.
motor. 362.
mount frame blinder. 362.
movable condenser. 361.
neckstrap lug. 353.
negative carrier. 361.
objective. 355.
objective lens. 357.
on/off witch. 368.
pan handle. 359.
panoramic and tilting head. 359.
paper easel. 360.
paper safe. 360.
parabolic reflector. 358.
pearl screen. 362.
pentaprism. 353.
perforation. 356.
photoelectric cell. 356.
photographic accessories. 359.
photographic picture. 362.
photography. 353, 354, 355, 356,
357, 358, 359, 360, 361, 362.
pocket instamatic camera. 354.
polarizing filter. 355.
Polaroid Land camera. 356.
press camera. 354.
print drying rack. 360.
print washer. 360.
printed circuit. 356.
processing rollers. 356.
projection lamp. 362.
projection screen. 362.
projector. 362.
projector zoom lens. 368.
pull bail. 362.
push-button. 362.
rangefinder. 354.
recording reproducing head. 368.
recording switch. 368.
red safelight filter. 361.
reel. 360.
reflecting screen. 358.
reflector. 359.
release button. 353.
remote control. 362.
remote control socket. 368.
resin-coated paper dryer. 360.
rewing lever. 353.
right angle finder. 355.
saddle. 362.
safelight. 360.
screen case. 362.
self timer. 353.
semi-fish-eye lens. 355.
setting ring. 355.

shoe. 362.
shoe bracket. 357.
shutter. 353.
shutter button. 356.
shutter release. 353.
shutter speed selector. 353.
side-tilt lock. 359.
single-lens reflex camera. 353.
sink. 360.
slide. 362.
slide changer. 362.
slide projector. 362.
slide tray. 362.
softlight reflector. 358.
sound camera. 368.
sound-on-sound control. 368.
sound projector. 368.
speaker. 368.
spot projector attachment. 358.
spotmeter. 357.
stand. 358, 359.
standard lens. 355.
stereo camera. 354.
still cameras. 354.
stop bath. 360.
studio accessories. 359.
studio lighting. 358.
subminiature camera. 354.
supply reel. 368.
switch. 357.
sync cable. 358.
synchro cord. 357.
take-up reel. 368.
take-up spool. 353.
taking mirror. 356.
tele-converter. 355.
telephoto lens. 355.
telescoping leg. 359.
timer. 360.
tone control. 368.
transfer scale. 357.
transparency slide. 362.
trigger. 368.
tripod. 359.
tripod. 362.
tube. 362.
twin-lens reflex camera. 354.
umbrella diffuser. 358.
view camera. 354.
viewfinder. 353, 368.
voltage stabilizer. 361.
volume control. 368.
wide angle adapter. 357.
wide-angle lens. 355.
zoom lens. 355.

PLUMBING

access panel. 263.
adjustable spud wrench. 266.
aerated filter. 267.
aerator. 261.
air chamber. 257, 262.
anode. 263.
ball assembly. 261.
ball-cock supply valve. 258.
base elbow. 265.
basin wrench. 266.
bathroom. 259.
bathtub. 259.
body. 261.
bonnet. 261.
branch. 257.
brass ball faucet. 261.
brass floor frange. 258.
building sewer. 257.
cabinet. 259.
cap. 265.
cartridge stem. 261.
chain pipe wrench. 266.
check valve. 267.
circuit vent. 257.
clamp. 267.
cleanout. 260.
closet bend. 257.

cold-water line. 258, 263.
cold-water riser. 257.
cold-water shutoff valve. 263.
cold-water supply line. 262.
compression coupling. 260.
compression fitting. 264.
conical washer. 258.
copper pipe. 264.
copper to plastic. 265.
copper to steel. 265.
cover. 259.
disc seat. 261.
disc seat ring. 261.
discharge line. 267.
dishwasher. 262.
distribution field. 267.
diverter valve. 259.
double kitchen sink. 257.
drain. 257.
drain elbow. 260.
drain hose. 262.
drain valve. 263.
elbow. 265.
electric supply. 263.
electric water-heater tank. 263.
escutcheon. 260.
examples of branching. 262.
faucet. 261.
faucet body. 261.
filler tube. 258.
fitting. 264.
fittings. 265.
fixture drain. 257.
flange bolt. 258.
flange nut. 264.
flare joint. 264.
flare nut. 264.
flexible hose. 259.
flexible rubber hose. 262.
float. 267.
float ball. 258.
float clamp. 267.
flush bushing. 265.
garbage disposal sink. 260.
garbage disposal unit. 260.
gasket. 261, 264.
gravel. 267.
grease trap. 267.
grooved sleeve. 261.
grounded receptacle. 267.
hacksaw. 266.
handle. 261.
hexagon bushing. 265.
high-temperature cutoff. 263.
hot-water heater. 257.
hot-water supply. 262.
hot-water supply line. 262, 263.
house drain. 262.
inspection chamber. 267.
inspection plug. 267.
insulation. 263.
lever. 260, 261.
lever cover. 261.
locking nut. 258.
locknut. 260.
lower heating element. 263.
lower thermostat. 263.
main cleanout. 257.
mechanical connectors. 264.
metal washer. 261.
monkey wrench. 266.
nipple. 265.
o-ring. 261.
offset. 265.
outdoor sill cock. 257.
overflow. 259.
overflow bend. 257.
overflow pipe. 263.
overflow tube. 258.
["p[" trap. 257.
packing. 261.
packing nut. 261.
packing retainer ring. 261.
perforated pipe. 267.
pipe. 264.
pipe coupling. 265.

pipe threader. 266.
pipe wrench. 266.
plumbing. 257, 258, 259, 260, 261, 262, 263, 264, 265, 266, 267.
plumbing system. 257.
plumbing tools. 266.
plunger. 266.
pressure relief valve. 263.
public water main. 257.
pump motor. 267.
pump suction head. 267.
reducing coupling. 265.
refill tube. 258.
removable lid. 267.
retainer nut. 261.
ring nut. 264.
roof flashing. 257.
roof vent. 265.
rubber gasket. 260.
rubber washer. 260.
screen. 261.
scum. 267.
seal. 263.
seat. 259.
septic tank. 267.
septic tank compartment. 267.
shower and tub fixture. 257.
shower head. 259.
shutoff switch. 267.
shutoff valve. 257, 258, 260, 262.
single-handle kitchen faucet. 261.
single-handle kitchen faucet. 260.
sink. 260.
sink. 259.
sink strainer. 260.
slotted wall bracket. 259.
sludge. 267.
soap dish. 259.
soil-or-waste stack. 257.
spindle. 261.
spout. 261.
spout assembly. 260.
spray head. 260.
spray hose. 260.
spring. 261.
square head plug. 265.
stack vent. 257.
standpipe. 262.
steel to plastic. 265.
stem faucet. 261.
strainer. 261.
strainer body. 260.
strainer coupling. 260.
strainer plug. 261.
strainer sleeve. 260.
strap wrench. 266.
stub out. 258.
sump. 267.
sump pump. 267.
supply line. 257.
supply riser. 257.
supply tube. 260.
tailpiece. 261.
tank ball. 258.
tank lid. 259.
tee. 262, 265.
telephone shower head. 259.
thread. 261.
threaded cap. 265.
tipping valve faucet. 261.
tissue holder. 259.
toilet. 258.
toilet. 259.
toilet bowl. 258, 259.
toilet tank. 259.
torch. 266.
towel bar set. 259.
transition fittings. 265.
trap. 260, 267.
trap and drain auger. 266.
trap coupling. 260.
trip handle. 259.
trip lever. 258.
tube cutter. 266.
tube end. 264.
tube flaring tool. 266.

tumbler holder. 259.
U-bend. 265.
union. 264.
union nut. 264.
upper heating element. 263.
upper thermostat. 263.
valve seat. 261.
valve seat shaft. 258.
valve seat wrench. 266.
vent line. 265.
washer. 262.
washer. 261.
waste pipe. 258.
waste stack. 257.
waste tee. 262.
water meter. 257.
water service pipe. 257.
wax seal. 258.
wye branch. 265.

RAILROAD

adjustable seat. 407.
air conditioning. 407.
air intake. 404.
alternator. 404.
arrivals schedule. 412.
automatic gates. 410.
automobile car. 406.
axle. 404.
baggage check. 412.
baggage lockers. 412.
baggage room. 412.
ballast. 408.
base. 408, 409.
body. 407.
booking hall. 412.
bottom-end transverse member. 411.
bottom retainer. 405.
bottom side rail. 411.
box car. 405.
bulkhead flat car. 406.
bumper. 404, 410.
caboose. 406.
car. 411.
cars, types of. 406.
center-aisle. 407.
change machine. 412.
channel. 409.
check-rail. 408.
classification yard. 411.
closure rail. 408.
coach car. 407.
collector bow. 413.
container. 411.
container car. 406.
control stand. 404.
corner cap. 405.
corner fitting. 411.
corner structure. 411.
counterweight. 408, 409.
coupler head. 405.
coupler knuckle. 405.
coupler knuckle pin. 405.
crossbuck sign. 409.
crossing. 413.
crossing gate mechanism. 409.
currency exchange office. 412.
dating nail. 408.
delay indicator. 413.
departure time indicator. 413.
departures schedule. 412.
depressed-center flat car. 406.
destination indicator. 413.
diaphragm. 407.
diesel-electric locomotive. 404.
diesel engine. 404.
diesel shop. 410.
dining car. 407.
dining section. 407.
ditch light. 413.
door hasp. 405.
door hasp fastener. 405.
door stop. 405.

driver's cab. 404.
end door. 411.
end ladder. 405.
expansion space. 408.
flashing light. 409.
flat car. 406.
fold-out table. 407.
footbridge. 410.
fork pocket. 411.
freight station. 410.
frog. 408.
gate arm. 409.
gate arm lamp. 409.
gate arm support. 409.
gondola car. 406.
group retarders. 411.
hand brake gear housing. 405.
hand brake wheel. 405.
hand brake winding chain. 405.
hand truck. 413.
head. 408.
headlight. 413.
headrest. 407.
highway crossing. 409.
highway crossing bell. 409.
hold yard. 411.
hopper car. 406.
hopper ore car. 406.
horizontal end handhold. 405.
horn. 404.
hump. 411.
hump area. 411.
indicator board. 413.
information office. 412.
journal box. 404.
junction box. 409.
king pin. 404.
kitchen. 407.
level crossing. 410.
lifting lever. 405.
livestock car. 406.
locomotive. 404.
lower berth. 407.
main generator. 404.
main line. 410.
main running track. 411.
mast. 409, 410.
master retarders. 411.
number of tracks sign. 409.
nut. 408.
outbound. 411.
panoramic window. 407.
parcels office. 412.
passageway. 407.
passenger cars, types of. 407.
passenger platform. 413.
passenger station. 410.
peep hole. 409.
piggyback car. 406.
pinnacle. 409.
placard board. 405.
platform edge. 413.
platform entrance. 412.
platform number. 413.
platform roofing. 413.
platform shelter. 410.
platform truck. 413.
point wire. 409.
points motor. 409.
pull rod. 408.
radiator. 404.
rail. 408.
rail anchor. 408.
rail joint. 408.
railroad station. 410.
railroad track. 408, 409.
railway map. 412.
ramp. 410.
receiving yard. 411.
redcap. 413.
refrigerator car. 406.
roof. 411.
routing cardboard. 405.
running track. 411.
schedules. 412.
scissors crossing. 410.

semaphore. 410.
side door. 411.
side ladder. 405.
side ladder tread. 405.
side wall. 411.
signal background plate. 409.
signal gantry. 410.
signals. 409.
sill step. 405.
sleeping car. 407.
slide chair. 408.
sliding window. 407.
speaking window membrane. 412.
spike. 408.
spleeping compartment. 407.
splice bar. 408.
spring. 404.
spring washer. 408.
starting signal. 413.
station hall. 412.
station platform. 413.
station platform. 410.
station sign. 413.
stretcher bar. 409.
subsidiary track. 410.
suburban commuter railroad. 410.
switch. 410.
switch, manually-operated. 408.
switch, remote-controlled. 409.
switch engine. 411.
switch point. 408.
switch point lock. 409.
switch signal. 408, 409.
switch stand. 409.
switch tower. 410.
tank car. 406.
tarpaulin covered gondola. 406.
telescoping uncoupling rod. 405.
ticket counter. 412.
ticket office. 412.
tie. 408.
tie plate. 408.
toilet. 407.
top-end transverse member. 411.
track. 413.
track bolt. 408.
traction motor. 404.
traction motor ventilator. 404.
train delays notice board. 412.
train set. 410.
trolley wire. 413.
trough. 409.
truck. 404, 407.
truck frame. 404.
turbocharger. 404.
turnbuckle. 409.
upper berth. 407.
ventilating fan. 404.
vestibule. 407.
vestibule door. 407.
visor. 409.
waiting room. 412.
water tank. 404, 407.
web. 408.
wood chip car. 406.
yard. 411.
yard office. 411.

SEWING

alteration line. 489.
arm. 485.
balance wheel. 485.
balance wheel locking screw. 485.
ball. 488.
bias. 488.
blade. 486, 487.
bobbin. 486.
bobbin case. 486.
bobbin winder. 485.
buckle. 488.
button. 488.
column. 485.
crosswise grain. 488.
cutting line. 489.

dart. 489.
dressmaker's model. 487.
drive. 485.
edge. 487.
eye. 486, 487.
fabric structure. 488.
fasteners. 488.
feed dog. 486.
flat-bed. 485.
fold line. 489.
garment fabric. 488.
groove. 486.
handle. 487.
head. 485.
hemline. 489.
hinged presser foot. 485, 486.
hook. 486, 488.
hook and eyes. 488.
interfacing. 488.
interlining. 488.
latch lever. 486.
lengthwise grain. 489.
lengthwise grain. 488.
lining. 488.
magnet. 487.
marking dot. 489.
motor. 485.
needle. 486.
needle. 485, 487.
needle bar. 486.
needle clamp. 486.
needle clamp screw. 486.
needle plate. 485.
needle threader. 487.
needle threader. 486.
notch. 489.
pattern. 489.
pin. 487.
pin cushion. 487.
pinking shears. 487.
pivot. 487.
point. 486.
presser bar. 486.
presser foot. 486..
presser foot lifter. 485.
ring. 488.
round eye. 488.
safety pins. 487.
scissors. 487.
seam allowance. 489.
seam line. 489.
selvage. 488.
sew-through buttons. 488.
sewing. 485, 486, 487, 488, 489.
sewing machine. 485, 486.
sewing spool. 485.
sewing supplies. 487.
shank. 486, 487.
shank button. 488.
shuttle. 486.
skirt marker. 487.
slide. 488.
slide plate. 485.
snap. 488.
socket. 488.
spool pin. 485.
stitch length regulator. 485.
stitch selector. 485.
stop. 488.
straight eye. 488.
tab. 488.
tape. 488.
tape measure. 487.
teeth. 488.
tension block. 486.
tension block. 485.
tension check spring. 486.
tension dial. 486.
tension disc. 486.
thimble. 487.
thread guide. 485, 486.
thread take-up. 485.
thread trimmer. 486.
tongue. 488.
tracing wheel. 487.
underlining. 488.

underlying fabrics. 488.
wheel. 487.
zipper. 488.
zipper line. 489.

SKIING

Alaskan snowshoe. 549.
alpine skier. 545.
alpine skiing. 545, 546.
anti-friction pad. 546.
automatic cable pulley. 544.
axle. 548.
back crossbar. 549.
backstay. 548.
ball bearing. 548.
base plate. 546.
basket. 545, 547.
bear paw. 549.
beaver tail. 549.
blade. 548.
bobsleigh. 550.
body. 549.
body lacing. 549.
boot. 548.
bottom. 545.
brakeman. 550.
buckle. 546.
cabin. 544.
cable binding. 547.
cable car. 544.
camber. 547.
captain. 550.
chalet. 544.
clamp. 547.
counter. 548.
crash helmet. 545, 550.
Cree snowshoe. 549.
cross-country ski. 547.
cross-country ski. 547.
cross-country skier. 547.
cross-country skiing. 547.
crossbar. 544.
cushion. 544.
disc. 544.
double chair lift. 544.
edge. 545, 547, 548, 550.
elbow pad. 550.
eyelet. 548.
fanny pack. 545.
figure skate. 548.
flag. 544.
footrest. 544.
frame. 549.
front crossbar. 549.
front runner. 550.
gaiter. 545.
gate. 544.
glove. 547, 550.
goggles. 550.
groove. 545, 547.
handle. 545, 550.
harness. 549.
haulage cable. 544.
headband. 547.
heel. 548.
heel flange. 546.
heel lacing. 549.
heel piece. 545, 546.
heel release setting indicator. 546.
heelplate. 547.
height adjustment screw. 546.
hinge. 546.
hockey skate. 548.
hook. 544, 548.
inner boot. 548.
kingpin. 548.
knee pad. 550.
knee sock. 547.
knickers. 547.
lace. 548.
lining. 548.
lock nut. 548.
lower shell. 546.
manual release. 546.

master cord. 549.
Michigan snowshoe. 549.
mitten. 545.
mocassin. 549.
otter paw. 549.
parka. 547.
pivot. 548.
point. 548.
pole. 544.
pole grip. 547.
pole shaft. 547.
pole tip. 547.
poma lift. 544.
pullover sweater. 547.
pylon. 544.
rear runner. 550.
release setting screw. 546.
rider. 550.
roller skate. 548.
rucksack. 547.
runner. 550.
running surface. 547.
safety bar. 544.
safety binding. 546.
safety binding. 545.
safety strap. 546.
scarf. 545.
screw. 548.
seat. 544, 550.
shovel. 545, 547.
skate guard. 548.
skates, types of. 548.
skating. 548.
ski. 545.
ski boot. 546.
ski boot. 545.
ski goggles. 545, 547.
ski hat. 547.
ski instructor. 544.
ski jumper. 544.
ski jumping hill. 544.
ski pole. 545, 547.
ski resort. 544.
ski stop. 545, 546.
ski suit. 545.
ski tip. 547.
skiing. 544.
slalom course. 544.
slalomist. 544.
snowshoe types. 549.
snowshoer. 549.
snowshoes. 549.
sole. 546, 548.
sole plate. 548.
speed skate. 548.
stanchion. 548.
strap. 550.
strut. 550.
T-bar lift. 544.
tail. 545, 547, 549.
tendon guard. 548.
tip. 545, 549.
tip guard. 548.
toboggan. 550.
toe binding. 547.
toe box. 548.
toe hole. 549.
toe lacing. 549.
toe pick. 548.
toe piece. 545, 546.
toe-piece release setting indicator.
  546.
toe stop. 548.
toeplate. 547.
tongue. 546, 548.
touring boot. 547.
track. 544.
truck. 548.
turtleneck. 545.
upper. 546.
upper cuff. 546.
upper shell. 546.
wheel. 548.
wire. 546.
wrist strap. 547.

SOUND REPRODUCING SYSTEM

Ac cord. 363, 365.
amplifier-tuner. 364.
analog frequency meter. 364.
anti-skating device. 365.
arm elevator. 365.
arm rest. 365.
balance control. 364.
band. 365.
band selectors. 364.
base. 365.
base plate. 365.
bass tone control. 364.
cabinet. 363.
cassette holder. 366.
center hole. 365.
cone. 363.
connecting cable. 363.
corrugation. 363.
counter reset button. 366.
counterweight. 365.
diaphragm. 363.
digital frequency display. 364.
Dolby noise reduction switch. 366.
drive belt. 365.
dust cover. 365.
ear cushion. 363.
eject button. 366.
EP adaptor. 365.
equalizer. 363.
fast-forward button. 366.
FM mode selector. 364.
FM stereo indicator. 364.
frequency automatic control. 364.
function lever. 365.
grille. 363.
groove. 365.
ground lead. 365.
head shell. 365.
headband. 363.
headphone. 363.
headphone. 363.
headphone jack. 364, 366.
hinge. 365.
input selectors. 364.
jack. 363.
label. 365.
LED peak level meter. 366.
level controls. 363.
locked groove. 365.
loudness switch. 364.
loudspeaker. 363.
memory button. 364.
microphone. 363.
microphone jack. 366.
midrange. 363.
monitor indicator. 364.
motor pulley. 365.
output lead. 365.
pause button. 366.
platter. 365.
play button. 366.
power switch. 364, 366.
preamplifier-amplifier. 363.
preset tuning button. 364.
record. 365.
record button. 366.
record muting button. 366.
recording level button. 366.
rewing button. 366.
rubber mat. 365.
shaft. 365.
*sound reproducing system. 363,
  364, 365, 366.*
speaker. 363.
speaker selector. 364.
speed selector lever. 365.
spiral. 365.
spiral-in groove. 365.
stop button. 366.
supertweeter. 363.
system elements. 363.
tail-out groove. 365.

tape counter. 366.
tape deck. 366.
tape deck. 363.
tape monitor switch. 364.
tape selector. 366.
tape-type indicator. 366.
tone arm. 365.
treble tone control. 364.
tuner. 363.
tuning buttons. 364.
turntable. 365.
turntable. 363.
tweeter. 363.
volume control. 363, 364.
woofer. 363.

TELEPHONE

acoustic resistance. 372.
armored cord. 373.
auto answer indicator. 373.
call director telephone. 373.
calls indicator. 373.
carbon granules. 372.
clapper. 372.
coil. 372.
coin return bucket. 373.
coin return knob. 373.
coin slot. 373.
coinbox telephone. 373.
cord. 372.
cordless telephone. 373.
cradle. 372.
cup. 372.
dial. 372.
diaphragm. 372.
earpiece. 372.
electrode. 372.
erase button. 373.
fast forward button. 373.
finger stop. 372.
gong. 372.
handset. 372, 373.
handset cord. 372.
handsfree telephone. 373.
housing. 372.
incoming message cassette. 373.
listen button. 373.
microphone. 373.
mouthpiece. 372.
network. 372.
on/play button. 373.
outgoing announcement cassette.
  373.
permanent magnet. 372.
plunger. 372.
pole piece. 372.
push-button telephone. 373.
push buttons. 373.
receiver. 372.
record announcement button. 373.
rewind button. 373.
ringer coil. 372.
stop button. 373.
switchhook. 372.
*telephone answering machine.
  373.*
telephone cord. 373.
telephone set. 372.
telephones, types of. 373.
transmitter. 372.
varistor. 372.
volume control. 373.

TELEVISION

amplifier. 374.
audio console. 374.
audio control room. 374.
audio operator. 374.
base. 377.
blue beam. 377.
boom operator. 375.
brightness control. 377.
cabinet. 377.

camera. 376.
camera mount. 375.
cameraman. 375.
catwalk. 375.
clock. 376.
contrast control. 377.
control panel. 374, 375.
control rooms. 374.
cue screen. 376.
cyclorama. 375.
dimmer control. 374.
earphone jack. 377.
electron beam. 377.
electron gun. 377.
external conductive coating. 377.
faceplate. 377.
fine tuning knob. 377.
floodlight. 375.
floor crew. 375.
floor manager. 375.
funnel. 377.
green beam. 377.
hoisting apparatus. 375.
host. 375.
lighting and vision control room.
  374.
lighting director. 374.
loudspeaker. 375.
microphone boom. 375.
monitor. 376.
monitor bank. 376.
monitor pusher. 375.
monitor speaker. 376.
neck. 377.
off-on knob. 377.
output monitor. 376.
phosphor dot. 377.
picture tube. 377.
preview monitor. 376.
producer. 376.
production control room. 376.
production control room. 374.
propman. 375.
protective window. 377.
red beam. 377.
screen. 377.
script assistant. 376.
shadow mask. 377.
sound engineer. 374.
speaker. 377.
special effects. 376.
spotlight. 375.
strip light. 375.
studio. 374.
studio. 374.
studio crane. 375.
studio floor. 375.
switcher. 376.
technical director. 376.
teleprompter. 375.
telescopic antenna. 377.
television. 374, 375, 376, 377.
television set. 377.
test pattern. 376.
UHF channel selector. 377.
utility speaker. 376.
VHF channel selector. 377.
video technician. 374.
videotape recorder. 374.

VEGETABLES

artichoke. 73.
asparagus. 77.
autumn squash. 73.
bean sprouts. 77.
beet. 76.
black salsify. 76.
branch. 77.
broad beans. 77.
broad-leaved endive. 74.
broccoli. 73.
Brussels sprouts. 74.
bud. 75.
bulb. 77.

bulb, section of a. 75.
bulb vegetables. 75.
bulbil. 75.
bundle. 77.
cabbage lettuce. 74.
cantaloupe. 73.
cardoon. 77.
carrot. 76.
cauliflower. 73.
celery. 74.
chard. 74.
chick peas. 77.
chicory. 74.
Chinese cabbage. 74.
chive. 75.
cob. 77.
corn. 77.
corn salad. 74.
cucumber. 73.
curled endive. 74.
curled kale. 74.
dandelion. 74.
eggplant. 73.
Florence fennel. 77.
fruit vegetables. 73.
garden sorrel. 74.
garlic. 75.
green bean. 73.
green cabbage. 74.
green peas. 77.
head. 77.
horse-radish. 76.
hot pepper. 73.
husk. 77.
inflorescence vegetables. 73.
Jerusalem artichoke. 76.
kernel. 77.
kohlrabi. 76.
leaf. 77.
leaf vegetables. 74.
leek. 75.
lentils. 77.
muskmelon. 73.
okra. 73.
parsnip. 76.
pickling onion. 75.
potato. 76.
pumpkin. 73.
radish. 76.
rhubarb. 77.
rib. 77.
romaine lettuce. 74.
root. 75.
root vegetables. 76.
rutabaga. 76.
salsify. 76.
scale leaf. 75.
scallion. 75.
seed vegetables. 77.
shallot. 75.
silk. 77.
snow peas. 77.
soybeans. 77.
Spanish onion. 75.
spear. 77.
spinach. 74.
stalk. 77.
stalk vegetables. 77.
stem. 75.
string. 77.
summer squash. 73.
sweet pepper. 73.
sweet potato. 76.
Swiss chard. 77.
tip. 77.
tomato. 73.
tuber vegetables. 76.
turnip. 76.
vegetables. 73, 74, 75, 76, 77.
vine leaf. 74.
water cress. 74.
watermelon. 73.
white cabbage. 74.
zucchini. 73.

WATER SPORTS

air hose. 536.
arm position. 535.
armstand. 534.
armstand dive. 535.
assistant timer. 53 l.
back binding. 540.
backstroke. 533.
backstroke start. 533.
backstroke swimmer. 533.
backstroke turn indicator. 532.
backward. 534.
backward dive. 535.
ball. 531.
bathing trunks. 531.
batten. 537, 538.
batten pocket. 537, 538.
beam reach. 539.
bear away (to). 537.
binding. 540.
blade. 536.
block. 539.
blue cap. 531.
blue flag. 531.
board. 537.
boom. 538.
boom vang. 538.
boot. 536.
bottom. 540.
bottom of the pool. 531, 534.
bow. 537.
breastroke kick. 533.
breastroke swimmer. 533.
breastroke turn. 533.
breaststroke. 533.
breathing in. 533.
breathing out. 533.
broad reach. 539.
buoyancy compensator. 536.
butterfly kick. 533.
butterfly stroke. 533.
butterfly swimmer. 533.
butterfly turn. 533.
centerboard. 538.
chief timekeeper. 532.
clam-cleat. 537, 539.
cleat. 538, 539.
clew. 537.
close hauled. 539.
close reach. 539.
cockpit. 538.
compass. 536.
competitive course. 532.
competitor. 532.
compressed-air cylinder. 536.
crawl swimmer. 533.
crossbar. 531.
crosstree. 538.
daggerboard. 537.
daggerboard well. 537.
depth gauge. 536.
dinghy. 538.
diver. 535, 536.
dives, groups of. 535.
diving. 534.
diving installations. 534.
diving well. 534.
double handles. 540.
down wind. 539.
downhaul. 537.
end of the lap. 533.
end wall. 532.
entries. 534.
entry. 535.
fairlead. 539.
false strart rope. 532.
feet-first entry. 534.
figure ski. 540.
figure skiing handle. 540.
fin. 536, 537, 540.
flight. 535.
flights. 534.
flip turn. 533.
foot. 537.
foot pocket. 536.

forestay. 538.
forward. 534.
forward dive. 535.
front binding. 540.
front crawl stroke. 533.
fulcrum. 534.
full and by. 539.
glove. 536.
goal. 531.
goal judge. 531.
goal line. 531.
goalkeeper. 531.
half-distance line. 531.
handle. 540.
handles, types of. 540.
hank. 538, 539.
harness. 536.
head-first entry. 534.
head of sail. 537.
headwind. 539.
heel piece. 540.
height. 534.
height of the dive. 535.
hood. 536.
inhaul. 537.
inward dive. 535.
jib. 538.
jib halyard. 538.
jibsheet. 538.
jump ski. 540.
kick. 533.
knife. 536.
lane number. 532.
lane rope. 532.
lane timekeeper. 532.
leech. 537.
leg position. 535.
length. 534.
light. 536.
luff. 537.
luff (to). 537.
main halyard. 538.
mainsail. 538.
mainsheet. 538.
mask. 536.
mast. 537, 538.
mast foot. 537.
mast sleeve. 537.
masthead. 537.
mono-ski. 540.
mouthpiece. 536.
on the wind. 539.
outhaul. 537.
pike position. 534.
placing judge. 532.
platform. 534.
platform diver. 534.
player. 531.
playing area, water polo. 531.
point of sailing. 539.
port tack. 539.
post. 531.
purge valve. 536.
rail. 536.
recorder. 532.
red cap. 531.
red flag. 531.
referee. 531, 532.
reverse dive. 535.
rudder. 538.
sail. 537.
sail panel. 538.
sailboard. 537.
scuba diver. 536.
secretary. 531.
shackle. 539.
sheet lead. 539.
shroud. 538.
side wall. 532.
sidestroke. 533.
skin diving. 536.
skis, types of. 540.
snap shackle. 539.
snorkel. 536.
speargun. 536.
spinnaker boom. 538.

spinnaker sheet lead. 538.
springboard. 534.
springboard diver. 534.
start wall. 532.
startboard tack. 539.
starter. 532.
starting block. 532.
starting dive. 532.
starting grip. 532.
starting position. 532.
starting position. 535.
starting positions. 534.
stem. 538.
stern. 537.
straight position. 534.
stroke judge. 533.
strokes, types of. 533.
submersible watch. 536.
substitute. 531.
surface of the water. 534.
swimmer. 532.
swimming. 532.
swimming competition. 532.
swimming pool. 531.
tack. 537.
tail. 540.
team bench. 531.
telltale. 538.
tiller. 538.
timekeeper. 531.
tip. 540.
toe piece. 540.
toe strap. 540.
tow bar. 540.
towrope. 540.
traveler. 539.
tuck position. 534.
turnbuckle. 539.
turning judge. 532.
twin skis. 540.
twist dive. 535.
uphaul. 537.
upperworks. 539.
water polo. 531.
water skiing. 540.
weight belt. 536.
wet suit. 536.
white cap. 531.
white flag. 531.
width. 534.
winch. 539.
wind. 539.
wind abeam. 539.
wind indicator. 538.
window. 537.
wishbone boom. 537.

WEAVING

back beam. 494.
ball. 496.
ball winder. 496.
beater. 494.
beater handtree. 494.
beater sley. 494.
bobbin. 495, 496.
bobbin winder. 496.
breast beam. 494.
clamp. 496.
cloth beam. 494.
comb. 495.
crossbar. 495.
crossbeam. 494.
crosspiece. 494.
driving wheel. 496.
eye. 495.
flat shuttle. 495.
frame. 494.
gear. 496.
handle. 494.
harness. 494.
harnesses. 494.
hatching. 497.
head roller. 494.
heddle. 494, 495.

Specialized Indexes

heddle rod. 495.
heddles. 495.
high warp loom. 495.
interloop. 497.
knot. 497.
lam. 494.
lease stick. 494, 495.
loom. 494, 495.
low wrap loom. 494.
nails. 495.
peg. 496.
plain weave. 497.
post. 494.
ratchet. 494.
ratchet wheel. 494.
reed. 494.
reed hooks. 496.
release treadle. 494.
rod. 495.
satin weave. 497.
screw eye. 494.
shaft. 496.
shed rod. 495.
shuttle. 495.
slit. 497.
spool rack. 496.
support. 495.
swift. 496.
take-up handle. 494.
tapestry bobbin. 495.
temple. 495.
thread guide. 496.
treadle. 494.
treadle cord. 494.
twill weave. 497.
upright. 494, 495.
vertical frame. 495.
warp. 494, 495.
warp beam. 494.
warp thread. 497.
warping reel. 496.
weaves, basic. 497.
weaving. 494, 495, 496, 497.
weaving accessories. 495.
weaving principle, diagram of. 497.
weft. 494.
weft thread. 497.
winder. 496.
worm. 496.

WOMEN'S CLOTHING

accordion pleat. 294.
anklet. 301.
arm slit. 291.
armhole. 296.
baby doll. 301.
back. 294.
back belt. 290.
barrel cuff. 296.
bateau neck. 299.
bathrobe. 301.
batwing sleeve. 296.
bellows pocket. 294, 297.
beret. 304.
Bermuda shorts. 300.
bertha collar. 298.
bib. 300.
bikini. 303.
bishop sleeve. 296.
blazer. 297.
blouses. 295.
boa. 299.
boater. 304.
body shirt. 295.
body suit. 302.
bolero. 297.
bottom of collar. 295.
bow collar. 298.
box pleat. 294.
bra. 303.
brassiere cup. 303.
break line. 298.
breast pocket. 295.
briefelette. 302.

briefs. 303.
brim. 304.
broad welt. 290.
broad welt side pocket. 294.
buttoned placket. 291, 295.
camisole. 302.
cap. 304.
cap sleeve. 296.
cape. 291.
cardigan. 297.
cartwheel hat. 304.
classic. 295.
cloche. 304.
coat dress. 292.
coats. 290, 291.
collar. 298.
collar point. 298.
collaret. 298.
collars, types of. 298.
corselet. 302.
corset. 303.
cowl collar. 298.
crew sweater. 297.
crotch piece. 295.
crown. 304.
crusader cap. 304.
crusader hood. 304.
culotte. 293.
cutaway armhole. 296.
décolleté bra. 303.
dog ear collar. 298.
doubel breasted buttoning. 291.
draped neck. 299.
draped neckline. 299.
dresses. 292.
drop waist dress. 292.
epaulet sleeve. 296.
fall. 298.
felt hat. 304.
flap pocket. 294.
fly front closing. 290.
footstrap. 300.
foundation slip. 302.
French cuff. 296.
frog. 298.
front top pocket. 300.
garter. 302, 303.
garter belt. 303.
gather. 295.
gather skirt. 293.
gauchos. 300.
gob hat. 304.
golf hose. 301.
gored skirt. 293.
half-slip. 303.
hand warmer pocket. 291.
hand warmer pouch. 294.
hat vell. 304.
head band. 304.
headwear. 304.
hose. 301.
hoses. 301.
inset pocket. 294.
inverted pleat. 294.
jabot. 298.
jeans. 300.
jewel neck. 299.
jumper. 292.
jumpsuit. 300.
kerchief. 304.
kick pleat. 294.
kilt. 293.
kimono. 301.
kimono sleeve. 296.
knickers. 300.
knife pleat. 294.
lapel. 298.
leading edge. 294, 298.
leg-of-mutton sleeve. 296.
loosely tied bow. 299.
mandarin collar. 298.
maternity dress. 292.
middy. 295.
midriff band. 303.
mini shirtdress. 295.
mob-cap. 304.

mock pocket. 291.
modesty. 298.
narrow cuff. 296.
necklines. 299.
necks. 299.
negligee. 301.
net stocking. 301.
nightgown. 301.
nightwear. 301.
notched lapel. 291, 298.
over-blouse. 295.
overalls. 300.
overcoat. 290.
pagoda sleeve. 296.
pajama. 301.
palazzo pants. 300.
panel. 303.
pants. 300.
panty girdle. 303.
panty hose. 301.
patch pocket. 290, 294.
pea jacket. 291.
pedal pusher. 300.
pelerine. 290.
Peter Pan collar. 298.
pillbox hat. 304.
pinafore. 292.
placket. 298.
pleat skirts. 294.
plunging neckline. 299.
pockets. 294.
pointed tab end. 296.
polo collar. 298.
polo shirt. 295.
pompom. 304.
poncho. 291.
princess dress. 292.
princess seaming. 302.
puff sleeve. 296.
pullover. 297.
pullovers. 297.
push up bra. 303.
raglan. 290.
raglan sleeve. 290, 296.
redingote. 290.
ribbing. 297.
ridge. 294.
right side. 294.
roll. 298.
roll line. 298.
ruffled skirt. 293.
safari. 297.
sailor collar. 298.
sarong. 293.
seam pocket. 290, 294.
seaming. 290.
set-in sleeve. 296.
shawl collar. 298.
sheath dress. 292.
sheath skirt. 293.
shirt collar. 295, 298.
shirt sleeve. 295.
shirttail. 295.
shirtwaist dress. 292.
shirtwaist sleeve. 296.
shorts. 300.
shoulder-strap. 303.
shrink. 297.
skirts. 293.
sleeves. 296.
slims. 300.
slip. 302.
smock. 295.
sock. 301.
southwester. 304.
spencer. 297.
square neck. 299.
stand. 298.
stand-up collar. 298.
steel. 303.
stitched pleat. 294.
stocking cap. 304.
straight skirt. 293.
strapless brassiere. 303.
string. 304.
sundress. 292.

sweater. 297.
sweetheart neckline. 299.
T-shirt dress. 292.
tailored collar. 291, 298.
tailored sleeve. 296.
tam o'shanter. 304.
thigh-high stocking. 301.
three-quarter sleeve. 296.
top stitched pleat. 294.
toque. 304.
tunic. 292, 295.
turban. 304.
turn-down flap. 290.
turn-up. 300.
turtleneck. 297, 298.
twin-set. 297.
underwear. 302, 303.
underwiring. 303.
unmounted sleeve. 296.
V-shaped neck. 299.
vest pocket. 297.
vests. 297.
waistband. 291.
welt pocket. 294.
weskit. 297.
windbreaker. 291.
women's clothing. 290, 291, 292, 293, 294, 295, 296, 297, 298, 299, 300, 301, 302, 303, 304.
wrap dress. 292.
wrap over top. 295.
wraparound skirt. 293.
yoke. 295.
yoke skirt. 293.

SELECTIVE BIBLIOGRAPHY

Dictionaries:

Gage Canadian Dictionary, Toronto, Gage Publishing Limited, 1983, 1313 p.

Larousse Illustrated International, Paris, Larousse, McGraw-Hill, 1972.

The New Britannica/Webster Dictionary and Reference guide, Encyclopedia Britannica, 1981.

The Oxford Illustrated Dictionary, Oxford, Clarendon Press, 1967.

The Random House Dictionary of the English Language, the unabridged Edition, 1983, 2059 p.

Webster's New Collegiate Dictionary, Springfield, G. @ C. Merriam Company, 1980, 1532 p.

Webster's New Twentieth Century Dictionary of the Language, unabridged, Cleveland, Collins World, 1975.

Webster's new world dictionary of the American language, New York, The World Pub., 1953.

French and English Dictionaries:

Belles-Isle, J.-Gerald. *Dictionnaire thématique général anglais-français*, Paris, Dunod, Montréal, Beauchemin, 2e édition, 1977, 553 p.

Collins-Robert. *French-English, English-French Dictionary*, London, Glasgow, Cleveland, Toronto, 1978, 781 p.

Dubois, Marguerite-Marie. *Dictionnaire moderne français-anglais*, Paris, Larousse, 1960.

Harrap's *New Standard French and English Dictionary*, part one, French-English, London, 1977, 2 vol., part two, English-French, London, 1983, 2 vol.

Harrap's *Shorter French and English Dictionary*, London, Toronto, Willington, Sydney, George G. Harrap and Company, 1953, 940 p.

Encyclopedias:

Academic American Encyclopedia, Princeton, Arete Publishing Company, Inc., 1980, 21 vol.

Chamber's Encyclopedia, New rev. edition, London, International Learning Systems, 1969.

Collier's Encyclopedia, New York, Macmillan Educational Company, 1984, 24 vol.

Compton's Encyclopedia, F.E. Compton Company, Division of Encyclopedia Britannica Inc., The University of Chicago, 1982, 26 vol.

Encyclopedia Americana, Danbury, International ed., Conn.: Grolier, 1981, 30 vol.

Encyclopedia Britannica, E. Britannica, Inc., USA, 1970.

How it works — The illustrated science and invention encyclopedia, New York, H.S. Stuttman, Co., Inc. publishers, 1974.

McGraw-Hill Encyclopedia of Science @ Technology, New York, McGraw-Hill Book Company, 1982, 5th edition.

Merit Students Encyclopedia, New York, Macmillan Educational Company, 1984, 20 vol.

New Encyclopedia Britannica, Chicago, Toronto, Encyclopedia Britannica, 1985.

The Joy of Knowledge Encyclopedia, London, Mitchell Beazleg Encyclopedias, 1976, 7 vol.

The Random House encyclopedia, New York, Random House, 1977, 2 vol.

The World Book Encyclopedia, Chicago, Field enterprises educational Corporation, 1973.

CONTENTS

Table of Contents 7
Preface 15
Introduction 17
Usage Guide 23

THEMES

ASTRONOMY 25
GEOGRAPHY 37
VEGETABLE KINGDOM 59
ANIMAL KINGDOM 79
HUMAN BEING 103
FOOD 133
FARM 149
ARCHITECTURE 157
HOUSE 175
HOUSE FURNITURE 197
GARDENING 235
DO-IT-YOURSELF 245
CLOTHING 279
PERSONAL ADORNMENT 313
PERSONAL ARTICLES 325
COMMUNICATIONS 343
TRANSPORTATION 381
OFFICE SUPPLIES AND EQUIPMENT 445
MUSIC 459
CREATIVE LEISURE ACTIVITIES 483
SPORTS 509
MEASURING DEVICES 589
OPTICAL INSTRUMENTS 603
HEALTH 613
ENERGY 619
HEAVY MACHINERY 659
WEAPONS 673
SYMBOLS 693

General Index 711
Thematic Indexes 745
Specialized Indexes 781
Selective Bibliography 795

423.1   Corbeil, Jean
COR   Claude.

        The Facts on File
        visual dictionary

    $29.95

DATE			